TechnoMarine

WATCHES 2003 INTERNATIONAL®

THE ORIGINAL ANNUAL OF THE WORLD'S FINEST WRISTWATCHES®

First published in the United States of America in 2003 by

Tourbillon International, LLC.
11 West 25th Street, 8th floor
New York, NY 10010
Tel: +1 (212) 627-7732 - Telefax +1 (212) 627-9093
Website: www.watches-2003.com

CHAIRMAN
Joseph Zerbib

CHIEF EXECUTIVE OFFICER & PUBLISHER
Caroline Childers

PRODUCTION DIRECTOR
Maurizio Zinelli

TECHNICAL DIRECTOR
Renata Pescatori

U.S. EDITOR
Roberta Naas

MANAGING EDITOR
Elizabeth Kindt

ART DIRECTOR
Mutsumi Hyuga

In association with **RIZZOLI** INTERNATIONAL PUBLICATIONS INC.

300 Park Avenue South, New York, NY 10010

Distributed by:
St. Martin's Press, c/o VHPS Order Department
16365 James Madison Highway,
Gordonsville, VA 22942-8501
T: 888 330 8477   F: 800 672 2054

ISBN: 0-8478-2526-4

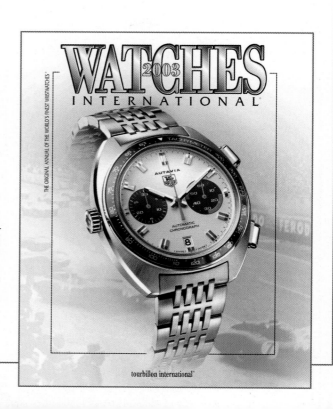

tourbillon international®

ZENITH

SWISS WATCH MANUFACTURE

SINCE 1865

Movements of pure simplicity and timeless beauty. ZENITH calibers are sheer
mechanical marvels, exposed to the scrutiny of the most discerning eyes.

DEAR READER,

Seasons change; time flies by. But in the end, it seems nothing really changes. Every day we forge ahead with our lives and plan for our futures and our children's futures. We plan based on time—precious time that the world's finest watchmakers allow us to track so perfectly. Indeed, we are surrounded by clocks on computers, microwaves, car dashboards, etc., yet we turn to wristwatches as our true measure of time—and perhaps even comfort.

In this world of factory production and high technology, it's hard to believe that hand craftsmanship still exists. But the world's best watchmakers continue to create by hand these intricately small items which miraculously house hundreds of tiny mechanical pieces fitted together to work for centuries to come.

For this reason, today more than ever before, luxury watches are great investments. They are works of art, prized possessions that someone has spent painstaking hours of craftsmanship and creativity producing. Some of the world's most magnificent watches are masterpieces as dear and coveted as a Renaissance painting or a piece of Louis XIV furniture. Witness to this are the myriad of incredible watch museums that have been opened by esteemed brands. Also witness to this are the wealth of watch-specific auctions that are held around the world and the record-breaking bids that some special timepieces draw.

Some of the best auction houses have begun to break down the category of watches by likening the concept to art. There are historical watches from Patek Philippe, Breguet and Audemars Piguet, for instance, that are akin to the world's finest historical art and command top dollar; there are newer timepieces that fetch bold prices as the counterparts of today's modern art; there are even behind-the-scenes objects of the trade (letters, notes and tools from the forefathers of watchmaking) for sale that are likened to the famed painters' brushes and palettes.

What most people seek when purchasing these limited-edition and special timepieces is a part of history—yesterday's and today's. Watches embody rich heritages and are grand legacies to leave to the next generation. Even as we retire the last of the world's great ocean liners, the QEII, we remember the heady times of ocean travel, elite socializing and grandeur. Similarly, complex luxury watches hold the lives of generations of watchmakers—their challenges, endeavors and accomplishments—within their cases.

As we pass on these elite timepieces to our loved ones for generations to come, we pass on great memories of our times and our lives. These handmade masterpieces not only represent an international spirit of authenticity and achievement, but also they represent a shared emotion of value and respect for beauty and heritage.

With these thoughts in mind, I express my deep appreciation for your support of this publication and of this amazing industry. I would also like to take this opportunity to dedicate *Watches International 2003* to peace and the preservation of heritage and history in all corners of the world.

Caroline Childers

Caroline Childers
Publisher & CEO

The legend reveals a new dimension

Reverso Septantième

For seventy years, the Reverso's legendary revolving case has been turning to reveal one innovation after another. And for this auspicious birthday, our craftsmen are unveiling a new, larger case, designed to house a landmark complicated movement. The limited-edition Reverso Septantième is fitted with a brand-new calibre, manually wound movement featuring an eight-day power-reserve, an exploit in that it combines this unusually long duration with uncompromising accuracy. The imposing case swivels to present a sapphire crystal case-back revealing details of the solid-gold, hand-decorated movement in all their beauty. The Reverso Septantième's generous size adds a new dimension to its owner's pleasure.

de GRISOGONO®
GENEVE

INTRODUCING

INSTRUMENTO
DOPPIO TRE
by de GRISOGONO

GENEVA - PARIS - LONDON - GSTAAD - ROME - HONG KONG - KUWEIT

www.degrisogono.com

de GRISOGONO®
GENEVE

INSTRUMENTO
DOPPIO TRE
by de GRISOGONO

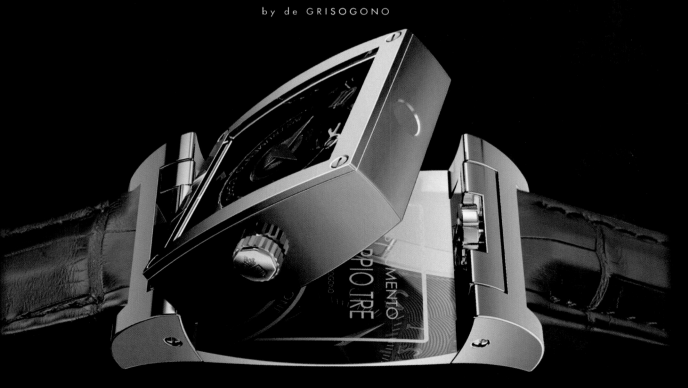

WORLD PREMIERE : STAINLESS STEEL WATCH WITH DUAL TIME ZONE AND LARGE DATE ON ONE SIDE.
INDEPENDENT THIRD TIME ZONE WITH A COAXIAL SET OF HANDS ON THE OTHER SIDE.
SINGLE BLACKENED AUTOMATIC MOVEMENT. REVOLVING CASE. WATERPROOF UP TO 50 M.

WATCHES 2003 INTERNATIONAL®

THE ORIGINAL ANNUAL OF THE WORLD'S FINEST WRISTWATCHES®

TOURBILLON INTERNATIONAL, LLC

ADMINISTRATION, ADVERTISING SALES, EDITORIAL, SUBSCRIPTIONS
11 West 25th Street, 8th Floor, New York, NY 10010
T: +1 (212) 627-7732   Fax: +1 (212) 627-9093
info@tourbillon-watches.com
sales@tourbillon-watches.com

EUROPEAN DISTRIBUTION
Via Pietro Maestri 3
00191 Rome Italy
T: +39 (06) 3294-977   Fax: +39 (06) 3294-976
tourbillon@tourbillon.it

CHAIRMAN   Joseph Zerbib

CHIEF EXECUTIVE OFFICER & PUBLISHER
Caroline Childers   cchilders@tourbillon-watches.com

PRODUCTION DIRECTOR
Maurizio Zinelli   zinelli@tourbillon.it

TECHNICAL DIRECTOR
Renata Pescatori   pescatori@tourbillon.it

U.S. EDITOR
Roberta Naas   roberta@tourbillon-watches.com

MANAGING EDITOR
Elizabeth Kindt   elizabeth@tourbillon-watches.com

ART DIRECTOR
Mutsumi Hyuga   mutsumi@tourbillon-watches.com

CONTRIBUTING EDITORS
Alan Downing, Roland G. Murphy, Barbara Notarangelo,
Maria Teresa Steri, Alessandro Lodolini, Stanley Drucker,
Caroline Ruiz, Kurt R. Schmidt

TRANSLATIONS   Igino Schraffl

PRE-PRESS & COLOR TECNICIAN   Andrea D'Autilia

PHOTOGRAPHERS
PHOTOGRAPHIC ARCHIVES, PROPERTY OF EDITORIALE TOURBILLON SRL

WEBMASTER
Marcel Choukroun   webmaster@tourbillon-watches.com

DISTRIBUTION
Rizzoli International Publications
Marco Ausenda, Executive Vice President
Rizzoli Bookstores; St. Martin's Press

TOURBILLON INTERNATIONAL ACCOUNTING
Maria Aprile, The Videre Group

WEB DISTRIBUTION   www.amazon.com

SUBSCRIPTIONS DEPARTMENT   Massimo Centrone

EDITORIAL

For centuries, timepieces have evolved to accommodate man's increased demands for time at a glance—finally resulting in the wristwatch. From there, invention ticked on to the point where those wristwatches can now time the tiniest fraction of a second—an important function in today's fast-paced life. There is no telling how frequently in a day we glance at the watch on our wrist, or how often we time ourselves and our meetings to the exact minute.

Despite our need to track time to the second, watches are about so much more than timing. They are about passion, about meticulous—often painstaking—craftsmanship, and sometimes they are about generations of secrets discreetly passed on and later improved upon. These virtues and venues are the impetus for some of the most luxurious and complex watches in the world.

A watch is one of the premier items by which we suppress our hunger for self-expression. These highly visible instruments allow us to quietly (or not so quietly) make our own statements—statements about our interests, our loves, our places in life, our ambitions. For this reason, the selection of watches in the world is vast.

Complex works of mechanical prowess exist side by side with high-jeweled masterpieces. Watches that offer split-second timing or measurement of speed or altitude have their places in the sun, as do watches that are built around designer names or fashion influences. There are colorful watches, there are black and white watches; there are big watches and little watches; neck, ring and wristwatches. Indeed, there are no limits.

We have freedom of creativity to thank for the watch industry's grand versatility. Indeed, ingenuity reigns supreme in today's watches—timepieces that are masterful blends of tradition and modernity, of heritage and technology. The pages of *Watches International 2003* pay homage to the innovation that brings so much more than timing to our wrists.

This annual must-have tool of the industry brings to you the history and lineage of so many of the world's finest brands. It presents insights into the newest products that will this year grace the wrists of people around the world.

Indeed, it is a compendium consisting of in-depth profiles of 70 premier watch brands. It offers a look at the newest movements developed by the world's finest makers, and gives complete technical descriptions of complex watches, haute joaillerie watches, classically elegant watches and high-tech sport watches. A glossary was added this year to benefit those new to watch collecting (page 64) as we continue to provide our readers with the most comprehensive presentation of the newest masterpieces in the world of fine watchmaking.

Roberta Naas

VINTAGE 1945

AUTOMATIC TOURBILLON WITH GOLD BRIDGE

Inspired by a watch dating from 1945, the GIRARD-PERREGAUX Manufactory is adding a new jewel to its Haute Horlogerie collection by housing the Tourbillon with one gold Bridge in the refined case of a VINTAGE model. An opening in the dial reveals the Tourbillon under a pink gold Bridge. Naturally, this new model is equipped with the Manufactory's own patented automatic winding mechanism.

GP
GIRARD-PERREGAUX

For the distinguished dealer nearest you, call 1-877 TIME 4 GP or 1-877-846-3447
Visit GIRARD-PERREGAUX at www.girard-perregaux-usa.com

www.fpjourne.com

F.P.JOURNE
Invenit et Fecit

Invenit et Fecit: "Invented and made".
The motto of a contemporary brand
building its own history.

The first resonance wristwatch

Chronomètre à Résonance

F.P.JOURNE
Invenit et Fecit

CHRONOMETRE A RESONANCE

Westime

LOS ANGELES, CALIFORNIA

Westime has good reason to bill itself as the store with "extraordinary watches and jewelry." Providing an elegant setting for the world's finest timepieces, this mega-retailer on the West Coast (arguably the premier jeweler in the west) has a luxurious store fully stocked with the most prestigious watch and jewelry brands.

Westime is an authorized retailer for the most elite watch brands, including but not limited to: Audemars Piguet, Blancpain, Breguet, Chopard, Chronoswiss, Concord, Franck Muller, Girard-Perregaux, Glashütte Original, IWC, Omega, Richard Mille, Vacheron Constantin, and Zenith. Esteemed jewelry brands include Chopard, Damiani, Fred and others.

Founded and owned by a second-generation watchmaker and connoisseur with a passion for mechanical timepieces and a true love of the business, Westime began 15 years ago in Los Angeles. It has since developed a most illustrious following—from Hollywood celebrities to sports stars to international business travelers. All of this is thanks to the store's superior selection and unparalleled service.

Westime prides itself on offering the rarest and most sought after timepieces. Indeed, limited editions and unique pieces are snapped up immediately on a regular basis. In some

instances, the store has even commissioned major brands to create custom models for them and, in other cases, Westime has been selected by brands to carry certain extremely complicated watches on an exclusive basis.

Genuinely warm and affable, the owner and staff of this special dealership insist on exemplary personal service and regularly goes above and beyond the call of duty. At Westime, if one needs a watch hand-delivered-across town or across the country-it's done. To accommodate its sophisticated clientele, Westime educates its staff not only about the brands it carries, but also about the intricacies of watchmaking and the specifics of compli-

cations. What's more, most of the sales associates speak at least two languages—with as many as 10 languages proficient among them—a definite plus in the cosmopolitan city.

What truly sets Westime apart from most other watch stores is that they are not only focused on selection and service before the sale, they are dedicated to after-sales service as well. Two full-time master watchmakers are on site at all times and utilize state-of-the-art equipment for service and repairs. Westime not only offers regular maintenance of mechanical watches, but also offers everything from testing for water resistance to changing straps and bracelets.

Westime also hosts unique customer events to introduce preferred clientele to the newest brand offerings or to meet owners, presidents and even master watchmakers of some of the key brands.

Truly an innovator and trendsetter in the world of luxury watch retailing, Westime offers an inviting atmosphere for its discerning clientele. Within the 6,000-square-foot showroom are expansive showcases, comfortable seating arrangements and even two specialty boutiques: Chopard and Audemars Piguet. For those to whom convenience and security are not mere luxuries but basic necessities, Westime even offers front-door valet service.

In addition to its great location at the Westside Pavilion, a new showroom on Rodeo Drive in Beverly Hills will open this year. Additionally, Westime has built a very informative and user friendly website (www.westimewatches.com) that includes a list of services and brands that the store offers, as well as an extensive glossary of horological terms and a guide to choosing and buying the perfect watch.

When in Southern California, a visit to Westime is a must-see destination for any self-respecting watch aficionado!

10800 W. Pico Blvd., #197, Los Angeles, CA 90064
Tel: 310 470 1388   Fax: 310 470 0628
www.westimewatches.com

BRANDS CARRIED

ALAIN SILBERSTEIN
AUDEMARS PIGUET
BAUME & MERCIER
BLANCPAIN
BREGUET
BREITLING
CHOPARD
CHRONOSWISS
CONCORD
CORUM
DANIEL JEANRICHARD
EBEL
FRANCK MULLER
GIRARD-PERREGAUX
GLASHÜTTE
HARRY WINSTON
IWC
LONGINES
MOVADO
OMEGA
PARMIGIANI FLEURIER
PAUL PICOT
PIERRE KUNZ
RICHARD MILLE
TAG HEUER
TUTIMA
VACHERON CONSTANTIN
ZENITH

SUMMARY

WEBSITE DIRECTORY

Antoine Preziuso:	www.antoine-preziuso.com	Fred:	www.fred-paris.com	Raymond Weil:	www.raymond-weil.ch
Audemars Piguet:	www.audemarspiguet.com	Frédérique Constant:	www.frederique-constant.com	RGM:	www.rgmwatches.com
Baume & Mercier:	www.baume-et-mercier.com	Gevril:	www.gevril.ch	Richemont Group:	www.richemont.com
Bédat & C°:	www.bedat.com	Girard-Perregaux:	www.girard-perregaux.ch	Rolex:	www.rolex.com
Bell & Ross:	www.bellross.com	Glashütte Original:	www.glashuette.de	Scatola del Tempo:	www.scatoladeltempo.com
Bertolucci:	www.bertolucci-watches.com	Goldpfeil:	www.goldpfeil-geneve.com	Sven Andersen:	www.andersen-geneve.ch
Blancpain:	www.blancpain.com	Gucci:	www.gucci.com	Swatch Group:	www.swatchgroup.com
Boucheron:	www.boucheron.com	Harry Winston:	www.harry-winston.com	TAG Heuer:	www.tagheuer.com
Breguet:	www.breguet.com	Hermès:	www.hermes.com	TechnoMarine:	www.technomarine.com
Breitling:	www.breitling.com	Hublot:	www.hublot.ch	Tiffany & Co.:	www.tiffany.com
Bvlgari:	www.bulgari.it	Ikepod:	www.ikepod.com	Tissot:	www.tissot.ch
Cartier:	www.cartier.com	IWC:	www.iwc.ch	Ulysse Nardin:	www.ulysse-nardin.com
Certina:	www.certina.com	Jaeger-LeCoultre:	www.jaeger-lecoultre.com	Universal:	www.universal.ch
Chanel:	www.chanel.com	Jean-Mairet & Gillman:	www.jean-mairetgillman.com	Vacheron Constantin:	www.vacheron-constantin.com
Charriol:	www.philippe-charriol.com	Jean Marcel:	www.jeanmarcel.com	Van der Bauwede:	www.vdb.ch
Chaumet:	www.chaumet.com	L. Leroy:	www.l-leroy.com	Versace:	www.versace.com
Chopard:	www.chopardgeneve.com	Locman:	www.locman.com	Vianney Halter:	www.vianney-halter.com
Christian Dior:	www.dior.com	Longines:	www.longines.com	Vincent Calabrese:	www.vincent-calabrese.ch
Chronoswiss:	www.chronoswiss.de	Mauboussin:	www.mauboussin.com	Xantia:	www.xantia.ch
Clerc:	www.clercwatches.com	Maurice Lacroix:	www.mauricelacroix.com	Xemex:	www.xemex.ch
Concord:	www.concord.ch	Michele Watches:	www.michelewatches.com	Zannetti:	E-mail: zannettiwatches@yahoo.it
Corum:	www.corum.ch	Montres Allison:	www.montresallison.ch	Zenith:	www.zenith-watches.ch
Daniel JeanRichard:	www.danieljeanrichard.ch	Movado:	www.movado.ch		
Daniel Mink:	www.danielmink.com	Olivier Roux:	www.olivier-roux.com		
David Yurman:	www.davidyurman.com	Omega:	www.omega.ch	**RELATED SITES**	
de GRISOGONO:	www.degrisogono.com	Panerai:	www.panerai.com	Tourbillon International:	www.watches-2003.com
Delaneau:	www.fhs.ch	Parmigiani Fleurier:	www.parmigiani.com	Association Interprofessionnelle de la Haute Horlogerie:	www.aihh.com
de Witt	www.dewitt.ch	Patek Philippe:	www.patekphilippe.com	Fédération de l'Industrie Horlogére Suisse:	www.fhs.com
Dubey & Schaldenbrand:	www.dubeywatch.com	Paul Picot:	www.paulpicot.ch	Salon Mondial de l'Horlogère:	www.baselshow.com
Ebel:	www.ebel.ch	Perrelet:	www.perrelet.com	Auctions:	www.christies.com www.sothebys.com
Eberhard & Co.:	www.eberhard-co-watches.ch	Piaget:	www.piaget.com	Museums:	www.thewatchmuseum.com www.uhrenmuseum.ch www.bhi.co.uk/museum.htm
Franck Muller:	www.franckmuller.com	Quinting:	www.quinting-watches.com		
F.P. Journe:	www.fpjourne.com	Rado:	www.rado.ch		

She hides her time, for experts all agree, that what a man desires the most, is what he cannot see.

DELANEAU
GENĒVE

ACKNOWLEDGMENTS

This book could not have been produced without the assistance and kindness from the many people who shared with us their keen knowledge and experience from the watchmaking industry. My special thanks to:

Ms. Terry Meier from A. Lange & Söhne Germany; Ms. Carole Augsburger, Mr. Eric Loth from The British Masters Switzerland for Arnold & Son; Mr. Olivier Bacher, Mr. Georges-Henri Meylan, Ms. Elisabeth Schneider from Audemars Piguet Switzerland; Mr. Sam Gabbas from Babylone Switzerland; Mr. Christian Bedat, Ms. Simone Bedat from Bedat & Co. Switzerland; Ms. Lisa Newman from Bedat & Co. New York; Mr. Jean Paul Gaillard, Ms. Beatriz Rossel Tür, Ms. Jutta Stienen from Bertolucci Switzerland; Mr. Tomasso Galli, Mr. Frédéric Lejosne from Luxury Goods International for Boucheron; Ms. Murielle Blanchard, Ms. Stephanie Lebadezet from Boucheron Paris; Ms. Kimberly Grogan from Breitling USA; Mr. Theodore Schneider from Breitling Switzerland; Ms. Maresa Laino from Cartier New York; Mr. Cédric Johner, Ms. Christine Johner from Cédric Johner Switzerland;

TOP LEFT
Eric Loth

LOWER LEFT
Georges-Henri Meylan

BOTTOM LEFT
Christian Bédat

BOTTOM CENTER
Jean Paul Gaillard

BELOW
Sam Gabbas

BOTTOM RIGHT
Cédric Johner

THERE IS AS MUCH ELEGANCE
IN ONE HOUR AS IN 24.

BERTOLUCCI

MANUFACTURE DE MONTRES NEUCHÂTEL SUISSE

NOW OR TOMORROW

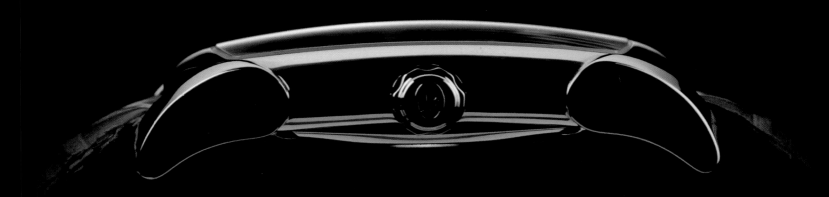

PARMI

Parmigiani Fleurier SA
Temple 11 • CH-2114 Fleurier • Switzerland
Telephone: (41) 32 862 66 30 • Fax: (41) 32 862 66 31

GIANI

TIME IS MEASURED,
TIME IS HEARD, TIME IS SEEN.
PARMIGIANI FORMA HEBDOMADAIRE

A GOOD TIME WILL BE HAD BY ALL.
Shop our exclusive selection of handmade,
complicated watches in the Precious Jewels Salon.

ACKNOWLEDGMENTS

Mr. Camille Berthet, Mr. Jean-Louis Merandet from Charles Oudin Paris; Mr. Philippe Charriol, Mr. Jack D. Zemer, Ms. Sandy Zemer, Ms. Laura Spielman from Charriol USA; Mr. Thierry Fritsch, Mr. Lionel Giraud, Ms. Evelyne Menager, Ms. Blandine Castaigne, Ms. Sandrine Atamaniuk from Chaumet Paris; Ms. Caroline Gruosi-Scheufele, Mr. Karl-Friedrich Scheufele from Chopard Switzerland; Ms. Annick Benoit-Godet from K&K Promotions for Chopard Switzerland; Mr. Thierry Chaunu from Chopard New York; Ms. Muriele Wormser, Ms. Catherine Lamy, Ms. Emilie Roy from LVMH Group for Christian Dior Paris; Mr. Gerd-R. Lang, Ms. Josephine Müller, Ms. Veronika Riggauer from Chronoswiss Germany; Mr. Stephen Butler, Ms. Christine Sullivan from Bellport Time Group for Chronoswiss USA;

FAR LEFT
Camille Berthet

BOTTOM LEFT
Thierry Fritsch

BOTTOM CENTER
Caroline Gruosi-Scheufele

BELOW
Karl-Friedrich Scheufele

BOTTOM RIGHT
Thierry Chaunu

WEMPE
NEW YORK, NEW YORK

This year marks the 125th anniversary of Wempe—world-renowned German jeweler extraordinaire. Indeed, this company's stellar success stems from an illustrious path rich with superb quality standards, very selective product assortment, and excellent customer service.

Founded in 1878 in Elsfleth, Germany, Wempe was the dream of 21-year-old watchmaker, Gerhard D. Wempe. He began his company with an initial capital of just 80 marks and with it, created a legacy. Wempe focused on crafting and selling beautiful timepieces—a tradition it has continued for 125 years. The company later delved into the world of luxurious diamond and gemstone jewelry, and ultimately put together an exquisite collection of European designed pieces.

In the late 20th century, nearly 100 years after its founding, Wempe began its international expansion and opened stores in some of the most prominent cities of the world—including New York, Paris, London, Madrid and Vienna. Still under family ownership today, the retailer remains dedicated to preserving its superior quality, selection and reputation.

In each of its 25 locations around the world, Wempe offers its signature watch and jewelry creations, and carries the finest brand names in these categories.

In addition to its own series of watches, Wempe offers such illustrious brands as Patek Philippe, Vacheron Constantin, Jaeger-LeCoultre, Breitling, Chopard, Cartier, Rolex and more. In fact, Wempe is one of a very elite group of jewelers authorized to sell the famed A. Lange & Söhne brand as well as Cartier's Collection Privée. At Wempe New York, a collector can choose from 100 different Patek Philippe watches in a comfortable, relaxed atmosphere. The company also backs its brands with an extended warranty of up to three years.

Wempe's flagship store in New York boasts the highest sales performance of all Wempe locations. Under the astute management of Ruediger Albers, president of Wempe in America, the 2,500-square-foot Fifth Avenue salon practically has become a New York landmark for elite shoppers. Holding a master's degree in watchmaking, Albers genuinely understands his collector clientele and its needs, and offers

32

selection and service of the highest order. The key to his success is the passion and level of experience of his loyal staff, many of whom have been with the company for over 20 years.

Regularly Wempe has maintained the highest level of commitment to excellent customer service. This facet has also helped Wempe forge incredibly solid relationships with each of the premier brands it carries. In fact, Wempe has such a sterling reputation that several of the world's finest watch brands are creating exclusive anniversary watches in conjunction with the retailer. Brands such as Patek Philippe, Cartier, IWC, A. Lange & Söhne, Jaeger-LeCoultre, Chopard and Breitling have each developed special timepieces that are both technically and visually advanced for the 125th anniversary collection.

Among the anniversary pieces that will make their debut in Wempe stores beginning in May 2003 is a Patek Philippe annual calendar watch with two casebacks and a commemorative coin. It is housed in a special presentation box and is being created in a limited edition of 100 pieces in platinum and 125 pieces in each color of gold. Called the W125, the gold timepieces will retail from $25,470 to $36,230. Nomos has also created a special model for Wempe that features a clear back depicting the symbol of each city where Wempe is located. The New York version is limited to 125 pieces and features the Statue of Liberty.

"Wempe does not want to be something for everybody," says Albers, "We want to be everything to somebody."

BRANDS CARRIED
A. LANGE & SÖHNE
AUDEMARS PIGUET
BAUME & MERCIER
BREGUET
BREITLING
CARTIER
CHOPARD
GLASHÜTTE ORIGINAL
IWC
JAEGER-LECOULTRE
NOMOS
OMEGA
PANERAI
PATEK PHILIPPE
ROLEX
VACHERON CONSTANTIN

700 Fifth Avenue at 55th Street, New York, NY 10019
Tel: 212 397 9000   toll-free: 1 866 WEMPE NY   Fax: 212 397 7235
www.wempe.com

CÉDRIC JOHNER

for more than a decade, Cédric Johner worked within the hallowed halls of horological excellence for some of the world's finest brands. Originally trained as a jeweler, Johner developed a keen interest in timepieces and pursued an education in the fine art of Swiss watchmaking.

Initially, Johner designed and produced special timepieces on a made-to-order basis, working out of his family home. In 1997, he opened his own workshops in a turn-of-the-century manor outside of Geneva and began creating one-of-a-kind timepieces. His wife helped run the company that bore his name and, in 1998, the two presented Johner's watches at the Basel Fair for the first time. Watch connoisseurs were intrigued by his innovative designs and impressive craftsmanship, and by the 1999 Basel Fair, Johner had developed an elite and loyal following.

Each of Johner's creations is housed in his striking Abyss case—a design that spent two years in the research and development stages. A brilliant combination of tonneau and round, the Abyss features an inset hexagonal edge around the watch dial. Each case is shaped by hand in one of three sizes and is a sensual blend of elegance and technical prowess.

Having his own case did not satiate his passions for long, however, and Johner went on to develop his own movements: the caliber 10, upon which many complications have been added (including the tourbillon, chronograph and minute repeater), and the caliber 01 for women.

All of Johner's timepieces are created with the utmost attention paid to every detail. Dials, movements and bracelets have been designed and created by Johner and all are hand assembled to Johner's most specific demands. In 2000, Johner moved his workshops to Vandoeuvers, just outside of Geneva. He then applied for and obtained the Geneva Hallmark; the elegant seal depicting this achievement is hand engraved on his most desirable timepieces.

Johner recently integrated the production of his own watchcases into his repertoire—improving his already high standards of quality. This in-house production gives each piece its own uniqueness: each is hand filed, hand finished and hand engraved in-house.

GENEVE

CEDRIC JOHNER

ACKNOWLEDGMENTS

Mr. Gérald Clerc, Ms. Nathalie Clerc from Clerc New York; Mr. Gedalio "Gerry" Grinberg, Mr. Efraim Grinberg, Ms. Barbara Binner, Ms. Jeanne Massaro, Ms. Diana Moran, Ms. Naomi Mansbach, Ms. Jill Golden from Movado Group USA for Concord; Mr. Chris Koeppel from Corbis USA; Dr. Gino "Luigi" Macaluso, Ms. Sylvie Rumo, Mr. Bernard Fleury from Daniel JeanRichard Switzerland; Mr. Ronald R. Jackson from Daniel JeanRichard USA; Mr. Jim Watson, Ms. Nancy Watson from Digital Color; Mr. David Yurman, Ms. Sybil Yurman, Ms. Angeline Urie from David Yurman USA; Mr. Fawaz Gruosi, Ms. Corinne Celeyron, Ms. Michele Reichenbach from de GRISOGONO Switzerland; Ms. Robin Davis from The Townsend Group USA for de GRISOGONO;

TOP LEFT
Gérald Clerc

BOTTOM LEFT
Nathalie Clerc

CENTER
Efraim Grinberg

TOP RIGHT
David and Sybil Yurman

BOTTOM RIGHT
Fawaz Gruosi

LOCMAN
ITALY

NU●VO

Carbon Fiber and Titanium
The only carbon fiber watch in the world

LOCMAN S. p. a. - Isola d'Elba - Tel +39. 0565. 979002/3 - Fax +39.0565. 979707 - mail@locman.it

www.locman.it

LOCMAN USA - 444 Madison Ave. Suite 2300 New York NY 10022 - Tel 212.371.1888 - 888.5.LOCMAN - Fax 212.371. 9985
sales@locman.com

GEVRIL

AVENUE OF AMERICAS GLAMOUR COLLECTION
AUTOMATIC * 25 JEWELS * 316L STAINLESS STEEL * TOP WESSELTON DIAMONDS, 2.10 CTS. * LTD EDITION, 100 PCS
TOLL FREE: (USA) 866.425.9882 PHONE: 845.425.9882 WWW.GEVRIL.CH

ACKNOWLEDGMENTS

Mr. Le Conte de Witt, Mr. Giorgio Bernasconi from de Witt Switzerland; Ms. Cristina Thévenaz from Delaneau Switzerland; Mr. Roberto Cristobal from Delaneau New York; Ms. Cinette Robert from Dubey & Schaldenbrand Switzerland; Ms. Amélie Berger, Ms. Karine Marie, Ms. Miriam Di Ninni, Mr. Guillaume Brochard, Mr. Xavier Gauderlot from Ebel Switzerland; Mr. Dennis Phillips from Ebel USA; Ms. Laetitia Sidler from Eberhard & Co. Switzerland; Mr. Albert Ganjei from European Watch Co.; Mr. Franck Muller from Franck Muller Switzerland; Mr. Hratch Kaprelian, Ms. Jenny Arakelyn from Franck Muller USA; Mr. François-Paul Journe, Ms. Natalia Signoroni, Ms. Hân Nguyen from F.P. Journe Switzerland; Mr. Pierre Halimi Lacharlotte for F.P. Journe;

FAR LEFT
Cristina Thévenaz

BOTTOM LEFT
Cinette Robert

TOP CENTER
Guillaume Brochard

BOTTOM CENTER
Xavier Gauderlot

BOTTOM RIGHT
François-Paul Journe

DANIEL JEANRICHARD

"TV SCREEN"
Retrograde Seconds

Faces of time®

EXCLUSIVELY FROM

THE WORLD'S FINEST

WATCH & JEWELRY

STORES.

It is not often that one can reach out and touch an historical landmark.

It is even less frequent to be able to caress and turn over one

of today's most striking "Faces of time",

to admire it from all angles, and even wear it on the wrist

as a daily companion.

Such is the unique privilege offered to the fortunate purchasers

of an exclusive series watch by Goldpfeil Genève.

esulting from an unprecedented competition among seven members of the prestigious

cadémie Horlogère des Créateurs Indépendants (AHCI),

hese models represent the highest level of watchmaking creativity and craftsmanship

nd carry the distinctive "golden arrow" sign of recognition.

y the time all the stunning timekeepers

vere unveiled, the jury simply could not choose between them.

he only question is, can you?

ACKNOWLEDGMENTS

Mr. Peter Stas from Frédérique Constant Switzerland; Mr. Alan Swierk, Mr. Jim Kennedy from International Time Group for Frédérique Constant USA; Mr. Pasquale Gangi, Mr. René Schmidlin, Ms. Aurélie Simone, Ms. Valerie Borghana from Gangi International Switzerland for Georges V; Mr. Samuel Friedmann, Ms. Monica Friedmann, Mr. Steven Pachtinger from Gevril USA; Dr. Gino "Luigi" Macaluso, Ms. Anne Biéler, Ms. Sylvie Rumo, Ms. Aline Ischer, Ms. Hannie Kyriacos, Mr. Dennis Schnegg from Girard-Perregaux Switzerland; Mr. Ronald R. Jackson from Girard-Perregaux USA; Ms. Missy Farren from Farren Communications for Girard-Perregaux;

TOP LEFT
Peter Stas

TOP CENTER
Pasquale Gangi

TOP RIGHT
Dr. Luigi Macaluso

BOTTOM LEFT
Aletta Stas

BOTTOM CENTER
René Schmidlin

BOTTOM RIGHT
Ronald R. Jackson

L.U.C - A proud watchmaking tradition
L.U.C Quattro. Chronometer, 4 spring barrels, 9½-day power-reserve,
"Geneva Seal"

Louis-Ulysse Chopard

Mr. Heinz J. Heimann, Ms. Caroline Vogt from Goldpfeil Switzerland; Mr. Eric Loth, Ms. Carole Augsburger from The British Masters Switzerland for Graham; Mr. Tomasso Galli, Mr. Massimo Machi, Ms. Simonetta Ruggeri, Ms. Paola Chopard, Mr. Tom Ford from Luxury Goods International for Gucci; Ms. Mireille Cabezas, Mr. Gianluca Maina from Harry Winston Switzerland; Mr. Guillaume de Seynes, Mr. Vincent Moesch, Ms. Natacha Guinnard from La Montres Hermès Switzerland; Mr. Karl F. Kreiser from La Montres Hermès USA; Mr. Carlo Crocco from MDM for Hublot Switzerland; Mr. Pascal Savoy from MDM for Hublot USA; Ms. Sandrine-Lise Taboada, Ms. Erdme Palkus, Ms. Corinne Paget-Blanc, Ms. Simone Prévalet, Ms. Mathilde Michel, Mr. John-Henry Belmont, Ms. Lydie Clement, Ms. Nathalie Micheletto from Jaeger-LeCoultre Switzerland; Mr. Ronald Wolfgang from Jaeger-LeCoultre New York; Mr. Cèsar Jean-Mairet, Mr. Montse Margalef from Jean-Mairet & Gillman Switzerland; Mr. Ricardo Guadalupe, Ms. Léa Petersell from Leonard Switzerland;

TOP LEFT
Heinz J. Heimann

FAR LEFT
Guillaume de Seynes

BOTTOM LEFT
Carlo Crocco

BOTTOM CENTER
Cèsar Jean-Mairet

BOTTOM RIGHT
Ricardo Guadalupe

PERPETUATING ELEGANCE IS GIVEN
ITS FULL VALUE BY THE PASSAGE OF TIME.

BERTOLUCCI

MANUFACTURE DE MONTRES NEUCHÂTEL SUISSE

NOW OR TOMORROW

ACKNOWLEDGMENTS

Mr. Marco Mantovani from Locman Italy; Mr. Ben Feigenbaum, Ms. Elizabeth Torovin from Locman USA, Ms. Linda Miller from Panda Communications for Locman; Mr. Walter von Känel, Ms. Yolande Peroulaz from Longines Switzerland; Mr. Philippe Pascal, Mr. Albert Bensoussan from LVMH Group Watch and Jewelry Paris; Mr. Jack Barouh, Ms. Michele Barouh, Mr. Michael Miarecki, Ms. Lola Garcia from Michele Watches USA; Mr. Terry L. Allison II, Mr. Walt Orenstein from Montres Allison USA; Mr. Mark Marshall, Ms. Annie Neslage from Neiman Marcus USA; Mr. Olivier Roux from Olivier Roux Switzerland; Mr. Michel Parmigiani, Mr. Jean Bernard Maeder, Mr. Alberto Caccia, Ms. Sylvie Humbert-Droz from Parmigiani Fleurier Switzerland; Mr. Donald R. Loke from Parmigiani Fleurier USA;

TOP LEFT
Ben Feigenbaum and Marco Mantovani

CENTER LEFT
Michele Barouh

BOTTOM LEFT
Terry L. Allison II

BOTTOM CENTER
Olivier Roux

BOTTOM RIGHT
Michel Parmigiani

EUROPEAN WATCH CO.

BOSTON, MASSACHUSETTS

Specializing in vintage and pre-owned timepieces, European Watch Co. has a great deal to offer its customers. Wisely located on Boston's prestigious Newbury Street, European Watch Co. dresses its showcases with high-grade luxurious Swiss and European brands.

A career in watch retailing was not the original aspiration of owner Albert Ganjei. A corporate executive in the world of engineering, Ganjei was a born watch-lover. Passionate about fine timepieces, Ganjei became an avid collector and, for the past decade-plus, has traveled regularly to Switzerland to witness the newest product unveilings at the most prestigious shows in the industry and also to visit factories and workshops.

About eight years ago, Ganjei began dabbling in buying and selling vintage watches and then ventured into the pre-owned and trade-in services. He has built an international following and his business has boomed. Because Ganjei understands what goes into the making of a complicated timepiece, and because he procures many limited-edition and hard-to-find pieces, European Watch Co. has a discerning clientele of wealthy notables and celebrities.

With his discerning customers in mind, Ganjei scours the world to find the perfect timepieces. Passionate about the mechanical wonders that the finest brands produce, Ganjei stocks perpetual calendars, tourbillons, rattrapantes and a wealth of other complexities. Watches retail anywhere from $2,000 to $50,000. In addition to a vast inventory, European Watch Co. has a master watchmaker on premises and offers servicing and watch repairs for all brands.

Decorated with mahogany and marble, the store has an inviting club-like atmosphere where many customers come just to peruse the merchandise, garner advice and plan their next watch purchases. What's more, customers around the world can enjoy a slide show of the store's complete stock on the comprehensive website; EuropeanWatch.com is updated daily and orders are shipped overnight.

232 Newbury Street, Boston, MA 02116
Tel: 617 262 9798   Fax: 617 247 0480
www.europeanwatch.com

ACKNOWLEDGMENTS

Mr. Henry Stern from Patek Philippe Switzerland; Ms. Tania Edwards from Patek Philippe USA; Mr. Flavio Audemars, Mr. Carlo Munari, Ms. Stefania Tiso from Perrelet Switzerland; Mr. Pascal Berclaz from Quinting Switzerland; Mr. Raymond Weil, Mr. Olivier Bernheim, Mr. Eric Viscont, Ms. Thérèse Legerer, Ms. Karin Soller, Ms. Caroline Dayen, Ms. Elisabeth Delannoy from RAYMOND WEIL Switzerland; Mr. Richard Mille from Richard Mille Switzerland; Mr. Alan Rutsky, Ms. Sheilah Ledwidge from Rizzoli International; Mr. Roland G. Murphy, Mr. Richard Baugh from RGM USA; Mr. Carlo Diaz from Roger Dubuis Switzerland; Mr. William Sullivan from Rolex New York; Ms. Dominique Tadion from Rolex Switzerland; Ms. Barbara Colarieti from Scatola del Tempo Italy; Mr. Harry Benitah from Season Graphics USA; Ms. Anne Biéler from SIHH Genève; Mr. Nicolas G. Hayek from Swatch Group Switzerland;

FAR LEFT
Henry Stern

LEFT
Carlo Munari

CENTER
Pascal Berclaz

BELOW
Richard Mille

BOTTOM RIGHT
Nicolas G. Hayek

BOTTOM LEFT
Flavio Audemars

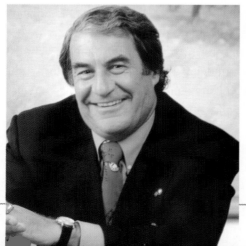

www.hublot.com

ACKNOWLEDGMENTS

Mr. Thierry Huron, Ms. Sandrine Segato from TAG Heuer Switzerland; Mr. Franck Dubarry, Mr. Pierre Halimi Lacharlotte, Ms. Eileen Barzola from TechnoMarine USA; Mr. Michael Kowalski, Ms. Linda Buckley, Mr. Jon M. King from Tiffany & Co. USA; Mr. Scott Rosen from Vacheron Constantin USA; Ms. Donatella Versace from Versace Italy; Mr. Giovanni Mattera from Versace USA; Mr. Ruediger Albers from Wempe USA; Mr. John Simonian from Westime USA; Mr. Riccardo Zannetti, Ms. Claudia Zerbe from Zannetti Italy; Mr. Thierry Nataf, Ms. Francoise Bezzola, Mr. Antoine Pin, Ms. Eliana Golay from Zenith International Switzerland.

TOP LEFT
Thierry Huron

LOWER LEFT
Franck Dubarry

BOTTOM LEFT
Michael Kowalski

TOP CENTER
Marco Giovanelli

BOTTOM CENTER
Giovanni Mattera

TOP BOTTOM
Donatella Versace

BOTTOM RIGHT
Thierry Nataf

EBEL

BELUGA TONNEAU IN STAINLESS STEEL,
CASE SET WITH 34 DIAMONDS,
SILVER DIAL WITH 13 DIAMONDS.
5 YEAR INTERNATIONAL WARRANTY.

BELUGA

ACKNOWLEDGMENTS

Thank you to our associates Ms. Renata Pescatori, Mr. Maurizio Zinelli, Mr. Andrea D'Autilia, Mr. Massimo Centrone from Editoriale Tourbillon Italy; and Mr. Marco Giovanelli from La Cromografica Italy Ms. Roberta Naas, Ms. Elizabeth Kindt, Ms. Mutsumi Hyuga, Mr. Alan Downing, Mr. Marcel Choukroun, Ms. Caroline Ruiz, Mr. Kurt R. Schmidt for Tourbillon International New York; Mr. Igino Scraffl from the University of Rome for Tourbillon International; Yael and Esther from Frenchway Travel, who make the impossible travel possible. And, of course, my special heartfelt thanks goes to Mr. Joseph Zerbib, a tireless source of strength who supports our team every step of the way!

Caroline Childers

TOP LEFT
Mutsumi Hyuga

TOP CENTER
Elizabeth Kindt

TOP RIGHT
Kurt R. Schmidt

BOTTOM LEFT
Caroline Ruiz

BOTTOM CENTER
Andrea D'Autilia

BELOW
Maurizio Zinelli

BOTTOM RIGHT
Yael and Esther

INTRODUCTION

Watches International 2003's 400-plus pages of editorial coverage pay homage to the world's finest watchmaking houses, their heritages and the craft they have perpetuated and strengthened from generation to generation.

In an effort to offer as much information as possible to the savvy reader, *Watches International 2003* brings together technology and design, cutting-edge innovation and rich history. Indeed, the timepieces featured in these pages represent the most recent unveilings in a long line of time-honored work from the world's most prestigious watchmakers.

The newest timepieces on the market offer a wealth of choices for watch connoisseurs around the globe. From cutting-edge styling to sports precision pieces, from diamond and gemstone bedecked masterpieces to complex technological innovations, the watches featured in this catalog represent a commitment to achievement and advancement.

Each company profiled traces its respective brand's roots and heritage, and then highlights the newest offerings and collections. When possible, we have provided the most up-to-date company news and information on the new models. Arranged alphabetically by brand, the profiles are often accompanied by technical descriptions of the new mechanical watches—the forefather and backbone of the Swiss watchmaking tradition.

We are confident that the information provided in this annual will offer many hours of enjoyable reading and that this catalog will be an invaluable reference in the coming year.

Technical Descriptions

The technical descriptions are thorough—offering all of the information needed to evaluate and compare the timepieces. In each case, we provide the movement information and functions of the watch, and list the aesthetic details, including case size, diameter and height, dial base and finish, and bracelet descriptions. Additionally, where other models or versions are available, we have so noted.

For watch movements that have been built upon a base caliber, we have indicated the base caliber wherever possible. In these instances, we attempt to indicate the difference between the caliber and the execution mounted on the watch shown therein—differences that are technical—functional rather than those that are based on decoration and further hand finishing.

(Gerd-R. Lang, master watchmaker and founder of Chronoswiss, with his daughter Natalie, an apprentice watchmaker)

CHRONOSWISS

Faszination der Mechanik

Chronoscope

"My watches are symbols of time." They bridge the gap between the past and the present and have been created for the future. It's wonderful for me to be accompanied on my journey through time by a person who shares my enthusiasm for this ageless handicraft. Rather than jumping on the bandwagon of short-lived trends, we prefer to progress together through the classical tradition of bygone days. You can learn more about our visions in "Signs of the Times."

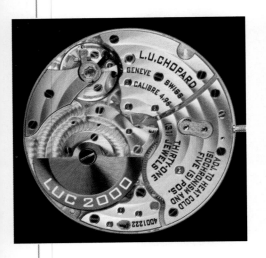

Movements

This year, too, *Watches International 2003* offers an in-depth look at the nuances of different movement types. Outlined in these pages are multi-complication watches, including tourbillons, perpetual calendars, minute repeaters, equations of time, and jump hours. Movements with invaluable functions such as alarms, GMT readouts and split-second chronograph timers are covered, as are movements with multiple indications, including dual- and triple-time-zone readouts, tachometer readings and dive watches. Beginning on page 84, these 22 pages detail the complexities of various functions and indications built into the world's finest watches.

Glossary

A glossary of terms has been included in *Watches International 2003* to make the reading more enjoyable and informative. We have made every effort to ensure technical accuracy, while offering layman's terminology. The glossary includes 17 pages of watch-related entries, beginning on page 64.

Photography

When photographing the watches depicted in the Technical sections of the book, the staff of *Watches International 2003* took great care to capture the details. Each timepiece was placed on the same background, and each photograph was taken from the same angle under the same lighting to assure unbiased presentation and consistency. Unless noted, the proportions between one watch and another have been maintained, enabling readers to make their own comparisons between different models.

Babylone

Genève

Babylone

Distribution by Sam Gabbas
Tel: +33 6 16 02 22 71 or +41 79 304 37 47

REGROUPING

The luxury holding companies play a vital role in perpetuating the growth of some of the finest brands in the world. The following is a comprehensive list (as of spring 2003) of the brands owned by each of the premier groups.

GUCCI GROUP

Bedat & Co (acquired 2000)
Boucheron (acquired 2000)
Gucci (acquired 1977)
Yves Saint Laurent (acquired 1999)

LVMH GROUP

Chaumet (acquired 1999)
Christian Dior(acquired 1999)
Ebel (acquired 1999)
Fred (acquired 1999)
Omas (acquired 2001)
TAG Heuer (acquired 1999)
Zenith (acquired 1999)

MOVADO GROUP

Coach
(launched 1998 as result of exclusive licensing agreement)
Concord (acquired 1970)
ESQ (launched 1992)
Movado(acquired 1983)
Tommy Hilfiger
(launched 2001 as result of exclusive licensing agreement)

THE RICHEMONT GROUP

A. Lange & Söhne (acquired 2000)
Baume & Mercier (acquired 1988)
Cartier (fully acquired between 1972 and 1974)
Dunhill (acquired 1989)
IWC (acquired 2000)
Jaeger-LeCoultre (acquired 2000)
Montblanc (acquired 1989)
Panerai (acquired 1997)
Piaget (acquired 1988)
Vacheron Constantin (acquired 1996)
Van Cleef & Arpels (acquired 1999)

THE SWATCH GROUP

Blancpain (acquired 2000)
Breguet (acquired 1999)
cK Watch (founded 1997)
Certina (acquired 1983)
FlikFlak (launched by SMH Group in 1987)
Glashütte (acquired 2000)
Hamilton (existed under original SSIH organization)
Jacquet-Droz (acquired 2000)
Leon Hatot (acquired 1999)
Longines (existed under original ASUAG organizatio
Mido (existed in formation of Swatch Group)
Omega (existed under original SSIH organization)
Pierre Balmain (acquired exclusive license in 1987)
Rado (existed under original ASUAG organization)
Swatch (launched by SMH Group in 1982)
Tissot (existed under original SSIH organization)

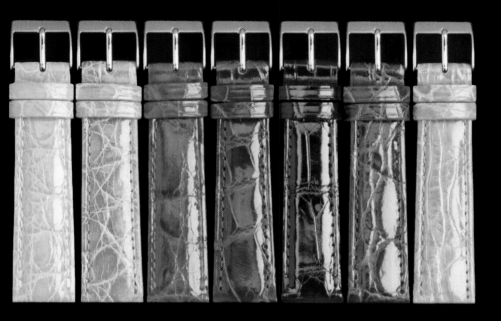

The Bands Your Watch Deserves

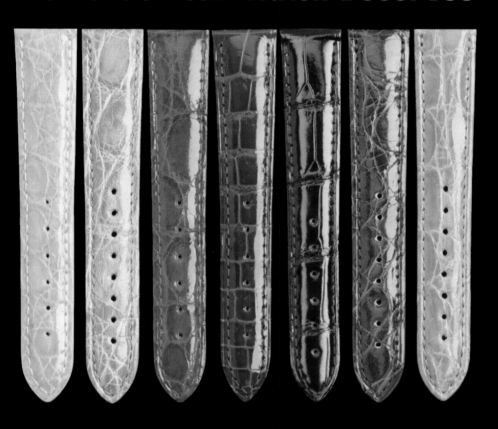

the Frenchway travel

we do it ... with passion

thanks to our clients for believing in the frenchway travel for seventeen years

AZZEDINE ALAIA • ALLEGRA MAGAZINE • AMICA MAGAZINE • ART DEPARTMENT • ART PARTNER • ART PRODUCTION • ENRIQUE BADULESCU • STEPHEN BALDWIN • BRADLEY CURRY MANAGEMENT • BRIAN HOWARD PROD • BW PUBLICATIONS • CALYPSO • CARLYN CERF • JUDY CASEY • CITY MODELS • COMPANY MODELS • ELYSE CONNOLLY • COSMOPOLITAN (GERMANY) • PATRICK DEMARCHELIER • DNA MODELS • ELLE (GERMANY) • ELLE (ITALY) • FINANCO • FRAME • FRANCOIS HALARD • STEPHEN GAN • HAMID BECHERI • HARPER'S BAZAAR • MARC HISPARD • IZAK • RITA JAEGER • VERNON JOLLY • CHRISTOPHE JOUANY • KARIN MODELS • TCHEKY KARYO • JEAN GABRIEL KAUSS • LA PAC • DAVID LACHAPELLE • LAZARD FRERES • LE BOOK • CHRISTIAN LOUBOUTIN • MADISON MODELS • MARIE CLAIRE (FRANCE) • MARILYN MODELS • MEGA MODELS • JULIAN MEIJER PRODUCTIONS • LAURA MERCIER • MODEL TEAM • NEXT MANAGEMENT • SERGE NORMANT • NOVA MODELS • OPRAH MAGAZINE • PAULINE AGENCY • RESERVOIR PROD • SATOSHI SAIKUSA • JULIAN SCHNABEL • SCOR INSURANCE • PEGGY SIROTA • VINCENT PEREZ • MIRA SORVINO • STREETERS • SUCCESS TAPESTRY • THE AGENCY • MARIO TESTINO • VAN KASPER & CO • ANTOINE VERGLAS • VISION MODELS • VISIONNAIRE • VIVA MODELS • VOGUE (FRANCE) • DIANE VON FURSTENBERG • WHY NOT • WOMEN MODELS • CAROLINE CHILDERS

11 west 25 street 8th floor • NEW YORK • N.Y. 10010
Tel: 212 243 35 00 Fax: 212 243 35 35.

www.FrenchwayTravel.com

Glossary

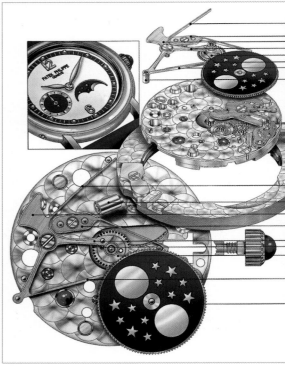

ALARM WATCH
A watch provided with a movement capable of releasing an acoustic sound at the time set. A second crown is dedicated to the winding, setting and release of the striking-work; an additional center hand indicates the time set. The section of the movement dedicated to the alarm device is made up by a series of wheels linked with the barrel, an escapement and a hammer (s.) striking a gong (s.) or bell (s.). Works much like a normal alarm clock.

ANALOG or ANALOGUE
A watch displaying time indications by means of hands.

ANTIMAGNETIC
Said of a watch whose movement is not influenced by electromagnetic fields that could cause two or more windings of the balance-spring to stick to each other, consequently accelerating the rate of the watch. This effect is obtained by adopting metal alloys (e.g. Nivarox) resisting magnetization.

ANTIREFLECTION, ANTIREFLECTIVE
Superficial glass treatment assuring the dispersion of reflected light. Better results are obtained if both sides are treated, but in order to avoid scratches on the upper layer, the treatment of the inner surface is preferred.

ARBOR
Bearing element of a gear (s.) or balance, whose ends—called pivots (s.)—run in jewel (s.) holes or brass bushings.

AUTOMATIC
A watch whose mechanical movement (s.) is wound automatically. A rotor makes short oscillations due to the movements of the wrist. Through a series of gears, oscillations transmit motion to the barrel (s.), thus winding the mainspring progressively.

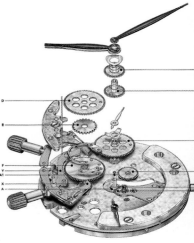

AUTOMATON
Figures, placed on the dial or case of watches, provided with parts of the body or other elements moving at the same time as the sonnerie (s.) strikes. The moving parts are linked, through an aperture on the dial or caseback, with the sonnerie hammers (s.) striking a gong.

BALANCE
Oscillating device that, together with the balance spring (s.), makes up the movement's heart inasmuch as its oscillations determine the frequency of its functioning and precision.

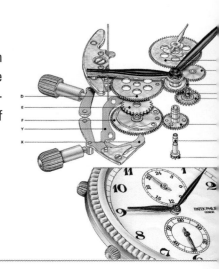

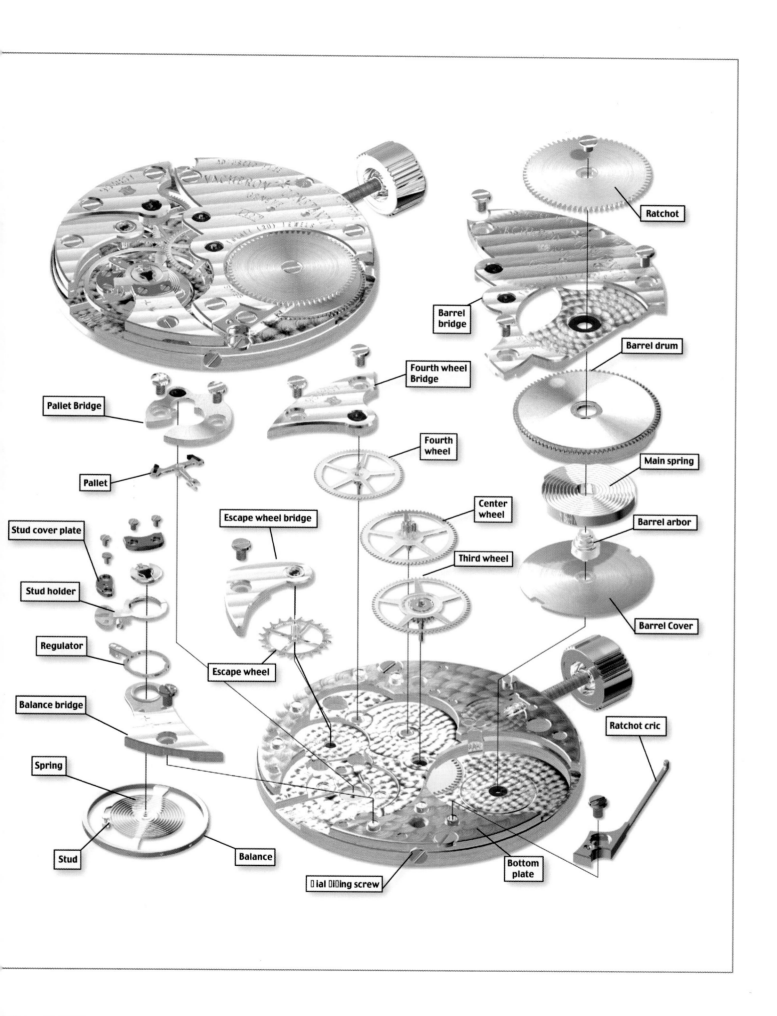

Ratchot

Barrel bridge

Barrel drum

Fourth wheel Bridge

Pallet Bridge

Fourth wheel

Main spring

Pallet

Center wheel

Barrel arbor

Stud cover plate

Escape wheel bridge

Third wheel

Stud holder

Barrel Cover

Regulator

Escape wheel

Balance bridge

Ratchot cric

Spring

Stud

Balance

Dial fiiling screw

Bottom plate

BALANCE SPRING

Component of the regulating organ (s.) that, together with the balance (s.), determines the movement's precision. The material used is mostly a steel alloy (e.g. Nivarox, s.), an extremely stable metal compound. In order to prevent the system's center of gravity from continuous shifts, hence differences in rate due to the watch's position, some modifications were adopted. These modifications included Breguet's overcoil (closing the terminal part of the spring partly on itself, so as to assure an almost perfect centering) and Philips curve (helping to eliminate the lateral pressure of the balance-staff pivots against their bearings). Today, thanks to the quality of materials, it is possible to assure an excellent precision of movement working even with a flat spring.

BARREL

Component of the movement containing the mainspring (s.), whose toothed rim meshes with the pinion of the first gear of the train (s.). Due to the fact that the whole—made up of barrel and mainspring—transmits the motive force, it is also considered to be the very motor. Inside the barrel, the mainspring is wound around an arbor (s.) turned by the winding crown or, in the case of automatic movements, also by the gear powered by the rotor (s.).

BEVELING

Chamfering of edges of levers, bridges and other elements of a movement by 45∞, a treatment typically found in high-grade movements.

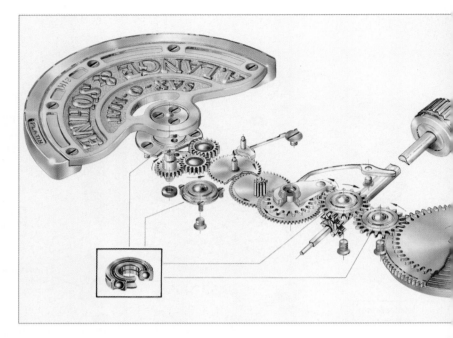

BEZEL

Top part of case (s.), sometimes holds the crystal. It may be integrated with the case middle (s.) or a separate element. It is snapped or screwed on to the middle.

BRACELET

A metal band attached to the case. It is called integral if there is no apparent discontinuity between case and bracelet and the profile of attachments is similar to the first link.

BRIDGE

Structural metal element of a movement (s.)—sometimes called cock or bar—supporting the wheel train (s.), balance (s.), escapement (s.) and barrel (s.). Each bridge is fastened to the plate (s.) by means of screws and locked in a specific position by pins. In high-quality movements the sight surface is finished with various types of decoration.

BRUSHED, BRUSHING
Topical finishing giving metals a line finish, a clean and uniform look.

CABOCHON
Any kind of precious stone, such as sapphire, ruby or emerald, uncut and only polished, generally of a half-spherical shape, mainly used as an ornament of the winding crown (s.) or certain elements of the case.

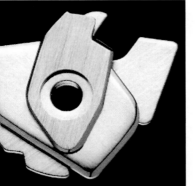

CALENDAR, ANNUAL
An intermediate complication between a simple calendar and a perpetual calendar. This feature displays all the months with 30 or 31 days correctly, but needs a manual correction at the end of February. Generally, date, day of the week and month, or only day and month are displayed on the dial.

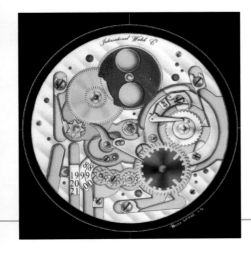

CALENDAR, FULL
Displaying date, day of the week and month on the dial, but needing a manual correction at the end of a month with less than 31 days. It is often combined with the moonphase (s).

CALENDAR, PERPETUAL
This is the most complex horology complication related to the calendar feature, as it indicates the date, day, month and leap year and does not need manual corrections until the year 2100 (when the leap year will be ignored).

CALIBER
Originally it indicated only the size of a movement (s.), but now this indication defines a specific movement type and shape (e.g. round caliber) and combines it with the constructor's name and identification number. Therefore the caliber identifies the movement.

CARRIAGE or TOURBILLON CARRIAGE
Rotating frame of a tourbillon (s.) device, carrying the balance and escapement (s.). This structural element is essential for a perfect balance of the whole system and its stability, in spite of its reduced weight. As today's tourbillon carriages make a rotation per minute, errors of rate in the vertical position are eliminated. Because of the widespread use of transparent dials, carriages became elements of aesthetic attractiveness.

CASE
Container housing and protecting the movement (s.), usually made up of three parts: middle, bezel, and back.

CENTER SECOND HAND, s.
Sweep second hand.

CHAMPLEVÉ

Hand-made treatment of the dial or case surface. The pattern is obtained by hollowing a metal sheet with a graver and subsequently filling the hollows with enamel.

CHRONOGRAPH

A watch that includes a built-in stopwatch function, i.e. a timer that can be started and stopped to time an event. There are many variations of the chronograph.

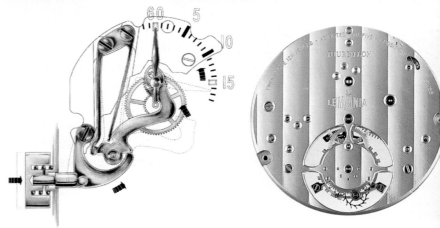

CHRONOMETER

A high-precision watch. According to the Swiss law, a manufacture may put the word "chronometer" on a model only after each individual piece has passed a series of tests and obtained a running bulletin and a chronometer certificate by an acknowledged Swiss control authority, such as the COSC (s.).

CIRCULAR GRAINING

Superficial decoration applied to bridges, rotors and pillar-plates in the shape of numerous slightly superposed small grains, obtained by using a plain cutter and abrasives. Also called Pearlage or Pearling.

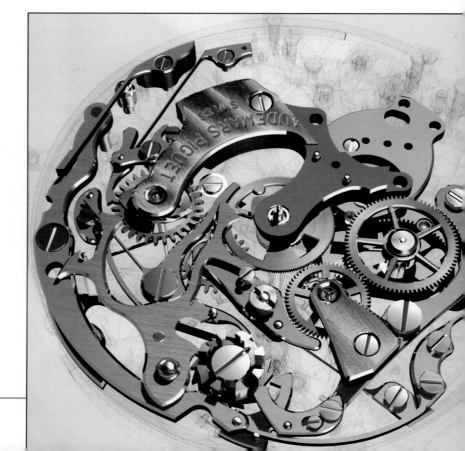

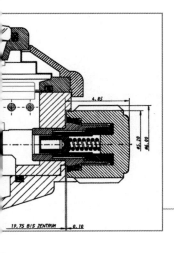

CLOISONNÉ
A kind of enamel work— mainly used for the decoration of dials—in which the outlines of the drawing are formed by thin metal wires. The colored enamel fills the hollows formed in this way. After oven firing, the surface is smoothed until the gold threads appear again.

CLOUS DE PARIS
Decoration of metal parts characterized by numerous small pyramids.

COCK, s. Bridge.

COLIMAÇONNAGE, s. Snailing.

COLUMN-WHEEL
Part of chronograph movements, governing the functions of various levers and parts of the chronograph operation, in the shape of a small-toothed steel cylinder. It is controlled by pushers through levers that hold and release it. It is a very precise and usually preferred type of chronograph operation.

COMPLICATION
Additional function with respect to the manual-winding basic movement for the display of hours, minutes and seconds. Today, certain features, such as automatic winding or date, are taken for granted, although they should be defined as complications. The main complications are moon-

phase (s.), power reserve (s.), GMT (s.), and full calendar (s.). Further functions are performed by the so-called great complications, such as split-second (s.) chronograph, perpetual calendar (s.), tourbilon (s.) device, and minute repeater (s.).

CORRECTOR
Pusher (s.) positioned on the case side that is normally actuated by a special tool for the quick setting of different indications, such as date, GMT (s.), full or perpetual calendar (s.).

COSC
Abbreviation of "Contrôle Officiel Suisse des Chronomètres," the most important Swiss institution responsible for the functioning and precision tests of movements of chronometers (s.). Tests are performed on each individual watch at different temperatures and in different positions before a functioning bulletin and a chronometer certificate are issued, for which a maximum gap of -4/+4 seconds per day is tolerated.

CÔTES CIRCULAIRES
Decoration of rotors and bridges of movements, whose pattern consists of a series of concentric ribs.

CÔTES DE GENÈVE
Decoration applied mainly to high-quality movements, appearing as a series of parallel ribs, realized by repeated cuts of a cutter leaving thin stripes.

COUNTER

Additional hand on a chronograph (s.), indicating the time elapsed since the beginning of the measuring. On modern watches the second counter is placed at the center, while minute and hour counters have off-center hands in special zones (s.), also called subdials.

CROWN

Usually positioned on the case middle (s.) and allows winding, hand setting and often date or GMT hand setting. As it is linked to the movement through the winding stem (s.) passing through a hole in the case. For waterproofing purposes, simple gaskets are used in water-resistant watches, while diving watches adopt screwing systems (screw-down crowns).

DIAL

Face of a watch, on which time and further functions are displayed by markers (s.), hands (s.), discs or through windows (s.). Normally it is made of a brass—sometimes silver or gold.

DIGITAL

Said of watches whose indications are displayed mostly inside an aperture or window (s.) on the dial.

ENDSTONE

Undrilled jewel, placed on the balance jewel with the tip of the balance-staff pivot resting against its flat surface, to reduce pivot friction. Sometimes used also for pallet staffs and escape wheels.

ENGINE-TURNED, s. Guilloché.

EQUATION OF TIME

Indication of the difference, expressed in minutes, between conventional mean time and real solar time. This difference varies from -16 to +16 seconds between one day and the other.

ESCAPEMENT

Positioned between the train (s.) and the balance wheel and governing the rotation speed of the wheel-train wheels. In today's horology the most widespread escapement type is the lever escapement. In the past, numerous types of escapements were realized, such as: verge, cylinder, pin-pallet, detent and duplex escapements. Recently, George Daniels developed a so-called "coaxial" escapement.

FLINQUÉ

Engraving on the dial or case of a watch, covered with an enamel layer.

FLUTED

Said of surfaces worked with thin parallel grooves, mostly on dials or case bezels.

FLY-BACK

Feature combined with chronograph (s.) functions, that allows a new measurement starting from zero (and interrupting a measuring already under way) by pressing down a single pusher, i.e. without stopping, zeroing and restarting the whole mechanism. Originally, this function was developed to meet the needs of air forces.

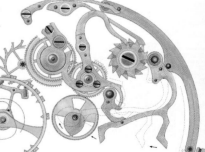

FOLD-OVER CLASP

Hinged and jointed element, normally of the same material as the one used for the case. It allows easy fastening of the bracelet on the wrist. Often provided with a snap-in locking device, sometimes with an additional clip or push-piece.

FREQUENCY, s. Vibration

Generally defined as the number of cycles per time unit; in horology it is the number of oscillations of a balance every two seconds or of its vibrations per second. For practical purposes, frequency is expressed in vibrations per hour (vph).

GENEVA SEAL, s. Poinçon de Genève.

GLUCYDUR

Bronze and beryllium alloy used for high-quality balances (s.). This alloy assures high elasticity and hardness values; it is non-magnetic, rustproof and has a very reduced dilatation coefficient, which makes the balance very stable and assures high accuracy of the movement.

GMT

Abbreviation for Greenwich Mean Time. As a feature of watches, it means that two or more time zones are displayed. In this case, the second time may be read from a hand making a full rotation in a 24-hour ring (thereby also indicating whether it is a.m. or p.m. in that zone).

GONG

Harmonic flattened bell in a steel alloy, generally positioned along the circumference of the movement and struck by hammers (s.) to indicate time by sounds. Size and thickness determine the resulting note and tone. In watches provided with minute-repeaters (s.), there are often two gongs and the hammers strike one note to indicate hours, both notes together to indicate quarters and the other note for the remaining minutes. In more complex models, equipped also with en-passant sonnerie (s.) devices, there may be up to four gongs producing different notes and playing even simple melodies (such as the chime of London's Big Ben).

GUILLOCHÉ

Decoration of dials, rotors or case parts consisting of patterns made by hand or engine-turned. By the thin pattern of the resulting engravings—consisting of crossing or interlaced lines—it is possible to realize even complex drawings. Dials and rotors decorated in this way are generally in gold or in solid silver.

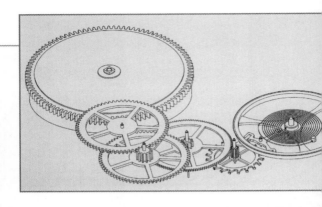

HAMMER
Steel or brass element used in movements provided with a repeater or alarm sonnerie (s.). It strikes a gong (s.) or bell (s.).

HAND
Indicator for the analogue visualization of hours, minutes and seconds as well as other functions. Normally made of brass (rhodium-plated, gilded or treated otherwise), but also steel or gold. Hands are available in different shapes and take part in the aesthetic result of the whole watch.

HEART-PIECE
Heart-shaped cam (s.) generally used to realign the hands of chronograph counters.

HELIUM VALVE
Valve inserted in the case of some professional diving watches to discharge the helium contained in the air mixture inhaled by divers.

HEXALITE
An artificial glass made of a plastic resin.

INCABLOC, s. Shockproof.

JEWEL
Precious stone used in movements as a bearing surface. Generally speaking, the steel pivots (s.) of wheels in movements turn inside synthetic jewels (mostly rubies) lubricated with a drop of oil. The jewel's hardness reduces wear to a minimum even over long periods of time (50 to 100 years). The quality of watches is determined mainly by the shape and finishing of jewels rather than by their number (the most refined jewels have rounded holes and walls to greatly reduce the contact between pivot and stone).

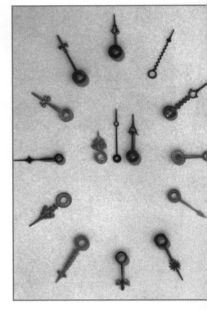

JUMPING HOUR
Feature concerning the digital display of time in a window. The indication changes almost instantaneously at every hour.

LINE
Ancient French measuring unit maintained in horology to indicate the diameter of a movement (s.). A line (expressed by the symbol ''') equals 2.255mm. Lines are not divided into decimals; therefore, to indicate measures inferior to the unit, fractions are used (e.g. movements of 13'''3/4 or 10'''1/2).

LUBRICATION
To reduce friction caused by the running of wheels and other parts. There are points to be lubricated with specific low-density oils such as the pivots (s.) turning inside jewels (s.), the sliding areas between levers, and the spring inside the barrel (requiring a special grease), as well as numerous other parts of a movement.

LUG
Double extension of the case middle (s.) by which a strap or bracelet is attached. Normally, straps and bracelets are attached with removable spring bars.

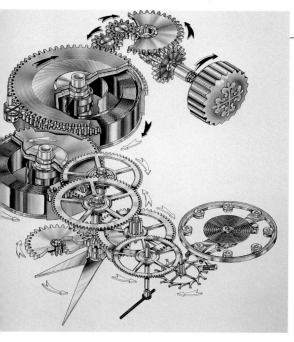

LUMINESCENT
Said of materials applied on markers (s.) and/or hands (s.), emitting the luminous energy previously absorbed as electromagnetic light rays. Tritium is no longer used and was replaced by other substances having the same emitting powers, but with virtually zero radioactivity, such as Super-LumiNova and Lumibrite.

MAINSPRING
This and the barrel (s.) make up the driving element of a movement (s.). It stores and transmits the power force needed for its functioning.

MANUAL
A mechanical movement (v.) in which winding is performed by hand. The motion transmitted from the user's fingers to the crown is forwarded to the movement through the winding stem (s.), from this to the barrel (s.) through a series of gears (s.) and finally to the mainspring (s.).

MARKERS
Elements printed or applied on the dial, sometimes they are luminescent (s.), used as reference points for the hands to indicate hours and fifteen- or five-minute intervals.

MICROMETER SCREW
Element positioned on the regulator, allowing to shift it by minimal and perfectly gauged ranges so as to obtain accurate regulations of the movement.

MICRO-ROTOR, s. Rotor.

MINUTE REPEATER, s. Repeater.

MODULE
Self-contained mechanism, independent of the basic caliber (s.), added to the movement (s.) to make an additional function available: chronograph (s.), power reserve (s.), GMT (s.), perpetual or full calendar (s).

MOONPHASE
A function available in many watches, usually combined with calendar-related features. The moonphase disc advances one tooth every 24 hours. Normally, this wheel has 59 teeth and assures an almost perfect synchronization with the lunation period, i.e. 29.53 days (in fact, the disc shows the moonphases twice during a single revolution). However, the difference of 0.03 days, i.e. 44 minutes each month, implies the need for a manual adjustment every two and a half years to recover one day lost with respect to the real state of moonphase. In some rare case, the transmission ratio between the gears controlling the moonphase are calculated with extreme accuracy so as to require manual correction only once in 100 years.

MOVEMENT

The entire mechanism of a watch. Movements are divided into two great families: quartz and mechanical; the latter are available with manual (s.) or automatic (s.) winding devices.

NIVAROX

Trade name (from the producer's name) of a steel alloy, resisting magnetization, used for modern self-compensating balance springs (s.). The quality level of this material is indicated by the numeral following the name in decreasing value from 1 to 5.

OSCILLATION

Complete oscillation or rotation movement of the balance (s.), formed by two vibrations (s.).

PALLETS

Device of the escapement (s.) transmitting part of the motive force to the balance (s.), in order to maintain the amplitude of oscillations unchanged by freeing a tooth of the escape wheel at one time.

PILLAR-PLATE OR MAIN PLATE

Supporting element of bridges (s.) and other parts of a movement (s).

PINION

Combines with a wheel and an arbor (s.) to form a gear (s.). A pinion has less teeth than a wheel and transmits motive force to a wheel. Pinion teeth (normally 6 to 14) are highly polished to reduce friction to a minimum.

PIVOT

End of an arbor (s.) turning on a jewel (s.) support. As their shape and size can influence friction, the pivots of the balance-staff are particularly thin and, hence, fragile, so they are protected by a shockproof (s.) system.

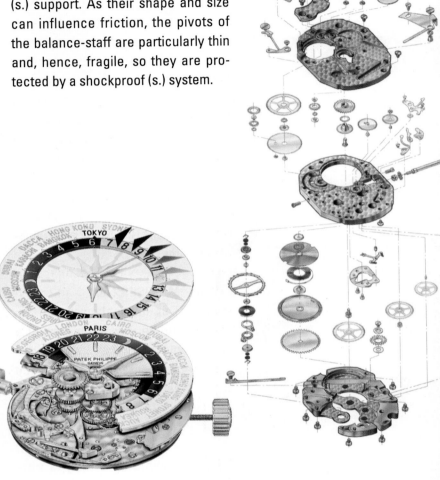

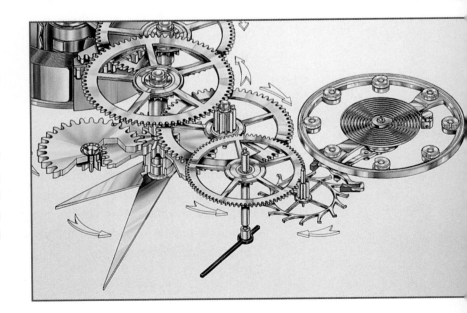

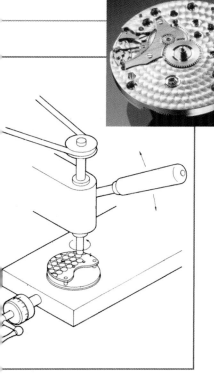

PLATED

Said of a metal treated by a galvanizing procedure in order to apply a slight layer of gold or another precious metal (silver, chromium, rhodium or palladium) on a brass or steel base.

PLEXIGLAS

A synthetic resin used for watch crystal.

POINÇON DE GENÈVE

Distinction assigned by the Canton of Geneva to movements produced by watchmaker firms of the Region and complying with all the standards of high horology with respect to craftsmanship, small-scale production, working quality, accurate assembly and setting. The Geneva Seal is engraved on at least one bridge and shows the Canton's symbol, i.e. a two-field shield with an eagle and a key respectively in each field.

POWER RESERVE

Duration (in hours) of the residual functioning autonomy of a movement after it has reached the winding peak. The duration value is displayed by an instantaneous indicator: analog (hand on a sector) or digital (through a window). The related mechanism is

made up of a series of gears linking the winding barrel and hand. Recently, specific modules were introduced which may be combined with the most popular movements.

PULSIMETER CHRONOGRAPH

The pulsimeter scale shows, at a glance, the number of pulse beats per minute. The observer releases the chronograph hand when starting to count the beats and stops at the 30th, the 20th or the 15th beat according to the basis of calibration indicated on the dial.

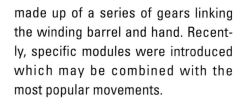

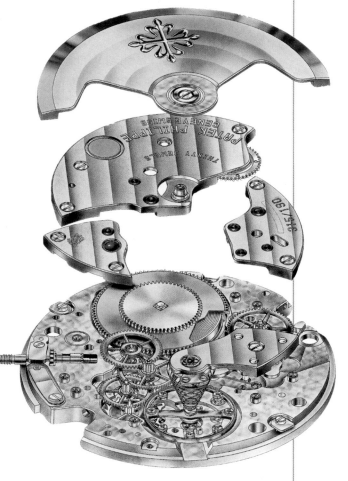

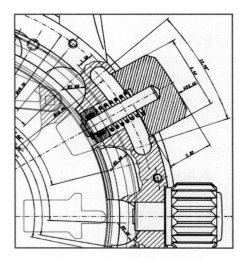

PUSHER, PUSH-PIECE or PUSH-BUTTON

Mechanical element mounted on a case (s.) for the control of specific functions. Generally, pushers are used in chronographs (s.), but also with other functions.

PVD

Abbreviation of Physical Vapor Deposition, a plating process consisting of the physical transfer of substance by bombardment of electrons.

REGULATING UNIT

Made up by balance (s.) and balance spring (s.), governing the division of time within the mechanical movement, assuring its regular running and accuracy. As the balance works like a pendulum, the balance spring's function consists of its elastic return and starting of a new oscillation. This combined action determines the frequency, i.e. the number of vibrations per hour, and affects the rotation speed of the different wheels. In fact the balance, by its oscillations, at every vibration (through the action of the pallets), frees a tooth of the escape wheel (s. Escapement). From this, motion is transmitted to the fourth wheel, which makes a revolution in one minute, to the

third and then the center wheel, the latter making a full rotation in one hour. However, everything is determined by the correct time interval of the oscillations of the balance.

REGULATOR

Regulating the functioning of a movement by lengthening and shortening the active section of the balance spring (s.). It is positioned on the balance-bridge and encompasses the balance spring with its two pins near its fixing point on the bridge itself. By shifting the index, the pins also are moved and, by consequence, the portion of the balance spring capable of bringing the balance back is lengthened or shortened by its elastic force. The shorter it is, the more reactive it tends to be and the more rapidly it brings the balance back and makes the movement run faster. The contrary happens when the active portion of the balance spring is lengthened. Given today's high frequencies of functioning, even slight index shifts entail daily variations of minutes. Recently, even more refined index-regulation sys-

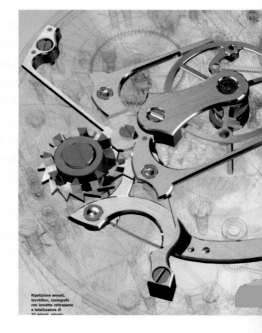

Ripetizione minuti, tourbillon, cronografo con lancetta rattrapante e totalizzatore di 30 minuti, piccola

tems were adopted (from eccentric (s.) to micrometer screws (s.)) to limit error margins to very few seconds per day.

REPEATER

Mechanism indicating time by acoustic sounds. Contrary to the watches provided with en-passant sonnerie (s.) devices, that strike the number of hours automatically, repeaters work on demand by actuating a slide (s.) or pusher (s.) positioned on the case side. Repeaters are normally provided with two hammers and two gongs: one gong for the minutes and one for the hours. The quarters are obtained by the almost simultaneous strike of both hammers. The mechanism of the striking work is among the most complex complications.

RETROGRADE

Said of a hand (s.) that, instead of making a revolution of 360∞ before starting a new measurement, moves on an arc scale (generally of 90∞ to 180∞) and at the end of its trip comes back instantaneously. Normally, retrograde hands are used to indicate date, day or month in perpetual calendars, but there are also cases of retrograde hours, minutes or seconds. Unlike the case of the classical indication over 360∞, the retrograde system requires a special mechanism to be inserted into the basic movement.

ROTOR

In automatic-winding mechanical movements the rotor is the part that, by its complete or partial revolutions and the movements of human arm, allows winding of the mainspring (s.).

SCALE

Graduation on a measuring instrument, showing the divisions of a whole of values, especially on a dial, bezel. The scales mostly used in horology are related to the following measuring devices: tachometer (s.) (indicating the average speed), telemeter (s.) (indicating the distance of a simultaneously luminous and acoustic source, e.g. a cannon-shot or a thunder and related lightning), pulsometer (to calculate the total number of heartbeats per minute by counting only a certain quantity of them). For all of these scales, measuring starts at the beginning of the event concerned and stops at its end; the reading refers directly to the chronograph second hand, without requiring further calculations.

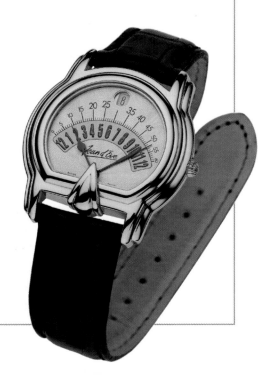

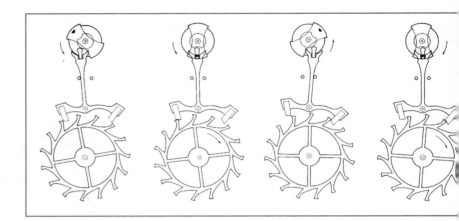

SECOND TIME-ZONE INDICATOR, s.
GMT and World Time.

SECTOR, s. Rotor.

SELF-WINDING, s. Automatic.

SHOCKPROOF or SHOCK-RESISTANT
Watches provided with shock-absorber systems (e.g. Incabloc) help prevent damage from shocks to the balance pivots. Thanks to a retaining spring system, it assures an elastic play of both jewels, thus absorbing the movements of the balance-staff pivots when the watch receives strong shocks. The return to the previous position is due to the return effect of the spring. If such a system is lacking, the shock forces exert an impact on the balance-staff pivots, often causing bending or even breakage.

SKELETON, SKELETONIZED
Watches whose bridges and pillar-plates are cut out in a decorative manner, thus revealing all the parts of the movement.

SLIDE
Part of a mechanism moving with friction on a slide-bar or guide.

SMALL SECOND
Time display in which the second hand is placed in a small subdial.

SNAILING
Decoration with a spiral pattern, mainly used on the barrel wheel or on big-sized full wheels.

SONNERIE (EN PASSANT)
Function consisting of an acoustic sound, obtained by a striking work made up of two hammers (s.) striking gongs (s.) at set hours, quarter- and half-hours. Some devices can emit a chime (with three or even four hammers and gongs). By a slide (s.) or an additional pusher (s.) it is possible to exclude the sonnerie device and to select a so-called grande sonnerie.

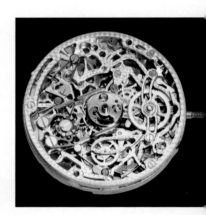

SPLIT-SECOND CHRONOGRAPH
Chronographs with split-second mechanisms are particularly useful for timing simultaneous phenomena which begin at the same time, but end at different times, such as sporting events in which several competitors are taking part. In chronographs of this type, an additional hand is superimposed on the chronograph hand. Pressure on the pusher starts both hands, which remain superimposed as long as the split-second mechanism is not blocked. This is achieved when the split-second hand is stopped while the chronograph hand continues to move. After recording, the same pusher is pressed a second time, releasing the split-second hand, which instantly joins the still-moving chronograph hand, synchronizing with it, and is thus ready for another recording. Pressure on the return pusher brings

the hands back to zero simultaneously, provided the split-second hand is not blocked. Pressure on the split pusher releases the split-second hand, which instantly joins the chronograph hand if the split-second hand happens to be blocked.

STAFF or STEM, s. Arbor.

STRIKING WORK, s. Sonnerie and Repeater.

SUBDIAL, s. Zone.

SUPER-LUMINOVA, s. Luminescent.

SWEEP SECOND HAND
A center second hand, i.e. a second hand mounted on the center of the main dial.

TACHOMETER or TACHYMETER
Function measuring the speed at which the wearer runs over a given distance. The tachometer scale is calibrated to show the speed of a moving object, such as a vehicle, over a known distance. The standard length on which the calibration is based is always shown on the dial, e.g. 1,000, 200 or 100 meters, or—in some cases—one mile. As the moving vehicle, for instance, passes the starting-point of the measured course whose length corresponds to that used as the basis of calibration, the observer releases the chronograph hand and stops it as the vehicle passes the finishing point. The figure indicated by the hand on the

tachometer scale represents the speed in kilometers or miles per hour.

TELEMETER
By means of the telemeter scale, it is possible to measure the distance of a phenomenon that is both visible and audible. The chronograph hand is released at the instant the phenomenon is seen; it is stopped when the sound is heard, and its position on the scale shows, at a glance, the distance in kilometers or miles separating the phenomenon from the observer. Calibration is based upon the speed at which sound travels through the air, viz. approximately 340 meters or 1,115 feet per second. During a thunderstorm, the time that has elapsed between the flash of lightning and the sound of the thunder is registered on the chronograph scale.

TONNEAU
Particular shape of a watchcase, imitating the profile of a barrel, i.e. with straight, shorter, horizontal sides and curved, longer, vertical sides.

TOURBILLON
Device invented in 1801 by A. L. Breguet. This function equalizes position errors due to changing positions of a watch and related effects of gravity. Balance, balance spring and escapement are housed inside a carriage (s.), also called a cage, rotating by one revolution per minute, thus compensating for all the possible errors over 360∞. Although this device is not absolutely necessary for accuracy purposes today, it is still appreciated as a complication of high-quality watches.

VIBRATION

Movement of a pendulum or other oscillating bodies, limited by two consecutive extreme positions. In an alternate (pendulum or balance) movement, a vibration is a half of an oscillation (s.). The number of hourly vibrations corresponds to the frequency of a watch movement, determined by the mass and diameter of a balance (s.) and the elastic force of the balance spring. The number of vibrations per hour (vph) determines the breaking up of time (the "steps" of a second hand). For instance, 18,000 vph equals a vibration duration of 1/5 second; in the same way 21,600 vph = 1/6 second; 28,800 vph = 1/8 second; 36,000 vph = 1/10 second. Until the 1950s, wristwatches worked mostly at a frequency of 18,000 vph; later, higher frequencies were adopted to produce a lower percentage of irregularities to the rate. Today, the most common frequency adopted is 28,800 vph, which assures a good precision standard and less lubrication problems than extremely high frequencies, such as 36,000 vph.

WATER RESISTANT or WATERPROOF

A watch whose case (s.) is designed in such a way as to resist infiltration by water (3 atmospheres, corresponding to a conventional depth of 30 meters; 5 atmospheres, corresponding to a conventional depth of 50 meters.)

WHEEL

Circular element, mostly toothed, combines with an arbor (s.) and a pinion (s.) to make up a gear (s.). Wheels are normally made of brass, while arbors and pinions are made of steel. The wheels between barrel (s.) and escapement (s.) make up the so-called train (s.).

WINDING STEM

Element transmitting motion from the crown (s.) to the gears governing manual winding and setting.

WINDOW

Aperture in the dial, that allows reading the underlying indication, mainly the date, but also indications concerning a second zone's time or jumping hour (s.).

WORLD TIME

Additional feature of watches provided with a GMT (s.) function, displaying the 24 time zones on the dial or bezel, each zone referenced by a city name, providing instantaneous reading of the time of any country.

ZONE

Small additional dial or indicator that may be positioned, or placed off-center on the main dial, used for the display of various functions (e.g. second counters).

MULTICOMPLICATION WATCHES

Multipurpose watches—as a "summa" of watchmakers' art, the messages of their dials charged with significance—narrate the eternal struggle for supremacy in the world of time. Sophisticated complications are combined in different manners in dozens of models, all of which are produced in limited series (some are even one-of-a-kind pieces); and some are worthy of entering history. Highlighted are the tourbillon device; minute repeater; grande and petite "en passant" sonnerie; perpetual calendar; and chronograph (also in the split-seconds version). Horological complications, developed to equip the most important pocket watches of the past and today, are prime examples of Swiss watchmakers' precision and skill. To create these complications, they miniaturize hundreds of components within the extremely small diameter of a wristwatch and apply multiple data on dials measuring just a few square-centimeters. Such functions increase the value and prestige of the whole class.

"Great Complications" are watches that combine inside their movements: perpetual calendar; split-second chronograph; minute repeater; and the grande and petite "en passant" sonnerie. All others are defined as "watches with multiple indications."

■ **TOP**: dial part of the **Star Caliber 2000 by Patek Philippe**, a multipurpose pocket watch which ranks third in the world with its number of complications. Apart from numerous subdials, the drawing discloses the mechanism for sunrise- and sunset-time indications with two transparent segments representing the horizon in two blue tones for day and night.

■ **RIGHT**: Caliber RTO 27 PS by Patek Philippe with minute repeater and tourbillon device. A manual-winding movement with 48-hour autonomy, performing the hours, minutes, small second and minute repeater functions. As with all Patek Philippe movements, it uses a Gyromax balance, characterized by 8 regulating inertia-blocks, and avails itself of a tourbillon device with an antimagnetic carriage making one revolution in a minute. Hallmarked with the Geneva Seal, it features decorations of outstanding beauty: the pillar-plate is decorated with a circular graining pattern, the bridges with a concentric circles pattern; the latter are also beveled. The Calatrava cross, the House⫪s symbol, is skeletonized and gilded. This movement consists of approximately 400 parts, 84 of which belong just to the tourbillon device. This movement, combined with the 126 perpetual calendar module with retrograde date, becomes caliber RTO 27 PS-QR.

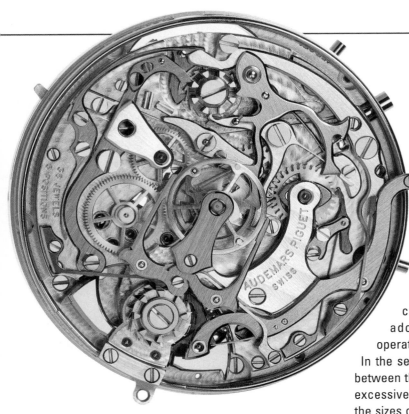

■ **ABOVE**: rear-side view (with the winding stem at 3:00) of the caliber used for the **Jules Audemars model by Audemars Piguet** (see photograph on right), an automatic movement provided with tourbillon, minute-repeater and split-second chronograph functions. This complex movement is not equal to the sum of the additional modules mounted on the basic movement, because to realize it, the watchmakers started from scratch by integrating the components in a homogeneous and harmonious whole. Shown in the center foreground are the complex levers of the split-second chronograph with its column-wheel at 7:00, aligned with the "clam" stopping and releasing the central wheel for the split-second feature; the levers of the minute repeater with its hammers (at 7:00 as well); and the annular gongs surrounding the circumference. The tourbillon is positioned on the dial side, where it is visible through an aperture. The gongs of the repeater are particularly accurate because the quality of sound depends on their precision. Each of their two elements is realized as a single piece: the thread (round section) and the block (square section). Thanks to this solution, vibrations, as the source of sound, are not diminished by the weldings performed; thus intensity is increased. The remarkable acoustic improvement is increased by the further transmission of vibrations to the case through a small tab connecting the block area and the case middle. Furthermore, to assure an absolutely constant sonnerie cadence, an "escapement" was developed that is provided with an inertial mass whose design regulates the amount of energy transmitted to the hammers when they are working by imposing upon them a constant rhythm. The minute-repeater mechanism supposes a strict coincidence of the number of strokes and the time indicated by the hands. Perfect harmony and reliability are continued during time setting or when actuating the repeater device. In the first case, mechanical safety systems were adopted to synchronize the time-setting operation with the working of cams and sonneries. In the second case, in order to avoid possible shifts between the sonnerie and the hands' display due to an excessively energetic pressure exerted on the slide, the sizes of some components were increased in such a way as to prevent them from bending. If, on the contrary, the slide is not moved along its whole trip, the risk of a gap occurring between the cams and hands is eliminated by the so-called "all-or-nothing device." The latter, normally cut off at the end of the actuation procedure, remains still and the system refuses winding of the sonnerie device. The movement (Ø 29.90mm, height 8.85mm) contains 474 pieces, 40 of which are jewels and 115 are screws. All of the components of brass alloy are rhodium plated, the steel parts are hand polished and beveled; bridges are decorated with a Côtes de Genève pattern; and the pillar-plate is decorated with a circular-graining pattern. The working autonomy covers a range of 48 hours. The tourbillon has a polished and beveled steel carriage (Ø 10.9mm), with polished escape wheel and pallets; balance with compensating screws; 21,600 vibrations/hour (3Hz) Breguet balance-spring.

■ **RIGHT: The IWC "Schaffhausen Steed" movement (cal. 1868).** In this dial-side view—between the original chronograph caliber (ETA/Valjoux 7760) and the classic IWC perpetual calendar module—are all of the components dedicated to the minute repeater. The radical modification of the rear part includes adopting a tourbillon device with a titanium carriage (at 1:00) and the spectacular closing bridge that integrates the device controlling the splitting function of the center chronograph seconds (clam at 7:00). In this case, the starting complex consists of the classic basic movement, chronograph, tourbillon, and repeater. The monetary value of a timepiece is based on the number of radical modifications of the basic elements (tourbillon, split-second chronograph, automata, and so on). The value applied to a watch depends on the information provided by the watch's module or modules. In addition to the work required to design, produce, finish, and decorate the micro-components by hand, a watchmaker must also devote himself to installing an incredible number of parts and to the very demanding final regulation testing that can be performed only by very few specialists in the world. The results of these operations also greatly increase a product's final value.

Equation of time

The time displayed by a watch is not the "real" time, which is dictated by the position of the sun. This is due to the fact that one mean time is used in each zone—but each zone can include a span of hundreds of miles east to west, thereby making it impossible for everyone in the zone to have the same perspective of the sun at any given moment. To know the exact time as indicated by the sun during its motion in the sky, among the different complications used in horology, the "Equation of time" feature must be employed. This function is expressed via an additional hand indicating the difference in minutes between conventional mean time and real time as indicated by the sun's motion instant by instant. The annual difference varies from -16 to +16 minutes. This complication is achieved on the dial by adding another hand, combined with a scale in minus or plus minutes with respect to civil time (visible on the drawing of the **Star Caliber 2000 movement by Patek Philippe** are the two coaxial-hands and the traditional watch's minute scale with its sixty division markers). The hand related to the Equation of time is moved by a bean-shaped cam, whose shape is specially gauged, and a taster transforming the oscillating motion from the bean-shaped cam directly into the indication of the hand on the dial. In order to make the cam turn, a cascade of gears borrows motion from the hour wheel and reduces it until it achieves one revolution per year. Also shown on the drawing of the Star Caliber 2000 are the two coaxial-hands on the dial; the taster lever usurping motion from the eccentric cam (under the toothed wheel on the left); and the device at the center that transforms the movement of the taster lever into a motion of the hand indicating the real sun-time with respect to the one related to conventional time during their respective daily revolutions.

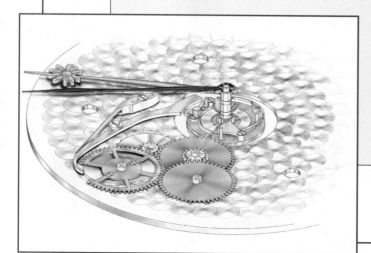

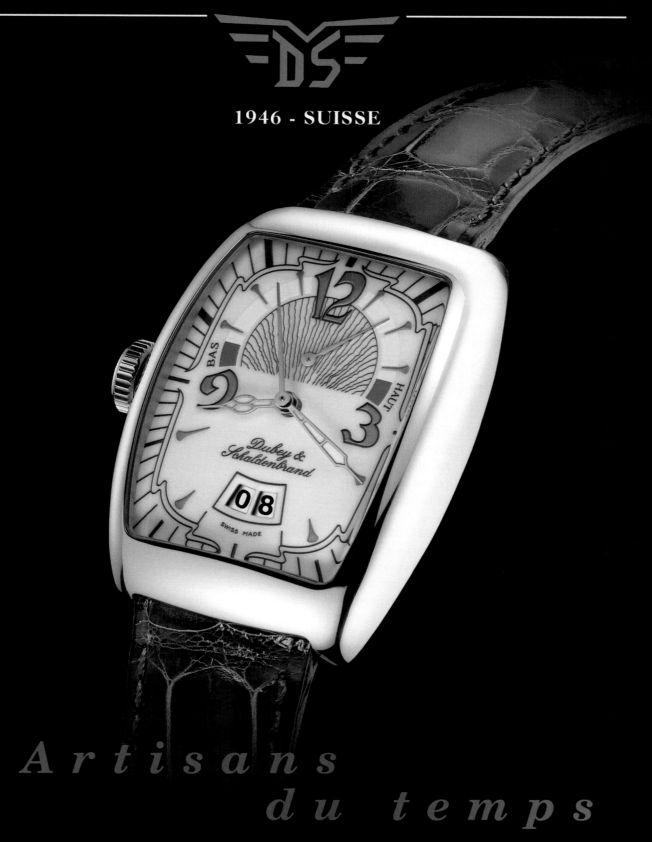

PERPETUAL CALENDAR

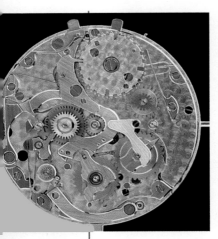

In 1795, Abraham-Louis Breguet claimed his patent for a Quantième Perpétuel, the first pocket watch that automatically registered the correct passage of the months with 28, 29, 30 or 31 days every four years according to the rules introduced by the Gregorian calendar in 1582. Far from being considered merely a virtuoso exercise, the watch provided with a perpetual calendar represents one of the most refined achievements of micro-mechanics. Even during the last decades it maintained its incorruptible fascination to the extent that, in spite of its high cost and the great deal of time required to design and set up its operations, many manufacturing firms exhibit one or more models, obeying definite market logic. On the one hand, there is a steady demand from the most tasteful clients less influenced by present economic recession, as well as from impatient members of the long waiting lists for other models. On the other hand, it is to be pointed out that, for a firm, presenting a Quantième Perpétuel means investing very much in terms of image.

Secular years are bisextile only if they are divisible by 400. In 2100 all perpetual calendars shall be manually advanced by one day, from the 28th of February to the 1st of March.

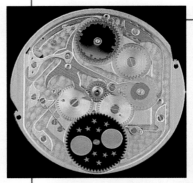

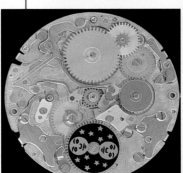

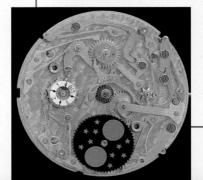

■ **TOP**: For some of its perpetual calendar watches, **Patek Philippe** uses the **caliber 240 Q**, automatic, with a 22-karat gold off-center micro-rotor, provided with a perpetual calendar module with: date, day, month, leap year, moonphase (4 fast correctors) and 24-hour display. Visible at 12:00 is the months' wheel that is coaxial with the 4-year cam; at 6:00, the star wheel for the date; at 9:00, the 24-hour wheel and the star wheel for the days of the week.

■ **LEFT, TOP**: **Caliber 8840**, marketed by **Lemania**, uses the 8815 automatic movement with two barrels as a base. Shown on the module side are the following elements, all driven by their respective wheels and synchronized by different levers and springs: at 12:00, the big wheel with 48 teeth (one tooth for each month of the four-year cycle) coaxial with cam that, via the long taster, controls the month change on Day 28, 30, or 31(or Day 29 every 4 years); at 3:00, the star wheel with 31 teeth for the date; at 6:00, the moonphase disc (59 teeth for two cycles of 29.5 days); at 9:00, the small star for the days of the week. The perpetual-calendar modules, according to the time or to the "philosophy" of the design, can be corrected usually by advancement only, by means of correctors and crown or just by the crown (unidirectional, IWC and Jaeger-LeCoultre; bidirectional, Ulysse Nardin).

■ **LEFT, CENTER**: **Frédéric Piguet's module 54** is designed in such a way as to be suitable for mounting on 11'''1/2 calibers combined with non-chronograph movements. For chronographs, the 55 module usually is used; with its hollow pivots, it allows the use of two coaxial hands for each subdial. It displays the following indications: date, day, month, leap year, moonphase.

■ **LEFT, BOTTOM**: the **ETA** module (mounted on the automatic caliber 2890A9). Date, day, month, leap year, moonphase, with 3 fast correctors. Visible at 12:00 is the date wheel with 31 teeth; at 9:00, the subdial with the four-year cycle display above the months' wheel (12 teeth); at 6:00, the disc with the moonphases; at 3:00, the small wheel with 7 teeth for the days of the week.

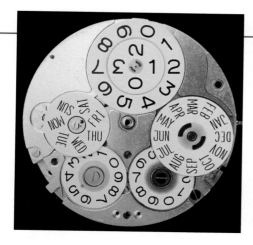 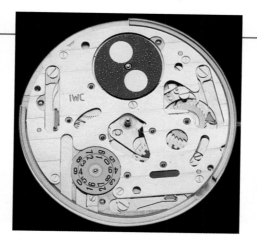 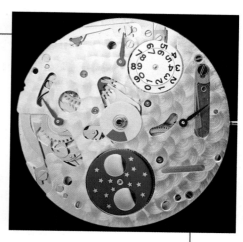

■ **TOP LEFT**: The perpetual-calendar movement **Ulysse Nardin Caliber UN 33** (an automatic movement with a gold rotor, today produced only in the version UN 32 with a center hand for a second time zone). All indications are shown via discs and windows: big-sized date (two concentric discs) above; day and month are readable on both sides of the pivot of the hour and minute hands, two-digit year below. This movement uses the train (barrel-balance) and the automatic-winding system of Lemania 1370 caliber. These elements are fastened directly to the pillar-plate produced by Ulysse Nardin, bearing the components of the perpetual calendar on the opposite face. By adjusting the crown, both forward and backward, it is possible to make all necessary corrections. In fact, it is the first movement to use only wheelworks—traditional and epicyclical—to activate and control the calendar functions (instead of levers, rocking bars, and various traditional non-rotating components, obliging to make only forward corrections).

■ The module adopted for perpetual calendars by IWC and Jaeger-LeCoultre is the result of an innovative common project, later developed through different executions. One of its outstanding features is the simple setting of the whole calendar, easily performed by actuating the winding crown as for a normal date correction by means of a fast corrector.

■ **TOP CENTER**: In the version developed by IWC it is possible to perceive the moonphase feature at 12:00 (at 3:00 on the rectangular Novecento model) with the exclusive, digital four-digit year display. Unfortunately, the photograph does not show the cursor indicating the first two displays (millennium and century).

■ **TOP RIGHT**: In the photograph of the module by Jaeger-LeCoultre, all indicators are set in place: three hands for day, date and month; four discs for the year (two-digit), moonphase, and for the useful two-color indicator of calendar-setting consent.

A perpetual calendar in its different executions (by hands, by windows, mixed, with or without leap-year indicator, with digital year display etc.) is generally realized on an additional pillar-plate housing all of the components. This is fastened to the dial-side face of the pillar-plate of the basic movement and closed on top by the watch dial. The perpetual calendar function is combined preferably with automatic movements that allow correct date storage when they are not in use, by adopting the usually available motorized supports or casings. The value of this complication (independent of its real usefulness in everyday life) is due to the difficulty of miniaturizing the diameter and especially the thickness of so many moving parts. After a long and expensive route to manual synchronization, it is necessary to assure correct indications on the dial, as well as to allow for updates to be made by the user after a long period of non-use. Generally, in the models provided with small correctors on the case middle, this operation is possible only in certain positions of the hour hands because the elements involved must not mesh with the others (as occurs during the date change).

MINUTE REPEATER
EN PASSANT SONNERIE

Sound and Time are enclosed in objects of great rarity and extreme complication, very achievements of the art of micro-mechanics, executions deserving admiration. With a minute repeater and an en passant sonnerie, a watch enters another sphere of expression—a musical one. Originated by the need to read time in the dark, without lighting a candle or waiting for the strokes of the nearby church tower, the minute repeater was invented during the 16th century—first appearing on coach clocks—and further developed during the subsequent centuries in pocket watches. The famous Abraham-Louis Breguet, at the end of the 18th century, focused his genius on this complication and transformed the resonance bell (then used inside the case) into very thin, bent steel strips on which the hammers struck the hours, like on gongs. The repeater appeared in wristwatches during the first half of the 20th century and came again into fashion some years ago, thanks to the creations by some prestigious Houses.

Recently, this example was followed by other important watchmaker firms thus enriching an extremely restricted sector with extreme models that—in addition to striking the hours, quarters and minutes at request—indicate time acoustically when the minute hand passes over the hours and quarters. Grande sonnerie strikes the (a) hours; and (b) hours + quarters. Petite sonnerie strikes the (a) hours; and (b) quarters only.

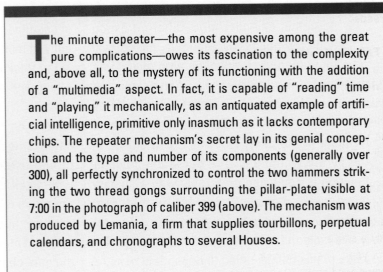

The minute repeater—the most expensive among the great pure complications—owes its fascination to the complexity and, above all, to the mystery of its functioning with the addition of a "multimedia" aspect. In fact, it is capable of "reading" time and "playing" it mechanically, as an antiquated example of artificial intelligence, primitive only inasmuch as it lacks contemporary chips. The repeater mechanism's secret lay in its genial conception and the type and number of its components (generally over 300), all perfectly synchronized to control the two hammers striking the two thread gongs surrounding the pillar-plate visible at 7:00 in the photograph of caliber 399 (above). The mechanism was produced by Lemania, a firm that supplies tourbillons, perpetual calendars, and chronographs to several Houses.

■ **TOP LEFT**: **Patek Philippe Star Caliber 2000**, pocket watch with two dials, ranks-with 21 complications-in third place among the most complex watches in the world. The drawing shows the "orchestra" reproducing the Westminster bell sound, a system protected by patent CH 689 337 A5: the transmission mechanism visible on opposite page represents the "conductor," while all of the other components (minute and quarter racks, hammers and gongs) play their respective roles as "musicians."

■ **TOP RIGHT**: (The same caliber seen from the side that is generally hidden by the dial.) In the middle, one can appreciate the four-arm minute cam, one for each quarter of an hour, with the 14 steps on which the taster of the minute rack (the toothed ring visible at 5:00) "reads" the strikes to give.

■ **FAR RIGHT AND BOTTOM**: the **Grande Sonnerie by Philippe Dufour**, one of the major events in horology, was realized and first presented at the World Watch and Jewelry Fair in Basel in 1992. It is worked entirely by hand by the Swiss master watchmaker. Given its complexity with regard to both its construction and regulation, only a single piece is produced in a year. The caseback view shows two barrels, the bigger of

which is dedicated to accumulating the energy necessary to activate the mechanisms of the (grande and petite) sonnerie at every passage of hours and quarters. The bridges are designed in an unusual shape, determined by the different requirements needed to perform the particular functions.

On his latest timepiece, the n° 6, Philippe Dufour wanted to hide the cursors for the GS/PS and Sonnerie/Mute mode switch (traditionally positioned on the case middle, as shown in the photograph) below a mobile bezel hinged on the dial side.

TOURBILLON

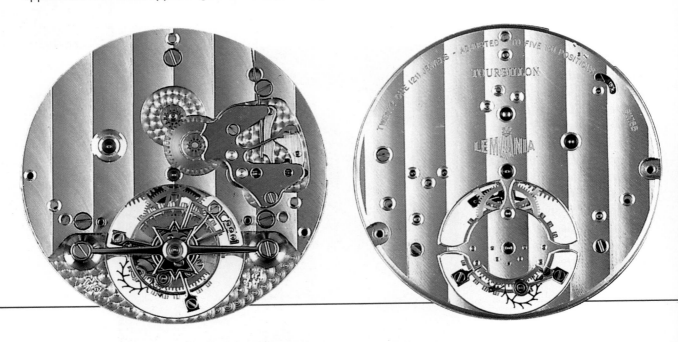

The tourbillon is one among the most fascinating complications of mechanical horology. Its invention dates back to 1795 but became known officially only in 1801 when the great French watchmaker Abraham-Louis Breguet claimed a patent for his Régulateur à Tourbillon (a name synonymous with the planetary system and referring to the scientific name used at the time.) The first piece was sold in 1805 but it was presented formally to the great public during the Parisian show of French industrial products in 1806. The aim of this device was to increase the average precision of the regulating organ. According to the inventor, the solution existed in housing the escapement inside a cage rotating within a regular time interval. Today it generally makes a complete revolution around itself in a minute. For this reason, watchmakers often bind it to the small-seconds hand. Because of the objective technical difficulties met when producing such mechanisms, very few firms engage in the output of their own tourbillons, thus increasing both the fascination and mystery characterizing this spectacular achievement in the past. Audemars Piguet developed an automatic movement with a hammer-shaped oscillating mass and a titanium carriage; Jaeger-LeCoultre proposed a movement in a rectangular shape; Girard-Perregaux miniaturized the components of its famous Tourbillon Sous Trois Ponts for pocket watches to the reduced sizes of a wristwatch and, today, has added an automatic-winding system with a micro-rotor coaxial with the barrel; Patek Philippe introduced its famous Gyromax balance; and Blancpain proposed a "tourbillon volant" with an autonomy of 8 days. Other firms use movements produced by Houses specializing in "ébauches," i.e. movement-blanks, and complications. In the following pages we present "pure" pieces, i.e. the ones that lack further complications, in order to fully appreciate the vortex appearing under the special aperture existing on almost all dials.

■**TOP**: The bridge of the **Pasha Tourbillon by Cartier**.

■**BOTTOM**: The movement provided with the tourbillon, produced and marketed by **Lemania** (in a limited number of pieces). This firm realizes a vast series of calibers available for high-quality watches in the versions Luxe, Grand Luxe and Haut-de-Gamme. The latter class of movements (tourbillon, minute repeater, and chronograph) includes the most important pieces of modern horology. The only firm producing movements with tourbillon devices for third-party clients (Frédéric Piguet produces one, but exclusively for Blancpain), proposes it in a standard version or in a version specially developed according to the buyer's specifications. In the photograph on the left it is evident that, in order to display the tourbillon device during its revolution through the glass, the pillar-plate underwent a wide découpage. This assures an easier mounting of the thin carriage-bridge directly onto the inner face of the rear closing-bridge, the only one adopted. By consequence, the latter lacks any mechanical fascination (see photograph on the right). It is partially skeletonized to give the tourbillon further "light" on watches provided with a crystal caseback. The finish, in this case the traditional Côtes de Genève pattern, with the constructor's short technical data indication, is replaced with beautiful hand-engravings.

THIS PAGE:
■**BELOW**: **caliber 76061** realized by **IWC** for the version with the tourbillon of the very famous DaVinci model.

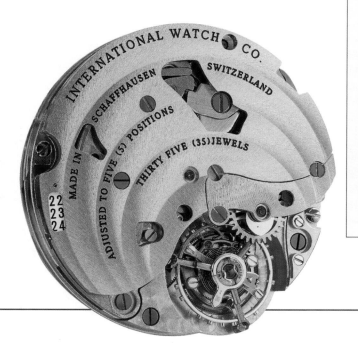

At the beginning of the 19th century, the construction of movements by Breguet achieved such an accuracy level that he considered (but was only partly right) the perfect balancing of balance and balance-spring to be a given. (The balance-spring element, realized according to the famous Breguet curve, makes it virtually concentric in its expansions and contractions with respect to the balance axis). However, his initial pocket models were not as accurate as they might have been. Later he observed that regular functioning was influenced to a great extent by the watch's position. In fact, when putting a watch in a horizontal or vertical position with the pendant positioned upwards or downwards, not only diverging but also opposite precision values were obtained. Therefore, the Parisian master concluded that the cause of such variations ought to be the influence of gravitation on the balance's inertial movements (eventually it was discovered that the real problem was the balancing of the balance and, only in the second place, its friction). The problem was solved according to Breguet's style with a great creative invention: a device making the escapement and balance turn continuously by placing them into a rotating cage and, in this way, disconnecting them from the pillar-plate. Thus, it was possible to take advantage of a steady variation of positional errors of the balance itself and, hence, of unbalances. This constant sequence of positive and negative errors led to their natural compensation and, by consequence, to a high-precision performance of watches.

The tourbillon, with respect to the time when it was developed, should have allowed the achievement of another important result: less frequent maintenance interventions. In 19th-century portable watches, which were without any exception pocket watches, because of the almost constantly held vertical position of the movement, the balance pivot rested only on one side of its seat. Therefore, friction—which was considerable given the materials used, the surface finish, and the lubricants adopted at that time—caused a strong wear on both seat and pivot and made frequent assistance necessary. The innovation introduced by Breguet, consisting of a continuous rotation of the support carriage of the balance-escapement system, allows distributing wear over the whole circumference of seat and pivot to achieve better lubrication results. This assured a more regular working performance, as the inventor himself described in a letter addressed to his son in 1795. "I succeeded in eliminating the anomalies due to the different positions of the center of gravity and movements of the balance, by distributing the function over all the pieces of the balance and pivot holes, so as to assure an equal lubrication of the friction surfaces." —Abraham-Louis Breguet

In today's wristwatches the tourbillon is in a position similar to a Ferrari car stuck in rush-hour traffic—nobody can resist a look.

JUMPING-HOURS

Two centuries ago, the tendency to consider the existing already as "old" led to very eccentric solutions, such as jumping-hour watches that eliminated the old dial which became boring with just two hands. This type of watch derived its name from a particular device designed to release each hour digit instantaneously inside a small aperture. Normally, the twelve hours are printed on a turning disc. This system, adopted for some pocket models already in early 19th century, was further developed by the Swiss engineer J. Pallweber (English Patent no. 5863 of 8.12.1882) who realized a jumping-hour and -minute watch with two separate windows. It was adopted almost immediately by IWC (first for pocket watches and later for wristwatches) and produced in very small series at the beginning of the 20th century, even though the manufacturing firm defined digital display as an "error regretted a long time ago by IWC." In any case, this kind of watch launched the fashion of the double window—one for the hours and the other for the minutes. Thanks to this complex mechanism and its curiously sophisticated nature, after the initial successes, this complication appeared again in some refined mechanical models during the 1930s, which now represent popular collection pieces.

Proposed first by Audemars Piguet, Patek Philippe and Rolex, followed by Cartier and other firms, they were pushed aside again by the upcoming quartz watches with their digital dials so much in vogue during the 1970s. However, some firms continue to produce them in a variety of models ranging from the most classic to the most fashion forward.

THIS PAGE

■ **RIGHT**: The famous **John Shaeffer by Audemars Piguet**, a manual-winding movement with minute repeater, displaying time by two discs, with the respective hours and minutes windows cut out on the piece covering the whole dial.

FACING PAGE

■ **TOP LEFT**: The **Breguet Ref. 3620**, provided with a double barrel, one among the first automatic-winding movements indicating time by jumping hours with a digital display. This Breguet combines the jumping-hour function with the aesthetics of the old pocket watches signed by the great French watchmaker.

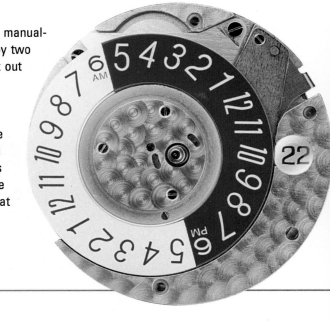

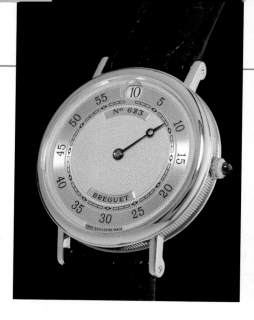

■ **TOP CENTER**: the jumping-hour piece by **Vacheron Constantin Ref. 43040**, an automatic-winding movement, proposes a pocket model of the 1930s in a wristwatch version. The dial shows a harmonious entity of refined and discrete details—delicate etchings with a "basket" pattern; small applied markers; and a Malta cross (the symbol of Vacheron Constantin) visible at 12:00—provide the background of an original minute display. Just the tip of the minute hand appears behind the dial window.

■ **TOP RIGHT**: The mythical **Star Wheel by Audemars Piguet** in its first wristwatch version, featuring an arabesque gold dial and a genial time dance representation. Three sapphire discs bear, respectively, a four-hour indication and indicate by turn the hours and minutes on the upper part of the dial. Automatic movement.

■ **RIGHT CENTER**: dial-side view of **cal. C 124** of the Delphis model by **Chronoswiss**. Connoisseurs can appreciate the extensive amount of work spent to achieve the digital display of jumping hours and the retrograde minute indication on a half-circle scale of 180°. To assure the instantaneous return of the minute hand to zero, a device was designed (the first on a wristwatch, as far as we know, for which a patent was claimed) allowing "jumps" in both ways-forward for the hours and backward for the minutes—without influencing the watch's regularity.

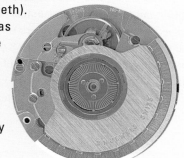

Contemporary jumping-dial watches that display time inside an aperture undergo a modification normally performed on former movements of the same Houses or supplied by external firms. One of the most popular movements adopted for committing complications, as far as friction requirements are concerned, is the ETA 2892A2 (see photograph below). The components, fastened on a dedicated pillar-plate (module) or directly to the main pillar-plate on the dial side, entail an increase of the total thickness of a movement, as a classic movement for window date-display does. The hour disc turns by steps, controlled (on a star wheel with 12 teeth integrated on its lower part) by a click actuated in its turn by a snail cam making one revolution in an hour (derived from the minute wheel). Stopping elements (like bending springs) prevent accidental time shifts. Jumping hours are still proposed with both digital and—albeit more rarely—hands display. In reality, the latter system—now considered a sort of simpler solution with respect to the aperture version—is very important historically because it was Breguet who used it with high-quality repeater watches at the beginning of the 19th century. Unfortunately, in these models hands required three minutes to pass to the following hour, thus causing momentary lapses in time availability. Various anecdotes tell of famous historical personalities who missed important appointments because of these types of watches.

The photograph on the right shows the old movement GMT by Ulysse Nardin displaying jumping hours by disc and aperture for an independent second time zone on a 24-hour scale (star wheel with 24 teeth). A small lens was added on the module in order to assure easier readability of the date displayed inside an aperture, featured already by the basic caliber.

ALARM WATCHES

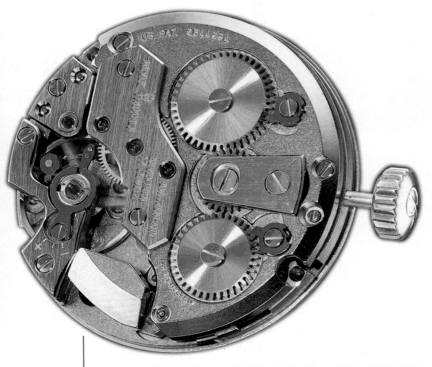

Alarm functions appeared for the first time in the wristwatches realized by Eterna, patented in 1908 and presented at the national Swiss Exhibition of Bern in 1914. It seems that the alarm-function concept, obviously in a pocket watch version, dates back to the great philosopher Jean-Jacques Rousseau, a son of the Genevan watchmaker Isaac Rousseau, a close friend of Henri Breguet and great-uncle of the famous "master." However, industrial series production did not begin before 1947 with the Cricket by Ditisheim, marketed by Vulcain and Revue Thommen. This watch became quite famous because it was used by the presidents of the United States of America Truman, Eisenhower and Johnson, as well as by the members of the expedition that conquered the K2 (the second highest mountain of the world after Mount Everest) in 1954.

Just as important were the Memovox by Jaeger-LeCoultre dated 1950 (the alarm watch by Movado of the same period) and the subsequent models by Cartier, Ebel, Baume & Mercier, and Girard-Perregaux.

Alarm watches, though still often snubbed by contemporary manufacturers despite their usefulness, can meet high standards with such perfection that they really could be considered "complicated." In any case, it seems that recently some firms rediscovered the fascination of such watches. The most traditional versions of modern alarm watches with manual- or automatic-winding movements are provided with two independent winding barrels and two crowns: one for general winding and adjusting; the other to wind up (by the second barrel), set and control the sonnerie device. As in the original movements, some houses prefer a single winding-barrel and crown, designating a pusher for the selection of specific functions. Among the models presented in the following pages, the one by Ulysse Nardin winds alternately both the watch and sonnerie barrels in both directions of the rotor. Jaeger-LeCoultre's Master Réveil and Memovox models have very refined sounds thanks to an annular tempered steel resonator mounted under the movements. Almost all the other brands use a caseback or a double bottom functioning as an acoustic membrane.

Mechanical alarm watches lost their place in the market rather quickly (except with the most appreciative connoisseurs) when multipurpose quartz watches were introduced with much lower production costs and higher performance reliability (more sonnerie options, more time displays and/or tones). Few manufacturers competed in this field because it requires developing not only a module or a modification, but rather an entirely new movement to integrate different winding, energy distribution and striking-work control systems. Among these watchmakers, we must mention A. Schild S.A. of Grenchen, inventor of caliber 1475, a manual-winding movement. The subsequent version, caliber 1568 Alertic with 11'''1/2, featured a date display and is still used today—sometimes with interesting modifications—by many brands. All the machines involved in the construction of the alarm movement by A. Schild were sold by ETA, who in the meantime—as for Peseux—had taken over the property of a Russian enterprise, which had created a certain (probably very high) number of such movements. Other firms that had produced movements for alarm watches were: Angelus with its caliber 240 RR with 14''' and power reserve of 8 days; Movado with its caliber 85 Alarm with 8''' 3/4; Vulcain Watch Factory with its calibers 120 and 401 with 12''' (the latter also in a version with calendar functions) and caliber 406 with 8'''3/4; and Venus S.A. with its caliber 230 Alertic with 12'''1/2.

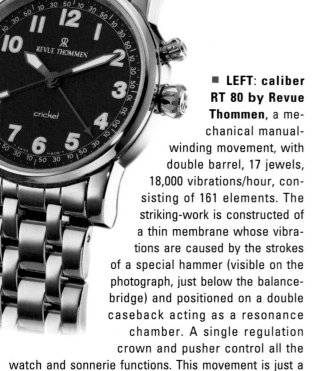

■ **LEFT**: caliber **RT 80 by Revue Thommen**, a mechanical manual-winding movement, with double barrel, 17 jewels, 18,000 vibrations/hour, consisting of 161 elements. The striking-work is constructed of a thin membrane whose vibrations are caused by the strokes of a special hammer (visible on the photograph, just below the balance-bridge) and positioned on a double caseback acting as a resonance chamber. A single regulation crown and pusher control all the watch and sonnerie functions. This movement is just a "modern" version of the caliber realized by Revue Thommen and used for its Cricket (the photograph below shows the modern piece) already in 1947.

■ **RIGHT**: automatic winding **918 caliber by Jaeger-LeCoultre** mounted on the Master Réveil. This movement is derived from caliber 914 with a manual-winding system, mounted on the Master Memovox. The hammer striking the steel-thread-gong (fastened on the caseback) is visible just above the balance. The difficulty of overcoming the hindrance represented by the rotor was solved, without increasing the overall volume, by providing the rotor with a special ball bearing, hollow at the center, so that the gong's end struck by the hammer protrudes inside the movement. The movement caliber 909 used for the Master Grande Memovox, stemming from the Grande Réveil, as the only alarm watch with a perpetual calendar of our time, is also worth mentioning.

■ The movement mostly used within today's alarm-watch class is **caliber 5008 by A. Schild**, an automatic movement born in the 1960s as the last evolution stage of a watch type very popular at that time. The movement is proposed in two different configurations, with 17 or 31 jewels (the photograph shows the jewels of the automatic-winding wheels in settings, while the pivots of the calibers with 17 jewels are placed directly in brass bushings). Another variant derived from this caliber is the one produced by G. P. Manufacture, sold also to other brands, to which Girard-Perregaux adds the GMT function displayed in an aperture on the dial. Caliber 5008, 28,800 vibrations/hour, is provided with a double barrel: one for the basic movement and the other for the alarm function.

GMT

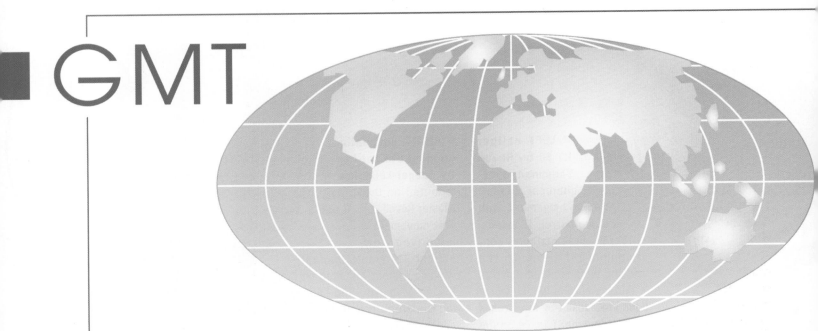

Ideally, our sense of time begins and ends at the central meridian (0°/360°) passing through Greenwich, the place, where an observatory with the same name was founded in 1675, and chosen as an official point of reference for the measurement of longitude in maritime calculations in 1884. The term GMT (Greenwich Mean Time) used aeronautics indicates a time respected by every pilot in every part of the world and upon which the calculations of flying times are based. (Although at a professional level the term UTC (Universal Time Coordinated)—corresponding to the GMT—is preferred to, for instance, prepare and coordinate all international flight schedules). GMT was adopted to define watches allowing more than a single time-zone reading. Many multi-time-zone watches are provided with one or more additional dials on a 12- or 24-hour basis and indicate several local times.

From the most elementary GMTs with simple 12-hour turning rings (movements without any modification) to the World Time models to those which supply a requested time via manual selection of a time zone, more than ten solutions were adopted. Each solution contains more or less radical modifications of the basic movement.

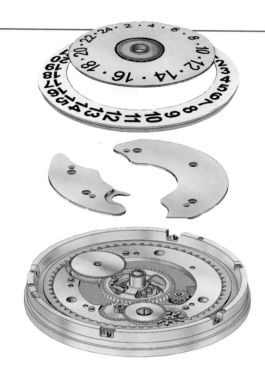

The most common GMT type is one equipped with an additional hour hand which makes one complete rotation every 24 hours; a coaxial with the main hand adjustable independently by actuating the crown; 24 markers on the ring or dial for the time reading in each zone. Since the relevant modification does not require the design of specific movements, it is performed on the pillar-plate on the dial side, by using existing movements. In other cases, information is placed off-center on one or more 24-hour dials (or on 12-hour dials, preferably with a day/night indicator) with or without a minute hand. A particularly interesting solution is represented by the World Time feature, which displays the times in all 24 zones at once on a flange bearing 24 markers and a ring with the names of the zones' reference towns (to turn by hand for the basic setting). Recently, very practical GMTs were presented, provided with pushers on the case middle, which allow selection of a time zone in one-hour increments at a time. Some feature the indication of the names of reference towns in an aperture; in this case, local time is displayed immediately when the town is selected.

FACING PAGE

■**BOTTOM LEFT**: the left shows the unusual mechanism controlling the functioning of **caliber 240/188 by Patek Philippe** used for the World Time model. By pressing down the corrector pusher and rotating the hands with the crown pulled out, it is possible to proceed to the first setting of the watch, by setting the town of one's zone to the local time. Later, to jump from one time zone to another, it is sufficient to press only the corrector pusher to obtain the indications of the time and reference town of a new destination.

THIS PAGE

■ The photograph above shows an enlarged view of the automatic-movement **caliber 37526** of the Flieger UTC World Time model by **IWC**. It allows, simply with the actuation of the crown, both the adjustment of the main hands and the moving of only the hour hand in hourly advancements, in order to set it at a different zone's time independently of the UTC time indicated by the 24-hour disc.

■ In 1993 **Ulysse Nardin** created the GMT± model that, by its "plus" and "minus" pushers, allows the instantaneous adjustment of the hour hand to another zone's time while retaining the home time when one is abroad through the home-time aperture (patent No.

CH685965). The GMT± can be set at different zones' times, without taking it off and without interfering with the watch's functioning. This device was developed in calibers UN 20, UN 22 with big-sized date, and UN 32 with a perpetual calendar. The photograph on the right shows caliber **UN 20** in a dial-side view (the functioning of the GMT feature is the same for all). The module realized by Ulysse Nardin and mounted on the basic caliber is decorated with a circular-graining pattern. It displays two independent zones' times; the disc of the main time zone works on a 24-jumping-hour basis (with 2 day-night sectors); time is displayed through an aperture at 11:00. The hands, normally set at the same time, can be moved in two directions when the time zone changes, simply by pressing down the two pushers positioned on the case middle. If one wants to keep a different zone's time stored, it is possible to set it by the crown inside the aperture and to adjust the hands by means of the pushers by setting them at the local hour for easier reading.

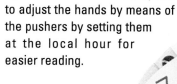

DIVING WATCHES

Protecting watches from outside agents was one of the major problems to solve when progressing from pocket watches to wristwatches, as the latter are exposed to the severity of the weather, dust and body moisture. It was a rather important obstacle to overcome; the stakes were high and concerned the reliability of a watch as a whole and its working capacity in various environmental conditions. The solution was derived in stages during the 1920s. First, glasses were realized in plastic resin and snapped on to the bezels. Then, casebacks were no longer snapped on, but screwed in and protected by gaskets (the first of which were made of smooth silver). Finally, the waterproofing of crowns had to be improved. The first brand to reach a suitable solution for industrial production was Rolex in 1926, sparking its success. In fact, all the subsequent technical evolutions—even those due to Rolex—aimed at improving production techniques and performance standards. However, for almost three decades the importance of waterproofing was vastly underestimated inside the civil sector (on the contrary, military milieus already valued its significance, as was confirmed by the production of some interesting models by Waltham, Longines and, of course, Panerai). The demand for diving watches became stronger in the late 1950s when, thanks to the diffusion of cylinders and breathing apparatuses, people really started diving. Modern watchmaker technicians developed waterproofing systems for cases, crowns and even chronograph pushers, based on reliable and surprising solutions. Some watchmaking firms developed real "professionals" of marine abysses: small bathyscaphs featuring ideal proportions and clear dials. Others combine strong and reliable cases, constructed according to the most rigorous water-resistance criteria, with a touch of elegance making them perfect accessories for any occasion.

Obviously, the key element of a diving watch is that it must protect the movement from water and moisture. To this end, gaskets (generally O-rings) are used to join together all case parts. These rubber rings are fastened between the surfaces of the parts to be joined, such as glass/bezel, bezel/case and caseback/case. The gaskets surrounding winding stems (this is always the case with screw-down crowns) and pushers in diving chronographs are microscopic in size and are used in a variable number (depending on the respective patents). The Swiss watch industry established severe standards that watches must meet if they are to be certified as diving watches, thus providing a guarantee to the buyer that the water-resistance rate declared by the manufacturer is in fact true.

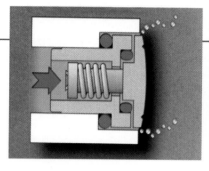
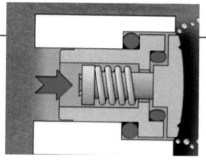
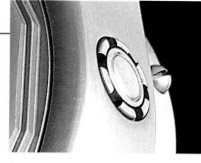

■ A device mounted exclusively on some professional models is the so-called helium valve. Divers work under water for long periods of time—sometimes days—inside pressurized tanks, breathing a mixture of oxygen and helium. This gas does not cause health problems at those pressure values, but is so volatile that it enters even watchcases through gaskets and steel porosities. Thus, the internal pressure inside a watch progressively matches the external pressure of the air inside the tank and of deep-sea water. When divers come back to the surface, however, internal pressure may pop the watch glass like a champagne cork; in this case, the special valve positioned on the side of some models releases the gas directly, thus preventing damage to the case structure.

The only mechanical (automatic-winding) watch equipped with a depth-gauge on the market today is IWC's Deep One, the newest model in the brand's GST family. It is provided with a sophisticated mechanical instrument gauged for immersions down to 45 meters. It works thanks to an admitting valve positioned on the case middle, a feeler/actuator around the movement and a series of wheelworks with levers and cams positioned on the caseback side. During immersions, the mechanism is in contact with the surrounding water (and, hence, subject to its pressure) and transmits pressure variation values to two hands (one for the real-time indication of the depth measure, the other for the maximum measure reached). It works in the following way. The depth-gauge hand positioned at the dial center starts moving as soon as the diver starts working. This hand makes the other coaxial hand move, which registers depth and stops as soon as this reaches its peak value, without coming back. The main hand registers every pressure variation until it goes back to zero when the diver comes back to the surface. Contrary to the rare mechanical wristwatches with depth gauges realized in the past, the measuring of water pressure is not performed by means of a membrane on the caseback but through the "reading" of the dilatation or contraction of a feeler having the shape of a half-circle tube. The variations of this element's volume (caused by changes in water-pressure) are converted into the motion of the depth-gauge hands like this: the admitting valve, provided with micro-holes positioned at 4:00, is used simultaneously with the depth-gauging crown before immersion, and the crown at 2:00 controls the inner minutes-ring and the zeroing mechanism of the maximum depth indicator.

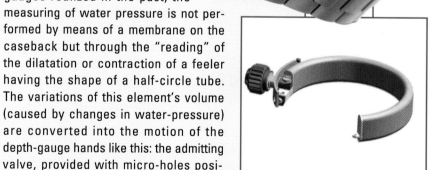

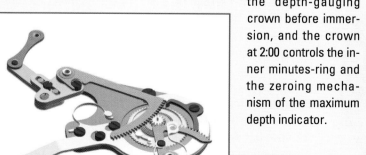

SPLIT-SECOND CHRONOGRAPH

The "split-second" chronograph is an evolution of the traditional chronograph movements that originated from the necessity to measure actions having common start-time but different durations, typically sporting events. An additional hand, positioned below the chronograph seconds hand, can be stopped to measure an intermediate time elapsed and subsequently re-aligned with the main hand by covering the space crossed by the latter in the meantime.

The magic of the additional hand, split and re-aligned at request, raised these watches to the status of "objects of desire" on the first- and second-hand market. Split-second chronographs were produced in very limited quantities due to the high production costs determined by the considerable difficulty of setting up the relevant mechanism. Today, we are facing an increased demand and, thanks to the production of strong movements by specialized workshops and suppliers of chronograph movements, today's supply tries to meet the market's requests.

■ **BOTTOM**: original caliber **Venus 179**, dating from the 1940s, reproduced here on the basis of a technical drawing of that time. It is a manual-winding movement with an autonomy of approximately 45 hours with two counters (center seconds, 45 or 30 minutes at 3:00) and small seconds at 9:00. The derived caliber 185 was also provided with an hour counter (12) at 6:00 and the minute counter had a scale of just 30 minutes. Diameter 31.00mm and thickness 7.20mm; 19 jewels; two-arm balance with compensating screws, flat balance-spring, 18,000 vibration/hour. This movement uses two column-wheels: a classic one for the distribution of traditional chronograph functions; and the other—positioned between the clam arms—to activate the latter.

■ **TOP**: **Venus 179/185** was recently "revitalized" by some Houses (in the few pieces left up to now) and inserted into the base of important collections' chronographs. The photograph shows the one used by **Girard-Perregaux**, duly modified as to some essential components such as the balance (having a greater diameter), the balance-spring (now it is of the Breguet type), the regulating device (with swan-neck retaining spring for the index), and the shock-absorber system (Incabloc). The Manufacture of La Chaux-de-Fonds applied new finishes: the pillar-plate is decorated with a circular-graining pattern, bridges are decorated with a Côtes de Genève pattern and beveled, as are all the levers and springs.

■ **TOP RIGHT**: the drawing (Frédéric Piguet caliber 1186) shows the detail of the open split-second clam (5) when the additional chronograph hand runs hidden under the main one. The column-wheel (3) is positioned in such a way as to keep the two clam arms open. In this case, the automatic-return system of the split-second hand under the main hand is active. A heart-piece (8) and a finger (7) pushed by a spring (9) control this system.

■ **BOTTOM RIGHT**: with the column-wheel rotated by one step (corresponding to a single pressure on a dedicated pusher, activating lever 1), the clam is closed and locks the wheel on which the split-seconds hand is fixed. In this phase, the split-seconds hand stops in order to indicate an intermediate time, while the chronograph seconds continue to run independently.

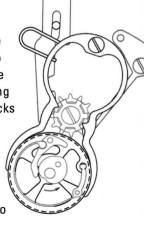

The mechanism governing the splitting function of the superposed chronograph-seconds hands and the realignment of the main time of the hand which stopped the intermediate measuring time was always positioned on the rear part of the movement, easily identified in watches provided with sight movements. Recently, some new chronograph movements were transformed into split-second chronographs, some of which are placed on the dial side. The number of components is small. The actuating pusher, normally positioned on the case middle and in some cases coaxial with the crown, governs a lever generally driving a column-wheel dedicated to the activation of the clam provided with long arms with very small teeth. These lock the split-seconds wheel, which is also equipped with small teeth complementary to those of the clam. The driving and realignment device placed on the hidden face of the wheel activates the heart-shaped cam integral with the main chronograph-seconds wheel. The drawing on the right shows an exploded view of the automatic caliber 1186 by Frédéric Piguet, made up by a basic integrated chronograph movement and two modules added for the automatic-winding function (above) and the split-seconds feature (center). Below the transmission wheelworks of the automatic-winding system it is possible to identify, from top to bottom: the bridge supporting the elements of split-seconds function; the main seconds wheel (gilded); the split-seconds wheel; the blocking and releasing clam; and the column-wheel of the split-seconds device.

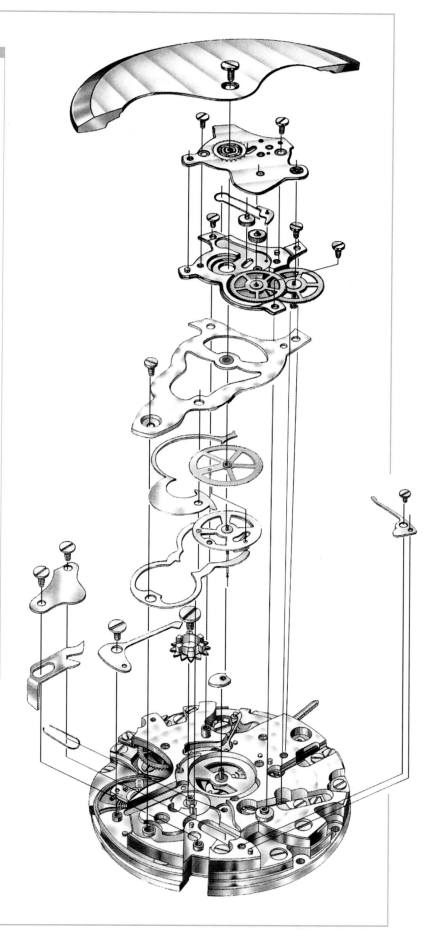

CHRONOGRAPH

A chronograph—a technical watch par excellence and the only "complicated" popular watch—bears in itself centuries of experiences and culture. In fact, at the beginning of the 18th century, English watchmaker George Graham constructed the first apparatus capable of measuring the duration of an event. This was the predecessor of modern chronographs, whose development began the following century in 1821 when Parisian watchmaker Rieussec built a watch registering the time elapsed. Around the same time, Breguet—together with Fatton—realized an ink-counter similar to Rieussec's invention. (The dispute over the true originator remains open.) As their production, mounting and regulation is rather complex, today's chronographs are very popular and several versions are available from prestigious houses. There is a great choice among manual- or automatic-winding pieces or the so-called "hybrid" models; waterproof and antimagnetic watches or the ones certified as chronometers by the Swiss supervisory authority are all much more reliable than in the past.

The following selection represents the best of mechanical horology to be unveiled in the marketplace.

■ **LEFT**: the **chronograph module** used by **Girard-Perregaux** (Ø 23.0mm, thickness 6.28mm together with the basic caliber) for some of its watches. The distinguishing element that classifies this chronograph module at the highest rank, is the functional distributing system working by means of a **column-wheel** (see photograph right). The latter is realized starting from a small single block of steel. The lower reel (Ø 3.85mm) shows Breguet-type wolf teeth; the upper part consists of a typical annular column row (Ø 3.08mm) which is perpendicular to the reel up to the component's total height of 1.45mm. As far as we know, this is the first and only chronograph module other than the basic caliber to have such features.

Fly-back chronographs

The fly-back function is certainly a fashionable one. This function was developed during World War II with the aim of improving the synchronization operations of take-off and landing procedures of entire flight formations. Blancpain utilized the fly-back function on its 2100 model and Zenith implemented it on its Rainbow before it became a standard feature for a considerable number of new pieces

The explanation of fly-back functioning is rather simple. Virtually, this fast-return feature allows zeroing of the chronograph hands during a timing operation by a single push of the zeroing pushpiece; the hands start running again as soon as the same pusher is released. Thus, three operations-stop, zeroing, and restart-become a single timesaving operation with a considerable gain in terms of precision. The "fly-back" feature is particularly useful in traditional aerial navigation. In fact, it allows pilots to easily control flight times calculated between each route change or during holding procedures before landing. It also can be used in sport-timing procedures such as repeated lap times. Quickly this feature became synonymous of a "complication within the complication" and for this reason it enjoys high prestige among manufacturing firms and popularity among the public.

To use it, two chronograph pushers must be actuated. Just two years after these were invented and patented (by Breitling in 1933 and further developed in 1935) the Fabrique des Longines Francillon & Co. SA in St.-Imier claimed a patent (no. 183262) in 1936 for a chronograph equipped with two pushers. In this instance, the second pusher, when pressed down during a timing operation, sets the chronograph to zero; as soon as it is released, the seconds-counting hand starts running again automatically. This was the birth of the fly-back watch. The drawing reproduced here shows the functioning scheme of the fly-back system in the new Datograph by A. Lange & Söhne (the photograph above shows the movement). The levers involved in this function are represented by dashed lines while their motions—initiated by the actuation of the chronograph; engaging the seconds wheel at the center; the coupling wheel; the driving wheel; and the hammer lever—are represented symbolically by the arrows.

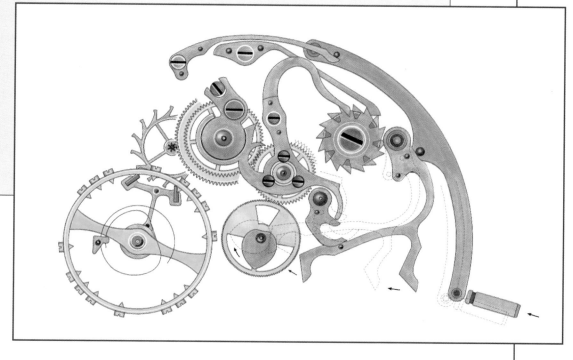

A. LANGE & SÖHNE

Superb craftsmanship—both inside and out—defines A. Lange & Söhne. This full-fledged German manufacturer of its own movements and finished timepieces adheres to superior horological standards in each of the complex and elegant timepieces it creates.

While its current production of timepieces dates back to only 1990, A. Lange & Söhne's roots rest in the 1800s. Founded in 1845 by Ferdinand Adolph Lange, the brand created fine German watches in the Saxony region for more than 100 years. However, World War II bombings decimated the workshops, and the subsequent expropriation of the company in 1948 by the socialist regime forced A. Lange & Söhne to cease operations altogether. Fourth-generation Walter Lange fled to the west with the communist takeover.

When the Berlin Wall fell in 1989, Walter Lange vowed to reestablish the family brand and tradition. A year later, with the help of IWC and the Richemont Group, this great German watchmaker reopened its doors in the city of Glashütte. The manufacture set about creating its own movements and so it was not until 1994 that the new generation of A. Lange & Söhne watches appeared. Once again, the great German watchmaking tradition flourished. In 1997, the Manufacture unveiled the Sax-o-Mat and a year later the brand opened the Lange Watchmaking School in Glashütte. In 2000, the company reacquired its original headquarters.

Today, the brand creates its own movements and assembles its timepieces from start to finish in its Glashütte workshops—creating just a few thousand fine mechanical watches annually. The brand crafts only in 18-karat gold or platinum, and offers just a few important collections.

This year, to reinforce its commitment to technical prowess and complicated watchmaking, Lange focused on enriching its Lange 1 Moonphase watch with technological advancements. Indeed, the brand's watchmakers spent many months devising a waxing and waning moon that never stands still as long as the watch is wound. While most moonphases click into position and don't move again until a certain segment of time has passed (typically one day), the Lange 1 Moonphase offers the most reliable depiction of moon time because it is always in motion.

Essentially, the moonphase disc is connected to the continuum of the hour wheel and emulates the moon's orbit with a deviation of merely .002 percent. The new Lange 1 Moonphase errs by only 1.9 seconds per day, or 57 seconds per lunar orbit (a total of about 11 minutes per year) as compared to other moonphase watches whose inaccuracies result in approximately 44 minutes per year. Indeed the Lange 1 Moonphase is a true horological accomplishment—indicative of A. Lange & Söhne's masterful craftsmanship.

HIGHLIGHTS

- Production of the new A. Lange & Söhne Lange 1 Moonphase watch with continual movement of the moonphase disc is in full swing. Created in 18-karat yellow or pink gold, or in platinum, the watch houses the Caliber L901.5 movement, consisting of 398 individual parts.

- In the Lange 1 Moonphase watch, the company combines its patented Lange outsize date with a shock-resistant screw balance timed to 21,600 semi-oscillations per hour.

- A. Lange & Söhne has also added models to its highly successful Arkade collection. One of the first four watches to be introduced upon the brand's revival, the Arkade is characterized by its elegant, curved rectangular case shape that emulates the arcades in the courtyards of Dresden's royal palace.

- The new Grande Arkade manually wound watch with patented outsize date is now available in four exclusive case versions crafted in platinum or in the three colors of gold.

ARNOLD & SON

One of the famed British names in horology and invention, Arnold & Son has roots dating back nearly 250 years. Indeed, the watchmaker for whom the brand is named played a significant role in developing the perfect marine chronometer in the 1760s. Today, the brand pays homage to the watchmaking prowess initiated by its forefather.

The Arnold & Son dynasty began in **1764** when John Arnold, a young clockmaker in London, first became noticed for his talents by King George III—who asked Arnold to join his courts. Throughout his career, Arnold was intent on trying to solve the problem of finding longitude at sea, and worked diligently on creating seafaring timepieces. From **1767** on, he ran several trials with clocks on board ships at sea. Each one led him to new horological inventions, including the spring detent escapement, the bimetallic spring and the helical balance spring. He even produced a pocket chronometer watch.

John Arnold's technical expertise was superb, and he dedicated himself to creating timepieces for the ships of His British Majesty. In **1787**, with the help of his son, he founded Arnold & Son. Their timepieces accompanied some of the most illustrious English explorers—Sir Ernest Shackelton, Captain Cook and Captain Phipps—on their famed expeditions.

Today, Arnold's dream of perfection is accessible through the Swiss manufacturer The British Masters SA. This company dedicated three years of relentless work to the rejuvenation of the English luxury watchmaking. In **1998**, The British Masters presented the Arnold & Son collection to the world.

Arnold & Son watches recall the world of the Navy with their precision timekeeping and complicated movements. Inspired by adventure and the challenges of navigation, Arnold & Son watches ...bine the legendary English efficiency with a ...assically elegant appeal.

The technicians of The British Masters—the company responsible for restoring several other forefathers of British horology to their former glory—insist that each of the timepieces presented by Arnold & Son offers the complexities that are necessary to the worldly traveler. Among the timepieces are a tourbillon, a Deck Marine Timekeeper, a GMT, a triple-time-zone watch and a Longitude Timekeeper— all created in the tradition of technical ingenuity and innovation. Every watch in the Arnold & Son collection is produced in a limited edition using only the finest materials—platinum, 18-karat gold or steel.

The brand is built on technical prowess. Its Longitude Timekeeper (launched in 1999) set the standards for all Arnold & Son watches of the future. It remains one of the strongest timepieces in the line. Essentially, the Longitude Timekeeper enables the user to determine a position at sea, to find the North-South axis and to resolve the equation of time. It houses the Arnold & Son A1714 caliber automatic mechanical movement with a mobile lon-
...de scale. The watch is a COSC-certified
...nometer and incorporates an anti-shock
...stem and a power reserve of 45 hours.

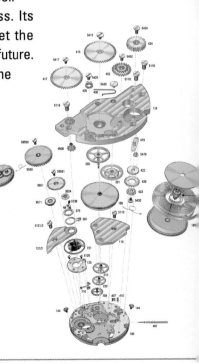

HIGHLIGHTS

To celebrate the 200th anniversary of the tourbillon, and to pay homage to the mutually respectful relationship between John Arnold and Abraham-Louis Breguet, Arnold & Son created an exclusive one-minute tourbillon with GMT dedicated to Breguet. Called the GMT Master Tourbillon, the watch is equipped with a manual-winding mechanical movement and a power reserve of 110 hours. It also consists of two 24-hour GMT counters, making it a double GMT tourbillon. The watch is crafted in a limited edition of 25 pieces in 18-karat red gold, 25 pieces in white gold, and 10 pieces in platinum. The tourbillon escapement is visible at 6:00 and the two GMT readouts are in subdials at 2:00 and 10:00.

Expanding its Timekeeper family of watches, Arnold & Son has unveiled the 7 Day Timekeeper III—a miniature version of a marine chronometer for the wrist. The watch features a 7-day movement with date at 3:00, a small seconds hand at 6:00 and a power-reserve indicator at 12:00. In typical British style, the power reserve indicates the time elapsed rather than the time remaining in the watch before it needs to be rewound. The watch is available in rose gold only and features a transparent caseback to view the manual movement.

Recognizing that travel today has moved from the sea to the air—with most people crossing time zones—Arnold & Son has unveiled the GMT II. This watch offers universal time and the time in two zones. It is fitted with a COSC-certified automatic chronometer movement, is water resistant to 160 feet, and is offered in steel and in 18-karat pink gold.

TOP LEFT
The Timekeeper III houses a 7-day movement with power-reserve indicator. It was developed after Arnold & Son spent a significant amount of time researching a four-day movement.

TOP CENTER
The 7 Day Timekeeper III features a transparent sapphire caseback.

TOP RIGHT
The GMT II is a COSC-certified automatic chronometer with double time-zone indicators and an oversized crown.

BOTTOM
This HMS stainless steel watch houses an automatic movement that is COSC-certified.

AUDEMARS PIGUET

a rguably among the finest luxury watch manufacturers in the world, Audemars Piguet boasts a history that is rich with tradition. One of a handful of watch companies that produces and assembles its own movements and complete timepieces, this illustrious brand has built an international following with its technical prowess and complex masterpieces.

The roots of Audemars Piguet date back nearly 130 years to **1875** when two great watchmakers—Jules-Louis Audemars and Edward-Auguste Piguet—formed a partnership to create complicated watches. Dedicated to excellence in performance and craftsmanship, the two regularly turned out coveted masterpieces. In **1882**, they unveiled the Grande Complication watch with minute repeater, perpetual calendar, moonphase and chronograph. In **1889**, the next Grande Complication included all of the functions of the previous watch, but also included a split-seconds chronograph—not an easy feat for that era. Four years later in **1892**, Audemars Piguet introduced its first wristwatch—complete with a minute repeater. By the turn of the century, the brand had firmly established itself as a leader in technology and design.

Indeed, throughout the entire **20**th century, Audemars Piguet turned out invention after invention and was regularly lauded for its contributions to the world of watchmaking. In **1915**, the company presented the smallest watch movement with minute repeater inside. Ten yeas later, the slimmest pocket watch was introduced by the company, followed twenty years later by the slimmest manual-winding wristwatch in the world. In **1967**, the slimmest automatic movement made its debut and in **1972**, Audemars Piguet unveiled the now-famed Royal Oak watch to the delight of collectors around the world. In **1992**, the Triple Complication appeared, followed in **1994** by the Grande Sonnerie, which houses one of the most complex movements comprised of 410 individual pieces.

In **1999**, Audemars Piguet began a series called the Tradition of Excellence. The first watch unveiled was the Tourbillon Minute Repeater Split Second Chronograph Jules Audemars watch. The next edition of the series was released in **2000** with two extremely complex masterpieces that incorporated such mechanics as the tourbillon escapement and the Equation of Time. In **2001**, the Tradition of Excellence III introductions included the Edward Piguet Tourbillon with power reserve, chronograph and dynamograph, and the Jules Audemars Metropolis Perpetual Calendar—the first watch to combine a perpetual calendar with a display of local time in each of the 24 key zones.

Producing no more than 17,000 timepieces annually, Audemars Piguet is committed to exclusivity. As a result, many of the pieces it unveils are created as limited editions. Such is the case with some of the special commemorative pieces it has introduced in the Royal Oak line. The year 2002 marked the 30th anniversary of the Royal Oak and Audemars Piguet has infused the collection with several inventions and has smartly aligned itself and this chic, bold sports watch with the America's Cup 2003.

The Royal Oak has not only become a signature collection for the brand and a coveted must-have for watch connoisseurs around the world, but also it has come to represent a particular standard of accomplishment in the luxury sport watch arena. Powerful in design, the Royal Oak was named in tribute to the British Royal Navy's HMS Royal Oak battleship—whose steel plates and octagon-shaped gun ports inspired the designers of the watch. Even today, this design tradition is evident in all Royal Oak watches.

Among the new Royal Oaks is the striking Royal Oak Concept watch, created in a limited edition of just 150 pieces. More than two years in the making, this resolutely futuristic watch houses a titanium hand-wound movement, complete with tourbillon and dynamograph. The watch also features a power-reserve display that is expressed in remaining going-barrel revolutions rather than hours.

The complex dynamograph allows the mainspring of the watch to be maintained within ideal winding limits by indicating exactly when the movement should be rewound. A winding gauge on the barrel determines the position of the dynamograph pointer on the dial—supplying the wearer with immediate information about the current mainspring stress and power. Rewinding the movement when the pointer moves beyond the zone of ideal stress shown on the indicator keeps the watch at peak precision. This accurate and rugged watch is housed in a case made of alacrite 602, a tungsten alloy borrowed from the aeronautical industry.

Another specialty is the Royal Oak City of Sails chronograph for navigators and sailors. Audemars Piguet has become a key co-sponsor of Team Alinghi (the Swiss Challenge for the America's Cup 2003), and has dedicated the Royal Oak City of Sails to this team. The world's oldest sporting trophy, the America's Cup (born in 1851) is a symbol of tradition and excellence, a hallmark of challenge, innovation and spirit—attributes that drew the attention of Audemars Piguet. This preeminent venue provides the perfect opportunity for Audemars Piguet to unveil the special-edition Royal Oak City of Sails chronograph.

Issued in 2003, the Royal Oak City of Sails is a chronograph equipped with a self-winding mechanism and 40 hours of power reserve. Water resistant to 50 meters, the Royal Oak City of Sails is created with an integrated rubber strap. Only 50 pieces will be crafted in platinum, and 200 pieces will be made in 18-karat pink gold. Audemars Piguet will also issue a limited series of 1,250 models in steel. In honor of the Challenge, the watch features an hour-counter adorned with the bright red Alinghi logo and a caseback that is intricately engraved with two racing sailboats.

ABOVE

This elegant Promesse watch is one of 7 watches packaged in a Colin Cowie-designed handbag.

TOP CENTER

The Jules Audemars Equation of Time watch is crafted in 18-karat pink gold and houses a self-winding movement with sunrise and sunset times, and perpetual calendar.

TOP RIGHT

The Edward Piguet No.3 of the Tradition of Excellence collection is a hand-wound mechanical chronograph with mainspring torque indicator, tourbillon mechanism and 70-hour power-reserve indicator. It is crafted in platinum.

BOTTOM RIGHT

Stunning in its beauty, this Edward Piguet Sapphire Tourbillon features a tourbillon mechanism and manual-wind movement. The transparent sapphire crystal of the plate reveals the sophistication of the high-precision mechanism and its functions.

- Continuing its alliance with the world of golf, Audemars Piguet has unveiled the Royal Oak Nick Faldo Special Series of watches. Produced in a limited edition of 450 pieces, the newest interpretation is dedicated to Europe's golf champion Nick Faldo. The oscillating weight of the watch echoes the texture of a golf ball and bears Faldo's signature. The watch is crafted with a platinum bezel to offset the steel of the case and bracelet. The watch houses a self-winding movement with date display and features a textured midnight-blue dial.

- Women's Royal Oak watches have also donned an elegant freshness as they are newly bedecked with diamonds and sapphires. The new Precious Royal Oak watches for women include a chronograph that is set in a platinum case and spectacularly enhanced by more than a thousand diamonds.

- In a unique alliance, Audemars Piguet in America has joined forces with Estée Lauder and Colin Cowie in a spectacular luxury and charity venture to benefit The Breast Cancer Research Foundation. To launch its all new Promesse ladies' collection of watches, Audemars Piguet turned to lifestyle guru Colin Cowie to design the unusual packaging: handbags. There are four different handbag styles, each holding a differently priced range of Promesse watches. The ultimate watch/bag combo is the diamond Promesse watch, which will be sold in a diamond-adorned handbag. Estée Lauder has created seven exclusive compacts to be sold along with the watches and handbags. The goal is to raise $1.5 million for The Breast Cancer Research Foundation through the sales of these watches and compacts.

AUDEMARS PIGUET

ROYAL OAK CONCEPT WATCH — REF. 25980AI

Movement: mechanical, manual-winding tourbillon; Audemars Piguet caliber 2896; all components manufactured and decorated by hand: chamfering, polishing and sapphire-blasting of the main plate, bars and bridges.
Functions: hours, minutes, small seconds; power-reserve indicator showing the number of barrel turns (1 turn every 6 hours); mainspring torque indicator (Dynamographe); crown function selector.

Case: Alacrite 602; transparent sapphire caseback; bezel in titanium (grade 1); case resistance to pressure: 50 bar (water resistant to 500 meters, about 1,650 ft.); max. case thickness: 17.51mm, max. thickness of sapphire crystal above: 4.58mm, max. thickness of sapphire crystal below: 4.13mm. The tourbillon is mounted on shock absorbers.
Dial: the bottom plate of the movement serves as a dial face; Dynamographe at 12; linear-shaped power-reserve indicator at 3; sub-dial for the seconds at 6; tourbillon visible at 9.
Strap: synthetic fiber with AP deployment clasp in titanium and stainless steel. **Also available:** limited series of 150 pieces in Alacrite 602, marking the 30th anniversary of the Royal Oak.

ROYAL OAK CONCEPT WATCH — REF. 25980AI

Representing a microcosm of innovations, the Royal Oak Concept, a hand-wound tourbillon model, is equipped with a dynamographe, a power-reserve display expressed in remaining going-barrel revolutions (in linear form) and a function selector for the crown. A particularly vulnerable complex watch mechanism, the tourbillon of this watch has been designed to withstand extreme conditions, thanks to several anti-shock devices. Until now, the winding-crown had to be pulled out in order to provide access to the various functions. For the Royal Oak Concept watch, a crown has been designed to remain flush with the case. A push-piece at 4, driving a column-wheel mechanism, provides a choice of three positions: Neutral, Rewinding, and Hour and minutes; adjustments are made by turning the crown. This system reduces wear and tear of the joints inside the crown and thereby enhances the water-resistance of the watch. The Royal Oak, which revolutionized the world of high-end sports watches thirty years ago, enters the third millennium with a resolutely futuristic version: the Royal Oak Concept.

ROYAL OAK CITY OF SAILS — REF. 25979OR

Movement: mechanical, automatic-winding, Audemars Piguet caliber 2385. Hand-decorated components: beveling, circular-graining pattern on the plates and Côtes de Genève on the bars and bridges. Diameter 11,5 lignes, height: 6.15mm; 37 jewels, 304 components; power reserve: 40 hours, cadence of the balance: 21,600 vph.
Functions: hours, minutes, small seconds; date; chronograph, 30-minute counter and 12-hour counter.

Case: 18K pink-gold; bezel and caseback secured by 8 screws; caseback is engraved with two sailboats racing against each other. Water resistant to 5atm.
Dial: decorated with "extra Grande Tapisserie" pattern; hour-counter is adorned with the flamboyant Alinghi logo.
Strap: notched, convex rubber with AP folding clasp.
Also available: Case in steel (series limited to 1,250 pieces); in 950 platinum (series limited to 50 pieces).

ROYAL OAK CITY OF SAILS — REF. 25979OR

Since 1972, the Royal Oak has been issued in many different versions with movements and "complications" ranging from the simplest to the most sophisticated. It has also accompanied important events via special-edition watches such as that dedicated to the Swiss Challenge for the America's Cup 2003. For sailors seeking to clip times to gain precious seconds, Audemars Piguet sought to provide a genuine competition watch. This chronograph is equipped with an innovative self-winding mechanism, designed to meet a primary criterion: to remain extremely thin despite the number of available functions. With a power reserve of 40 hours, water resistance to 50 meters, and a strap fashioned from an exclusive rubber, the Royal Oak City of Sails Chronograph reiterates the spirit of innovation governing the Manufacture. Crafted in 950 platinum, steel or 18K pink-gold, the chronograph features the new ultra-large "tapestry-work" pattern and, in honor of the Challenge, its hour-counter is adorned with the flamboyant Alinghi logo. The caseback is engraved with two sailboats racing against each other.

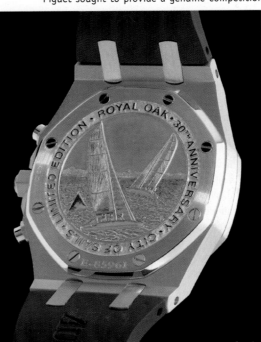

ROYAL OAK NICK FALDO   REF.15190SP

Movement: mechanical, automatic-winding, Audemars Piguet caliber 2225 with bi-directional automatic-winding; special "Nick Faldo" oscillating weight, oscillating weight segment in 21K gold; Diameter: 11,5 lignes (26mm), thickness: 3.25mm; 36 jewels, 422 parts; Power-reserve: 38 hours, cadence of the balance: 28,800 vph; Finish: movement handcrafted-decoration on all parts: beveling, circular-graining on the plate and Côtes de Genève on the bridges and bars.
Functions: hours, minutes, large seconds hand; date display.
Case: steel with bezel in 950 platinum; sapphire crystal and caseback. Water resistant to 5atm; engraving on the back.
Dial: midnight-blue with "Grande Tapisserie" motif in the center; luminescent numerals and hands.
Bracelet: steel with AP folding clasp.
Also available: limited series of 450 pieces.

ROYAL OAK NICK FALDO   REF.15190SP

With a special limited series of 450 watches dedicated to the most titled European golf champion, the Royal Oak Nick Faldo provides a new interpretation of a legendary watch: a model whose oscillating weight segment echoes the texture of a golf ball and carries the signature of the famous sportsman. Moreover, each purchaser will receive an Audemars Piguet leather golf bag, embroidered with Nick Faldo's signature, as well as a set of ten clubs. Playing with materials, the Royal Oak Nick Faldo special series uses 950 platinum for the bezel to offset the steel of the case and bracelet. This combination of metals creates a particularly subtle contrast, highlighted by alternating polished- and satin-brushed surfaces. 950 platinum illuminates the midnight-blue dial with exceptional elegance and refinement. Its luminescent Arabic numerals stand out around the center featuring the "Grande Tapisserie" motif. Finally, as one would expect from a limited series, the Royal Oak Nick Faldo special series is fitted with a sapphire crystal and caseback.

RUBBER-CLAD ROYAL OAK OFFSHORE CHRONOGRAPH   REF. 25940OK

Movement: Caliber 2226/2840 bi-directional automatic-winding; oscillating weight segment in 21K gold; Diameter: 11,5 lignes (26mm), thickness: 6.15mm; 54 jewels, 370 parts; Power-reserve: 38 hours, cadence of the balance: 28,800 vph; Finish: all parts decorated by hand: beveling, circular-graining pattern on the main plate and Côtes de Genève on the bridges.
Functions: hours and minutes, small seconds, numerical calendar display, chronometer, 1000-based tachometric scale.
Case: 18K pink-gold; rubber-clad 18K pink-gold bezel; rubber guards for the crown and push-pieces.
Dial: slate-gray with "extra Grande Tapisserie" pattern; Arabic numerals and white luminescent hour-markers.
Strap: black rubber, notched and padded, with steel reinforcements and AP folding clasp in 18K pink-gold.
Also available: in steel.

ROYAL OAK OFFSHORE CHRONO RUBBER   REF. 25940SK

Synthetic materials ever since played an outstanding role in Royal Oak Offshore models from a functional and aesthetic point of view. In fact, compounds such as Therban, used for gaskets (visible or hidden), and Silicone, used for the coating of crowns and pushers, characterize this family, created as a hypertechnical evolution of the classical Royal Oak collection. In the new chronograph, rubber constitutes the dominant aesthetic element. The bezel consists of a steel core, fastened on the case back by the usual through screw and nut system, and coated with a layer of black rubber. Years of studies and experiments allowed to achieve an optimal union between steel and rubber and to preserve the latter from wear. The whole is completed by a rubber strap and a dial characterized by the "Grande Tapisserie" decoration; on the anthracite background it is possible to distinguish silvered zones and highly luminescent embossed markers.

AUDEMARS PIGUET

ROYAL OAK AUTOMATIC   REF. 14790ST

Movement: mechanical, automatic-winding, Audemars Piguet 2125 caliber. Manufactured and finished by hand, decorated with Côtes de Genève pattern and beveled. **Functions:** hour, minute, second; date.
Case: stainless steel, two-piece case (Ø 37mm, thickness 8.2mm), polished and brushed finish; flat sapphire crystal; octagonal bezel with gasket and 8 recessed hexagon nuts in white gold fastening the 8 white-gold through screws of the case back; hexagonal screw-down crown. Water resistant to 5atm.

Dial: black, decorated with Grande Tapisserie pattern; luminescent applied steel bâton markers; luminescent steel bâton hands; printed minute track with 5 minute progression.
Indications: date at 3.
Bracelet: brushed steel; double fold-over clasp with safety pusher.
Also available: with Grande Tapisserie" cosmos" blue, silvered or Clous de Paris dark-gray dial; Pilot black dial, leather strap, bracelet; steel/yellow gold, Clous de Paris dark gray or silvered Grande Tapisserie dial, bracelet; yellow-gold, silvered Grande Tapisserie dial; with Pilot black dial, luminescent Arabic numerals, leather strap.

ROYAL OAK CHRONOGRAPH   REF. 25860ST

Movement: mechanical, automatic-winding, Audemars Piguet 2385 caliber (Frédéric Piguet 1185 base). Manufactured and finished by hand, decorated with Côtes de Genève pattern and beveled.
Functions: hour, minute, small second; date; chronograph with 3 counters.
Case: stainless steel, three-piece case (Ø 39mm, thickness 11mm), polished and brushed finish; flat sapphire crystal; octagonal bezel with gasket and 8 recessed

white-gold hexagon nuts fastening the 8 white-gold through screws of the case back; hexagonal screw-down crown; pushers with case protection. Water resistant to 5atm.
Dial: silvered, decorated with Grande Tapisserie pattern; counters decorated with circular beads; luminescent applied markers; luminescent bâton hands.
Indications: minute counter at 3; date between 4 and 5; small second at 6; hour counter at 9; center second counter; minute track.
Bracelet: stainless steel, brushed finish; fold-over clasp with safety pusher.
Also available: with black or "cosmos" blue or silvered dial; yellow gold with silvered or blue Clous de Paris dial; white gold with silvered dial.

ROYAL OAK DUAL TIME   REF. 25730ST

Movement: mechanical, automatic-winding, Audemars Piguet 2129/2845 caliber. Manufactured and finished by hand, decorated with Côtes de Genève pattern and beveled.
Functions: hour, minute, date; second time zone; power reserve.
Case: stainless steel, two-piece brushed case (Ø 36mm, thickness 9.5mm); flat sapphire crystal; octagonal bezel with gasket and 8 recessed white-gold hexagon nuts fastening the 8 white-gold through screws of the case back; hexagonal screw-down crown. Water resistant to 5atm.

Dial: "Cosmos" blue, decorated with Grande Tapisserie pattern; luminescent applied white-gold bâton markers; luminescent white-gold bâton hands.
Indications: date at 2; second time-zone with double hand at 6; power reserve between 8 and 11.
Bracelet: stainless steel, brushed finish; fold-over clasp with safety pusher.
Also available: black or silvered Grande Tapisserie dial; in steel/yellow gold with silvered Grande Tapisserie dial; in yellow gold with silvered Grande Tapisserie dial.

ROYAL OAK PERPETUAL CALENDAR   REF. 25820ST

Movement: mechanical, automatic-winding, extra-thin, Audemars Piguet 2120/2802 caliber. White-gold skeleton rotor. Hand-finished and hand-decorated.
Functions: hour, minute; perpetual calendar (date, day, month, year, moonphase).
Case: stainless steel, two-piece case (Ø 38.5mm, thickness 9.5mm), polished and brushed finish; flat sapphire crystal; octagonal bezel with gasket and 8 recessed hexagon nuts in white-gold, fastening the 8 white-gold through screws of the case

back; back displaying the movement through a sapphire crystal; 4 correctors on the middle; hexagonal screw-down crown. Water resistant to 2atm.
Dial: gray; applied white-gold bâton markers; white-gold bâton hands; printed minute track. **Indications:** date at 3; moonphase at 6; day at 9; month and four-year cycle at 12.
Bracelet: brushed stainless steel; fold-over clasp with safety pusher.
Also available: with sapphire blue dial; yellow-gold gilded dial; platinum and stainless steel black Grande Tapisserie dial; platinum Tuscany blue dial. Medium size with blue Clous de Paris dial Ref. 25800: in stainless steel; in yellow gold. Skeleton Ref. 25829: in steel; yellow gold; in platinum.

EDWARD PIGUET SAPPHIRE TOURBILLON — REF. 25924PT

Movement: Audemars Piguet caliber 2888, manual-winding; tourbillon regulator; quartz movement with rutile inclusions; Dimensions: 28.80 x 21.80mm, height: 6.51mm; 19 jewels, 167 parts; power reserve: 48 hours, cadence of the balance: 21,600 vph; Finish: rhodium-plated movement with Côtes de Genève decorative pattern, circular graining and hand engraving.
Functions: hours, minutes, small seconds.
Case: in 950 platinum; sapphire crystal and caseback.
Dial: tourbillon-bridge inspired by the shape of Galileo's pendulum.
Strap: full-grain crocodile leather with AP folding clasp.

EDWARD PIGUET CABINET 3 — REF.25958PT

Movement: mechanical, automatic-winding, Audemars Piguet caliber 2894 Maillechort (50% cuivre; 30% zinc; 20% nickel); Dimensions: 36.8 x 30.40mm, thickness: 8.90mm; 37 jewels, 323 parts and components; power reserve: in excess of 70 hours, cadence of the balance: 21,600 vph; Finish: all parts decorated by hand: beveling, circular-graining on the main plate and Côtes de Genève on the bridges.
Case: 950 platinum with sapphire crystal and caseback. Water resistant to 2atm.
Functions: hours and minutes; chronograph watch with sweep-seconds chronograph hand; tourbillon regulator; power reserve and Dynamographe.
Strap: black crocodile leather hand-stitched with AP folding clasp in 950 platinum.
Note: third piece of the "Tradition d'Excellence" collection (Limited Series of 20 pieces for sale plus one for the Audemars Piguet Museum).

EDWARD PIGUET CHRONOGRAPH — REF. 25925OR

Movement: mechanical, automatic-winding, Audemars Piguet 2385 caliber (Frédéric Piguet 1185 base). Manufactured and finished by hand, decorated with Côtes de Genève pattern and beveled.
Functions: hour, minute, small second, date, chronograph with 3 counters.
Case: 18K pink-gold, two-piece rectangular case (size 35.5 x 28.7mm, thickness 12mm); curved sapphire crystal; pink-gold crown; pink-gold oval pushers; case back attached by 4 screws. Moisture protection.
Dial: black, engine-turned (guilloché) hour ring; luminescent applied pink-gold markers and printed gilded Arabic numerals; luminescent pink-gold bâton hands.
Indications: minute counter at 3; date between 4 and 5; small second at 6; hour counter at 9; center second counter; white railway minute track.
Strap: crocodile leather, hand-stitched; pink-gold fold-over clasp in the shape of the firm's logo.
Also available: in white gold.

EDWARD PIGUET TOURBILLON — REF. 25956OR

Movement: mechanical, manual-winding, Audemars Piguet caliber 2871 with tourbillon device. Manufactured and finished by hand, decorated with Côtes de Genève pattern and beveled.
Functions: hour, minute, small second.
Case: 18K pink-gold, two-piece rectangular case (size 37.6 x 28.8mm, thickness 12.5mm), polished and brushed finish; curved sapphire crystal; pink-gold crown; case back attached by 4 screws, displaying the movement through a sapphire crystal. Moisture protection.
Dial: silvered, engine-turned (guilloché) with "flamed" pattern and aperture on the tourbillon; applied pink-gold bâton markers and Arabic numerals; pink-gold leaf style hands.
Indications: small second at 6 integrated in the tourbillon carriage.
Strap: crocodile leather, hand-stitched; pink-gold clasp.
Also available: in white gold; with engine-turned dial (guilloché with sun pattern): in pink gold; in platinum.

AUDEMARS PIGUET

MILLENARY CHRONOGRAPH   REF. 25822OR

Movement: mechanical, automatic-winding, Audemars Piguet 2126/2840 caliber. Rotor with 21K gold segment. Manufactured and finished by hand, decorated with Côtes de Genève pattern and beveled.
Functions: hour, minute, small second, date, chronograph with 3 counters.
Case: 18K pink-gold, three-piece oval case (size 37 x 41mm, thickness 11mm), polished and brushed finish; flat sapphire crystal; pink-gold crown with sapphire cabochon; case back attached by 6 screws. Water resistant to 2atm.
Dial: silvered; printed luminescent Arabic numerals; luminescent burnished gold bâton hands.
Indications: date with magnifying glass at 3; hour counter at 6; minute counter at 9; small second at 12; center second counter; scroll tachometer scale; telemeter scale on the flange.
Strap: crocodile leather; pink-gold clasp.
Also available: with black Arabic numerals; in stainless steel, white dial, luminescent Arabic numerals.

JULES AUDEMARS GRANDE COMPLICATION   REF. 25806OR

Movement: automatic-winding, A. Piguet 2885 caliber, consisting of more than 600 elements. Hand-made and hand-finished (Côtes de Genève pattern and beveled). **Functions:** hour, minute, small second, perpetual calendar (date, day, month, year, week, moon-phase), minute repeater, split-second chronograph with 2 counters.
Case: 18K pink-gold, three-piece case (Ø 42mm, thickness 13.5mm); flat sapphire crystal; middle with 5 correctors and slide repeater on case side; pink-gold crown and pushers (with coaxial split-second pusher); snap-on back. Moisture protection.
Dial: silvered; applied pink-gold bâton and cabochon markers; burnished gold leaf style hands.
Indications: minute counter and day of the week at 3; month and four-year cycle at 6; date and small second at 9; week and moonphase at 12; center split-second counters; minute track with divisions for 1/5 of a second.
Strap: crocodile leather; pink-gold fold-over clasp. Limited edition of 5 pieces a year.
Also available: in yellow gold and platinum.

JULES AUDEMARS METROPOLIS PERPETUAL CALENDAR   REF. 25919PT

Movement: automatic, extra-thin, A. Piguet, 2120/2804 caliber. Rotor with 21K gold segment, 42 jewels, 19,800 vph. Realized and finished by hand, decorated with Côtes de Genève and beveled. **Functions:** hour, minute, perpetual calendar (date, day, month, year), world time.
Case: platinum, three-piece case (Ø 39, thickness 10mm), polished and brushed finish; curved sapphire glass; middle with 3 correctors; white-gold crown; pusher for the independent hour correction of world time at 4; back attached by 5 screws, displaying the movement through a sapphire glass. Water resistant to 2atm.
Dial: silvered, engraved meridians and parallels, zones decorated with circular beads, with gold rim; applied white-gold Arabic numerals and cabochon markers; printed minute track with 5-minute progression; white-gold leaf style hands.
Indications: date at 3; world time at 6; day at 9; month and four-year cycle at 12.
Strap: crocodile leather; platinum fold-over clasp shaped with the firm's logo.
Also available: in pink gold.

JULES AUDEMARS TIME EQUATION   REF. 25934BA

Movement: automatic, extra-thin, A. Piguet 2120/2808 caliber, Realized and finished by hand. **Functions:** hour, minute, perpetual calendar (date, day, month, year, moon-phase), equation of time, sunrise and sunset hours.
Case: 18K yellow-gold, three-piece case (Ø 39, thickness 11.7mm), polished and brushed finish; curved sapphire glass; polished bezel with engraved digits for the equation of time indication (difference between solar and civil time in minutes); middle with 3 correctors; gold crown; back attached by 5 screws, displaying the movement through a sapphire glass. Water resistant to 2atm.
Dial: silvered, center and zones decorated with circular beads, with gold rim; applied faceted gold bâton and triangular markers; printed minute track with 5-minute progression; skeletonized burnished gold Alpha hands. **Indications:** four-year cycle between 1 and 2; sunset hour at 3; date and day of the week at 6; sunrise hour at 9; month and moonphase at 12; time equation center hand with sun.
Strap: crocodile leather; gold fold-over clasp shaped with the firm's logo.
Also available: in pink gold, black dial; white gold, dark gray dial.

CHRONOGRAPH ROYAL OAK OFFSHORE DAME   REF. 25986CK

Movement: automatic-winding chronograph watch with Audemars Piguet caliber 2385, with date calendar; rhodium-plated movement with Côtes de Genève decorative pattern and circular-graining pattern with 18K gold rotor; Diameter: 25.60mm, thickness: 5.50mm; 37 jewels; power reserve: 40 hours, cadence of the balance: 21,600 vph.
Functions: hours and minutes, small seconds, date, chronograph with 3 counters.
Case: 18K white-gold; rubber-clad gem-set bezel (32 diamonds, in total 1.28 carats) with gemstones certificate; sapphire crystal. Water resistant to 50 meters.
Dial: exclusive, traditional "extra Grande Tapisserie" decorative pattern.
Strap: rubber, notched and padded, with steel reinforcements and AP folding clasp in 18K white-gold.
Also available: in 18K yellow-gold with gray rubber strap.

JULES AUDEMARS REPETITION CARILLON DAME   REF. 25818OR

Movement: mechanical, manual-winding, Audemars Piguet 2873 caliber, consisting of 340 elements (enclosed in 2 ccm), 33 jewels, 21,600 vph, 48 hours power reserve. Hand-finished (Côtes de Genève and beveled).
Functions: hour, minute, small second; minute repeater.
Case: 18K pink-gold, three-piece case (Ø 28mm, thickness 8.65mm); curved sapphire crystal; repeater slide on the middle; pink-gold crown; closed snap-on back.
Dial: silvered, engine-turned (guilloché) hour ring; brushed center disc, additional zone decorated with circular beads; applied pink-gold bâton markers and Roman numerals; printed minute track with 5 minute progression; pink-gold bâton hands, blued bâton small second hand.
Indications: small second at 6.
Strap: crocodile leather; pink-gold clasp.
Model out of stock.
Also available: in platinum.

PROMESSE   REF. 67259ST

Movement: quartz; Audemars Piguet caliber 2508; manufactured and finished by hand; rhodium-plated movement with Côtes de Genève decorative pattern and circular graining.
Functions: hours and minutes.
Case: stainless steel set with diamonds and water resistant to 20 meters (over 65 feet); anatomically curved; two rows of diamonds; curved sapphire crystal; crown is tipped with a sapphire cabochon; Gemstones certificate; 12 diamonds (0.21 carats); Crown: 1 sapphire (0.14 carats).
Dial: sky-blue curved; two embossed Arabic numerals (6 and 12) tone-on-tone.
Bracelet: stainless steel.
Also available: in various sizes and color combinations of dial and strap; in many other jeweled-versions.

PROMESSE   REF. 67346BA

Movement: quartz; Audemars Piguet caliber 2508; manufactured and finished by hand; rhodium-plated movement with Côtes de Genève decorative pattern and circular graining.
Functions: hours and minutes.
Case: 18K yellow-gold; bezel and dial set with diamonds and water resistant to 20 meters (over 65 feet); anatomically curved; curved sapphire crystal; crown is tipped with a sapphire cabochon; Gemstones certificate; 78 diamonds (0.21 carats); Crown: 1 sapphire (0.14 carats).
Dial: two Arabic numerals (6 and 12) set with diamonds.
Bracelet: 18K yellow-gold.
Also available: in various sizes and color combinations of dial and strap; with bracelet; in many other jeweled-versions.

AUDEMARS PIGUET

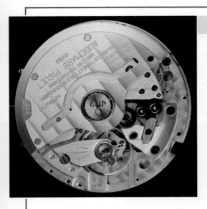

CALIBER 2124

Automatic movement, 45-hour autonomy, two-piece rotor with a 21K gold sector, on a ball bearing. **Functions:** hours, minutes, date. **Shape:** round. **Diameter:** 26.00mm. **Thickness:** 3.25mm. **Jewels:** 33. **Balance:** smooth, with two arms, in Glucydur. **Frequency:** 21,600 vph. **Balance-spring:** flat, Nivarox 1, with micrometer screw regulating device. **Shock-absorber system:** Kif. **Notes:** Pillar-plate decorated with a circular-graining pattern, bridges and rotor decorated with a Côtes de Genève pattern and beveled. **Derived calibers:** 2125 (center second); 2124/2825 (day-date; moonphase); 2126/2840 (chronograph; date); 2126/2841 (chronograph); 2127/2827 (hand date, day and month by discs and windows); 2129/2845 (date; p-reserve; two time zones); 2224, 2225, 2226 (28,800 vph); 2224/2814 (annual calendar); 2224/2811 (Star Wheel).

CALIBER 2120

Automatic-winding movement, 45-hour autonomy; three-piece rotor whose parts are connected by 4 screws: bearing ring rotating on 4 jewel rollers, steel main body, 21K gold sector. **Functions:** hours, minutes. **Shape:** round. **Diameter:** 28.00mm. **Thickness:** 2.45mm. **Jewels:** 36. **Balance:** smooth, with three arms, in Glucydur. **Frequency:** 19,800 vph. **Balance-spring:** flat, Nivarox 1. **Shock-absorber system:** Kif for both balance and escape wheel. **Notes:** Pillar-plate decorated with a circular-graining pattern, bridges decorated with a Côtes de Genève pattern and beveled. **Derived calibers:** 2120 QP (2120 + modules 2801 or 2802 perpetual calendar; thickness: 4.00mm, 38 jewels); 2120/2804 (perpetual calendar and world time); 2121 (2120 with date; thickness: 3.05mm).

CALIBER 2120/2808

Automatic-winding movement, 40-hour autonomy; three-piece rotor whose parts are connected by 4 screws: bearing ring rotating on 4 jewel rollers, 21K gold sector. **Functions:** hours, minutes; perpetual calendar (date, day, month, year, moonphase); dawn and sunset time; equation of time. **Shape:** round. **Diameter:** 28.00mm. **Thickness:** 5.35mm. **Jewels:** 41. **Balance:** smooth, with three arms, in Glucydur, with regulation masses. **Frequency:** 19,800 vph. **Balance-spring:** flat, Nivarox 1. **Shock-absorber system:** Kif for both balance and escape wheel. **Notes:** Pillar-plate decorated with a circular-graining pattern, bridges decorated with a Côtes de Genève pattern and beveled, skeletonized and chased rotor.

MODULE 2808

Module 2808, view on the dial side. This module, adopted for Jules Audemars Equation of time, displays perpetual calendar indications (date, day, month, four-year cycle and moonphase along a vertical line), dawn and sunset time (respectively at 9 and 3) and equation of time (by center hand with a scale engraved on the bezel). For both dawn/sunset time and equation of time, Audemars Piguet offers models set on the meridians of 16 towns or, at request, on any other place chosen by a client. This is a world premiere for wristwatches, derived from an Audemars Piguet pocket model from 1925.

MODULE 2840 (CHRONOGRAPH)

Functions: chronograph with three counters (center seconds, minutes and hours). **Shape:** round. **Diameter:** 30.00mm. **Thickness:** 2.90mm. **Jewels:** 19. **Notes:** Module base and bridge are decorated with a circular-graining pattern, levers are beveled. The photograph shows the Module without the upper bridge.

MODULE 2845

Functions: date; power reserve; two time zones. **Shape:** round. **Diameter:** 26.00mm. **Thickness:** 1.60mm. **Jewels:** 2. **Notes:** the base is decorated with a circular-graining pattern, the bridges with a Côtes de Genève pattern. Screw heads are finished by specular polishing. Combined with the Caliber 2129 in watches with hand subdial for hours and minutes of a second time zone.

MODULE 2801 (PERPETUAL CALENDAR)

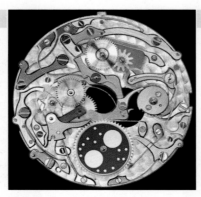

Functions: perpetual calendar (day, date, week and leap year by hands; moonphase by disc). **Shape:** round. **Diameter:** 28.00mm. **Thickness:** 1.85mm. **Jewels:** 2. **Notes:** the base is decorated with a circular-graining pattern, the levers and spring are brushed and beveled. Screw heads are finished by specular polishing. Combined with the Caliber 2120 within the "Millenary" family. **Derived modules:** 2802.

MODULE 2802

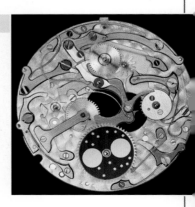

Functions: perpetual calendar (day, date, month and leap year by hands; moonphase by disc). **Shape:** round. **Diameter:** 28.00mm. **Thickness:** 1.85mm. **Jewels:** 2. **Notes:** the base is decorated with a circular-graining pattern, the levers and spring are brushed and beveled. Screw heads are finished by specular polishing. Combined with the Caliber 2120 within the "Royal Oak" and classical "Perpetual calendar" watch families.

CALIBER 2140

Automatic-winding movement with 45-hour autonomy, two-piece rotor with a 21K gold sector, mounted on a ball bearing. **Functions:** hours, minutes, seconds; date. **Shape:** round. **Diameter:** 20.00mm. **Thickness:** 3.95mm. **Jewels:** 31. **Balance:** smooth, two arms, in Glucydur. **Frequency:** 28,800 vph. **Balance-spring:** flat, Nivarox 1, with micrometer screw regulating device. **Shock-absorber system:** Kif.
Notes: bridges and rotor are decorated with a Côtes de Genève pattern and beveled.
Derived calibers: 2141 (without center seconds, to be combined with the Module 2806).

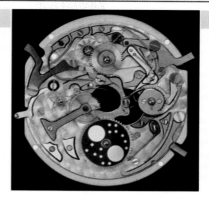

MODULE 2806 (PERPETUAL CALENDAR)

Functions: perpetual calendar (day, date, month and leap year by hands; moonphase by disc). **Shape:** round. **Diameter:** 20.80mm. **Thickness:** 1.55mm. **Jewels:** 2. **Notes:** the base is decorated with a circular-graining pattern, the levers and spring are brushed and beveled. Screw heads are finished by specular polishing. Combined with the Caliber 2141 in medium-sized Royal Oak, in Quantième Perpétuel Cambré and combined with the Caliber 2866 in the John Shaeffer Minute Repeater, Perpetual Calendar.

CALIBER 2003

Manual-winding movement, with 45-hour autonomy. **Functions:** hours, minutes. **Shape:** round. **Diameter:** 20.80mm. **Thickness:** extra-thin, 1.64mm. **Jewels:** 18 (escape wheel with end-stones). **Balance:** with compensating screws, in Glucydur. **Frequency:** 18,000 vph. **Balance-spring:** flat. **Shock-absorber system:** Kif.
Notes: the pillar-plate is decorated with a circular-graining pattern, bridges are decorated with a Côtes de Genève pattern and beveled.

CALIBER 2385

Automatic-winding movement with 45-hour autonomy, 18-karat-gold rotor. **Functions:** hours, minutes, small seconds; date; chronograph with three counters (center seconds, minutes and hours). **Shape:** round. **Diameter:** 25.60mm. **Thickness:** 5.40mm. **Jewels:** 37.
Balance: smooth, with three arms, in Glucydur. **Frequency:** 21,600 vph. **Balance-spring:** flat, Nivarox 1, with micrometer screw regulating device. **Shock-absorber system:** Kif.
Notes: the pillar-plate and bridges are decorated with a circular-graining pattern. The balance-bridge's winding device and

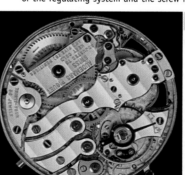

the rotor are decorated with a Côtes de Genève pattern and beveled. The components of the regulating system and the screw heads are finished by specular polishing.

CALIBER 2875

Automatic-winding movement, 60-hour autonomy; oscillating inertial hammer mass and elastic shock absorbers at trip end. **Functions:** hours, minutes; date; power reserve. **Shape:** round. **Diameter:** 30.00mm. **Thickness:** 5.70mm. **Jewels:** 41. **Balance:** two arms, with compensating screws, in Glucydur and tourbillon device with titanium carriage. **Balance-spring:** flat. **Notes:** the pillar-plate is decorated with a circular-graining pattern, bridges are decorated with circular graining and Côtes de Genève patterns and beveled. The oscillating mass and the thin titanium carriage of the tourbillon are brushed and beveled. The regulation

crown is positioned on the rear side. The photograph shows the dial side. The tourbillon is placed at 6, the hour and minute pivots at 12, the date pivot at 3, the reserve pivot at 9.

CALIBER 2877

Basic caliber: 2866. Manual-winding movement, 70-hour autonomy. **Functions:** hours, minutes, small seconds; hour, quarter and minute repeater; power reserve of the sonnerie. **Shape:** round. **Diameter:** 24.25mm. **Thickness:** 5.00mm. **Jewels:** 33. **Balance:** with compensating screws, with two arms, in Glucydur. **Frequency:** 21,600 vph. **Balance-spring:** flat, first quality. **Shock-absorber system:** Kif. **Notes:** the pillar-plate is decorated with a circular-graining pattern, bridges are decorated with a Côtes de Genève pattern. The balance-spring regulation system and the screw heads are finished by specular polishing and beveled. The movement shown in the photograph is the Caliber 2866 (34 jewels and 45-hour autonomy) which originated the 2877, displaying the sonnerie power reserve as well as the sonnerie status.

CALIBER 2866

Caliber 2866, view on the dial side. The pillar-plate is decorated with a circular-graining pattern; the levers and springs are brushed and beveled. Screw heads are finished by specular polishing. On the John Shaeffer Minute Repeater Skeleton model, today out of production and on which this Caliber was mounted, the dial had been eliminated (time indications were printed directly on the sapphire crystal) to allow following the "life" of this fascinating feature, when the repeater was activated.

CALIBER 2865

Basic caliber: 2866. Manual-winding movement with the same technical features as Caliber 2866 from which it derives, except for the greater thickness due to the modification, on the dial side (shown here), for the jumping hour and minute discs with a window. The basic caliber was used exclusively for the John Shaeffer Minute Repeater series in four versions: basic (Caliber 2866) also with sight movement on the dial side: "Squelette" with a traditional hand display; with jumping hours and minutes: "Saltarello" (Caliber 2865); with a jumping display "Star Wheel" (Caliber 2867) with a big-sized arc window

in which hours appear printed on rotating sapphire discs; and finally, a perpetual calendar (Caliber 2866 + Module 2806).

AUDEMARS PIGUET

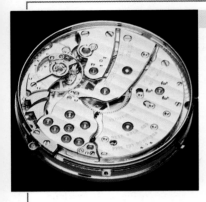

CALIBER 2868

Manual-winding movement, autonomy of 48 hours. **Functions:** hours, minutes, seconds; hour and quarter repeater; grande and petite "au passage" sonneries.
Shape: round. **Diameter:** 28.60mm. **Thickness:** 5.20mm. **Jewels:** 51 (escape wheel with end-stones).
Balance: with compensating screws, two arms, in Glucydur.
Frequency: 18,000 vph.
Balance-spring: flat, first quality.
Shock-absorber system: Kif.
Notes: the pillar-plate is decorated with a circular-graining pattern, bridges are decorated with a Côtes de Genève pattern and beveled. The balance-spring regulation system, the repeater hammers and the screw heads are beveled and finished by specular polishing.

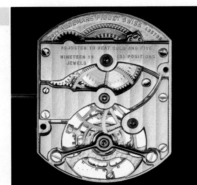

CALIBER 2868

Caliber 2868 dial-side view. The photograph shows the great complexity of the movement, consisting of 410 pieces. A three-year planning work and over 1,000 construction drawings were needed for its realization. In this case, the hour and quarter repeater—a complication almost as difficult to realize as the hours-quarters-minutes repeater—is combined with the "au passage" sonnerie allowing for three options: "Grande sonnerie" (hours and quarters); "Petite sonnerie" (just hours); or "Mute" that may be selected by means of a cursor positioned on the case middle. The Grande sonnerie has autonomy of 10 hours, the Petite sonnerie of 32 hours and the watch of 48 hours. A special device eliminates the noise of the regulating system, when the sonnerie is working.

CALIBER 2871

Manual-winding movement, autonomy of 48 hours.
Functions: hours, minutes, small seconds.
Shape: rectangular with arc-shaped pole sides. **Size:** 21.45x28.20mm. **Thickness:** 6.10mm. **Jewels:** 19.
Balance: with compensating screws, two arms, in Glucydur, with tourbillon device.
Frequency: 21,600 vph.
Balance-spring: Breguet.
Notes: the pillar-plate is decorated with a circular-graining pattern and gilded, bridges are decorated with a Côtes de Genève pattern, beveled and gilded. The bridge and tourbillon carriage are brushed and beveled.
Derived calibers: 2878 (2871 with power reserve).

CALIBER 2871

Caliber 2871 dial-side view. The pillar-plate is decorated with a circular graining (concentric circle) pattern. Screw heads are finished by specular polishing. In the complete watch (Tourbillon Cambré) the tourbillon device is visible through a round aperture on the dial and through the sapphire crystal back, which seconds the movement's shape.

CALIBER 2869

Manual-winding movement, autonomy of 48 hours. **Functions:** hours, minutes, small seconds; hour, quarter and minute repeater; perpetual calendar (big-sized date with double disc, day, month, four-year cycle). **Shape:** round. **Diameter:** 29.30mm. **Thickness:** 7.60mm. **Jewels:** 38.
Balance: with compensating screws, two arms, in Glucydur, with tourbillon device.
Frequency: 21,600 vph.
Balance-spring: Breguet.
Notes: the pillar-plate is decorated with a circular-graining pattern, bridges are decorated with a Côtes de Genève pattern and beveled. The tourbillon bridge and repeater hammers are beveled and finished by specular polishing. Screw heads are polished and levers are brushed and beveled. Consists of 443 elements.

CALIBER 2869

Caliber 2869 dial-side view. Outstanding features of this Caliber are the combination of the three most valuable complications (tourbillon, repeater and perpetual calendar), the unusual double-disc big date and the four-year cycle display by a complete circle and three circle arcs (the number of visible marks on the dial indicates the current year). The tens disc of the big-sized date indicates also the digits 10, 20 and 30, which makes the 0 useless on the units disc.

CALIBER 2891

Manual-winding movement, autonomy of 48 hours. **Functions:** hours, minutes, small seconds; hour, quarter and minute repeater; grande and petite chime sonneries with a dynamograph; power reserve of the sonnerie. **Shape:** round. **Diameter:** 29.30mm. **Thickness:** 5.80mm **Jewels:** 57 (escape wheel with end-stones). **Balance:** with compensating screws, two arms, in Glucydur. **Frequency:** 21,600 vph.
Balance-spring: flat, first quality.
Shock-absorber system: Kif.
Notes: the pillar-plate is decorated with a circular-graining pattern, bridges are decorated with a Côtes de Genève pattern and beveled. The balance-spring regulation system, the repeater hammers and the screw heads are beveled and finished by specular polishing.

CALIBER 2891

Caliber 2891 dial-side view. The special technical feature—a novelty for the whole horology sector—introduced in this movement is represented by the dynamograph, i.e. the indication of the force transmitted by the barrel to the movement. When the spring is completely wound or almost uncoiled, the movement's functioning may be impaired. By controlling the force transmitted, it is possible to wind the movement manually so that the spring tension always is correct and, hence, the transmission-force optimal. By turning the crown clockwise, the movement's barrel is wound; by turning it counterclockwise, the sonnerie's barrel is wound. The autonomy is 22 hours for the Grande sonnerie, 60 hours for the Petite sonnerie, 48 hours for the watch.

DISTRIBUTORS

 GERMANY

Audemars Piguet Deutschland
Bahnhofstrasse 44/46
65185 Wiesbaden
Tel: 49 611 341 750
info@audemarspiguet-gmbh.de

 FRANCE

Audemars Piguet France
19, rue Marbeuf
75008 Paris
Tel: 33 1 44 94 97 64
Fax: 33 1 44 94 97 98

 MEXICO

Raconli SA de CV
Periferico Sur 4349, Local 18
Col. Jardines de la Montaña
Mexico D.F.C.P
Tel: 525 645 22 12
Fax: 525 645 20 90

 SPAIN

Catol SA
Paseo de Gracia 95, 6 – 1
08008 Barcelona
Tel: 34 932 720 250
Fax: 34 932 720 251

 NORTH AMERICA

Audemars Piguet North America
545 Madison Avenue
New York 10022, NY USA
Tel: 1 212 758 8400
Fax: 1 212 758 8538

 GREECE

Chrono Hellas Ltd.
9 Zalokosta Street
10671 Athens
Tel: 301 0363 82 86
Fax: 301 0362 29 77

 MIDDLE EAST

Audemars Piguet Moyen Orient
Sinelfil Horch Tadet
Immeuble Tamer
Beyrouth
Tel: 961 1 499 851
Fax: 961 1 499 843

 SWITZERLAND

Audemars Piguet Switzerland
Av. Auguste Forel 6
1110 Morges
Switzerland
Tel: 41 21 811 22 80
Fax: 41 21 802 49 57

 AUSTRALIA

Desco Australia Ltd
154 Elizabeth Street, Level 3
NSW 2000
Sydney
Tel: 612 92 64 78 22
Fax: 612 92 61 4067

 HONG KONG

Desco Hong Kong Ltd
901 Chinachem Golden Plaza
77 Mody Road
Tsimshatsui East
Kowloon
Tel: 852 2 369 12 21
Fax: 852 2 369 54 83

 NETHERLANDS

Bagijn BV
Alkmaardermeer 49
3068 Rotterdam
Tel: 31 10 420 44 59
Fax: 31 10 455 44 46

 TAIWAN

All Prestige Ltd.
21/F-A N° 216 Section 2
Tun Hua South Road
Taipei, Taiwan ROC
Tel: 886 2 2377 39 79
Fax: 886 2 2377 87 96

 BELGIUM

Elteger SA
523, Chaussée de Louvain
1380 Lasne
Tel: 32 2 351 44 40

 ISRAEL

JB Jewelers
71 Ibn Gvirol Street
Gan Ha'ir
61164 Tel Aviv
Tel: 972 3 523 01 10
Fax: 972 3 523 11 27
jb@jb-jewelers.com

 PORTUGAL

Relogios & Companhia Lda
Avenida de França 256- 3°
Sala 3.1. / Edificio Capitolio
4050 Porto
Tel: 351 22 834 99 60
Fax: 351 22 830 18 13

 TURKEY

Cogex SA
78, rue du Rhône
1204 Geneva
Tel: 41 22 311 38 32
Fax: 41 22 311 60 31

 CARIBBEAN

Bay Distributors Inc.
Bulkeley Great House
Bulkeley
St George
Barbades, West Indies
Tel: 1 246 437 7509
Fax: 1 246 435 6184
info@baydistributors.com

 ITALY

Audemars Piguet Italia
Via Melchiorre Gioia, 168
20125 Milan
Tel: 39 02 66 98 50 54
Fax: 39 02 66 98 40 03

 RUSSIA

Ego Elite
15, Bolchaia Polanka
109180 Moscow
Tel: 70 95 95 90 120
Fax: 70 95 95 90 129

UNITED KINGDOM

Time Products PLC
23, Grosvenor Street
London W1K 4QL
Tel: 44 207 416 41 60
Fax: 44 207 416 41 61

 EASTERN EUROPE

La Boutique Suisse AG
Mittelstrasse 24
2560 Nidau, Switzerland
Tel: 41 32 332 82 82
Fax: 41 32 332 82 32

 JAPAN

Desco Japon Ltd
Sanko Bldg, 13-1
Ginza 1-chome, Chuo-Ku
Tokyo 104 -8201
Tel: 81 3 3562 1281
Fax: 81 3 3562 1285
dj.audemarspiguet@desco-group.com

 SINGAPORE

Audemars Piguet Singapore
501 Orchard Road
03-10/11 Wheelock Place
23880 Singapore
Tel: 65 278 54 50
Fax: 65 273 25 09

125

BAUME & MERCIER

With its watchmaking roots planted in the 1500s, Baume & Mercier is a brand teeming with tradition. Formally founded in the early 1830s as the Société Baume Frères, the company was making table and pocket watches to export throughout Europe, Australia and New Zealand. The brand's ingenuity in design and prowess in technical craftsmanship earned it a wealth of international accolades and awards over the decades.

In the early 1900s, William Baume established a close friendship with watchmaker Paul Mercier and in 1918 the two formed Baume & Mercier, headquartered in Geneva. At the height of the wristwatch craze, the two devoted their energies to creating fashion-forward watches that housed technological advancements. Throughout the ensuing decades, Baume & Mercier unveiled thin automatic timepieces, tuning fork watches, and a stunning octagon-shaped watch line that won the company a Golden Rose prize at an international exhibition in 1973.

In the mid-1980s, Baume & Mercier formed an alliance with Piaget Watch Company and became part of the Vendôme Luxury Group in 1988. Today, under the auspices of this holding company, Baume & Mercier continues to turn out fashion-forward watches of glamour and strength. Among its top collections are the sleek Linea, the high-styled Hampton, and the bold and sporty CapeLand.

Recently, the brand added to all three of these key collections with several exciting new models. The Hampton Spirit recalls Baume & Mercier's first electronic watch movement with a dial that evoked the shape of the television screens of the early 1970s. The bold rectangular watch features cushioned accents on case corners and edges and is undeniably masculine. It is available in two models—18-karat white gold or pink gold. Each version is available in a limited edition of just 172 pieces. The Hampton Spirit houses an automatic movement that is COSC certified. It features a sapphire caseback and a dial with striking guilloché tapestry decoration.

FACING PAGE

FAR LEFT

This Hampton Spirit screen-shaped watch is crafted in 18-karat white gold and houses an automatic movement with 42 hours of power reserve. It is a COSC-certified chronometer and is water resistant to 50 meters.

TOP RIGHT

Called the CapeLand S Titanium, this automatic watch with chronograph functions is crafted in titanium and features a titanium and steel bracelet. It is water resistant to 200 meters and each watch is individually numbered on the caseback.

BOTTOM RIGHT

Written by Dominique Flèchon, *Baume & Mercier* describes the poignant ambitions and the growth of the company.

THIS PAGE

TOP RIGHT

The Linea variations for women are set with stunning Top Wesselton VVSI diamonds.

CENTER RIGHT

The new Hampton Mini watches for women are adorned with varying degrees of Top Wesselton diamonds.

BOTTOM LEFT

The CapeLand PM watch for women dons new elegance with a diamond-set bezel.

Baume & Mercier has also added a COSC-certified chronometer to its strong CapeLand series of timepieces. The bold new CapeLand S Titanium is crafted in high-tech titanium and the watch features a rotating bezel with graduated 15 minutes readout. The watch crown is covered and the timepiece is water resistant to 200 meters for professional use. Combining luxury and sport, Baume & Mercier has dressed the watch with a dark gray dial and anthracite counters, as well as luminescent hands and indexes. It is equipped with a steel and titanium bracelet for rugged durability.

HIGHLIGHTS

- Baume & Mercier has added some important models for women. The new Linea versions of interchangeable bracelet and strap watches are now adorned with diamonds. Crafted in 18-karat gold, these Linea models are set with 104 Top Wesselton diamonds on the bezel.

- Similarly, Baume & Mercier has unveiled the CapeLand PM watch for women. The round stainless steel case is set with 28 VVS1 Top Wesselton diamonds. Water resistant to 100 meters, it is fitted with a domed scratch-resistant sapphire crystal. There is also a new series of Hampton Mini watches that are set with diamonds and feature an 18-karat gold, elegantly integrated bracelet.

- A new book has been published that traces the history of the Baume Brothers, the Baume Frères watchmaking house and the Baume & Mercier brand. *Baume & Mercier* offers an insight into the minds and ambitions of the forefathers of this prestigious brand.

BEDAT & Cº

t he first Bedat & Cº watches were unveiled to the world six years ago. Refined and elegant in nature, this entirely Swiss-made brand offered a timeless yet modern design that was an immediate international success.

Designed by Christian Bedat, who formed the company with his watch-veteran mother Simone, Bedat & Cº watches offer distinct personality and originality. Each watch is designed and crafted with precision and meticulous care. Indeed, when the company was in its development stages, the Bedats had already delineated a strict code of ethics and quality standards for their timepieces.

In the year 2000, the distinguished Gucci Group took a profound interest in Bedat & Cº and by the end of the year purchased 85 percent of the brand. With Christian Bedat still at the helm as CEO and Creative Director, Bedat & Cº continues its legacy of luxury and authenticity.

There are four key collections in the Bedat & Cº line, each identified by a number. Arguably the premier collection, the Nº 7 collection has received the most attention this past year. In fact, Bedat & Cº has rolled out a host of new and exciting models in the Nº 7 series.

Determined to expand the men's watch business, Bedat ocused his attentions on adding complexities to the line. While the Nº 7 already includes a ChronoAutomatic and an Annual Calendar watch, Bedat has now added an elegant dual-time-zone watch.

Christian Bedat

FACING PAGE

TOP RIGHT

This elongated Nº 7 watch features a brown dial on a brown leather padded strap. The watch is set in 18-karat yellow gold with pink-gold bezel and lugs.

FAR LEFT

This Dual Time watch with tawny dial and sapphire crystal features an 18-karat yellow-gold case with an 18-karat pink-gold bezel.

BOTTOM LEFT

This elegant Dual Time watch features a silver dial and brilliant blue hands. The strap is fully padded hand-stitched alligator.

THIS PAGE

TOP LEFT

This stunning 18-karat pink-gold bezeled watch is set with 162 carats of diamonds. It features a white dial and a cranberry fully padded fully padded hand-stitched alligator.

TOP CENTER

Crafted in steel with a supple bracelet, the Nº 7 shown here is set with 162 diamonds on the case.

TOP RIGHT

The dial of this steel Nº 7 watch is a new brown guilloché that is offset by the beauty of fully padded a hand-stitched alligator strap.

BOTTOM LEFT

For classic elegance, this Annual Calendar watch is crafted in 18-karat yellow gold and features an 18-karat pink-gold bezel. The white dial is accented with bright blue hands.

BOTTOM RIGHT

Crafted in steel, this Annual Calendar watch features a striking black dial with bright orange accents.

HIGHLIGHTS

■ The striking new Dual Time watch features a round main dial to indicate local time, with a round subdial at 6:00 to indicate the second time zone. Classically elegant, the dial is offered in an array of colors, including white, black and a tawny shade. The watch is crafted in either steel or in a combination of 18-karat rose and yellow gold.

■ Bedat also added new versions to the Annual Calendar watch, with the addition of a black sunburst guilloché dial and an antique-ivory dial. In addition to the existing steel cased version, Bedat unveils an 18-karat yellow-gold model with an 18-karat pink-gold bezel and brilliant blue hands. This timepiece is an elegant mix of past and present with its chocolate brown crocodile strap. There are also some new bracelet versions and some diamond-adorned models that have joined the mix.

■ All Bedat & Cº timepieces are engraved with an individual serial number that identifies its origin. Additionally, each watch is accompanied by the brand's A.O.S.C. certificate—the company's own seal that guarantees that all watch parts are of Swiss origin. The A.O.S.C. identifies all materials used in the watch, including metal choice, gemstone choice and carat weight.

BEDAT & CO

BEDAT & C° N°3 — REF B314.010.100

Movement: automatical, ETA calibre 8 ¾ 2000/1
Functions: hour, minute, center seconds, date at 6 o'clock with BEDAT & C° logo replacing the date 8.
Case: stainless steel, barrel shaped. Curved sapphire crystal. Steel crown identified with BEDAT & C° logo and trademarks. Inside casing ring in metal. Water resistant to 5 atm.

Strap: orange alligator fully padded hand stitched with BEDAT & C° lining. Regular steel buckle.
Dial: BEDAT & C° guilloche, white, roman numerals makers. BEDAT & C° own designed hands. Logo at 8 o'clock.
Note: Swiss origin of each component certified with the BEDAT & C° trademark Swiss AOSC and the hallmark.

BEDAT & C° N°3 — REF. B314.050.100

Movement: automatical, ETA calibre 8 ¾ 2000/1
Functions: hour, minute, center seconds, date at 6 o'clock with BEDAT & C° logo replacing the date 8.
Case: stainless steel, barrel shaped. Curved sapphire crystal. Steel crown identified with BEDAT & C° logo and trademarks. Inside casing ring in metal. Water resistant to 5 atm.

Diamonds: set on the bezel and the sides with 173 Top Wesselton VVSI diamonds. (1.95 cts).
Strap: alligator fully padded with BEDAT & C° lining. Regular steel buckle.
Dial: BEDAT & C° guilloche, white, roman numerals makers. BEDAT & C° own designed hands. Logo at 8 o'clock.
Note: Swiss origin of each component certified with the BEDAT & C° trademark Swiss AOSC and the hallmark.

BEDAT & C° N°7 — REF B727.050.109

Movement: automatical, ETA calibre 8 ¾ 2000/1,
Functions: Automatic, hour, minute, second, date at 4 o'clock with BEDAT & C° logo replacing the date 8.
Case: stainless steel case, sapphire crystal. Steel crown identified with BEDAT & C° logo and trademarks. Water resistant to 5 atm.
Diamonds: 151 diamonds on bezel and dial (2.12cts).

Strap: fully padded hand stitched alligator with BEDAT & C° lining. Regular buckle in steel.
Dial: BEDAT & C° guilloche, steel, diamond makers. BEDAT & C° own designed hands..
Also available: on stainless steel bracelet
Note: Swiss origin of each component certified with the BEDAT & C° trademark Swiss AOSC and the hallmark.

BEDAT & C° N°7 — REF B727.310.800

Movement: automatical, ETA calibre 8 ¾ 2000/1,
Functions: Automatic, hour, minute, second, date at 4 o'clock with BEDAT & C° logo replacing the date 8.
Case: yellow gold case, rose bezel gold case back, sapphire crystal. Yellow gold crown identified with BEDAT & C° logo and trademarks. Water resistant to 5 atm.

Strap: Burgundy fully padded hand stitched alligator with BEDAT & C° lining. Regular buckle in yellow gold.
Dial: BEDAT & C° guilloche,. BEDAT & C° own designed hands.
Also available: with diamonds on case and bezel (1.62 cts).
Note: Swiss origin of each component certified with the BEDAT & C° trademark Swiss AOSC and the hallmark.

BEDAT & Cº N. 7   REF B777.010.310

Movement: mechanical, automatic winding. Annual Calendar calibre.
Functions: hour, minute, small second at 4 o'clock, date at 12 o'clock with Bedat & Cº logo replacing the date 8, month at 8 o'clock.
Case: stainless steel, three pieces, rectangular shaped, curved case (satin and polished finish). Curved and bevelled sapphire crystal. Case back attached by screws. Crown identified with Bedat & Cº logo and trademarks. Inside casing ring in metal. Water resistant to 5 atm.
Strap: fully padded hand stitched alligator with Bedat & Cº lining. Bedat & Cº steel expansion clasp.
Dial: Bedat & Cº guilloche, black, indexes. Bedat & Cº own designed hands. Logo at 8 o'clock.
Also available: silver, indexes or antique white, roman numerals.
Note: Swiss origin of each components certified with the Bedat & Cº trademark SWISS A.O.S.C. and the hallmark.

BEDAT & Cº N°7   REF B787.010.710

Movement: automatical, ETA calibre 2004/1,
Functions: Duo Time complication by Antoine Preziuso, hour, minute, date at 12 o'clock with BEDAT & Cº logo replacing the date 8.
Case: stainless steel case, bevelled sapphire crystal. Steel crown identified with BEDAT & Cº logo and trademarks. Water resistant to 5 atm.
Strap: fully padded hand stitched alligator with BEDAT & Cº lining. Steel expansion clasp.
Dial: BEDAT & Cº guilloche, steel, diamond makers. BEDAT & Cº own designed hands. Logo at 8 o'clock.
Also available: In yellow and pink gold with brown or silver dial
Note: Swiss origin of each component certified with the BEDAT & Cº trademark Swiss AOSC and the hallmark.

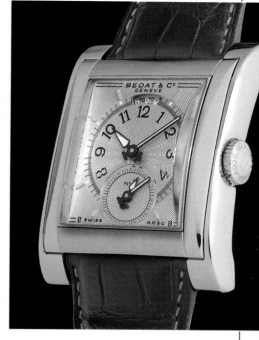

BEDAT & Cº N. 7   REF B768.310.800

Movement: automatic winding, ETA calibre 12 1/2 2894.
Functions: hour, minute, center second, date at 4 o'clock with Bedat & Cº logo replacing the date 8. Chronograph functions: recorder of second, minute (30) and hour (12).
Case: yellow and rose gold, three pieces, rectangular shaped, curved case (satin and polished finish). Curved sapphire crystal. Case back attached by screws. Crown identified with Bedat & Cº logo and trademarks. Inside casing ring in metal. Water resistant to 5 atm.
Strap: fully padded hand stitched alligator. Bedat & Cº steel folding clasp.
Dial: Bedat & Cº guilloche, antique white, roman numerals. Bedat & Cº own designed hands. Logo at 8 o'clock.
Note: Swiss origin of each components certified with the Bedat & Cº trademark SWISS A.O.S.C. and the hallmark.

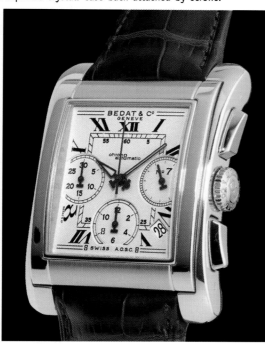

BEDAT & Cº N°7   REF B737.310.410

Movement: automatical, ETA calibre 8 _ 2000/1
Functions: hour, minute, center seconds, date at 6 o'clock with BEDAT & Cº logo replacing the date 8.
Case: yellow gold case, white gold case back, pink gold bezel and lugs, sapphire crystal. Pink gold crown identified with BEDAT & Cº logo and trademarks. Water resistant to 5 atm.
Strap: fully padded hand stitched leather with BEDAT & Cº lining. Yellow gold expansion clasp.
Dial: BEDAT & Cº guilloche, brown, diamond makers. BEDAT & Cº own designed hands. Logo at 8 o'clock.
Also available: gold or silver, indexes.
Note: Swiss origin of each component certified with the BEDAT & Cº trademark Swiss AOSC and the hallmark.

BERTOLUCCI

When Bertolucci launched its watch collection 16 years ago, no one could have foreseen the tremendous success the brand would have. A leading designer of distinct style, Bertolucci has consistently unveiled timepieces that set trends and remain on the cutting edge of creativity.

Italian Remo Bertolucci unveiled his first collection of timepieces to the world in **1987**. Individualistic in style, the Vir timepiece series featured elegantly sculpted bracelets that emulated the water-caressed pebbles found on the shores of Neuchâtel's lake. This concept embodied a simple purity and the beautiful design was luxurious to the touch. Bertolucci was an instant hit. Since then, the brand has turned out creative designs for men and women that are always in step with the latest fashions.

In **1998**, with spectacular fanfare, Bertolucci launched the now-famed Serena collection. Designing with a younger audience in mind, Bertolucci blended brilliant colors with ergonomic styling. The haute couture watch featured a curved oval case set directly onto a custom-created strap. Feminine and futuristic, the Serena has grown to be one of the most sensual and successful Bertolucci collections.

In **2001**, a luxury group of private investors purchased the Bertolucci brand and resolved to increase distribution in key markets around the world and to further enhance the brand's development. Remaining true to the original philosophy of distinctive styling, Bertolucci's owners made important moves.

Under the vigilant eye of Jean-Paul Gaillard, Bertolucci's managing director, the brand was carefully repositioned. Gaillard has adopted an all-new marketing concept for Bertolucci and has evolved the product—adding significantly to the key collections. Gaillard also turned his attentions to the all-important American market.

Gaillard entered into a joint venture with Bellport Time Group in **2001** to open Bertolucci North America LLC. Under the direction of entrepreneur Stephen Butler, the year **2002** was one of excitement for the brand in America. Today, Bertolucci is well poised for even further growth.

New ideas, approaches and products are propelling the Bertolucci brand to new levels of elegance and beauty. The structural and strategic innovations put into place in 2001 by the brand's new owners have placed it on sound economic footing.

The new leadership has provided the company with a new corporate communications strategy and a solid structure. This tour de force has enriched Bertolucci with new marketing openings and enhancements to the product's key collections.

Bertolucci's three core lines, Serena, Vir and Uomo, are crafted in the finest materials—steel, 18-karat gold and with precious stones. Each has a reference number engraved on the caseback and the dials are crafted of mother of pearl or guillochéd metal. The Neuchâtel watchmaker uses fine movements for its timepieces, including automatics and chronometers.

In 2002, Bertolucci made great strides with its collections—adding strikingly oversized chronograph chronometers to the Uomo series and presenting jeweled versions of varying degrees to the Serena and Vir collections.

Women factor high on Bertolucci's scale, and the brand has devoted much time to the feminine aspects of its collections. Once again the Serena takes center stage with breathtaking new models.

Perhaps top among them is the Serena Steel with bracelet. Its innovative, state-of-the-art design blends perfectly with the Serena concept of sensual, flowing curves and supple elegance. The integrated steel bracelet is perfectly contoured to match the dial and creates a feeling of harmony. The Serena with bracelet is available with mother-of-pearl dials in a variety of colors and is set elegantly with diamonds to varying degrees. The launch of the first Serena bracelet watch brings monumental opportunities to the line in terms of future growth into precious metals and gemstone settings.

While the custom-made leather strap has always been at the heart of the Serena collection, this year the line has incorporated lizard. The depth and texture of lizard give a very light and sophisticated appeal to the Serena.

BERTOLUCCI

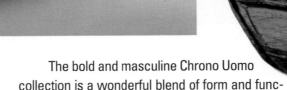

The bold and masculine Chrono Uomo collection is a wonderful blend of form and function. Forceful and balanced in design, the stainless steel case is matte-finished and accented with a high-polished bezel. Crowns, pushers and case-to-bracelet attachments are also polished for a dramatic finish. The automatic watch is a COSC-certified chronometer and the chronograph offers three counters. The Chrono Uomo is also available with a diamond-set bezel. Water resistant to 100 meters, the watch features all of the appropriate aspects of a sport timepiece—screw-down crown and caseback, and double-sided anti-glare sapphire crystal.

Also joining the Uomo lineup is a new large-sized watch with a diameter of 42mm. Distinguished and sporty, the Uomo Large is a voluminous watch that houses a COSC-certified automatic chronometer movement. It is also available with a diamond-set bezel and can be purchased in either steel or in 18-karat gold with a matching bracelet.

- Bertolucci has added to Vir, its most famous timepiece series. Among the new models is a Vir Lady crafted in steel with highly polished pebble-like bracelet links. The bezel of this watch is set with a single row of diamonds and the stones adorn the case-to-bracelet attachment. Similarly, the mother-of-pearl dial is set with 11 diamond markers.

- Recognizing that some women still prefer gold, Bertolucci offers the new diamond-bezel Vir Lady in 18-karat yellow or pink gold and in a combination steel-and-gold version.

- Bertolucci has also unveiled a stunning Mini Vir Jewelry watch. The case and bracelet links of this sumptuous beauty are set with 2.28 carats of diamonds and the dial is totally paved. To add to the luster, the watch is offered only in 18-karat pink gold.

RIGHT
Bedecked with more than 2 carats of diamonds on the dial, bezel, case and bracelet, this Mini Vir Jewelry watch is crafted in 18-karat white gold for shimmering beauty.

FAR RIGHT
Color reigns supreme in this elegant Serena with antique rose dial.

BLANCPAIN

In 1988, Blancpain—a brand with historical connections dating back more than two and a half centuries—unveiled a complete watch collection dedicated to complicated mechanical watchmaking. Born on the premise that it would never make a quartz watch, Blancpain has regularly mastered the most complex horological feats of excellence.

Indeed, the first Blancpain collection included the six most difficult timekeeping legacies: the ultra-slim watch, the moonphase, split-seconds chronograph, perpetual calendar, tourbillon and minute repeater. Every timepiece the brand creates is dedicated to the master watchmaker that bears its name, and pays homage to the traditional art of watchmaking begun by him. Blancpain's expansive history is inextricably tied to the rural village of Villeret, nestled in the Jura Mountains, where Jehan-Jacques Blancpain set up shop in 1735 in a farmhouse—and gradually built a full-fledged watchmaking atelier. Blancpain's work was steeped in invention and innovation. These are the benchmarks of the brand even today.

Blancpain garnered international acclaim in 1991, when it unveiled the now-famed "1735" model—one of the most complex timepieces in the world. Six years in the making, the 1735 housed a movement comprised of 740 parts and offering a wealth of different functions. Other critical accomplishments of the 1990s included creating the smallest self-winding chronograph, and creating the ultra-complicated Self-Winding Tourbillon Split-Seconds Flyback Chronograph watch.

In the year 2000, The Swatch Group acquired Blancpain and CEO Nicholas Hayek vowed to continue in the brand's rich tradition. Following this creed in 2001, Blancpain unveiled the Quattro platinum watch—an elegant self-winding timepiece housing a tourbillon regulator, perpetual calendar, flyback chronograph, and split-seconds chronograph. The 39-jeweled movement features a platinum rotor and consists of 432 parts—each hand finished to exacting detail.

In 2002, Blancpain unveiled a very classic new watch collection—appropriately named Villeret. Bold in size and endowed with signature Blancpain aesthetic references (including long hands, a slender bezel and a stepped case), the Villeret series of timepieces combines the beauty of a clean, uncluttered face with the technical sophistication of complex automatic movements.

The most recently unveiled Villeret watch, referred to as the 4040, is a 40mm-wide case of 18-karat white or red gold that houses an extra-slim self-winding movement with hour and minute displays and a power-reserve indicator. Water resistant to 30 meters, the watch features a silvered opaline dial with Roman numerals and long, leaf-shaped hands.

FACING PAGE

TOP LEFT

Crafted in 18-karat white gold, the Villeret, ref. 4040, houses an extra-slim self-winding movement with power-reserve indicator at 9:00.

BOTTOM RIGHT

Jehan-Jacques Blancpain.

THIS PAGE

TOP LEFT

The Léman Automatic Moonphase Calendar watch, ref. 2360, is created in 18-karat red gold and offers 100 hours of power reserve.

TOP RIGHT

The Le Brassus full-calendar GMT watch offers day, date, moonphase, and a subseconds hand at 6:00.

BOTTOM RIGHT

The Grande Date features 100 hours of power reserve and a two-digit date readout that is double the size of most standard dates.

HIGHLIGHTS

- Blancpain has rounded out many of its collections and recently added a new Léman Automatic Moonphase Calendar watch. The Léman collection, noted for its contemporary appeal, includes timepieces that offer such complexities as multiple time zones and flyback chronograph functions. The newest Léman watch houses an automatic movement consisting of 254 parts and 30 jewels. It offers a complete calendar and a moonphase indicator at 6:00.

- Crafted in 18-karat red gold, the Léman timepiece is bedecked with a shimmering mother-of-pearl dial that is set discreetly with six brilliant-cut diamonds as markers. The watch is offered in steel, and comes with or without a diamond-set bezel.

- Blancpain has added a full-calendar GMT watch to its Le Brassus collection of highly elaborate, highly technical timepieces. The new watch houses a hand-decorated, hand-assembled 289-piece movement that offers 100 hours of power reserve. The full calendar displays the day, date and month and the GMT indicator displays the time of day in all 24 zones.

- The Le Brassus calendar GMT watch, ref. 4276, is being created in 18-karat red gold and in a limited edition of 200 pieces in platinum.

BOUCHERON

f or 145 years, this fine French brand has been designing precious jewelry and watches for the world's most elite clientele. Indeed, since 1858 when Frédéric Boucheron opened his first shop in Paris, the brand name has been synonymous with innovation and daring designs in the luxury field.

Throughout the late 1800s, Boucheron specialized in nature-inspired motifs, florals and incredible fashion-forward jewels that garnered it international acclaim. Generation after generation since, the Boucheron family remained dedicated to the standards or perfection and invention set forth by its founder. Throughout the entire 20th century, Boucheron enjoyed the position of jeweler to czars, maharajahs, princes, kings and queens. With each creation, Boucheron's jewels and timepieces sparkle with articulated elegance.

In the year 2000, the Gucci Group took an avid interest in the brand's accomplishments and by year-end had purchased Boucheron. Today, under this luxury conglomerate, Boucheron continues its remarkable expertise, forging a new chapter in its legacy. What's more, it is the Gucci Group's intention to increase the number of Boucheron boutiques around the world from the current five to 50 within the next three years.

While Boucheron remains dedicated to producing exclusive jewelry that reflects its dynamic heritage, it is equally committed to its timepiece production. Since its inception, the brand has created delicate works of art and time in the form of chatelaines, pendants and, later, wristwatches.

Boucheron's signature timepiece collection—and the one with the most innovation this year—is the Reflet. The striking steel and 18-karat gold Reflet watches are rectangular in shape with the Boucheron signature ridged pattern—called gadroons—across the case. The elegant watch features a patented sliding-clasp bracelet system that enables the wearer to easily and quickly change straps.

Recent additions to the Boucheron Reflet include the Reflet Icare and the Reflet Parallèle. The Reflet Icare is a sleek, seductive reinterpretation of the rectangular Reflet. The base of the rectangular case is several millimeters wider than

FACING PAGE

TOP LEFT
The Reflet Parallèle is a stunning oversized watch that is bold and beautiful in its classic gadroon-adorned presentation.

BOTTOM LEFT
The Reflet Icare watch is slightly asymmetrical, with a wider case base than top.

THIS PAGE

TOP
The Gold Reflet Icare watches are also available in medium and small sizes and house quartz movement with water resistance up to 30 meters.

FAR RIGHT
Colorful and scintillating, these snake rings are elegantly set with diamonds and rubies.

BOTTOM
This stunning snake necklace is from the La Beauté Dangereuse collection.

the top of the case—offering a subtle asymmetrical pattern. The gleaming dial of this new piece features a satin-finished sun pattern. The new Refelt Icare is available in four versions, polished- and satin-finished gold, gold and diamonds, polished- and satin-finished steel, and steel and diamonds.

The Reflet Parallèle is a striking oversized piece whose opulence is reflected in the grand 45mm length of the case. In typical Reflet styling, the Reflet Parallèle features the gadroons running across the case and dial. Like the Reflet Icare, this Reflet is also offered in either 18-karat gold or in steel.

HIGHLIGHTS

■ Boucheron has unveiled a new jewelry collection. Called La Beauté Dangereuse, the line is at once seductive and dramatic. In this series, glittering diamond snakes coil and curl around the neck, finger, or ear.

■ For this daring collection, Boucheron turns to sapphires, emeralds and rubies in addition to diamonds to bring color and life to the snake. These jewels are meant to be worn draped on the body like sensual clothing.

BREGUET

Perhaps no other name in watchmaking is as famous or as highly revered as the name Abraham-Louis Breguet. Credited as the father of watchmaking, Breguet has given us a legacy of technical inventions and advancements thanks to his innovative nature and his tireless dedication to perfecting timekeeping.

A master watchmaker with an insatiable desire to build the finest timepieces in the world, Breguet acquired numerous patents and awards for his legendary work. Breguet founded his watchmaking company in 1775 and quickly became jeweler to the French Royal family. Still, he continued to create timepieces and develop technological inroads on his own. Amongst his most famed inventions is the tourbillon escapement, unveiled to the world in 1801. Considered one of the most important—and difficult—horological

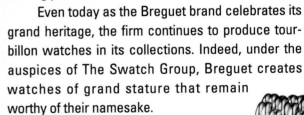

feats, the tourbillon remains a pinnacle of watchmaking prowess.

Even today as the Breguet brand celebrates its grand heritage, the firm continues to produce tourbillon watches in its collections. Indeed, under the auspices of The Swatch Group, Breguet creates watches of grand stature that remain worthy of their namesake.

In addition to the spectacular Tourbillon Classique that the brand created in celebration of the 200th anniversary of the tourbillon, Breguet continues to enhance its Classique collection of limited-edition timepieces. Among them is the Classique Ref. 5237 hand-wound mechanical chronograph with column-wheel device. Crafted in 18-karat yellow gold with a finely fluted case, the watch houses a 21-jeweled movement that is numbered and bears the Breguet signature. The watch offers a subdial for the seconds at 9:00 and presents a 30-minute totalizer at 3:00.

The Classique Ref. 5140 watch is a definitive recollection of the brand's heritage. The 18-karat gold case features a cambered sapphire crystal and is fitted with a classically elegant

oven-fired enamel dial. The extra-thin movement (2.4mm) is a self-winding mechanical caliber with 35 jewels and offers 46 hours of power reserve. The watch features an off-centered subdial for the seconds at 5:00. Additionally, Breguet has unveiled a self-winding mechanical Classique with date aperture at 6:00. This timepiece features a 28-jeweled, four-day power-reserve movement.

For women, Breguet introduces the Classique Ref. 8101 timepiece. Crafted in 18-karat white gold and featuring an off-centered dial, the watchcase is partially fluted and is set with crescent-shaped diamonds weighing just over 1.26 carats. The exquisite dial is pale blue mother of pearl with an iridescent finish and diamond accents. The movement is a self-winding mechanical caliber with 21 jewels and 40 hours of power reserve.

HIGHLIGHTS

- In a salute to women, Breguet has launched a selection of fine jewelry timepieces. Embodying aesthetic refinement and horological precision, Breguet's ladies' timepieces incorporate mechanical movement with precious metals and superbly set diamonds.

- Among the models is the Classique Ref. 8561. The round 18-karat yellow-gold watch with 18-karat gold dial and bracelet is set with diamonds on the case-to-bracelet attachment and on the bezel. The watch is water resistant to 100 feet and is also available in white gold.

- Part of the Heritage Collection, another women's model is the fascinating tonneau-shaped Ref. 8671. Crafted in 18-karat gold, the watch features a curved case with fluting and a bezel that is meticulously set with diamonds. The curved dial, crafted in silvered gold, is engine turned by hand and set with 77 diamonds.

BREITLING

Steeped in technical expertise, Breitling is a company ripe with achievement. For nearly 120 years, this brand has been building instruments for professional divers, drivers, pilots and astronauts. From its first chronographs and stopwatches of the late 1880s to its cutting-edge Emergency Mission watch that has made headlines around the world, this brand is synonymous with professional sports in general and aviation in particular.

Founded in 1884 by Léon Breitling, this family-owned and -operated company has long been making history. In 1934, the brand patented a wristwatch chronograph with second return-to-zero function—the forerunners of today's modern chronograph. By the late 1930s, the brand was already producing flight chronographs for the British Royal Air Force. Decades after decades since, it has unveiled timepieces of extreme importance to industries that rely on precision timing and navigation.

In the 1950s, the company launched the Navitimer chronograph for aviators—capable of measuring speed and fuel-consumption levels. In 1969, the brand unveiled the Caliber 11 Chronomat watch with all-new modular construction. In 1979, Breitling made an agreement with Ernest Schneider to ensure the continuation of the company—which today is run by the Schneider family with the same dedication to the professional spirit of the company. In 1995, the brand unveiled the renowned Emergency watch (which saved the lives of 13 people aboard the raft Mata-Rangi). In 2001, Breitling released its SuperQuartz™ technology with ultra-sophisticated movement.

It can be difficult to keep up with the overwhelming multitude of advancements made by this firm in the professional sports arena. Most recently, the company unveiled the Avenger Seawolf watch—water resistant to 10,000 feet. This technical treasure is crafted of a titanium case and houses a Breitling Caliber 17 self-winding, 25-jeweled chronometer movement. The watch was months in the making and required extensive testing and retesting to achieve such high-performance results. The screw-locked crown is a patented system and the watch crystal is 4.8mm thick to ensure such dramatic water resistance.

FACING PAGE

LEFT

The Avenger Seawolf, built on the sturdy platform of Breitling's original Avenger watch, is water resistant to an impressive 10,000 feet. The chronometer movement is housed in a titanium case and features a patented screw-locked crown.

THIS PAGE

TOP

Celebrating the 50th anniversary of the famed Navitimer, Breitling has unveiled a new model that is an updated rendition of the original. The exclusive edition carries the emblem of the first watch and features chronograph counters arranged in their original configuration. The watch is cased in steel and features a lacquered silvered dial designed exclusively for this commemorative piece.

BOTTOM

The newest Emergency Mission watch is housed in steel and features the Breitling SuperQuartz Caliber 73 chronometer-certified movement. It offers chronograph function, calendar and quick time-zone change in addition to the built-in miniature transmitter that operates on the 121.5MHz aviation distress frequency. Available on a steel bracelet or leather strap.

HIGHLIGHTS

■ In celebration of the 50th anniversary of the Navitimer, Breitling has also unveiled an emblematic model—a special version of the oldest chronograph in uninterrupted production. This self-winding chronograph with slide-rule bezel houses Breitling's Caliber 41 high-frequency, 38-jeweled chronometer movement.

■ The chronograph of the new Navitimer anniversary watch offers 12-hour, 30-minute and 1/5-of-a-second totalizers. The re-edition is crafted in steel or in limited editions in 18-karat white or yellow gold.

■ Breitling has also issued a new version of the life-saving Emergency Mission watch. Housing the SuperQuartz Caliber 73 chronometer movement, the watch is created in steel and is water resistant to 100 meters.

CARTIER

this is the name of which dreams are made. For more than a century and a half this legendary brand has been creating jewelry and timepieces in the most magnificent and enduring style. Using only the finest gems of the world, creating truly innovative designs, and crafting to the most exacting of standards, Cartier has become a standard of measure for most others in this industry.

In 1847 Louis-François Cartier began creating elegant jewelry in his Parisian workshops. Commissioned by French royalty, he designed some of the most regal jewelry in history and quickly earned a French-court following. Over the century-plus since the first Cartier piece was designed, the brand has built a reputation for engineering some of the most exotic and unique jewelry in the world.

This preeminent House has created jeweled pieces for some of the world's wealthiest families, has procured some of the most fascinating and famed gems on earth, and has garnered international acclaim for its scintillating designs. In the early 1900s, when wristwatches were just coming into their own, Cartier made history by creating a multitude of watches—including a wristwatch for famed inventor and flyer Alberto-Santos Dumont and later, the world-renowned Tank watch.

While the Cartier family stepped down from the family business in the early 1970s, the brand has nonetheless retained its famed positioning thanks to luxury owner the Richemont Group. Under the auspices of this prestigious conglomerate, Cartier continues to excite the senses with its exquisite works. Indeed, the brand recently unveiled a significant array of luxury timepieces from mega-diamond-adorned watches, to impressive technical innovations, to specialty watches.

Adding significantly to its Collection Privèe series (available in Cartier boutiques only), the House has introduced several new Tank à vis models. The Tank watch has become an icon in styling and timing and Cartier regularly unveils evolutions of this rectangular wonder. The new Tank à vis two time-zone watch has a modernized shape and houses a unique rectangular movement designed entirely by Cartier. The 9901 MC mechanical move-

FACING PAGE

FAR LEFT

This elegant jeweled
watch combines gold,
diamonds and enameling
to bring life to the tiger
on the dial.

TOP CENTER

The Tank à vis watch
features a two time-zone
indicator and is crafted in
18-karat white gold. It
houses an 18-jeweled
mechanical movement.

TOP RIGHT

The new Tank a`vis watch
with hour and date apertures
is a striking rendition of an
early 1900s model. It houses
a 24-jeweled mechanical
movement and is water
resistant to 30 meters.

BOTTOM

The elegant Pasha watch,
crafted in 18-karat rose
gold, houses an automatic
movement with tourbillon
escapement.

THIS PAGE

TOP LEFT

The striking Divan watch
is bold and classy.

TOP RIGHT

The elegant Lanières
watch features individual
strands of gold or leather
as the strap.

BOTTOM RIGHT

This 18-karat gold Roadster
watch is also fitted with an
interchangeable strap and
houses an automatic-
winding mechanism.

ment with manual-wind mechanism is composed of 161 parts with special finishes and decoration. The elegant watch dial tracks two time zones with a single adjustment of the stem.

The Tank à vis Aperture watch, with hour and date apertures, is also a striking rendition of classic appeal. With this watch, the minutes are read off of the main dial, and the hour and date are read from crescent-shaped apertures at 12:00 and 6:00. The watch houses Cartier's 9902 MC movement, which is composed of 185 parts. The case and movement of each watch share the same number. Both of the Tank à vis watches are created in a choice of rose, yellow or white gold.

The famed Pasha series is now joined by a Pasha de Cartier watch in rose gold with automatic tourbillon and single bridge in the form of a grill. This watch features a platinum oscillating weight and is created in a limited edition of just 25 pieces. The highly successful Tortue collection now has a rose-gold counterpart. The 18-karat gold watch with guilloché dial features a workshop-crafted mechanical movement with manual-wind mechanism.

HIGHLIGHTS

- Cartier has unveiled the new Divan watch collection. Impressive with its bold, rectangular curved case, the watch is a fascinating combination of past and future. The extra-wide precision design of this timepiece makes it immediately captivating for both men and women. Crafted in either steel or 18-karat gold, this watch houses a quartz movement.

- Cartier's newest jeweled timepieces offer an enchanting respite from the real world. Of particular note is a collection of enamel watches that celebrate the animal kingdom. Deftly combining gold, diamonds and enamel, Cartier creates a splendidly rich panther, zebra or tiger on each of these watches. These designs are handcrafted onto dials for the Pasha, Tortue, or Basculante.

- Another elegant jeweled collection is the Lanières Collection. This geometrically inspired series features ribbons of gold as bracelets or individual strands of leather as straps.

- Cartier displays its sporty side in new renditions of the Roadster series, including an 18-karat gold version with mechanical movement. The watch features an interchangeable strap or an 18-karat gold bracelet for chic appeal.

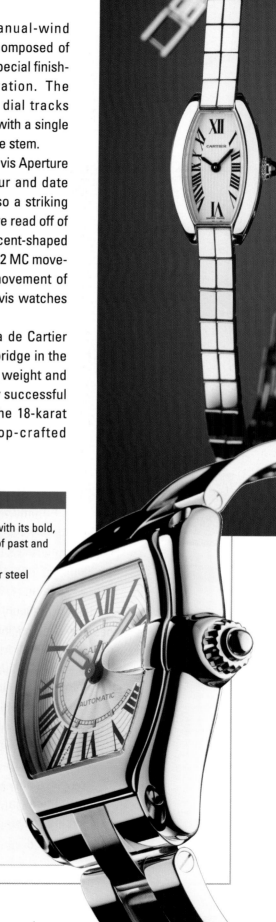

CÉDRIC JOHNER

Watchmaker extraordinaire, Cédric Johner has been creating timepieces of distinction under his own name for eight years— and is constantly inspired to set new standards of excellence and precision in all he creates.

A master jeweler for more than a decade, Johner began his illustrious career working for some of the finest houses in Geneva. In **1992**, he resolved to pursue his dreams and opened a small workshop in his home. From **1992** until **1995**, he regularly turned out exceptional pieces under their names. Johner worked tirelessly using wax to sculpt an all-new case shape and design.

In **1997**, the Abyss watchcase was born and drew immediate attention. An unusual design of geometric and spherical harmony that is both round and squared, the Abyss is singularly distinctive. By **1997** Johner had four complex timepieces in his collection, including a regulator and a jumping hour. He officially established his name Cédric Johner as a brand and a year later made his debut at the **1998** Basel Fair. His creations included women's watches in the Abyss case, as well as complications— and they were global hits with critics. His unique cases and extraordinary craftsmanship garnered him a key spot in the horological limelight.

In **2000**, Johner established new workshops, hired his own watchmakers, unveiled a variety of limited-edition chronographs and perpetual calendars, and ventured into the world of one-of-a-kind pieces. In **2001**, Cédric Johner received permission to use the L.U.C from Chopard. To this caliber, Johner added a perpetual calendar and a bi-retrograde. Called the caliber 10, the automatic movement with micro-rotor has 65 hours of power reserve. That same year he introduced the caliber 01 automatic movement for women—establishing himself as a true manufacture of exclusive timepieces from the inside-out.

In the style of a true master watchmaker, Johner insists on producing all of his watches by hand—a tradition he has honored since the inception of his brand. This dedication to preserving Swiss watchmaking heritage has propelled Johner to the forefront of independent watchmakers.

Just recently, Johner wisely brought the production of his gold watchcases in-house to further ensure that his already high standards of production remain unscathed. Now, the cases in gold and some in steel are hand filed, hand finished and hand engraved directly under his vigilant eye. With this move, Johner has come full circle as a complete Manufacture of watchcases and bracelets.

In Johner's workshops, master watchmakers execute his designs for tourbillons, column-wheel chronographs and perpetual calendar watches to exacting standards of perfection. Only the finest artisans hand-engrave the movements and only premier gemsetters and jewelers are recruited to spend painstaking hours setting diamonds and precious stones on dials, bezels and cases of Johner's haute joaillerie timepieces.

For Johner, personalization is key. His clientele may choose the precious metal color, engraving, dial face, strap or buckle of their watches. What's more, they can choose from a variety of movements ranging from small subseconds to dual time, biretrograde perpetual calendar, fly-back chronograph, minute repeater and others. Indeed, the combinations are virtually limitless.

Because of the time-consuming nature of hand craftsmanship, Johner and his team of watchmaking experts and artisans produce approximately 300 exceptional timepieces this year.

TOP LEFT
This 18-karat red-gold chronograph houses Johner's caliber 05 movement with column-wheel chronographs. A monopulsant watch, the start, stop, and return-to-zero all function from the crown.

TOP RIGHT
This new chronograph houses the caliber 71 Valjoux movement with column wheel and offers double counters on the exquisite dial

BELOW
The Abyss Two Time Zone watch houses an automatic movement and offers hour, minute and seconds readout in additon to the second time-zone time in 24-hour format.

BOTTOM
This striking ladies' Abyss watch is adorned with rubies and features color-coordinated markers and strap. It is powered by Johner's caliber 01 movement

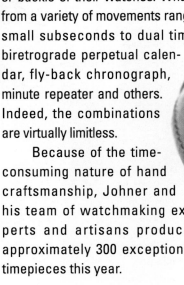

- In true Johner style, complications hold center stage. Among the newest models is an elegant minute repeater with a dial aperture to reveal the ringing racks. Housed in a striking 18-karat white-gold Abyss case, this mechanical masterpiece rings the hours, quarters and minutes. It also offers 45 hours of power reserve and features a sapphire caseback for viewing of the entire movement.

- Another scintillating complication is Johner's new platinum tourbillon, whose movement is entirely blued. The bridges, barrel and carriage bar have been designed by Johner and are unique because of the bluing technique that is further embellished with a delicate hand-guillochéd pattern. The tourbillon's mechanical movement is designed by Cédric Johner and Christophe Claret, and features 110 hours of power reserve.

- Two new chronographs also grace the Johner line. The Chronograph caliber 05 for women is crafted in 18-karat red gold and features a mother-of-pearl dial. The mechanical Chronograph caliber 71, with column wheels and two counters, is the result of specialized teamwork and is a technical feat for Johner. The chronograph is offered in 18-karat white gold and each of these two new chronograph models is engraved with the Côtes de Genève.

TOP LEFT
Reference 5310 with elegant subseconds dial at 6:00 houses Johner's caliber 10 movement.

RIGHT
The Bi-Retrograde Abyss watch houses Johner's new Automatic Caliber 10 movement.

BOTTOM RIGHT
Reference 4891 is a spectacular perpetual calendar watch with moonphase readout housed in 18-karat white gold and bedecked in diamonds.

CÉDRIC JOHNER

ABYSS MINUTE REPEATER   REF. 5388/4

Movement: mechanical, manual-winding, Christophe Claret base modified by Cédric Johner, 45 hours autonomy, 18,000 vph.
Functions: hour, minute, small second, minute repeater.
Case: 18K pink-gold, two-piece case in curved tonneau shape (size 47 x 39mm, thickness 12mm); hexagonal curved sapphire crystal; repeater slide on the middle and pink-gold crown; back attached by 4 screws, displaying the movement through a sapphire crystal.
Dial: beige, center engine-turned (guilloché) by hand; brushed hour ring, blanked on the movement; applied pink-gold Roman numerals and cabochon on the printed minute track; pink-gold leaf-style hands.
Indications: small second at 9.
Strap: crocodile leather; pink-gold fold-over clasp.
Also available: in yellow gold; in white gold; in platinum with blue dial. With brilliants (on request).
Note: all versions are available with specific dials on request.

ABYSS MINUTE REPEATER

This model was launched in 2001 and subsequently this variant was added with a dial displaying the repeater wheelwork. Thus, on this side it is possible to look at the cam motion and through the back the hammer working. All the components of this watch are in gold, including the slide and crown. In the jewel versions, the slide is adorned with diamonds and the crown with a sapphire cabochon.

ABYSS TOURBILLON   REF. 5280/4

Movement: mechanical, manual-winding, Cédric Johner 80 caliber (Christophe Claret caliber base caliber elaborated by Cédric Johner), with tourbillon device; autonomy 110 hours, 21,600 vph.
Functions: hour, minute.
Case: 18K yellow-gold, two-piece case, in tonneau shape (size 47 x 39mm, thickness 12mm); hexagonal, curved sapphire crystal; yellow-gold crown; back attached by 4 screws, displaying the movement through a sapphire crystal. Water resistant to 3atm.
Dial: replaced with the upper surface of the engine-turned (guilloché Petit Panier) silver pillar-plate and bridges; yellow-gold leaf-style hands.
Strap: crocodile leather; yellow-gold fold-over clasp.
Also available: in pink or white gold; in platinum.

ABYSS TOURBILLON   REF. 2080/4

Pillar-plate and bridges of the Claret movement are metalized blue and guilloché in this version signed by Cédric Johner. Big-sized windows on the dial side display the barrel and tourbillon, components, while through the back it is possible to view the mechanisms of the winding and setting system. This watch is entirely made by craftsmen. The name Abyss evokes the immense sea and the watch's shape reminds us the changing surfaces of the sea.

The photograph shows the platinum model with a metalized blue and engine-turned (guilloché Petit Panier) movement.

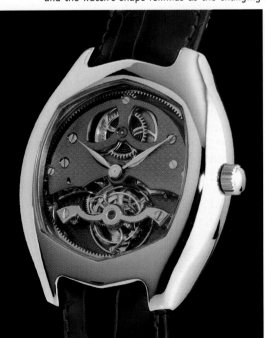

CÉDRIC JOHNER

ABYSS PERPETUAL CALENDAR BI-RETRO   REF. 5397/4

Movement: mechanical, automatic-winding, 97 caliber (Chopard L.U.C 4.96 caliber base + Agenhor calendar module).
Functions: hour, minute; perpetual calendar (retrograde date and day, month, year, moonphase).
Case: 18K pink-gold, two-piece case, in tonneau shape (size 47 x 39mm, thickness 12mm); hexagonal curved sapphire crystal; four correctors on the middle; pink-gold crown; back attached by 4 screws, displaying the movement through a sapphire crystal. Water resistant to 3atm.
Dial: silvered, engine-turned (guilloché) with sun pattern; printed Roman numerals; pink-gold leaf-style hands.
Indications: date and day of the week with retrograde hands at 3 and 9; moonphase at 6; month and four-year cycle at 12.
Strap: crocodile leather; pink-gold clasp.
Also available: with silvered engine-turned (guilloché) dial: in yellow or white gold; in platinum with engine-turned (guilloché) ruthenium dial.
Note: all versions are available with specific dials on request.

ABYSS PERPETUAL CALENDAR BI-RETRO   REF. 2097/4

Strongly characterized by the fan-shaped day and date indicators, the dial of the Bi-Rétrograde model, protected by a characteristic hexagonal curved sapphire glass, alternates arabesque and grained parts and is proposed in a silvered (on a gold case), and a ruthenium version (on a platinum case).

ABYSS PERPETUAL CALENDAR   REF. 5391/4

Movement: mechanical, automatic-winding, 91 caliber (Chopard L.U.C 4.96 caliber base + Agenhor calendar module).
Functions: hour, minute, second; perpetual calendar (date, day, month, year, moonphase).
Case: 18K white-gold, two-piece case, in tonneau shape (size 47 x 39mm, thickness 12mm); hexagonal curved sapphire crystal; 3 correctors on the middle; white-gold crown; back attached by 4 screws, displaying the movement through a sapphire crystal. Water resistant to 3atm.
Dial: silvered with engine-turned (guilloché) center; printed Roman numerals; pink-gold leaf-style hands.
Indications: date at 3; moonphase at 6; day of the week at 9; month and four-year cycle at 12.
Strap: crocodile leather; white-gold clasp.
Also available: with blue, black or ruthenium dial; in pink or yellow gold; in platinum.
Note: all versions are available with specific dials on request.

ABYSS PERPETUAL CALENDAR

An elegant architecture based on the oval shape characterizes the Abyss collection. The Perpetual model uses the prestigious automatic L.U.C caliber and a calendar module produced by Agenhor. It is realized in Large Size and with a classical arrangement of the indications on a guilloché solid-gold dial.

CÉDRIC JOHNER

ABYSS SPLIT-SECOND CHRONOGRAPH   REF. 4879/4

Movement: mechanical, manual-winding, Venus 185 caliber. Entirely assembled and finished by the House. Decorated with circular graining and Côtes de Genève patterns, beveled.
Functions: hour, minute, small second; split-second chronograph with three counters.
Case: 18K white-gold, two-piece case, in tonneau shape (size 47 x 39mm, thickness 15mm); hexagonal curved sapphire crystal; white-gold crown; drop-shaped white-gold pushers; back attached by 4 screws, displaying the movement through a sapphire crystal. Water resistant to 3atm.

Dial: silvered, engine-turned (guilloché); brushed hour ring; printed Roman numerals; blued leaf-style hands.
Indications: minute counter at 3; hour counter at 6; small second at 9; center split-second counter; minute track with divisions for 1/5 of a second.
Strap: crocodile leather; white-gold clasp.
Note: limited edition of 5 pieces.

ABYSS SPLIT-SECOND CHRONOGRAPH

Realized in only 5 pieces, the Abyss Rattrapante is the result of a lenghty process in Cédric Johner's workshop. The craftsmen used one of the first wristwatch movements with the split-second feature, the manual-winding Venus 185, displayed through the caseback, entirely finished and fitted for the usual white-gold tonneau-shaped case. The solution adopted for the splitting function consists of a pusher coaxial with the crown.

ABYSS CHRONOGRAPH   REF. 5371/4

Movement: mechanical, manual-winding, Valjoux 71 caliber, 14'''', 18,000 vph. Entirely assembled and finished by the House. Decorated with circular graining and Côtes de Genève patterns, beveled.
Functions: hour, minute, small second; chronograph with two counters.
Case: 18K pink-gold, two-piece case, in tonneau shape (47 x 38.5mm, thickness 13.5mm); hexagonal curved sapphire crystal; pink-gold crown; drop-shaped pink-gold pushers; back attached by 4 screws, displaying the movement through a sapphire crystal. Water resistant to 3atm.

Dial: gray, ruthenium-plated, engine-turned (guilloché) with a central sun pattern; subdials with a basket pattern; brushed hour ring; printed Roman numerals; pink-gold leaf-style hands.
Indications: minute counter at 3; small second at 9; center second counter; minute track with divisions for 1/5 of a second.
Strap: crocodile leather; pink-gold clasp.
Also available: in yellow gold; in white gold; in platinum.
Note: all versions are available with a specific dial on request.

ABYSS CHRONOGRAPH SINGLE PUSHER   REF. 4805/2

Movement: mechanical, manual-winding, Jacquet 5000 caliber, 10 1/2''', 21,600 vph. Entirely assembled and finished by the House. Decorated with circular graining and Côtes de Genève patterns, beveled.
Functions: hour, minute, small second; chronograph with two counters.
Case: 18K white-gold, two-piece case, in tonneau shape (size 37 x 30mm, thickness 9.5mm); hexagonal curved sapphire crystal; white-gold crown; with

coaxial chronograph pusher; back attached by 4 screws, displaying the movement through a sapphire crystal. Water resistant to 3atm.
Dial: silvered, engine-turned (guilloché) with a central sun pattern; subdials with a basket pattern; brushed hour ring; printed Roman numerals; black enameled leaf-style hands.
Indications: minute counter at 3; small second at 9; center second; minute track with divisions for 1/5 of a second.
Strap: crocodile leather; white-gold clasp.
Also available: in yellow or pink gold; in platinum; with rosé dial.
Note: limited edition of 250 pieces. All versions are available with specific dials on request.

ABYSS RÉGULATEUR LARGE SIZE   REF. 5350/4

Movement: mechanical, automatic-winding, Jacquet 876500 caliber.
Functions: hour, minute, small second, regulator.
Case: 18K pink-gold, two-piece tonneau-shaped case (size 47 x 39mm, thickness 11mm); hexagonal curved sapphire crystal; pink-gold crown; back attached by 4 screws. Water resistant to 3atm.
Dial: ivory with brown printed markers, round markers on the printed railway minute track; black enameled leaf-style hands.
Indications: off-center hours at 12 with Roman numerals; small seconds at 6; center minutes.
Strap: crocodile leather; pink-gold fold-over clasp.
Also available: in yellow or white gold; in stainless steel; in platinum; in Medium Size: in yellow, pink or white gold; in stainless steel; in platinum.
Note: all versions are available with a specific dial on request.

ABYSS SMALL SECONDE POINÇON DE GENÈVE   REF. 5310/4

Movement: mechanical, automatic-winding, Chopard L.U.C 1.96 caliber.
Functions: hour, minute, small second.
Case: 18K pink-gold, two-piece tonneau-shaped case (size 47 x 39mm, thickness 12mm); hexagonal curved sapphire crystal; pink-gold crown; back attached by 4 screws, displaying the movement through a sapphire crystal. Water resistant to 3atm.
Dial: ivory, engine-turned (guilloché) central part; grained hour ring with brown printed markers; printed Arabic numerals and brilliants set on the printed railway minute track; pink-gold leaf-style hands.
Indications: small seconds at 6.
Strap: crocodile leather; pink-gold fold-over clasp.
Also available: in yellow or white gold; in platinum; in Medium Size (on request).
Note: all versions are available with a specific dial on request.

ABYSS AUTOMATIC "PETITE"   REF. 4801/2

Movement: automatic, Piguet 951 caliber.
Functions: hour and minute.
Case: 18K white-gold, two-piece tonneau-shaped case (size 37 x 30mm, thickness 9mm); orange sapphires set on the bezel; hexagonal curved sapphire crystal; white-gold crown; back attached by 4 screws. Water resistant to 3atm.
Dial: mother-of-pearl with orange nuances; printed Arabic numerals and railway minute track; black enameled leaf-style hands.
Strap: crocodile leather; white-gold fold-over clasp.
Also available: without diamants, with basic painted dial: in yellow or pink gold, in stainless steel or in platinum.
Note: all versions are available with a specific dial on request.

ABYSS AUTOMATIC "PETITE"   REF. 4801/2

Movement: automatic, Piguet 951 caliber.
Functions: hour and minute.
Case: 18K white-gold, two-piece tonneau-shaped case (size 37 x 30mm, thickness 9mm); hexagonal curved sapphire crystal; white-gold crown; back attached by 4 screws. Water resistant to 3atm.
Dial: silvered, engine-turned (guilloché) central part; hour ring decorated with a basket pattern; printed and cabochon Arabic numerals and railway minute track; black enameled leaf-style hands.
Strap: crocodile leather; white-gold fold-over clasp.
Also available: in yellow or pink gold; in stainless steel; in platinum. With other dials.
Note: all versions are available with a specific dial or with bezel set with precious stones on request.

CHARLES OUDIN PARIS

THIS PAGE

TOP LEFT
This stunning Royal watch is set with sapphires and diamonds in a random, modern motif.

BOTTOM
Camille Berthet, owner of Charles Oudin Paris.

FACING PAGE
Diamonds with Russian demantoïd garnets and sapphire and ruby accents bring this Royal watch to life.

Nearly two centuries ago, French watchmaker extraordinaire Charles Oudin made his mark on history with a glorious collection of timepieces. His reputation for fine watchmaking was quickly spread and he became chronometer-maker to the French navy and watchmaker by appointment to the leading dynasties of 18th-century Europe.

Today, the name Charles Oudin has reemerged with consummate elegance to revive the French capital's talents in jewelry- and watchmaking. Although the recognized home of fine watchmaking is now in Switzerland, there was a time when the masters of horology hailed from France and England. Abraham-Louis Breguet, for example, worked for some time in France, and it was with Breguet that the young Charles Oudin (born in Clermont in **1772**) apprenticed for several years. Charles Oudin's apprenticeship with Breguet instilled in him an extraordinary sense of aesthetics and a creative capacity that he asserted constantly.

In **1804**, Oudin set up shop at number 52 Palais Royal. Surrounded by the Paris Opera, the Carnavalet Museum, the Louvre, and the Comédie Française, the Palais Royal had a turbulent history but remained a cultural center where members of refined society could meet talented artists and craftsmen. Oudin soon became the darling of Europe's royal families for whom he created original and valuable timepieces. Among his clientele: the czar and czarina of Russia, the king and queen of Spain, the king of Portugal, and the empress Josephine.

Oudin's timepieces, with their unique, custom-made styling, were the products of great talent. Oudin won awards and honorable mentions at international fairs and exhibitions. In **1859**, Oudin invented the first crucifix watch and in **1860** became watchmaker to the Pope.

Throughout the ensuing decades, the Oudin name shone in the world of haute horology. Charles Oudin watches were known for their elegant styling and technical advancement. Many timepieces bearing his signature are featured in auction sales and even in the private museums of prestigious Swiss watch manufacturers.

In **1998**, the Berthet family, which has been involved in watchmaking for more than five generations, revived the Charles Oudin name, and the family has assumed the task of restoring French watchmaking in general—and Charles Oudin Paris in particular—to its former leading role.

Commemorating the life and work of a great watchmaker, today's Charles Oudin Paris collection renews its ties with Parisian expertise. Attracting artists and craftsmen of considerable talents, Paris remains one of the last world capitals in which exceptional objects are designed and created in their entirety.

The Charles Oudin Paris collection subtly weaves an aesthetic nature-themed link between the past and the present. Their typically Parisian nature gives Charles Oudin timepieces an instantly recognizable style. Although inspired by the classic creations of the past, the bold originality of their manufacture makes them resolutely contemporary.

The platinum and gold cases are made by one of the few remaining Parisian manufactures whose craftsmen possess the finely honed skills and experience that attracts orders from the greatest names in luxury for the realization of precious cases for limited-series timepieces. The gemstones are set by the expert hands of craftsmen accustomed to meeting the standards of the city's prestigious jewelry houses.

Inspired by the Palais Royal, the models in the Charles Oudin Paris collection are named for the flowers growing in its magnificent gardens or in honor of cultural and architectural features of the building. The Lily, Pansy, Tulip, and Rose models, for example, emulate the shapes of these flowers while the period models recall the feminine elegance typical of Paris. They are fitted with a choice of straps in every color, in plain or moiré satin, leather or shagreen.

The Precious collection is inspired by nature's rarest gemstones—sapphires, rubies, emeralds and diamonds—that adorn time with outstanding elegance. Each is produced in a limited series and exemplifies the skills of the most talented craft-masters. The Art Déco collection features mother-of-pearl dials, which are masterpieces of meticulous decoration.

TOP

The entire Charles Oudin Paris collection is inspired by the Palais Royal in Paris, as evidenced by these diamond, emerald and ruby Royal watches.

BOTTOM

Designed in an antique floral motif, the curved cases of the Royal watches offer ergonomic beauty to complement the diamond, emerald and ruby settings.

For women as for men, the Fontaine or Palais models, inspired by the fountains and the magnificent architecture of the Palais Royal, have regal bearings. The wide rectangular case allows every extravagance. Set with black or white diamonds, rubies and emeralds, these elegant creations express, in their most simple versions, the fashion-transcending quality that contributes to their long-term values.

The pure and structured lines of the Column models recall the celebrated Buren pillars of the Palais Royal forecourt, while the Historique collection evokes the prestigious past of the naval horologist with the Régulateur watch, designed for lovers of bygone watchmaking techniques.

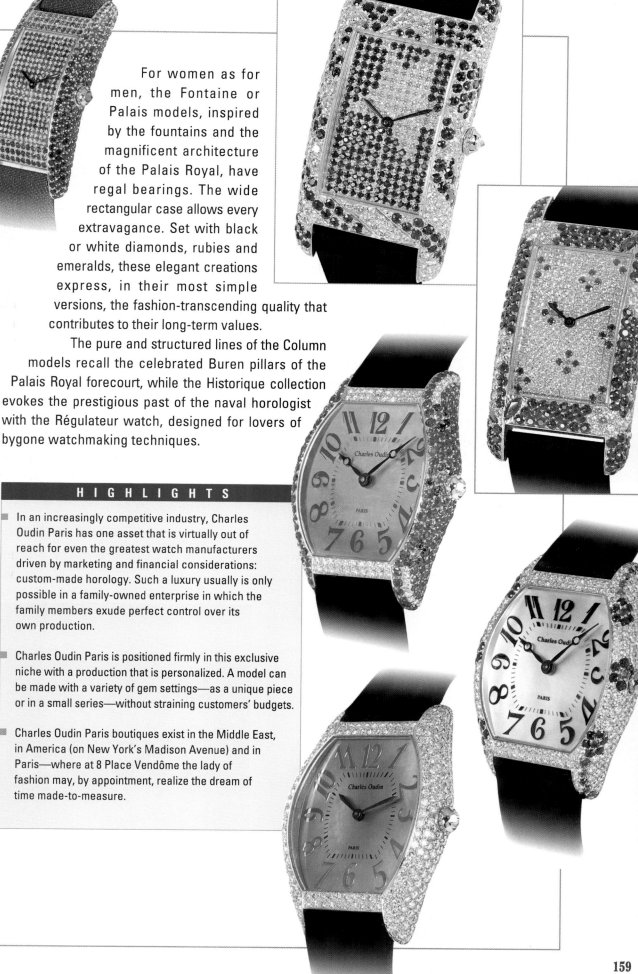

ABOVE
The Royal collection is designed to reflect the many fountains of Paris, with rivulets of diamonds and sapphires.

TOP RIGHT
A delicate work of art and beauty, this women's watch represents the American flag, with stars and stripes of rubies, sapphires and diamonds.

FAR RIGHT
A tribute to women, the Florale watch exudes a retro appeal that is subtly enticing with this diamond and ruby dial.

BOTTOM RIGHT
These three elegant tortue-shaped watches combine retro styling with magnificent beauty. Crafted in either 18-karat white or yellow gold, these watches are meticulously set with sapphires, rubies or emeralds in a floral motif reminiscent of classic elegance. The all-diamond version has modern appeal with its stunning blue mother-of-pearl dial.

HIGHLIGHTS

- In an increasingly competitive industry, Charles Oudin Paris has one asset that is virtually out of reach for even the greatest watch manufacturers driven by marketing and financial considerations: custom-made horology. Such a luxury usually is only possible in a family-owned enterprise in which the family members exude perfect control over its own production.

- Charles Oudin Paris is positioned firmly in this exclusive niche with a production that is personalized. A model can be made with a variety of gem settings—as a unique piece or in a small series—without straining customers' budgets.

- Charles Oudin Paris boutiques exist in the Middle East, in America (on New York's Madison Avenue) and in Paris—where at 8 Place Vendôme the lady of fashion may, by appointment, realize the dream of time made-to-measure.

CHARLES OUDIN

WD/DD — REF. 202

Movement: Swiss mechanical, manual winding or quartz.
Functions: hour, minute.
Case: 18K white-gold, two-piece case, rectangular curved; size: 23x46mm, thickness: 8mm; curved sapphire glass, framed by set diamonds; back attached by 8 screws; gold crown with faceted diamond.
Dial: set diamonds, blued-steel bâton-style hands.

Strap: satin, white-gold and diamonds clasp.

W/BAGUETTE — REF. 215

Movement: Swiss mechanical, manual winding or quartz.
Functions: hour, minute.
Case: 18K white-gold, two-piece case, rectangular curved; size: 20x41mm, thickness: 8mm; curved sapphire glass, framed by set baguette-cut diamonds; back attached by 4 screws; gold crown with faceted diamond.
Dial: mother of pearl, printed with Roman numerals, blued-steel bâton-style hands.

Strap: satin, white-gold and diamonds clasp.

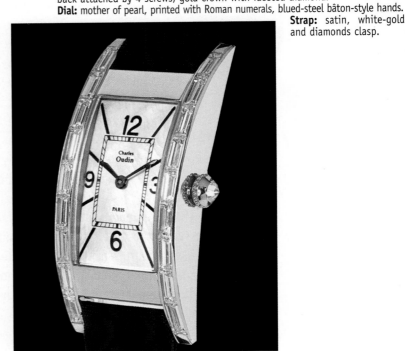

W/AMAZONE — REF. 203

Movement: Swiss mechanical, manual winding or quartz.
Functions: hour, minute.
Case: 18K white-gold, two-piece case, rectangular curved; size: 23x46mm, thickness: 8mm; curved sapphire glass, framed by set Urals Russian demantoïd garnets, diamonds, rubies, sapphires; back attached by 8 screws; gold crown with faceted diamond.

Dial: white guilloché, printed with Arabic numerals, blued-steel bâton-style hands.
Strap: satin, white-gold and diamonds clasp.

FLORALE/RUBIES — REF. 203

Movement: Swiss mechanical, manual winding or quartz.
Functions: hour, minute.
Case: 18K yellow-gold, two-piece case, rectangular curved; size: 23x46mm, thickness: 8mm; curved sapphire glass, framed by set rubies, white and yellow diamonds, emeralds; back attached by 8 screws; gold crown with faceted diamond.
Dial: yellow guilloché, printed with Arabic numerals, blued-steel bâton-style hands.

Strap: satin, yellow-gold and diamonds clasp.

W/BLUE FLORAL — REF. 303

Movement: Swiss mechanical, automatic winding or quartz.
Functions: hour, minute.
Case: 18K white-gold, two-piece case, tonneau shape; size: 32x42mm, thickness: 7.5mm; sapphire glass, framed by set sapphire and diamonds; back attached by 6 screws; gold crown with faceted diamond.
Dial: mother of pearl, printed with Arabic numerals, blued-steel bâton-style hands.
Strap: satin, white-gold and diamonds clasp.

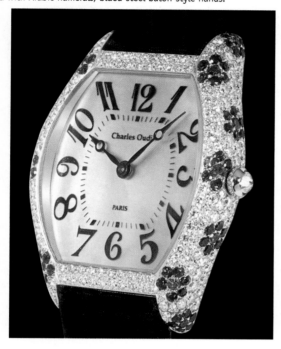

BRANCARD WD/WD — REF. 401

Movement: Swiss mechanical, automatic winding or quartz.
Functions: hour, minute.
Case: 18K white-gold, two-piece case, rectangular curved; size: 25x47mm, thickness: 8.5mm; curved sapphire glass, framed by set diamonds; back attached by 8 screws; gold crown with faceted diamond.
Dial: white guilloché, printed with Arabic numerals, blued-steel bâton-style hands.
Strap: satin, white-gold and diamonds clasp.
Also available: yellow-gold and red-gold.

Y/FALCON — REF. 430

Movement: Swiss mechanical, automatic winding or quartz.
Functions: hour, minute.
Case: 18K red-gold, two-piece case, rectangular; size: 26x42mm, thickness: 8mm; sapphire glass, framed by set diamonds; back attached by 8 screws; gold crown with faceted diamond.
Dial: red guilloché, blued-steel bâton-style hands.
Strap: satin, red-gold and diamonds clasp.

W/FALCON/DD — REF. 440

Movement: Swiss mechanical, automatic winding or quartz.
Functions: hour, minute.
Case: 18K white-gold, two-piece case, rectangular; size: 26x33mm, thickness: 8mm; sapphire glass, framed by set diamonds; back attached by 4 screws; gold crown with faceted diamond.
Dial: set diamonds, blued-steel bâton-style hands.
Strap: satin, white-gold and diamonds clasp.

CHARRIOL

the Charriol® collection of timepieces and jewelry is imbued with a vigor and freshness that is at once enlightening and alluring. Turning to color and shapes, Charriol deftly blends attention to detail with artistic influences in each watch series.

It was 21 years ago in 1982 that Philippe Charriol created the Philippe Charriol brand of luxury products. A man of many talents (Charriol is an avid automobile racer and ice racer, as well as an astute businessman), Charriol turned to his love of the arts and antiquity when designing his first collection of watches and jewelry. The result was the Celtic collection of stunning twisted cable designs reminiscent of the ancient Celtic cultures. This series has become a signature for the brand.

So well received was Charriol's line that he quickly expanded—in all directions. Indeed, within 16 years, Charriol had built a small empire. He designs and produces watches, jewelry, leathergoods, accessories and eyewear. Additionally, he has opened more than 40 boutiques internationally and has established a worldwide network of more than 600 Charriol corners in key retail jewelry outlets.

Always on the cutting edge of style and elegance, Charriol regularly unveils pieces that enhance his collection and enthrall the consumer. Recently, Charriol launched the Colvmbvs Round watch—built on the success of its rectangular predecessor. Designed with the same creative characteristics—clean edges, graphic lines, dramatic volume—as the initial watch, the new round versions add a touch of classic appeal. Crafted in steel with a bold bezel—sometimes set with two rows of diamonds—the Colvmbvs Round is offered with a new cascading bracelet and a redesigned push-button release on the folding crown.

Expanding its impressive tonneau-shaped Jet Set collection—which the brand unveiled years ago for men and just one year ago for women—Charriol has added new colors to its selection of dials and straps. The Jet Set Chronograph—softly enhanced by a dual row of diamonds on each side of the gently curved case—now includes pink, blue, and white mother-of-pearl dials accented by contrasting colored mother-of-pearl subdials for the chronograph counters.

FACING PAGE

TOP RIGHT
The Colvmbvs Tonneau Chronograph features a patented integrated hinged crown to ensure water resistance.

LEFT
The new Colvmbvs watch is round—bringing classic elegance to its rectangular predecessor.

BOTTOM RIGHT
Philippe Charriol.

THIS PAGE

TOP LEFT
The Jet Set Chronograph watch is a refreshing combination of diamonds and color.

TOP RIGHT
The Colvmbvs rectangular curved watch houses an automatic movement and embodies the innovative spirit of its namesake.

BOTTOM LEFT
These pieces from Charriol's 18-karat white-gold Flamme Blanche collection are set with stunning pavé diamonds.

BOTTOM RIGHT
Charriol Megeve watch with diamonds.

HIGHLIGHTS

- Known for the stunning diamond jewelry that complements its watch collections, Charriol has added color to these jeweled beauties. Precious stones such as amethyst citrine, blue topaz and Rhodolite garnet blend with diamonds for artistic luxury.

- In the typical philanthropic style of Charriol, the brand continues its Charriol Foundation work. Designed to help budding young artists, the Charriol Foundation sponsors a competition each year to determine who will win the grand prize—a scholarship to study in Paris. Presently, the foundations (established by Charriol) exist in Hong Kong, Singapore, the Philippines and Thailand.

CHAUMET

arguably one of the most romantic jewelry companies in the world with a history rich with intrigue and grandeur, Chaumet has been delighting jewelry lovers for centuries. Chaumet's rise to success ran parallel to Napoleon's glory, and firmly set the stage for the brand as leader of regal beauty, daring splendor and originality.

Founded in **1780** by Marie-Etienne Nitot, who set up shop in Paris, Chaumet quickly became the official jeweler to emperor Napoleon I—who greatly admired the brand's magnificent work. From tiaras to swords, Chaumet deftly combined the world's finest gems with creative designs that would last for centuries. Indeed, the innovative spirit of Chaumet's designs reflected some of the most romantic periods in history with an individuality and flair reserved for the brand.

In **1875**, the House of Chaumet was launched to new heights by the distinct style of the brilliant Joseph Chaumet, who married the daughter of the head of the jewelry firm and officially registered the name of Chaumet. Throughout the late **1800**s and early **1900**s, Chaumet led the world with its art nouveau designs of flora and fauna. With the transition into the art deco era, Chaumet made even greater strides—leading with its geometric wonders. Indeed, Chaumet has remained a leader in designs of every epoch and era since its inception.

In a bold and timely move, the brand launched into the world of timepieces in **1995**—unveiling the Khésis collection of diamond and steel watches. In the ensuing years, Chaumet launched a diverse collection of timepieces, including the Style de Chaumet, Class One diver's watch, Night Spirit and Mihewi—each with its own theme of passion and perfection.

TOP CENTER
Crafted in stainless steel and adorned with diamonds, this Class One is fitted with a rubber strap and is water resistant to 100 meters.

FAR LEFT
Demonstrating its sense of fashion and function, this Class One dive watch in rich burgundy is bedecked with pink sapphires.

BELOW
The Khésis is crafted with a link bracelet and diamonds. It features a white dial with Roman numerals.

A brand committed to stirring emotions and fulfilling dreams, Chaumet regularly offers intriguing styles that scintillate the soul. Such is the case with the bold Class One watch collection. The first dive watch collection created by Chaumet, the Class One was unveiled in 1998 and has been enjoying phenomenal success ever since. A noteworthy presence, the Class One combines steel, mother of pearl, and a choice of black or white diamonds with a round dial and a rotating bezel. Colored gemstones also adorn some Class One watches—with sapphires being the prime choice.

A striking instrument of elegance and function, the Class One is a unisex watch that is water resistant to 100 meters and can suit every mood or occasion. The newest Class One watches include a silver dial with diamond markers, a burgundy dialed watch outlined with a double row of pink sapphires, and a striking pale blue mother-of-pearl-dialed model with pale sapphires on the bezel.

Chaumet also continues the romance with its signature Khésis collection of watches with luxuriously supple bracelets and sleek elegance. Created in steel as well as in 18-karat gold, the Khésis is set with diamonds and is available in a choice of dials: tone-on-tone gray, black with diamond hour indicators, or white with Roman numerals. The 18-karat gold versions are even more sumptuous, especially the yellow-gold version with complete pavé diamonds on dial and case, and the white-gold versions with one model that is set totally with princess-cut diamonds.

Indeed, each collection of Chaumet watches has been joined recently by a scintillating and sumptuous sibling—the telltale sign that Chaumet remains forever on the cutting edge of style and beauty.

HIGHLIGHTS

■ Star ballerina of the Opera National de Paris, Aurélie Dupont has associated her image with the collections of this famed Parisian jeweler. A prima ballerina who has appeared in some of the finest international productions, Dupont wears a Chaumet Class One watch.

■ Renewing its ties with its magical past, this famed Place Vendôme jeweler retraces the making and progressions of some of its most famed tiaras and headbands in a book titled *Timeless Tiaras*. Written by Diana Scarisbrick and published by Editions Assouline, the book offers a host of illustrations, drawings and photographs from Chaumet's archives.

■ Inspired by its own illustrious history and regal involvements, Chaumet is unveiling a totally new collection of "Haute Joaillerie" featuring tiara, barrettes, combs and brooches in 2003.

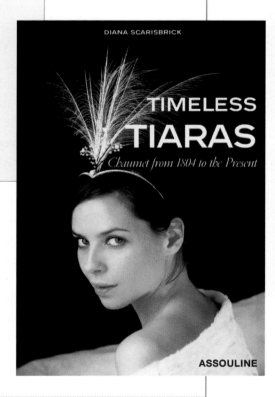

CHOPARD

for 143 years, Chopard has stood for quality and creativity. Excellence and ingenuity—the hallmarks of this illustrious jewelry and watch brand—reign supreme in all the firm produces. Indeed, high technology and traditional craftsmanship blend beautifully at Chopard to create a world where dreams come true.

Intent on producing pocket watches and chronometers of stature, Louis-Ulysse Chopard founded his company in **1860**, and the brand has continually turned out masterpieces. Just about a century into its legacy, Chopard was purchased by jewelry entrepreneur Karl Scheufele in **1963**. It was his vision to unite his jewelry company with watchmaking under one brand and to propel both areas to greater levels of accomplishment in design and technology.

In **1975**, Scheufele built a production facility in Meyrin-Geneva, marking a new era for the brand. In **1976**, Chopard unveiled the now-famed Happy Diamonds collection to the world, and in the **1980**s the brand launched the Gstaad collection of timepieces. In **1988**, Chopard teamed with the Mille Miglia as an official partner and began creating the annual special-edition Mille Miglia watch—an icon of vintage automobile racing.

In the early **1990**s, Karl and Karin Scheufele's children became integral players in the family business. Caroline took over the jewelry design and Karl-Friedrich headed up the watch division. In **1996**, the brand established itself as a complete Manufacture with the opening of a movement factory in Fleurier. The L.U.C movement made its debut that year and was the impetus for other movements to come.

In **1999**, Chopard unveiled the L.U.C Sport 2000 collection, and a year later presented the L.U.C Quattro watch—equipped with a new caliber with four barrels and nine days of power reserve—in **2000**. Chopard presented the L.U.C Tonneau in **2001**.

Chopard is also a major supporter of charitable causes and is a devoted patron of the arts. In **2001**, Chopard began supporting the Elton John AIDS Foundation, creating limited-edition Elton John timepieces whose sales would benefit the foundation. Chopard is also intimately involved with such high-profile events as the Cannes International Film Festival.

CHOPARD

TOP LEFT
Designed by de Grisogono
for Chopard, this Ice Cube
necklace is set with more
than 80 carats of
diamonds.

TOP RIGHT
From the Rainbow
collection, these heart-
shaped pendants are
crafted in 18-karat white
gold and set with white or
black diamonds, blue
topaz, spinels, or blue or
pink sapphires.

Chopard's collections of ladies' jewelry and watches are amazing and inviting. From Happy Diamonds to Happy Sport with free-flowing diamonds, from the 1950s-inspired chic La Strada to the innovative Pushkin and Ice Cube collections, rich colors, seductive shapes and innovation are prominent driving forces.

With creativity at an all-time high, Chopard has grown at a faster rate than the market as a whole while preserving its independence—a rarity amongst watch and jewelry companies today. Caroline's exquisite designs continually impress and excite the senses.

All of Chopard's magnificent jewelry is created with the utmost attention to details. Each stone is hand picked and every design is completed by painstaking hand-craftsmanship. From gem selection to setting and polishing, master jewelers work long hours to ensure smooth, sensual finished pieces.

For the past decade, Chopard jewels have glistened on the necks and wrists of celebrities from all corners of the earth. Partnering with the Cannes International Film Festival, Chopard is jeweler to the stars for 12 days each year at this exciting gala of heady days and wild nights. In addition to adorning the stars as they parade down the red carpet, Chopard produces all of the Palme d'Or trophies in its own workshops.

CENTER
Celebrities at the Interna-
tional Film Festival in Cannes:
from left to right
Virginie Ledoyen;
Paz Vega, laureate of the
Chopard Trophy; Gong Li;
Sharon Stone; Rebecca
Romjin-Stamos; Rosanna
and Patricia Arquette.

LEFT
This exquisite Haute
Joaillerie necklace is set
with 64 pear-shaped
diamonds and 991
brilliants. It weighs more
than 70 carats.

HIGHLIGHTS

For both men and women, Chopard creates timepieces of technical excellence and sophisticated design. Utilizing its own caliber, the brand has unveiled the L.U.C GMT watch. A new mechanical masterpiece for Chopard, this is the first time the brand offers a GMT. Fitted with the Chopard self-winding caliber L.U.C 4.96/1-H1 movement with microrotor, the watch offers a second time-zone on a subsidiary dial at 6:00. It also features a jumping date at 3:00 and is an officially certified chronometer. Housed in 18-karat white, rose or yellow gold, the watch movement is distinguished by its two stacked mainspring barrels.

Similarly, Chopard's new diver's watch, the Pro One, houses the L.U.C 4.96 caliber. Housed in steel, the professional sports instrument is water resistant to 300 meters. The watch features a screwed in caseback and crown designed to withstand deep pressure. The COSC-certified watch is offered with a natural rubber strap or with a leather or steel bracelet.

Determined to offer tailored glamour to the refined woman of taste, Chopard has unveiled a new rectangular timepiece that harks back to the elegant Art Deco era. Its sleek lines and gently curved profile have made it an alluring addition to Chopard's already scintillating ladies' watch lines.

CHOPARD

L.U.C QUATTRO   REF. 16/91863

This new manual-winding movement of the L.U.C family by Chopard leaves the constructive qualities and technical sophistication of the 1.96 caliber unchanged, which are essential for the quality standard recognized by the "Geneva Seal." In the present movement, the space left free by the removal of the winding micro-rotor and related elements is used to introduce a second couple of superimposed barrels, linked with the first one. Thus the working autonomy is increased up to the

prestigious target of 216 hours, i.e. 9 days. However, in order to exploit always the best part of the motive force produced by the four barrels, before its drop causes a reduction of the amplitude of the balance vibrations, it is recommended to proceed to manual winding once a week.

The photograph shows a piece with platinum case and blue dial.

L.U.C QUATTRO   REF. 16/1863

Movement: mechanical, manual-winding, L.U.C 1.98 caliber produced by Chopard's workshops at Fleurier. Mounted, decorated and finished entirely by hand (Côtes de Genève pattern) and beveled. Officially certified chronometer (COSC). Hallmarked with the "Geneva Seal."
Functions: hour, minute, date, small second, power reserve.
Case: 18K pink-gold, three-piece case (Ø 38mm, thickness 9.6mm); curved sapphire glass; pink-gold

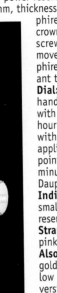

crown; back attached by 8 screws, displaying the movement through a sapphire glass. Water resistant to 3atm.
Dial: silvered, center hand-turned (guilloché) with sun pattern, brushed hour ring, zone decorated with circular beads; applied faceted pink-gold pointed markers; printed minute track; pink-gold Dauphine-style hands.
Indications: date and small seconds at 6, power-reserve indicator at 12.
Strap: crocodile leather; pink-gold clasp.
Also available: in white gold (same price); in yellow gold; in platinum. All versions are available with black, blue or silvered dial.

L.U.C TONNEAU 6.96   REF. 16/2267

Movement: automatic, tonneau-shaped, L.U.C 6.96 caliber produced by Chopard's workshops at Fleurier. Mounted and finished entirely by hand; bridges decorated with Côtes de Genève pattern. Officially certified chronometer (COSC).
Functions: hour, minute, date, small second.
Case: 18K white-gold, three-piece tonneau-shaped, anatomically curved case (size 38.5 x 40mm, thickness 10mm); curved sapphire glass; white-gold crown;

back attached by 8 screws, displaying the movement through a sapphire glass. Water resistant to 3atm.
Dial: black, center hand-turned (guilloché) with sun pattern, brushed hour ring; applied faceted white-gold pointed markers; printed railway minute track; white-gold Dauphine-style hands.
Indications: date and small seconds at 6.
Strap: crocodile leather; white-gold clasp.
Limited edition of 1860 pieces (this number recalls the anniversary of the House's creation), dedicated to its founder Louis-Ulysse Chopard.
Also available: with silvered dial; in pink or yellow gold.

L.U.C 1.96   REF. 16/1860/2

Movement: mechanical, automatic-winding, L.U.C 1.96 caliber produced by Chopard's workshops at Fleurier. Mounted and finished entirely by hand. Hallmarked with the "Geneva Seal". **Functions:** hour, minute, small second, date.
Case: 18K pink-gold, three-piece case (Ø 36mm, thickness 8mm); curved sapphire crystal; pink-gold crown; caseback attached by 8 screws, displaying the movement through a sapphire crystal. Water resistant to 3atm.

Dial: silvered gold, center hand-turned (guilloché), brushed hour ring; applied pink-gold pointed markers; printed minute track; pink-gold Dauphine-style hands.
Indications: small second and date display at 6.
Strap: crocodile leather; pink-gold clasp.
Numbered edition of 1860 pieces, a homage to Louis-Ulysse Chopard who founded the firm in 1860.
Also available: with black dial; in white gold with silvered, black, gilded or coppered dial (same price); in yellow gold with black or silvered dial; in platinum with silvered, black, gilded or coppered dial. With L.U.C 3.96 movement (without "Geneva Seal"), white or coppered dial and silvered zone 1860 pieces; in white or pink gold; in yellow gold.

MILLE MIGLIA 2000 CHRONOGRAPH — REF. 16/8407

Movement: mechanical, automatic-winding, ETA 2892A2 caliber plus Dubois Dépraz chrono module. Officially certified "chronometer" (COSC).
Functions: hour, minute, small second, date, chronograph with 3 counters.
Case: titanium, three-piece brushed case (Ø 40mm, thickness 13mm); curved sapphire crystal with antireflective treatment on both sides; caseback attached by 8 screws, displaying the movement through a sapphire crystal. Water resistant to 5atm.

Dial: anthracite gray with circular graining finish (the same used in the 1930s for the instrument panels of sport cars), silvered flange and counters, decorated with circular beads, luminescent Arabic numerals; luminescent rhodium-plated brass bâton-style hands.
Indications: small seconds at 3 (with the famous red arrow as a symbol for racing), date between 4 and 5, hour counter at 6, minute counter at 9, center second counter, minute track with divisions for 1/5 of a second and triangular markers, tachometer scale on the flange. **Strap:** rubber (reproducing the tread of Dunlop Racing tires of the 1960s); titanium clasp.
Also available: in yellow gold, 250 pieces; in white gold 250 pieces.

MILLE MIGLIA 2002 CHRONOGRAPH — REF. 16/8920

Movement: mechanical, automatic-winding, ETA 2892A2 caliber plus Dubois Dépraz chronograph module. Officially certified "chronometer" (COSC).
Functions: hour, minute, small second, date, chronograph with 3 counters.
Case: stainless-steel, three-piece polished case (Ø 40.5mm, thickness 12.5mm); curved sapphire crystal with antireflective treatment on both sides; caseback attached by 8 screws, showing the embossed race run and displaying the movement through a sapphire crystal. Water resistant to 5atm.

Dial: black; zones decorated with circular beads; luminescent Arabic numerals; luminescent rhodium-plated brass bâton-style hands.
Indications: small seconds at 3 (with the famous red arrow as a symbol for the race), date between 4 and 5, hour counter at 6, minute counter at 9, center second counter, minute track with divisions for 1/5 of a second on the flange.
Strap: rubber (reproducing the tread of the Dunlop Racing tires of the 1960s); steel clasp. Created as a limited edition of 1,000 numbered pieces.
Also available: in yellow gold, 250 pieces.

L.U.C SPORT — REF. 15/8200

Movement: mechanical, automatic-winding, L.U.C 4.96 caliber produced by Chopard at the workshops in Fleurier. Mounted and finished entirely by hand, double barrel. Screw heads and rotor with "black nickel" finish. Officially certified "chronometer" (COSC). **Functions:** hour, minute, second, date.
Case: stainless steel, three-piece brushed case (Ø 40mm, thickness 10mm); curved sapphire crystal; screw-on crown; caseback attached by 8 screws, displaying the movement through a sapphire crystal. Water resistant to 10atm.

Dial: black, center hand-turned (guilloché) with lozenge pattern, hour ring decorated with circular beads; applied pointed rhodium-plated brass markers; printed minute track with luminescent square markers on the flange; luminescent rhodium-plated brass Dauphine-style hands.
Indications: date display at 3.
Bracelet: brushed stainless steel, double fold-over clasp. Limited edition of 2000 numbered pieces.
Also available: with rubber strap; in yellow gold with rubber strap; in white gold with rubber strap. All versions available with blue, black, white or pearl-gray dials.

L.U.C PRO ONE — REF. 16/8912

Movement: mechanical, automatic-winding, L.U.C 4.96 caliber produced by Chopard at the workshops at Fleurier. Mounted and finished entirely by hand. Officially certified "chronometer" (COSC).
Functions: hour, minute, second, date.
Case: stainless steel, three-piece polished and brushed case (Ø 42mm, thickness 13.3mm); curved sapphire crystal; counter-clockwise-turning brushed and knurled ring with a graduated scale and luminescent pointer and polished raised chapters; screw-on crown with case protection; screwed-on back with raised rose. Water resistant to 30atm.

Dial: silvered, brushed; center decorated with a raised wave pattern, hour ring decorated with circular beads; luminescent applied rhodium-plated brass lozenge markers; printed minute track with five-minute divisions on the flange; luminescent rhodium-plated brass sport-style hands.
Indications: date between 4 and 5.
Strap: rubber with a raised wave pattern; steel clasp.
Also available: with blue or black dial.

CHOPARD

CHRONOGRAPH RATTRAPANTE   REF. 34/1243

Movement: mechanical, automatic-winding, Frédéric Piguet 1186. Beveled, Côtes de Genève and circular graining finish. 18K-gold rotor.
Functions: hour, minute, small second, date, split-second chronograph with 3 counters.
Case: 18K white-gold, three-piece case (Ø 38mm, thickness 11.7mm); antire-flective curved sapphire crystal; white-gold crown and rectangular pushers (for the split-second feature at 10); caseback attached by 8 screws, displaying the movement through a sapphire crystal. Water resistant to 3atm.
Dial: gold, silvered; zones with circular beads; printed Arabic numerals; white-gold luminescent bâton-style hands.
Indications: minute counter at 3, date between 4 and 5, small seconds at 6, hour counter at 9, center split-second counters, minute track with divisions for 1/5 of a second.
Strap: crocodile leather; hand-engraved white-gold clasp.
Also available: in yellow gold. Both versions available with white or silvered dial.

IMPERIAL CHRONOGRAPH   REF. 37/3168-23.

Movement: mechanical with electric drive controlled by a quartz crystal, Frédéric Piguet 1270 caliber.
Functions: hour, minute, small second, date, chronograph with 3 counters.
Case: 18K white-gold, four-piece case (Ø 37mm, thickness 9mm); flat sapphire crystal; bezel and central attachment with brilliant-cut set diamonds (3.36 carats); brand and progressive number engraved on the left middle side; white-gold octagonal crown, pushers and lugs with sapphire cabochons; back attached by 8 screws. Water resistant to 3atm.
Dial: white, silvered counters; applied round faceted markers, white-gold lozenge-style hands.
Indications: hour counter at 3, date between 4 and 5, small seconds at 6, minute counter at 9, center second chronograph counter, railway minute track with divisions for 1/5 of a second.
Strap: crocodile leather, central attachment with brilliants; white-gold clasp.
Also available: with sapphire cabochons in yellow, pink or white gold; with sapphire cabochons on bezel and central attachment Ref. 37/3168-23 in yellow or white gold; with ruby cabochons: in yellow, pink or white gold.

ST. MORITZ CHRONOGRAPH   REF. 26/8390

Movement: mechanical, automatic-winding, Frédéric Piguet 1185 caliber. 21K-gold rotor.
Functions: hour, minute, second, date, chronograph with 3 counters.
Case: stainless steel, three-piece case (Ø 37.5mm, thickness 10.7mm); antire-flective flat sapphire crystal; bezel fastened by 8 steel screws; screw-on crown; rectangular pushers; caseback attached by 8 screws, displaying the movement through a sapphire crystal. Water resistant to 10atm.
Dial: blue, counters decorated with circular beads; applied stainless steel bâton markers (12 in Roman numerals); luminescent bâton-style hands.
Indications: minute counter at 3, date between 4 and 5, small seconds at 6, hour counter at 9, minute track with divisions for 1/5 of a second and luminescent dots on the flange.
Strap: Kevlar fiber; double fold-over steel clasp.
Also available: with single clasp with bracelet; black or white dial. Automatic (white, gray, blue or coppered dial, bracelet): in stainless steel; yellow gold; white gold; steel/yellow gold ladies' size.

HAPPY SPORT CHRONOGRAPH   REF. 28/8267-23

Movement: electromechanical, Frédéric Piguet 1270 caliber.
Functions: hour, minute, small second, date, chronograph with 3 counters.
Case: stainless steel, three-piece case (Ø 38.5mm, thickness 10.5mm); 7 Top Wesselton quality brilliants (totaling 0.39 carats) individually set and fluctuating between two flat sapphire crystals; sapphire cabochons on crown, pushers and lugs; caseback attached by 8 screws. Water resistant to 3atm. **Dial:** white, silvered counters decorated with circular beads; printed Roman numerals; blued steel bâton-style hands.
Indications: hour counter at 3, date between 4 and 5, small seconds at 6, minute counter at 9, center second counter, railway minute track.
Bracelet: steel; double fold-over clasp.
Also available: iolite cab., strap, brac.; sapphire cab., strap; ruby cab., strap; ruby cab., mother-of-pearl dial, brac. Mother-of-pearl dial: yellow gold, sapphire cab., strap, brac.; yellow gold, ruby cab., strap, brac.; white gold, sapphire cab., strap, brac.; white gold, ruby cab., strap, brac. Bezel with brilliants: yellow gold, mother-of-pearl dial, sapphire cab., strap, brac.; white gold, sapphire cab., strap, brac.; in other jewel versions.

TONNEAU PERPETUAL CALENDAR — REF. 36/92249

Movement: mechanical, automatic-winding, Jaeger-LeCoultre 888 caliber base and perpetual calendar module developed by Chopard.
Functions: hour, minute, 24-hour indication, perpetual calendar (date, day, month, year, moonphase).
Case: platinum, three-piece tonneau-shaped case (size 36.50 x 34.40mm, thickness 8.85mm); flat sapphire crystal; 4 correctors on the middle; white-gold crown; caseback attached by 8 screws. Water resistant to 3atm.
Dial: silvered, engine-turned (guilloché); printed Roman numerals and railway minute track; blued steel Breguet-style hands.
Indications: month and four-year cycle at 3, moonphase at 6, day and 24-hour display at 9, date with retrograde hand at 12.
Strap: crocodile leather, hand-stitched; platinum clasp.
Also available: white dial: in yellow gold; pink or white gold.

CLASSIC FOR GENT — REF. 17/3450

Movement: mechanical, manual-winding, produced by Frédéric Piguet, 6.10 caliber. Bridges finished with Côte de Genève and beveled, pillar-plate with circular graining.
Functions: hour, minute.
Case: 18K white-gold, two-piece rectangular-shaped case, curved (size 31.5 x 28mm, thickness 7.5mm); curved sapphire glass; bezel and lugs set with brilliants; back attached by 4 screws. Water resistant to 3atm.
Dial: white; printed Roman numerals; blued steel leaf-style hands.
Strap: lizard skin; white-gold clasp.
Also available: yellow gold.

ICE CUBE — REF. 13/6858/42

Movement: mechanical, automatic-winding, ETA 2000 caliber.
Functions: hour, minute.
Case: 18K burnished white-gold, two-piece anatomically curved case (size 31.5 x 31.3mm, thickness 8.5mm); entirely studded with square-cut pink sapphires; curved sapphire crystal; recessed burnished gold crown; curved caseback attached by 4 screws. Water resistant to 3atm.
Dial: white gold, studded with brilliants, blued steel bâton-style hands.
Strap: pink satin; white-gold clasp.
Also available: with blue sapphires; entire brilliant pavé; dial with black brilliants.

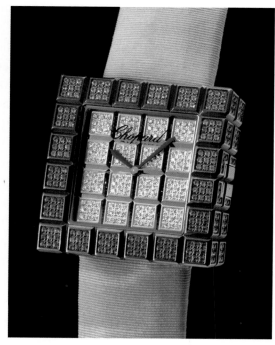

LA STRADA — REF. 41/6866/8

Presented in 1997, the La Strada collection consists of necklaces, bracelets, rings and earrings characterized by big-sized elements in half-moon shapes; of course this is also the motive met in the watches of the same family. The La Strada timepieces, proposed in numerous combinations according to the subtle psychology of the feminine universe, have two case sizes, while the movement can be manual—the Omega 730 old-timer—or quartz.
The photograph shows the bigger version (size 39.5x32mm, thickness 9.8mm) in 18K white-gold with three rows of diamonds on bezel sides and a mother-of-pearl dial with a small second zone driven by a quartz movement.

CHRISTIAN DIOR

today, watches are crucial accessories at the heart of the Dior brand. They combine creativity and quality representative of the Couture house, and all of the expertise of fine Swiss watchmaking. Enhanced more than ever by the brand dynamic in terms of image, distribution and communication, Christian Dior watches have an additional advantage to ensure their success thanks to the integration into LVMH Watches and Jewelry division.

The objective of Dior Watches is to be Number One in the market of luxury fashion watches, with their work focused on exclusivity and quality. John Galliano and the brand's studio supervise the creation of all the watches, which are totally also integrated with the substance of the brand.

Sparkling timepieces light up Dior Watches

Dior watches are the perfect combinations of beautiful watchmaking, precious settings and fashionable allure. With the Sparkling watch collection, jewelry enters the fashion world for a true world premiere.

The Riva Chrono Sparkling houses an ETA Swiss movement and features a scratch-proof sapphire crystal on a watch that is water resistant to 30 meters—three utterly demanding criteria worthy of a luxury watchmaking brand.

Outside: a totally new design with a unique three-strand setting. The stones are set diagonally across the case, creating an original and poetic shower of diamonds.

Ultra-trendy through the marriage of sport and jewelry: the XL (extra large) square steel case has a bold allure that is utterly feminine with 43 scintillating diamonds.

Captivating, the Sparkling collection represents wholly impertinent watches for today's young, urban fashion lovers.

Riva Chrono Sparkling Dior Admit it: daring in black and white. Indeed, for spring 2003, it adopts the Dior Admit it high- fashion look, provocative and ultra-sexy with its strap crafted in laced leather.

Christian Dior
WATCHES

FACING PAGE

Riva Chrono Sparkling
Dior Admit it.

THIS PAGE

The Chris 47 Steel is
shown here on a red
leather strap.

HIGHLIGHTS

▪ The new Chris 47 Steel is an urban, exclusive and highly fashionable design which has preserved all the finest assets that made the Chris 47 aluminum so successful when it was launched in 2001: the superbly designed curves and Dior engraved recesses on the side; the vertical asymmetry of its case; the highly stylized dials; and the time adjustment hidden discreetly on the rear of the case.

▪ The Chris 47 Steel has also won acclaim for its new characteristics that bring luxury and sophisticated design to the finest details: a polished 316L steel case, the traditional material for high-end timepieces; a screwed back for a perfect finish; refined lacquered or sun-brushed dials; and scratch-proof sapphire glass.

▪ Chris 47 Steel has a supremely slender profile (only half the thickness of the original model Chris 47 Steel), and an interchangeable strap system matching the latest line of Dior leather goods, and features a Dior engraved unfolding buckle. Perfectly adaptable to every kind of wrist for optimal comfort, all of these are visible signs of quality for a luxury watch ideally suited to both men and women.

▪ The permanent collection of timeless timepieces. Now belonging to the High-Watchmaking category, the Chris 47 Steel has also adopted a new color code with a series of decisive, authentic shades—white, red and black. It is available in four matching versions: white dial and white bracelet; red dial and red bracelet; black dial and black bracelet; silver dial and black bracelet.

Christian Dior
WATCHES

CHRONOSWISS

Currently celebrating its 20th anniversary, Chronoswiss's unique timepieces have captured the hearts and souls of collectors around the world thanks to their mechanical majesty. According to founder, Gerd-R. Lang, Chronoswiss is a brand "whose time has come."

Even as a child, German-born Lang had a passion for mechanical things. He pursued a career in watchmaking and was obsessed with tracking time precisely. In **1983**, this watchmaker extraordinaire founded Chronoswiss in Munich, Germany, and embarked on a quest to make the most extraordinary mechanic timepieces. He purchased limited-edition- and out-of-use movements that he could embellish and improve. His watches were immediately recognized for their classical elegance and technical prowess.

In **1988**, Chronoswiss surprised the world when it unveiled its stunning regulator wristwatch—which carried the oversized regulator dial that heretofore had only graced the faces of pocket watches and clocks. In **1990**, the brand began to manufacture its own models and in **1992**, it again caused an international stir when it presented its patented two-handed Rattrapante.

Indeed, Chronoswiss has regularly unveiled mechanical masterpieces that have garnered the brand international acclaim. Among them are the patented, reversible Cabrio watch, which was launched in **1993**, followed a year later by the patented Grand Regulateur. In **1995**, the Opus automatic skeletonized chronograph made its debut and in **1996**, the Delphis watch with a unique system of analog, digital and retrograde time-displays made a profound impression on the world of mechanical watchmaking. The first skeletonized self-winding fly-back chronograph, called the Pathos, made its debut in **1998** and in **2001**, the Tourbillon Regulator stole the limelight with its beauty and technically advanced movement. Each of these creations has won at least one international award, with many winning multiple honors.

Lang relentlessly pursues the fine art of mechanical watchmaking and has thereby propelled his brand into the **21**st century with a gusto that is, perhaps, unmatched. Chronoswiss believes in exclusivity and produces only about **7,000** watches per year for global distribution. Every component of Chronoswiss watches is produced in Switzerland and watches are hand finished to Lang's exacting specifications.

Obsessed with the measurements of time intervals, Lang has affectionately been called "Mr. Chronograph" by friends and colleagues. For decades he has restored many exotic chronograph movements, and he has regularly imbued these treasures of timing with additional functions and complexities.

In his most recent unveiling—the Chronoscope—Lang pays homage to the pioneering achievements of 19th-century watchmakers who dedicated themselves to developing split-second timing. For this first chronograph with regulator dial, Chronoswiss has reworked the plate of the movement in order to mount the switching mechanism at the front. The three chronograph functions (start, stop and return to zero) are triggered via a pushpiece that is integrated into the winding crown rather than by separate pushers. To create this system, 38 components were specially made. The self-winding movement enables the Chronoscope to measure intervals of time to a sixth-of-a-second accuracy.

The lacquered dial of the Chronoscope is a work of beauty and harmony. The scale for the chronograph hand is subdivided into exactly 360 strokes. There is a separate subdial at 12:00 for the hours readout and another subdial at 6:00 for the minutes. The hands of the watch have been specially developed to be extremely slender and elegant, and they are crafted in a reddish-blue hue to emulate the dials of 19th-century chronographs.

The 38mm case of the Chronoscope is assembled from 23 individual parts and is water resistant to 30 meters. The sapphire crystal is antireflective on both sides to enhance readability. Chronoswiss has developed 17 different renditions of the Chronoscope—with cases created of gold or steel and dials of various colors. Every Chronoscope is hand signed by Lang.

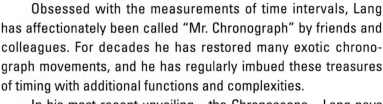

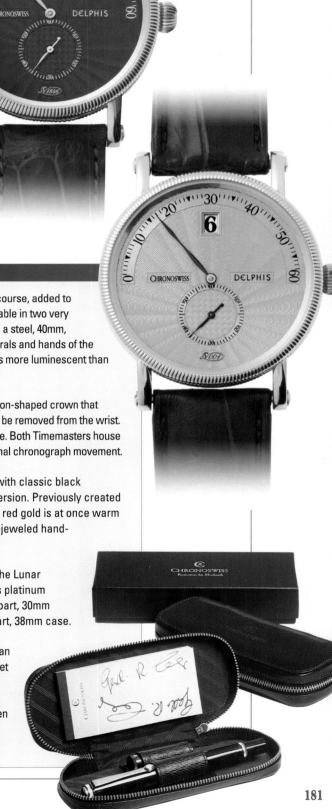

ABOVE

Both the Lunar Triple
Date and the Lunar
Chronograph are now
available in platinum
cases in a limited edition
of 99 pieces.

TOP RIGHT

Fitted with the well-known
round Chronoswiss case,
these two new Delphis
models unite three contrasting display methods on an
aesthetically balanced dial:
"retrograde" for the minutes,
"digital" for the hours, and
standard for the seconds.

BOTTOM RIGHT

The Styloscope fountain
pen features a transparent
green acrylic barrel that
allows the owner to view
the piston mechanism
inside the pen. The nib is
hand-engraved with a
bicolor rhodium décor on
18-karat gold. It is created
in a limited edition of
999 pieces.

HIGHLIGHTS

■ In addition to the spectacular Chronoscope, Chronoswiss has, of course, added to
its other very successful collections. The Timemaster is now available in two very
sporty self-winding versions. Each Timemaster watch is housed in a steel, 40mm,
29-part case with rotating bezel and ultra-luminous dial. The numerals and hands of the
Timemaster are made with Super-LumiNova C3, which is 100 times more luminescent than
conventional zinc sulfide treatments.

■ Each Timemaster watch features Chronoswiss's characteristic onion-shaped crown that
protrudes out far enough so that it can be wound without having to be removed from the wrist.
There is also a model for lefties, with the crown on the opposite side. Both Timemasters house
automatic movements, but one version is equipped with an additional chronograph movement.

■ The Orea watch series—known for its enamel dial calibrated with classic black
numerals—is now joined by a spectacular 18-karat red-gold version. Previously created
only in steel, yellow gold, or a combination thereof, the Orea in red gold is at once warm
and inviting. Created in two case sizes, the watch houses a 17-jeweled hand-
wound movement and is water resistant to 30 meters.

■ Orea isn't the only series to don a new precious metal case. The Lunar
Chronograph and the Lunar Triple Date now come in luxurious platinum
cases. The automatic-wind Lunar chronograph features a 23-part, 30mm
case, while the Lunar Triple Date is housed in a massive 27-part, 38mm case.

■ Chronoswiss has expanded its selection of accessories to include an
elegant fountain pen in a limited edition of 999 exclusive sets. The set
contains an individually numbered Styloscope pen with solid 925
sterling silver fittings, an additionally 18-karat gold nib and a
notepad—delivered in a Chronoswiss-green cowhide case. The pen
is made by Pelikan and is based on the 1992 Demonstrator fountain
pen with which Lang signs each of his guarantee certificates.

CHRONOSWISS

CHRONOGRAPH RATTRAPANTE   REF. CH 7321

Movement: automatic, Chronoswiss C 732 caliber, Valjoux 7750 caliber base modified to support the split-second chronograph and off-center hours and minutes functions. Rolled gold skeletonized rotor; blued screws, Côtes de Genève and circular graining finish. **Functions:** hour, minute, small second; split-second chronograph with 3 counters.
Case: 18K yellow-gold, three-piece case (Ø 38mm, thickness 15.5mm);

antireflective curved sapphire crystal; screwed-on knurled bezel; brushed middle, crown and splitting pusher at 10; gold rim; screwed-on knurled back, displaying the movement through a sapphire crystal. Water resistant to 3atm.
Dial: silvered; off-center hour and minute with printed Roman numerals and blued stainless steel Stuart hands.
Indications: hour counter at 6; small seconds at 9; minute counter at 12; center second and split-second counters; minute track with divisions for 1/5 of a second and 5-second progression.
Strap: crocodile leather; screwed attachment; gold clasp.
Also available: in yellow gold & stainless steel; in steel; with bracelet.

CHRONOGRAPH OPUS   REF. CH 7520 S BL

Movement: mechanical, automatic-winding, Chronoswiss C741S caliber, Valjoux 7750 caliber base, modified to position the hand date indicator at 3. Hand-skeletonized, rhodium-plated pillar-plate and bridges; blued screws; skeletonized rotor. **Functions:** hour, minute, small second; date; chronograph with 3 counters.
Case: platinum, three-piece case (Ø 38mm, thickness 14.8mm); antireflective curved sapphire crystal; screwed-on knurled bezel; brushed middle; platinum

crown and pushers; screwed-on knurled back, displaying the movement through a sapphire crystal. Water resistant to 3atm.
Dial: solid silver, blued and grained, skeletonized; printed minute track; rolled white-gold Breguet hands. **Indications:** date at 3; hour counter at 6; small seconds at 9; minute counter at 12; center second counter; minute track with divisions for 1/5 of a second. **Strap:** crocodile leather, hand stitched; screwed attachment; platinum clasp.
Also available: with bracelet and silvered skeleton dial, unlimited edition; in stainless steel; in yellow or pink gold & stainless steel; in yellow, pink or white gold.
Note: created as a limited edition of 99 numbered pieces.

CHRONOGRAPH TORA   REF. CH 7421 R

Movement: automatic, Chronoswiss C.742 caliber, Valjoux 7750 caliber base. Côtes de Genève and circular graining decoration; skeletonized gilded rotor.
Functions: hour, minute, small second; date; second time-zone time; 24-hour indication; chronograph with 3 counters. **Case:** 18K pink-gold, three-piece case (Ø 38, thickness 15.5mm); antireflective curved sapphire crystal; screwed-on knurled bezel, brushed middle; pushers with non-skid finish (at 10 for fast second time-zone time cor-

rection, blued); screwed-on knurled back, displaying the movement through a sapphire crystal. Water resistant to 3atm.
Dial: solid silver, silvered, engine-turned (guilloché); printed Arabic numerals; rolled pink-gold Breguet lozenge hands.
Indications: date at 3; hour counter at 6; small seconds and second time zone 24-hour (day-night) at 9; minute counter at 12; center second; minute track with divisions for 1/4 of a second.
Strap: crocodile leather; screwed attachment; pink-gold clasp.
Also available: pink gold; white gold; in stainless steel and pink or yellow gold; platinum, 99 pieces; in stainless steel with silver or black enameled dial; with bracelet.

CHRONOGRAPH LUNAR   REF. CH 7523 L SW

Movement: mechanical, automatic-winding, Chronoswiss C755 caliber, Valjoux 7750 caliber base. Rolled gold skeletonized rotor, blued screws.
Functions: hour, minute, small second; date; moonphase; chronograph with 3 counters.
Case: stainless steel, three-piece case (Ø 38mm, thickness 15mm); antireflective curved sapphire crystal; screwed-on knurled bezel; brushed middle;

screwed-on knurled back, displaying the movement through a sapphire crystal. Water resistant to 3atm.
Dial: solid silver, black enameled, engine-turned (guilloché); printed Arabic numerals; white enameled Breguet lozenge hands.
Indications: moonphase at 3; hour counter at 6; small seconds at 9; minute counter at 12; center second; minute track with divisions for 1/4 of a second; red-tip center arrow-shaped date hand.
Strap: crocodile leather; screwed attachment; stainless steel clasp.
Also available: with silver dial; in yellow or pink gold & stainless steel, with silver dial; in yellow, white or pink gold, silver dial; in platinum, silver dial, 99 pieces; with bracelet.

DELPHIS   REF. CH 1423 BL

Movement: mechanical, automatic-winding, Chronoswiss C 124 caliber, Enicar base modified to support digital jumping hour display and retrograde minute. Gilded rotor.
Functions: jumping hour, minute, small second.
Case: stainless steel, three-piece case (Ø 38mm, thickness 11mm); flat antireflective sapphire crystal; knurled screwed-on bezel; brushed middle; screwed-on knurled back, displaying the movement through a sapphire crystal. Water resistant to 3atm.
Dial: blue enameled, hand-turned (guilloché) with sun pattern.
Indications: jumping hour in a window at 12; minute track and printed markers; steel center retrograde Stuart hand; small seconds at 6.
Strap: crocodile leather; screwed attachment; steel clasp.
Also available: in pink gold; yellow or pink gold & stainless steel; steel; yellow gold, white gold silver dial; platinum silver dial, 99 pieces; steel, pink gold with mother of pearl dial; with bracelet.

LUNAR   REF. CH 9323

Movement: mechanical, automatic-winding, Chronoswiss C931 caliber, ETA 2892A2 caliber base + full calendar module. Gilded skeletonized rotor.
Functions: hour, minute, second; full calendar (date, day, month, moon-phase).
Case: stainless steel, three-piece case (Ø 37mm, thickness 10.7mm); antireflective flat sapphire crystal; screwed-on knurled bezel; brushed middle with 4 correctors; screwed-on knurled back, displaying the movement through a sapphire crystal. Water resistant to 3atm.
Dial: solid silver, silvered, engine-turned (guilloché), zone decorated with old-basket pattern; brushed hour ring; printed Arabic numerals and minute track with 5-minute progression; blued steel Breguet lozenge hands.
Indications: date and moon phase at 6; day and month at 12.
Strap: crocodile leather; screwed attachment; steel clasp.
Also available: in stainless steel and yellow or pink gold, yellow or pink gold silver dial; in white gold, silver dial; in platinum, silver dial, 99 pieces; with bracelet.

CHRONOSCOPE   REF. CH 1521 R

Movement: automatic, Chronoswiss C125 caliber, Enicar base modified by addition of a chronograph module, 11'''3/4 (Ø 26.80mm, thickness 6.80mm), 30 jewels, 21,600 vibrations per hour. Pink gilded skeletonized rotor.
Functions: hour, minute, small second; chronograph with one counter.
Case: 18K pink-gold, three-piece case (Ø 38mm, thickness 12.4mm); antireflective curved sapphire glass; knurled screwed-on bezel; brushed middle; pink-gold crown with coaxial chronograph pusher; screwed-on knurled back displaying the movement through a sapphire glass. Water resistant to 3atm.
Dial: white enameled; steel Stuart hands "lie de vin" (from the typical color of young wine).
Indications: off-center hour at 12 with printed Roman numerals; small seconds at 6; center minute and second counters; internal railway minute track and external 360° scale to measure fractions of a second with divisions for 1/6 of a second.
Strap: crocodile leather; screwed attachment; pink-gold clasp.
Also available: in white or yellow gold; steel and yellow or pink gold; steel; platinum, 99 pieces; with bracelet.

KAIROS MEDIUM   REF. CH 2823 K MD SW SBL

In 1995 Chronoswiss presented two new sizes of the most classical watch in its catalog: the Kairos. The medium size, whose dimensions are limited to 34 millimeter in diameter and 8.3 in thickness is driven by the automatic ETA 2892A2 movement, that drives also the larger-size model. It is assembled and finished entirely by hand by the House's watchmaker masters. This movement has 21 jewels, a diameter of 25.6mm and a thickness of 3.6mm. The balance is provided with an Incabloc shock-absorber system and is in Glucydur; its frequency is 28,800 vph; its spring is of the first-quality Nivarox type. It is equipped with a skeletonized rolled gold rotor. The photograph shows a version with stainless steel case and bracelet, a bezel with a row of set brilliants and a back enameled dial.
Also available: with silver dial; leather strap; without brilliants: in stainless steel, black or silvered dial; in steel and yellow gold, silver dial; in yellow gold, silver dial; with bracelet.

CHRONOSWISS

RÉGULATEUR À TOURBILLON REF. CH 3121 R

Movement: mechanical, automatic-winding, with tourbillon "volant" device, Chronoswiss C361 caliber, Progress 6361.101 caliber base. Decorated with Côtes de Genève and circular graining.
Functions: hour, minute.
Case: 18K pink-gold, three-piece case (Ø 38mm, thickness 10.5mm); antireflective flat sapphire crystal; knurled bezel; brushed middle; crown with gold rim; screwed-on knurled back, displaying the movement through a sapphire crystal. Water resistant to 3atm.
Dial: solid silver, silvered, engine-turned (guilloché) by hand (hour zone decorated with old-basket pattern); aperture on the tourbillon; blued steel Poire hands.
Indications: off-center hour at 12 with printed Roman numerals; center minute with printed track and 5-minute progression
Strap: crocodile leather; screwed attachment; pink-gold clasp.
Also available: in yellow or white gold; in steel and yellow or pink gold; in steel; in platinum, 99 pieces; with bracelet.

RÉGULATEUR REF. CH 1223 KU

Movement: mechanical, automatic-winding, Chronoswiss C122 caliber.
Functions: hour, minute, small second.
Case: stainless steel, three-piece case (Ø 38mm, thickness 10.3mm); antireflective flat sapphire crystal; knurled screwed-on bezel; brushed middle; screwed-on knurled back, displaying the movement through a sapphire crystal. Water resistant to 3atm.
Dial: coppered; printed railway track with 5-minute progression; blued steel Stuart hands.
Indications: off-center hour at 12 with Roman numerals; center minutes; small seconds at 6.
Strap: ostrich skin; screwed attachment; steel clasp.0
Also available: with silver or black enameled dial; in steel and yellow gold, silver dial; in yellow gold, silver dial; with bracelet.

CHRONOGRAPH KLASSIK REF. CH 7401 BL

Movement: mechanical, automatic-winding, Chronoswiss, C741 caliber, Valjoux 7750 caliber base, modified to position the hand date at 3.
Functions: hour, minute, small second; chronograph with 3 counters.
Case: stainless steel, three-piece case (Ø 37mm, thickness 14.3mm); horn-shaped lugs; antireflective curved sapphire crystal; rectangular pushers; snap-on back, displaying the movement through a sapphire crystal. Water resistant to 3atm.
Dial: blue enameled, engine-turned (guilloché) by hand with a sun pattern, counters decorated with circular beads; applied steel square markers and Roman numerals; steel Railway hands.
Indications: date at 3; hour counter at 6; small seconds at 9; minute counter at 12; center second; tachometer scale; minute track with divisions for 1/5 of a second.
Strap: crocodile leather; steel clasp.
Also available: in pink gold & stainless steel; in pink gold; silver or black or blue enameled dial (only steel version); with a pulsometer scale.

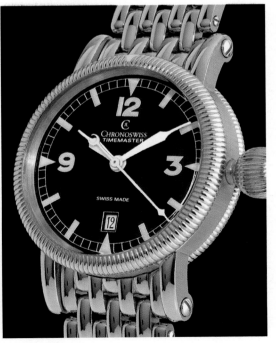

TIMEMASTER REF. CH 2833 SW SBL

Movement: mechanical, automatic-winding, ETA 2892A2 caliber improved by Chronoswiss. **Functions:** hour, minute, second; date.
Case: stainless steel, three-piece case (Ø 40mm, thickness 12mm); antireflective curved sapphire crystal; knurled bezel turning in two ways with luminescent marker; brushed middle; oversized and jutting crown on the left (the related tube is integrated in the case) allowing operations also with gloves; screwed-on knurled back, displaying the movement through a sapphire crystal. Water resistant to 10atm.
Dial: black enameled; luminescent bâton and triangular markers and Arabic numerals; printed railway minute track; white enameled Railway hands.
Indications: date at 6.
Bracelet: in steel, screwed attachment; recessed double fold-over clasp; furnished with a case containing spare accessories and an additional cowhide leather strap allowing to wear it on a pilot's suit.
Also available: with luminescent dial, printed Arabic numerals; strap. Version for left-handers (with crown on the left, same versions); bracelet only in steel.

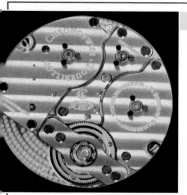

CALIBER C.361

Basic caliber: Progress cal. 6361.101. Manual-winding movement with two barrels and 72-hour autonomy.
Functions: hours (off-center), minutes. **Shape:** round. **Diameter:** 30mm (13'''3/4). **Thickness:** 5.40mm. **Jewels:** 23. **Balance:** in Glucydur, with three arms, flying tourbillon device. **Frequency:** 28,800 vph. **Balance-spring:** flat.
Shock-absorber system: Incabloc.
Notes: the tourbillon carriage shows an exclusive Chronoswiss design; the pillar-plate is decorated with a circular-graining pattern, bridges are decorated with a Côtes de Genève pattern and beveled; three gold settings fastened by blued screws.

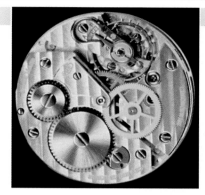

CALIBER C.672

Basic caliber: ETA/Unitas 6497-1. Manual-winding movement, autonomy of 50 hours.
Functions: hours, minutes, seconds. **Shape:** round. **Diameter:** 36.6mm (16'''1/2). **Jewels:** 18. **Balance:** with compensating screws, two arms, in Glucydur. **Frequency:** 18,000 vph. **Balance-spring:** flat, Nivarox 1. **Shock-absorber system:** Incabloc.
Notes: the basic movement was modified by adding indirect center seconds, a micrometer screw index regulating device and swan-neck retaining spring. The pillar-plate is decorated with a circular-graining pattern, bridges are decorated with a Côtes de Genève pattern.

CALIBER C.1722 R

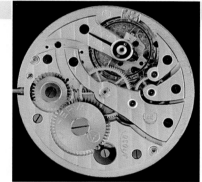

Basic caliber: Minerva 1722. Manual-winding movement, 36-hour autonomy.
Functions: hours (off-center), minutes, small seconds. **Shape:** round. **Diameter:** 38.35mm (17'''). **Jewels:** 15.
Balance: with compensating screws, with two arms. **Frequency:** 18,000 vph.
Balance-spring: Breguet. **Notes:** Caliber C.1722 is realized as a limited series by using a Lépine type pocket watch movement produced by the Minerva manufacture in 1921. This is completely disassembled, finished and modified by Chronoswiss for the off-center hour display at 12. The watch derived in this way is proposed only in the transformable pocket/wrist version under the name Grand Régulateur, as a series limited to 300 pieces for worldwide distribution.

CALIBER C.122

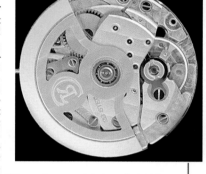

Basic caliber: C. 121 (Enicar, center hours/minutes, small sec.). Automatic mov., autonomy of 40h, skeletonized and gilded rotor, mounted on a ball bearing.
Functions: off-center hours, minutes, small sec. **Shape:** round. **Diameter:** 26.80mm (11'''3/4) **Thickness:** 5.30mm. **Jewels:** 29.
Balance: smooth, with three arms, in Glucydur. **Frequency:** 21,600 vph. **Balance-spring:** flat, Nivarox 1, with an eccentric regulating device. **Shock-absorber system:** Incabloc. **Notes:** pillar-plate decorated with a circular-graining pattern, bridges with circular graining and Côtes de Genève patterns and beveled, rotor with a Côtes de Genève pattern. **Derived calibers:** C.123 (C.122 + center second, independent 24-hour 2nd time zone); C.124 (C.122 + jumping hours, retrograde minutes, small second).

CALIBER C.124

Caliber C.124, derived from C.122, hides behind its dial the remarkable work performed by Chronoswiss's technicians to combine the display of jumping hours and retrograde minutes. This movement was one among the first assuring, thanks to a patented device, the actual simultaneity of the hour change inside the relevant window and the return to zero of the minutes hand, and all this without interfering with the proper working of the movement.

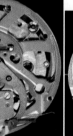

CALIBER C.741S

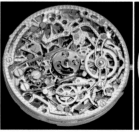

Basic caliber: ETA 7750. Automatic mov., autonomy of 44h, skeletonized rotor mounted on a ball bearing. **Functions:** hours, minutes, small sec.; date; chronograph with 3 counters (center sec., minutes, hours). **Shape:** round. **Diameter:** 30.00mm (13'''1/4). **Thickness:** 7.90mm. **Jewels:** 25. **Balance:** smooth, with 3 arms, in Glucydur. **Frequency:** 28,800 vph. **Balance-spring:** flat, Nivarox 1, with fine regulation device. **Shock-absorber system:** Incabloc. **Notes:** skeletonized pillar-plate and bridges, with fine circular graining and beveled. C.741S differs from ETA 7750 by the analogue and off-center date display. Other basic Chronoswiss 7750 calibers without calendar: C.753 (3 counters, hours/minutes at 3); C.754 (3 counters, COSC).

CALIBER C.732

Basic caliber: ETA 7750. Automatic-winding movement, autonomy of 44 hours, skeletonized and gilded rotor mounted on a ball bearing.
Functions: hours and minutes (off-center at 3), small seconds; split-second chronograph with three counters (center seconds, minutes and hours).
Shape: round. **Diameter:** 30.00mm (13'''1/4). **Thickn.:** 8.20mm. **Jewels:** 27.
Balance: smooth, three arms, in Glucydur. **Frequency:** 28,800 vph. **Balance-spring:** flat, Nivarox 1, with fine regulation device. **Shock-absorber system:** Incabloc.
Notes: the pillar-plate is decorated with a circular-graining pattern, the upper bridge and the rotor with a Côtes de Genève pattern.

DIAL-SIDE CALIBERS C.732S - C.741S (SKELETONIZED)

Left: the picture shows the column-wheel (on the left side) for the regulation of the movement of the steel clams locking and releasing—by actuating the third pusher—the gear on which the second seconds hand is mounted on the right, the sinuous, aesthetically agreeable bridge that holds the off-center hours and minutes wheelwork in place. On the opposite side, this caliber appears identical to the C.741S because the modifications made by Chronoswiss (split-second chronograph and off-center hours) are concentrated under the dial. **Right:** complete dial side. In the original cal. ETA 7750, the analogue date display at 3 is by the center hand or inside an aperture.

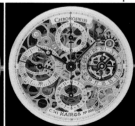

CLERC

heir to a longstanding family tradition handed down from one generation to the next, Clerc has been cultivating a taste for exceptional watchmaking for more than 125 years.

Since **1874**, the watches bearing this well-recognized signature have consistently been known for their avant-garde design and exceptional quality. The new collection designed by Gérald Clerc pursues the path laid by the original founders of the family firm in Paris—namely a will to create unique and sophisticated watches.

Clerc has always been skilled in capturing the spirit of the times. In the aftermath of World War I, the popularity of wristwatches inspired the brand to design new creations combining precious stones and time display. During successive periods, they developed jewelry watches and classic models. Gérald Clerc continues to draw inspiration for his own collections from this rich heritage, thereby perpetuating the founders' goals: the pursuit of elegance and unwavering standards of craftsmanship.

Throughout its history, Clerc has signed prestigious creations for highly recognized personalities. The Clerc name is associated with crowned heads such as Princess Grace of Monaco; heads of state such as General Charles de Gaulle, Khrushchev, Sheikh Abdullah El Zawir; artists including Salvador Dali, Paco Rabanne, Francoise Hardy, and Maurice Chevalier; and more recently, Michael Douglas, Jack Scalia and Ewan McGregor.

THIS PAGE

ABOVE
Clerc's original flagship location after its inception in 1874.

TOP LEFT
Gérald Clerc oversees every aspect of design and development.

BOTTOM LEFT
This one-of-a-kind Clerc bangle bracelet watch, circa 1920, is crafted in platinum and bedecked in diamonds.

FACING PAGE

Michael Douglas and Catherine Zeta-Jones.

CLERC

TOP CENTER

Water resistant to 300 meters, this CXX Chronograph features automatic movement, annual date function, and 44 hours of power reserve.

LEFT

Gentlemen's steel automatic power-reserve watch.

BOTTOM

This stainless steel automatic men's watch is an officially certified Swiss chronometer and each is individually numbered and handcrafted in Switzerland.

For sporty appeal, Clerc offers the CXX Chronograph®. Designed for extreme conditions and professional use, this diving watch features mechanical complications in several combinations. Water resistant to 300 meters and fitted with a rotating bezel, screw-locked crown and natural rubber strap, this diving watch is made to confront the elements. The CXX Chronograph was designed and developed in cooperation with a team of diving professionals well acquainted with the underwater world. Handcrafted in Switzerland, each Clerc CXX Chronograph is individually numbered and comes with a 3-year international warranty.

The C125® bracelet design is graced with a natural, flowing feel, encircling the wrist so gently that its touch could almost go unnoticed. The C125 rectangular cuff watch is enhanced by a fine row of diamonds on the case, and is also available as a stunning piece of jewelry with diamonds spilling over the case and bracelet.

TOP LEFT
This striking pink sapphire watch attests to the technical prowess in gemsetting mastered by Clerc.

TOP RIGHT
C125 rectangular cuff watch is available in vibrantly colored leather straps.

BOTTOM
From the C125 collection of ladies' watches, this steel bracelet with diamonds houses a precision quartz movement.

From the Haute Joaillerie collection, this 18-karat gold chronograph is crafted with 438 diamonds and 85 rubies.

LEFT

The officially certified C-Collection chronograph chronometer.

BELOW

This ladies' 18-karat gold jewelry watch with diamonds and sapphires features an automatic movement, and the Cie de Geneve quality hallmark.

The C-Collection® of timepieces is a powerful modern design combined with a level of excellence and quality synonymous with Clerc. A perfect blend of elegance and technology, the watches in this series are fashioned and sculpted from solid steel or 18-karat gold. Gold versions are stamped with the prestigious Cie de Geneve quality hallmark. Handcrafted in Geneva, each Clerc C-Collection watch is individually numbered and comes with a 3-year international warranty.

As an extension of the C-Collection, Clerc has unveiled the C-Collection Complications series, which includes a men's steel automatic Power Reserve and Two-Timer Power Reserve.

HIGHLIGHTS

■ Montres Clerc created a precedent by opening the path into the delicate art of marrying precious stones with the chilled elegance of steel.

■ In addition to rubies, diamonds and blue sapphires that grace the well-known Red, White & Blue® collection, Clerc has turned to black diamonds and pastel colored sapphires to the series.

■ Handcrafted in Switzerland, each Clerc watch is individually numbered and comes with a 3-year international warranty.

CONCORD

truly one of the most innovative watch companies, Concord has been creating timepieces of distinction for nearly a century. From the beginning, Concord focused on technical prowess and aesthetic advancements, quickly propelling itself to a premier position within the world of fine watchmaking.

Since its founding in Bienne, Switzerland, in **1908**, Concord has regularly turned out masterpieces. Within the first decade of its existence, the brand carved out a niche for itself as a producer of luxury timepieces, crafting in platinum and accenting its watches with diamonds, rubies, emeralds and sapphires.

In the **1920**s, Concord moved into the realm of clock design and unveiled the now-famed Concord Ring Clock—the first portable eight-day winding travel alarm clock. Nearly two decades later this clock was still so impressive that president Harry Truman presented it to several heads of state in **1945**, including Winston Churchill.

In **1969**, visionary businessman Gedalio Grinberg purchased Concord Watch Company and incorporated it into North American Watch Corporation in New York—which is known today as Movado Group Inc. Under Grinberg's vigilant eye, the Concord brand flourished. Groundbreaking research resulted in the launch of the quartz-powered Delirium in **1979**. The world's thinnest watch, the Delirium measured 1.98mm. Within a year, the brand broke its own record with the Delirium IV—measuring just under 1mm.

A year later, in **1980**, Concord introduced its Mariner sports watch, and in **1986** unveiled the Saratoga—an icon for the brand even today. A trendsetter in the sophisticated art of watch design, Concord went on to launch the Saratoga Exor in **1995**. Created in three versions, including a perpetual calendar, minute repeater and tourbillon, each of the Exor watches was so elaborately decorated with gemstones that they ranked among the world's most expensive jeweled creations.

Today, Concord's impressive roster includes not only the Saratoga, but the sophisticated Veneto watch (launched in **1996**), the daring 18-karat gold geometric La Scala (launched in **1997**), and the bold La Scala Stainless Steel Chronograph (launched in **2001**). In typical Concord style, the brand regularly adds new models to these collections—offering fresh intrigue and excitement.

TOP LEFT
Crafted in steel with 18-karat gold accents, this Saratoga features a date window at 3:00.

TOP RIGHT
The Mini Saratoga in steel with gold accents is set with 24 diamonds on the bezel.

BOTTOM LEFT
This elegant men's Saratoga is crafted in steel and features a charcoal hand-engraved dial.

Determined to adhere to the highest standards in watchmaking, Concord creates all of its timepieces with scrupulous attention to detail, performance and originality. Such is the case with the superb Saratoga line. First launched 17 years ago, the Saratoga was a sophisticated, elite timepiece that earned international praise. It has remained an important signature collection for the brand and was recently reinterpreted to reflect today's lifestyles and designs.

The new Saratoga is the culmination of nearly a century of Concord watchmaking excellence. Its casually elegant beauty is emphasized by the eight-sided bezel—a hallmark of the watch—and by the striking modernistic scallop-engraved dials. The faces are graced with alpha hands, applied markers and numerals, with a date at 3:00.

A precision sports watch, the Saratoga is sleek and bold—a true expression of individuality. The newly designed Saratoga watches are crafted in solid stainless steel, 18-karat white or rose gold, and stainless

steel with 18-karat yellow-gold or rose-gold accents. They feature a distinctive woven-link bracelet with deployment clasp and elegantly engineered, patented crown protector that securely latches shut to ensure water resistance to 50 meters. The newest models feature embossed casebacks with an equestrian design, recalling the original sport for which the watch was created. New variations include diamond-adorned bezels and dials.

Paying homage to its heritage, Concord has unveiled a one-of-a-kind Saratoga Tourbillon that is crafted harmoniously in 18-karat white gold. This spectacular piece is a work of art and old-world craftsmanship. It features a tourbillon escapement, minute repeater, chronograph, and power reserve. The watch features a sapphire caseback to view the magnificent movement.

I am not late,
you are.

The New Concord Saratoga.

CONCORD

FAR LEFT
The square La Scala is elegantly crafted in 18-karat yellow gold with a fully set diamond bezel and textured dial with a diamond-set minute track.

CENTER LEFT
The square La Scala is also exquisite in 18-karat white gold with a fully set diamond bezel and textured dial with a diamond-set minute track.

TOP LEFT
Crafted in 18-karat rose gold, this La Scala Fashion watch features a mother-of-pearl dial. The bezel and dial center are set with 1.22 carats of diamonds.

TOP RIGHT
Fully set with 5.77 carats of diamonds, this 18-karat white-gold La Scala Fashion is a shimmering beauty.

BELOW LEFT
The striking La Scala Stainless Steel Square Chronograph is highlighted by a lilac mother-of-pearl dial set with diamond markers, diamond case and corner accents, and a matching alligator strap.

BELOW RIGHT
The La Scala Stainless Steel Square Chronograph is also available with a white mother-of-pearl dial, black alligator strap, and fully set bezel.

Concord's smoothly sculpted, incredibly elegant La Scala collection dons newness with color and gemstones. First introduced at the 1997 World Watch and Jewelry Fair in Basel, the La Scala stole hearts with its sleek design and bold beauty.

Already rich with variation, the La Scala collection of round and square timepieces boasts chronograph models bedecked in diamonds (colorless and black) or in gemstones (sapphires of all hues). The straps of these watches are interchangeable and are made of alligator or rubber in many colors and shades. Bracelets of these architecturally inspired timepieces feature deployment clasps and are crafted either in steel or in 18-karat gold.

New square models include a stainless steel chronograph with two rows of diamonds on the top and bottom case-to-bracelet attachments, with a lustrous mother-of-pearl dial in pastel hues of either lilac, mango or yellow with color-coordinated straps. There also is a full diamond-set model.

For a more fashionable appeal in the world of luxury, Concord has unveiled the striking 18-karat white-gold La Scala Fashion manchette model that wears like a cuff bracelet. Featuring a panoply of diamonds in varying settings, the watch is reminiscent of a fine piece of sculpted jewelry. It is available with either 122 diamonds weighing just over 1 carat, or with 328 diamonds with a total weight of just over 3 carats.

I am yesterday,
today, tomorrow.

The Concord La Scala.

I am the dream.
You are the dreamer.

The Concord La Scala Chronograph.

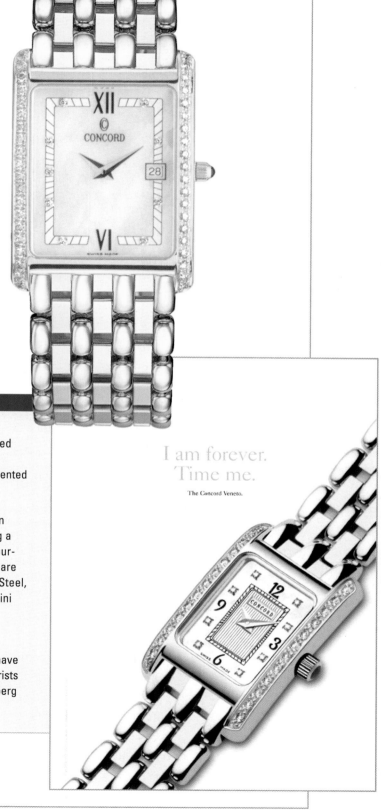

I am forever.
Time me.

The Concord Veneto.

HIGHLIGHTS

- Concord has added several new pieces to its Veneto collection of round and rectangular-shaped watches. New models feature bezels, dials and bracelets set with brilliant-cut diamonds, and accented with either white or mother-of-pearl dials.

- An alluring new advertising campaign has been developed and launched by the brand. Featuring a single watch as the star of each, there are six four-color single-page ads. The six watches depicted are the La Scala pink Chrono, the La Scala Stainless Steel, the Veneto, the men's Steel Saratoga and two mini steel Saratogas—one with diamonds and one without diamonds.

- So captivating are Concord timepieces that they have made their way to the Academy Awards on the wrists of celebrities such as Geena Davis, Whoopi Goldberg and Allison Janney.

197

CONCORD

CONCORD SPORTIVO   REF. 14-H1-0610.1-R37-1/0114

Movement: quartz, ETA.
Functions: hour, minute, small second; date; chronograph (up to 30 minutes) with 3 counters.
Case: stainless steel case (size 29.5 x 40mm); curved sapphire crystal; crown with case protection; water resistant to 3atm.
Dial: silver engraved dial; applied pointed markers; 12 applied Arabic numeral.

Indications: tenths of a second at 2; date at 4; small second at 6; minute counter (up to 30 minutes) at 10; center second counter.
Bracelet: stainless steel; deployment clasp.

CONCORD SPORTIVO   REF. 14-36-0622.1-2324-1/0113-BK

Movement: quartz, ETA.
Functions: hour, minute, center second; date.
Case: stainless steel case (size 26 x 38mm); curved sapphire crystal; crown with case protection; water resistant to 3atm.
Dial: silver engraved dial; applied pointed markers; 12, 6 and 9 applied Arabic numerals.

Indications: date at 3.
Strap: black calfskin; stainless steel deployment clasp.

CONCORD SARATOGA   REF. 14-C2-1894-A040-1/0113

Movement: quartz, ETA.
Functions: hour, minute, center second; date.
Case: stainless steel case (size 38mm); 8-sided bezel; flat sapphire crystal; crown with signature patented latched crown protector; back attached with screws; water resistant to 5atm.
Dial: silver engraved dial; applied triangular markers; 12, 6 and 9 applied Arabic numerals.
Indications: date at 3.
Bracelet: stainless steel; deployment clasp.

CONCORD SARATOGA   REF. 14-E1-1855-A040-71/0113S-S

Movement: quartz, ETA.
Functions: hour, minute, date.
Case: stainless steel case (size 27.50mm); flat sapphire crystal; 8-sided bezel set with 16 brilliants; crown with signature patented latched crown protector; caseback attached with screws; water resistant to 5atm.
Dial: white mother-of-pearl; 8 brilliant markers; 12, 6 and 9 applied Arabic numerals.
Indications: date at 3.
Bracelet: stainless steel; deployment clasp.

CONCORD LA SCALA STEEL SQUARE CHRONOGRAPH
REF. 14-H1-1371-2306-75/0108S-S71RD

Movement: quartz, ETA.
Functions: hour, minute, small second; date; chronograph (up to 30 minutes) with 3 counters.
Case: stainless steel square case (size 29.95mm); strap attachments set with 12 brilliants; bezel corners set with 16 brilliants; flat sapphire crystal; octagonal crown; brand engraved on the side of the case; water resistant to 3atm.
Dial: orange mother-of-pearl; 5 brilliant markers; 12 applied Arabic numeral.
Indications: tenths of a second at 2; date at 4; small second at 6; minute counter (up to 30 minutes) at 10; center second counter; minute track.
Strap: orange matte alligator; stainless steel deployment clasp.

CONCORD LA SCALA STEEL SQUARE CHRONOGRAPH
REF. 14-H1-1371-2308-71/0108S-S31BK

Movement: quartz, ETA.
Functions: hour, minute, small second; date; chronograph (up to 30 minutes) with 3 counters.
Case: stainless steel square case (size 29.95mm); strap attachments set with 12 brilliants; bezel set with 54 brilliants; flat sapphire crystal; octagonal crown; brand engraved on the side of the case; water resistant to 3atm.
Dial: white mother-of-pearl; 5 brilliant markers; 12 applied Arabic numeral.
Indications: tenths of a second at 2; date at 4; small second at 6; minute counter (up to 30 minutes) at 10; center second counter; minute track.
Strap: black matte alligator; stainless steel deployment clasp.

CONCORD LA SCALA SQUARE CHRONOGRAPH
REF. 14-H1-1371-A0092-71/0108S-S71

Movement: quartz, ETA.
Functions: hour, minute, small second; date; chronograph (up to 30 minutes) with 3 counters.
Case: stainless steel square case (size 29.95mm); strap attachments set with 12 brilliants; bezel corners set with 16 brilliants; flat sapphire crystal; octagonal crown; brand engraved on the side of the case; water resistant to 3atm.
Dial: white mother-of-pearl; 5 brilliant markers; 12 applied Arabic numeral.
Indications: tenths of a second at 2; date at 4; small second at 6; minute counter (up to 30 minutes) at 10; center second counter; minute track.
Bracelet: polished and brushed stainless steel; deployment clasp.

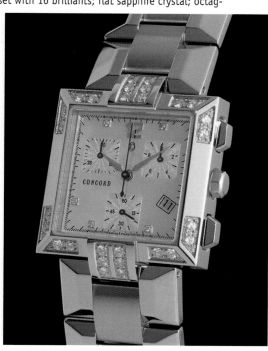

CONCORD LA SCALA CHRONOGRAPH
REF. 52-C5-0205-2325BRN-1/0003

Movement: quartz, ETA.
Functions: hour, minute, small second, date, chronograph (up to 30 minutes) with 3 counters.
Case: 18K rose-gold case (size 38mm); flat sapphire crystal; octagonal rose-gold crown; brand engraved on the side of the case; water resistant to 3atm.
Dial: silver engraved dial; triangle markers; 12 applied Arabic numeral.
Indications: tenths of a second at 2; date at 4; small second at 6; minute counter (up to 30 minutes) at 10; center second counter; minute track.
Strap: brown matte alligator strap; deployment clasp.

CONCORD

LA SCALA CHRONOGRAPH   REF. 61-C5-0205-2328BLU-72/0121S-S

Movement: quartz, ETA.
Functions: hour, minute, small second; date; chronograph (up to 30 minutes) with 3 counters.
Case: 18K white-gold case (size 38mm); bezel set with 38 blue baguette-cut sapphires; flat sapphire crystal; octagonal white-gold crown; brand engraved on the side of the case; back attached by screws; water resistant to 3atm.

Dial: blue mother-of-pearl set with pavé diamonds; 12 applied Arabic numeral.
Indications: tenths of a second at 2; date at 4; small second at 6; minute counter (up to 30 minutes) at 10; center second counter; minute track.
Strap: blue matte alligator strap; deployment clasp.

LA SCALA CHRONOGRAPH   REF. 14-C5-1891.1-2297-4/0004S-S317R

Movement: quartz, ETA.
Functions: hour, minute, small second; date; chronograph (up to 30 minutes) with 3 counters.
Case: stainless steel coated with black PVD case (size 38mm); flat sapphire crystal; octagonal crown; bezel set with 42 diamonds; brand engraved on the side of the case; water resistant to 3atm.

Dial: black engraved dial; 7 brilliant markers; 12 applied Arabic numeral.
Indications: tenths of a second at 2; date at 4; small second at 6; minute counter (up to 30 minutes) at 10; center second counter; minute track.
Strap: red alligator strap; deployment clasp.

LA SCALA STEEL CHRONOGRAPH REF. 14-C5-1891-2327-71/0004S-S242

Movement: quartz, ETA.
Functions: hour, minute, small second; date; chronograph (up to 30 minutes) with 3 counters.
Case: stainless steel case (size 38mm); bezel set with 30 blue sapphires; flat sapphire crystal; octagonal crown; brand engraved on the side of the case; water resistant to 3atm.

Dial: white mother-of-pearl dial; 7 brilliant markers; 12 applied Arabic numeral.
Indications: tenths of a second at 2; date at 4; small second at 6; minute counter (up to 30 minutes) at 10; center second counter; minute track.
Strap: blue alligator strap; deployment clasp.

LA SCALA CHRONOGRAPH

Movement: quartz, ETA.
Functions: hour, minute, small second; date; chronograph with 3 counters.
Case: stainless steel, two-piece case; 30 black brilliants set on the strap attachments; flat sapphire glass; rectangular pushers; octagonal crown; brand engraved on the middle; back attached by screws. Water resistant to 3atm.
Dial: silvered, engine-turned (guilloché) with sun pattern; 7 brilliant markers,

12 applied rhodium-plated Arabic numeral; rhodium-plated Alpha hands.
Indications: tenths of a second at 2; date at 4; small second at 6; minute counter at 10; center second counter; minute track with divisions for 1/5 of a second.
Strap: crocodile leather; central attachment; steel fold-over clasp.

CONCORD

LA SCALA CHRONOGRAPH

Movement: quartz, ETA.
Functions: hour, minute, small second; date; chronograph with 3 counters.
Case: 18K yellow-gold, two-piece case; bezel with 22 set brilliants; flat sapphire glass; yellow-gold rectangular pushers; yellow-gold octagonal crown with sapphire cabochon; brand engraved on the middle; back attached by screws. Water resistant to 3atm.
Dial: yellow gold; center disc in mother-of-pearl; gold ring with brilliant pavé; hour ring in mother-of-pearl with 12 brilliant markers on the printed minute track; gold Dauphine hands.
Indications: tenths of a second at 2; date at 4; small second at 6; minute counter at 10; center second counter.
Bracelet: yellow gold with brilliants set on the central links; fold-over clasp.

LA SCALA CHRONOGRAPH

Movement: quartz, ETA.
Functions: hour, minute, small second; date; chronograph with 3 counters.
Case: stainless steel, two-piece case; flat sapphire glass; rectangular pushers; octagonal crown; brand engraved on the middle; back attached by screws. Water resistant to 3atm.
Dial: black with blue zones, engine-turned (guilloché) with sun pattern; bâton markers, 12 applied rhodium-plated Arabic numeral; rhodium-plated Alpha hands.
Indications: tenths of a second at 2; date at 4; small second at 6; minute counter at 10; center second counter; minute track with divisions for 1/5 of a second.
Bracelet: polished and brushed stainless steel; fold-over clasp.

LA SCALA CHRONOGRAPH

The new La Scala Chronograph versions use stainless steel as the advanced material par excellence. Concord, after having presented the model in yellow gold in 1997, is looking out for a vaster public, still using the same quartz movement and the same design elements in a modern and unconstrained interpretation. For gentlemen, dials have silver or black-blue tones with sun-pattern engravings and bracelets or rubber straps; for ladies, the chronograph becomes also an accessory both elegant and useful. Pastel colors coat dials and straps as well, but more precious variants have brilliants on bezels and markers. On the other hand, the series with stainless steel cases and bezels bordered by black and white diamonds is particularly sophisticated and conspicuous. In fact, the union of these two stones, accurately cut by Concord's craftsmen, generates mysterious and fascinating versions in both men's and ladies' sizes.
The photograph shows the sober version for gentlemen with a silvered dial.

LA SCALA STEEL   REF. 14-G4-1843-A009-1/0060S

Movement: quartz, ETA.
Functions: hour, minute.
Case: stainless steel case (size 26mm); flat sapphire crystal; hexagonal crown; brand engraved on the side of the case; water resistant to 3atm.
Dial: silver engraved dial; 10 diamond markers; 12 and 6 applied Arabic numerals.
Bracelet: polished and brushed stainless steel; deployment clasp.

CONCORD

LA SCALA

Movement: quartz, ETA.
Functions: hour, minute.
Case: 18K white-gold with 22 set brilliants, two-piece case; flat sapphire glass; octagonal white-gold crown; brand engraved on the middle; back attached by screws. Water resistant to 3atm.
Dial: white gold, high-polished; 1 row of brilliants around the central disc, 1 row of mother-of-pearl pieces and embossed logo below 12; 2 rows of brilliants on the external ring with embossed white-gold Roman numerals at quarters; white-gold Dauphine hands.
Bracelet: white gold and brilliants set in central links; fold-over clasp.

LA SCALA

Movement: quartz, ETA.
Functions: hour, minute.
Case: stainless steel, two-piece case; bezel with 22 set brilliants; flat sapphire glass; hexagonal crown; brand engraved on the middle; back attached by screws. Water resistant to 3atm.
Dial: mother-of-pearl; 10 brilliant markers, 12 and 6 applied rhodium-plated Arabic numerals; rhodium-plated Dauphine hands.
Bracelet: stainless steel; fold-over clasp.

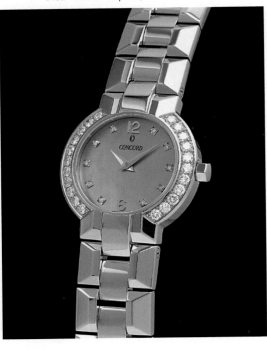

LA SCALA

The polished case with its rounded shape, characterizing the La Scala family, many years after its launching, becomes again the protagonist in a series of both extra-luxury proposals in gold and less sophisticated and modern versions in stainless steel or combined with rubber straps. For the latter, that are in no way inferior to the others in terms of elegance, Concord chose dials in silvered tones for men (also with diamonds), while white and blue mother-of-pearl, also luckily combined with set brilliants as hour markers, were reserved for ladies. "Luxury" versions are meant for more sophisticated and selected customers who prefer (yellow or white) gold as a symbol for elegance and brilliants set on cases, dials and bracelets, within artistic geometries. Precious details also distinguish dials in white, blued or pink mother-of-pearl decorated with sun pattern to make it particularly luminous, while bracelets have jointed links of the same material as the case. They come in numerous variants, among which the precious example shown in the photograph in yellow gold with brilliant and white mother-of-pearl.

LA SCALA

Movement: quartz, ETA.
Functions: hour, minute.
Case: 18K yellow-gold, two-piece case with 22 set brilliants; flat sapphire glass; octagonal white-gold crown; brand engraved on the middle; back attached by screws. Water resistant to 3atm.
Dial: white gold, high-polished; 1 row of brilliants around the central disc, 1 row of mother-of-pearl pieces and embossed logo below 12; 2 rows of brilliants on the external ring with embossed white-gold Roman numerals at quarters; white-gold Dauphine hands.
Bracelet: yellow-gold and brilliants set in central links; fold-over clasp.

LA SCALA   REF. 54-G4-1843-A0095-31/0125S-S32

Movement: quartz, ETA.
Functions: hour, minute.
Case: 18K rose-gold case (size 26mm); bezel set with 32 brilliants; flat sapphire crystal; hexagonal rose-gold crown; brand engraved on the side of the case; back attached with screws; water resistant to 3atm.
Dial: white mother-of-pearl dial set with pavé diamonds; 12 and 6 applied Arabic numerals.
Bracelet: 18K rose-gold set with 36 brilliants in center links; deployment clasp.

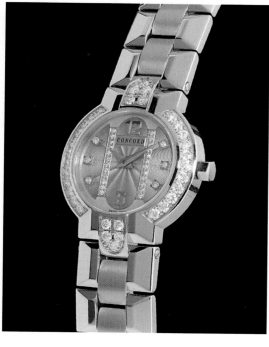

LA SCALA   REF. 61-H5-1442.0-A0365-31/0123S-S44

Movement: quartz, ETA.
Functions: hour, minute.
Case: 18K white-gold case (size 18.5 x 25mm); bezel set with 26 sapphire baguettes; sapphire crystal; hexagonal white-gold crown; brand engraved on the side of the case; back attached with screws; water resistant to 3atm.
Dial: pavé dial with white mother-of-pearl center zone.
Bracelet: 18K white-gold set with 180 brilliants and 10 round-cut sapphires; deployment clasp.

CONCORD LA SCALA   REF. 61-25-1440.1-2353BLU-31/0130S-S21

Movement: quartz, ETA.
Functions: hour, minute.
Case: 18K white-gold case (size 24.5 x 42.4mm); bezel set with 40 diamonds; curved sapphire crystal; hexagonal white-gold crown; back attached with screws; water resistant to 3atm.
Dial: off-center mother-of-pearl dial with pavé "C" design; 12 applied Arabic numeral.
Strap: blue satin; 18K white-gold buckle.

CONCORD LA SCALA   REF. 60-25-1440-2360BLK-1/0113

Movement: quartz, ETA.
Functions: hour, minute.
Case: 18K white-gold Clous de Paris case (size 24.5 x 42.4mm); curved sapphire crystal; hexagonal white-gold crown; water resistant to 3atm.
Dial: off-center silvertone dial; applied markers; 12, 3, 6 and 9 applied Arabic numerals.
Strap: black alligator strap; 18K white-gold buckle.

DANIEL JEANRICHARD

a legend in Swiss watchmaking history, Daniel JeanRichard is a name long synonymous with quality and innovation. Today, under the vigilant eye of Dr. Luigi "Gino" Macaluso, who more than a decade ago determined to restore this brand to its former glory, Daniel JeanRichard remains committed to the principles of its namesake: originality and perfection.

In the late **17**th century, young goldsmith apprentice Daniel JeanRichard (born in **1665**) became enthralled with the world of watchmaking. A meticulous perfectionist, JeanRichard was among the first to create machinery to make watch parts, and was instrumental in bringing watch production to the region of Neuchâtel, Switzerland—now famous for this craft. Committed to creating superior timepieces, JeanRichard began training others as watchmakers and, for decades, produced fine pocket instruments. Even after his death in **1741**, his name and contributions to the field held steadfast and are well-documented in Swiss watchmaking journals.

In the early **1980**s, Macaluso purchased the Daniel JeanRichard name and determined to set up production according to a strict code of excellence worthy of the legacy. He brought the brand under the Sowind Group umbrella (which also owns Girard-Perregaux) and set up shop in La Chaux-de-Fonds. The first Daniel JeanRichard watches made their debut in the early **1990**s and, by **1996**, the brand was sold in some of the world's key markets.

In **1998**, Daniel JeanRichard introduced its striking TV Screen watch to the world. Inspired by the 1940s' television sets, the cushioned-square design was an immediate hit. In **1999**, Daniel JeanRichard unveiled a series of special limited-edition TV Screen Chronographs and Chronoscopes and established itself as a producer of top-quality sporty-chic timepieces. With retro-inspired cases and fine movements, the brand had carved out a niche for itself and a strong signature look. In **2000**, Daniel JeanRichard added the flyback chronograph and a GMT to its line and presented its first collection for women, the TV Screen Lady, in **2001**.

DANIEL JEANRICHARD

Designed for those with discerning taste, the Daniel Jean-Richard collection is comprised of four main collections including the TV Screen, the Chronoscope, Diverscope and Bressel. Each of these houses an automatic movement and offers complex functions.

Of all the collections, it is the TV Screen watch that has made the most prolific impact on this brand. Its large size and impressive styling have kept it in high demand and Daniel JeanRichard continually adds new complications and accents to the collection. Among the newest models are the Grand TV Screen Tourbillon, the TV Screen Retrograde Seconds watch and the Grand TV Screen Calendar. There is also a new striking jeweled TV Screen Lady series that will surely scintillate the senses.

The TV Screen Tourbillon watch is crafted in 18-karat rose gold and houses the tourbillon movement. An aperture on the delicately engine-turned dial reveals the refined mechanism.

Highly distinctive, the TV Screen Retrograde Seconds watch features a striking fan-shaped retrograde seconds indicator at the 6:00 position. The seconds hand sweeps smoothly back and forth across a 30-second guilloché zone. Available in a variety of sizes, the automatic mechanical watch is crafted in steel or in 18-karat pink gold, with an anthracite or white dial.

The Grand TV Screen Calendar watch is crafted in steel and features a black or beige matte dial with red accents. The automatic mechanical movement features a small seconds subdial at 6:00 and a double window at 12:00 to depict the day and month. The date is read via a pointer hand that revolves around an inner ring on the dial.

The TV Screen Lady is sophisticated in its gemstone versions. Available in steel, or in 18-karat yellow or pink gold, the watch comes with a choice of distinct sunburst guilloché dials or pastel mother-of-pearl dials, each featuring brightly colored applied numerals. The bezel of each watch is set with a single row of brilliant diamonds or sapphires.

TOP

The Grand TV Screen Calendar watch houses an automatic mechanical movement and features a small seconds subdial at 6:00.

BOTTOM LEFT

The TV Screen Retrograde Seconds watch houses an automatic movement with retrograde seconds readout on the bottom of the dial in a fan-shaped pattern.

HIGHLIGHTS

- Daniel JeanRichard regularly enhances its lines with superb new models. Recently, the brand added to its highly successful Chronoscope collection with a 40mm version.

- The automatic mechanical movement of this reduced-size Chronoscope chronograph is housed in a steel case and comes with a sable dial with a blue or black exterior zone. This elegant version offers three chronograph counters, is water resistant to 100 meters, and features a crocodile strap.

- There is a new Bressel chronograph in the series that offers sporty-chic elegance. Designed with a black dial and black crocodile strap set in a steel case, the automatic watch offers telemeter and tachometer functions.

- A new Diverscope has also emerged with sportier spirit. Crafted in steel with a black dial and black neoprene strap, the Diverscope features two screwed crowns and an inner rotating bezel. Water resistant to 330 meters, it houses an automatic movement.

DANIEL JEANRICHARD

GRAND TV SCREEN CHRONOSCOPE   REF. 25030

Movement: automatic, DJR 25 caliber, 13'''1/4 (ETA 2824-2 caliber base + Dubois Dépraz 2020 caliber chronograph module), 51 jewels, 28,800 vph.
Functions: hour, minute, small second; date; chronograph with three counters.
Case: stainless steel, three-piece case, in cambered square shape (size 43 x 43mm, thickness 14.7mm), brushed and polished finish; curved sapphire crystal; rectangular pushers; screw-down winding crown at 3, screw-down

crown at 9 for the regulation of the two-way turning flange with case protection; back attached by 4 screws. Water resistant to 5atm.
Dial: mat black; flange with scale for the calculation of diving time, with luminescent markers; luminescent Arabic numerals; luminescent white enameled bâton hands.
Indications: small seconds at 3; hour counter at 6; minute counter at 9; center second counter; minute track with divisions for 1/5 of a second.
Strap: leather; steel clasp.
Also available: with silvered dial, applied markers; rubber or leather strap or bracelet.

GRAND TV SCREEN TOURBILLON SOUS PONT D'OR   REF. 96016

Movement: mechanical, automatic-winding, DJR 960 caliber, 12'''3/4 (G.P. Manufacture 9600 caliber base), with tourbillon device mounted on a pink-gold bridge, 48 hours autonomy, 30 jewels, 21,600 vph.
Functions: hour, minute, small second.
Case: 18K pink-gold, three-piece case, in cambered square shape (size 41 x 39mm, thickness 12.35mm); curved sapphire crystal; pink-gold crown; back

attached by 4 screws. Water resistant to 3atm.
Dial: silvered, guilloché with a ray pattern, with an aperture on the tourbillon; applied gold-plated brass Arabic numerals; printed railway minute track; blued Poire hands.
Indications: small seconds at 6 integrated in the tourbillon carriage.
Strap: crocodile leather; pink-gold clasp.
Unique version.

GRAND TV SCREEN TRIPLE DATE   REF. 52016

Movement: mechanical, automatic-winding, DJR 52 caliber, 11'''1/2 (ETA 2824-2 caliber base + Jacquet 3105 caliber calendar module).
Functions: hour, minute, second; full calendar (date, day, month).
Case: stainless steel, three-piece case, in cambered square shape (size 41 x 38.5mm, thickness 13mm); curved sapphire crystal; three correctors on the middle; back attached by 4 screws. Water resistant to 5atm.

Dial: ivory; luminescent black printed Arabic numerals and bâton at quarters; printed railway minute track; luminescent black enameled lozenge hands.
Indications: small seconds at 6; day and month below 12; date with red enameled half-moon center hand for center reading.
Strap: crocodile leather; steel clasp.
Also available: with black dial; bracelet.

TV SCREEN RETROGRADE SECOND   REF. 45006

Movement: mechanical, automatic-winding, DJR 45 caliber, 11'''1/2 (ETA 2824-2 caliber base + AGH 2302 caliber retrograde small-second module), 31 jewels, 28,800 vph.
Functions: hour, minute, retrograde second; full calendar (date, day, month).
Case: 18K pink-gold, three-piece case, in cambered square shape (size 37 x 35mm, thickness 13mm); curved sapphire crystal; pink-gold crown; back

attached by 4 screws, displaying the movement through a sapphire crystal. Water resistant to 3atm.
Dial: silvered, central part guilloché with a honeycomb pattern, with a sun pattern in the small-second sector; grained hour ring; applied gold-plated brass Arabic numerals; printed railway minute track; gold-plated brass Dauphine hands.
Indications: small seconds at 6 with retrograde hand and indicating sequences of 30 seconds.
Strap: crocodile leather; pink-gold clasp.
Also available: in stainless steel with anthracite dial with silvered sector, strap or bracelet.

TV SCREEN MEDIUM — REF. 24006

Movement: mechanical, automatic-winding, DJR 24 caliber, 11'''1/2 (ETA 2824-2 caliber base), 25 jewels, 28,800 vph.
Functions: hour, minute second. **Case:** stainless steel, three-piece case, in cambered square shape (size 37 x 35mm, thickness 12.4mm); curved sapphire crystal; back attached by 4 screws. Water resistant to 3atm.
Dial: glossy black; printed sand-color raised Arabic numerals; white printed railway minute track; luminescent white enameled leaf-style hands.
Indications: date at 3.
Strap: crocodile leather; steel fold-over clasp.
Also available: with leather strap and buckle; bracelet; silvered dial, black or brown Arabic numerals, pink with pink Arabic numerals, blue with blue Arabic numerals.

TV SCREEN LADY — REF. 26006Q01

Movement: mechanical, automatic-winding, DJR 26 caliber, 7'''1/2 (ETA 2671 caliber base), 25 jewels, 28,800 vph.
Functions: hour, minute, second; date.
Case: stainless steel, three-piece case, in cambered square shape (size 28.5 x 27.5mm, thickness 9.6mm); curved sapphire crystal; crown with sapphire cabochon; back attached by 4 screws. Water resistant to 3atm.
Dial: pink mother of pearl; luminescent applied Roman numerals and set brilliants; printed railway minute track; rhodium-plated brass Dauphine hands.
Indications: date at 3, framed.
Strap: crocodile leather; steel fold-over clasp.
Also available: with satin strap and buckle; bracelet; natural, green, anthracite or yellow mother of pearl dial.

CHRONOSCOPE 40MM — REF. 25022R

Movement: automatic, DJR 25 caliber, 13'''1/4 (ETA 2824-2 cal. base + D.Dépraz 2020 chrono module), 51 jewels (13'''1/4), 28,800 vph. **Functions:** hour, minute, small second; chronograph with 3 counters. **Case:** shot-blasted steel, 3-piece case (Ø 40, thick. 14.3mm); curved mineral crystal; pushers with case protection; screw-down winding crown at 3 with case protection, screw-down crown at 9 for the adjustment of the two-way turning flange, with case protection; screwed-on back. Water res. to 10atm.
Dial: mat black, counters with circular beads; flange with minute track for diving times, with luminescent markers; printed square markers, luminescent at quarters; luminescent white bâton hands.
Indications: small seconds at 3; hour counter at 6; minute counter at 9; center second counter; minute track with divisions for 1/2 of a second. **Strap:** crocodile leather; steel fold-over clasp. **Also av.:** sand-color dial, silvered counters, blue flange, Arabic numerals; leather or rubber strap or bracelet; Ø 40mm: mat titanium rubber strap; mat steel leather or crocodile or rubber strap or bracelet; polished steel silvered or black dial and white subdials, blue dial and silvered subdials, leather or rubber or crocodile strap or bracelet.

DIVERSCOPE 40MM — REF. 24022Q02

Movement: mechanical, automatic-winding, DJR caliber 24, 11'''1/2 (ETA caliber 2824-2 base), 38 jewels, 28.800 vph.
Functions: hour, minute, second, date.
Case: stainless steel, three-piece case (Ø 40mm, thickness 14.4mm), polished and brushed finish; curved mineral crystal; screw-down crowns at 3 (for hour and date corrections) and 9 (for the adjustment of the two-way turning flange) with case protection; screwed-on back. Water resistant to 30atm.
Dial: sand-color; blue flange with minute track, for the calculation of diving times with luminescent markers and five-minute progression; luminescent Arabic numerals; printed railway minute track; luminescent rhodium-plated brass bâton hands.
Indications: date at 3.
Strap: rubber; steel fold-over clasp.
Also available: with crocodile leather strap; black dial, luminescent Arabic numerals; bracelet. Ø 43mm: steel, black dial, rubber strap or bracelet.

DAVID YURMAN

Nearly 25 years ago, David Yurman and his wife Sybil made their dream a reality when they founded their own jewelry company. Through hard, hands-on work and creative genius, the couple forged a new frontier into the world of branding, and within just a few years David Yurman had become a global standard of excellence in luxury designer jewelry.

It was in **1979** that David Yurman was established. Up to this point, no designer had yet to build his own brand image. Yurman was to be leader of the pack. Focusing on innovative and stylish designs, he developed fashion-forward jewelry that immediately caught the eyes of discerning customers. He then backed his artistic creations with a splendid marketing concept that made Yurman's designer name a brand name.

In **1983**, Yurman unveiled the now-famed Cable collection of jewelry that has become the brand's signature motif. Throughout the **1980**s and **1990**s, the company's growth was phenomenal. Yurman moved from sterling silver to gold and combinations thereof; he introduced gemstones and diamonds and in **1995**, he introduced the Cable Watch Collection®—an expressive interpretation of his cable bracelets. Two years later he unveiled the extensive Thoroughbred™ collection of cushion-shaped watches.

Four years ago in **1999**, the Yurmans opened their first retail store on prestigious Madison Ave in New York City. Also that year, the company created a bronze Angel Statue to honor individuals who donate time and energy to humanitarian and charitable causes. In **2000**, Yurman launched the Women's Thoroughbred watch series and in **2001**, they teamed with acclaimed photographer Peter Lindbergh to launch the first lifestyle campaign. That same year, the David & Sybil Yurman Humanitarian and Arts Foundation was established to formalize the company's dedication to supporting charitable efforts.

The second flagship Yurman retail store was opened in **2002** in Costa Mesa, California at South Coast Plaza. In this elegant setting—designed with some of David's early sculptures and works of art—Yurman offers a limited-edition couture collection of jewelry and watches. Also in **2002**, Yurman opened his own watch manufacturing operation in La Chaux de Fonds, where all Yurman timepieces are meticulously produced and assembled according to the highest standards.

DAVID YURMAN

By deftly combining quality craftsmanship, artistic innovation and the concept of branding jewelry, Yurman has built a world-recognized empire. His ability to fuse art and technology has made him a true phenomenon in the fine jewelry and watchmaking arena.

All Yurman timepieces house only the finest Swiss automatic and quartz movements, all crystals are sapphire, and dials are either porcelain, lacquer, mother of pearl, or guilloché. Some pieces even feature interchangeable bezels. Keeping today's lifestyles in mind, all Yurman watches are water resistant to 30 meters.

Yurman crafts only in the finest metals, including platinum, gold, surgical-grade stainless steel and high-tech titanium. Diamonds and gemstones of the highest quality adorn many of Yurman's timepieces. Every Yurman collection is created in a limited series ranging from 500 to 1,500 pieces per model and the timepieces are sold only in 220 retail outlets (versus the 425 stores that carry Yurman's jewelry).

Both the Cable and Thoroughbred Watch collections have grown proportionately thanks to Yurman's unstoppable innovation. The newest timepieces unveiled are naturally of superb quality and further attest to the brand's pursuit of technical excellence and superlative design.

The Cable Watch Collection has grown in scope to encompass numerous limited editions and special models. The Thoroughbred series now includes more than 25 important style variations, including the Limited Edition Artist's Series Chronograph and the DualTime™ watch.

Recognizing the success of and demand for the Thoroughbred Chronograph (previously crafted only in platinum or 18-karat gold), Yurman has unveiled two new versions in steel. Each of the new models houses a 37-jeweled automatic movement and features a transparent exhibition sapphire caseback. Both the sculpted rubber strap and the steel bracelet are impressive in their powerful statements. The watchcase is 41mm—oversized for bold, dramatic appeal. It is available with either a white or black enamel dial.

LEFT
These exquisite Thoroughbred watches for women are particularly alluring thanks to their shimmering diamond-adorned bezels.

BELOW LEFT
The women's elegant Cable collection of watches includes mother-of-pearl dials and gemstone accents

BELOW RIGHT
The Thoroughbred Chronograph automatic watch is available on a bold steel bracelet with white dial

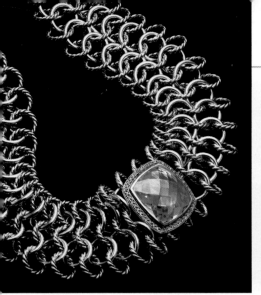

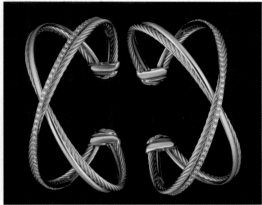

HIGHLIGHTS

■ Yurman continues to add to his successful jewelry series. Recently he unveiled chains, charms and lockets made of individual cable links. These new collections move naturally with the curves of the body and are both romantic and modern. Included in the series is a striking rendition of medieval chain maille in updated styling with five rows of twisted and polished silver links woven together for supple beauty.

■ Yurman has also unveiled the new Albion collection of cable necklaces interspersed with gemstones that feature a new patented cut by David Yurman. Dramatic large gems on hand-linked chain, Yurman weaves a wondrous statement of color and elegance.

■ In the new Crossover™ collection of jewelry, bold cuff bracelets, sleek stick earrings, pendants, and rings are crafted of polished 18-karat gold juxtaposed with woven cable crafted in sterling silver.

■ Adding to the growing family of David Yurman fine jewelry and timepieces, the prolific designer has launched the Cable Kids line of jewelry for children and teens and has added various baby gifts. The Cable Kids collection features delicately scaled cable bracelets, necklaces, earrings, rings and pendants in sterling silver accented with 18-karat gold. The Cable Fables collection of baby keepsakes includes rattles, teething rings, spoons, cups, hair combs and brushes.

■ In 2003, Yurman makes the move to a new 65,000-square-foot headquarters facility in New York's TriBeCa neighborhood—marking a momentous occasion of growth.

DAVID YURMAN

MEN'S LARGE THOROUGHBRED — REF. T3071AL-SS-BRACR

Movement: mechanical, automatic winding ETA 2892/A2, 21 jewels, 28,8000 vph.
Functions: hour, minute, sweep second, date.
Case: oxidized and high-polished sterling silver and high-polished steel 6-piece case (Ø 35mm, thickness 11mm); domed, antireflective sapphire crystal; caseback attached by 4 screws; water resistant to 3atm.

Dial: black enamel dial with center guilloché zone; feuille hands; applied baton markers; applied David Yurman logo.
Indications: date at 3.
Strap: brushed and polished steel with black rubber bracelet; recessed deployant clasp.
Also available: gold case; alligator strap.
Price: upon request.

LADIE'S THOROUGHBRED — REF. T3146QS-ST-BKGRD

Movement: quartz movement, ETA 956.032, long life, 7 jewels.
Functions: hour, minute.
Case: oxidized and high-polished sterling silver and high-polished steel 6-piece case (Ø 25mm, thickness 7mm); domed, antireflective sapphire crystal; bezel set with diamonds (43 stones); caseback attached by 4 screws; water resistant to 3atm.

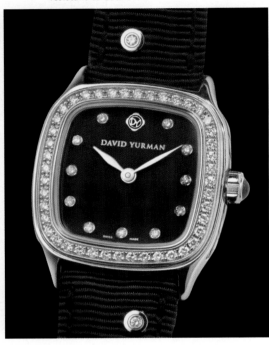

Dial: black enamel dial with 11 applied markers; feuille hands; applied David Yurman logo.
Strap: grosgrain strap with diamond accents.
Also available: steel or gold bracelet.
Price: upon request.

LADIES THOROUGHBRED — REF. T3144QS-88-BRACD

Movement: quartz movement, ETA 956.032, long life, 7 jewels.
Functions: hour, minute.
Case: high-polished 18K yellow-gold 6-piece case (Ø 25mm, thickness 7mm); domed, antireflective sapphire crystal; bezel set with diamonds (43 stones); caseback attached by 4 screws; water resistant to 3atm.
Dial: natural white mother-of-pearl dial; applied markers set with diamonds;

applied Arabic numerals and David Yurman logo; feuille hands.
Bracelet: high-polished 18K yellow-gold bracelet with pavé set diamonds (56 stones); recessed deployant clasp.
Also available: calf, alligator, or grosgrain strap; gold bracelet.
Price: upon request.

CABLE CAPRI — REF. T9514M-88-ADIBKGR

Movement: quartz movement, ETA 280.002, 7 jewels.
Functions: hour, minute.
Case: high-polished 18K yellow-gold 6-piece case (Ø 21mm, thickness 9mm); sapphire crystal; bezel and lugs set with diamonds (80 stones); water resistant to 3atm.
Dial: natural white mother-of-pearl dial; applied markers set with diamonds;

applied markers; feuille hands.
Strap: black grosgrain and leather strap with gold buckle.
Also available: alligator or moiré strap.
Price: upon request.

CLASSIC CABLE   REF. T1010M-SS-GG

Movement: quartz movement, ETA 280.002, 5 jewels.
Functions: hour, minute.
Case: high-polished 18K yellow-gold 2-piece case (Ø 21mm, thickness 9mm); sapphire crystal; water resistant to 3atm.
Dial: natural white mother-of-pearl dial; applied Roman numerals and markers; feuille hands.
Bracelet: oxidized and high-polished sterling silver and high-polished 18K yellow-gold cable bracelet.
Also available: gold cable bracelet; gold cable bracelet accented with precious and semiprecious stones.
Price: upon request.

LIM. EDIT. THOROUGHBRED CHRONOGRAPHE   REF. T3065AC-SP-BRACR

Movement: mechanical, automatic winding, ETA 2894, 37 jewels, 28,800 vibrations per hour.
Functions: hour, minute, second, date, chronograph with 3 counters.
Case: high-polished steel with brushed platinum bezel 8-piece case (Ø 41mm, thickness 13mm); domed, antireflective sapphire crystal; caseback displays the movement through a sapphire crystal; caseback attached by 4 screws; water resistant to 3atm; limited edition of 50, signed and numbered on caseback.
Dial: brushed platinum dial; feuille hands; applied Arabic numerals and David Yurman logo.
Indications: center flyback second counter; small second at 3; date between 4 and 5; hour counter (12h) at 6; minute counter (30') at 9.
Bracelet: brushed and high-polished steel with black rubber bracelet; recessed deployant clasp.
Also available: black alligator strap.
Price: upon request.

LIM. EDIT. THOROUGHBRED CHRONOGRAPHE   REF. T3066AC-88-BKMA

Movement: mechanical, automatic winding, ETA 2894-2, 37 jewels, 28,800 vibrations per hour.
Functions: hour, minute, second, date, chronograph with 3 counters.
Case: high-polished 18K yellow-gold 8-piece case (Ø 41mm, thickness 13mm); domed, antireflective sapphire crystal; caseback displays the movement through a sapphire crystal; caseback attached by 4 screws; water resistant to 3atm; limited edition of 50, signed and numbered on caseback.
Dial: black enamel dial applied in 12 layers; feuille hands; applied Arabic numerals and David Yurman logo.
Indications: center flyback second counter; small second at 3; date between 4 and 5; hour counter (12h) at 6; minute counter (30') at 9.
Strap: black alligator strap with deployant clasp.
Price: upon request.

THOROUGHBRED DUALTIME ®   REF. T3062AD-ST-BRAC

Movement: mechanical, automatic winding, ETA 2893-2, 21 jewels, 28,800 vibrations per hour.
Functions: hour, minute, sweep second.
Case: oxidized and high-polished sterling silver and high-polished steel 6-piece case (Ø 41mm, thickness 13mm); domed, antireflective sapphire crystal; caseback displays the movement through a sapphire crystal; caseback attached by 4 screws; water resistant to 3atm.
Dial: white enamel dial applied in 12 layers with gray guilloché subdial; feuille hands; applied baton markers and David Yurman logo.
Indications: date at 3; red painted center second-time-zone 24-hour hand.
Bracelet: high-polished and brushed steel bracelet; recessed deployant clasp.
Also available: alligator strap; black dial on alligator strap or steel and rubber bracelet.
Price: upon request.

de GRISOGONO

One of the most prolific designers of our time, Fawaz Gruosi has captured hearts and souls with his creativity and ingenuity in design. Regularly turning out masterpieces, Gruosi has deftly channeled his passion for originality to watches.

Born in Syria in **1952**, Gruosi lived the majority of his early life in Lebanon, and then in Florence, Italy, where he lived until the age of 18. Gruosi was greatly inspired by the aesthetics and beauty of the city of Florence and he took a keen interest in the art of jewelry making—a career that he pursued with zeal.

Over the ensuing decades, Gruosi created magnificent gems for some of the finest international jewelers. Nonetheless, his undying passion had always been to open his own shop and create jewels under his own name.

In **1996**, at the age of 44, Gruosi followed his dream and opened his first de GRISOGONO boutique in Geneva. He filled his cases with magnificent one-of-a-kind pieces and unveiled a collection of black diamond jewelry that would become his signature statement. Indeed, Gruosi—who had for several years been captivated by the 190-carat Black Orlov diamond—created one of the most unique collections around these scintillating black gems that have since become his hallmark.

Responding to international acclaim, Gruosi opened his second de GRISOGONO boutique in **1997**, this one in London. A year later, Gruosi opened a shop at the Palace Hotel in Gstaad, and in **1999**, he selected Rome's Hotel de Russie as de GRISOGONO's fourth location.

Gruosi unveiled his first timepiece collection in **2000**. Called the Instrumento Nº Uno, the collection was an instant success thanks to its bold case and modern design. This series was followed in **2002** by the unveiling of the Instrumento Doppio—a sizzling collection housed in a square case that echoes the stylistic design of the successful Nº Uno signature case.

THIS PAGE

TOP LEFT
The Instrumento Nº Uno watch shown here is elegantly crafted in 18-karat rose gold and is set with 478 black diamonds weighing almost 9 carats. It is also set with nearly one carat of rubies. The mechanical watch with automatic wind features dual time zone and oversized date.

BELOW
Fawaz Gruosi.

FACING PAGE

The all-new Instrumento Doppio is a double-faced watch. One side of the mechanical face displays the chronograph with oversized date and the second dial displays a second time zone.

Credited today as the man who initiated the black diamond craze and who sparked the exotic relationship between the stone and women around the world, Gruosi continually endeavors to find new cuts and settings that enrapture and mystify. In the seven years that he has been working with black diamonds, Gruosi has created bolder, daring, more intriguing designs collection by collection.

Deftly blending black diamonds with other gemstones such as rubies, emeralds, pearls and even turquoise, Gruosi has achieved a new sense of color and light. What's more, he infuses his designs with a sense of whimsical attitude and sensual overtones. Feminine shapes flow with the movement of the wearer, exotic animals such as panthers and snakes emerge in sinful beauty and flowers and hearts are incredibly supple and stunning.

So prolific has Gruosi become in his work with black diamonds that, to date, he has designed and created more than 4,000 mystical black diamond masterpieces and has earned a reputation as the "king of black diamonds." The de GRISOGONO symbol of perfection and creativity, the black diamond remains one of the most enticing passions of Gruosi's work.

LEFT
This exquisite black panther is meticulously set with black diamonds and dramatic emerald eyes.

BELOW
Galuchat leather is offset with pear-shaped and marquise-cut white diamonds for striking contrast and beauty in this one-of-a-kind piece by Gruosi.

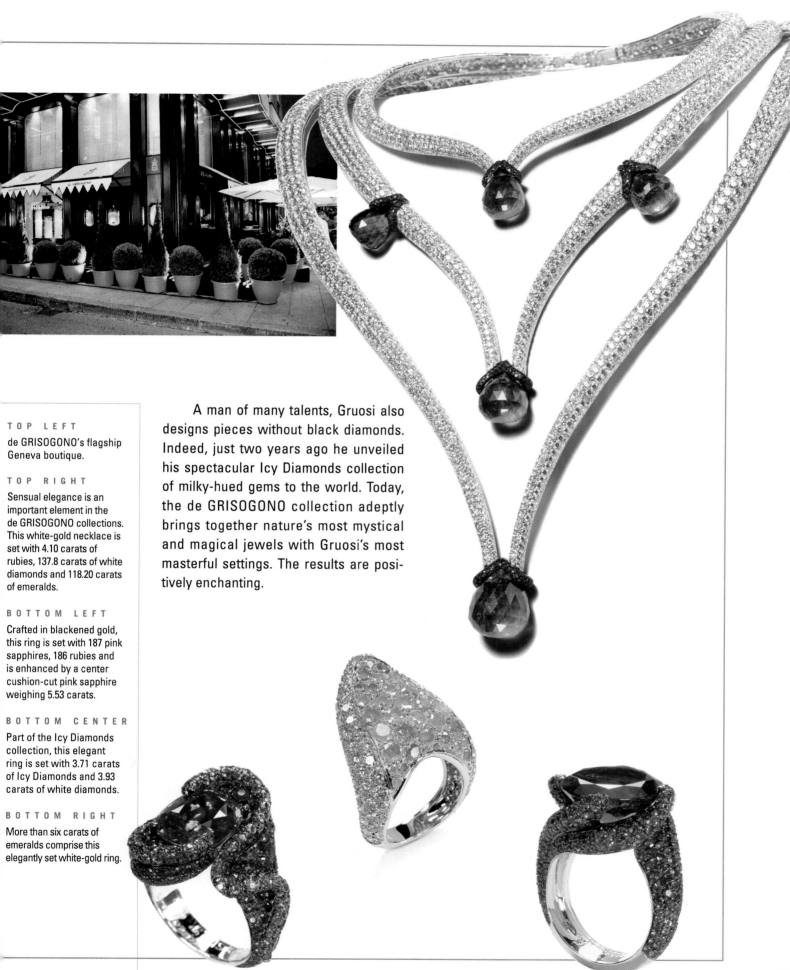

TOP LEFT

de GRISOGONO's flagship Geneva boutique.

TOP RIGHT

Sensual elegance is an important element in the de GRISOGONO collections. This white-gold necklace is set with 4.10 carats of rubies, 137.8 carats of white diamonds and 118.20 carats of emeralds.

BOTTOM LEFT

Crafted in blackened gold, this ring is set with 187 pink sapphires, 186 rubies and is enhanced by a center cushion-cut pink sapphire weighing 5.53 carats.

BOTTOM CENTER

Part of the Icy Diamonds collection, this elegant ring is set with 3.71 carats of Icy Diamonds and 3.93 carats of white diamonds.

BOTTOM RIGHT

More than six carats of emeralds comprise this elegantly set white-gold ring.

A man of many talents, Gruosi also designs pieces without black diamonds. Indeed, just two years ago he unveiled his spectacular Icy Diamonds collection of milky-hued gems to the world. Today, the de GRISOGONO collection adeptly brings together nature's most mystical and magical jewels with Gruosi's most masterful settings. The results are positively enchanting.

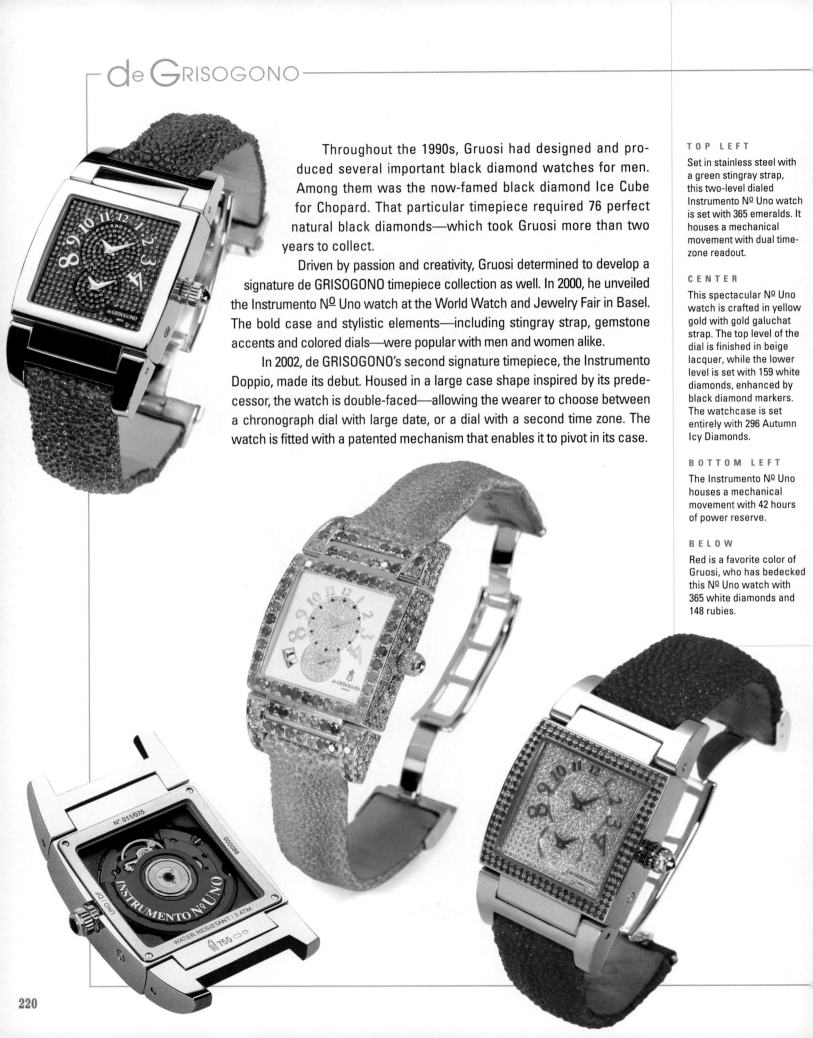

Throughout the 1990s, Gruosi had designed and produced several important black diamond watches for men. Among them was the now-famed black diamond Ice Cube for Chopard. That particular timepiece required 76 perfect natural black diamonds—which took Gruosi more than two years to collect.

Driven by passion and creativity, Gruosi determined to develop a signature de GRISOGONO timepiece collection as well. In 2000, he unveiled the Instrumento N⁰ Uno watch at the World Watch and Jewelry Fair in Basel. The bold case and stylistic elements—including stingray strap, gemstone accents and colored dials—were popular with men and women alike.

In 2002, de GRISOGONO's second signature timepiece, the Instrumento Doppio, made its debut. Housed in a large case shape inspired by its predecessor, the watch is double-faced—allowing the wearer to choose between a chronograph dial with large date, or a dial with a second time zone. The watch is fitted with a patented mechanism that enables it to pivot in its case.

TOP LEFT
Set in stainless steel with a green stingray strap, this two-level dialed Instrumento N⁰ Uno watch is set with 365 emeralds. It houses a mechanical movement with dual time-zone readout.

CENTER
This spectacular N⁰ Uno watch is crafted in yellow gold with gold galuchat strap. The top level of the dial is finished in beige lacquer, while the lower level is set with 159 white diamonds, enhanced by black diamond markers. The watchcase is set entirely with 296 Autumn Icy Diamonds.

BOTTOM LEFT
The Instrumento N⁰ Uno houses a mechanical movement with 42 hours of power reserve.

BELOW
Red is a favorite color of Gruosi, who has bedecked this N⁰ Uno watch with 365 white diamonds and 148 rubies.

HIGHLIGHTS

- The Instrumento Doppio was born under the numeral two: the second in a timepiece series; unveiled two years after the first watch line; featuring two faces.

- Technically sophisticated and elegantly intriguing, the Instrumento Doppio houses a mechanical movement with sweep second hand, chronograph and dual-time-zone reference.

- An easy-to-turn octagonal crown enhances the curved case of the Instrumento Doppio. Pushpieces are aligned with the curved case via an intricate system of invisible hammers within the watch.

- The two analog displays of the watch function on the basis of a single movement to which the chronograph module has been added. The watch required the specific creation of 83 new movement components out of the nearly 300 total parts.

- The timepiece is patented, and represents the first occasion that a double analog display is combined with a system of hands passing through the oscillating weight.

- The Instrumento Doppio is quite exclusive—produced in a series of 500 pieces each in steel or in 18-karat yellow, white or red gold.

DELANEAU

delaneau offers a surprising alternative for those who think jewelry watches are just watches set with gemstones.

Delaneau is an independent Swiss company founded in **1880** that provides a small but loyal clientele with extremely sophisticated jewelry watches. Delaneau has a reputation for exotic, and even eccentric, pieces that always stand out.

Making fewer than 1,500 watches a year—including unique objects to customer order—Delaneau cannot afford to be a slave to fashion or addicted to advertising. Instead, it has to invest its resources in creating sensational products that signal the brand's sexy and provocative image.

THIS PAGE

BELOW
Cristina Thévenaz, creative director of a brand with strong signaling powers.

FACING PAGE

The double-hinged gold case of the Marlene watch allows women to dress up from a leather strap to a 29mm-wide gold brickwork bracelet with a tassel with pearls and an onyx tassel. The lid on concealed hinges reveals a baguette watch and its reflection.

Marlene White gold, totally paved. 18-karat white-gold case set with 314 diamonds (1.58 carats). Off-white dial with dark blue Arabic numerals and black minutes and signs. Quartz movement. 18-karat white-gold bracelet with pearls and onyx tassel, set with 680 diamonds (3.55 carats) + 1 interchangeable leather strap with 18-karat white-gold clasp.

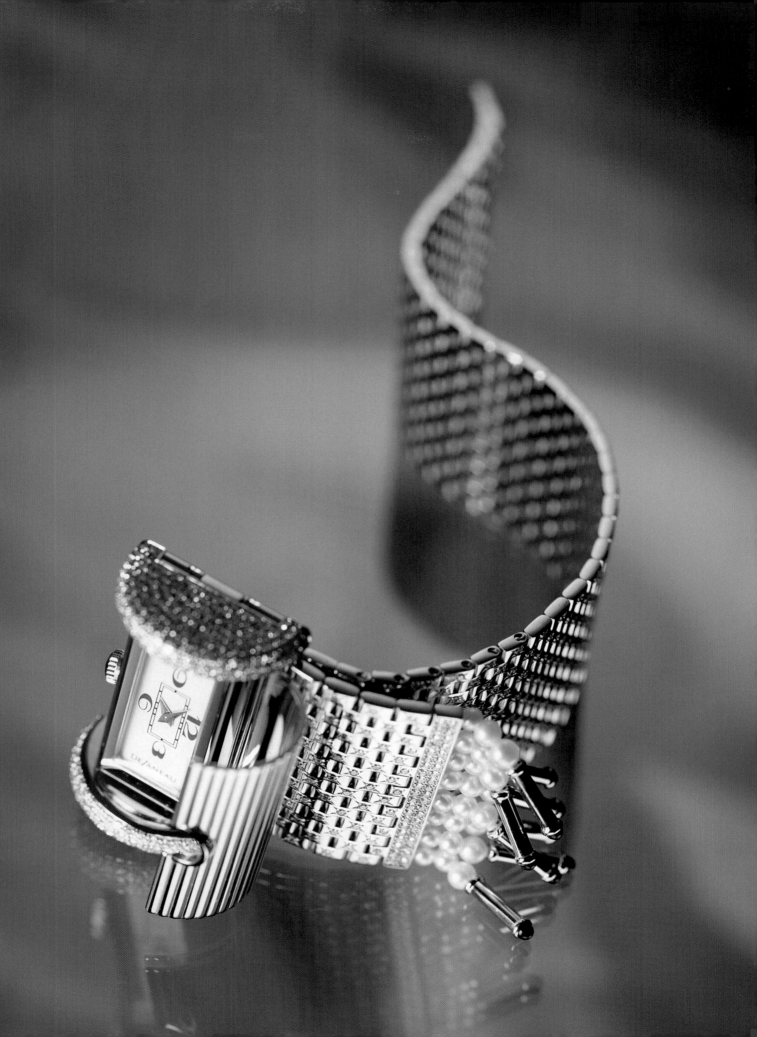

Delaneau's clients are women who have seen it all before and crave excitement, originality and wit. The latest watches, entitled "Les Capricieuses," (for those who need to know the time only so that they can be late, according to Delaneau's brochure) are highly individualistic pieces retailing from more than $25,000 to $120,000 for the sumptuous Josephine sautoir watch. A unique triangular diamond watch entitled "Eternity" sold for $400,000 last year in Hong Kong, but Delaneau does have watches for under $10,000.

Delaneau is also famous for its Butterfly watches of color-coordinated sapphires. Each creation finds a dazzling new way to bring a butterfly to a woman's wrist.

TOP LEFT
The Marlene's original design finds a new direction in the Lilli Marlene. It hides the time in a diamond-set treasure chest, secured twice around the wrist on a double-length strap.

Lilli Marlene 18-karat white-gold case set with 322 diamonds (1.87 carats). Off-white dial with dark blue Arabic numerals and black minutes and signs. Quartz movement. Black crocodile strap with 18-karat white-gold buckle.

BELOW
The Marlene in its most sober yet sophisticated attitude.

Marlene in 18-karat white-gold case. Off-white dial with 4/4 dark blue Arabic numerals. Quartz movement. Burgundy ostrich strap.

The latest are made in five series, each limited to 29 numbered watches, in pink, blue or yellow sapphires, in a combination of any two colors or set entirely with 566 diamonds. For each Butterfly, Delaneau's jewelers match sapphires in five different hues of a single color, grading them into 12 sizes to create a unique chromatic palette.

Once in the avant-garde of luxury fashion, Delaneau had lost some of its creative impulse, but none of its reputation for high quality, when it was taken over by private investors in 1997. Under the creative direction of Cristina Thévenaz, Delaneau has rediscovered its role as producer of extraordinary jewelry watches for people with sophisticated taste.

TOP

Delaneau's Three Time Zone watch, patented in 1987 for time-management on a global scale. The automatic chronograph or calendar watch is flanked by two independent quartz movements.

Three Time Zones
(Quantième). 18-karat white-gold case set with 246 diamonds (1.99 carats) and attachments set with 4 blue sapphire cabochons (1.32 carats). Three movements: 1x automatic movement + 2x mini quartz movements. One main blue galvanic dial 3/4, 6/8 appliqué indexes and one white mother-of-pearl month counter at 6:00 + two small white mother-of-pearl dials with 4/4 indexes and 8/8 dots. Black crocodile strap with 18-karat white-gold buckle. Water resistant to 30 meters.

"We have inherited some of the best jewelry craftsmen in Switzerland. They have always liked working for Delaneau because we give them challenging designs," says Thévenaz. She likes jewelry that moves—a tassel of gold and ruby pearls, a lid or a shutter that reveals the time, or a clever clasp. "Each watch must have its own accessory," she declares.

Delaneau makes the most of its privileged access to specialized talent by demanding a lot of technical and creative effort in everything it produces. The results are unique technical solutions—a jalousie watch with a shutter that rolls on rubies, the double-hinged Marlene watch that migrates from strap to bracelet, or a three-dialed watch for global time.

FACING PAGE

BOTTOM

Art Deco gets a dramatic dimension in the First Lady, a classic Delaneau design combining gold, diamonds, fancy-cut gemstones and mother of pearl in imaginative new ways. First Lady watches are also made for pearl bracelets or gold Milanese bracelets, as well as colored straps in soft leather.

First Lady
18-karat white-gold case set with 18 pink sapphire baguettes (1.33 carats) and 64 diamonds (0.23 carats). Quartz movement. Pink mother-of-pearl dial set with 32 diamonds (0.08 carats). 18-karat white-gold bracelet set with 12 pink sapphire baguettes (1.50 carats) and 498 diamonds (3.20 carats).

THIS PAGE

TOP

Josephine sautoir watch features a gold shutter running on ruby bearings, a Delaneau-patented invention of 1989.

Josephine Tourmaline
Chain-watch in 18-karat yellow gold with one tourmaline cabochon on the shutter knob. Bell-shaped attachment in 18-karat yellow gold with tassel of Akoya pearls and tourmaline and 18-karat yellow-gold beads. Off-white dial with burgundy Roman numerals. Quartz movement.
Necklace of Akoya pearls, lilac and green tourmalines, and 18-karat yellow-gold beads. Clasp in 18-karat yellow gold.

The creative effort is as apparent in Delaneau's latest watches presented at this year's Basel Show—a series of five impressive sculpted ring watches made by the sculptor André Chéca and a new collection called Dôme, which is quite unlike the extravagant and baroque Les Capricieuses models. Yet, it is just as stunning in its geometrical simplicity—an arch and a square—that forms the clasp as well as the watch.

With the new models, the company has launched a new advertising campaign reflecting the wit and sophistication of a brand that can never make an ordinary watch.

HIGHLIGHTS

- In the year 2000, Delaneau launched the Les Capricieuses collection consisting of the Marlene, Ginger and Josephine. This collection definitely positions Delaneau as "the" jeweler of watches.

- Sold in Europe, Asia and the Middle East for years, only recently has Delaneau branched into the United States market. Just about 15 stores across the country, including some Neiman Marcus locations and a core of independent retailers, will be authorized to sell Delaneau timepieces.

- Among the most sought-after of Delaneau's creations, the First Lady jewelry watches combine fancy-cut gems or diamonds with a choice of either gold bracelets or soft leather straps—each of which are interchangeable. This series also offers the option of an alluring pearl bracelet.

- Delaneau uses only the finest materials for its timepieces. Precious metals are 18-karat gold and platinum, and gemstones include Burmese rubies, VVSI top-quality diamonds, and lustrous cultured pearls.

DUBEY & SCHALDENBRAND

dubey & Schaldenbrand produces some 5,000 watches a year with the simple aim of giving people pleasure. — Cinette Robert

Georges Dubey, teacher at the La Chaux-de-Fonds Watchmaking School, developed a simple and ingenious device called the Index Mobile in the early **1940**s. It performed the functions of the split-seconds chronograph by linking the twin chronograph hands with a coiled spring. In **1946**, Georges Dubey and fellow watchmaker René Schaldenbrand officially founded the company to exploit the Index Mobile and to expand the line of watches. The Index Mobile was patented worldwide in **1947-48** and was well-received, but its commercial success was limited. In the ensuing two decades, from **1950-1970**, watch production reached a peak of around 2,000 pieces a year—mainly automatics and chronographs for men and women.

In **1960**, Cinette Robert, aged 16, joined a local watch-supplies company as a business apprentice. Throughout the late **1970**s and early **1980**s, the series production of watches ceased as Dubey & Schaldenbrand declined to convert to quartz. Instead, the company concentrated on specialized watchmaking—restoring antique watches and building sophisticated pieces such as minute repeaters and tourbillons. In **1985** Robert began collecting old watch movements and became an independent dealer.

Georges Dubey finished his 17th tourbillon pocket watch in **1990** and upon his retirement in **1995**, Robert acquired Dubey & Schaldenbrand with the aim of selling high-quality watches worldwide. Today, more than 5,000 watches are exported to 30 countries.

THIS PAGE

TOP LEFT
Cinette Robert spent many years in the watch industry before acquiring Dubey & Schaldenbrand.

BOTTOM LEFT
Georges Dubey taught watchmaking at the La Chaux-de-Fonds horological school.

BOTTOM RIGHT
The original Index Mobile performed the functions of a split-seconds chronograph.

FACING PAGE

The automatic Gran'Chrono Astro combines triple calendar and moonphase with a chronograph.

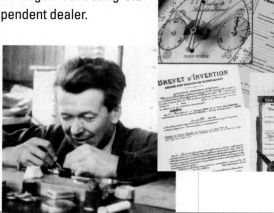

228

DUBEY & SCHALDENBRAND

TOP LEFT

The Spiral One is equipped with the Valjoux 7750 automatic shuttle-chronograph movement. The coiled spring in the center recalls that of Dubey & Schaldenbrand's original Index Mobile watch, but in this model it is entirely non-functional, simply rotating with the chronograph hand. This is the only watch in the Dubey & Schaldenbrand collection with a conventional round case.

TOP RIGHT

An Art Nouveau dial distinguishes the Vintage Caprice, fitted with a large date. The crown has been strategically placed at 9:00 instead of 3:00 for visual enhancement.

BOTTOM LEFT

Each Aerodyn chronometer is sold with a COSC certificate showing the individual performance of its ETA 2895 movement.

BELOW

This sleek Jump Hour watch features an offset seconds-hand subdial at 6:00 and is created in a limited edition.

Dubey & Schaldenbrand, headquartered in the village of Les Ponts-de-Martel in the Jura foothills, maintains its workshops in nearby Les Brenets. The brand specializes in dressy watches—with retro-inspired cases that are fashionable today. Typical of this styling is the Vintage Caprice model with an Art Nouveau dial, up/down power-reserve indicator and large date.

Almost all of the watches are automatic and many have practical complications—calendars, large dates, power-reserve indicators, time zones. Most of the movements are ETA or Valjoux calibers, but the company also issues limited editions housing classic movements that are no longer in production. Some movements are transformed with gilt and engraved openwork, blued screws and burnished steel; others are COSC-certified chronometers.

Dubey & Schaldenbrand watches have all the attributes of value—fine workmanship, distinctive styling and rarity. The basic version of the Aerodyn model is enhanced with diamond and gemstone accents, and the Gran'Chrono Astro chronograph features a full calendar with moonphase indicator.

Dubey & Schaldenbrand watches are popular in Asia and Europe, which together account for 80 percent of production. The other 20 percent of the watches are sold primarily in the United States. Hong Kong and New York are Dubey & Schaldenbrand's biggest city markets.

■ This past year, Dubey & Schaldenbrand unveiled several new timepiece collections.

■ Among the collections: the striking Lady Acier with a choice of three distinct dials (white, blue or black), and crocodile straps or a supple chain-linked bracelet; and the Lady Celebrity with new dial colors.

■ Additionally, the brand has unveiled the newest evolution of its highly successful Gran'Chrono. Called the Gran'Chrono Astro, the watch features a triple date combined with the phases of the moon. These added complications are fitted into the same ergonomic case of its predecessor. The making of this case requires 90 operations and the exclusive guilloché of the new dial for the Astro was achieved in no less than 85 steps.

■ A new limited-series Jumping Hour watch has also been unveiled. It features a striking jump-hour window with offset seconds-hand subdial on a striking guilloché-patterned dial. It is accompanied by a new Sonnerie-GMT watch that combines these complications in an elegantly engraved case.

TOP LEFT
The Carré Cambré Calendar model has a cushion-shaped case, popular in the 1920s. The large date, based on the cross-and-disc model, is in a divided window to disguise the overlap between the tens and the units.

TOP RIGHT
The Sonnerie GMT alarm watch shows the hour in second time-zone with a 24-hour disc appearing through an aperture at 6:00. The crown at 4:00 sets the alarm and winds its spring.

BOTTOM
The Aerodyn Celebrity watch in a pink-gold tonneau case for women has an ETA automatic movement and a finely engine-turned dial. The jeweled version, limited to 100 pieces, is set with 173 diamonds totaling 2.6 carats.

DUBEY & SCHALDENBRAND

GRAN'CHRONO ASTRO

Movement: mechanical, automatic winding, modified Valjoux 7751 caliber. Gilded and engraved; skeletonized rotor.
Functions: hour, minute, full calendar (day, date, month), moonphases, chronograph with 2 counters.
Case: stainless steel, two-piece case in curved tonneau shape (size: 49 x 37.5mm, thickness: 15.3mm); curved sapphire crystal; drop-shaped pushers; back attached by 6 screws, displaying the movement through a sapphire crystal; water resistant to 3atm.
Dial: silvered, engine turned (guilloché); printed markers on a railway minute track.
Indications: moonphase and hour counter at 6; day, month and minute counter at 12; center counter and date.
Strap: crocodile leather; stainless steel fold-over clasp.
Also available: with simple clasp; with stainless steel bracelet; in pink gold with leather strap. All versions are available with silvered, black or blue dials.

AERODYN DUO

Movement: mechanical, automatic winding, modified ETA 2892-2A caliber (exclusive model D&S), with 23 jewels. Balance with 28,800 vibrations per hour.
Functions: hour, minute, second, date, second time-zone indicator, 24 hours.
Case: stainless steel, two-piece case in curved tonneau shape (size: 43 x 32.5mm, thickness: 11.5mm); curved sapphire glass; crown for regulation of all functions (winding, adjustment of the second time zone, date correction, main time correction); back attached by 7 screws; water resistant to 3atm.
Dial: bright blue; printed white Arabic numerals and luminescent dots on the printed railway minute track; luminescent steel Sports hands.
Indications: date at 6; 24 hour at 9; a second time zone with double hand at 12.
Bracelet: steel; fold-over clasp.
Also available: with leather strap (with simple fold-over clasp); in pink gold, leather strap. All versions are available with silvered dial and pink numerals or black and white numerals.

AERODYN DATE

Movement: mechanical, automatic winding, modified ETA 2892 caliber.
Functions: hour, minute, small second, big-sized date.
Case: stainless steel, two-piece case in curved tonneau shape (size: 43 x 32.5mm, thickness: 11.7mm); curved sapphire in crystal, antireflective on both sides; back attached by 7 screws; water resistant to 3atm.
Dial: silvered, engine turned (guilloché), zones decorated with circular beads; printed Roman numerals and railway minute track; blued-steel leaf-style hands.
Indications: small second at 6; big-sized date at 12.
Strap: crocodile leather.
Also available: in pink gold.

SONNERIE ALARM GMT

Movement: self-winding, automatic, 31 jewels, 28,800 oscillations, A-quality escapement, Glucydur balance, Nivarox I hairspring, 2 barrels (one for the watch function, the other for the alarm).
Functions: alarm, hour, minute, second, date, GMT.
Case: double curvature tonneau-shaped case (size: 50 x 38mm; thickness: 15.4mm); transparent sapphire caseback attached by polished, blued-steel screws; bridge is decorated with a circular-grain pattern and rhodium-plated Côtes de Genève finish; water resistant to 30 meters.
Dial: Arabic numerals; printed inside minute track.
Indications: alarm (which is easy to read and set due to its interior 15-minute scale); a second time-zone indicator at 6; and a date indicator at 3.
Strap: crocodile leather.
Also available: 316L stainless steel with a choice of white, blue or black enamelled dials, a crocodile strap or metal bracelet.

DUBEY & SCHALDENBRAND

SPIRAL ONE

Movement: automatic chronograph, Valjoux 7750, 25 jewels, Incabloc, hand-engraved, skeletonized rotor.
Functions: hour, minute, small second, date.
Case: stainless steel (316L), (size: 40 x 46.5mm, thickness: 14.3mm), blued-steel screws, transparent sapphire crystal caseback.
Dial: guilloché, Roman numerals, luminescent hour and minute hands, large second hand with "Isoval" spiral recoil spring.
Indications: 3 counter subdials; date calendar window at 4:30.
Strap: crocodile leather with deployable buckle.
Also available: silver or black guilloché dial.

VINTAGE CAPRICE

Movement: self-winding, automatic, ETA 2892-2A (modified exclusively for D&S), 22 jewels, Incabloc, Glucydur balance wheel, hairspring type 1,
Functions: power reserve, hour, minute, second, big-sized date.
Case: 18K rose-gold, tonneau-shaped case; domed sapphire crystal, antireflective on both sides; water resistant to 3atm.
Dial: Arabic numerals 3, 9 and 12.
Indications: big date window at 6; power-reserve indicator at 12; crown at 9.
Strap: crocodile leather
Also available: stainless steel (316L) in 500-piece limited edition; 18K rose gold in 200-piece limited edition; dials available in black enamel, white or blue.

LADY CELEBRITY

Movement: automatic, 28,800 vph, 25 jewels, 37-hour power reserve.
Functions: hour, minute, second.
Case: Barrel-shaped, 18K rose-gold case set with 173 brilliants (2.6 carats) in a limited series of 100 watches.
Dial: guilloché base; four Arabic "gold-powdered" numerals, outside minute track.
Strap: crocodile leather.
Also available: 18K rose-gold case without diamonds in a limited series of 300 watches; steel case with silvered, black or white dial on a crocodile strap or steel bracelet.

CARRE CAMBRE DIPLOMATIC

Movement: mechanical, automatic winding, modified ETA 2892-A2 caliber (exclusive model D&S), with 23 jewels; balance with 28,800 vph.
Functions: hour, minute, second, date, second time-zone indicator, 24 hours.
Case: stainless steel, two-piece curved cambered shape (size: 34 x 34mm, thickness: 9.5mm); antireflective curved sapphire glass; crown for the regulation of all functions; back attached by 4 screws; water resistant to 3atm.
Dial: white; printed black Arabic numerals and railway minute track; blued leaf-style hands.
Strap: crocodile leather; steel clasp.
Also available: with fold-over clasp; in pink gold. Both versions available with white dial and black numerals, black dial and silvered numerals, or blue dial and silvered numerals.

E BEL

Eugène Blum founded Ebel in 1911 with his wife Alice Lévy. The Blums symbolically used their initials to name their new company: E(ugène) B(lum) E(t) L(évy). This formation spelled the beginning of a long family tradition: for three generations the Blums were to remain at the head of Ebel, making it one of the greatest houses in the famous Neuchâtel region of watchmaking.

Since its founding in **1911**, Ebel has acquired and demonstrated considerable know-how in the haute-joaillerie domain. From the outset, the House was renowned for its daring originality and exceptional inventiveness, earning praise around the world.

Ebel's creativity has received numerous accolades: The gold medal at the National Exposition in Bern (**1914**); Grand Prize Commemorative Diploma at the Exposition of Decorative Arts in Paris for the originality and beauty of geometric design of its watch bracelets (**1925**); The Diploma of Honour at the Universal Exposition in Barcelona for its collection of watches for ladies (**1929**); The First Prize at the Swiss National Exposition in Lausanne for its haute-joaillerie watch with off-centered bezel (**1964**). The **1920**s and **1980**s were among the most important periods for Ebel. During these decades, remarkable gem-set, etched and enameled pieces were created.

Continuing this tradition of prestigious haute-joaillerie, in **2002** Ebel launched an exceptional new collection: Gems of the Ocean.

This new collection consists of four new haute-joaillerie timepiece lines, each named after a Polynesian

island. The brand-new and aptly named coral setting used for the Gems of the Ocean is based on a bed of brilliant-cut diamonds set by hand, topped by a superposed colored gemstone. These are unique handcrafted creations, numbered from 1 to 50.

Each woman may choose her gemstone: Topaz (blue), Tourmaline (green or pink), Amethyst (purple), Palmeira Orange Citrine (orange), and Rock Crystal (white).

All the models are crafted in 18-karat white gold and feature white-gold hour and minute hands, a dial set entirely with brilliant-cut diamonds and a crown cut from a precious colored stone.

All models are water resistant to 30 meters (3atm) and house an Ebel quartz movement, caliber 057.

EBEL

1911

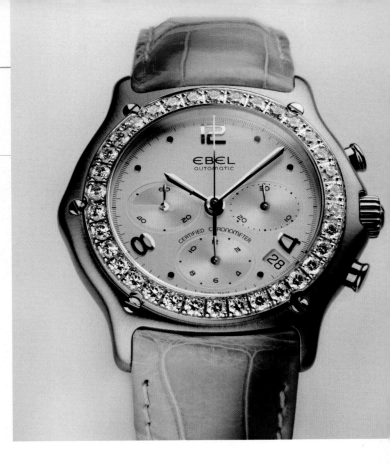

New oval counters, gem-set versions of the chronograph and new strap colors have been added to the ladies' models. Such sophisticated touches are reflections of the particular attention devoted to this line whose name recalls Ebel's historic legacy-much to the delight of connoisseurs of prestigious timekeepers.

The 1911 Chronograph models now feature a silvered dial enhanced by oval counters. A closer look reveals that the left one carries an extremely light impression of the E for Ebel, providing a subtle reminder of the brand's logo. Tremendous care has been lavished upon even the slightest details, all carrying the hallmark of Ebel's undeniable taste for excellence.

The models with black or sand-colored alligator leather straps feature a bezel set with 34 diamonds totaling 2.04 carats, an unusual characteristic for such a resolutely masculine model and which is likely to make borrowing an even stronger temptation for women. All are driven by Ebel's COSC-certified movement, caliber 137.

Beluga

Since 1985, Beluga-an exclusive feminine line with beautifully rounded case and wrist-hugging bracelet-has become a great classic, radiating unmistakable sensuality, but in a subtle, gentle manner.

Nature's bounty as revealed in the world around us has inspired the latest dials displayed by Beluga: two delicate pastel shades of mother-of-pearl.

Mini or Lady Beluga in steel is adorned with a pink mother-of-pearl dial providing a glowing reminder of life's rosiest moments, while the blue mother-of-pearl dial draws the gaze into a cloudless sky. Both are precious new expressions of the essence of femininity.

Classic Wave

Launched in 2001, Classic Wave rapidly asserted both its renowned heritage-drawn from the Sport Classic—and its own distinctively novel character.

In 2002, Classic Wave unlocked fresh potential and revealed new depths within each of its watch lines via two new dials and two gem-setting variations.

In addition to existing dial-colors, the steel and two-tone models of the Senior Classic Wave are treated to a galvanic silver engine-turned dial with 11 Roman numerals. An imprint of the attractive guilloché pattern-hand-crafted by a specialized engraver-is made on the dial plates, thereby creating a raised effect that catches the light and gives added character to the face of this forcefully elegant watch.

Beluga Tonneau

Ebel proudly introduces its interpretation of the tonneau watch, inspired by and continuing the strong success of the Beluga line: Beluga Tonneau.

Named after a French term referring to the voluptuous "tonneau" or barrel shape of this watchcase, Beluga Tonneau is the latest addition to the Ebel family of finely crafted Swiss timepieces. This elegant design, originally a popular style in the early 19th century, remains a classic, timeless favorite today, and complements the company image and tradition.

HIGHLIGHTS

■ Reaffirming its dedication to technical excellence and its status as a complete Manufacture, Ebel has unveiled the Chronograph Automatic Perpetual Calendar. Crafted in 18-karat gold and housing the self-winding mechanical caliber 136, the watch represents the high end of Ebel's collection. The perpetual calendar takes into account the months and leap years, and offers moonphase display. The chronograph measures time from 1/10th of a second to 12 hours.

■ Retaining all the signature features of the Classic Wave, Ebel has added new versions that include two new dials and two gem-set models. Blue and galvanic silver now grace the line, as well as models with diamond bezels or diamond bezels and bracelet links.

■ Similarly, the striking Beluga line has new pink or blue mother-of-pearl dials and has also been set with several different natural-stone dials including hematite or lepidolite, a crystal that contains sparkling mica. Additionally, the Beluga has been set with varying degrees of diamonds for stunning appeal. The Beluga Manchette also dons three new mother-of-pearl dials, including pink, green and mauve.

■ Demonstrating remarkable refinement and elegance, the 1911 has been slightly revamped with oval counters on the chronograph models and sparkling diamond bezels on both the Chronograph and Lady models. Ebel's COSC-certified chronometer movement 137 powers all of the 1911 watches.

EBEL

CHRONOGRAPH, PERPETUAL CALENDAR   REF. 3136901/35

Movement: mechanical, automatic-winding, Ebel 136 caliber (40.0 caliber + perpetual calendar module realized by Ebel).
Functions: hour, minute, small second; perpetual calendar (date, day, month, year, moonphase); chronograph with 3 counters.
Case: 18K yellow-gold, three-piece brushed case (Ø 40mm, thickness 12mm); flat sapphire glass with antireflective treatment; polished bezel fastened with 5 white-gold screws; 4 correctors on the middle; hexagonal white-gold crown with case protection. Water resistant to 3atm.
Dial: ivory; applied yellow-gold Roman numerals, yellow-gold bâton-style hands.
Indications: minute counter and date display at 3; moonphase and hour counter at 6; small seconds and week day at 9; four-year cycle and month at 12; center second counter; minute track with divisions for 1/5 of a second; tachometer scale on the flange.
Strap: crocodile leather; yellow-gold, triple-blade folding clasp.
Also available: with yellow-gold bracelet.

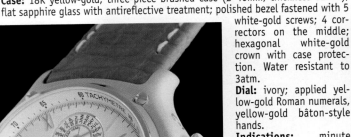

CHRONO 1911   REF. 9137240/26735135

Movement: mechanical, automatic-winding, Ebel 137 caliber. Officially certified "chronometer" (COSC).
Functions: hour, minute, small second; date.
Case: stainless steel, three-piece brushed case; flat sapphire glass with antireflective treatment; polished bezel fastened with 5 screws; steel crown. Water resistant to 3atm.
Dial: gray with sun pattern; zones decorated with circular beads; cabochon markers and applied curved steel Roman numerals, luminescent dots on the flange; luminescent steel bâton-style hands.
Indications: minute counter at 3; date display between 4 and 5; hour counter at 6; small seconds at 9; center second counter; minute track with divisions for 1/5 of a second.
Strap: crocodile leather; screwed attachment; stainless steel fold-over clasp.
Also available: with stainless steel bracelet; with black dial; in steel and gold with strap or steel and gold bracelet, silvered or black dial; in yellow gold with strap or yellow-gold bracelet and silvered dial.

1911 BIG DATE   REF. 9125241/15635152

Movement: mechanical, automatic-winding, Ebel 125 caliber, autonomy 48 hours, 21 jewels, 11'''1/2 (Ø 25.6mm, thickness 4.90mm). Balance with 28,800 vph.
Functions: hour, minute, small second, date.
Case: stainless steel, three-piece brushed case (Ø 38mm, thickness 9.8mm); flat antireflective sapphire glass; polished bezel fastened with 5 white-gold screws; crown with case protection; back fastened with 8 screws. Water resistant to 10atm.
Dial: matte black; applied curved steel Roman numerals and luminescent dots; printed minute track on the flange; luminescent steel bâton-style hands.
Indications: double-disc big-sized date at 6.
Strap: crocodile leather; screwed attachment; steel fold-over clasp.
Also available: with stainless steel bracelet; with black or white dial.

MINI CLASSIC WAVE   REF. 8157F14/9725

Movement: quartz, Ebel 157 caliber. **Functions:** hour, minute. **Case:** 18K yellow-gold, single-piece brushed case; domed sapphire glass with antireflective treatment; bezel with set diamonds, fastened with 5 screws; gold crown. Water resistant to 5atm. **Dial:** mother-of-pearl; applied curved gold Roman numerals and 10 set diamonds; round domed hands. **Bracelet:** gold; triple-blade folding clasp.
Also available: bezel with diamonds or simple bezel; mother-of-pearl dial applied Roman numerals; in steel and yellow gold (stainless steel bracelet with PVD treatment) matte white, matte ivory or mother-of-pearl dial applied Roman numerals, matte white, black enameled or mother-of-pearl dial diamond markers; in steel and yellow gold, diamond bezel, mother-of-pearl dial applied Roman numerals, matte white or mother-of-pearl dial applied Roman numerals, matte white or mother-of-pearl dial: in steel with matte black, silvered, blue galvanized, blue guilloché or mother-of-pearl dial applied Roman numerals, matte white or mother-of-pearl dial, diamond markers, matte white or mother-of-pearl dial applied Roman numerals, mother-of-pearl dial, diamond markers.

CALIBER 124

Basic caliber: ETA 2892A2.
Automatic-winding movement, 42-hour autonomy, Etarotor rotor mounted on a ball bearing.
Functions: hours, minutes, seconds; date (with fast corrector); world time.

Shape: round.
Diameter: 25.60mm (11'''1/2).
Thickness: 4.80mm.
Jewels: 21.
Balance: smooth, with three arms, in Glucydur.
Frequency: 28,800 vph.
Balance-spring: flat, Nivarox, with Etachron regulating device.
Shock-absorber system: Inca-bloc.
Notes: the pillar-plate and bridges are decorated with a circular-graining pattern, the rotor with a concentric circle pattern.

CALIBER 124

Caliber 124, dial-side view. The special plate mounted on the basic movement allows housing, with minimal friction, the rotating flange with the engraved 24 hour-indications facing the dial together with the turning bezel on the watchcase. The names of 24 reference cities for the 24 time zones appear on the bezel, thus allowing the world-time reading (Voyager). The central work-driving wheel is dismounted in order to show the structure of the modification introduced on the basic caliber.

CALIBER 136

Basic caliber: Zenith 40.0.
Automatic-winding movement, autonomy of 50 hours, rotor mounted on a ball bearing.
Functions: hours, minutes, small seconds; chronograph with three counters (center seconds, minutes and hours); perpetual calendar (date, day, month, leap year, moonphase, with 4 fast correctors).
Shape: round. **Diameter:** 30.00mm (13'''1/4). **Thickness:** 8.10mm. **Jewels:** 31.
Balance: smooth, in Glucydur.
Frequency: 36,000 vph.
Balance-spring: flat, with eccentric screw regulating device.
Shock-absorber system: Kif.
Notes: the rotor is decorated with a concentric circle pattern, the calendar module with a circular-graining pattern.

CALIBER 136

The caliber is shown on its dial side. The complex module combined with the basic movement does not only display calendar information on a perpetual basis, but also allows chronograph indications to be displayed on the dial. To this end, the chronograph hand and calendar pivots are coaxial at the 3, 6 and 9 positions. Furthermore, it is possible to identify the calendar's four fast correctors with their levers, return springs and trip end limits, all brushed and beveled. The Zenith 40.0 caliber is totally finished and assembled by Ebel; when it is not combined with the perpetual calendar module, it results in the Caliber 134. In both cases the lubrication system adopted for the mounting operations is patented by Ebel.

CALIBER 137

Automatic-winding movement with autonomy of over 48 hours, rotor mounted on a ball bearing. **Functions:** hours, minutes, small seconds; date in an aperture; chronograph with three counters (center seconds, minutes and hours).
Shape: round. **Diameter:** 31.00mm (13'''3/4). **Thickness:** 6.40mm. **Jewels:** 27.

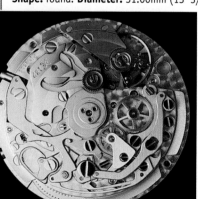

Balance: smooth, with three arms, in Glucydur. **Frequency:** 28,800 vph. **Balance-spring:** flat, Nivarox 1, with micrometer screw regulating device (Triovis).
Shock-absorber system: Inca-bloc.
Notes: the pillar-plate is decorated with a circular-graining pattern, bridges are decorated with a concentric circle pattern, the rotor (dismounted in the photograph) shows guilloché engraved patterns. Screw heads are finished by specular polishing, the levers and springs of the chronograph mechanism are brushed and beveled.

CALIBER 137

Caliber 137, dial-side view. Consisting of more than 200 elements, this movement was first developed by Ebel in 1989 after purchasing a former project by Lemania. The thickness was reduced from the original 8mm to the present 6.40mm by exploiting the most recent knowledge in the field of both materials and production techniques. In its versions as officially certified "chronometer" (COSC), this movement is used exclusively by Ebel. The derived caliber 135 is marketed by Lemania.

EBERHARD & CO.

f or more than a century, Eberhard & Co. has been creating professional instruments of the highest quality. By paying strict attention to performance, the brand has built an international reputation for its chronographs and chronometers.

Young watchmaker Georges-Emile Eberhard opened his watchmaking shops in La Chaux-de-Fonds in 1887. The technical quality and elegant beauty of his pocket watches garnered him popularity amongst the most discerning clientele of the time. Eberhard & Co. became a family business when Georges-Emile's sons followed in their father's footsteps.

In 1919, Eberhard unveiled its first chronograph wristwatch. Five years later, the firm launched its chronograph with two pushbuttons and in 1939 it unveiled the distinctive chronograph rattrapante. Decade after decade since, Eberhard has continued to demonstrate its technical prowess and design innovation.

Eberhard's collection of timepieces is rich with diversity. Among its watch lines are the patent-pending Chrono 4 series; Extra Forte; Replica; and Tazio Nuvolari—each with sporty appeal. The sophisticated 8 Days collection of technically refined watches with a patented power-reserve device offers chic elegance, as does the Traversetolo collection of oversized timepieces with transparent caseback exposing the movement with pearl-finished embellishments.

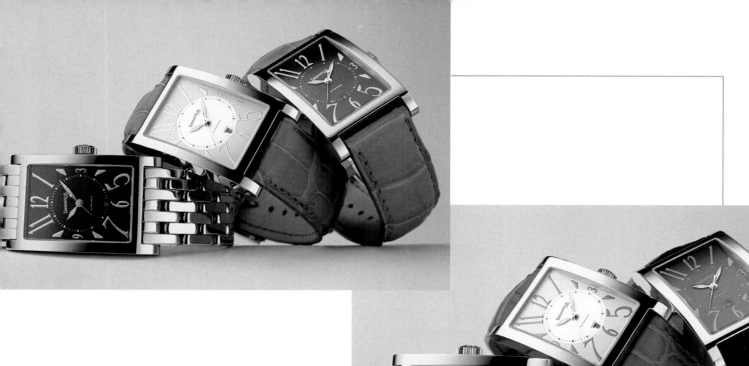

FACING PAGE

TOP LEFT

The striking and technically advanced Chrono 4 watch changes the way one reads the chronograph.

TOP RIGHT

These Chrono 4 watches feature chronograph subdials set horizontally across the watch face, offering progressive readout of counters.

BOTTOM LEFT

The Boucanier Grande Date offers oversized date window at 12:00 and is a mechanical watch with automatic wind.

THIS PAGE

TOP LEFT

The Les Courbées collection comes with either bracelet or strap with new dials featuring stylized Arabic numerals.

TOP RIGHT

Water resistant to 30atm, the Les Courbées timepieces offer chic appeal.

BOTTOM RIGHT

Color adds beauty and elegance to the Gingi Date watches.

HIGHLIGHTS

■ Eberhard's new Chrono 4 watch revolutionizes chronograph readability. This is the first chronograph whose counters are arranged in one row across the bottom of the dial. With its chronograph counters lined up horizontally, information is provided in a natural progression: the first subdial displays the minutes elapsed, followed by the hours elapsed. The next subdial displays the 24 hours and the fourth features a small-seconds/date readout.

■ The Chrono 4 Bellissimo watch, offered in a 40mm case, houses an automatic movement and comes in steel or in 18-karat pink gold with either a blue or white dial. A genuine innovation of function and aesthetics, the Chrono 4 has met with international success.

■ Eberhard has rounded out its successful Les Courbées collection of mechanical watches by adding steel and 18-karat pink-gold models with dials of blue, black or white.

FRANCK MULLER

e xactly 11 years ago in 1992, master watchmaker Franck Muller launched his own collection of mechanical timepieces. Marvelous both inside and outside, Muller's line of complicated watches was an immediate international hit. Packed with such complex timepieces as tourbillons, minute repeaters and perpetual calendars, the Franck Muller brand has been creating technical sensations ever since.

Most noted is the Tourbillon Revolution watch—a timepiece that was several years in the making. Protected by several patents, the new mechanism enables the wearer to simply push a button to allow the tourbillon case to rise up to the sapphire crystal for better viewing. When the tourbillon's rising function is engaged, the hour and minute hands almost magically sweep to the 12:00 position to make room for the hanging tourbillon case to come to the surface. An extremely complex mechanism, this timepiece also offers power reserve of approximately 70 hours. It is crafted in the Cintree Curvex 7850 case in platinum only.

Another complicated marvel is the Perpetual Calendar Retrograde Equation watch, Ref. 7850 QPE. The watch houses a self-winding movement with 47 hours of power reserve. Available in yellow, red, or white gold, or in platinum, it offers the perpetual calendar function with leap-year display, date display and moonphase display. Additionally, it houses the complex retrograde equation of time function that indicates the time difference between the true solar day and the mean solar day.

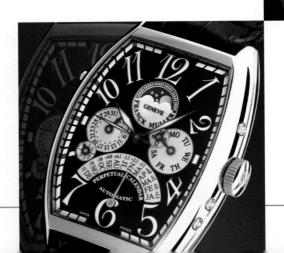

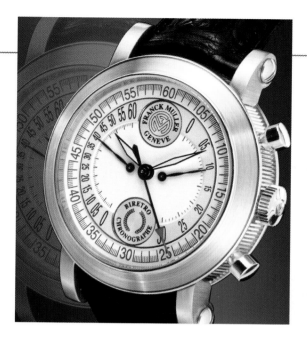

FACING PAGE

FAR LEFT

The Tourbillon Revolution is an extraordinary watch wherein the tourbillon escapement is housed in a free-style case that can rise up to the surface of the watch crystal at the touch of a button.

RIGHT

Offering classic elegance, the Cintree Curvex Grand Guichet Chronograph watch houses a self-winding movement with a 950 platinum rotor.

BOTTOM

Featuring the complex retrograde equation of time function, this Perpetual Calendar Retrograde Equation watch is crafted in platinum or 18-karat red, white or yellow gold.

THIS PAGE

TOP LEFT

The Bi-Retrograde Chronograph, Ref. 7000 CCB, allows timing in hours, minutes and fractions of a second by means of a seconds hand that can be activated, stopped and returned to zero.

TOP RIGHT

The Long Island Master Calendar watch offers moonphase readout, date, day and month readout.

FAR RIGHT

Crafted in 18-karat gold, this stunning black-dialed Long Island Perpetual Calendar watch houses an automatic movement with 47 hours of power reserve and a platinum rotor.

BOTTOM

Diamonds on the dial and the case enhance this colorful Long Island Diamond watch for women.

Franck Muller has also unveiled a Cintree Curvex Chronograph Grand Guichet, Ref. 7850 CCGG. The watch, crafted in all three colors of gold, platinum or steel, houses a self-winding movement with platinum rotor. It offers the hours and minutes readout, as well as the chronograph function with 60-seconds counter, hour counter and 30-minutes counter.

HIGHLIGHTS

Franck Muller has also added significantly to its Long Island collection of distinctive timepieces. Among the new models is an art deco interpretation of time, the Long Island Master Calendar Moon, Ref. 1200 MCL. This automatic watch, housing the FM 2800 caliber, has 47 hours of power reserve and is water resistant to 30 meters. It offers hour and minute indicators, as well as days and months through two display windows at 12:00. A hand in the center of the watch indicates the date and there is a moonphase aperture at 6:00.

Another version is the Long Island Perpetual Calendar watch. This horological complication was previously available only from Franck Muller in the Classiques or Cintree Curvex lines. Muller now incorporates it into the rectangular Long Island series. The automatic watch is crafted in 18-karat yellow, rose or white gold.

For women, Franck Muller unveiled the Long Island Date Diamond watch, a self-winding timepiece designed in art deco style. Crafted in platinum or 18-karat red, yellow or white gold, the watch is bedecked with a double row of diamonds on the case and a center circle of diamonds on the dial.

F.P. JOURNE-INVENIT ET FECIT·

Other watchmakers recognize François-Paul Journe as one of the most inventive independent horologists working today. His field is classic watchmaking, but his watches are unlike any other.

François-Paul Journe has inhabited the upper echelon of horology since **1976**, when he graduated from the Paris School of Watchmaking. He immediately joined forces with his uncle, a noted restorer of antique timepieces, and created his first tourbillon pocket watch in **1978**. Indeed, before creating his own complete line of wristwatches, Journe restored some of the world's most important historical timepieces, devised and built unique pocket watches to order, and designed and made complications for prestigious watch brands.

In **1983** he first attempted to apply resonance to achieve precision in a watch. Journe was constantly striving for perfection and building one-of-a-kind timepieces in the style of Abraham-Louis Breguet. In **1985**, he built his first Planetary pocket watch, and in **1987**, he created the Pendule Sympathique clock and watch combination in pink coral for John Asprey. The piece won him the Bleustein-Blanchet prize. Two years later, in **1989**, he won the Balancier d'Or award, followed a few years later by the Gaïa prize for the best watchmaker for the year **1994**.

In **1996**, Journe established TIM S.A. workshops in Geneva, designing and making watch mechanisms for other brands. Three years later, in **1999**, he launched his own watches under the F.P. Journe Invenit et Fecit label. Among his first timepieces were the resonance wristwatch and the tourbillon wristwatch with constant-force remontoir. In **2001**, he partnered with Harry Winston to create the first in the Harry Winston Opus series.

Journe's watchmaking is influenced by the golden-age ideals of scientific watchmaking of the 18th and 19th centuries when precision and mechanical elegance were the major objectives of horological research.

Indeed, Journe's craftsmanship has a depth and sophistication that appeals to the knowledgeable enthusiast. His watches easily range in price up to half a million dollars or more for a custom-made piece.

In 1999, Journe opened his workshops in downtown Geneva to build a wristwatch that won immediate public attention. The "tourbillon à remontoir d'égalité" combined the most intricate compensation devices known to horology: the tourbillon and a remontoir to feed it constant force. The following year, the resonance wrist chronometer achieve unprecedented mechanical precision by using resonance to lock twin movements onto a common frequency.

Montres F.P. Journe's Latin motto proclaims its products are of Journe's own invention and creation. The F.P. Journe workshops build around 700 pieces a year. Each watchmaker assembles and adjusts one watch at a time, spending several weeks on the most complicated. Great care is taken to reflect the highest standards of workmanship in every detail.

TOP

The twin dials of Journe's resonance-system chronometer can be set separately by the crown at 12:00 to times in different zones.
The symmetrical twin movements of the resonance watch. The rack to the right of the mid-point moves the right-hand balance to within half a millimeter of its twin. When resonance sets in, the two balances beat in counter-phase at the same frequency.

CENTER LEFT

This Octa instant-restart chronograph features 60-minute counter and large date. The mechanism is flattened to three mechanical levels measuring less than 1mm high.

CENTER RIGHT

The most sophisticated Octa is an annual calendar that automatically adjusts for date corrections.

BOTTOM

In this Tourbillon Souverain, the remontoir delivers a constant force to the tourbillon to compensate for the declining mainspring. Together they attain the limits of mechanical precision. (Limited Series produced in ruthenium, numbered 1 to 99.)

TOP LEFT

François-Paul Journe (left) in his Geneva workshops with his chief watchmaker, Georges Alessio. To date, he has built 10 unique pieces, which are all in private collections.

CENTER

Inspired by the complicated watch that Abraham-Louis Breguet made for Queen Marie-Antoinette (she lost her head before it was finished), F.P. Journe's one-of-a-kind piece reveals its mechanical magic through a dial of rock crystal.

RIGHT

The latest in F.P. Journe's unique pieces is a minute-repeating clock-watch that strikes the time to the nearest minute, quarter-hour and hour. Journe has inverted the conventional chiming mechanism to display the twin hammers through the face.

BOTTOM

Journe's Sympathique clock-watch, built for Asprey in 1987, is decorated with an inlay of 3,000 pieces of pink coral.

HIGHLIGHTS

■ F.P. Journe's latest Octa watches belongs to a series of automatics with power reserve of five days. The Octa caliber incorporates different complications within the movement without changing its size.

■ Among the Octa complex movements are the instant-restart chronograph with 60-minute counter and large date, and the annual calendar that features automatic adjustments for months with 29, 30 or 31 days.

■ Another complex innovation from F.P. Journe is the oversized minute-repeating watch. On demand, it strikes the hours, quarters and minutes in Grand or Small Strike mode.

■ F.P. Journe has added a twist to this inventive repeater watch. The chiming mechanism has been reversed so that the twin hammers are displayed through the watch face, while the cams and racks can be seen through the caseback.

F. P. JOURNE INVENIT ET FECIT

SONNERIE SOUVERAINE UNIQUE PIECE — SOUVERAINE COLLECTION

Movement: world exclusivity mechanical, manual-winding. Original concept and production by F.P. Journe, 1996 caliber.
Functions: hour, retrograde minute; power reserve; minute repeater; grande and petite sonnerie.
Case: platinum, numbered two-piece case (Ø 38mm, thickness 11mm); curved sapphire crystal; knurled crown and pushers (for the repeater at 2, for the selection of the

grande or petite sonnerie and mute at 4); snap-on back displaying the movement through a sapphire crystal. Water resistant to 3atm.
Dial: 18K gold; solid silver engine-turned (guilloché) shaped center zone and applied brushed solid silver minute ring; printed Arabic numerals; blued steel hands in an exclusive shape.
Indications: power reserve at 2; mute; petite or grande sonnerie at 4; retrograde center minute with 5-minute progression.
Strap: crocodile leather; platinum clasp.
Note: unique piece.

TOURBILLON SOUVERAIN — SOUVERAINE COLLECTION

Movement: world exclusivity mechanical, manual-winding, with tourbillon and constant force remontoir. Original concept and production by F.P. Journe, 1498 caliber (patented system). **Functions:** hour, minute; power reserve of 42 hours.
Case: platinum, two-piece numbered case (Ø 38.3mm, thickness 9.1mm); curved sapphire crystal; knurled crown; back attached by 6 screws displaying the movement through a sapphire crystal. Water resistant to 3atm.

Dial: 18K gold, aperture on the tourbillon; solid silver engine-turned (guilloché) zones; blued steel hands in an exclusive shape.
Indications: off-center hour and minute at 3 with printed Arabic numerals and railway minute track with five-minute progression; power reserve at 12.
Strap: crocodile leather; platinum clasp.
Also available: case in pink gold; with bracelet in platinum or gold; dial in white, yellow and pink gold.
Note: Journe's Tourbillon Souverain is equipped with a constant force device (partly visible through the aperture at 6) that compensates the force of the escapement, thus allowing a more accurate balance isochronism.

CHRONOMETRE A RESONANCE — SOUVERAINE COLLECTION

Movement: world exclusivity mechanical, manual-winding. Original concept and production by F.P. Journe. Working with resonance phenomenon.
Functions: hours and minutes of two different time zones, small second; power reserve of 40 hours.
Case: platinum, numbered two-piece case (Ø 38.3mm, thickness 9,20mm); curved sapphire crystal; knurled crowns (at 12 for winding and time adjustment on both

dials, at 4 for the automatic synchronization of the seconds hands); back attached by 6 screws displaying the movement through a sapphire crystal. Water resistant to 3atm.
Dial: 18K gold; symmetric solid silver engine-turned (guilloché) zones; printed Arabic numerals and railway minute track with five-minute progression; blued steel hands in an exclusive shape.
Indications: symmetric off-center double time display (hour; minute; small second); power reserve at 12.
Strap: crocodile leather; platinum clasp.
Also available: case in pink gold; with bracelet in platinum or gold; dial in white, yellow or pink gold.

CHRONOMETRE A RESONANCE — SOUVERAINE COLLECTION

F. P. Journe is a skillful watchmaker, capable of designing and entirely realizing all of the components of a watch, distinguishing himself because of the highly original technical and creative solutions chosen. That is also the case of this world premiere. Today more than 20 years of research into the phenomenon of resonance have resulted in the first twin-movement, resonance-system wrist-chronometer — the first timekeeper in 100 years of wristwatches designed specifically for precision on the wrist.

F.P. Journe uses mechanical resonance to get two independent balance-wheels to vibrate at the same frequency — the constant average of their individual natural frequencies. The objective is to achieve a steady rate in a watch exposed to shocks and accelerations on the wrist.
The synchronised balances support one another to develop greater inertia. External forces on wristwatches such as shocks and sudden movements are absorbed because they have opposite effects on the rate of each balance — if one speeds up, the other slows correspondingly. The balances then return to their common frequency.
The twin independent movements indicate times on two dials. The crown at 12 o'clock winds both movements and sets the hours and minutes of each dial independently, to different times if desired.

OCTA RESERVE DE MARCHE — OCTA COLLECTION

Movement: world exclusivity mechanical, automatic-winding. Entirely designed and produced by F. P. Journe. 22K gold rotor, personalized and engine-turned (guilloché).

Functions: hour, minute, small second; date; power reserve 120h.

Case: platinum, numbered two-piece case (Ø 38.3mm, thickness 10mm); curved sapphire crystal; knurled crown; back attached by 6 screws displaying the movement through a sapphire crystal. Water resistant to 3atm.

Dial: 18K gold; solid silver engine-turned (guilloché) zones; blued steel hands in an exclusive shape.

Indications: off-center hour and minute at 3 with printed Arabic numerals and railway minute track with five-minute progression; small second between 4 and 5; power reserve at 9; patented big-sized date with double disc below 11.

Strap: crocodile leather; platinum clasp.

Also available: in pink gold; with bracelet in platinum or gold; dial in white, yellow or pink gold.

OCTA CHRONOGRAPHE — OCTA COLLECTION

Movement: world exclusivity mechanical, automatic-winding. Entirely designed and produced by F. P. Journe. 22K gold rotor; power reserve 120h; personalized and engine-turned (guilloché). Three level chronograph mechanism, flattened to just 1mm, combines zero-stop and zero-restart features.

Functions: hour, minute, small second; large date; chronograph with two counters. **Case:** platinum, numbered, two-piece case (Ø 38.3mm, thickness 10.30mm); curved sapphire crystal; knurled crown and pushers; back attached by 6 screws, displaying the movement through a sapphire crystal. Water resistant to 3atm.

Dial: 18K gold; solid silver engine-turned (guilloché) zones; blued steel hands in an exclusive shape.

Indications: off-center hour and minute at 3 with printed Arabic numerals and railway minute track with five-minute progression; small second between 4 and 5; minute counter at 9; large date at 11; center second counter.

Strap: crocodile leather; platinum clasp.

Also available: case in pink gold; with bracelet in platinum or gold; dial in white, yellow or pink gold.

OCTA CALENDRIER — OCTA COLLECTION

Movement: world exclusivity mechanical, automatic-winding. Entirely designed and produced by F. P. Journe. 22K gold rotor, personalized and engine-turned (guilloché). The calendar which displays the day and month through two separate windows advances instantaneously and is self-adjusting for the months of 29, 30 and 31 days.

Functions: hour, minute, small second; retrograde date; day and month in two separate windows; power reserve of 120 hours. **Case:** platinum, numbered two-piece case (Ø 38.3mm, thickness 10mm); curved sapphire crystal; knurled crown; back attached by 6 screws, displaying the movement through a sapphire crystal. Water resistant to 3atm.

Dial: 18K gold; solid silver engine-turned (guilloché) zones; blued steel hands in an exclusive shape.

Indications: off-center hour and minute at 3 with printed Arabic numerals and railway minute track with five-minute progression; small second between 4 and 5; day window at 11; month window at 7; retrograde date hand in the center.

Strap: crocodile leather; platinum clasp.

Also available: in pink gold, with bracelet in platinum or pink gold, dial in white, yellow and pink gold. Special award of the "Jury Grand Prix d'Horlogerie de Genève 2002."

LIMITED SERIE IN RUTHENIUM — OCTA COLLECTION

The movements of the Octa Reserve de Marche and Octa Chronographe have been proposed in 2002 in a new 40mm-diameter size with ruthenium-clad dials and movements. Both mechanical automatic-winding wristwatches are produced in a limited series of 99 pieces each and both have a power reserve of 120 hours with day and night window for the Octa Réserve de Marche. Available also for the models: "Tourbillon Souverain" and "Chronomètre à Résonance."

FRÉDÉRIQUE CONSTANT

deftly combining elegance and technology in a striking collection, Frédérique Constant offers cutting-edge timepieces with complex movements and sophisticated designs.

It was in the **1980**s that Dutch businessman Peter Stas traveled regularly to Switzerland, visiting watch factories and feeding his personal passion for luxury timepieces. Employed in an unrelated field, Stas's genuine interest in watch production heightened and he began developing his own ideas for a brand. Having been transferred by his employer to the Far East, Stas cultivated new relationships with watch experts and began the actual creation of his own watches—building several dozen prototypes.

In **1988**, with the help of colleague Aletta Bax (who would later become his wife), Stas started his own company. The name Frédérique Constant was derived from both families' histories (Frédérique was Bax's great-grandmother and Constant was Stas's great-grandfather—a maker of clock dials in the early **1900**s). The couple spent three years exchanging and developing ideas and in **1991**, they opened a small office for the fledgling firm. After showing their timepieces at one exhibition, Frédérique Constant garnered nearly 400 orders and official watchmaking commenced.

In **1992**, the brand's first automatic mechanical wristwatches made their debut. Two years later, the innovative Heart Beat was unveiled to international markets. This collection of mechanical timepieces was an instant hit thanks to its visible three-spoke balance wheel that continuously rotates clockwise and counter-clockwise—giving it the name Heart Beat.

Frédérique Constant made its official appearance at the World Watch and Jewelry Fair in Basel in **1995**. Orders poured in. Within two years, a larger office was established outside of Geneva and by year-end **1997**, the brand was producing 24,000 watches annually. In the ensuing five years, Frédérique Constant regularly expanded its collections, adding a Yacht Timer, as well as several important limited-edition designs, and developing the Highlife™ collection. In **2001**, the brand presented its watches to entertainers at the Cannes Film Festival and launched a global advertising campaign encouraging passion and individuality.

Frédérique Constant's extensive collection of timepieces is created in Switzerland and sold in 36 countries around the world. Production is currently up to 40,000 pieces annually and revolves around three main lines: Highlife Heart Beat, Persuasion, and an 18-karat gold jewelry series (in which each model is created in an edition of only 99 pieces). Designed for both men and women, Frédérique Constant watches often include complex functions and complicated movements—ranging from tourbillons to day/night indicators and calendars.

Most recently, Frédérique Constant unveiled several new Highlife watches, including a Highlife Tourbillon and a Moonphase Chronograph. The exceptional Highlife Tourbillon is crafted in platinum and features an aperture at 6:00 for viewing the tourbillon escapement. The mechanical movement consists of 23 rubies and its bridges are decorated with the Côtes de Genève markings. The Highlife Moonphase Chronograph, which houses a mechanical movement with 42 hours of power reserve, offers the hours, minutes, seconds, chronograph functions, moonphase indicator, and date pointer.

As additions to the Persuasion collection of men's timepieces (first unveiled in 2001 and sold internationally in 2002), Frédérique Constant has introduced the Persuasion Business timer, a round watch with perpetual calendar and dual time-zone indicator, and the Persuasion Carree—a sophisticated square calendar-watch with moonphase indicator.

HIGHLIGHTS

■ Constantly evolving its impressive Highlife collection, Frédérique Constant has developed a premiere model: the Highlife Heart Beat Retrograde watch. An automatic-winding mechanism on a mechanical model, the movement offers a 30-second retrograde subdial at 6:00.

■ The Highlife Heart Beat Retrograde watch features 42 hours of power reserve and is designed in the true Frédérique Constant style of elegance and sophistication. The bridges are decorated with the Côtes de Genève design and the case is crafted in 18-karat rose gold. A stainless steel version is also available. The watch, with sapphire crystal and screw-down crown, is water resistant to 50 meters.

■ In typical Frédérique Constant tradition, the Highlife Heart Beat Retrograde watch features an elegant dial with the brand's emblem appliquéd by hand at 3:00. The watch is fitted with either a Louisiana crocodile strap, a hand-sewn ostrich strap or a specially designed bracelet.

■ Frédérique Constant also continues with its highly successful Live Your Passion advertising campaign on an international basis.

253

FREDERIQUE CONSTANT

HIGHLIFE AUTOMATIC MOONPHASE CHRONOGRAPH   REF. FC-395ABS4H6B

Movement: automatic caliber FC-395 with Dubois-Dépraz, 28,800 vph, 42-hour power reserve, 25 rubies, Incabloc anti-shock system, Côtes de Genève pattern, Anglage finished.
Functions: hour, minute; date; moonphase; chronograph with 2 counters.
Case: three-piece stainless steel; 42x14.8mm; convex sapphire crystal, transparent sapphire crystal caseback with 6 screws; water resistant to 100 meters. Each case is numbered individually.
Dial: black; 18K solid gold Frederique Constant Crest applied to dial; Frederique Constant Highlife registered Arabic numerals; translucent Frederique Constant Crest in center background.
Indications: date and moonphase at 6; minute counter at 12; central second counter.
Bracelet: signature Highlife stainless steel.
Price: US $4,000 retail.

HIGHLIFE HEART BEAT AUTOMATIC DAY-DATE   REF. FC-610AB3H6

Movement: automatic caliber FCO610 with Dubois-Dépraz, 28,800 vph, 42-hour power reserve, 27 rubies, Incabloc anti-shock system, Côtes de Genève pattern, Anglage finished.
Functions: hour, minute, second; day-date.
Case: stainless steel, three-piece case with 6 screws; 39x11mm; convex sapphire crystal, transparent crystal caseback; water resistant to 60 meters. Each case is numbered individually.
Dial: black; 18K gold Frederique Constant Crest applied to dial; translucent Frederique Constant Crest in center background; Frederique Constant Highlife registered Arabic numerals; day-date scale with engraved concentric circles; diamond-cut around Heart Beat opening.
Indications: day-date at 6; heart beat at 12.
Strap: waterproof, genuine leather.
Price: US $3,200 retail.

HIGHLIFE GENTS' HEART BEAT AUTOMATIC RETROGRADE REF. FC-680AS3H6

Movement: automatic caliber FC-680 with Agenhor, 28,800 vph, 42-hour power reserve, 27 rubies, Incabloc anti-shock system, Côtes de Genève pattern, Anglage finished.
Functions: hour, minute, retrograde second.
Case: three-piece stainless steel; 39x10.5mm; convex sapphire crystal, transparent crystal caseback with 6 screws; water resistant to 60 meters. Each case is numbered individually.
Dial: silvered guilloché; 18K gold Frederique Constant Crest applied to dial; translucent Frederique Constant Crest in center background; Frederique Constant Highlife registered Arabic numerals.
Indications: 30-second jump retrograde at 6.
Strap: waterproof, genuine ostrich leather.
Price: US $4,200 retail.

HIGHLIFE LADIES' BLACK ROMAN CARREE   REF. FC-202RB1C6B

Movement: ultra-slim caliber FC-202-2, 1.95mm thick, controlled by integrated circuit and quartz, 7 jewels.
Functions: hour, minute.
Case: two-piece stainless steel; 24.5x27x6mm; curved caseback, curved glare-proof sapphire crystal, water resistant to 30 meters. Each case is numbered individually.
Dial: black; Roman numerals; translucent Frederique Constant Crest in center background.
Bracelet: stainless steel.
Price: US $950 retail.

HIGHLIFE LADIES' DIAMOND ALURE — REF. FC-203MPWD2LD6B

Movement: ultra-slim caliber FC-203-H3, 1.95mm thick, controlled by integrated circuit and quartz, 7 jewels.
Functions: hour, minute.
Case: two-piece stainless steel; 21x29x10mm; curved glare-proof sapphire crystal; water resistant to 30 meters. Each case is numbered individually.
Dial: white mother of pearl; 86 diamonds on bezel and hour markers.
Bracelet: signature Alure curved stainless steel.
Price: US $2,200 retail.

PERSUASION MOONPHASE CARREE — REF. FC-265EG3C6

Movement: caliber FC-265-3, controlled by integrated circuit and quartz, 5 jewels.
Functions: hour, minute; full calendar (day-date-month, moonphase).
Case: two-piece stainless steel; 36x34x8mm; curved glare-proof sapphire crystal; water resistant to 30 meters. Each case is numbered individually.
Dial: white enamel.
Indications: date at 3; moonphase at 6; day at 9; month at 12.
Strap: waterproof, genuine leather.
Price: US $600 retail.

PERSUASION HEART BEAT AUTOMATIC — REF. FC-310MP3P6

Movement: automatic caliber FC-310-3, 28,800 vph, 38-hour power reserve, 25 rubies, Glucydur Balance, Nivarox spring, Incabloc anti-shock system, Côtes de Genève pattern.
Functions: hour, minute, second.
Case: three-piece stainless steel; 38x10mm; sapphire crystal, transparent caseback; water resistant to 60 meters. Each case is numbered individually.
Dial: silver guilloché.
Strap: waterproof, genuine leather.
Price: US $1,000 retail.

CLASSIC HEART BEAT AUTOMATIC ART DECO — REF. FC-310M4T6

Movement: automatic caliber 310-3, 28,800 vph, 38-hour power reserve, 25 rubies, Glucydur Balance, Nivarox spring, Incabloc anti-shock system, crown with two O-rings.
Functions: hour, minute, second.
Case: two-piece stainless steel; 47x36x11.2mm; sapphire crystal; water resistant to 30 meters. Each case is numbered individually.
Dial: silver guilloché.
Strap: waterproof, genuine leather.
Price: US $1,000 retail.

GEORGES V

launched in 2000, Georges V has an advantage that few young brands enjoy—its own manufacturing capacity and its exclusive watch movement.

On **August 28, 2000**, Pasquale Gangi and René Schmidlin (then the head of a private-label manufacturer) entered into a partnership to produce and market high-end watches under the Georges V label, previously registered by Schmidlin.

The first watches appeared on the market in **2002**, including tourbillons and other striking multi-complications. The collections of mostly dress watches are positioned in the luxury sector with prices beginning around $10,000 for the chronograph, while the perpetual-calendar combinations at the highend of the V collection for men are worth much more.

Says Gangi, "Georges V is a niche brand for people who want exclusive products, a watch that is out of the ordinary."

GEORGES V

Georges V watches are full of interesting design details. Most notable is the original moon indication, with the ages of the waxing or waning moon shown on scales. The lugless cases in the Q collection are also unusual. A fingernail-friendly, quick-release device changes from gold bracelet to leather straps or stiff bangles in exotic leathers. In this collection, men's and women's watches are the same size—only the styling determines the gender.

Georges V's exclusive movement, the GV1, is one of the smallest automatics made and took five years to develop. Today it's the jewel inside the Q collection of watches.

Georges V's technical and manufacturing capacities give it privileged access to the greatest complications. Thus it enters the top league with a tourbillon with power-reserve indicator and day date. Also under development is a travel watch with three time-zone indicators.

In these few short years, Georges V has demonstrated impressive high-end watchmaking. "I consider it something of an exploit," says Gangi.

TOP
The bands on the Q watches can be changed at whim from a chunky gold bracelet to a semi-rigid bangle in exotic skins. The quartz chronograph measures to the tenth of a second while changing easily across time zones.

CENTER
The V1001 watch houses an automatic movement and is crafted in steel, gold, or platinum, on a leather strap.

RIGHT
While most V2012 chronographs feature a black dial, this yellow-gold model sports a white dial with open-worked gladiator hands.

BOTTOM LEFT
The gray-gold V3015 model with blue dial is a practical annual calendar that shows the conventional day, date and month as well as the number of weeks.

BOTTOM RIGHT
The perpetual calendar in the V 4018 tracks the leap-year cycle. The escapement, which advances every eighth of a second, regulates a cam that rotates once every four years inside a gray-gold case.

- One of the most striking design elements in Georges V's Q collection is its interchangeable watchstraps and bracelets. With a simple maneuver, one can quickly and easily change from leather to metal, from chain-link bracelets to cuffs.

- Unique in style and form, the Q collection is a signature series of sleekly curved automatic watches in one bold rectangular size that dons feminine characteristics such as diamond accents and pastel colored dials and straps.

- There is also an exciting V collection of softly cushioned square watches that offers a wealth of complicated movement options.

- The V collection includes chronographs and fly-back chronographs, calendars and perpetual calendar watches housed in pink, white or yellow 18-karat gold or in platinum.

- In 2003, Georges V plans to launch two more collections and to extend the brand to other luxury goods including leather, jewelry and cigars.

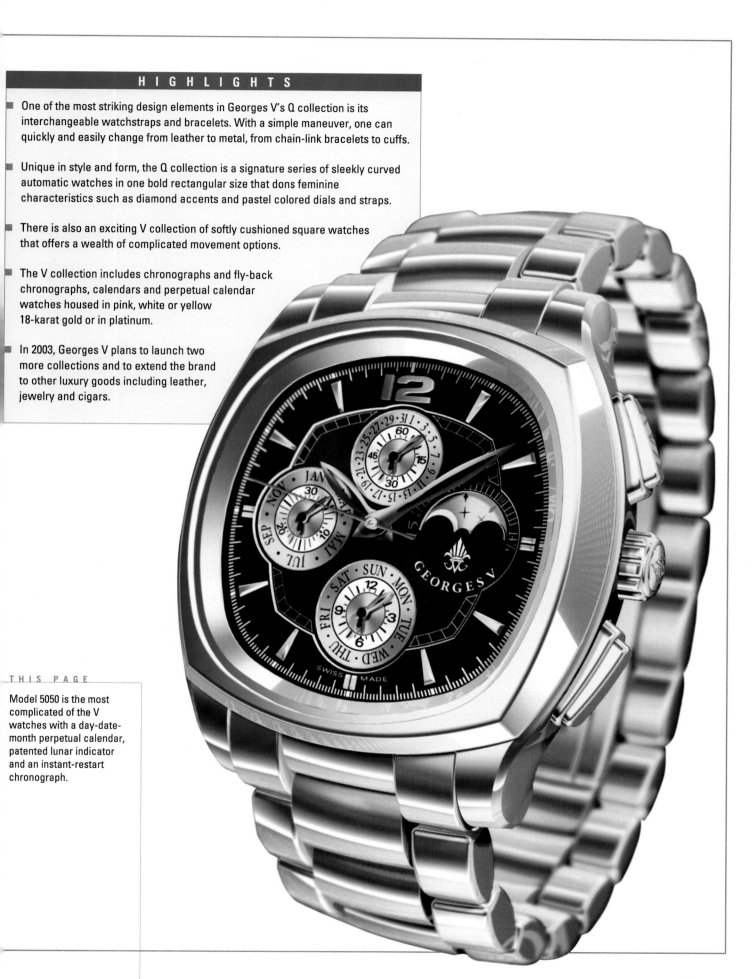

THIS PAGE

Model 5050 is the most complicated of the V watches with a day-date-month perpetual calendar, patented lunar indicator and an instant-restart chronograph.

GEVRIL

resplendent in their honoring of time, Gevril watches are works of style, art and craftsmanship. The brand, as it exists today, blends tradition with a rich new spirit of modernity and passion.

While the roots of this brand can be traced to the mid-**18**th century, it was in **2001** that a determined young entrepreneur breathed fresh life and excitement into Gevril. With family ties to the watchmaking business, Samuel Friedmann was eager to break out on his own and build a brand of mechanical watches that would rival the finest in history and leave its mark for generations to come.

In **2000**, Friedmann was presented with the opportunity to purchase the Gevril brand. Intrigued by its horological ancestry, Friedmann did his research. Jacques Gevril had been among the first Swiss watchmakers of distinction who developed important innovations for the field. In **1744**, he built the first Repetition dial and in **1758**, he became the first exporter of Swiss watches—crafting for the King of Spain. Friedmann decided that this illustrious history deserved an illustrious future, and he bought the brand.

With earnest determination to restore the name to its proper status, Friedmann focused on creating timepieces of technical innovation and exceptional design. In just a short year and a half, Friedmann has made monumental moves with the brand. In fact, by **2002** Friedmann had a complete line of impressive mechanical timepieces with complex functions and unique patented systems built into them.

THIS PAGE

TOP LEFT
This elegant 18-karat rose-gold GMT Power Reserve watch features numerals raised from the dial metal.

BOTTOM
This pocket watch from the museum in LeLocle, Switzerland, was created by Jacques Gevril.

FACING PAGE

The Avenue of Americas GMT Power Reserve watch is crafted in steel and in an edition of just 500 pieces.

TOP LEFT

These elegant Avenue of Americas watches feature Automatic Date movements. Crafted in steel, they are set with 2.10 carats of Top Wesselton diamonds.

TOP RIGHT

The Gramercy (left) automatic regulator watch offers 40 hours of power reserve. The Chelsea (top) is crafted in steel and houses a 25-jeweled automatic movement. This yellow-gold Madison (right) is shown on a leather strap. The elegant Soho Deluxe (bottom) depicts day, date, month and moonphase readout.

BOTTOM

This striking Madison watch houses a 30-jeweled automatic movement and features a seconds subdial at 6:00. An exhibition caseback allows viewing of the movement.

A perfectionist dedicated to boosting the Gevril name, Friedmann has worked tirelessly with his team of professionals to unveil a collection that recalls the original inspirations of Jacques Gevril. Unlike most other Swiss watch brands, Gevril is headquartered in America—in a spectacular 6,000-square-foot villa replicating Switzerland's finest ateliers. From this location just outside of New York City, Friedmann personally handles all of the logistics of the company. The watchmaking, however, takes place on the outskirts of Bienne, Switzerland. In a traditional watchmaking factory in Tramelan, the movements of Gevril's watches are modified and enhanced, and assembly of the final timepieces is done by hand.

Only 6,000 Gevril watches are created annually in order to maintain exceptional quality throughout the brand. The watches that are crafted in steel are limited to 500 pieces of each model, while those made of 18-karat gold are produced in editions of 100 pieces of each model. Gevril uses only natural mother-of-pearl dials when that is the dial venue of choice, and when choosing diamonds, only Top Wesseltons will do. The crocodile straps on Gevril's watches are cut expertly from the same Louisiana crocodile skin to offer uniform graining.

Among the key lines in the new Gevril collection, the Avenue of Americas incorporates many unique technical innovations including a curved sapphire crystal, curved case, curved dial, comfort beveled back, and raised (not applied or painted) numerals. The Soho is the foundation of the Gevril collection; it is a stunning example of the complete calendar that never goes out of style. The Chelsea is another example of a fabulous, classic day-date-moonphase, and the Gramercy is an updated version of the Regulator, known as one of the most accurate of all automatic timepieces. The Madison features a sub-date with a striking guilloché dial. In a sportier motif, the Sea Cloud line of GMT and chronograph watches prevails, and for women, the elegant Lafayette series of watches with interchangeable straps is individualistic in style.

ABOVE

This chronograph Avenue of Americas watch offers 30-minute and 12-hour counters, and is powered by a 51-jeweled automatic movement.

CENTER

This Avenue of Americas Day-Date-Moonphase watch is crafted in steel and houses a 25-jeweled automatic movement with 40 hours of power reserve.

TOP RIGHT

These two elegant Lafayette timepieces are automatic chronographs equipped with 51-jeweled movements and set with Top Wesslton diamonds.

HIGHLIGHTS

- Building on its premier Avenue of Americas collection of timepieces, Gevril has added several striking new models. Among them: an automatic date watch with a 25-jeweled movement and 45 hours of power reserve; a Day-Date-Month and Moonphase watch; and a GMT.

- Adding to its popular Sea Cloud line of rugged yet chic sports watches, Gevril unveils the GMT date watch or a Chronograph version with anti-glare treatments on both sides of the sapphire crystal.

- Recognizing the impact of color, Gevril has added exotic new hues to the straps and dials of its impressive Lafayette series of bold chronographs for women. Currently, the brand offers more than 25 interchangeable straps for diversity and elegance. The Lafayette Chronograph is now available with a diamond bezel, as well.

- In dedication to the inventions by Jacques Gevril, the brand is creating a special limited-edition tourbillon. After more than a year in research and development, the tourbillon will be produced in an extremely limited series of just 26 pieces to be completed over a two-year period.

- The brand continues to gain international popularity and sports celebrities and film stars are among those taking notice. Plans are in the works for Gevril timepieces to grace actors' wrists on the silver screen.

GEVRIL

LAFAYETTE CHRONOGRAPH — REF. 2911

Movement: automatic, GV-993; 51 jewels; 40-hour autonomy.
Functions: chronograph.
Case: stainless steel 316L; diameter 37mm; bezel set with 56 Top Wesselton diamonds; hesalite crystal; water resistant to 10atm.
Back: decorated stainless steel 316L.
Dial: pink natural mother-of-pearl, raised metallic numerals.

Strap: Louisiana crocodile.
Note: limited edition of 500 pieces.
Suggested Retail: $7,495

LAFAYETTE CHRONOGRAPH — REF. 2916

Movement: automatic, GV-993; 51 jewels; 40-hour autonomy.
Functions: chronograph.
Case: stainless steel, 316L; diameter 37mm; bezel set with 56 Top Wesselton diamonds; water resistant to 10atm.
Back: decorated stainless steel 316L.
Dial: blue natural mother-of-pearl with 8 diamonds.

Strap: Louisiana crocodile.
Note: limited edition of 500 pieces.
Suggested Retail: $8,295

MADISON — REF. 2502

Movement: automatic, GV-834; 30 jewels; 40-hour autonomy.
Functions: subdial second date.
Case: 316L stainless steel; diameter 39mm; sapphire crystal; water resistant to 5atm.
Back: exhibition.
Dial: guilloché silvered.

Strap: Louisiana crocodile.
Also available: 18K gold.
Note: limited edition of 500 pieces.
Suggested Retail: $2,495

MADISON — REF. 2515

Movement: automatic, GV-834; 30 jewels; 40-hour autonomy.
Functions: subdial second date.
Case: 18K yellow gold; diameter 39mm; 18K yellow-gold bezel; sapphire crystal; water resistant to 5atm.
Back: exhibition.
Dial: guilloché silvered.

Bracelet: 18K yellow gold.
Note: limited edition of 100 pieces.
Suggested Retail: $14,495

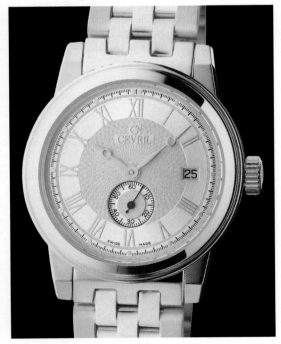

LAFAYETTE CHRONOGRAPH REF. 2919

Movement: automatic, GV-993; 51 jewels; 40-hour autonomy.
Functions: chronograph.
Case: stainless steel 316L; diameter 37mm; bezel set with 56 Top Wesselton diamonds; hesalite crystal; water resistant to 10atm.
Back: decorated stainless steel 316L.
Dial: white natural mother-of-pearl with 8 diamonds.
Strap: Louisiana crocodile.
Note: limited edition of 500 pieces.
Suggested Retail: $8,295

SEA CLOUD DATE AUTOMATIC REF. 3101

Movement: automatic, GV- 1X321; 25 jewels; 40-hour autonomy.
Functions: date.
Case: stainless steel 316L; diameter 40mm; unidirectional stainless steel bezel with raised minutes to control the diver timing; sapphire crystal with anti-glare treatment on both sides; water resistant to 20atm.
Back: screwed back, stainless steel 316L.
Dial: appliques/luminous on black.
Bracelet: stainless steel.
Note: limited edition of 500 pieces.
Suggested Retail: $2,995

SEA CLOUD CHRONOGRAPH REF. 3103

Movement: automatic, GV-7B89; 51 jewels; 40-hour autonomy.
Functions: chronograph.
Case: stainless steel 316L; diameter 40mm; unidirectional stainless steel bezel with raised minutes to control the diver timing; sapphire crystal with anti-glare treatment on both sides; water resistant to 20atm.
Back: screwed back, stainless steel 316L.
Dial: appliques/luminous on black.
Bracelet: stainless steel.
Note: limited edition of 500 pieces.
Suggested Retail: $4,995

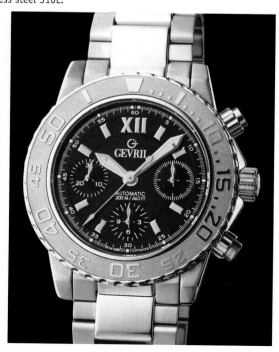

LAFAYETTE CHRONOGRAPH REF. 2913

Movement: automatic, GV-993; 51 jewels; 40-hour autonomy.
Functions: chronograph
Case: stainless steel 316L; diameter 37mm; bezel set with 56 Top Wesselton diamonds; hesalite crystal; water resistant to 10atm.
Back: decorated stainless steel 316L.
Dial: green natural mother-of-pearl, raised metallic numerals.
Strap: Louisiana crocodile.
Note: limited edition of 500 pieces.
Suggested Retail: $7,495

GEVRIL

SEA CLOUD GMT   REF. 3102

Movement: automatic, GV-813Z2; 21 jewels; 40-hour autonomy.
Functions: GMT; date.
Case: stainless steel 316L; diameter 40mm; screwed back; unidirectional stainless steel bezel with raised 24 hours for third time-zone; sapphire crystal with and anti-glare treatment on both sides; water resistant to 20atm.
Dial: appliques/luminous on black.

Bracelet: stainless steel.
Note: limited edition of 500 pieces.
Suggested Retail: $3,995

SEA CLOUD DATE AUTOMATIC   REF. 3104

Movement: automatic, GV-1X321; 25 jewels; 40-hour autonomy.
Functions: date.
Case: stainless steel 316L; diameter 40mm; screwed back; unidirectional 18K gold bezel with raised minutes to control the diver timing; sapphire crystal with anti-glare treatment on both sides; water resistant to 20atm.
Dial: appliques/luminous on black.

Bracelet: stainless steel with logo in 18K gold.
Note: limited edition of 500 pieces.
Suggested Retail: $3,995

SEA CLOUD GMT   REF. 3106

Movement: automatic, GV-813Z2; 21 jewels; 40-hour autonomy.
Functions: GMT; date.
Case: stainless steel 316L; diameter 40mm; screwed back; unidirectional 18K gold bezel with raised 24 hours for third time-zone; sapphire crystal with anti-glare treatment on both sides; water resistant to 20atm.
Dial: appliques/luminous on black.

Bracelet: stainless steel with logo in 18K gold.
Note: limited edition of 500 pieces.
Suggested Retail: $4,995

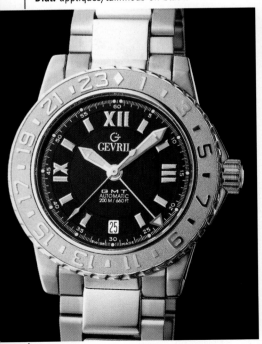

SEA CLOUD CHRONOGRAPH   REF. 3107

Movement: automatic, GV-7B89; 51 jewels; 40-hour autonomy.
Functions: chronograph.
Case: stainless steel 316L; diameter 40mm; unidirectional 18K gold bezel with raised minutes to control diver timing; sapphire crystal with and anti-glare treatment on both sides; water resistant to 20atm.
Dial: appliques/luminous on black.

Bracelet: stainless steel with logo 18K gold.
Note: limited edition of 500 pieces.
Suggested Retail: $5,995

GRAMERCY — REF. 2401

Movement: automatic, GV-182; 31 jewels; 40-hour autonomy.
Functions: regulator automatic.
Case: stainless steel 316L; diameter 39mm; stainless steel bezel; sapphire crystal; water resistant to 5atm.
Back: exhibition.
Dial: guilloché silvered.
Bracelet: stainless steel.
Note: limited edition of 500 pieces.
Suggested Retail: $3,995

GRAMERCY — REF. 2402

Movement: GV-182; 31 jewels; 40-hour autonomy.
Functions: regulator automatic.
Case: 18K yellow gold; diameter 39mm; 18K yellow-gold bezel; sapphire crystal; water resistant to 5atm.
Back: exhibition.
Dial: guilloché silvered.
Strap: Louisiana crocodile.
Note: limited edition of 500 pieces.
Suggested Retail: $3,495

CHELSEA — REF. 2305

Movement: automatic, GV-934; 25 jewels; 40-hour autonomy.
Functions: complete calendar, day/date/month; moonphase.
Case: 18K yellow gold; diameter 39mm; 18K yellow-gold bezel; sapphire crystal; water resistant to 5atm.
Back: exhibition.
Dial: guilloché silvered.
Strap: Louisiana crocodile.
Note: limited edition of 100 pieces.
Suggested Retail: $8,495

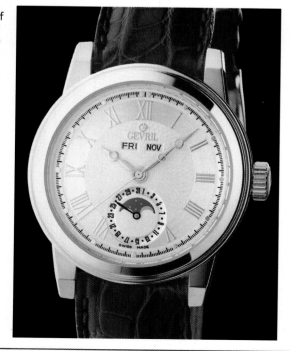

CHELSEA — REF. 2302

Movement: automatic, GV-934; 25 jewels; 40-hour autonomy.
Functions: complete calendar, day/date/month; moonphase.
Case: stainless steel 316L; diameter 39mm; stainless steel bezel; sapphire crystal; water resistant to 5atm.
Back: exhibition.
Dial: guilloché silvered.
Strap: Louisiana crocodile.
Note: limited edition of 500 pieces.
Suggested Retail: $3,995

GEVRIL

SOHO DELUXE   REF. 2605

Movement: automatic, GV-613; 25 jewels; 40-hour autonomy.
Functions: complete calendar, day/date/month; moonphase.
Case: 18K yellow gold; diameter 39mm; 18K yellow-gold bezel; sapphire crystal; water resistant to 5atm.
Back: exhibition.
Dial: guilloché silvered.

Strap: Louisiana crocodile.
Note: limited edition of 100 pieces.
Suggested Retail: $9,995

SOHO DELUXE   REF. 2602

Movement: automatic, GV-613; 25 jewels; 40-hour autonomy.
Functions: complete calendar, day/date/month; moonphase.
Case: stainless steel 316L; diameter 39mm; stainless steel bezel; sapphire crystal; water resistant to 5atm.
Back: exhibition.
Dial: guilloché silvered.

Strap: Louisiana crocodile.
Note: limited edition of 500 pieces.
Suggested Retail: $4,495

AVENUE OF AMERICAS DATE AUTOMATIC   REF. 5004

Movement: automatic, GV-AOM3J1; 25 jewels; 40-hour autonomy; Incabloc, Adouci and engraved.
Functions: date.
Case: stainless steel 316L; size 44mm x 34mm; polished steel bezel; exclusive sapphire crystal; water resistant to 5atm.
Back: sapphire crystal.

Dial: blue with luminous numerals.
Strap: Louisiana crocodile.
Note: limited edition of 500 pieces.
Suggested Retail: $4,595

AVENUE OF AMERICAS DATE AUTOMATIC   REF. 5101

Movement: automatic, GV-AOM3J1; 25 jewels; 40-hour autonomy; Incabloc, Adouci and engraved.
Functions: date.
Case: 18K rose gold; size 44mm x 34mm; 18K rose-gold bezel; exclusive sapphire crystal; water resistant to 5atm.
Back: sapphire crystal.

Dial: black with raised rose-gold numerals.
Strap: Louisiana crocodile with 18K rose-gold buckle.
Note: limited edition of 00-99.
Suggested Retail: $8,495

AVENUE OF AMERICAS GMT POWER RESERVE   REF. 5024

Movement: automatic, GV-AOAX32; 25 jewels; 40-hour autonomy; Incabloc, Adouci and engraved.
Functions: GMT; power reserve; date.
Case: stainless steel 316L; size 44mm x 34mm; sapphire crystal caseback; polished steel bezel, exclusive sapphire crystal.
Dial: blue with luminous numerals.
Strap: Louisiana crocodile.
Note: limited edition of 500 pieces.
Suggested Retail: $7,995

AVENUE OF AMERICAS GLAMOUR DATE AUTOMATIC   REF. 6207V

Movement: automatic, GV-AOM3J1; 25 jewels; 40-hour autonomy; Incabloc, Adouci and engraved.
Functions: date.
Case: stainless steel 316L with 2.10 carats of Top Wesselton diamonds on polished steel bezel and sides; size 44mm x 34mm; exclusive sapphire crystal; water resistant to 5atm.
Back: sapphire crystal.
Dial: silver with blue mother-of-pearl, raised stainless steel numerals and hands.
Strap: Louisiana crocodile.
Note: limited edition of 100 pieces.
Suggested Retail: $14,995

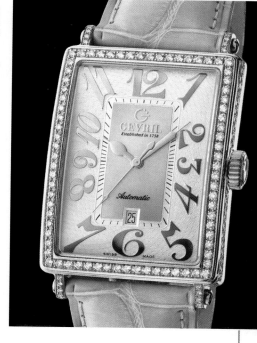

AVENUE OF AMERICAS GLAMOUR DATE AUTOMATIC   REF. 6205V

Movement: automatic, GV-AOM3J1; 25 jewels; 40-hour autonomy; Incabloc, Adouci and engraved.
Functions: date.
Case: stainless steel 316L; diameter 44mm x 34mm; sapphire crystal caseback; polished steel bezel with 2.10 carats of Top Wesselton diamonds on bezel and sides; exclusive sapphire crystal; water resistant to 5atm.
Dial: silver with pink mother-of-pearl, raised rose-gold numerals and hands.
Strap: Louisiana crocodile.
Note: limited edition of 100 pieces.
Suggested Retail: $14,995

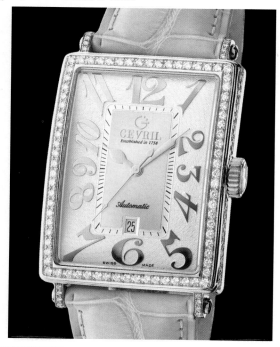

AVENUE OF AMERICAS GMT POWER RESERVE   REF. 5025

Movement: automatic, GV-AOAX32; 25 jewels; 40-hour autonomy; Incabloc, Adouci and engraved.
Functions: GMT; power reserve; date.
Case: stainless steel 316L; size 44mm x 34mm; polished steel bezel; exclusive sapphire crystal; water resistant to 5atm.
Back: sapphire crystal.
Dial: Silver with raised rose-gold numerals and hands.
Strap: Louisiana crocodile.
Note: limited edition of 500 pieces.
Suggested Retail: $7,995

GEVRIL

AVENUE OF AMERICAS GMT POWER RESERVE — REF. 5121

Movement: automatic, GV-AOAX32; 25 jewels; 40-hour autonomy; Incabloc, Adouci and engraved.
Functions: GMT; power reserve; date.
Case: 18K rose gold; size 44mm x 34mm; 18K rose-gold bezel; exclusive sapphire crystal; water resistant to 5atm.
Back: sapphire crystal.

Dial: black with raised rose-gold numerals.
Strap: Louisiana crocodile with 18K rose-gold buckle.
Note: limited edition of 00-99.
Suggested Retail: $12,995

AVENUE OF AMERICAS DATE AUTOMATIC — REF 5005

Movement: automatic, GV-AOM3J1; 25 jewels; 40-hour autonomy; Incabloc, Adouci and engraved.
Functions: date.
Case: stainless steel 316L; size 44mm x 34mm; polished steel bezel; exclusive sapphire crystal; water resistant to 5atm.
Back: sapphire crystal.

Dial: Silver with raised rose-gold numerals and hands.
Strap: Louisiana crocodile.
Note: limited edition of 500 pieces.
Suggested Retail: $4,595

AVENUE OF AMERICAS DAY-DATE-MOONPHASE — REF. 5035

Movement: automatic, GV-AOA71L; 25 jewels; 40-hour autonomy; Incabloc, Adouci and engraved.
Functions: day/date/month; moonphase.
Case: stainless steel 316L; size 44mm x 34mm; polished steel bezel; exclusive sapphire crystal; water resistant to 5atm.
Back: sapphire crystal.

Dial: Silver with raised rose-gold numerals and hands.
Strap: Louisiana crocodile.
Note: limited edition of 500 pieces.
Suggested Retail: $9,495

AVENUE OF AMERICAS DAY-DATE-MOONPHASE — REF. 5131

Movement: automatic GV-AOA71L; 25 jewels; 40-hour autonomy; Incabloc, Adouci and engraved.
Functions: day/date/month; moonphase.
Case: 18K rose gold; size 44mm x 34mm; 18K rose-gold bezel; exclusive sapphire crystal; water resistant to 5atm.
Back: sapphire crystal.

Dial: black with raised rose-gold numerals.
Strap: Louisiana crocodile with 18K rose-gold buckle.
Note: limited edition of 00-99.
Suggested Retail: $15,995

AVENUE OF AMERICAS DAY-DATE-MOONPHASE — REF. 5034

Movement: automatic, GV-AOA71L; 25 jewels; 40-hour autonomy; Incabloc, Adouci and engraved.
Functions: day/date/month; moonphase.
Case: stainless steel 316L; size 44mm x 34mm; polished steel bezel; exclusive sapphire crystal; water resistant to 5atm.
Back: sapphire crystal.
Dial: blue with luminous numerals.
Strap: Louisiana crocodile.
Note: limited edition of 500 pieces.
Suggested Retail: $9,495

AVENUE OF AMERICAS CHRONOGRAPH — REF. 5015

Movement: automatic, GV-AOAWZ1; 51 jewels; 40-hour autonomy; Incabloc, Adouci and engraved.
Functions: chronograph, 30-minute, 12-hour counters.
Case: stainless steel 316L; size 44mm x 34mm; polished steel bezel; exclusive sapphire crystal; water resistant to 5atm.
Back: sapphire crystal.
Dial: silver with raised rose-gold hands and numerals.
Strap: Louisiana crocodile.
Note: limited edition of 500 pieces.
Suggested Retail: $6,995

AVENUE OF AMERICAS CHRONOGRAPH — REF. 5111

Movement: automatic, GV-AOAWZ1; 51 jewels; 40-hour autonomy; Incabloc, Adouci and engraved.
Functions: chronograph, 30-minute, 12-hour counters.
Case: 18K rose gold; size 44mm x 34mm; 18K rose-gold bezel; exclusive sapphire crystal; water resistant to 5atm.
Back: sapphire crystal.
Dial: black with raised raised rose-gold numerals.
Strap: Louisiana crocodile with 18K rose-gold buckle.
Note: limited edition of 00-99.
Suggested Retail: $10,995

AVENUE OF AMERICAS CHRONOGRAPH — REF. 5014

Movement: automatic, GV-AOAWZ1; 51 jewels; 40-hour autonomy; Incabloc, Adouci and engraved.
Functions: chronograph, 30-minute, 12-hour counters.
Case: stainless steel 316L; size 44mm x 34mm; polished steel bezel; exclusive sapphire crystal; water resistant to 5atm.
Back: sapphire crystal.
Dial: blue with luminous numerals.
Strap: Louisiana crocodile.
Note: limited edition of 500 pieces.
Suggested Retail: $6,995

GIRARD-PERREGAUX

e ngineering and architecture define the style of Girard-Perregaux, a highly respected yet relatively low-profile manufacturer in the upper echelons of watchmaking known as Haute Horlogerie.

THIS PAGE

TOP LEFT
Girard-Perregaux made watchmaking history in 1867 with a spectacular precision movement on three bridges that holds the barrel, the train and the balance. The original tourbillon chronometer won a first-class rating and a prize from the Neuchâtel Observatory.

BOTTOM LEFT
Dubbed the "ww.tc," this striking watch displays the time around the world and features a day/night ring.

BOTTOM RIGHT
In 1854, Constant Girard married Marie Perregaux; two years later the pair established Girard-Perregaux.

FACING PAGE
Girard-Perregaux has fitted its elegant Tourbillon with three gold Bridges into this rectangular Vintage 1945 case.

This venerable company, with associations dating to the famous Geneva horologist Jean François Bautte in the late **18**th century, has had its ups and downs since watchmaker Constant Girard married watchmaking heiress Marie Perregaux and established a factory in La Chaux-de-Fonds in **1856**.

The company's most remarkable product was first launched in **1867** and remains an integral player in Girard-Perregaux's creations. The Tourbillon with three gold Bridges is a stunning rendition of supreme watchmaking technique that exemplifies horology's highest ideals.

Girard-Perregaux survived the quartz shock, largely because it had a reputation for realizing far-sighted ideas, like producing 2,000 wristwatches for the Kaiser's navy in **1880**, and creating the first balance to chop the second into tenths. In **1969** it out-paced Switzerland's Beta project in the race to develop the first popular quartz movement by establishing the now standard frequency for quartz oscillators—32.768Hz.

Despite the esteem with which it had been regarded, Girard-Perregaux was at low ebb when it was acquired in **1992** by a minority shareholder, Italian architect Dr. Luigi "Gino" Macaluso.

Almost immediately, Macaluso embarked upon a huge and costly luxury—the design, construction, production engineering, and series manufacture of the brand's own automatic watch movements. To the rest of the watch industry, it made about as much economic sense as an airline building its own planes. But to Macaluso, Girard-Perregaux could only be credible as a complete manufacturer.

His gamble has paid off. Girard-Perregaux was a $12-million company when Macaluso acquired the brand; today annual sales exceed $100 million on a production of some 20,000 watches.

The majority of the brand's production line is equipped with the company's own movements. Girard-Perregaux's 3000 series automatic caliber is in its second generation (serving a range of models from simple watches to split-seconds chronographs) and now the brand is producing the 1900 series—a new, bigger caliber. Only a handful of watch brands can claim the status of "Manufacture" and Girard-Perregaux is the smallest and most recherché of this horological elite.

Macaluso's office is a shrine to the obsessions that have driven the company for the past decade—Ferrari engines and the architecture of Le Corbusier (1887-1965), La Chaux-de-Fonds's most celebrated son. Perfect half-scale models of Ferrari's celebrated V-12s, including the legendary 250 3-liter, line the walls. His office is in the eaves of the company's 1948 factory building, sharing the privileged domain of the "gods." This is where Girard-Perregaux's elite watchmakers are housed, each of whom will spend the best part of a year building and adjusting a single three-bridge tourbillon comprising horology's most fascinating complications.

Despite its small size, Girard-Perregaux strives to make the widest variety of models available to enthusiasts. A watch is a very personal object and the brand does not wish to impose a single design identity, even with the company's best selling model. The Vintage 1945 rectangular watch, based on a 1940s style, meets the current vogue for a period look. Likewise inspired by a former model—a 1970s dress watch—the Classique Elégance collection meets the needs of business travel with time-zone indicators, alarms and chronographs.

Among the most spectacular Girard-Perregaux watches are the models dedicated to the Scuderia Ferrari, especially the three-button split-seconds chronograph foudroyante. A red hand (driven by an additional escapement) flies around a one-second dial and stops on the nearest eighth of a second.

In styling his watches, Macaluso seeks to achieve the restrained and studied elegance of Le Corbusier's machine aesthetic. "You don't wear a Girard-Perregaux to show off," he says. "It's more a state of mind than a status symbol."

Macaluso has restored one of La Chaux-de-Fonds's finest buildings—the 1918 Villa Marguerite—into a Girard-Perregaux museum to showcase two centuries of original watchmaking.

Today, Girard-Perregaux is secure in its position as a cultural symbol of a town that produces the world's most precise electronic and micro-mechanical components for watches, aerospace and medical instruments.

TOP LEFT
Dr. Luigi Macaluso.

LEFT
Girard-Perregaux's slim automatic caliber, launched in 1994, maintains the company's credibility as a Manufacture that designs and builds the movements of its watches.

ABOVE
This elegant Lady's chronograph has been intricately set with diamonds for ultimate appeal.

BOTTOM LEFT
This elegant Vintage Grand Date watch is crafted in 18-karat gold and features a date aperture at 12:00 and an exquisite moonphase dial at 6:00.

BOTTOM RIGHT
In classic styling, this Vintage Power Reserve watch offers a date window in an off-centered position at the top of the dial, the seconds readout is displayed at 9:00 and the power reserve indicator spans from 3:00 to 6:00 in all its glory.

- Focused on haute horlogerie—the roots of its being—Girard-Perregaux recently unveiled stunning new masterpieces including a limited-edition set of platinum watches. Only 50 sets will be created. Each watch is set and sold in a spectacular wood presentation case, and consists of three different platinum timepieces: a flyback chronograph, a perpetual calendar watch with moonphase display, and a power reserve with grand date.
Each of these exquisite watches houses Girard-Perregaux's sophisticated mechanical movements—hand engraved and hand finished to perfection.

- The brand has also unveiled the Tourbillon with three gold Bridges in its highly distinctive Vintage 1945 case. It is created in 18-karat yellow, pink or white gold, and in an exclusive platinum version.

- To its elegant Classique collection, the brand has added the Classique 2002 automatic watch with moonphase indicator and large date.

- The brand has also unveiled several Sea Hawk II models. First registered by Girard-Perregaux in 1959, the Sea Hawk trademark designates the brand's marine products. The Sea Hawk II, available in either a 40- or 42mm size, is equipped with a Girard-Perregaux automatic movement with 50+ hours of power reserve, and is crafted in either steel or titanium.

- The "Sea Hawk II to John Harrison" watch is dedicated to the 18th-century watchmaker who developed the ship's chronometer for determining longitude at sea. Crafted in 18-karat white, yellow or pink gold and in stainless steel, the watch features a power-reserve indicator, small subseconds hand and date window.

- For women, the new Lady Richeville Chronograph houses an automatic movement and features a sapphire caseback for viewing of the column-wheel chronograph mechanism with gold rotor.

TOP LEFT
The Classique 2002 model houses the company's own 3000 series automatic caliber with moonphase and a large date with separate digits.

TOP CENTER
The Richeville chronograph houses Girard-Perregaux's automatic movement and offers date aperture at 4:00.

TOP RIGHT
This striking XXL Split Seconds Chronograph watch featurse an extremely precise movement with flyback function for multiple timing. It is housed in an extra large case for dramatic boldness.

RIGHT CENTER
The Sea Hawk II is a fully functional diver's watch with large luminous markings, water-resistance to 300 meters and a unidirectional bezel.

BOTTOM RIGHT
The Sea Hawk II to John Harrison chronograph features power-reserve indicator and date window.

GIRARD-PERREGAUX

VINTAGE 1945 TOURBILLON with THREE GOLD BRIDGES   REF. 008PR2002

Movement: mechanical, automatic-winding, GP 9600 caliber, with tourbillon device mounted on three 18K pink-gold bridges, over 40 hours' autonomy; 21,600 vph. Platinum micro-rotor mounted under the winding barrel (patented system). Rhodium-plated and chased pillar-plate and barrel cover. Realized, finished and decorated entirely by hand by the firm's watch-makers. **Functions:** hour, minute, small second.

Case: 18K pink-gold, three-piece square, anatomically curved case (size 32x32mm, thickness 12.5mm); antireflective curved sapphire crystal; pink-gold crown; snap-on back. Water resistant to 3atm.
Dial: made up of the silvered rhodium-plated brass pillar-plate with vertical engravings, the three arrow-shaped tourbillon bridges in solid pink gold, cut out on the chased barrel and the tourbillon, pink-gold Dauphine hands.
Indications: small seconds at 6 integrated with the tourbillon carriage.
Strap: crocodile leather, hand-stitched; pink-gold fold-over clasp.
Also available: in yellow and gray gold; in platinum.

VINTAGE 1945 CHRONOGRAPHE À RATTRAPANTE FOUDROYANTE   REF. 90210

Movement: automatic, GP 8020 caliber (Valjoux 7750 base + foudroyante Jacquet Baume module), 45 hours power reserve, 13''', 40 jewels; 28,800 vph. Decorated with Côtes de Genève pattern and beveled. Modified, finished and decorated by hand by the firm's watchmakers.
Functions: hour, minute; split-second chronograph with three counters and "foudroyante" feature.

Case: 18K yellow-gold, rectangular anatomically curved three-piece case (size 36.8x36mm, thickness 15.3mm), antireflective curved sapphire crystal; gold crown and rectangular pushers (splitting pusher coaxial with the crown); back attached by 4 screws. Water resistant to 3atm.
Dial: matte ivory; applied gold-plated brass Arabic numerals; gold-plated brass leaf-style hands.
Indications: minute counter at 3; eighths-of-a-second counter with red "foudroyante" hand at 9; center split-second counters; minute track with divisions for 1/5 of a second.
Strap: crocodile leather, hand-stitched; gold fold-over clasp.
Also available: pink or white gold; black dial, luminescent markers and hands.

VINTAGE 1945 CHRONOGRAPH   REF. 02599

Movement: automatic, GP 3080 caliber (Ø 23.3, thickn. 6.28mm, base + chronograph module with column wheel), 36 hours' autonomy; 38 jewels; 28,800 vph. Finished and decorated by hand by the firm's watchmakers.
Functions: hour, minute, small-second; chronograph with two counters.
Case: 18K white-gold, rectangular anatomically curved three-piece case (size 31x30, thickness 13mm); bezel with set brilliants; antireflective curved sapphire

crystal; white-gold crown and rectangular pushers; snap-on back attached. Water resistant to 3atm.
Dial: natural solid mother-of-pearl; cambered, applied white-gold-plated brass Arabic numerals; white-gold-plated brass Dauphine hands, railway minute track. **Indications:** minute counter at 3; small-seconds at 9; center second counter; minute track. **Strap:** crocodile leather, hand-stitched; white-gold fold-over clasp. **Also available:** without brilliants in yellow, pink or white gold with strap or bracelet; in pink gold with anthracite or silvered guilloché dial, applied numerals; in yellow, pink or white gold with anthracite or silvered dial and applied markers or black with applied Arabic numerals.

VINTAGE 1945 GRAND DATE   REF. 25800

Movement: mechanical, automatic-winding, GP 3330 caliber with 50 hours' autonomy; 12'''1/2, 32 jewels. Balance for 28,800 vph. Decorated with Côtes de Genève pattern and beveled. Modified, mounted, adjusted, finished and decorated by hand by the firm's watchmakers.
Functions: hour, minute, small-second; date; moonphase.
Case: 18K pink-gold, square anatomically curved two-piece case (size 32x32mm, thickness 11.6mm), antireflective

curved sapphire crystal; pink-gold crown; one corrector on the middle; back attached by 4 screws, displaying the movement through a sapphire crystal. Water resistant to 3atm.
Dial: blue, brushed with sun pattern; luminescent Arabic numerals; white printed railway minute track; pink-gold-plated brass Dauphine hands.
Indications: small-seconds and moonphase at 6; oversized double-disc date at 12.
Strap: crocodile leather, hand-stitched; pink-gold fold-over clasp.
Also available: in pink or yellow gold; black or cream-colored dial, 3 applied markers; in white gold with silvered dial.

VINTAGE 1945 POWER RESERVE   REF. 25850

Movement: mechanical, automatic-winding, GP 33R0 caliber, 50 hours' autonomy; 27 jewels, 11'''1/2; 28,800 vph. Beveled and decorated with Côtes de Genève pattern. Modified, mounted, adjusted, finished and decorated entirely by hand by the firm's watchmakers. **Functions:** hour, minute, small second; date; power reserve. **Case:** 18K yellow-gold, three-piece square anatomically curved case (size 32x32mm, thickness 11.7 mm); antireflective curved sapphire crystal; yellow-gold crown; back fastened by 4 screws, displaying the movement through a sapphire crystal. Water resistant to 3 atm.
Dial: black, engine-turned (guilloché), flat reserve sector; silvered small-second counter decorated with circular beads; luminescent Arabic numerals, white printed railway minute track; luminescent gold-plated brass Dauphine hands.
Indications: date with lens between 1 and 2; power reserve between 4 and 5; small seconds at 9.
Strap: crocodile leather, hand-stitched; yellow-gold fold-over clasp.
Also available: in white gold with slate-gay dial; in yellow, pink and white gold with black or silvered dial and applied Arabic numerals.

VINTAGE 1945 DATE, SMALL SECOND   REF. 25830

Movement: mechanical, automatic-winding, GP 3200 caliber 10'''1/2), 42 hours' autonomy; 27 jewels; 28,800 vph. Beveled and decorated with Côtes de Genève pattern. Finished and decorated by hand by the firm's watchmakers.
Functions: hour, minute, small second; date.
Case: stainless steel, three-piece square anatomically curved case (size 32x32mm, thickness 11.3mm); antireflective curved sapphire crystal; steel crown; back fastened with 4 screws, displaying the movement through a sapphire crystal. Water resistant to 3atm.
Dial: matte black, luminescent bâton markers, 6 and 12 luminescent Arabic numerals, white printed circular railway minute track with divisions by five minutes; white enameled brass Sports hands.
Indications: date between 1 and 2; small seconds at 9.
Strap: crocodile leather, hand-stitched; steel fold-over clasp.
Unique version.

VINTAGE 1945 DATE, SMALL SECOND   REF. 25960

Movement: automatic, GP 3200 caliber, 42 hours' autonomy; 27 jewels, 10'''1/2; 28,800 vph. Beveled and decorated with Côtes de Genève pattern. Finished and decorated by hand by the firm's watchmakers.
Functions: hour, minute, small second; date.
Case: 18K yellow-gold, two-piece square anatomically curved case (size 28x28mm, thickness 8.9mm); antireflective curved sapphire crystal; gold crown; snap-on back displaying the movement through a sapphire crystal. Water resistant to 3atm.
Dial: silvered, engine-turned (guilloché) center, curved; applied gold-plated brass Arabic numerals and triangular markers, printed minute track; gold-plated brass Dauphine hands.
Indications: date at 6; small seconds at 9.
Strap: crocodile leather, hand-stitched; gold clasp.
Also available: with bracelet; with black dial and luminescent or applied Arabic numerals; with anthracite dial and applied markers; in pink gold; in white gold with pink, yellow, green, blue dial and applied Arabic numerals, leather strap or bracelet.

VINTAGE 1945 LADY   REF. 25730

Movement: mechanical, automatic-winding, GP _____ caliber (ETA _____ caliber base), 36 hours' autonomy; 17 jewels; 21,600 vph. Beveled and decorated with Côtes de Genève pattern. Finished and decorated by hand by the firm's watchmakers.
Functions: hour, minute, second.
Case: 18K pink-gold, two-piece rectangular anatomically curved case (size 22.5x26.5mm, thickness 9.65mm); antireflective curved sapphire crystal; steel crown; back fastened with 4 screws, displaying the movement through a sapphire crystal. Water resistant to 3atm.
Dial: matte slate-gray, cambered, luminescent pink-gold-plated brass Roman numerals applied at quarters and eight round markers with set brilliants, black printed rectangular railway minute track; luminescent pink-gold-plated brass leaf-style hands.
Strap: crocodile leather, hand-stitched; pink-gold fold-over clasp.
Also available: in yellow or white gold. With quartz movement in yellow, pink or white gold or in steel.

GIRARD-PERREGAUX

OPERA TWO   REF. 99740

Movement: mechanical, manual-winding, GP 9897 caliber, with tourbillon device mounted on three 18K pink-gold bridges, 37 jewels; 21,600 vph. Westminster Carillon sonnerie with four hammers and four gongs tuned to the notes E-C-D-G. Realized, finished and decorated totally by hand by the firm's watchmakers. **Functions:** hour, minute; minute repeater; chime; perpetual calendar (date, day, month, year). **Case:** platinum, polished and brushed three-piece case (Ø 41.5mm,

thickness 14.5mm); antireflective curved sapphire crystal; repeater slide on the middle; white-gold crown; cambered back attached by 6 screws, displaying the movement through a sapphire crystal.
Dial: grained, silvered; aperture on the tourbillon and on three carillon hammers G, C, D (E is hidden); applied white-gold pointed markers; white-gold subdial crowns; white-gold-plated brass Dauphine hands; printed railway minute track.
Indications: date at 3; day at 9; month and four-year cycle at 12.
Strap: crocodile leather, hand-stitched; white-gold fold-over clasp.
10 pieces produced per year. **Also available:** in yellow, pink or white gold.

TOURBILLON WITH THREE GOLD BRIDGES AUTOMATIC   REF. 99250

Movement: mechanical, automatic-winding, GP Manufacture 9600 caliber, with tourbillon device mounted on three 18K pink-gold bridges, over 40 hours' autonomy; 21,600 vph. Platinum micro-rotor mounted under the winding barrel (patented system). Rhodium-plated and chased pillar-plate and barrel cover. Realized, finished and decorated entirely by hand by the firm's watchmakers.

Functions: hour, minute, small second.
Case: 18K pink-gold, three-piece case (Ø 38mm, thickness 10mm), polished and brushed finish; antireflective flat sapphire crystal; pink-gold crown; back attached by 6 screws. Water resistant to 3atm.
Dial: 3 solid gold tourbillon bridges, arabesqued pillar-plate, barrel and tourbillon are all visible; pink-gold Dauphine hands.
Indications: small second at 6 integrated in the tourbillon carriage.
Strap: crocodile leather, hand-stitched; pink-gold clasp.
Also available: in yellow or white gold; in platinum.

PETIT TOURBILLON   REF. 99020

Movement: mechanical, automatic-winding, GP 9700 caliber, with tourbillon device mounted on three 18K pink-gold bridges, 75 hours' autonomy; 21,600 vph; 20 jewels. Silvered and chased pillar-plate. Realized, finished and decorated entirely by hand by the firm's watchmakers.
Functions: hour and minute.
Case: 18K pink-gold, three-piece case (Ø 31mm, thickness 9mm); antireflec-

tive curved sapphire crystal; pink-gold crown; back attached by 7 screws. Water resistant to 3atm.
Dial: 3 solid gold tourbillon bridges, guilloché pillar-plate, barrel and tourbillon are all visible; blued steel leaf-style hands.
Strap: crocodile leather, hand-stitched; pink-gold clasp.
Also available: in yellow or white gold; in platinum.

CLASSIQUE ELEGANCE CHRONO WW.TC   REF. 49800

Movement: automatic, GP 3387 cal. (GP 3100 base + chronograph and world-time modules), 45 hours' autonomy; 63 jewels. 18K gold rotor. Decorated with Côtes de Genève pattern and beveled. Realized and finished by hand by the firm's watchmakers. **Functions:** hour, minute, small second; date; world time, 24 hours; chronograph with 3 counters. **Case:** titanium three-piece case (Ø 43mm, thick. 14mm), brushed finish; antireflective curved sapphire crystal; screw-down

Reduced by 5%

crowns (at 9 for town disc control) and rectangular titanium pushers; back attached by 6 screws, displaying the movement through a sapphire crystal. Water resistant to 3atm.
Dial: matte black; luminescent applied white-gold-plated cabochon markers (Arabic 12); luminescent white-gold-plated leaf-style hands.
Indications: date between 1 and 2; small second at 3; hour counter at 6; minute counter at 9; center sec. counter; minute track; day-night 24-hour ring turning together with the main time; turning ring with reference-town names for 24 time zones.
Strap: crocodile leather, hand-stitched; titanium clasp. **Also available:** with titanium bracelet; in yellow, pink or white gold with strap or bracelet.

SPORT CLASSIQUE CHRONOGRAPH RETOUR EN VOL   REF. 49580

Movement: mechanical, automatic-winding, GP 337A caliber (GP 3100 base + fly-back chronograph module developed on an exclusive basis by Dubois Dépraz), 13''', autonomy 50 hours, 63 jewels; 28,800 vph. Decorated with Côtes de Genève pattern and beveled. Modified, mounted, regulated, finished and decorated by hand by the firm's watchmakers. **Functions:** hour, minute, small second; date; fly-back chronograph with 3 counters. **Case:** stainless steel, three-piece case (Ø 40mm, thickness 13mm); antireflective curved sapphire crystal; steel crown and pushers; back attached by 7 screws, displaying the movement through a sapphire crystal. Water resistant to 3atm.

Dial: glossy black; subdials decorated with circular beads, applied rhodium-plated brass bâton markers (Arabic 12); luminescent rhodium-plated brass leaf-style hands.

Indications: small second at 3; date between 4 and 5; hour counter at 6; minute counter at 9; center fly-back second counter; minute track; tachometer scale.

Strap: crocodile leather, hand-stitched; steel clasp.

Also available: with steel bracelet: in pink or white gold with strap or bracelet; with black or cream-colored dial.

GP POUR FERRARI S.F. FOUDROYANTE   REF. 90200

Movement: automatic, GP 8020 caliber, 13''', 45 hours' autonomy; 40 jewels; 28,800 vph. Decorated with Côtes de Genève pattern and beveled. Modified, hand-finished and decorated by the firm's watchmakers. **Functions:** hour, minute; split-second chronograph with two counters and "foudroyante" feature. **Case:** 18K yellow-gold, three-piece case (Ø 40mm, thickness 14.6mm), polished and brushed finish; antireflective curved sapphire crystal; gold crown and pushers (splitting pusher coaxial with the crown); back attached by 7 screws with engraved "1929-1999." Water resistant to 3atm. **Dial:** ivory; applied gold-plated brass triangular markers and Arabic numerals; gold-plated brass leaf-style hands.

Indications: minute counter at 3; eighths-of-a-second counter with "foudroyante" hand at 9; center split-second counters; minute track with divisions for 1/5 of a second; tachometer scale.

Strap: crocodile leather, hand-stitched; gold fold-over clasp. Limited ed. of 750 numbered pcs; delivered in a special case.

Also available: pink or white gold; platinum, leather strap; black dial, applied markers or luminescent Arab. numerals; titanium, carbon fiber dial.

GP POUR FERRARI "275 LE MANS"   REF. 80900.0.11.6741

Movement: mechanical, automatic-winding, GP 2280 caliber (ETA base + chronograph module by Dubois Dépraz), autonomy 36 hours, 48 jewels; 28,800 vph. Modified, mounted, regulated, finished and decorated by hand by the firm's watchmakers.

Functions: hour, minute, small second; 24 hour; chronograph with 3 counters. **Case:** stainless steel, three-piece case (Ø 40mm, thickness 14mm) with polished and brushed finish; antireflective curved sapphire crystal; back attached by 8 screws. Water resistant to 5atm.

Dial: matte black; silvered subdials decorated with circular beads, luminescent bâton markers (Arabic 12); luminescent white enameled bâton hands.

Indications: small second at 3; hour counter at 6; 24 hours at 9; center minute counter (with red arrow-tip hand) and second counter; minute track with divisions for 1/5 of a second; tachometer scale.

Strap: crocodile leather, hand-stitched; steel clasp.

Also available: with rubber strap; with steel bracelet.

Note: total edition of 2,000 pieces.

GP POUR FERRARI "F1-2000"   REF. 49590.0.11.1749

Movement: automatic, GP 3370 caliber (GP 3300 + chronograph module), 13''', auton. 45h, 57 jewels; 28,800 vph. Decorated with Côtes de Genève pattern and beveled. Realized and finished by hand by the firm's watchmakers. **Functions:** hour, minute, small second; date; chronograph with 3 counters. **Case:** stainless steel, 3-piece case (Ø 40, thick. 13mm); antireflective curved sapphire crystal; back fastened by 8 steel screws with an engraving showing the car that won the 2000 Formula 1 World Championship. Water resistant to 3atm.

Dial: silvered, red enameled zones; luminescent rhodium-plated brass bâton markers (12 Arabic) and hands.

Indications: small sec. at 3; between 4 and 5; hour counter at 6; minute counter at 9; center second counter; minute track with divisions for 1/5 of a sec. and tachometer scale.

Strap: rubber; steel buckle. 2,001 pieces in total. Wooden case with "Ferrari red" lacquer.

Also av: carbon fiber or silvered dial with black zones; yellow, rubber or crocodile strap, bracelet; in white gold with ivory or anthracite dial and silvered zones; coconut fiber strap or white-gold bracelet; in yellow gold with cream-colored or anthracite dial with silvered zones, in pink gold with cream-colored dial, crocodile strap or bracelet.

GIRARD-PERREGAUX

THE SEA HAWK II TO JOHN HARRISON

As a special version meant as a tribute to John Harrison, this model features a dial reminiscent of a marine chronometer. John Harrison (1693–1776), a carpenter's son, was a self-taught watchmaker living at a time when the British were building their empire based on their military and commercial maritime power. Like every other navy of the period, however, the British had its Achilles heel: the inability of mariners to determine their exact positions at sea. By using the sun and stars, they were able to calculate latitude but not longitude. The

Admiralty realized that it could no longer sustain the massive losses in human life and cargo brought about by this deficiency. In 1714, Queen Anne's Government offered a high reward to whomever invented a reliable method to calculate longitude. John Harrison discovered that the precise reading of a ship's longitude depended on knowing the exact time. He therefore undertook the construction of clocks and then watches that were far more accurate than any in use at the time, and had them tested at sea by, among others, Captain Cook. Experiments proved Harrison's original thesis to be correct. Thus, the marine chronometer had been born. After numerous trials, Harrison's invention was accepted by the Government.

SEA HAWK II ®   REF. 49900.0.11.2042

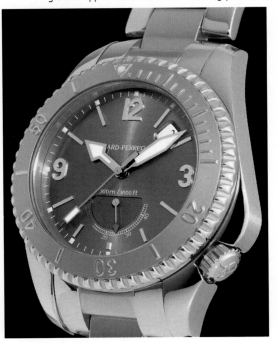

Movement: mechanical, automatic-winding. Modified, mounted, regulated and decorated by hand by the firm's watchmakers. **Functions:** hour, minute, second; date; power reserve. **Case:** stainless steel, three-piece case (Ø 42mm, thickness 13.65mm) with polished and brushed finish; antireflective flat sapphire crystal; counter-clockwise-turning white-gold ring with polished or knurled rim and grained upper face with a scale showing polished embossments; recessed screw-down crown at 4 with raised case protection; back attached by 6 screws. Water resistant to 30atm. **Dial:** ruthenium gray, brushed with a sun pattern; guilloché reserve subdial; applied rhodium-plated brass bâton markers and Arabic numerals; luminescent rhodium-plated brass Sports hands; luminescent dots on the printed minute track. **Indications:** date between 1 and 2; power reserve at 6. **Bracelet:** stainless steel with brushed central link; double fold-over recessed clasp. **Also available:** with matte white or sapphire blue dial; steel, rubber strap, fold-over clasp; titanium, black dial, luminescent markers, rubber strap or bracelet. Ø 40mm in steel, strap or bracelet.

CLASSIQUE ELEGANCE TRAVELLER II 40 MM   REF. 49350

Movement: automatic, GP 2291 caliber (A. Schild 5008 base modified by GP), 31 jewels; 28,800 vph. Realized and finished by hand by the firm's watchmakers. **Functions:** hour, minute, second; date; second time-zone time; 24-hour indication; alarm. **Case:** stainless steel, three-piece case (Ø 4 mm, thickness 13.8mm), polished and brushed finish; antireflective curved sapphire crystal; winding crown at 2 for hour, second time-zone and date setting; at 4 for alarm winding

and setting; back attached by 6 screws. Water resistant to 3atm. **Dial:** matte black; luminescent bâton markers, 12 Arabic; printed minute track; luminescent white enameled brass bâton hands. **Indications:** date at 6 (referred to central time); second time-zone time 24-hour display below 12; sonnerie with luminescent red arrow-pointed center hand and dedicated minute track with divisions for quarters. **Strap:** crocodile leather, hand-stitched; steel clasp. **Also available:** in yellow or pink gold with strap; in white gold, strap; black, anthracite, blue dial with applied Arabic numerals. Ø 38mm Ref. 49400 in steel, strap or bracelet; in yellow, pink or white gold, strap or bracelet.

SPORT CLASSIQUE CHRONO 7000   REF. 70300

Movement: mechanical, automatic-winding, GP 2280 caliber (ETA base + Dubois Dépraz chronograph module), autonomy 46 hours, 57 jewels, 13'''; 28,800 vph. Beveled and decorated with Côtes de Genève pattern. Modified, mounted, adjusted, finished and decorated by hand by the firm's watchmakers. **Functions:** hour, minute, small second; date; chronograph with 3 counters. **Case:** stainless steel, two-piece case (Ø 38mm, thickness 11.8mm); antireflective flat sapphire crystal;

bezel with engraved tachometer scale; teardrop pushers; back attached by 6 screws. Water resistant to 5atm. **Dial:** matte black, subdials decorated with circular beads; luminescent bâton markers, 12 in Arabic numerals; luminescent white enameled Sports hands. **Indications:** small second at 3; date between 4 and 5; hour counter at 6; minute counter at 9; center second counter; railway minute track. **Bracelet:** stainless steel; recessed double fold-over clasp. **Also available:** with leather strap; pink gold and stainless steel, leather strap or bracelet. White or black dial, luminescent markers or silvered dial, applied Arabic numerals.

RICHEVILLE TONNEAU CHRONOGRAPH   REF. 27650.0.53.6151

Movement: mechanical, automatic-winding, GP 3370 caliber (GP Manufacture 3300 base + Dubois Dépraz chronograph module). Finished and decorated entirely by hand by the firm's watchmakers.
Functions: hour, minute, small second; chronograph with three counters.
Case: 18K white-gold, two-piece tonneau-shaped case (size 37x37mm, thickness 12.7mm); antireflective curved sapphire crystal; oval pushers; back attached by 4 screws, displaying the movement through a sapphire crystal. Water resistant to 3atm.

Dial: matte black, silvered subdials decorated with circular beads; flush white printed markers (12 Arabic) and minute track; luminescent white enameled brass lozenge hands.
Indications: small second at 3; hour counter at 6; minute counter at 9; center second counter; date between 4 and 5; track with divisions for 1/5 of a second.
Strap: crocodile leather; white-gold clasp.
Also available: in yellow or pink gold with strap, silvered dial.

RICHEVILLE TONNEAU CHRONOGRAPH LADY   REF. 26500.0.52.72M7

Movement: mechanical, automatic-winding, GP 30GC caliber (base + GP Manufacture module). Realized, mounted, adjusted, finished and decorated by hand by the firm's watchmakers.
Functions: hour, minute, small second; chronograph with two counters.
Case: 18K pink-gold, two-piece tonneau-shaped case (size 30x30mm, thickness 12.2mm); antireflective curved sapphire crystal; oval pushers; back attached by 4 screws, displaying the movement through a sapphire crystal. Water resistant to 3atm.

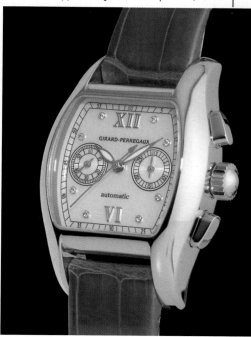

Dial: mother-of-pearl, subdials decorated with circular beads; luminescent applied pink-gold-plated brass markers, 8 with set brilliants, 6 and 12 Roman numerals; printed railway minute track; luminescent pink-gold-plated brass leaf-style hands.
Indications: minute counter at 3; small seconds at 9; center seconds; minute track.
Strap: crocodile leather; pink-gold clasp.
Also available: in yellow, pink or white gold with white dial, mixed printed markers and Arabic numerals, blued Poire hands.

PETIT CHRONO 32 MM   REF. 08046D1A11.11M7

Movement: mechanical, automatic-winding, GP 30GC caliber (base + GP Manufacture module). Realized, mounted, adjusted, finished and decorated by hand by the firm's watchmakers. **Functions:** hour, minute, small second; chronograph with 2 counters. **Case:** stainless steel, 3-piece case (Ø 31.7, thickness 12mm); bezel with a row of set brilliants, antireflective curved sapphire crystal; back attached by 5 screws, displaying the movement through a sapphire crystal. Water resistant to 3atm.

Dial: silvered, grained, subdials in mother-of-pearl; luminescent applied rhodium-plated markers, 8 with set brilliants, 6 and 12 in Roman numerals; luminescent blued steel leaf-style hands.
Indications: minute counter at 3; small sec. at 9; center second counter; minute scale with divisions for 1/5 of a second.
Bracelet: steel, brushed central link, recessed double fold-over clasp.
Also available: in yellow, pink or white gold; without brilliants in yellow, pink or white gold. Black dial, luminescent Arabic numerals or silvered dial, mother-of-pearl counters, 8 brilliant markers; or all mother-of-pearl, 8 brilliant markers; skeletonized dial in: yellow, pink or white gold.

GRAND CLASSIQUE BIG DATE MOONPHASE   REF. 49530.0.51.1121

Movement: mechanical, automatic-winding, GP 3300 caliber, autonomy 50 hours, 27 jewels, 11'''1/2; 28,800 vph. Beveled and decorated with Côtes de Genève pattern. Modified, mounted, adjusted, finished and decorated by hand by the firm's watchmakers.
Functions: hour, minute, small second; oversized date; moonphase.
Case: 18K yellow-gold, three-piece polished and brushed case (Ø 40mm, thickness 10.6mm); antireflective curved sapphire crystal; one corrector on the middle; yellow-gold crown; back attached by 6 screws, displaying the movement through a sapphire crystal. Water resistant to 3atm.

Dial: silvered, brushed with a sun pattern, subdials decorated with circular beads; applied yellow-gold-plated brass bâton markers, 6 and 12 in Roman numerals; printed minute track; yellow-gold-plated brass leaf-style hands.
Indications: oversized date with complanar double disc at 12; small seconds and moonphase at 6.
Strap: crocodile leather, hand-stitched, yellow-gold clasp.
Also available: in pink gold, gray dial; in white gold, blue dial.

GIRARD-PERREGAUX

CALIBER 3000

Automatic-winding movement, autonomy of 40 hours.
Functions: hours, minutes, center seconds (seconds stopping device); date with instantaneous change (with fast corrector).
Shape: round.

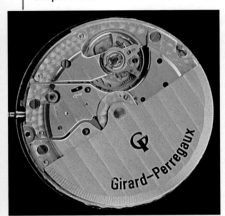

Diameter: 23.90mm.
Thickness: 2.98mm.
Jewels: 27.
Balance: smooth, with three arms, in Glucydur.
Frequency: 28,800 vph.
Balance-spring: flat, Nivarox 1, with micrometer screw regulating device.
Shock-absorber system: Kif.
Notes: pillar-plate decorated with a circular-graining pattern, bridges and rotor with a Côtes de Genève pattern.
Derived caliber: 3100.

CALIBER 3000

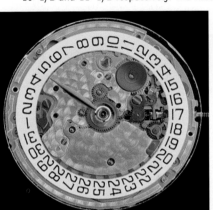

Caliber 3000, dial-side view.
The GP Manufacture started production in 1994 with the movements 3000 and 3100, both representing concepts of very high quality with diameters of 10‴1/2 and 11‴1/2 respectively. The first allows realizing automatic watches with limited outer sizes, the second can be adapted as a perpetual calendar or for other sophisticated complications in cases that may have any shape, refined and elegant, of strongly reduced thickness, as the movement's height measures only 2.98mm.

CALIBER 3100

Basic caliber: 3000. Automatic-winding movement, autonomy of 50 hours.
Functions: hours, minutes, center seconds (seconds stopping device); date with instantaneous change (with fast corrector).
Shape: round. **Diameter:** 26.20mm. **Thickness:** 2.98mm. **Jewels:** 27.
Balance: smooth, with three arms, in Glucydur. **Frequency:** 28,800 vph. **Balance-spring:** flat, Nivarox 1, with micrometer screw regulating device. **Shock-absorber system:** Kif.
Notes: pillar-plate decorated with a circular-graining pattern, bridges and (two-piece) rotor with a Côtes de Genève pattern.
Derived calibers: 3200 (with small seconds at 9 and date at 6); 3300 (with small seconds at 9); 33R0 (with small seconds at 9, date at 2 and power reserve); 3330 (32 jewels, with small seconds at 6, big date with double disc and moonphase).

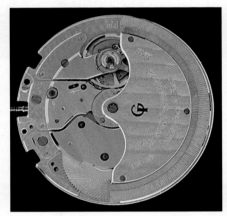

CALIBER 3170

Basic caliber: 3100 + chronograph plate and perp. calendar module. Automatic movement, autonomy of 50 hours, two-piece rotor with heavy metal sector. **Functions:** hours, minutes, small seconds; 24 hour; perp. calendar (day, date, four-year cycle—48 months—leap year, moonphase); chronograph with 3 counters (seconds, minutes, hours). **Shape:** round. **Diameter:** 30.00mm. **Thickness:** 7.10mm. **Jewels:** 44. **Balance:** in Glucydur, smooth, with 3 arms. **Frequency:** 28,800 vph. **Balance-spring:** flat, Nivarox 1, with micrometer screw regulating device. **Shock-absorber system:** Kif. **Notes:** pillar-plate with a circular-graining pattern, bridges and rotor with a Côtes de Genève pattern and beveled. The picture shows a perpetual calendar module to be mounted on the chronograph plate. The wheels supporting the calendar hands (at 3-6-9-12) are perforated to let the long pivots of the chronograph plate pass through, that house the relevant coaxial hands as well as the calendar hands ("F50").

CALIBER 3100 "SQUELETTE"

Basic caliber: 3100.
Automatic-winding movement, autonomy of 50 hours.
Functions: hours, minutes, center seconds (seconds stopping device).
Shape: round.

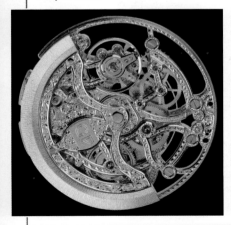

Diameter: 26.20mm.
Thickness: 2.98mm.
Jewels: 27.
Balance: smooth, with three arms, in Glucydur.
Frequency: 28,800 vph.
Balance-spring: flat, Nivarox 1, with micrometer screw regulating device.
Shock-absorber system: Kif.
Notes: pillar-plate, bridges and (two-piece) rotor skeletonized, chased and beveled by hand.

CALIBER 3080

Basic caliber: 3000 plus chronograph plate with column-wheel. Automatic-winding movement, 36-hour autonomy. **Functions:** hours, minutes, small seconds (seconds stopping device); date with instantaneous change (with fast corrector); chronograph with three counters.

Shape: round. **Diameter:** 23.30mm. **Thickness:** 6.28mm. **Jewels:** 38.
Balance: smooth, with three arms, in Glucydur.
Frequency: 28,800 vph.
Balance-spring: flat, Nivarox 1, with micrometer screw regulating device.
Shock-absorber system: Kif.
Notes: pillar-plate decorated with a circular-graining pattern, bridges and (two-piece) rotor decorated with a Côtes de Genève pattern, chronograph levers brushed. This data refers to the whole Caliber 3080, featuring a 3000 base plus the plate.

CALIBER 9892-070A

Basic caliber: GP 9890.
Manual-winding movement with 45-hour autonomy.
Functions: hours, minutes; hour, quarter and minute repeater.
Shape: round. **Diameter:** 28.00mm. **Thickness:** 7.60mm.

Jewels: 38.
Balance: with compensating screws, with two arms, in Glucydur, with tourbillon device.
Frequency: 18,000 vph.
Balance-spring: Breguet, Nivarox 1.
Shock-absorber system: Kif.
Notes: pillar-plate decorated with a circular-graining pattern. Three pink-gold bridges hand-engraved and beveled. Tourbillon carriage finished by specular polishing and beveled. Screw heads finished by specular polishing.
Derived caliber: GP 9892-070S (Squelette).

CALIBER GP 9892-070A

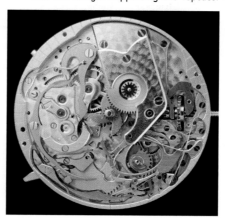

In this dial-side view, one perceives the components controlling the repeater activation and regulation. Levers, springs and racks are brushed and beveled. Screw heads are finished by specular polishing. In the 070S version, the base and the bridges supporting the repeater components are further decorated with engravings. The three rear bridges are skeletonized. In this case, in the assembled watch both sides of the movement are at sight.

CALIBER 9981

Basic caliber: 9900 with chronograph plate.
Manual-winding movement, autonomy of 70 hours.
Functions: hours, minutes, small seconds; chronograph with three counters (center seconds, minutes and hours).
Shape: round.
Diameter: 30.00mm.
Thickness: 9.80mm.
Jewels: 46.
Balance: with compensating screws, with two arms, in Glucydur; with tourbillon device.
Frequency: 21,600 vph.
Balance-spring: Breguet.
Shock-absorber system: Kif.
Notes: the pillar-plate and barrel are hand-engraved and rhodium-plated. The three bridges (characterizing also the watch's name) are in pink gold, hand-engraved and beveled. The tourbillon carriage is finished by specular polishing and beveled.

CALIBER 9981

View on the dial-side. The photograph shows the chronograph plate (mounted on Caliber GP 9900) in the specific version, decorated with a Côtes de Genève pattern and beveled on both bridges and levers. This component is checked, finished and assembled at the Girard-Perregaux factory.

The same plate is used also in other chronograph versions, combined with the House's automatic calibers. In this case, the finish of the upper bridge shows a circular-graining pattern. The date display window is at 3.
Data for the plate:
Functions: chronograph with three counters (chronograph center seconds, chronograph minutes at 9 and chronograph hours at 6).
Shape: round.
Diameter: 30.00mm.
Thickness: 2.90mm.
Jewels: 19.

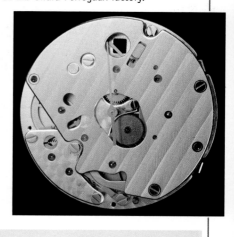

CALIBER 9780

Basic caliber: Venus 179. Manual-winding movement with 45-hour autonomy.
Functions: hours, minutes, small seconds; split-second chronograph with two counters (chronograph center seconds and minutes). **Shape:** round. **Diameter:** 31.00mm. **Thickness:** 7.20mm. **Jewels:** 26. **Balance:** with compensating screws, two arms, in Glucydur. **Frequency:** 18,000 vph.

Balance-spring: Breguet, with micrometer screw regulating device and swan-neck retaining spring.
Shock-absorber system: Incabloc.
Notes: pillar-plate decorated with a circular-graining pattern, bridges are decorated with a Côtes de Genève pattern and beveled. Levers and springs are brushed and beveled. The components of the regulation system are finished by specular polishing and beveled. Screw heads are finished by specular polishing. The chronograph functions are distributed by a column-wheel. Each movement is checked, finished, assembled and regulated by Girard-Perregaux.

CALIBER 751

Basic caliber: ETA 2660 (former FHF of the 1960s).
Manual-winding movement, autonomy of 35 hours.
Functions: hours, minutes.
Shape: baguette.

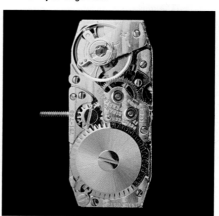

Length: 17.50mm.
Thickness: 3.50mm.
Jewels: 17.
Balance: smooth, with three arms, in Glucydur.
Frequency: 28,800 vph.
Balance-spring: flat, Nivarox 1.
Shock-absorber system: Incabloc.
Notes: bridges are decorated with a Côtes de Genève pattern, rhodium-plated, with gilded indications.

GLASHÜTTE ORIGINAL

a company with roots dating back to the 19th century, Glashütte Original creates complex mechanical timepieces of grand stature. Reclaiming its former position of glory, this brand is dedicated to horological excellence—producing watches that are beautiful both inside and out.

Originally founded as "Glashütte" in 1845, the brand produced some of the finest timepieces in Germany's history. But in 1951 the company's business was stifled by the East German government, which merged the Saxony region's various watch brands into one company. However, following the German reunification in 1990, Glashütte proudly reestablished itself.

In 1994, Glashütte Original was formed and two years later the brand unveiled its first watches. Its timepieces met with marked satisfaction from collectors around the world thanks to the company's excellent craftsmanship and elegant designs. In the year 2000, The Swatch Group purchased Glashütte and vowed to continue in the company's traditions. All timepieces are created in limited editions and are mechanical masterpieces that blend state-of-the-art technology with traditional horology.

Among the shining stars created by Glashütte are a column-wheel chronograph movement and a caliber fitted with a tourbillon escapement. In fact, the company has 10 proprietary movements, a watch line comprised of five different collections, and a host of master complications—all created in limited editions.

Most recently the brand unveiled two new models inspired by its very successful, long-since sold-out PanoRetroGraph watch. The newest timepieces, the PanoReserve and the PanoGraph, take their design inspirations from the original model. The elegant dials feature an off-center hour and minute display and a subsidiary seconds hand. Glashütte developed new, exceptionally lavish, manually wound movements for these watches.

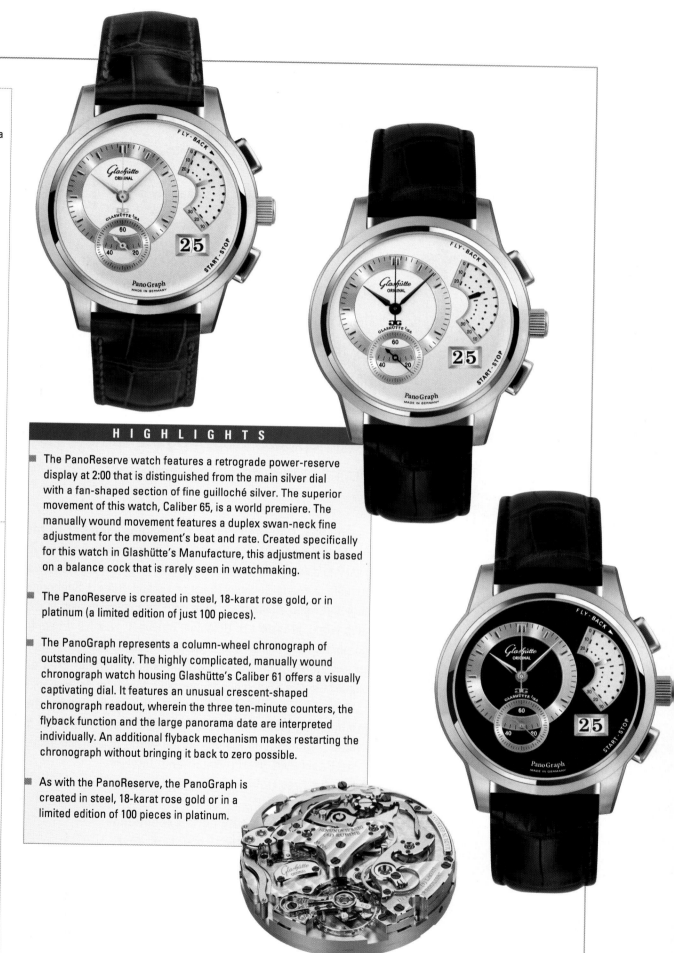

FACING PAGE

TOP LEFT

This 18-karat gold PanoReserve watch houses a manually wound movement, Caliber 65-01, and features a striking retrograde power-reserve display.

CENTER RIGHT

Classically elegant, the PanoReserve features a large date readout at 4:00. This model is crafted in steel and is fitted with a transparent caseback.

BOTTOM LEFT

Released in a limited edition of 100 pieces, this PanoReserve is crafted in platinum and offered with a hand-made Louisiana crocodile strap.

BOTTOM RIGHT

This 18-karat rose-gold PanoGraph watch houses a column-wheel chronograph movement.

THIS PAGE

TOP LEFT

Unique in its dial readouts, the PanoGraph displays the three ten-minute counters in a crescent-shaped aperture.

TOP RIGHT

The PanoGraph is fitted with a second flyback function that enables the wearer to reset without returning to zero first.

FAR RIGHT

Glashütte's Caliber 65-01 is a manually wound movement with 42 hours of power-reserve display and panorama date. It features a duplex swan-neck fine adjustment.

BOTTOM CENTER

The Caliber 61 is a classic column-wheel chronograph with flyback mechanism and panorama date. The winding wheels are decorated with a double sunburst pattern, and the balance cock and bridges are hand engraved.

HIGHLIGHTS

- The PanoReserve watch features a retrograde power-reserve display at 2:00 that is distinguished from the main silver dial with a fan-shaped section of fine guilloché silver. The superior movement of this watch, Caliber 65, is a world premiere. The manually wound movement features a duplex swan-neck fine adjustment for the movement's beat and rate. Created specifically for this watch in Glashütte's Manufacture, this adjustment is based on a balance cock that is rarely seen in watchmaking.

- The PanoReserve is created in steel, 18-karat rose gold, or in platinum (a limited edition of just 100 pieces).

- The PanoGraph represents a column-wheel chronograph of outstanding quality. The highly complicated, manually wound chronograph watch housing Glashütte's Caliber 61 offers a visually captivating dial. It features an unusual crescent-shaped chronograph readout, wherein the three ten-minute counters, the flyback function and the large panorama date are interpreted individually. An additional flyback mechanism makes restarting the chronograph without bringing it back to zero possible.

- As with the PanoReserve, the PanoGraph is created in steel, 18-karat rose gold or in a limited edition of 100 pieces in platinum.

GOLDPFEIL GENÈVE

for nearly a century and a half, the name Goldpfeil has been synonymous with luxury. Since 1856, this legendary leather goods brand has successfully cultivated a reputation for tradition and distinction. Now it has branched into the field of fine timepieces, displaying the same unparalleled pursuit of excellence.

In **1998**, Goldpfeil became a leading member of the international holding group Egana and the management dedicated itself to diversifying the brand into only the finest of categories. The head of Egana Goldpfeil Holdings Limited, Hans J. Seeberger appointed Heinz Heimann, a man with an extensive past in the watch world, President of Goldpfeil Genève. It was his dream to incorporate the tradition and heritage of Goldpfeil with the tradition and heritage of Swiss watchmaking. Heimann created Goldpfeil Genève SA and headquartered it smartly in Geneva.

Heimann established a unique partnership with the Watchmaking Academy of Independent Creators (AHCI) to develop a full-fledged identity in the world of watchmaking. At the Basel **2001** World Watch and Jewelry Show, the first Goldpfeil timepieces were unveiled to the world.

An original concept testifying to exceptional perfection, the Goldpfeil collection consists of seven one-of-a-kind and seven series watches—each created by seven different watchmakers of the AHCI.

The master watchmakers who partook in this first Goldpfeil Genève watch venture are Svend Andersen, Thomas Baumgartner, Vincent Calabrese,

TOP LEFT
Heinz J. Heimann.

LEFT CENTER
One-of-a-kind Mythos 7
This watch from Svend Andersen features a solid gold hand-engraved dial displaying the seven days of the week as they glide past the diamond at 12:00. From Sunday to Saturday, the dial features mythological engravings.

BOTTOM LEFT
**One-of-a-kind
Center Jumping Hours**
Vincent Calabrese developed this unique design with the hour positioned in the center of the watch and the Goldpfeil arrow representing the minute hand as it glides around the dial.

BELOW
One-of-a-kind Amphiscala
Inspired by a rediscovered 17th-century clock, this timepiece was designed by Thomas Baumgartner. The hour appears in the oval and the minute graduation is located under the oval, divided into five-minute intervals.

286

TOP LEFT

**One-of-a-kind
Gravitating Moon Phases**
Developed by Vianney Halter, this elaborate watch features three dials. Based on his Antiqua concept, it offers the time, a geometric display of the moonphase, and a thermometer.

TOP RIGHT

One-of-a-kind Tourbillon
By Frank Jutzi, this is a supreme example of artistry and complex craftsmanship. The mobile tourbillon carriage is crafted in filigree-worked steel and housed in a solid gold case with dial aperture to view the tourbillon.

RIGHT

**One-of-a-kind
Dual Time-Zone**
Antoine Preziuso's creation features a unique case design, merging round and oval shapes with slopes and domed elements. The second time-zone is displayed in a small subdial indicating hours and minutes.

BOTTOM

One-of-a-kind
This creation by Bernhard Lederer is a stylistic work of art. The hour is represented by the point of convergence of the guilloché waves on the large dial, while the minutes are read off at the tip of the arrow on the rotating subdial.

Vianney Halter, Frank Jutzi, Bernhard Lederer and Antoine Preziuso. It was Goldpfeil's commitment to the watchmakers that in their creations they would not sacrifice their intrinsic individual personalities. By perpetuating the inventive powers of these brilliant master watchmakers, Goldpfeil was guaranteed impressive and diverse results.

Goldpfeil gave the watchmakers carte blanche when it came to creating the seven exceptional one-of-a-kind pieces. Constituting highlights of ingenuity in movements, design, styling and even architecture, these watches spent a year touring the world—showcased at some of the finest luxury retail stores.

The first seven series watches are being created in very limited editions. These timepieces will be selectively distributed in the United States and Canada, as well as in certain countries in Europe, Asia and the Middle East. Each watch in the series production is a masterpiece of mechanical horology embodying the finest traditional values with a modern edge. Now, building upon the original series models, each watchmaker offers nuances with various materials, colors, dials or straps to expand the Goldpfeil selections.

The brand's advertising creed, "Faces of Time®," further underscores Goldpfeil's respect for these watchmakers and their individual talents. Every visual includes the watchmaker's photo and a photo of his Goldpfeil creation.

The overall concept is a watch, which one can caress, admire and wear on a daily basis.

The seven watch models from Goldpfeil represent the industry's highest level of creativity and craftsmanship, and each carries Goldpfeil's distinctive "golden arrow" logo.

PUPITRE

Born in Denmark and trained at the Danish Watchmaker's School, Svend Andersen has been creating timepieces for nearly 40 years. A member of the Royal Technological Institute of Copenhagen in the early **1960**s, Andersen moved to Geneva in **1963** to work in the esteemed company of Gubelin.

Andersen's artistic style and superb craftsmanship attracted the attention of Patek Philippe and earned him a privileged post in the complications workshop of the illustrious brand under the guidance of master watchmaker Max Berney.

In **1979**, Andersen struck out on his own—creating cases for antique pocket watch movements, restoring Patek Philippe watches, and developing movements for major brands. Not only was Andersen commissioned to create one-of-a-kind watches, he also began developing his own timepieces. In fact, in **1989** he unveiled his Communication World Time Watch and in **1992** he launched Christophorus Columbus.

In the ensuing years, Andersen unveiled such complications as the Perpetual calendar, the Hebraika and the Perpetual Secular calendar (which made its debut in **1996**). Committed to true watchmaking tradition, Andersen also has created a number of special automaton watches.

His Goldpfeil creation, called the Pupitre watch, features his own 24-hour mechanism. Driven by a self-winding movement, the watch houses a gold and platinum oscillating weight that is visible though the caseback.

THIS PAGE

LEFT
Svend Andersen.

BOTTOM
The original series watch created by Andersen sported a white dial.

FACING PAGE
The Pupitre watch houses an automatic movement and offers the 24-hour time display, minutes, date, and rapid correction of time and date. It is crafted in 18-karat yellow gold

CHRONOMETER WITH POWER-RESERVE INDICATOR

Just 35 years old, master watchmaker Thomas Baumgartner began his training in the watch industry when he was 15 years old. Born in **1968** in Geneva, Baumgartner spent his childhood in the German-speaking city of Schaffhausen, Switzerland. Fortunately for Baumgartner, IWC (International Watch Company) was also headquartered there.

From **1984** to **1988**, he served as an apprentice at IWC—guided by some of the finest master watchmakers in the world. In **1989** and **1990**, Baumgartner worked with Laurence Harvey, a specialist in 17th- and 18th-century British watches and clocks. From this experience he garnered unique knowledge of the history and tradition of fine watchmaking styles and became proficient with the tools used during these periods. These years had a profound effect on him and set the stage for the types of timepieces he would create.

Well into the **1990**s, Baumgartner worked with such fine companies as Reuge Music and Breguet, either restoring antiques or designing or refinishing automatons. In **1995**, he returned to Geneva and began working with his brother Felix and designer Martin Frei on the "Urwerk" watchmaking project. Together, the three associates developed an original mechanism based on a 17th-century Italian clock. Called the Amphiscala, the mechanism was unveiled in three prototypes in **1997**. This concept provided the foundation for Baumgartner to develop his one-of-a-kind Amphiscala watch for Goldpfeil.

The series watch that Baumgartner designed for Goldpfeil is a chronometer with power-reserve indicator. With a distinct, contemporary look, the mechanical manual-wind certified chronometer is housed in a striking square case with crown set at the bottom of the case rather than on the right side.

JUMPING HOURS

Unlike most of the other watchmakers selected to create Goldpfeil's first launch of timepieces, Vincent Calabrese is Italian. Born in the inspiring city of Naples, Calabrese is a predominantly self-taught artisan with an inherent sense of watchmaking. In Italy, he was already repairing watches after just three weeks as an apprentice. His keen ability to take apart and restore timepieces coupled with his love of mechanics and art were a blessing in his chosen career path.

When Calabrese moved to Switzerland, he worked first for Tissot and then managed a prestigious boutique for 10 years before deciding to launch his own watch collection. As with most talented and artistic Italians, aesthetics was the driving force for Calabrese. It was his goal that each of his watch designs epitomizes elegance and beauty. In fact, a watch "with no dial or case" earned him the gold medal at the Inventors Exhibition in Geneva. This system, purchased by Corum, gave rise to the famous Golden Bridge watch.

Calabrese certainly recognized, however, that aesthetics was not everything in watchmaking, and he went on to learn various important techniques such as case design, engraving, enameling, and jewelry making. In this way he was able to bring all of the elements of watchmaking together to launch his innovative—and sometimes whimsical—watches.

The timepiece Calabrese designed for Goldpfeil is a Jumping Hours watch, in which he uses large window apertures on a broad, thick case. The retro design, powerful in its appeal, offers the jumping hours at 12:00 and a date aperture at 6:00. The blue Goldpfeil arrow navigates the dial to indicate the minutes.

JUMPING HOURS WITH MOON PHASES

For the past 15 years, Vianney Halter has been involved in various fields in the watch industry. Trained as a watchmaker in Paris, he began his career by restoring antique clocks. In **1990**, he immigrated to Switzerland to entrench himself more firmly in the world of fine Swiss horology.

That same year, in conjunction with watchmaker François-Paul Journe, Halter developed a variety of projects for major Swiss brands. Later he teamed with watchmaker François Junod and traveled to Japan to study and create an entire collection of automatons. He was enthralled with the traditional watchmaking techniques and movements and was compelled to create timepieces of only the finest stature.

In **1994**, Halter founded his own company, Janvier SA, in the picturesque village of Sainte-Croix and unveiled his first major creation—a watch with striking mechanism and automatons designed for Jaquet-Droz. In **1998** he presented a very special watch to the world that he had created in cooperation with designer Jeffrey Barnes. Called the Antiqua, the concept was based on multiple dials that float together—each offering its own information to the wearer. It was upon this concept that Halter built his one-of-a-kind watch for Goldpfeil. The multiple dials offered the time, temperature and a geometrical depiction of the moon's phases.

For the Goldpfeil series production, Halter has created a Jumping Hours with Moon Phases watch. Crafted in 18-karat white gold, the rectangular watch offers three distinct display apertures. The hours jump in a rectangle in the upper left corner of the watch; the moonphases are depicted around a circle of geometrical icons; the minutes are marked by a blue Goldpfeil arrow hand and the seconds by a red hand—both of which rotate on a round dial set within a main square on the watch.

MOON PHASES

After studying at the Rudolf Steiner School and serving a watchmaking apprenticeship of several years, Frank Jutzi established his own restoration workshop in **1985**. He was anxious to get to work immediately upon completion of his education and devoted himself exclusively to restoring vintage clocks.

However, Jutzi was restless and eager to create new pieces—a powerful combination. Intent on developing his own creations, Jutzi quickly made a name for himself when he unveiled several original clocks. At the **1990** World Watch and Jewelry Fair in Basel, Jutzi presented a large clock with a three-day movement that had been inspired by a collector's item and for which he had developed his own mechanism.

Over the ensuing decade, he continually developed his own pieces while at the same time restoring clocks and wristwatches. It is only in the past few years that Jutzi has begun developing and crafting his own watches displaying impressive technical mastery. For the one-of-a-kind Goldpfeil watch, Jutzi created the supreme Tourbillon whose escapement is crafted in filigree-worked steel.

Jutzi's series watch for Goldpfeil is a striking Moon Phases timepiece crafted in 18-karat white gold and inspired by the regulators of yesteryear. The central hand marks the minutes while the hour can be read off a subdial at 2:00, and a subdial tracks the seconds at 6:00. The elegant moonphase indicator is set in a window at 10:00 for perfect symmetry on the solid silver dial.

DOUBLE TIME-ZONE WITH WEEK DISPLAY

Born in the town of Kornwestheim, Germany (near Stuttgart), Bernhard Lederer spent his apprenticeship in watchmaking at the Wuppertal Museum, where he became intimately familiar with all facets of the horological tradition.

A true watch enthusiast, Lederer further pursued his career goals by training for another three years at the Pforzheim Watchmaker's School—the German Mecca of watchmaking. He opened his own watchmaking workshops in the **1980**s and fulfilled his dreams of creating distinguished, traditional watches.

In the ensuing decades, Lederer was honored for several of his creations and was encouraged to venture further into the world of mechanical watchmaking. He has regularly focused primarily on creating complex watch movements in the finest cases and featuring the most elegant designs.

In the year **2000**, Lederer was commissioned by the Brazilian government to create a watch that would mark the 500th anniversary of the country's discovery. He created 28 monumental clocks—each of which stood more than 14 meters tall. While this was an incredible achievement for Lederer, he nonetheless remains committed to the world of wristwatches.

For Goldpfeil, the series production watch he has developed is a Double Time-Zone with week display. Inspired by the characteristic configuration of regulators, the watch features a central arrow hand that marks the minutes. The second central hand, in a half-moon shape, indicates the weeks around the outer edge of the dial. The hour is read off a small dial at 12:00, with a second time-zone indicator included on the dial at 6:00. Two windows show the day and the date.

THE LEATHER WATCH

Renowned as one of Switzerland's finest independent watchmakers, Antoine Preziuso was raised in Geneva and educated at the Geneva Watchmakers School. Talented and ambitious, Preziuso worked for Patek Philippe and for Antiquorum in their restoration workshops before opening his own facility in **1980**.

Preziuso acquired a strong following and a sterling reputation for his exquisite and exacting restoration of antique clocks and watches—a forte he continues to pursue to this day.

Still, Preziuso was obsessed with the desire to create his own watches, and in **1990**—after two years of research and development—unveiled a specially made perpetual calendar watch with minute-repeater mechanism that was controlled by the bezel. This exceptional watch earned him the prestigious Geneva Hallmark of quality and opened doors for him to work closely with such illustrious brands as Breguet and Harry Winston.

Under his own brand name, he has created significant timepieces and movements including the tourbillon and the Hours of the World GMT watch that demonstrate his blend of traditional techniques and artistic sensitivity. The one-of-a-kind watch he developed for Goldpfeil was a Dual Time-Zone watch of distinctive design.

The series watch Preziuso created for Goldpfeil is called The Leather Watch, a clean, sensual piece whose entire dial is covered with the same leather as the strap. The watch comes in eight refined colors. Crafted in 18-karat gold, the hands and the hour markers are also gold.

THIS PAGE

LEFT
Antoine Preziuso.

BOTTOM
At first, The Leather Watch was unveiled in only one color.

FACING PAGE

The newest Leather Watch extends the leather of the strap straight across the dial, and is available in eight striking natural hues.

GRAHAM

graham is one of the finest names in British watchmaking history. With roots dating back to the early 1700s, the name of George Graham was synonymous in British horological history with invention and advancement. Indeed, George Graham (who trained in the workshops of the famed Thomas Tompion) is credited with such watchmaking innovations as the deadbeat escapement, the cylinder escapement, and the mercury compensation pendulum.

Today, the brand has regained its rightful place in the world of precision watchmaking due to the commitment of its owners to follow in the traditional splendor and heritage to which Graham dedicated himself.

It was nearly six years ago that The British Masters SA presented its first Graham timepieces. Headquartered in La Chaux-de-Fonds and spearheaded by Eric A. Loth, CEO, The British Masters is a company dedicated to restoring the names of Britain's original horologers to their former glory. First on their list was the reintroduction of the fine George Graham and John Arnold names.

In tribute to Graham's innovations and contributions, the British Masters determined that all Graham watches would house complicated chronograph movements. In **1997**, the first timepiece introduced in the spirit of Graham was the Foudroyante chronograph—paying homage to George Graham's chronograph invention.

Following the launch of the Foudroyante, Graham unveiled the art-deco-styled SprintCounter with flyback mechanism in **1998**, and the striking Chronofighter was unveiled in **2000**. This self-winding mechanical watch is COSC certified and is a bold technical instrument that remains one of the brand's bestsellers.

THE BRITISH MASTERS SA

Graham's newest timepieces feature incredibly advanced precision functions and are resolutely elegant in design. The exceptional new Chronofighters are striking combinations of form and function. Essentially, the Chronofighter features a big release lever on the left side of the watchcase—offering purity of design on the right side (no crown or pushpieces are visible). The release lever is the type used by the British RAF pilots during World War II, enabling them to activate the chronograph easily with their right thumbs at an altitude of 8,000 meters. The Chronofighter is equipped with a Graham G. 1722 caliber self-winding mechanical movement. The COSC-certified movement features 25 jewels and a shock-resistant system.

The Silverstone Chronograph, dedicated to motor sports enthusiasts, is characterized by a design in harmony with the world of automobile racing. Its round case is inspired by the Formula One race car wheel and its dial features a black-and-white checkered 30-minutes counter. The watch also features a GMT hour circle and a big date aperture. The movement is a self-winding mechanical movement with flyback function and 42 hours of power reserve. Crafted in red gold or in steel, the watch is a chic combination of mechanical performance and British charm.

LEFT
The newest COSC-certified Chronofighter watch also comes with a stunning diamond-adorned case.

BOTTOM
The Chronofighter features a large release lever on the left side of the case, as well as the reset pushpiece.

TOP LEFT

The Collectors 132 watch commemorates Graham's horological mastery. Crafted in 18-karat red gold, the COSC-certified chronograph enables activation of all functions from a single pushpiece. This chronograph measures pulse rates in addition to other chronograph uses.

TOP RIGHT

Very stylish in its red-gold version, the Silverstone with steel bracelet is sleek and bold.

BOTTOM RIGHT

The Mastersplit in 18-karat red gold houses a mechanical movement with new split-second chronograph function.

HIGHLIGHTS

Graham has extended its very successful Foudroyante Chronograph, which was first created in 1997 to pay homage to George Graham and his chronograph innovations. This exceptional chronograph features a $1/8$th second jumping-seconds hand and a crown-operated coaxial flyback. Fitted with the Graham G. 1695 automatic caliber, the chronograph incorporates two column wheels and two barrels. It has 40 jewels and offers 42 hours of power reserve. The watch is water resistant to 160 feet.

Now the steel Foudroyante Chronograph is available in three versions, with a black, blue or silvered dial with triangular indexes. Each dial of the steel variations has an aperture revealing the start/stop column wheel. For better viewing, the sapphire crystal features a magnifying glass over the Foudroyante counter (which completes one 360 degree turn per second in eight consecutive steps).

Graham had watch lovers in mind when it created this piece and created a rose-gold version with silvered dial, pink indexes and rose-gold hands.

Graham also introduces a special, limited-edition watch that pays tribute to British great Winston Churchill. The watch commemorates the writing career of Churchill, which started with his first book published in 1902.

The Graham Silverstone is presented as a multi-complicated chronograph with flyback seconds, double-disc big date and second time-zone GMT. Produced in steel or gold, the Silverstone is also equipped with a steel bracelet. A true wrist machine for the automotive sports enthusiast.

The Churchill Special series watch is a COSC-certified mechanical chronograph housing the Graham G. 1722 caliber. The movement is engraved with the Côtes de Genève seal.

Several new Chronofighter timepieces join the original ranks. With its oversized release lever on the left side of the case, this chronograph is a bold instrument of precision and function. Each Chronofighter is equipped with a self-winding mechanical movement that is COSC certified.

GRAHAM

SILVERSTONE — REF. 2SIAR.S01A

Movement: mechanical, automatic winding, G-1721 caliber, 13" 1/4, 28,800 vibrations per hour, 28 jewels. Decorated with Côtes de Genève pattern and circular grained, blue steel screws, adjusted five (5) positions.
Functions: hour, minute, small second at 9, second time zone indicator in center, big date with double disc system at 6, chronograph with minute counter at 3 and center flyback second. **Case:** 18K red-gold 5N18, three-piece case, Ø 41.60mm,

curved sapphire crystal, back attached by 8 screws, engraved royal marine crown in the back. Water resistant to 160 feet.
Dial: silvered; luminescent applied red-gold plated bâton-style markers (Roman numeral XII), luminescent red-gold plated hands, luminescent red-gold plated second hand with red marker, red-gold plated second time zone hand.
Indications: small seconds at 9; big date display at 6; minute register at 3; second time zone in center; printed minute track.
Strap: black genuine crocodile or alligator leather with polished and engraved solid red-gold buckle.
Also available: in steel with black, silver or blue dial with leather strap or with steel bracelet.

SILVERSTONE — REF. 2SIAS.B01A

Movement: mechanical, automatic winding, G-1721 caliber, 13" 1/4, 28,800 vibrations per hour, 28 jewels. Decorated with Côtes de Genève pattern and circular grained, blue steel screws, adjusted five (5) positions.
Functions: hour, minute, small second at 9, second time zone indicator in center, big date with double disc system at 6, chronograph with minute counter at 3 and center flyback second. **Case:** low carbon high corrosion resistance stain-

less steel, three-piece case, Ø 41.60mm, curved sapphire crystal, back attached by 8 screws, engraved royal marine crown in the back. Water resistant to 160 feet.
Dial: black luminescent Arabic numerals; luminescent bâton-style hands, luminescent second hand with red marker; second time zone hand painted yellow.
Indications: small seconds at 9; big date display at 6; minute register at 3; second time zone in center; printed minute track.
Strap: black genuine crocodile or alligator leather with polished and engraved solid steel buckle.
Also available: in red gold with silver dial or in steel with blue or silver dial with steel bracelet or leather strap.

SILVERSTONE — REF. 2SIAS.U01A

Movement: mechanical, automatic winding, G-1721 caliber, 13" 1/4, 28,800 vibrations per hour, 28 jewels. Decorated with Côtes de Genève pattern and circular grained, blue steel screws, adjusted five (5) positions.
Functions: hour, minute, small second at 9, second time zone indicator in center, big date with double disc system at 6, chronograph with minute counter at 3 and center flyback second. **Case:** low carbon high corrosion resistance stain-

less steel, three-piece case, Ø 41.60mm, curved sapphire crystal, back attached by 8 screws, engraved royal marine crown in the back. Water resistant to 160 feet.
Dial: blue; luminescent Arabic numerals; luminescent bâton-style hands, luminescent second hand with red marker; second time zone hand painted yellow.
Indications: small seconds at 9; big date display at 6; minute register at 3; second time zone in center; printed minute track.
Bracelet: low carbon high corrosion resistance stainless steel bracelet with double fold-over clasp.
Also available: silver or black dial, with steel bracelet or leather strap; in red gold, silver dial with leather strap.

SILVERSTONE — REF. 2SIAS.S01A

Movement: mechanical, automatic winding, G-1721 caliber, 13" 1/4, 28,800 vibrations per hour, 28 jewels. Decorated with Côtes de Genève pattern and circular grained, blue steel screws, adjusted five (5) positions.
Functions: hour, minute, small second at 9, second time zone indicator in center, big date with double disc system at 6, chronograph with minute counter at 3 and center flyback second. **Case:** low carbon high corrosion resistance stain-

less steel, three-piece case, Ø 41.60mm, curved sapphire crystal, back attached by 8 screws, engraved royal marine crown in the back. Water resistant to 160 feet. **Dial:** silvered luminescent Roman numerals XII, luminescent applied markers; black counters, luminescent bâton-style hands, luminescent second hand with red marker; second time zone hand painted yellow.
Indications: small seconds at 9; big date display at 6; minute register at 3; second time zone in center; printed minute track.
Strap: black genuine crocodile or alligator leather with polished and engraved solid steel buckle. **Also available:** in red gold with silver dial or in steel with blue or black dial with steel bracelet or leather strap.

OXFORD · REF. 20XAS.B01A

Movement: mechanical, automatic winding, G-716 caliber, 8" 3/4, 28,800 vibrations per hour, 25 jewels. Decorated with Côtes de Genève pattern and circular grained, blue steel screws, adjusted four (4) positions.
Functions: hour, minute, second.
Case: low carbon high corrosion resistance stainless steel, three-piece case, 46.40 x 30.37mm, curved sapphire crystal, back attached by 8 screws, engraved royal marine crown in the back. Water resistant to 100 feet.
Dial: black, steel markers, steel Arabic numerals 6-12; steel hands.
Strap: black genuine crocodile or alligator leather with polished and engraved steel buckle.
Also available: in steel with silvered dial and steel markers.

SPRINT · REF. 2SPAR.S04A

Movement: mechanical, manual winding, G-715 caliber, 8" 3/4, 21,600 vibrations per hour, 21 jewels. Decorated with Côtes de Genève pattern and circular grained, blue steel screws, adjusted four (4) positions.
Functions: hour, minute, small flyback second counter at 6.
Case: 18K red-gold 5N18, three-piece case, 46,10 x 26,30mm, curved sapphire crystal, angle pusher at 4 for flyback function, curved back attached by 8 screws, engraved royal marine crown in the back. Water resistant to 100 feet.
Dial: silvered, red-gold plated Art Déco markers, red-gold plated Arabic numerals 3-9-12; red-gold plated hands.
Indications: small flyback second at 6.
Strap: black genuine crocodile or alligator leather with polished and engraved solid red-gold buckle.
Also available: with black dial, red gold plated Art Déco markers and silvered second counter.

FOUDROYANTE · REF. 2LIAS.B04A

Movement: mechanical, automatic winding, G-1695 caliber, 13" 1/4, 28,800 vph, 40 jewels. Decorated with Côtes de Genève pattern and circular grained, blue steel screws, adjusted five (5) positions. **Functions:** hour, minute, seconds, central split seconds, 1/8th jumping seconds "foudroyante" counter at 9, 30-minutes counter at 3. **Case:** low carbon high corrosion resistance stainless steel, three-piece case, Ø 41.60mm, sapphire crystal with "cyclop" magnifying glass on the "Foudroyante" counter at 9, back attached by 6 screws, engraved royal marine crown in the back. Water resistant to 160 feet.
Dial: black with silvered and black counters, with visible column wheel, luminescent markers with luminescent Arabic numerals 12-6; printed railway minute track; luminescent and silvered bâton-style hands, red central sweep seconds; white and red hands for small counters.
Indications: central split second for intermediary timing; central second corrected with 1/8th jumping second "foudroyante" at 9 to measure time at 1/8th a second. Counter 30 minutes at 3. **Strap:** black genuine crocodile or alligator leather with polished and engraved steel buckle. **Also available:** in steel with silvered dial; in pink gold with silvered dial.

FOUDROYANTE · REF. 2LIAS.S05A

Movement: mechanical, automatic winding, G-1695 caliber, 13" 1/4, 28,800 vibrations per hour, 40 jewels. Decorated with Côtes de Genève pattern and circular grained, blue steel screws, adjusted five (5) positions. **Functions:** hour, minute, seconds, central split seconds, 1/8th jumping seconds "foudroyante" counter at 9, 30-minutes counter at 3. **Case:** low carbon high corrosion resistance stainless steel, three-piece case, Ø 41.60mm, sapphire crystal with "cyclop" magnifying glass on the "Foudroyante" counter at 9, back attached by 6 screws, engraved royal marine crown in the back. Water resistant to 160 feet. **Dial:** silvered with silvered and blue counters, with visible column wheel, steel markers with steel Arabic numerals 12-6; printed railway minute track; steel hands, black central sweep seconds; white and steel blue hands for small counters. **Indications:** central split second for intermediary timing; central second corrected with 1/8th jumping second "foudroyante" at 9 to measure time at 1/8th a second. Counter 30 minutes at 3. **Strap:** black genuine crocodile or alligator leather with polished and engraved steel buckle. **Also available:** in steel with black dial; in pink gold with silvered dial.

GRAHAM

FOUDROYANTE PINK GOLD   REF. 2LIAP.S07A

Movement: mechanical, automatic winding, G-1695 caliber, 13" 1/4, 28,800 vibrations per hour, 40 jewels. Decorated with Côtes de Genève pattern and circular grained, blue steel screws, adjusted five (5) positions.
Functions: hour, minute, seconds, central split seconds, 1/8th jumping seconds "foudroyante" counter at 9, 30-minutes counter at 3. **Case:** 18K pink-gold 4N18, three-piece case, Ø 41.60mm, sapphire crystal; back attached by 6 screws, engraved royal marine crown in the back. Water resistant to 160 feet. **Dial:** silvered with silvered and black counters, pink-gold plated markers with pink-gold plated Arabic numerals 12-6; printed railway minute track; red-gold plated hands, light metal jumping seconds, central second in CuBe plated, split second and minutes counters painted white.
Indications: central split second for intermediary timing; central second corrected with 1/8th jumping second "foudroyante" at 9 to measure time at 1/8th a second. Counter 30 minutes at 3.
Strap: black genuine crocodile or alligator leather with polished and engraved solid red-gold buckle.
Also available: in steel with black or silvered dial.

COLLECTORS RED GOLD LIMITED EDITION OF 100 PCS   REF. 2COAR.S02A

Movement: mechanical, automatic winding, G-0450 caliber, 11" 1/5, 18,000 vibrations per hour, 17 jewels. Beveled and decorated with Côtes de Genève pattern and circular grained, visible column wheel, adjusted five (5) positions, counter one minute. **Functions:** hour, minute, small second at 9, central second counter, mono pusher for start, stop and reset functions.
Case: 18K red-gold 5N18, three-piece case, Ø 41.60mm, curved sapphire crystal, back attached by 8 screws, see-through back with sapphire crystal, engraved with limited edition numbering. Water resistant to 160 feet.
Dial: curved dial; silvered; triangular red-gold plated markers, red-gold Arabic numerals 3-6-12; red-gold plated hands, curved steel blue center counter with red indicator, steel blue hand for small seconds; printed minute track.
Indications: special graduation scale to measure heart beat frequency based on 15 heart pulsations.
Strap: black genuine crocodile or alligator leather with polished and engraved in solid red-gold 5N18 buckle.
Also available: Limited edition of 32 pieces in white gold, both limited edition with black or silvered dials.

AEROFLYBACK   REF. 2AFAS.S01A

Movement: mechanical, automatic winding, G-1723 caliber, 13" 1/4, 28,800 vibrations per hour, 28 jewels. Decorated with Côtes de Genève pattern and circular grained, blue steel screws, adjusted five (5) positions.
Functions: hour, minute, small second at 9, 30-minutes counter at 3, big date with magnifying "cyclope in sapphire" at 6, center flyback second.
Case: low carbon high corrosion resistance stainless steel, three-piece case, Ø 41.60mm, curved sapphire crystal, back attached by 6 screws, engraved royal marine crown in the back. Water resistant to 160 feet.
Dial: silvered, steel markers; luminescent and blue hands, steel second hand with luminescent indicator, printed railway minute track; blue hands for counters.
Indications: central second flyback; seconds counters at 9; 30-minutes counters at 3; magnified date display with cyclope at 6.
Strap: black genuine crocodile or alligator leather with polished and engraved steel buckle.
Also available: in steel with black dial.

CHRONOFIGHTER   REF. 2CFAS.B01A

Movement: mechanical, automatic winding, G-1722 caliber, 13" 1/4, 28,800 vibrations per hour, 30 jewels. Decorated with Côtes de Genève pattern and circular grained, blue steel screws, adjusted five (5) positions. Chronometer certified by the Chronometer Testing Institute (C.O.S.C.). **Functions:** hour, minute, small second, chronograph with 2 counters. Special system with mobile lever and coaxial command for fast action stop and start. **Case:** low carbon high corrosion resistance stainless steel, three-piece case, Ø 43mm, curved sapphire crystal, back attached by 8 screws, embeded royal marine crown in the back. Water resistant to 160 feet, lever mechanism in stainless steel. **Dial:** black with two silvered counters, luminescent applied markers, luminescent Arabic numerals 12-6, printed minute track, large luminescent bâton-style hands, luminescent center second with red marker, blue steel hands for counters. **Indications:** 30-minutes counter at 9; seconds counter at 3; printed minute track. **Strap:** aviator leather with special enlarged and engraved buckle. **Also available:** black or silvered dial with luminescent applied bâton-style markers. In red gold with white-gold lever and black or silvered dial.

CHRONOFIGHTER STICK SILVER — REF. 2CFAS.S01A

Movement: mechanical, automatic winding, G-1722 caliber, 13" 1/4, 28,800 vibrations per hour, 30 jewels. Decorated with Côtes de Genève pattern and circular grained, blue steel screws, adjusted five (5) positions. Chronometer certified by the Chronometer Testing Institute (C.O.S.C). **Functions:** hour, minute, small second, chronograph with 2 counters. Special system with mobile lever and coaxial command for fast action stop and start. **Case:** low carbon high corrosion

resistance stainless steel, three-piece case, Ø 43mm, curved sapphire crystal, back attached by 8 screws, embeded royal marine crown in the back. Water resistant to 160 feet, lever mechanism in stainless steel. **Dial:** silvered with two black/silvered counters, luminescent applied bâton-style markers, printed minute track, large luminescent bâton-style hands, luminescent center second with red marker, white hands for counters. **Indications:** 30-minutes counter at 9; seconds counter at 3; printed minute track.
Bracelet: aviator leather with special enlarged and engraved buckle.
Also available: black dial with luminescent applied bâton-style markers. In red gold with white-gold lever and black or silvered dial.

CHRONOFIGHTER STICK BLACK — REF. 2CFAS.B06A

Movement: mechanical, automatic winding, G-1722 caliber, 13" 1/4, 28,800 vibrations per hour, 30 jewels. Decorated with Côtes de Genève pattern and circular grained, blue steel screws, adjusted five (5) positions. Chronometer certified by the Chronometer Testing Institute (C.O.S.C). **Functions:** hour, minute, small second, chronograph with 2 counters. Special system with mobile lever and coaxial command for fast action stop and start. **Case:** low carbon high corrosion

resistance stainless steel, three-piece case, Ø 43mm, curved sapphire crystal, back attached by 8 screws, embeded royal marine crown in the back. Water resistant to 160 feet, lever mechanism in stainless steel. **Dial:** black with two silvered counters, luminescent applied bâton-style markers, printed minute track, large luminescent bâton-style hands, luminescent center second with red marker, white hands for counters. **Indications:** 30-minutes counter at 9; seconds counter at 3; printed minute track.
Bracelet: aviator leather with special enlarged and engraved buckle.
Also available: silvered dial with luminescent applied bâton-style markers. In red gold with white-gold lever and black or silvered dial.

CHRONOFIGHTER GOLD — REF. 2CFAR.B04W

Movement: mechanical, automatic winding, G-1721 caliber, 13" 1/4, 28,800 vibrations per hour, 28 jewels. Decorated with Côtes de Genève pattern and circular grained, blue steel screws, adjusted five (5) positions.
Functions: hour, minute, small second, chronograph with 2 counters. Special system with mobile lever and coaxial command for fast action stop and start.
Case: 18K red-gold 5N18 three-piece case, Ø 43mm, curved sapphire crystal,

back attached by 8 screws, mobile lever in white-gold, embeded royal marine crown in white-gold in the back. Water resistant to 160 feet.
Dial: black with two silvered/black counters, red-gold plated and luminescent square markers, printed minute track, red-gold plated skeletonized hands, red-gold plated center second and red-gold plated hands for counters.
Indications: 30-minutes counter at 9; seconds counter at 3; printed minute track.
Bracelet: crocodile or alligator leather with special enlarged and engraved solid red-gold buckle.
Also available: silvered dial with black counters or in steel with different dials.

AEROFLYBACK — REF. 2AFAS.B01A

Movement: mechanical, automatic winding, G-1723 caliber, 13" 1/4, 28,800 vibrations per hour, 28 jewels. Decorated with Côtes de Genève pattern and circular grained, blue steel screws, adjusted five (5) positions.
Functions: hour, minute, small second at 9, 30-minutes counter at 3, big date with magnifying "cyclope in sapphire" at 6, center flyback second.
Case: low carbon high corrosion resistance stainless steel, three-piece case,

Ø 41.60mm, curved sapphire crystal, back attached by 6 screws, engraved royal marine crown in the back. Water resistant to 160 feet.
Dial: two tones black and dark gray; luminescent and steel hands, printed railway minute track; white hands for counters.
Indications: central second flyback; seconds counters at 9; 30-minutes counters at 3; magnified date display with cyclope at 6.
Strap: black genuine crocodile or alligator leather with polished and engraved steel buckle.
Also available: in steel with silvered dial.

GUCCI

In 1921, Guccio Gucci opened a small luggage and saddle company in Florence, Italy, selling leather goods made by the best Florentine craftsmen. Soon Gucci's shop attracted a sophisticated international clientele and the business flourished into one of the world's most prolific luxury brands.

The overwhelming success of Gucci's first shop prompted the opening of a new store in **1938** on Via Condotti in Rome. In **1947**, Gucci's icon product—the bamboo-handle handbag—was introduced. During the **1950**s the trademark striped webbing, which was derived from the saddle girth, was launched with great success. The moccasin with metal bit was introduced that same decade and became another signature Gucci product. Guccio Gucci died in **1953** while the company was enjoying a period of great renown, building a global presence with the opening of its New York store. Subsequent stores soon opened in London, Paris and Palm Beach.

Grace Kelly, Peter Sellers and Audrey Hepburn helped make Gucci synonymous with Hollywood chic. Jackie Kennedy carried the Gucci shoulder bag, known today as the "Jackie O." At the end of **1960**s the company adopted the legendary GG logo.

The Far East was targeted for international expansion in the **1970**s, and stores were opened in Hong Kong and Tokyo. In **1972** Gucci was one of the first fashion brands to enter the watchmaking business through a licensing agreement with the Swiss company Severin Montres. The first model was a "bangle" watch with a solid bracelet and interchangeable color dials.

Tom Ford joined Gucci as Chief Women's Ready-to-Wear Designer in **1990**. Four years later, Domenico De Sole became CEO of Gucci Group NV and Ford was appointed Creative Director. Gucci took control of its watch business in **1997** by acquiring Severin Montres, one of the largest and most profitable watch companies in the world. That same year, Gucci launched the first gold and diamond timepiece collection featuring the iconic G watch. Gucci was named "European Company of the Year **1998**" by the European Business Press Federation for its economic and financial performance, strategic vision and management quality. In **1999**, Gucci entered a strategic alliance with Pinault-Printemps-Redoute and expanded from a single-brand company to a multi-brand group.

In **2000**, Gucci launched a successful model, inspired by the buckle of a famous icon bag, with a thin leather lace bracelet that wraps around the wrist. Gucci introduced mechanical hand-wound watches—a prestigious first for the brand—in **2001**, and in **2002**, launched a revisited design version of its classic bangle watch.

310

GUCCI

Gucci timepieces are high-quality watches directly aligned and connected with the Gucci fashion image. Their timepieces' presence is powerful and compelling in the highly dynamic and expanding sector of fashion and design watches—an area where creativity, combined with superior quality, is a key factor for success.

Gucci Group Watches, with its different brands, has built a credible and sustainable reputation and a solid experience in each of the most distinctive sectors of the watch industry. In fact, in the past two years Gucci Group has successfully regained control of Yves Saint Laurent's watch license. It also acquired Boucheron International S.A., one of the world's most prestigious and exclusive jewelry, watch and perfume brands, and Bédat & Cº, the Geneva-based Swiss watchmaker whose timepieces were introduced into the United States luxury market in 1997 and met with phenomenal success.

The future direction of Gucci timepieces is in line with this strategy centered on high quality and direct control. Under Tom Ford's creative direction, Gucci timepieces have been consistently repositioned in tandem with Gucci's luxurious image and quality standards. In fact, the close unity of the Gucci entity and its watchmaking operation is one of the most significant factors for the timepieces' success. This activity is becoming more and more intimate, leading to a clear positioning of the Gucci timepieces as fashion and design objects that benefit from the highest standards of the Swiss watch-making craftsmanship. Following this strategy, both male and female consumers are targeted, with a special emphasis on the quality of the materials, new developments in the diamond collection, and the further addition of special mechanical movements for each model of the new collection.

TOP LEFT

Called the G watch, this steel watch is set with 82 full-cut diamonds weighing just over one carat. The dial is available in black, silver or white mother of pearl, and the leather strap is fitted with a push-deployment clasp.

FAR RIGHT

This model is available in men's and women's sizes and is an updated interpretation of a 1950s' style. The square dial is softened by rounded edges and the recessed crown features the G logo.

BOTTOM RIGHT

This solid gold mechanical watch features a 40mm case and a silver dial with applied indexes. The crocodile strap is closed with an 18-karat gold tongue-buckle.

HIGHLIGHTS

- Iconic images, design pieces and the latest trends in Gucci fashion inspire the new collection with a special emphasis on diamonds, precious materials, and high-quality technical movements.

- Some of Gucci's best sellers are now presented with new colors and unconventional materials offering a wider choice of models in line with the Gucci fashion trends.

- An iconic timepiece has been introduced with the new collection, a classic design interpretation which appears in several versions ranging from glamorous with diamonds to a more technical model with an automatic mechanical movement.

HARRY WINSTON

harry Winston—the mere name conjures up glamorous images of diamonds and gemstones, of beautiful women and wonderful times. Indeed, the House of Harry Winston has been scintillating hearts and minds around the world for decades with its majestic jewelry. It's no wonder that this legendary brand can easily work the same magic with watches of ultimate distinction.

Since his very early teens, Harry Winston was consumed by a passion for diamonds and gems. He embarked on his career as a jeweler when he was just 15 and by **1920**—at age 24— he had started his first diamond company. A man with a vision and extraordinary talent, Harry Winston built a reputation for purveying some of the most celebrated gems in the world. In **1925** he caused a stir when he acquired the famous jewelry collection of Rebecca Darlington Stoddard. By the time he founded Harry Winston, Inc. in **1932**, he had already made several million-dollar transactions and was viewed as a shining star.

In **1946**, Winston met the Duke and Duchess of Windsor who became avid admirers of Winston's jewelry. In **1947** Winston was among the first to lend jewelry to the attendees of the Hollywood Oscars. Winston traveled the world to acquire famed stones, including the Hope Diamond and the sapphire of Catherine the Great. He began opening a series of salons around the world in **1955**—with the first neatly situated in Geneva.

Through the ensuing decades, Winston bought, sold and donated famous stones and continued to create the most magnificent masterpieces of diamonds and gems in the world.

The house of Harry Winston survived the founder's death in **1978**. Winston's son Ronald, at the helm today, masterfully continued in his father's tradition. In **1989** Ronald Winston established the brand's first collection of fine watches—called The Ultimate Timepiece series. Now focusing on haute horology as well as haute joaillerie, Winston has regularly unveiled spectacular timepieces. The Perpetual Calendar Minute Repeater made its debut in **1995** and the Ocean chronograph—the world's first platinum diving watch—came to fruition in **1998**. In **1999**, Winston unveiled the world-premiere Biretrograde complication and in the few years since, the brand has consistently offered remarkable timepieces of technical and aesthetic excellence to the world.

HARRY WINSTON

It is Harry Winston's Premier collection of watches that takes center stage when it comes to technical excellence. The newest addition to this series is the Excenter, which takes its name from the off-centered position of its two counters. The result of much technological research, the exclusive HW2811 module was specially designed for Excenter.

A world's first, the wristwatch boasts a bi-directional seconds display with a mechanical self-winding movement. The left counter tracks the seconds with a hand that moves down the semicircular indicator from 0 to 30 seconds and then back up again to 60 seconds. The larger counter on the right displays the hours and minutes.

Water resistant to 30 meters, the Excenter sports a bold round case of 18-karat white gold with double anti-reflection treatment on both the front and back sapphire crystal. In typical Harry Winston style, a jeweled version of the Excenter has also been created for women. It features a bezel and case-to-bracelet attachment that is set with Top Wesselton diamonds weighing more than three carats. The borders of the two counters on the natural mother-of-pearl dial are also framed with diamonds for added elegance.

New to the Harry Winston Avenue collection of Ultimate Time-pieces is the exquisite Golden Lady Avenue. This striking 18-karat yellow-gold watch is bedecked with stunning cognac colored diamonds that glow with lustrous sophistication. Decadent and daring, Harry Winston has created two versions of the Golden Lady Avenue. One is set with 28 golden diamonds and 25 white diamonds (weighing just under two carats), while the other is set with 36 golden diamonds and 26 white diamonds (weighing a total of 3.4 carats). A striking hand-stitched cognac satin strap further enhances the amber hue of this diamond beauty.

TOP
Two spectacular versions of the Golden Lady Avenue have been created, each with differing amounts of cognac and white diamonds.

BOTTOM
Steeped in legend and mystery, the Hope Diamond weighed about 112.19 carats when discovered in India more than 300 years ago. Cut several times, the now-45.52-carat gem was acquired by Harry Winston in 1949. Mr. Winston shared the Hope Diamond with the world in 1958 when he donated the deep-blue beauty to the Smithsonian Institution, where it became the single most-visited attraction in the world.

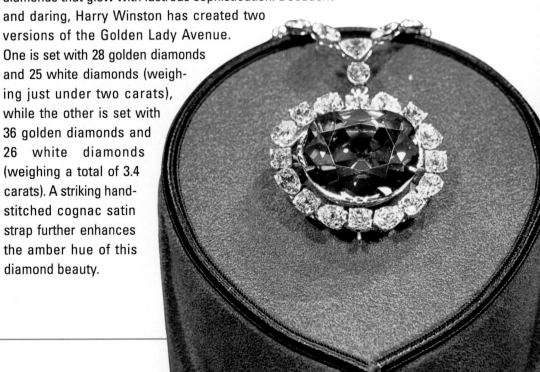

TOP

The Opus Two Perpetual
Calendar Tourbillon watch
is crafted in platinum and
features the day and date
readouts on the reverse
side of the watch with a
platinum cover.

BOTTOM

The Premier Excenter
is the world's first
wristwatch with a
bi-directional seconds
hand on a mechanical
self-winding movement.

HIGHLIGHTS

- The House of Harry Winston unveils the Opus Two, the second introduction in a series of joint creative ventures. The Opus Two was created in partnership with Geneva master watchmaker Antoine Preziuso, internationally known for his great complications.

- The Opus Two is a series of two platinum watches—each with tourbillon escapement. One is a tourbillon with 110 hours of power reserve and the other is a tourbillon with perpetual calendar. Just 12 pieces of each will be created.

- A jeweled version of the Opus Two also exists, with its bezels meticulously set with Harry Winston's flawless baguette diamonds. It is extremely rare for such an intricately engraved movement to be set with diamonds, but the motif of the movement is further enhanced with 157 miniature round diamonds—each a full brilliant cut with 57 facets—individually set into the spaces between the bridges of the movement.

- The Opus Two models are housed in one of the most technically complex cases that Harry Winston has ever created. It is based on the round Premier case, but now features a screw-in caseback. The Tourbillon with Perpetual calendar also features a solid platinum sprung-back cover with two apertures to reveal the day and date.

- The Opus Two follows Opus One (designed in 2001 by Winston and François-Paul Journe) and is unique to the watchmaking industry. The Opus concept is the brainchild of Ronald Winston and brings together two watchmakers to form a partnership in design and innovation. Working as equals, Harry Winston and the designated watchmaker in the Opus lineage, strive to create a valuable and rare timepiece worthy of the finest international collectors. With Opus, it is the intention of Harry Winston to intensify the brand's commitment to the future of fine Swiss Horology.

317

HARRY WINSTON

SEMIRAMIS   REF. 510/UQPL.D3/S03

Movement: quartz movement.
Functions: hour and minute.
Case: 950PT platinum case set with 24 baguette-cut diamonds on the bezel, 16 round-cut diamonds on the sides of the case and 1 round-cut diamond on the crown. Water-resistant to 3atm.
Dial: pavé-set diamonds.

Bracelet: satin strap with buckle set with 4 full-cut diamonds.
Carats: total weight of 7.35 carats of white diamonds.

SQUARE SIGNATURE   REF. 100/LQ18WW.D/DBC

Movement: quartz movement.
Functions: hour and minute.
Case: 18-karat white-gold square case set with diamonds on the bezel. Water-resistant to 3atm.
Dial: pavé-set diamonds.
Bracelet: 18-karat white-gold full-diamond set bracelet with 18-karat white-gold folding clasp.

Carats: total weight of 16.70 carats of white diamonds.
Also available: other versions available in 950PT platinum or 18-karat yellow gold with different types of settings and dials.

SQUARE SIGNATURE   REF. 100/LQ14WW.D01/DS02

Movement: quartz movement.
Functions: hour and minute.
Case: 18-karat white-gold square case set with baguette-cut pink sapphires on the bezel. Water-resistant to 3atm.
Dial: pavé-set diamonds.
Bracelet: 18-karat white-gold bracelet fully set with round-cut white diamonds and baguette-cut pink sapphires with 18-karat white-gold folding clasp.
Carats: total weight of 12.08 carats of white diamonds and 13.08 carats of pink sapphires.
Also available: other versions available with blue or yellow sapphires.

AVENUE C   REF. 330/LQGG31.M/D3.1/D2.1

Movement: quartz movement.
Functions: hour and minute.
Case: 18-karat yellow-gold rectangular case set with white diamonds on the bezel. Water-resistant to 3atm.
Dial: mother-of-pearl dial.
Bracelet: 18-karat yellow-gold captive bracelet set with white diamonds.
Carats: total weight of 4.78 carats of white diamonds.
Also available: other versions available in 18-karat white gold with various types of settings.

LADY AVENUE   REF. 310/LQWL.M/D3.2

Movement: quartz movement.
Functions: hour, minute and small second.
Case: 18-karat white-gold rectangular case set with white diamonds on the bezel. Water-resistant to 3atm.
Dial: mother-of-pearl dial.
Bracelet: croco strap with 18-karat white-gold folding clasp.
Carats: total weight of 1.20 carats of white diamonds.
Also available: other versions available in 18-karat yellow or pink gold with various types of settings and bracelets.

LADY AVENUE   REF. 310/LQRL.M/A04

Movement: quartz movement.
Functions: hour, minute and small second.
Case: 18-karat pink-gold rectangular case set with white diamonds and pink diamonds on the bezel. Water-resistant to 3atm.
Dial: mother-of-pearl dial.
Bracelet: satin strap with 18-karat pink-gold folding clasp.
Carats: total weight of 1.55 carats of white diamonds and 0.30 carats of pink sapphires.
Also available: other versions available in 18-karat white or yellow gold with yellow, "golden" or black diamonds, or blue sapphires and bracelets.

LADY AVENUE   REF. 310/LQGL.MD04/AB03

Movement: quartz movement.
Functions: hour, minute and small second.
Case: 18-karat yellow-gold rectangular case set with white diamonds and yellow baguette-cut sapphires on the bezel and on the sides of the case. Water-resistant to 3atm.
Dial: mother-of-pearl dial set with white diamonds on the index and the counter of the small second counter.
Bracelet: satin strap with 18-karat yellow-gold folding clasp.
Carats: total weight of 3.30 carats of white diamonds and 0.95 carats of yellow baguette-cut sapphires.
Also available: other versions available in 18-karat white or pink gold with blue or pink baguette-cut sapphires.

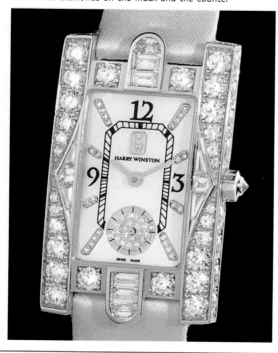

SWINGSECOND   REF. 310/UQSRWL.KD/D3.2

Movement: quartz movement.
Functions: hour, minute and bi-directional second.
Case: 18-karat white-gold rectangular case set with white diamonds on the bezel. Water-resistant to 3atm.
Dial: black dial set with white diamonds on the border of the bi-directional second.
Bracelet: croco strap with 18-karat white-gold folding clasp.
Carats: total weight of 1.55 carats of white diamonds.
Also available: other versions available in 18-karat yellow gold with various types of settings and bracelets.
Notes: A world's first.

HARRY WINSTON

PREMIER CHRONOGRAPH   REF. 200/UCQ32WL.KD/D3.1

Movement: FP1270 meca-quartz movement.
Functions: hour, minute, second and chronograph functions.
Case: 18-karat white-gold round case (32mm) set with white diamonds on the bezel and the lugs. Water-resistant to 3atm.
Dial: black dial set with diamonds on the counters of the chronograph.
Bracelet: croco strap with 18-karat white-gold folding clasp.

Carats: total weight of 2.35 carats of white diamonds.
Also available: other versions available in 18-karat yellow gold with various types of dials, bracelets and settings.

PREMIER CHRONOGRAPH   REF. 200/MCQ37WL.M/D3.1

Movement: FP1270 meca-quartz movement.
Functions: hour, minute, second and chronograph functions.
Case: 18-karat white-gold round case (37mm) set with white diamonds on the bezel and the lugs. Water-resistant to 3atm.
Dial: mother-of-pearl dial.
Bracelet: croco strap with 18-karat white-gold folding clasp.

Carats: total weight of 3.60 carats of white diamonds.
Also available: other versions available with various types of dials, bracelets and settings.

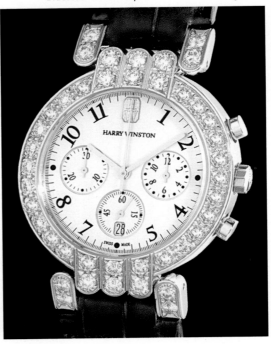

BIRETROGRADE   REF. 200/MABI37RL.W

Movement: GP3106 automatic movement with HW300 module.
Functions: hour, minute, retrograde second and retrograde day of the week.
Case: 18-karat pink-gold round case (37mm). Water-resistant to 3atm.
Dial: silvered white dial.
Bracelet: croco strap with 18-karat pink-gold folding clasp.
Also available: other versions available in 18-karat white gold with various types of dials, bracelets and settings.

BIRETROSECOND   REF. 200/MADSR37PL.A.

Movement: FP1160 automatic movement with HW 301 module.
Functions: hour, minute and double retrograde seconds.
Case: 950PT platinum round case (37mm). Water-resistant to 3atm.
Dial: anthracite dial.
Bracelet: croco strap with folding clasp.
Also available: other versions available with various types of bracelets and settings.
Notes: Limited edition of 100 pieces.

EXCENTER — REF. 200/MASR37WL.W

Movement: GP 3106 automatic movement with HW 2811 module.
Functions: hour, minute and bi-directional second.
Case: 18-karat white-gold round case (37mm). Water-resistant to 3atm.
Dial: silvered white dial with anthracite scales and off-center second.
Bracelet: croco strap with 18-karat white-gold folding clasp.
Also available: other versions available with various types of dials, bracelets and settings.
Note: A World's First.

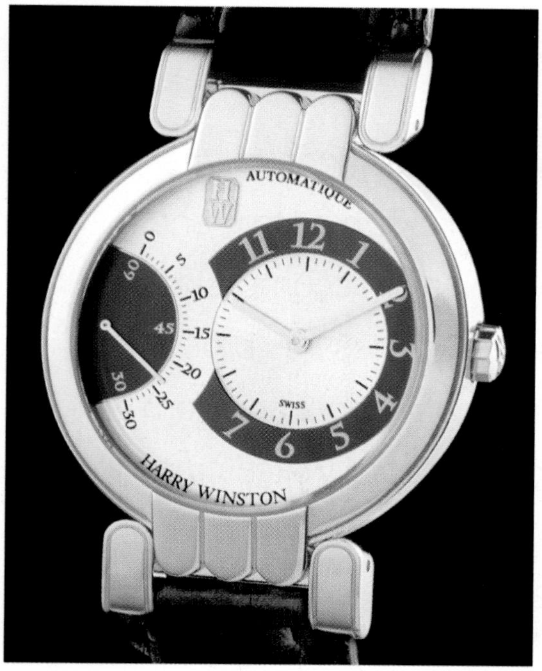

EXCENTER — REF. 200/MASR37WWC.MD/D3.1/D2.1

Movement: GP 3106 automatic movement with HW 2811 module.
Functions: hour, minute and bi-directional second.
Case: 18-karat white-gold round case (37mm) set with diamonds. Water-resistant to 3atm.
Dial: mother-of-pearl dial with scales and off-center second set with diamonds.
Bracelet: rubber and 18-karat white-gold bracelet set with diamonds and 18-karat white-gold folding clasp.
Carats: total weight of 5.46 carats of white diamonds.
Also available: other versions available with various types of dials, bracelets and settings.
Note: A World's First.

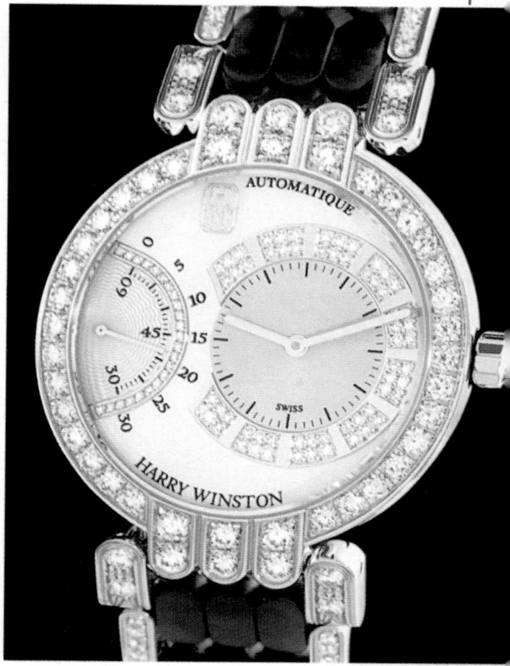

PREMIER PERPETUAL CALENDAR CHRONOGRAPH — REF. 200/MCAPC38PL.A.

Movement: FP 5688 chronograph automatic movement with perpetual calendar.
Functions: hour, minute, second, chronograph, month, date, day, moonphase, leap year.
Case: 950PT platinum round case (38mm). Water-resistant to 3atm.
Dial: anthracite dial.
Bracelet: croco strap with folding clasp.
Note: Limited edition of 100 pieces.

OCEAN AUTOMATIC CHRONOGRAPH — REF. 400/MCADV39PPC.K.

Movement: FP1185 chronograph automatic movement.
Functions: hour, minute and chronograph functions.
Case: 950PT platinum round case (39mm). Water-resistant to 10atm.
Dial: black dial.
Bracelet: rubber and 950PT platinum bracelet with folding clasp.
Also available: other versions available with various types of bracelets.
Notes: A world's first. Limited series of 200 pieces.

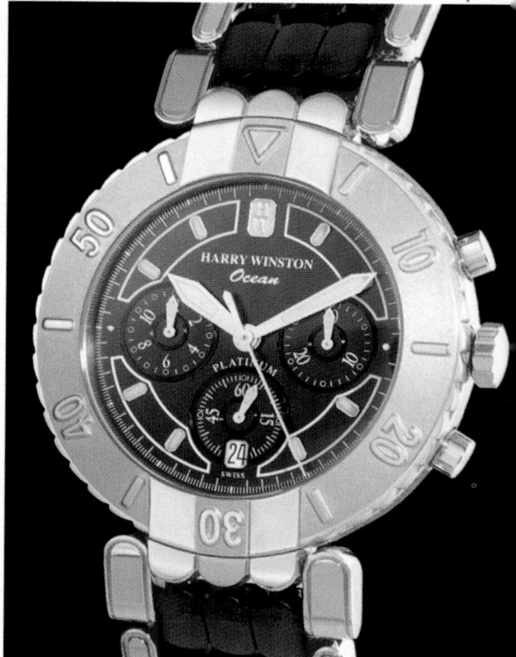

HERMÈS

time is limitless for Hermès. Indeed, the company is steeped in a rich history and tradition, in innovation and accomplishment. For more than a century, Hermès has brought to the world luxury items of distinction. From saddlebags to handbags, from watchstraps to watches, Hermès embodies the spirit of a world where expression is paramount.

Established in **1837** as a maker of fine saddles and harnesses, Hermès immediately gained a reputation for its luxurious leathers and quality craftsmanship. By the early **1900s**, the brand had acquired a very prestigious international following.

As times changed, Hermès kept pace. Moving from the equestrian field to the world of automobiles, Hermès began designing luggage, trunks, gloves and car accessories. Through the years, the company branched out into other areas. As wristwatches took the world by storm in the **1920s**, Hermès carved out its own niche creating elegant watchstraps for the finest companies.

In the **1930s**, the brand launched its handbags and in **1937**, unveiled its own custom silk scarves. In the ensuing decades, Hermès reveled in its position as a leader of the world's finest French products.

In **1975**, Hermès launched its Kelly watch—fashioned after its most famous Kelly handbag. Just three years later, Jean-Louis Dumas-Hermès reorganized the company and established La Montre Hermès SA in Bienne. This watchmaking factory gave rise to an entire collection of Hermès watches that embody the spirit and style of the brand.

Over the decades, Hermès has unveiled a variety of important watch collections, including the Clipper Cape Cod, Espace and H-Our signature watch line. In **1999**, the brand inaugurated its new state-of-the-art workshops in Bienne. Two years later, the Nomade collection of autoquartz watches made its debut in **2001**.

THIS PAGE

LEFT
The new Nomade Gent's watch dons a steel bracelet for boldness.

FACING PAGE

A true precision instrument, the Nomade autoquartz watch is offered with a compass.

FAR LEFT
The chronograph version of the Nomade offers three counters.

TOP CENTER
The Cape Cod Deux Zones is available for men or women. This ladies' model features a supple chain-link bracelet.

TOP RIGHT
This Cape Cod Chronograph offers hours, minutes and seconds, and date in addition to the counters.

BELOW
Crafted in steel and gold, the Oval Clipper watch features 12 porthole bolts on its bezel to indicate the hours.

Located in the heart of the traditional Swiss-watchmaking region, Hermès retains the advantage of its innovative Parisian spirit when it comes to watch styling. Regularly, this fine company adds novelties and new versions to its successful collections.

A watch that's built to withstand the elements, the Nomade is powered by an autoquartz movement, which requires no battery. By combining high-precision quartz with rotor technology, the autoquarz movement has 45 to 100 days of power reserve built into it. Now, Hermès has expanded the Nomade collection by adding a striking ladies' version, a chronograph, a men's bracelet model, and the precision-oriented compass watch. The Nomade Compass watch links time and space in avant-garde fashion. The anti-magnetic stainless steel case features a sapphire crystal and a hinged back cover that opens to reveal the compass beneath an optical mineral glass.

The elongated rectangular Cape Cod collection also inherits a sporty new member. The Cape Cod Deux Zones displays two time zones—each on a separate subdial on the gracefully curved watch face. Water resistant to 50 meters, the watch is incredibly versatile with its various colored offerings.

Constantly revisiting and reinterpreting its long-time bestsellers, Hermès can't resist adding new touches. The Paprika model from the 1970s has been reintroduced with a moveable H-shaped case-to-bracelet attachment that also offers a very modern appeal. Dedicated exclusively to women, this watch is named after the signature Hermès color.

Similarly, the Clipper—first designed in 1981—has become one of Hermès's leading models. Recognized by its distinctive round bezel decorated with six "bolts" designed to resemble the portholes of old sail boats, the round watch now has an oval sibling. The new oval Clipper features 12 bolts on its bezel, one for each hour. The clean dial is beautifully guillochéd and simply elegant in black, silver or white.

ABOVE

The Rallye watch is now available in a men's version. This steel model features a 31x38mm case.

TOP CENTER

Pastel hues brighten the signature H-Our collection of timepieces.

TOP RIGHT

Water resistant to 30 meters, the new Paprika is characterized by its flexible case-to-bracelet attachments.

RIGHT

The newest Kelly Clochette watch features a freestanding timepiece designed to nestle within a leather pendant necklace.

■ Hermès has added at least one new version to a half a dozen of its key collections—offering variety and newness.

■ The Cape Cod now features a chronograph version for men that measures the time on three different counters. The square case is crafted of steel and features a date window at 4:00.

■ First created in 1985 as a ladies' model, the cushion-cornered rectangle Rallye watch is now available as a men's model with a sleek subdial seconds display at 6:00.

■ Color—a vital element in Hermès's collections—refreshes the H-Our series as pastels join the collection. New watches feature dials and straps of matching hues in pale blue, green, orange and mauve.

■ The Kelly watch, linked historically to the Kelly bag and one of the most famous Hermès collections, is regularly updated and fused with invention in styling. The newest piece is the Kelly Clochette, which features the lock-shaped watch fitted inside a leather pouch worn around the neck.

HERMÈS

MEN'S AUTOMATIC CAPE COD   REF. CC1.710.220/ACO

Movement: automatic rewind, ETA 8 3/4 2000, autonomy 42 hours.
Functions: hour, minute, second, date.
Case: steel, sapphire glass, water resistant to 50 meters.
Also available: yellow-gold 750 (only for ladies' yellow-gold 750 with diamonds, white gold or white gold with diamonds).
Size: 34.00 x 29.00mm.

Thickness: 8.40mm.
Dial: silver, painted Arabic numerals.
Also available: black, white, ivory, white-mother-of pearl only for gold version.
Strap: cognac ostrich.
Also available: on Hermès leather strap (standard or double tour: bridle leather, gulliver, barenia calf, chamonix calf, ostrich, courchevel, box, smooth grained calf, lizard, crocodile), steel, yellow gold (only for ladies' with diamonds, white gold with or without diamonds).

LADIES' QUARTZ CAPE COD   REF. CC1.210.220/VBA2

Movement: quartz ETA 5 1/2 976.001.
Functions: hour, minute.
Case: steel, sapphire glass, water resistant to 30 meters.
Also available: yellow-gold 750 (only for ladies' yellow-gold 750 with diamonds, white gold or white gold with diamonds).
Size: 23.00 x 23.00mm.

Thickness: 6.45mm.
Dial: silver, painted Arabic numerals.
Also available: black, white, ivory, white mother-of-pearl only for gold version.
Strap: natural barenia calf double tour.
Also available: on Hermès leather strap (standard or double tour: bridle leather, gulliver, barenia calf, chamonix calf, ostrich, courchevel, box, smooth grained calf, lizard, crocodile), steel, yellow gold (only for ladies with diamonds, white gold with or without diamonds).

LADIES' QUARTZ CAPE COD   REF. CC1.293.213/4706

Movement: quartz ETA 5 1/2 976.001.
Functions: hour, minute.
Case: white gold with diamonds, sapphire glass, water resistant to 30 meters.
Also available: white gold, yellow gold or yellow gold with diamonds, steel
Size: 23.00 x 23.00mm.
Thickness: 6.45mm.

Dial: white mother-of-pearl, painted Arabic numeral.
Also available: black, white, ivory, silver.
Bracelet: white gold with diamonds.
Also available: without diamonds, yellow gold with or without diamonds, steel, or Hermès leather strap (standard or double tour: bridle leather, gulliver, chamonix calf, barenia calf, ostrich, courchevel, box, smooth grained calf, lizard, crocodile).

MEDIUM'S H-OUR   REF. HH1.510.260/CAR

Movement: quartz ETA 5 1/2 901.001.
Functions: hour, minute.
Case: steel, sapphire glass, water resistant to 30 meters.
Also available: steel with diamonds, yellow gold with or without diamonds.
Size: 26.00 x 26.00mm.
Thickness: 6.40mm.

Dial: silver.
Also available: blue jeans, black, orange, copper, white, gilt, mauve, pale orange, blue, green.
Strap: crocodile agate rousse.
Also available: on Hermès leather strap (crocodile, lizard, gulliver, courchevel, barenia calf, nepal calf) steel with or without diamonds, yellow gold with or without diamonds, white gold with or without diamonds.

MEDIUM'S AUTOQUARTZ NOMADE — REF. NO1.710.230/VRH

Movement: autoquartz ETA Cal. 11 ½ 205.911, autonomy 100 days.
Functions: hour, minute, second, date.
Case: steel, glare-proof sapphire glass, water resistant to 50 meters.
Size: 35.00 x 36.50mm.
Thickness: 8.75mm.
Dial: silver.
Also available: black.
Strap: red H chamonix.
Also available: natural bridle leather, black smooth grained calf, black barenia calf, black alligator matte, nepal calf, steel bracelet.

MEDIUM'S HARNAIS MODEL — REF. HA3.410.130/INA

Movement: quartz ETA 7 ¾ 956.112.
Functions: hour, minute, date.
Case: steel, domed sapphire glass, water resistant to 30 meters.
Size: diameter 30.50mm.
Thickness: 8.70mm.
Dial: white.
Strap: natural bridle leather.
Also available: black bridle leather.

LADIES' KELLY — REF. KE1.210.280/HNO

Movement: quartz ETA 5 ½ 901.001.
Functions: hour, minute.
Case: steel, mineral glass, non-water resistant.
Also available: gold, gold with diamonds and gold plated.
Size: 20.00 x 20.00mm.
Thickness: 8.48mm.
Dial: black.
Also available: white, red H, silver, gold, orange, blue jeans, gilt, green.
Strap: black courchevel.
Also available: on Hermès leather strap (standard: ostrich, fjord, gulliver, courchevel, box calf, crocodile, alligator, lizard, double tour: royal blue box, pale-beige nepal box, smooth red H grained calf, barenia calf).

MINI BELT — REF. BE1.130.160/CRY

Movement: quartz ETA 5 ½ 976.001.
Functions: hour, minute.
Case: steel with diamonds, sapphire glass, water resistant to 30 meters.
Also available: stainless steel without diamonds.
Size: 25.70 x 22.00mm.
Thickness: 7.50mm.
Dial: white.
Also available: ivory.
Strap: royal blue crocodile.
Also available: on Hermès leather strap (gulliver, box calf, grained calf, crocodile, alligator, ostrich, smooth cognac pigskin) steel bracelet.

HERMÈS

MEN'S SÉSAME — REF. SM1.710.220/MGO

Movement: skeleton mechanical, automatic winding, ETA 11 1/2 2892 A2, autonomy 42-hour power-reserve.
Functions: hour, minute, second.
Case: steel, sapphire glass face and back, water resistant to 30 meters, finally worked oscillating weight.
Also available: yellow gold and white gold.

Size: diameter 36.50mm.
Thickness: 7.75mm.
Dial: visible steel movement.
Strap: gold alligator.
Also available: red H alligator, black alligator matte.

MEN'S ESPACE — REF. ES1.710.330/ENO

Movement: quartz ETA 11 1/2 988.431.
Functions: analog hour and minute, digital hour, minute and second, date and second, date and day, countdown, second time zone, chronograph, alarm.
Case: steel, sapphire glass, water resistant to 30 meters.
Size: 36.50 x 37.70mm.
Thickness: 6.90mm.

Dial: black, white painted numeral, luminous points and hands.
Strap: coromandel goat.
Also available: alligator matte, steel bracelet.

MEN'S CHRONOGRAPH CLIPPER MODEL — REF. CL1.910.630/3753

Movement: quartz gent's chronograph ETA 13 1/4 251.262
Functions: hour, minute, small second, date, chronograph with 3 counters.
Case: steel, glare-proof sapphire glass, water resistant to 50 meters.
Also available: steel and yellow gold, yellow gold.
Size: diameter 38.50mm.
Thickness: 9.95mm.

Dial: blue with 3 counters.
Also available: white, ivory, black or gilt, dark gray, copper, blue.
Strap: steel bracelet.
Also available: on Hermès straps (buffalo, crocodile, smooth grained calf only for Clipper Oval) steel and yellow-gold bracelet, double-tour natural bridle leather, and barenia calf for automatic Clipper only.

LADIES' H-OUR — REF. HH1.286.270/4800

Movement: quartz ETA 5 1/2 901.001
Functions: hour, minute.
Case: yellow gold with diamonds, sapphire glass, water resistant to 30 meters.
Also available: yellow gold, white gold with or without diamonds, steel with or without diamonds.
Size: diameter 21.00 x 21.00mm.

Thickness: 6.20mm.
Dial: silver.
Also available: blue jeans, black, orange, copper, white, gilt, mauve, pale blue, orange, green.
Bracelet: yellow gold.
Also available: on Hermès leather strap (crocodile, courchevel, gulliver, barenia calf, lizard, nepal calf) yellow gold with diamonds, white gold with or without diamonds, steel with or without diamonds.

MEN'S CHRONOGRAPH NOMADE   REF. NO1.910.330/4932

Movement: autoquartz men's chronograph ETA Cal. 13 1/4 206.211, Autonomy 45 days.
Functions: hour, minute, small second, date, chronograph with three counters.
Case: steel, glare-proof sapphire glass, water resistant to 50 meters.
Size: 40.80 x 39.00mm.
Thickness: 12.45mm.
Dial: black.
Also available: silver.
Bracelet: steel.
Also available: on Hermès leather strap (natural bridle leather, black smooth grained calf, black barenia calf, black alligator matte, nepal calf, Red H chamonix).

LADIES' OVAL CLIPPER   REF. CO1.220.220/3787

Movement: quartz ETA 5 1/2 976.001.
Functions: hour, minute.
Case: steel and gold, sapphire glass, water-resistant to 50 meters.
Also available: steel.
Size: 27.00 x 22.00mm.
Thickness: 6.25mm.
Dial: silver.
Also available: white, black.
Bracelet: steel, yellow gold.
Also available: on Hermès strap, smooth grained calf, steel and yellow gold bracelet, double-tour natural bridle leather and barenia calf for automatic Clipper only.

MEN'S YELLOW GOLD TANDEM   REF. TA1.785.212/CNO

Movement: quartz ETA 7 3/4 956.032
Functions: hour, minute.
Case: yellow gold, beveled sapphire glass, water resistant to 50 meters.
Also available: steel with or without diamonds, yellow gold with diamonds, white gold, white gold with diamonds (only for ladies).
Size: 31.60 x 25.60mm.
Thickness: 7.38mm.
Dial: white mother-of-pearl.
Also available: blue, white mother-of-pearl, silver, black, copper.
Strap: etrusque crocodile.
Also available: fjord, barenia calf, crocodile, steel with or without diamonds, yellow gold with or without diamonds.

MEN'S CHRONOGRAPH CAPE COD   REF. CC1.910.330/SNO

Movement: quartz ETA 10 1/2 251.471
Functions: hour, minute, second, date, chronograph with three counters.
Case: steel, glare-proof sapphire glass, water resistant to 30 meters.
Also available: white gold with or without diamonds, yellow gold with or without diamonds (not for chronograph).
Size: 31.50 x 31.00mm.
Thickness: 10.00mm.
Dial: black.
Also available: silver, white, gilt, ivory, white mother-of-pearl (not for chronograph).
Strap: black smooth grained calf.
Also available: on Hermès leather strap (standard or double tour: bridle leather, gulliver, barenia calf, chamonix calf, ostrich, courchevel, box, smooth grained calf, lizard, crocodile), steel, yellow gold with or without diamonds, white gold with or without diamonds, bracelet (not for chronograph).

HUBLOT

barely 25 years old, Hublot is a brand that has made a rare mark on the world. Distinct in style and immediately recognizable, Hublot timepieces set the trend in watchmaking for marrying precious metals with rubber—a trend that, two decades later, is finally taking the watch world by storm.

In **1977**, Carlo Crocco established MDM Geneve. It was his dream to create the ultimate watch—a sporty, elegant piece that would rise above changing fashions and become an icon around the globe. In **1980**, after spending three years on their research and development, Crocco unveiled his Hublot timepieces to the world. Unprecedented in design, the watches were crafted in 18-karat gold and featured vanilla-scented rubber straps. While some people were aghast, others quickly embraced the concept. Within months, royalty and celebrities, tycoons and politicians were donning Hublot timepieces.

In **1985**, Crocco took the sporty side of the watch a step further with the Plongeur Professional—a diver's watch that was water resistant to 300 meters. This was followed two years later by the first automatic Hublot, which housed a Frédéric Piguet movement. In **1988**, the first Hublot chronograph was presented to the world. Housing an electro-mechanical Piguet movement, the watch was a technical advancement for the brand. Throughout the ensuing decade, Hublot continued to introduce special watches, including a GMT and a limited-edition automatic chronograph.

In **1999**, Hublot launched the Super Professional, a high-tech diver's watch that was water resistant to 45 atmospheres. The year **2000** marked the brand's 20th anniversary and Hublot celebrated by unveiling the Grand Quantième perpetual calendar watch. Today, Hublot continues to offer excellence in craftsmanship and design. Never abandoning its rubber roots, the brand has triumphed with shimmering accents such as mother-of-pearl dials, diamonds and gemstones.

Today, 23 years after their debut, Hublot watches remain true to their original concept. The original creator of today's fashion phenomenon, Hublot proceeds with its philosophy and long-established trademark. Focusing on freedom of creation and preservation of watchmaking excellence, Crocco regularly unveils Hublot timepieces of unique stature.

In addition to the rubber strap, Hublot's case design is also an original concept. No less than 160 manual operations are required to produce each Hublot watchcase with its porthole design. Every limited-edition watch is numbered and accompanied by a certificate designating its number within the series.

Among the newest pieces from Hublot are expansions of its chronograph line for women. Indeed, Hublot has taken great care to design a functional timepiece that offers all of the femininity and grace that women deserve. Inspired by the Elegant Chronograph 1810 watch, Hublot has designed a smaller case for women's wrists in the new Chrono Lady.

The Chrono Lady combines sensual beauty and technical prowess. Each watch features a colored mother-of-pearl dial and is adorned with eight diamond markers. A date aperture appears at the 6:00 position and the watch houses a Piguet 1270 movement.

Hublot has extended the Chrono Lady and unveiled the Diamond Chrono Lady. Crafted in steel, this watch is embellished with a dazzling double row of Top Wesselton diamonds set around the bezel and case.

HIGHLIGHTS

- Favoring color, Hublot has unveiled the natural mother-of-pearl Indigo dial. Inspired by the indigo hues of the Tuareg turbans and caftans of the Sahara desert, the dial is a rich blue/purple shade.

- The Indigo dial is available on three watches in the Hublot collection, the Elegant Chronograph, the Elegant Homme and the Elegant Femme. The registers of the Chronograph version are hollowed out to unveil a deeper shade of indigo for striking contrast.

- A new SuperB extra-wide chronograph has joined the Hublot lineup. Resolutely contemporary, the Chrono SuperB was developed on the basis of the Classic Chronograph, but its case has been widened considerably and Hublot has devised a new bezel with larger, easier to read numerals.

- The Chrono SuperB features new high-security lockable pushpieces made of natural rubber. The dial of the watch is a sun-brushed translucent lacquer elegantly applied by MDM Geneve's master artisans. The tobacco-colored dial features charcoal subdials for the chronograph counters.

- Housing an automatic movement, the Chrono SuperB is water resistant to100 meters.

TOP LEFT

The new Diamond Chrono Lady is crafted in steel and adorned with two rows of diamonds to accent the shimmering mother-of-pearl or black dial.

CENTER

The Chrono Lady features a pink mother-of-pearl dial with eight diamonds as markers. The 37mm case is crafted in steel and is water resistant to 50 meters.

RIGHT

Hublot specializes in creating one-of-kind watches.

HUBLOT

CHRONOGRAPH ELEGANT FLY-BACK
REF. 1810.910.4

Movement: automatic, ETA 2892A2 base + Dubois Dépraz 2021 caliber chronograph module, personalized for Hublot. **Functions:** hour, minute, small second; date; fly-back chronograph with 3 counters. **Case:** 18K white-gold, three-piece case (Ø 40mm, thickness 12.7mm), black brilliant pavé; flat sapphire crystal; bezel with set rubies; white-gold screw-down crown and olive-shaped pushers; back attached by 6 screws. Water resistant to 10atm. **Dial:** black gold, counters decorated with cir-

cular beads; applied burnished bâton markers, applied black-gold Hublot logo at 12; marks between 7 and 8, luminescent burnished steel leaf-style hands. **Indications:** small second at 3; date between 4 and 5; hour counter at 6; minute counter at 9; center fly-back counter; minute track with divisions for 1/5 of a second with luminescent dots and tachometer scale. **Strap:** rubber, reinforced with integrated steel blades and inserted in a patented attachment; white-gold double fold-over clasp. **Also available:** in pink gold with brilliant pavé and pink-gold dial, 25 pieces; without brilliants: in pink gold with pink-gold dial, 25 pieces; in white gold with black-gold dial; 199 pieces.
Note: created as a limited edition of 25 pieces.

CHRONOGRAPH ELEGANT
REF. 1810.844B.1

Movement: automatic, ETA 2892A2 base + Dubois Dépraz 2021 chronograph module, personalized for Hublot. **Functions:** hour, minute, small second; date; chronograph with 3 counters. **Case:** stainless steel, three-piece case (Ø 40, thickness 12.7mm); flat sapphire crystal; screw-down crown and olive-shaped pushers; back attached by 6 screws. Water resistant to 10atm. **Dial:** indigo mother-of-pearl, dark indigo counters decorated with circular beads; markers with set brilliants, applied

white-gold Hublot logo at 12; luminescent blued steel leaf-style hands. **Indications:** small second at 3; date between 4 and 5; hour counter at 6; minute counter at 9; center second counter; minute track with divisions for 1/5 of a second with luminescent dots and tachometer scale. **Strap:** rubber, reinforced with integrated steel blades and inserted in a patented attachment; double fold-over steel clasp. **Also available:** black, silvered, blue or bordeaux dial: steel; yellow, pink or white gold; bezel and markers with brilliants: steel or yellow gold; without brilliants, with black, silvered, blue, bordeaux or yellow dial, luminescent applied markers or Arabic numerals: steel, steel and yellow gold or yellow, pink or white gold, platinum.

CHRONOGRAPH ELEGANT LADY
REF. 1640.844M.1

Movement: electrical drive controlled by a quartz crystal and mechanical chronograph, Frédéric Piguet 1270 caliber.
Functions: hour, minute, small second; date; chronograph with 3 counters.
Case: stainless steel, three-piece case (Ø 37mm, thickness 9.8mm), polished and brushed finish; flat sapphire crystal; olive-shaped pushers; back attached by 6 screws. Water resistant to 5atm.

Dial: "borealis" pink mother-of-pearl; markers with set brilliants, applied white-gold Hublot logo at 12; skeleton steel leaf-style hands.
Indications: hour counter at 3; date and small second at 6; minute counter at 9; center second counter; minute track with divisions for 1/5 of a second and tachometer scale.
Strap: rubber, reinforced with integrated steel blades and inserted in a patented attachment; double fold-over steel clasp.
Also available: indigo mother-of-pearl dial; black dial, bezel and markers with brilliants with black dial; indigo or "borealis" mother-of-pearl dial; without brilliants, with silvered dial and blued markers.

ELEGANT POWER RESERVE
REF. 1830.130.1

Movement: mechanical, automatic-winding, ETA 2892A2 base + power reserve module.
Functions: hour, minute, second; date; power reserve.
Case: stainless steel, three-piece case (Ø 40mm, thickness 12mm); flat sapphire crystal; brushed bezel; screw-down crown; back attached by 6 screws. Water resistant to 10atm.

Dial: black; luminescent printed Arabic numerals, applied white-gold Hublot logo at 12; printed minute track; luminescent steel bâton hands.
Indications: date at 3; power reserve at 6.
Strap: rubber, reinforced with integrated steel blades and inserted in a patented attachment; double fold-over steel clasp.
Also available: with applied bâton markers; bordeaux dial with luminescent Arabic numerals or applied baton markers.

CLASSIC CHRONOGRAPH SUPER B   REF. 1920.440.1

Movement: mechanical, automatic-winding, ETA 2892A2 base + Dubois Dépraz 2021 caliber chronograph module, personalized for Hublot.
Functions: hour, minute, small second; date; chronograph with 3 counters.
Case: stainless steel, three-piece case (Ø 42.5mm, thickness 13.5mm); flat sapphire crystal; brushed bezel with engraved tachometer scale; screw-down steel crown with rubber cover and screw-down pushers (in steel with screw-down ring covered with rubber); back attached by 8 screws. Water resistant to 10atm.
Dial: silvered, counters decorated with circular beads; luminescent printed bâton markers, Hublot logo at 12; luminescent steel bâton hands.
Indications: small second at 3; date between 4 and 5; hour counter at 6; minute counter at 9; center second counter; minute track with divisions for 1/5 of a second.
Strap: rubber, reinforced with integrated steel blades and inserted in a patented attachment; double fold-over steel clasp.
Also available: black or "marron-glacé" dial and black subdials.

SUPER PROFESSIONAL 450MT   REF. 1850.F40.1

Movement: mechanical, automatic-winding, ETA 2892A2 caliber, personalized for Hublot.
Functions: hour, minute, second; date.
Case: stainless steel, three-piece case (Ø 41mm, thickness 12.5mm); flat sapphire crystal with magnifying lens on date; one-way turning bezel with additional locking device to maintain the selected position (causing a counter clockwise rotational force of the element placed between frame and ring acting upon the lateral juts, this shall snap in by approx. 5mm in the "safety" position, thus preventing any accidental rotation); engraved minute track, for the calculation of diving time; screw-down crown with case protection; back attached by 8 screws. Water resistant to 45atm.
Dial: fuchsia; luminescent round markers; printed logo and minute track; luminescent Index steel hands.
Indications: date at 3.
Strap: rubber, reinforced with integrated steel blades and inserted in a patented attachment; double fold-over steel clasp.
Also available: with blue or black dial.

CLASSIC GRAND QUANTIÈME   REF. 1840.BUR.8

Movement: mechanical, automatic-winding, Dubois Dépraz 14370 caliber, ETA 2892A2 base + big-date and day module.
Functions: hour, minute, second; day; date.
Case: 18K pink-gold, three-piece case (Ø 38.5mm, thickness 10.5mm); flat sapphire crystal; brushed bezel with 12 titanium screws at hour markers; pink-gold screw-down crown; back attached by 6 screws. Water resistant to 5atm.
Dial: bordeaux; applied pink-gold firm's logo at 12; luminescent pink-gold bâton hands.
Indications: day of the week at 6; big date in double window at 12.
Strap: rubber, reinforced with integrated blades and inserted in a patented attachment; double pink-gold fold-over clasp.
Also available: with black, white or blue dial; in yellow or white gold, steel; in pink gold with pink-gold dial, 200 pieces; white gold with black-gold dial, 100 pieces.

CLASSIC LARGE   REF. 1880.BUR.8

Movement: mechanical, automatic-winding, ETA 2892A2 caliber, personalized for Hublot.
Functions: hour, minute, second; date.
Case: 18K pink-gold, three-piece case (Ø 38.5mm, thickness 7.7mm); flat sapphire crystal; brushed bezel with 12 titanium screws at hour markers; pink-gold screw-down crown; back attached by 6 screws. Water resistant to 5atm.
Dial: bordeaux; applied pink-gold Hublot logo at 12; luminescent pink-gold bâton hands.
Indications: date at 3.
Strap: rubber reinforced by integrated steel blades and inserted in the patented central attachment; double fold-over pink-gold clasp.
Also available: in yellow gold with black dial; steel with white, black or blue dial; with quartz movement: in stainless steel; in steel/yellow gold, in yellow gold.

IWC International Watch Co.

for 135 years, IWC, International Watch Co., has been turning out masterpieces wrought with technical prowess and excellence in craftsmanship. The only Swiss brand to have the unique distinction of being founded by an American, IWC has continuously displayed unflagging vigilance in the field of precision timekeeping.

American watchmaker Florentine Ariosto Jones traveled from the New England region to Switzerland in the late 1860s, intent upon creating precision timepieces and bringing their production to America. Jones established IWC and set about creating his own caliber, a high-precision movement that was among the first to be wound from the crown. In 1890, IWC developed its first Grand Complication pocket watch, which incorporated more than 1,300 mechanical pieces.

Throughout the entire 20th century, IWC would regularly demonstrate its leadership in the field of luxury watchmaking. Its first wristwatches were produced for the British Royal Navy and the Imperial German Navy in 1900. By the early 1930s, the brand had produced advanced pilot's watches and by the early 1940s it had developed the world's first antimagnetic system. In the second half of the 20th century, IWC perfected its automatic-rewinding mechanisms and introduced the now-famed Ingenieur sports watch.

In 1985, IWC unveiled its revolutionary DaVinci perpetual calendar watch—the first to hold a mechanism that would retain accuracy for at least 500 years. Five years later, the brand released what was hailed as the most complicated wristwatch of the era—the Grande Complication with nine hands and 659 parts. In 1997, the GST collection of sports chronograph watches made its debut.

With such an illustrious profile, IWC drew the attention of the luxury giant Richemont Group, which purchased the brand in 2000. In 2001, IWC unveiled the Portuguese model with the patented Pellaton winding system and two new GST high-precision watches. Indeed, under the auspices of Richemont Group, IWC continues to flourish and to unveil masterpieces of technical perfection.

The recently unveiled Big Pilot's Watch houses a 7-day automatic movement equipped with IWC's patented Pellaton winding mechanism. With its imposing 46mm case, The Big Pilot's Watch (ref. 5002) becomes the new flagship model for the brand's Fliegerchronograph series of pilot's watches. Crafted from a solid block of steel, the case is bold and distinctive and houses an inner iron ring guaranteeing antimagnetism.

In its GST collection, where the brand recently unveiled the GST Chrono-Rattrapante and the GST Perpetual Calendar watches, freshness comes with new dials and accents. The GST Perpetual Calendar, which is programmed until the year 2499, is now available in either titanium or steel. It features luminous hands and markers and an antireflective convex sapphire crystal. Dial choices include white, silver and black. Similarly, the GST Chrono-Rattrapante is now available with either a rhodium-plated dial, or with a black, blue or white dial.

HIGHLIGHTS

- For the first time, IWC has teamed with a famous international fashion house to create a limited-edition timepiece. This past year, the brand established a creative partnership with Prada, and is producing a special series of 2000 GST Chrono-Automatic Prada watches. The high-tech sports watch is designed to withstand extreme stress and is created in honor of the Luna Rossa challenge-one of the toughest sailing races in the world and an event that Prada takes part in each year.

- The GST Chrono-Automatic Prada watch is crafted in steel and features "IWC for Prada" on the dial. It is also hand engraved on the caseback. The 40mm case houses an automatic mechanical movement and offers a calendar displaying the day and date.

- IWC now offers the Portuguese Chrono-Automatic watch in an 18-karat rose-gold, white-gold or yellow-gold version with hands and numerals color-coordinated in gold to match the case.

- In a particularly timely move, IWC has developed its own forum of watch collectors and has held virtual meetings via its website (www.iwc.ch). Devised as a platform for experts and connoisseurs of IWC watches from around the world to exchange knowledge, the Collectors' Forum represents a trend-setting dynamic for IWC.

JAEGER-LeCOULTRE

One of the few, prestigious watch Manufactures today, Jaeger-LeCoultre boasts a history rich with invention, innovation and quality craftsmanship. Easily setting standards of excellence by which others can measure their products, Jaeger-LeCoultre has been making significant contributions to watchmaking for more than 170 years.

The first timepieces made by Antoine LeCoultre in **1833** were exceptional mechanical movements. Among the wonders he produced, LeCoultre invented the first keyless winding system in **1847**, followed by other specialty timepieces that included minute repeaters and alarm clocks. LeCoultre's family followed in his footsteps—watchmakers by trade for generation after generation.

In **1903**, Antoine's grandson Jacques-David met the Parisian chronometer-maker Edmond Jaeger. In the ensuing decades, this firm would emerge as a strong leader in the elite world of horological masterpieces. In **1928**, the Atmos—the only clock powered by air—was perfected. In **1931**, the legendary Reverso watch was unveiled to the world and was an immediate hit. Jaeger-LeCoultre brand was officially registered in **1937**. In the **1950**s, the brand launched the Memovox, the first automatic wristwatch alarm and the Geophysic chronometer. To protect its watchmaking inventions and secrets, Jaeger-LeCoultre has garnered hundreds of patents over the years.

Continually making inroads in invention and craftsmanship, Jaeger-LeCoultre introduced a wealth of new timepieces in the **1990**s, ranging from the Master Control 1000 Hour watches to the Reverso 101—which holds the world's record for the smallest mechanical movement (Jaeger-LeCoultre's Caliber 101, first invented in **1929**).

In **2000**, Jaeger-LeCoultre was acquired by Richemont Group, which has upheld the virtues of the brand and compromised none of its sanctity. Today, Jaeger-LeCoultre continues to unveil masterpiece after masterpiece.

THIS PAGE

TOP LEFT
A true technical feat, the Master Compressor Memovox watch features an automatic movement whose crowns at 2:00 and 4:00 are equipped with compression keys. The watch is inspired by the Memovox from the 1960s.

CENTER LEFT
The limited-edition Septantième in 18-karat gold is housed in the large XGT Reverso case.

BELOW
Featuring a mechanical movement that is decorated by hand, this Reverso Gran'Sport Duo is a dual time-zone watch that is water resistant to 5atm.

FACING PAGE

The Reverso Septantième watch in platinum features an extraordinary 18-karat white-gold movement with eight-day power reserve.

This esteemed company is known for producing some of the finest timepieces in horological history—and its current unveilings are no exception. Focused on bringing its spectacular Reverso collection to even greater heights, Jaeger-LeCoultre has introduced the Reverso Septantième Limited Edition watch. Featuring the extra-large 18-karat gold XGT Reverso case, the precision timepiece houses a solid 18-karat gold movement consisting of 224 parts and 25 jewels, offering eight days of power reserve.

The uniqueness of this watch lies not in the eight days of power reserve, but in the fact that Jaeger-LeCoultre's master-watchmakers, after months of meticulous research and development, were able to achieve the eight days of power reserve without having to compromise precision. The balance of this movement oscillates at 28,800 vibrations per hour. To date, few watches with an eight-day power reserve have been able to achieve such a high frequency (simply because increasing the duration of the power reserve necessitates reducing the movement's energy consumption). The mechanical manually wound Jaeger-LeCoultre Caliber 879 at the heart of the Reverso Septantième is also the first wherein just a few turns of the crown are enough to wind the watch for more than a week. The Reverso Septantième is being created in a limited edition of 500 pieces in 18-karat rose gold with an 18-karat rose-gold movement (with a suggested retail price of $32,500), and 500 pieces in platinum with an 18-karat white-gold movement (with a suggested retail price of $45,000).

HIGHLIGHTS

■ In addition to the Reverso Septantième, Jaeger-LeCoultre has unveiled a variety of other magnificent Reverso watches. Among them is the Gran'Sport Duo (dual time-zone watch) for men and a collection of diamond-adorned Gran'Sport watches for women.

■ Jaeger-LeCoultre has also unveiled a series of incredible Haute Joaillerie Reversos featuring white or natural fancy colored diamonds on dials, cases and bracelets. The brand has also launched several radiant new renditions of the Reverso Duetto and Reverso Florale for women.

■ A new series of engraveable Reversos emerges both with and without diamonds.

MASTER GRANDE MEMOVOX   REF. 146.344.A

Movement: automatic-winding, Jaeger-LeCoultre 909 caliber, 45 hours power reserve. Tested over 1,000 hours. Constructed and decorated by hand with Côtes de Genève and circular graining patterns. Oscillating weight segment in 22K pink-gold. **Functions:** hour, minute, second, 24 hours, perpetual calendar (date, day, month, year, moonphase), alarm.
Case: 18K white-gold, 3-piece (Ø 41.5, thickness 15.7mm); curved sapphire crystal; white-gold setting crown at 4, for alarm at 2; calendar corrector at 8; back attached by 6 screws, numbered, with "1,000 hours" seal. Water resistant to 5atm.
Dial: ruthenium-gray with sun pattern; silvered zones with circular beads; applied pointed markers; printed minute track with luminescent dots at quarters; luminescent Dauphine hands.
Indications: week day at 3; moonphase and 24 hours (red-color display of the hours at which calendar corrections are not allowed) at 6; date at 9; month and two-digit year at 12; alarm with center arrow-pointed hand and scale with divisions for a quarter of an hour.
Strap: crocodile leather; white-gold fold-over clasp.
Also available: in pink gold with silvered dial.

MASTER GEOGRAPHIC   REF. 142.3470

Movement: automatic, Jaeger-LeCoultre 929/3 caliber. Rotor with a 22K pink-gold segment. Côtes de Genève and circular graining decoration. Tested over 1,000 hours. **Functions:** hour, minute, second, date, world time, 2nd time-zone, power reserve. **Case:** 18K white-gold, 3-piece case (Ø 38mm, thickn. 11.8mm); bezel fastened from behind with 4 through screws; curved sapphire crystal; winding crown at 3 for the synchronization of secondary zones with the main time-zone; world time white-gold crown at 10; date corrector at 2; back with sapphire crystal fastened by 4 screws. Water resistant to 5atm.
Dial: ruthenium-gray, grained, curved; silvered zones with circular beads; applied white-gold markers and printed minute track on the flange; luminescent rhodium-plated Dauphine hands. **Indications:** date at 2; 2nd time zone (night & day; two hands) and window with two-way disc for reference-town names of the 24 time zones at 6; power reserve at 10.
Strap: crocodile leather; fold-over white-gold clasp.
Also available: steel, strap, silvered dial, closed caseback or "Black" dial, sapphire caseback; pink gold, leather strap, silvered dial, closed caseback; in white gold, leather strap, gray dial, hinged cover.

MASTER PERPETUAL   REF. 149.347.A

Movement: automatic, Jaeger-LeCoultre 889/440/2 caliber, 36 jewels, 28,800 vph, 349 elements. "Master Control 1000 Hours" engraved on rotor. Decorated with Côtes de Genève and circular graining patterns. Tested over 1,000 hours. **Functions:** hour, minute, perpetual calendar (date, day, month, year, moonphase). **Case:** 18K white-gold, 3-piece case (Ø 37, thick. 10.6mm); bezel fastened from behind by 4 through screws; curved sapphire crystal; full calendar corrector at 8; white-gold crown; back fastened by 4 screws displaying the movement through a sapphire crystal, hinged cover and numbered medallion. Water resistant to 5atm. **Dial:** ruthenium-gray with sun pattern, curved; silvered zones with circular beads decoration; applied faceted white-gold pointed markers (Arabic numeral 6); luminescent dots on the printed minute track; faceted white-gold Dauphine hands, skeletonized on the "off hours."
Indications: week day at 3; moonphase at 6; date at 9; month and two-digit year at 12; central sector for the red-color display of the period in which calendar corrections are not allowed.
Strap: crocodile leather; white-gold fold-over clasp.
Also available: "Black" dial, sapphire back: in steel; pink gold; pink gold, silvered dial, closed caseback.

MASTER MOON   REF. 143.347.A

Movement: automatic, Jaeger-LeCoultre 891/448 caliber. Rotor with 22K pink-gold segment and gilded engraving "Master Control 1000 Hours." Côtes de Genève and circular graining decoration. Tested over 1,000 hours.
Functions: hour, minute, small second, full calendar (date, day, month, moonphase). **Case:** 18K white-gold, three-piece case (Ø 37mm, thickness 11.5mm); bezel fastened by 4 screws from behind; curved sapphire crystal; 3 correctors on the middle; white-gold crown; sapphire crystal back, fastened by 4 screws and protected by a hinged numbered cover. Water resistant to 5atm.
Dial: ruthenium-gray, grained, curved; silvered zone; applied white-gold pointed markers and Arabic numerals; 4 luminescent dots; luminescent white-gold Dauphine hands.
Indications: small second and moonphase at 6; center day and month; date with half-moon center hand.
Strap: crocodile leather; white-gold fold-over clasp.
Also available: "Black" or silvered dial, sapphire caseback without cover: steel, leather strap and fold-over clasp; pink gold, leather strap and fold-over clasp. Limited series of 250 pieces, platinum with "deep blue" dial, leather strap.

JAEGER-LeCOULTRE

MASTER GRANDE TAILLE	REF. 140.2420

Movement: mechanical, automatic-winding, Jaeger-LeCoultre 889/2 caliber. Côtes de Genève and circular graining decoration. Tested over 1,000 hours.
Functions: hour, minute, second, date.
Case: 18K pink-gold, three-piece case, with additional ductile iron non-magnetic back (Ø 37mm, thickness 9.8mm); bezel fastened from behind with 4 screws; curved sapphire crystal; pink-gold crown; back attached by 4 screws, numbered, with gold "1,000 hours" seal. Water resistant to 5atm.
Dial: silvered, curved; applied pink gold Arabic numerals and pointed markers; luminescent dots on the printed minute track; luminescent pink-gold Dauphine hands.
Indications: date at 3.
Strap: crocodile leather; pink-gold fold-over clasp.
Also available: in steel, leather strap with fold-over clasp.

MASTER COMPRESSOR MEMOVOX	REF. 170.8470

Movement: mechanical, automatic-winding, Jaeger-LeCoultre caliber 918, crafted and decorated by hand. 28,800 vph, 45-hour power reserve, 260 parts, 22 jewels.
Functions: hour, minute, center second, mechanical alarm, date. **Case:** stainless steel (Ø 41.5mm); 2 crowns with compression key: at 2 for winding, setting and alarm starting and stopping; at 4 for starting the watch and setting the hour, minute and date; crown at 10 for rotating bezel adjustment; Master Compressor seal set on the caseback, in 18K gold; cambered sapphire crystal. Water resistant to 100 meters. **Dial:** brilliant black with luminescent numerals and 8 hour markers; rotating bezel; rhodium-plated trapeze-shaped luminescent hours and minutes hands; white-lacquered bâton seconds hand with red arrow. **Indications:** date at 3; center alarm. **Strap:** caramel leather with double saddle-stitching and steel fold-over buckle. **Also available:** with anthracite or slate gray dial; in white gold, matte honey crocodile leather, double saddle-stitching, white-gold fold-over buckle or patented white-gold bracelet; in pink gold, matte chocolate crocodile leather, double saddle-stitching, pink-gold fold-over buckle or patented, 5 dual-axis links pink-gold bracelet.

MASTER ULTRA-THIN	REF. 145.3570

Movement: mechanical, manual-winding, Jaeger-LeCoultre 849 caliber, ultra-thin. Winding barrel with the engraving "Master Control 1000 Hours." Côtes de Genève and circular graining decoration. Tested over 1,000 hours.
Functions: hour, minute.
Case: 18K white-gold, three-piece case (Ø 34mm, thickness 6mm); bezel fastened from behind with 4 screws; curved sapphire crystal; white-gold crown; back fastened by 4 screws, displaying the movement through a sapphire crystal. Water resistant to 5atm.
Dial: ruthenium-gray, with sun pattern; applied faceted rhodium-plated Arabic numerals and pointed markers; faceted rhodium-plated Régate hands.
Strap: crocodile leather; white-gold fold-over clasp.
Also available: in steel with black dial and sapphire caseback or silvered dial and closed caseback with hinged cover; in pink gold, with silvered dial, closed caseback with hinged cover; in platinum with deep blue dial and sapphire crystal caseback, 250 pieces.

MASTER ULTRA-THIN	REF. 145.2401

Movement: mechanical, manual-winding, Jaeger-LeCoultre 849 caliber, ultra-thin. Winding barrel with the engraving "Master Control 1000 Hours." Côtes de Genève and circular graining decoration. Tested over 1,000 hours.
Functions: hour, minute.
Case: 18K pink-gold, three-piece case (Ø 34mm, thickness 6mm); bezel with double set brilliant row, fastened from behind with 4 screws; curved sapphire crystal; pink-gold crown; back fastened by 4 screws, displaying the movement through a sapphire crystal. Water resistant to 5atm.
Dial: silvered; applied pink-gold faceted pointed markers and printed Eastern-style Arabic numerals; pink-gold faceted Régate hands.
Strap: pink crocodile leather; pink-gold fold-over clasp.

REVERSO GRAN'SPORT CHRONOGRAPH   REF. 295.1620

Movement: manual, Jaeger-LeCoultre 859 caliber (derived from 829 caliber), 38 jewels, 28,800 vph, made up by 317 elements. Beveled and Côtes de Genève hand-decorated. **Functions:** hour, minute, second, date, chronograph with 2 counters, chronograph on/off indicator.
Case: 18K yellow-gold, barrel-shaped, reversible double-face case (with carrier size 43 x 28mm, thickness 11.5mm; only case size 32 x 28mm, thickness 10mm),

engraved with sand-blasted transverse grooves; curved sapphire crystal on both sides; gold crown and beveled rectangular pushers; back attached by 4 screws, carrier with brushed finish and circular graining decoration. Water resistant to 5atm.
Dial: solid silver, engine-turned (guilloché) with center panels; printed Arabic numerals; luminescent burnished gold hands.
Indications: chronograph on/off indicator at 5; date at 6; back face: silvered, black counter rings, engine-turned (guilloché) panels; minute counter with retrograde hand at 6; slightly off-center second counter.
Strap: rubber; yellow-gold double fold-over clasp and safety pushers (length adjustable by pushers).

REVERSO GRAN'SPORT DUO FACE   REF. 294.1601

Movement: manual, Jaeger-LeCoultre 851 caliber, 21 jewels, 21,600 vph, made up by 229 elements. Beveled and Côtes de Genève hand-decorated.
Functions: hour, minute, small second, 24-hour indicator; second time-zone time, 24-hour indicator. **Case:** 18K yellow-gold, barrel-shaped, reversible double-face case (with carrier size 43 x 28mm, thickness 11.25mm; only case size 32 x 28mm, thickness 10.4mm), engraved with sand-blasted transverse grooves; curved sap-

phire crystal on both sides; gold crown and beveled rectangular pusher; back attached by 4 screws, carrier with brushed finish and circular graining decoration. Water resistant to 5atm. **Dial:** front face: solid silver, engine-turned (guilloché) with center panels; back face: silvered, decorated with vertical rib pattern, black 12 and 24 hours rings; both with printed Eastern style Arabic numerals and luminescent burnished gold hands.
Indications: front face: date between 5 and 6, 24 hours at 11. **Rear face:** center second time zone, 24 hours at 6. **Strap:** rubber; yellow-gold double fold-over clasp and safety pushers (length adjustable by pushers). **Also available:** with yellow-gold bracelet; in steel with rubber strap or steel bracelet.

REVERSO GRAN'SPORT LADY   REF. 296.8120

Movement: manual, Jaeger-LeCoultre 864 caliber, 19 jewels, 21,600 vph, made up by 164 elements. Beveled and Côtes de Genève hand-decorated.
Functions: hour, minute, small second, date, day-night indicator, second time-zone, day-night. **Case:** stainless steel, barrel-shaped, reversible double-face case (only case size 27.5 x 24.5mm, thickness 9.5mm), engraved with sand-blasted transverse grooves; 32 diamonds set on the second face; curved sapphire crystal on both sides;

corrector for the adjustment of the second time-zone on the middle; carrier with brushed finish and circular graining decoration. Water resistant to 5atm.
Dial: silvered, guilloché; "Linton" Arabic numerals; printed minute track with 3 luminescent dots; burnished steel hands.
Indications: small second at 6; night-day at 12. **Rear face:** silvered, engine-turned (guilloché) panels; applied rhodium-plated drop-shaped markers and printed blue "flower" Arabic numerals; luminescent steel bâton hands; second time-zone, night-day at 6.
Strap: polished/brushed steel; double fold-over clasp and safety pushers.
Also available: in yellow gold with bracelet.

REVERSO GRAN'SPORT LADY   REF. 296.8650

The Reverso Gran'Sport Lady model proposes some technical and aesthetic characteristics typical for the Jaeger-LeCoultre production in a sportsman-like version, such as one with diamonds applied only on the caseback, like in the Reverso Duetto, and the display of two different time zones on the opposite dials. This models features for the first time the double day/night indication, respectively referring to the time of the related time zone. The

independent time setting on the second dial is made by actuating the corrector positioned on the case at 2, that makes the hours hand advance by one hour at each pressing. The particular time-correction mechanism is highly interesting inasmuch as this operation does not influence at all the corresponding minutes hand, as the latter is directly coupled with the opposite hand also during the correction of the additional time display.
Also available: in yellow gold.

JAEGER-LeCOULTRE

REVERSO CLASSIC
REF. 250.1420

Movement: mechanical, manual-winding, Jaeger-LeCoultre 846/1 caliber.
Functions: hour, minute.
Case: 18K yellow-gold, rectangular, reversible case (with carrier size 38.5 x 23mm, thickness 7.3mm; case only size 27 x 23mm, thickness 6.3mm) with engraved transverse grooves; curved sapphire crystal; gold crown; caseback attached by 8 screws, with gasket.

Dial: silvered; printed Arabic numerals and railway minute track; blued steel bâton hands.
Strap: ostrich skin; yellow-gold fold-over clasp.
Also available: with bracelet; in steel and yellow gold, leather strap and fold-over clasp or bracelet; in stainless steel, leather strap and fold-over clasp or bracelet; with quartz movement.
Reverso Lady: in stainless steel, leather strap and fold-over clasp or steel bracelet; in steel and yellow gold, leather strap and fold-over clasp or steel and yellow-gold bracelet; in yellow gold, leather strap and fold-over clasp or yellow-gold bracelet; with quartz movement.

REVERSO MEMORY
REF. 255.8470

Movement: manual-winding, Jaeger-LeCoultre 862 caliber. Modified with an original fly-back counter mechanism equipped with an "artificial release" device, which detects whether the pusher performed its function simply by touch.
Functions: hour, minute, small second, 60-minute fly-back "memento" counter.
Case: 18K yellow-gold, rectangular, reversible double-face case (with carrier size 38.5x23, thickn. 10mm; case only 27x23), made up by 50 elements, engraved transverse grooves; curved sapphire crystal; rectangular counter pusher at 4; caseback attached by 8 screws, with gasket.
Front dial: silvered, engine-turned (guilloché) center and zone; printed Arabic numerals and minute track; luminescent blued steel bâton hands; small second at 6. **Rear dial:** black, engine-turned (guilloché) center, luminescent bâton hand, for the continuous center 60-minute counter with simultaneous zeroing and restart by the pusher. **Strap:** crocodile leather; fold-over gold clasp. **Also available:** with bracelet; in steel, leather strap, fold-over clasp or bracelet; in steel and yellow gold, leather strap, fold-over clasp or bracelet.

REVERSO DUETTO CLASSIC
REF. 256.1420

Movement: mechanical, manual-winding, Jaeger-LeCoultre 865 caliber. Constructed and decorated by hand; 50 hours power reserve, 19 jewels, 21,600 vibrations per hour. **Functions:** double hour and minute indication, small second.
Case: 18K yellow-gold, rectangular, reversible, double-face (with carrier size 38.5 x 23mm, thickness 10mm; only case size 27 x 23mm) with engraved transverse grooves; 32 brilliant-cut diamonds set on the second face; curved sapphire crystal on both sides; yellow-gold crown with a recessed brilliant.
Front dial: solid silver, engine-turned (guilloché) center and zone; printed Eastern style Arabic numerals and minute track; blued steel bâton hands. **Rear dial:** silvered, with engine-turned (guilloché) center with rim, applied yellow-gold pointed markers and Arabic numerals; yellow-gold bâton hands. **Indications:** small second at 6.
Strap: crocodile leather; yellow-gold fold-over clasp.
Also available: with yellow-gold bracelet; in white gold, with leather strap and fold-over clasp or white-gold bracelet; in stainless steel (see right picture).

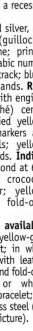

REVERSO DUETTO CLASSIC
REF. 256.8120

Movement: mechanical, manual-winding, Jaeger-LeCoultre 845 caliber, autonomy 50 hours, 19 jewels, 21,600 vph. Manufactured and decorated by hand.
Functions: double hour and minute display, small second.
Case: stainless steel, rectangular, reversible, double face case (with carrier size 38 x 23mm, thickness 10mm; case only size 27 x 23mm) with engraved transverse grooves; 32 brilliant-cut diamonds set on the back; curved sapphire crystal on both sides.

Font dial: solid silver, center and zones engine-turned (guilloché); printed Chinese-style Arabic numerals and minute track, blued steel bâton hands.
Rear dial: silvered, center engine-turned (guilloché) with rim; applied yellow-gold Arabic numerals and bâton markers; yellow-gold bâton hands.
Indications: small second at 6.
Bracelet: stainless steel; double fold-over clasp.
Also available: with leather strap and fold-over clasp.

REVERSO SEPTANTIÈME   REF. 300.2420

Movement: mechanical, manually wound, Jaeger-LeCoultre caliber 879, crafted and decorated by hand, in 18K white-gold for the platinum version and 18K pink-gold for the pink-gold version. 28,800 vph, 8-day power reserve, 224 parts, 25 jewels. **Functions:** hour, minute, small second, large date, day/night, power-reserve. **Case:** 18K pink-gold, reversible, XGT size; made up by more than 50 parts; transparent anti-glare sapphire crystal; crown for winding the watch and setting the hours, minutes, day/night indication and large date in intermediate positions; caseback displaying the movement.
Dial: guilloché solid silver, black Arabic numerals and applied gold-plated JL logo; blued steel hands.
Indications: small second at 5; large date at 7; day/night indicator at 2; power-reserve at 10.
Strap: chestnut brown matte crocodile leather; fold-over buckle in pink gold.
Also available: in platinum, ruthenium dial, with powdered floral silvered numerals. Limited edition of 500 pieces, also in 18K pink gold.

REVERSO DUOFACE   REF. 271.2470

Movement: mechanical, manual-winding, Jaeger-LeCoultre 854 caliber, patented. **Functions:** main time zone, minute and small second; second time-zone, minute and 24-hour.
Case: 18K pink-gold, rectangular, reversible, double-face case (with carrier size 42 x 26mm, thickness 9.8mm; case size 30.5 x 26mm, thickness 8.5mm); engraved sand-blasted transverse grooves; curved sapphire crystal on both sides; second time-zone corrector on the middle; pink-gold crown.
Front dial: in solid silver, Art Déco design, with engine-turned (guilloché) center, printed Arabic numerals and minute track, blued steel bâton hands; small second at 6.
Rear dial: black, engine-turned (guilloché), with luminescent applied pink-gold pointed markers and Arabic numerals, luminescent gold hands and 24-hour display at 6.
Strap: crocodile leather; pink-gold fold-over clasp.
Also available: both dials silvered; with bracelet; in yellow gold; in steel, ostrich-skin strap and fold-over clasp or bracelet; in white gold with black-silvered dials, leather strap and fold-over clasp or bracelet.

REVERSO PLATINUM NUMBER ONE   REF. 216.6401

Movement: mechanical, manual-winding, Jaeger-LeCoultre 849R-SQ caliber, 19 jewels, 21,600 vph. Made up by 128 elements. Skeletonized, chased and polished by hand. **Functions:** hour, minute.
Case: platinum, rectangular, reversible (with carrier size 42 x 26mm, thickness 8.8mm; only case size 30.5 x 26mm, thickness 7.5mm) with engraved sand-blasted transverse grooves; curved sapphire crystal; white-gold crown with set sapphire cabochon; back with a rectangular aperture displaying the movement through a sapphire crystal.
Dial: blued steel leaf-style hands.
Strap: crocodile leather; platinum fold-over clasp. Limited edition of 500 pieces.

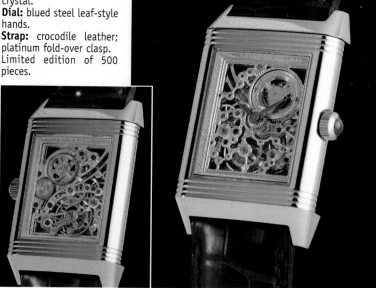

REVERSO SUN MOON   REF. 275.3170

Movement: mechanical, manual-winding, Jaeger-LeCoultre 823 caliber.
Functions: hour, minute, small second, night/day indicator, moonphase, power reserve.
Case: 18K white-gold, rectangular, reversible (with carrier size 42 x 26mm, thickness 9.8mm; only case size 30.5 x 26mm, thickness 8.5mm) with engraved transverse grooves; curved sapphire crystal; white-gold crown; back with a rectangular aperture displaying the movement through a sapphire crystal.
Dial: black; white painted Chinese-style Arabic numerals and railway minute track; luminescent white-gold leaf-style hands.
Indications: night & day display at 2; small second and moonphase at 6; power reserve between 10 and 11.
Strap: crocodile leather; white-gold fold-over clasp.
Also available: with white-gold bracelet; in pink gold with silvered dial, leather strap and fold-over clasp or pink-gold bracelet.

JAEGER-LeCOULTRE

REVERSO JOAILLERIE CABOCHONS "PASTEL" REF. 262.3402

Movement: mechanical, manual-winding, Jaeger-LeCoultre 846 caliber. Finished, assembled and decorated by hand.
Functions: hour, minute.
Case: 18K white-gold, rectangular, 116 brilliants (front and rear) and two pink sapphire cabochons, reversible case (with carrier size 33 x 21mm, thickness 8.5mm; only case size 22.5 x 21mm, thickness 7.5mm); curved sapphire crystal; white-gold crown with pink sapphire cabochon.
Dial: silvered hour ring, mother of pearl in the middle; printed Chinese-style Arabic numerals and minute track; blued steel bâton hands.
Strap: crocodile leather; white-gold fold-over clasp.
Also available: with blue or yellow sapphire cabochons.

REVERSO NEVA REF. 267.3404

Movement: quartz, Jaeger-LeCoultre caliber 608, crafted and decorated by hand, 7 jewels, 68 parts, 1.6mm thick.
Functions: hour and minute.
Case: reversible, ladies' size, in 18K white-gold; made up of more than 50 parts, cambered sapphire crystal; crown for setting the hours and minutes, set blue sapphire. Gemsetting: diamonds set according to the snow technique: Ø 0.5 to 1.6mm, F-G Top Wesselton, VVS1, full cut, totaling 2.5 carats; case set with more than 570 diamonds totaling approximately 2.3 carats; fold-over buckle set with more than 60 diamonds, totaling approximately 0.3 carats.

Dial: silvered with mirror-polished waves. Black transferred 6 and 12 numerals; blued steel hands, fan-shaped.
Strap: black satin with 18K white-gold gem-set fold-over buckle.

REVERSO DUETTO JOAILLERIE SERTIE NEIGE REF. 266.3405

Combining the techniques of "Haute Joaillerie" with the creativity and daring of the watchmaking art, the "snow" gemsetting undulates exquisitely over the rectangular case of the Reverso, playing on alternating glimpses of metal and diamonds. In creating the Reverso Neva, the master-gemsetters of Jaeger-LeCoultre are further establishing the incomparable mastery of their talent and creativity. Inspired by the word "neve" (meaning "snow" in Italian) and the river on which Saint-Petersburg is built, the name "Neva" evokes the fairytale beauty of a scintillating river amid a snowy landscape. Such is the beautiful sublime picture portrayed by the Reverso Neva. Following the flow of his inspiration, master-jeweler Sam Wühl has endowed it with the power to illuminate time. The technique of setting infinitely small brilliants represents a sublimation of the jeweler's art; "snow" gemsetting created by Alain Kirchof's team testifies to exceptional expertise. The term "snow" refers to the characteristic consisting of concealing entire sections of metal with individually cut and adjusted precious stones.

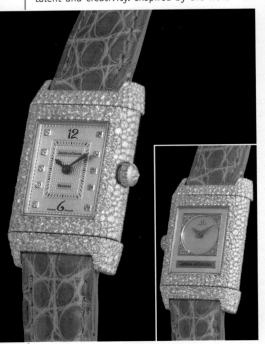

REVERSO DUETTO JOAILLERIE REF. 266.2413

Movement: mechanical, manual-winding, Jaeger-LeCoultre 844 caliber. Constructed and decorated by hand, 50 hours power reserve, 18 jewels, 21,600 vibrations per hour.
Functions: double hour and minute indication, small second.
Case: 18K pink-gold, rectangular, reversible, double-face; brilliant-cut diamonds set on both faces; curved sapphire crystal on both sides; pink-gold crown with a recessed diamond.

Front dial: solid silver, brushed, engine-turned (guilloché) perimeter, central part in mother-of-pearl; printed Eastern style Arabic numerals and minute track; blued steel bâton hands.
Rear dial: in mother of pearl and pink gold with 24 diamonds, pink-gold Dauphine hands.
Strap: in leather-lined satin; with pink-gold fold-over clasp.

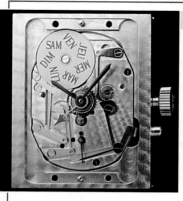

CALIBER 836 (1997)

Basic caliber: 822 (1992). Manual-winding movement, with autonomy of 45 hours. **Functions:** hours, minutes, small seconds; day, date. **Shape:** tonneau. **Size:** 17.20x22.60mm. **Thickness:** 4.14mm. **Jewels:** 21 (escape wheel with end-stones). **Balance:** in Glucydur, with two arms, with compensating screws, diameter: 8.50mm. **Frequency:** 21,600 vph. **Balance-spring:** flat, Nivarox 1, with Spirofin micrometer screw regulation device. **Shock-absorber system:** Kif for balance and escape wheel. **Notes:** pillar-plate and adapter are decorated with a circular-graining pattern, the bridges are decorated with a Côtes de Genève pattern and beveled. Screw heads are finished by specular polishing. In the dial-side view, on the module added to the basic movement, the date hand and the window day disc are put in place.

CALIBER 818/5 (1992)

Basic caliber: 818 (1959). Manual-winding movement, with 45-hour autonomy. **Functions:** hours, minutes, small seconds. **Shape:** round. **Diameter:** 21.10mm (9'''1/4). **Embedding diameter:** 2.80mm. **Thickness:** 2.94mm. **Jewels:** 21 (escape wheel with end-stones). **Balance:** with compensating screws, with two arms, diameter: 8.54mm, in Glucydur. **Frequency:** 21,600 vph. **Balance-spring:** flat, Nivarox 1. **Shock-absorber system:** Kif for balance and escape wheel. **Notes:** the pillar-plate is decorated with a circular-graining pattern, the bridges are decorated with a Côtes de Genève pattern and beveled. Screw heads are finished by specular polishing. **Derived caliber:** 819 (818 with center seconds).

CALIBER 844 (1997)

Basic caliber: 846/1 (1992). Manual-winding movement, 42-hour autonomy. **Functions:** hours, minutes. **Shape:** tonneau. **Size:** 13.00x15.20mm. **Thickness:** 3.45mm. **Jewels:** 18 (escape wheel with end-stones). **Balance:** smooth, with three arms, in Glucydur. **Frequency:** 21,600 vph. **Balance-spring:** flat, Nivarox 1, with Spirofin micrometer screw regulating device. **Shock-absorber system:** Kif. **Notes:** the pillar-plate is decorated with a circular-graining pattern, the bridges are decorated with a Côtes de Genève pattern and beveled. Screw heads are finished by specular polishing. This caliber is realized for the purpose of being mounted on the "Reverso Duetto." Its peculiarity is that it indicates the same time on both sides: in the middle of the main dial and slightly off-center towards 12 on the rear dial. **Derived calibers:** 865; 864.

CALIBER 846/1 (1992)

Basic caliber: 846 (1975). Manual-winding movement, 42-hour autonomy. **Functions:** hours, minutes. **Shape:** tonneau. **Size:** 13.00x15.20mm. **Thickness:** 2.90mm. **Jewels:** 18 (escape wheel with end-stones). **Balance:** smooth, three arms, in Glucydur. **Frequency:** 21,600 vph. **Balance-spring:** flat, Nivarox 1, with Spirofin micrometer screw regulating device. **Shock-absorber system:** Kif. **Notes:** the pillar-plate is decorated with a circular-graining pattern, the bridges are decorated with a Côtes de Genève pattern and beveled. Screw heads are finished by specular polishing.

CALIBER 849 (1994)

Basic caliber: 838 (1975). Manual-winding movement, autonomy of 35 hours. **Functions:** hours, minutes. **Shape:** round. **Diameter:** 21.10mm (9'''1/4). **Embedding diameter:** 20.80mm. **Thickness:** extra-thin, 1.85mm. **Jewels:** 18 (escape wheel with end-stones). **Balance:** smooth, with two arms, diameter: 8.40mm, in Glucydur. **Frequency:** 21,600 vph. **Balance-spring:** flat, Nivarox 1. **Shock-absorber system:** Kif for balance and escape wheel. **Notes:** the pillar-plate is decorated with a circular-graining pattern, the bridges are decorated with a Côtes de Genève pattern and beveled. Screw heads are finished by specular polishing.

CALIBER 854 (1994)

Basic caliber: 822 (1992). Manual-winding movement, with 45-hour autonomy. **Functions:** hours, minutes, small seconds; second time-zone (with fast corrector), 24 hours. **Shape:** tonneau. **Size:** 17.20x22.60mm. **Thickness:** 3.80mm. **Jewels:** 21 (escape wheel with end-stones). **Balance:** with compensating screws, with two arms, diameter: 8.50mm, in Glucydur. **Frequency:** 21,600 vph. **Balance-spring:** flat, Nivarox 1, with Spirofin micrometer screw regulating device. **Shock-absorber system:** Kif for balance and escape wheel. **Notes:** the pillar-plate and bridges are decorated with a circular-graining pattern and beveled. Screw heads are finished by specular polishing.

CALIBER 854

Caliber 854, dial-side view. This movement, realized for the purpose of being used in the "Reverso Duoface" model, has the peculiarity that it indicates the time of two different time zones on one of the two opposite dials: in the middle of the main dial and slightly off-center towards 12 on the rear dial. The complex mechanism (patented and consisting of 180 components) also allows quick adjustment of the local time on the main dial by actuating a small pusher positioned on the case middle. On the rear side (the one indicating the "home" time zone when travelling) there is the indispensable 24-hour display at 6.

CALIBER 889/1 (1994)

Basic caliber: 889 (1982). Automatic, 40 hours of power-reserve; 2-piece rotor mounted on a ball bearing, with a 21K gold sector. **Functions:** hours, minutes, center sec. (with stopping device), date (with fast corrector). **Shape:** round. **Diameter:** 26.60mm (11'''1/2). **Embedding diameter:** 26.00mm. **Thickness:** 3.25mm. **Jewels:** 36 (escape wheel with end-stones). **Balance:** smooth, with 2 arms, in Glucydur. **Frequency:** 28,800 vph. **Balance-spring:** flat, Nivarox 1, with Spirofin micrometer screw regulating device. **Shock-absorber system:** Kif. **Notes:** Pillar-plate with a circular-graining pattern, bridges and rotor with a Côtes de Genève pattern. Bridges beveled, screw heads polished and blued. **Derived caliber:** 891/2 (small sec.); 891/2-447; 891/2-448; 889-440/2; 928; 929/3. Caliber 889-440/2 (889/2+mod. 440) shown in the photograph.

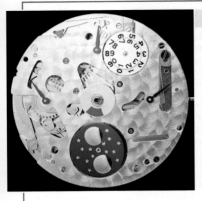

CALIBER 889-440/2 (1987/1996)

Basic caliber: 889/2. Same characteristics, decorations and finishing as Caliber 889/2 with some variants. **Functions:** hours, minutes, seconds (with stopping device); perpetual calendar (date, day, month, year, moonphase with fast corrections). Total diameter (base +.module): 28.00mm (12"'1/2). **Thickness:** 4.55mm. **Jewels:** 50. **Notes:** the photograph shows a dial-side view with all the components for the indications (except for hours, minutes, seconds) put in place. Day, date and month applied by hand respectively at 3, 9, 12; 2-digit year, moonphase and consent indicator (for calendar corrections) by discs and windows respectively at 1, 6 and at the center. The perpetual-calendar correction is possible by advancing only a single corrector.

CALIBER 891/2-448 (1997)

Basic caliber: 889/2.
Same characteristics, decorations and finishing as Caliber 889/2 with some variants.
Functions: hours, minutes, center seconds (with stopping device); full calendar (day, date, month and moonphase with fast corrections).
Thickness: 3.25mm.
Jewels: 36 (escape wheel with endstones).
Notes: the caliber derives from 891/2-447 (of 1993, without moonphase). The photograph shows a dial-side view with all the components for the indications (except for hours, minutes, seconds) put in place: center and date; day, month and moonphase by disc, respectively at 9, 3 and 6.

CALIBER 914 (1996)

Basic caliber: 916 (1969).
Manual-winding movement with 45-hour autonomy. **Functions:** hours, minutes, seconds; alarm.
Shape: round. **Diameter:** 30.40mm (13"'). **Embedding diameter:** 30.00mm. **Thickness:** 5.15mm. **Jewels:** 18.
Balance: smooth, with three arms, diameter 9.50mm, in Glucydur. **Frequency:** 28,800 vph. **Balance-spring:** flat, Nivarox 1, with Spirofin micrometer screw regulating device. **Shock-absorber system:** Kif.
Notes: the pillar-plate is shot-blasted, bridges are decorated with a Côtes de Genève pattern and beveled. Next to the balance is the alarm hammer striking a thread-gong in tempered steel (not visible in the photograph) fastened on the caseback.

CALIBER 918 (1994)

Basic caliber: 916. Same characteristics, decorations and finishing as Caliber 914 with the following variants: automatic winding with 45-hour autonomy, two-piece rotor mounted on a ball bearing, with a 21K gold sector.
Functions: hours, minutes, seconds; date; alarm.
Thickness: 7.45mm. **Jewels:** 17.
Notes: the cylindrical part of the gong struck by the hammer faces the latter through the thickness of the rotor in the middle of its supporting ball bearing.
Derived calibers: 909 used for "Grande Memovox" and combined with the 918 base for the 440 (perpetual calendar module, 24 hours, thickness: 8.30mm, 36 jewels).

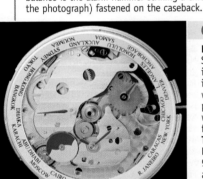

CALIBER 929/3 (1990/1996)

Basic caliber: 889/2.
Same characteristics, decorations and finishing as the 889 family with the following variants: date (with fast corrector); world time, second time-zone, 24 hours; power reserve; ring adapter for the disc with the indications of the reference cities for the 24 time zones.
Thickness: 4.85mm; **Jewels:** 38.
Notes: the photograph shows Caliber 929/3 on the dial side in the version adopted for the "Master Geographic" with all the components for the indications (except for hours and minutes) put in place. Outside the city disc, at 7 the two-color disc for day/night window display; respectively at 2 and 6; at 9 the hands of the date, second time-zone time and power-reserve displays.

CALIBER 960 (1995)

Automatic-winding movement, autonomy of 44 hours, two-piece rotor mounted on a ball bearing, with a 21K gold sector.
Functions: hours, minutes, seconds; date.
Shape: round. **Diameter:** 20.60mm. **Embedding diameter:** 20.00mm (9"'). **Thickness:** 3.95mm. **Jewels:** 31. **Balance:** smooth, with two arms, in Glucydur. **Frequency:** 28,800 vph. **Balance-spring:** flat, Nivarox 1, with Spirofin micrometer screw regulating device. **Shock-absorber system:** Kif. **Notes:** the pillar-plate is decorated with a circular-graining pattern on the dial side and shot-blasted on the rear surface. The rotor and bridges are decorated with Côtes de Genève patterns and beveled, Screw heads are finished by specular polishing and blued. **Derived caliber:** 960R on the Reverso Gran'Sport.

CALIBER 943 (1994)

Manual-winding movement, autonomy of 35 hours.
Functions: hours, minutes; hour, quarter and minute repeater.
Shape: rectangular. **Size:** 23.40 x 28.90mm. **Thickness:** 4.85mm.
Jewels: 38 (escape wheel with endstones).
Balance: smooth, with two arms, diameter: 8.40mm, in Glucydur.
Frequency: 21,600 vph.
Balance-spring: flat, Nivarox 1.
Shock-absorber system: Kif for balance and escape wheel.
Notes: the pillar-plate is decorated with a circular-graining pattern, the bridges are decorated with a Côtes de Genève pattern and beveled. Screw heads are finished by specular polishing.

CALIBER 943

Caliber 943, realized exclusively for the "Reverso Répétition Minutes," dial-side view.
The complex and numerous repeater components are clearly visible: at 12, the superposed hammers striking the hours (on request) with a low-pitched sound, the quarters with a shrill and a low sound and the minutes with a shrill sound on the two-tone thread-gongs superposed on the movement's perimeter; between 4 and 5, the strike-work regulator controlling the stroke sequence; the two 18K gold sectors visible through a bull's eye on the dial and turning at a speed of approximately 600 rpm. The Caliber 943, containing 306 elements, finished and assembled by hand, is realized in a series of 500 numbered pieces.

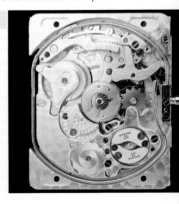

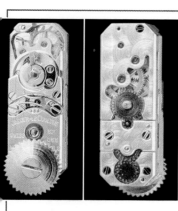

CALIBER 101/4 (1994)

Basic caliber: 101 (1929). Manual-winding movement, autonomy of 33 hours.
Functions: hours, minutes.
Shape: rectangular. **Size:** 4.80x14.00mm.
Thickness: 3.40mm.
Jewels: 19.
Balance: smooth, with two arms, in 14K gold.
Frequency: 21,600 vph.
Balance-spring: flat, Nivarox 1.
Shock-absorber system: Kif.
Notes: the pillar-plate is decorated with a circular-graining pattern, the bridges are decorated with Côtes de Genève and circular-graining patterns and beveled. Screw heads are finished by specular polishing. The winding crown is positioned on the rear of the dial side.

CALIBER 822 (1992)

Manual-winding movement, with 45-hour autonomy. **Functions:** hours, minutes, small seconds.
Shape: tonneau. **Size:** 17.20x22.60mm.
Thickness: 2.94mm.
Jewels: 21 (escape wheel with end-stones).
Balance: with compensating screws, with two arms, diameter: 8.50mm, in Glucydur.
Frequency: 21,600 vph. **Balance-spring:** flat, Nivarox 1, with Spirofin micrometer screw regulating device. **Shock-absorber system:** Kif for balance and escape wheel.
Notes: the pillar-plate is decorated with a circular-graining pattern, the bridges are decorated with a Côtes de Genève pattern and beveled. Screw heads are finished by specular polishing. **Derived calibers:** 822 AD; 824 (822 in pink gold with date and power reserve); 836; 854.

CALIBER 822 AD (1993)

Caliber 822 is used also in this very special version for the "Reverso Art Déco," through whose caseback—provided with a wide aperture protected by a sapphire crystal—it is possible to admire the peculiar hand-worked bridges. In fact, rather than a skeleton work carried out on the pillar-plate and barrel (with 4 cross-shaped emblems of the House), the shaping adopted is suitable for the creation (by reducing superfluous material) of a typical Art Déco pattern that continues also on the sight portion of the adapter. The whole is gilded in pink gold. Screw heads are finished by specular polishing and blued.

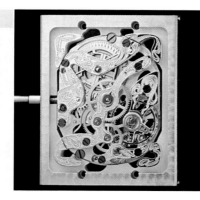

CALIBER 824 (1991)

Basic caliber: 822 (1992). Manual-winding movement, with 45-hour autonomy. **Functions:** hours, minutes, small seconds; center hand date (with fast corrector); power reserve. **Shape:** tonneau. **Size:** 17.20 x 22.60mm. **Thickness:** 4.14mm. **Jewels:** 23 (escape wheel with end-stones). **Balance:** with compensating screws, two arms, diameter: 8.50mm, in Glucydur. **Frequency:** 18,000 vph. **Balance-spring:** flat, Nivarox 1. **Shock-absorber system:** Kif for balance and escape wheel. **Notes:** pillar-plate, bridges and rectangular adapter are in 14K gold. **Notes:** the pillar-plate is decorated with a circular-graining pattern, bridges are decorated with a Côtes de Genève pattern and beveled. Screw heads are finished by specular polishing and blued. Caliber 824 was realized on the occasion of the 60th birthday of the Reverso model.

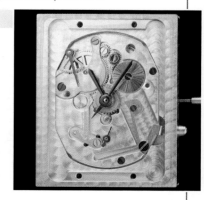

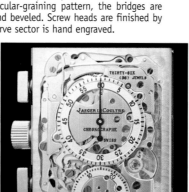

CALIBER 828 (1993)

Manual-winding movement, with 45-hour autonomy.
Functions: hours, minutes, small seconds; power reserve.
Shape: rectangular. **Size:** 23.40x28.90mm.
Thickness: 4.79mm. **Jewels:** 27.
Balance: with compensating screws, with two arms, in Glucydur, tourbillon device with a steel carriage turning once in a minute.
Frequency: 21,600 vph.
Balance-spring: Breguet, Nivarox 1.
Shock-absorber system: Kif.
Notes: the pillar-plate is decorated with a circular-graining pattern, the bridges are decorated with a Côtes de Genève pattern and beveled. Screw heads are finished by specular polishing and blued. The power-reserve sector is hand engraved.

CALIBER 828

Caliber 828, dial-side view. On the finished watch, the tourbillon device is visible only through the caseback, different from other competing makes. The carriage and bridge are finished by specular polishing, as are the ring with the power-reserve indicator (acting as a bridge for some wheel-work) and the heads of all screws, which are also blued on the rear side. At present a version without power reserve is being produced.

CALIBER 829 (1996)

Manual-winding movement, autonomy of 44 hours. **Functions:** hours, minutes; chronograph with two counters (seconds and minutes), state indicator (run/stop) of the device.
Shape: rectangular. **Size:** 23.30 x 28.80mm. **Thickness:** 4.62mm. **Jewels:** 36.
Balance: smooth, with two arms, in Glucydur. **Frequency:** 28,800 vph. **Balance-spring:** flat, Nivarox 1, with Spirofin micrometer screw regulating device. **Shock-absorber system:** Kif.
Notes: the pillar-plate is decorated with a circular-graining pattern, the bridges are decorated with a Côtes de Genève pattern and beveled. Screw heads are finished by specular polishing and blued.
Derived caliber: 859, 38 jewels.

CALIBER 829

Caliber 829, dial-side view. This particular movement, designated to fit the "Reverso Chronographe Rétrograde" model, is characterized by the positioning of the chronograph indications on the rear side of the movement and, hence, visible on the normally hidden dial. Thus, the watch features a sober main dial lacking traditional counters; except for the state indicator (run/stop) at 5, the chronograph functions are regulated by a column-wheel. The second counter is slightly off-center towards the top and the retrograde minute counter is positioned at 6.

Jean-Mairet & Gillman

I n 1999, young watchmaker César A. Jean-Mairet embarked on a mission to create mechanical watches of the most exclusive status. Drawing on a wealth of family tradition in watchmaking, Jean-Mairet has unveiled an elite collection of timepieces marked by quality and sobriety.

The Jean-Mairet & Gillman brand is just four years old, but the watchmaking roots of its founder, César A. Jean-Mairet, can be traced back to **1766** when Jean-Henry Mairet invented industry tooling. Decades later, horologist Sylvain Jean-Mairet began building precision timepieces. Over the years, he created a double stem-wind watch and perfected several lever devices. In fact, a carriage watch movement that he developed in **1884** resides today in the Musee d'Horlogerie in LeLocle.

The family's watchmaking heritage continued into yet another generation and, in the **1900**s, André Jean-Mairet was appointed chief of workshops at one of Switzerland's key watchmaking schools. A winner of more than 115 first prizes for creative watchmaking and technical advancements from the Neuchâtel Observatory, André Jean-Mairet excelled in the production of chronometers.

On the other side of César Jean-Mairet's ancestral tree are the Gillmans, who trace their roots back to a family of scientists who traveled the world during the Victorian period. In fact, César's great-great grandparents were Robert Gillmand and Caroline Bovet of the famous Bovet of Fleurier.

In **1999**, César Jean-Mairet began developing his own line of timepieces. A year later, in **2000**, he registered the name Jean-Mairet & Gillman (bringing together both sides of his family ancestry) and created the brand's first prototype. In **2001**, he unveiled two collections that would become icons of the brand, the Grand Voyageur and the Seven Days lines. In **2002**, the brand made its debut at the Basel Watch and Jewelry Fair.

My past is my history;
My present is my watches;
I embrace the future
with my arms.

—César Jean-Mairet

Today, César Jean-Mairet blends traditional Swiss craftsmanship with his own ideas of innovation and invention. Indeed, he draws on the Gillman side of his family roots for his design inspiration. The Gillmans were traveling scientists who made many contributions to their field during the Victorian era.

Jean-Mairet's watch collection embodies the spirit of these worldly explorers with timepieces offering such functions as day/date readouts, dual time zone, chronograph and GMT. All of the timepieces produced by Jean-Mairet & Gillman are handcrafted in the company's Geneva workshops. Created in limited numbers to ensure exclusivity, the Jean-Mairet & Gillman watches are all crafted of the finest materials and house mechanical movements.

The signature collection is the Grand Voyageur, which pays tribute to geographer Clement Gillman. These watch models feature a second time-zone aperture and a mechanical alarm. Crafted in 18-karat yellow, white or pink gold, it houses a 31-jeweled Jean-Mairet caliber 1999 movement.

The Seven Days watch is a sophisticated timepiece with seven days of power reserve—readable from a round subdial at 12:00 on the watch face. A second subdial at 6:00 displays the seconds and offers elegant symmetry to the design.

JMG
GENÈVE

HIGHLIGHTS

- After a great deal of research and development, Jean-Mairet & Gillman has unveiled a timepiece of exceptional design and quality. Called the Hora Mundi (simply translated as "hours of the world"), the watch offers GMT timing and mechanical alarm function.

- Housing Jean-Mairet & Gillman's complex caliber 1999 movement with 31 jewels, the Hora Mundi collection is crafted in 18-karat yellow, white or rose gold and is offered with a striking white porcelain dial with hand-applied 18-karat gold accents.

- The Hora Mundi features 24 key city names—one representing each of the world's time zones—in 18-karat gold in a circular pattern on the outer edges of the dial. Each piece is individually signed and numbered for authenticity and exclusivity.

TOP

Jean-Mairet & Gillman's headquarters in Geneva.

TOP RIGHT

The Seven Days watch shown here with a white lacquered dial is also available with a champagne dial and blued applied numerals. It is crafted in stainless steel, 18-karat yellow, white or pink gold and houses a manual-winding movement with seven days' power reserve.

BOTTOM

The Hora Mundi watch.

LEONARD

While the roots of this fine French fashion house date back nearly half a century, its watchmaking involvement is relatively young. Nevertheless, in just three short years the brand has made an impression on sophisticated consumers. Drawing on its French haute couture background and capitalizing on the rich talents of its designers, Leonard offers fashion-forward timepieces of quality and distinction.

Two men with a vision to produce exclusive, exciting fashions established the Leonard house in **1958**. The brand won immediate popularity first in Europe and then internationally with its bold prints, specially designed fabrics, and chic silhouettes. Just over a decade later in **1969**, Leonard unveiled its first fragrance (Fashion de Leonard), and in **1970** opened its first boutique in Paris. (Today, the brand has 123 boutiques internationally.)

Leonard's success soared thanks to the creative strengths of its designers and the quality of its goods. In **1979**, the brand branched out into porcelains, and later introduced a variety of accessories ranging from tabletop designs to silk scarves and men's ties.

In **2000**, the company Leonard SA was founded in Geneva, Switzerland for the creation, development, production and distribution of the Leonard watches. Just one year later, under the supervision of watchmaking veteran Ricardo Guadalupe, the brand launched its first collection at the **2001** Basel World Watch and Jewelry Fair. Based on the same bold principles of leadership in design, the watches are immediately identifiable by their bold cases and personalities.

LEFT
This bold red Sphere is bedecked with 40 Top Wesselton VVS quality diamonds.

FACING PAGE

This elegant Screen watch is chic and stylish in white rubber with diamond accents on the case. The bezel is set with 62 Top Wesselton VVS diamonds weighing .6 carats.

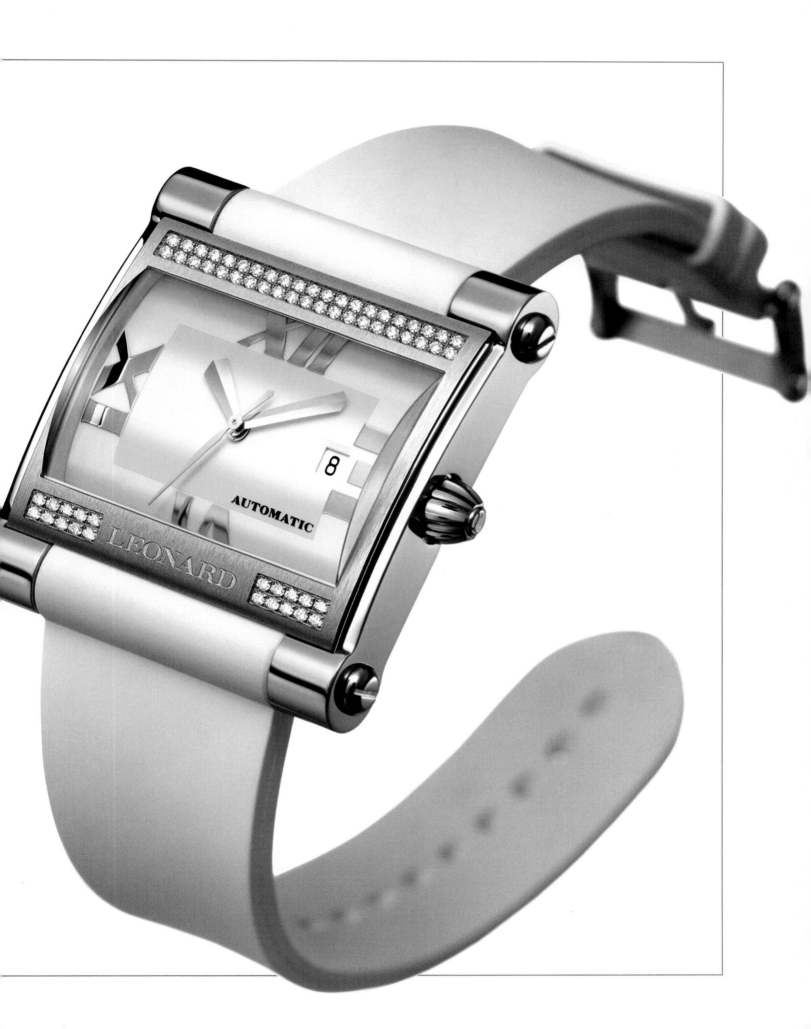

TOP
Leonard's latest haute couture collection.

LEFT
This exotic fuchsia Screen watch features a brightly painted dial.

BOTTOM LEFT
A side view of the Screen watch shows its domed crystal.

BOTTOM RIGHT
For men, this Screen watch houses an automatic movement with 40 hours of power reserve.

The Leonard SA collection of haute couture timepieces for men and women revolves around two key case shapes: square and round. The square collection, called the Screen, is actually based on a horizontal rectangular case that is curved and accented by a faceted crown.

The Sphere collection features a round case that is accentuated and seemingly elongated by a curved case-to-bracelet attachment that adds contemporary flair. A domed sapphire crystal further enhances it.

All Leonard watches are fitted with either striking integrated bracelets, or with chic straps that are color coordinated to the dials. The steel or 18-karat gold cases house either quartz or self-winding mechanical movements.

Some Leonard models feature diamond bezels, or high-tech embellishments such as rubber or synthetic fabric straps. All Leonard timepieces are water resistant to 50 meters. Distribution of Leonard watches is as exclusive as the timepieces—no more than 500 retailers worldwide ever will be authorized to sell the collection.

ABOVE
The Sphere watch is offered with an array of strap or bracelet choices.

TOP CENTER
A domed sapphire crystal enhances the geometry of the Sphere watch.

TOP RIGHT
This new Sphere features a steel case, a bezel set with 50 Top Wessleton VVS diamonds totaling .5 carats, and a smart blue dial.

BOTTOM RIGHT
The men's Sphere houses an automatic movement and is water resistant to 50 meters.

HIGHLIGHTS

- Recognized for originality in design, Leonard SA continues to unveil new models in its Screen and Sphere collections.

- Desirably stylish and chicly refined, the newest models match the spirit of the brand's ready-to-wear collection.

- The Men's Screen designs are fitted with self-winding movements and feature a glossy black dial with a satin-finished center.

- The Men's Sphere designs include self-winding models and mechanical chronograph models in steel or 18-karat gold.

- Both the Screen and Sphere for women have been bedecked with diamond bezels for added elegance.

- Leonard has also added a wealth of new straps to each of the collections. In addition to sleekly styled bracelets in steel or gold, rubber straps, fabric straps and exotic leather straps abound in a variety of trendy colors.

L. LEROY

this extraordinary Parisian enterprise has been creating timepieces of distinction for more than 250 years. Throughout the centuries, the brand has been favored by royalty, made incredible inroads in the world of scientific timing and chronometers, and has been the brand by which many observatories have set their clocks.

In **1751** Basile Leroy founded his company in Paris. Among his first timepieces were elegant table watches and clocks engraved and decorated in the finest French tradition. Throughout the **18**th century and into the **19**th century, a Leroy timepiece was considered to be a rare and precious possession—one coveted by royalty. In fact, the brand supplied such rulers as King Louis XVI, Queen Marie-Antoinette, Napoleon Bonaparte and countless others. In France, the brand was watchmaker to the king and abroad it enjoyed such appointments as watchmaker to the Queen of Spain, the King of Belgium, the King of Portugal and their Royal Highnesses of Wales.

Leroy has also excelled in technical advancements for centuries. In **1766**, Pierre Leroy conquered problems of timing at sea and presented King Louis XV with a chronometer timepiece that won him the appointment of Watchmaker to the French Navy. The excellence of Leroy's chronometers is evidenced by this and by the nearly 350 medals it has been awarded by the Observatory of Besancon—a record to this day.

In the late **1800**s, Louis Leroy worked diligently to design the first transmissions of time by radio signal from the top of the Eiffel Tower—accurate to $1/10$th of a second. Shortly thereafter Leroy perfected a clock that emitted signals with an accuracy of $1/100$th of a second. Known as the Constant Pressure Regulator, this clock was immune to variations in temperature and atmospheric pressure. In **1917**, three of these were installed in the catacombs beneath the observatory to serve as master clocks, and between **1917** and **1970**, a total of 64 Constant Pressure Regulators were supplied to 34 observatories around the world.

Leroy was also known as a maker of some of the world's most complicated watches. In **1900**, the brand unveiled a watch it called No. 1, which represented the culmination of three years of research. The elegantly engraved pocket watch featured 25 complications and housed 975 pieces. It was the world's most complicated timepiece until Patek Philippe surpassed its record in 1989.

Throughout the **20**th century, Leroy continued its tradition of developing art and technology, and has regularly unveiled stunning timepieces.

THIS PAGE

LEFT
This stunning Leroy pocket watch was unveiled in 1900 after three years of development. It was considered the most complicated watch of the time with 25 complex functions.

BELOW
This stunning table alarm clock, signed "Charles Leroy, Horloger du Roi," was given by Queen Marie-Antoinette as a gift to Count Hans Axel Von Fersen, marshal of the Royal Swedish Guard and Ambassador to France.

FACING PAGE

The Osmior Chronograph watch with date at 12:00 houses the self-winding L. Leroy caliber 5511. It is water resistant to 30 meters and cased in 18-karat gold.

L. LEROY

Today, the Leroy collection sustains the brand's traditions. Run by ninth-generation Philippe Leroy, the company is still rooted in Paris. However, its manufacturing facilities are now located in the Swiss Jura—ensuring that every watch is endowed with a double seal of excellence: French creativity and Swiss precision.

Like their predecessors, the watchmakers at Leroy strive to achieve harmony between design and technical excellence. The characteristics that distinguish a watch by Leroy include the ultra-thin construction, the smooth lines of the case, and the simple, uncluttered dials that are textured and tinted in old-world beauty.

The Leroy collection includes automatic watches, calendars, chronographs, moonphases, and power-reserve marine watches. Leroy's movements feature solid 18-karat gold rotors that are finely engine-turned and stamped in relief with the Leroy monogram.

Among the most coveted Leroy timepieces is the automatic watch with calendar that is fitted with twin spring barrels for exceptional power reserve, and the Automatic Chronograph watch that records elapsed time instantaneously to a precision of 1/5th of a second. Other timepieces of distinction include the Automatic Split-Seconds Chronograph and the Annual Calendar watch with Dual Time.

Recently, the brand returned to its Navy roots and introduced the Marine Automatic Watch with power-reserve indicator. The watch features a mechanical system designed to indicate the state of winding and the amount of power reserve. Fitted with the L. Leroy caliber 4711 self-winding movement, the watch offers a center seconds hand and power-reserve indicator at 12:00. Its watch case features bold lugs and the L. Leroy signature on the high-polished case.

TOP
The Marine Automatic watch with power-reserve indicator is crafted in 18-karat gold and features a self-winding movement.

LEFT
Classically elegant with its antique dial, this Osmior Mechanical watch is extra thin. It houses a manual-wind movement with 44 hours of power reserve.

BELOW
Offering full phases of the moon with date, this Grande Osmior watch houses a mechanical movement and features a silver dial pierced to reveal the blue night sky.

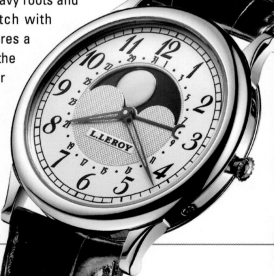

TOP LEFT
For an elegant touch, Leroy has added sapphires, emeralds, rubies or diamonds to the Grande Osmior watch.

TOP RIGHT
Housing a mechanical-wind movement, the Grande Osmior watch is 42mm in diameter.

BOTTOM RIGHT
Offering the utmost in precision timing, this Osmior Automatic Chronograph Rattrapante watch is crafted in gold and allows timing of two events simultaneously.

HIGHLIGHTS

■ Recently, Leroy significantly increased its offerings in the Osmior line. The all-new Osmior Mechanical Extra-Thin watch features the brand's pure styling and timeless distinction. Available with or without a small seconds hand located at 6:00, the watch is cased in 18-karat gold and houses the L. Leroy caliber 1025, complete with 44 hours of power reserve.

■ Leroy has also introduced several variations of the Osmior Mechanical Extra-Thin, including a Grande Osmior that is crafted in a 42mm 18-karat gold case, and the Grande Osmior with Jewels, which features sapphires, rubies, emeralds or diamonds set intricately into the sides of the 18-karat gold watch case.

■ There are several important automatic Osmiors, as well. The Osmior Automatic timepieces feature instantaneous date setting and twin barrels for three days of power reserve. Housing the L. Leroy caliber 3211, these watches offer either a center seconds hand or a subsidiary seconds readout.

■ The Osmior Chronograph Automatic heralds the company's rich tradition with perfect timing. This watch is fitted with the L. Leroy caliber 5511 movement that provides 45 hours of power reserve and measures elapsed time with 30-minute and 12-hour counters.

■ The split-seconds chronograph has been a specialty of Leroy since it was the first Official Timekeeper to Sports and Motor racing organizations in the early 1900s. The new Osmior Automatic Split Seconds Chronograph is fitted with the L. Leroy caliber 5511R self-winding movement and can time two events simultaneously.

■ The Grande Osmior with Phase of the Moon watch is a splendid moonphase calendar watch that is distinguished by its elegant dial design. The guilloché center is pierced to reveal a high-polished flamed blue disk reflecting the inky night sky. The watch, housing the L. Leroy caliber 1543 manually wound movement, features a concentric pointer to indicate the date.

LOCMAN ITALY

Locman Italy is taking the world by storm with its high-fashion, diamond-enhanced timepieces. Deftly mixing diamonds with such materials as aluminum, Locman has introduced collectors to a whole new realm of timekeeping.

Founded in **1986** by Marco Mantovani, Locman Italy has been on the cutting edge of design and style, sparking trends with its innovative timepieces. The brand was the first to set diamonds into aluminum, creating a whole new dazzling category of fun, diamond-embellished sports watches.

With its headquarters on the idyllic Island of Elba on the Tuscany coast, European offices in Milan and its new USA offices on New York City's Madison Avenue, Locman has positioned itself as a trend-setting leader.

The first watch introduced by Locman has since become a collectors' piece. Called Radica, the collection features bezels carved of rare Mediterranean Briarwood. The Radica was followed by the Aluminum Sport, a new concept of incorporating feather-light metal into boldly oversized watches.

It was in **2000**, though, that Locman made a tremendous impact and became a leader in style when it unveiled the Diamond Aluminum collection of tonneau-shaped aluminum watches with diamond-adorned cases. The brainchild of company co-owner Ben Feigenbaum, the Diamond Aluminum was the first watch to combine these two diverse materials. The collection, first unveiled with diamonds only on the top of the bezel (the Half Pavé), was an immediate hit and within months the diamond chronograph and the Full Pavé aluminum watches were launched.

In **2001**, the mother-of-pearl Full Pavé collection emerged onto the scene along with the Total Pavé. This was followed by the bold automatic "1970" series. In **2002**, the brand won the prestigious Premio Argo award for innovation in men's fashions in Italy.

LOCMAN ITALY

TOP

Locman's Signature Diamond Aluminum Collections retain their fame on the wrists of: Sir Elton John, Oprah Winfrey, Catherine Zeta-Jones, Madonna, Michael Jordan, Brad Pitt, Elizabeth Taylor, Sharon Stone and Barbara Walters, among others.

BELOW

Called Titanio, this striking chronograph sport watch is crafted of titanium, a first for Locman.

The year 2002 was a busy one for Locman. The brand rounded out and added to its already successful lines with a wealth of important new models, including Diamond Aluminum pieces with whiskey and fancy yellow diamonds. It also unveiled the "1970" watch for women, complete with some diamond-adorned versions and the "1970" chronograph in a variety of brilliant colors.

Above and beyond these launches, however, Locman has unveiled four new collections—each with its own futuristic yet elegant elements. A visionary company, Locman prides itself on creativity in design and material. The Nuovo Collections of aluminum- and steel-cased watches is a supreme example of Locman's abilities in European design. The bold oval-shaped watch is richly elongated at the top and bottom to further enhance the ergonomic shape.

Crafted in two sizes for men and women, the Nuovo Collections offer a host of nuances for Locman. The women's models are showered with 1.5 carats of diamonds on the aluminum case. Mother-of-pearl dials in white, pink, blue or champagne are available and are augmented with new pearlized alligator straps for enhanced elegance.

The men's Nuovo includes two limited-edition models geared for the collector. Both are crafted in steel and one offers a Tiger Eye dial, while the other three styles feature woven carbon-fiber bezels or dials. In addition to these two models, a Nuovo for men in aluminum with diamonds has been presented, as well as an Aluminum Chronograph Nuovo Sport.

Another new collection is the striking Quadrato line of oversized aluminum square watches. Bold and beautiful, the ladies' models are available with mother-of-pearl dials and bedecked with diamonds. There is also a chronograph version for men, with or without diamonds.

The bubble-design of the 1970s gets a makeover in this all-new Luna collection, embodying a bold and daring spirit sure to start a new Locman trend.

BELOW

The new beautifully shaped Quadrato is designed in models for both men and women. The men's version is available with or without diamonds and the ladies' model features a mother-of-pearl or colored dial.

Utilizing titanium for the first time, Locman has unveiled the Titanio line of watches and chronographs in sharp and classic colors. Crafted in a round case with interesting geometric complementary shapes, the watch is oversized and striking with a slightly domed crystal.

Incorporating an architectural spin, Locman introduces the Luna. An oversized round watch with domed crystal and domed aluminum case, the Luna resembles half a globe sitting on the wrist. It is offered in a diamond-cased version or with a single row of diamonds surrounding the face. It also comes without diamonds in bright, sporty colors such as hot pink, purple, turquoise, red and lime green.

- Highly revered in Italy, Prime Minster, Silvio Berlusconi, deemed Locman watches the gift of choice for delegates of the 2002 NATO-URSS Summit held in Rome. Receiving a Locman Aluminum Sports watch were such world leaders as United States President George W. Bush, and British Prime Minister Tony Blair.

- Locman watches are sold in the finest stores in the United States, including Bergdorf Goodman, Neiman Marcus, Mayors and Barney's. The company has a strong presence in the Middle East and is synonymous with creating watch trends in all European markets. In October 2002, Locman opened its own single-brand store in Tokyo, Japan in the Ginza quarter.

- With its island roots and sporty timepieces, Locman is a natural to pair with international yacht racing. The first annual Toscana Elba Cup Trophy Locman Regatta was held in 2002 on the picturesque waters of the Tirrenian Sea. Locman was one of several Italian sponsors of the race, which was opened to teams that competed in the America's Cup. The Cup prize was the highest in yacht racing history, E90,000.

- In less than three years, Locman has increased its product line from one model to six. Within each collection, several styles are available. Locman will expand its lines even further in 2003 with an emphasis on very sophisticated men's collections and new trend-setting ladies' sport watches with more diamond pizzazz for elegant fashion fun.

TOP

Locman was the first company to use aluminum as a high-fashion, cutting-edge and sexy material for watches. Setting it with diamonds and pairing it with the brightest of colors, the Aluminum Sports Collections are featherlight and hugely popular worldwide.

BOTTOM

The "1970" is available in two sizes and a large selection of colors. It's the company's first all steel watch and looks powerful with or without diamonds.

LONGINES

for more than 170 years, Longines has been creating timepieces that have demonstrated cutting-edge technological breakthroughs. Indeed, throughout the 19th and 20th centuries this Swiss brand won dozens of international awards, including 28 gold medals.

Today, under the auspices of The Swatch Group, this venerable brand continues to create chronographs and precision instruments of excellence, presented in beautiful elegance.

Most recently the company added to its incredibly successful DolceVita collection of stylish timepieces. First unveiled in 1997 as a rectangular watch and joined in 2000 by a square version, the DolceVita has come full circle with a round-cased watch. Superb in this bold rendition, the round DolceVita has a graceful curve that his accented by a discreet, supple bracelet or an elegant strap. This watch comes in five sizes: mini, ladies', midsize, men's, and a men's chronograph version. It is produced in steel and in 18-karat gold, with many models adorned with diamond-set bezels to varying degrees.

On the technical side, the brand has launched the Longines Avigation watch—a tribute to aviation pioneers. Based on the Weems Navigation aviation watch—developed in the 1920s by US naval officer Philip van Horn Weems and co-patented with Longines—the new Longines Avigation Maxi watch takes its inspiration from the past. Only 500 pieces of the Avigation Maxi will be created. The watches are fitted with the last of the remaining original L878 hand-wound Swiss mechanical movements (previously Longines 550 caliber).

Since there can be no further Avigation Maxi's after this production, Longines has also created a standard Avigation Maxi, which will house a hand-wound mechanical movement in the 47.5mm case. It is complemented by a standard-sized model (with a 38.5mm case) and by a chronograph version. There is also a GMT model available in the Avigation series that offers the world's 24 time zones on an outer rotating ring.

FACING PAGE

TOP LEFT

These watches are part of the Commemorative Collection of timepieces that celebrates Longines's 170 years of heritage. The watch on the left dates back to 1929 and houses a hand-wound movement; the middle watch dates back to 1928 and is enhanced with diamonds and sapphires; the watch on the right is crafted in 18-karat white gold and also dates back to 1928.

BOTTOM LEFT

The DolceVita round watch features a bold, sculpted case and houses a self-winding automatic movement with a date aperture at 3:00.

BOTTOM RIGHT

Crafted in steel, this ladies' DolceVita Round watch is set with 11 diamond markers and a diamond bezel with 100 Top Wesselton VVS diamonds weighing 0.5 carats.

THIS PAGE

TOP

A selection of A Heart for Children watches has been created by Longines to benefit the Audrey Hepburn CARES Team at the Children's Hospital Los Angeles.

FAR RIGHT

This Longines Avigation watch features an oversized crown and a subseconds dial at 9:00.

BOTTOM

The Longines Avigation Maxi recalls Longines's proud history with flight instruments that it created throughout the 1930s. This oversized watch houses a hand-wound mechanical movement.

HIGHLIGHTS

- The Audrey Hepburn Children's Fund and Children's Hospital Los Angeles, along with founding sponsor Longines, recently joined together to celebrate the A Heart for Children event. The charity benefits the Audrey Hepburn CARES Team at the hospital.

- The event was highlighted by a silent, private auction that featured nine unique 18-karat gold Longines watches designed especially for this charity. One watch up for auction was previously owned by Hepburn and was set with 218 diamonds. While the watch had an estimated worth of $9,950, it sold for $16,000.

- Additionally, Longines has created special models of the A Heart for Children watches that are being sold by select Longines retailers in the United States—the profits of which will benefit the CARES Team project.

369

MICHELE WATCHES

In the three short years since its USA launch, Michele Watches has experienced enormous global success with its collection thanks to its innovative product design and its clear message of individuality.

Michele Watches was created from the concept that a timepiece is an expression of an individual's place in life. The brainchild of Michele Watches President Jack Barouh, the brand reaps the benefits of the knowledge and insight of three generations of watchmaking tradition. Barouh is the son of a European watchmaker, and his son Jeremy and daughter Michele are the third generation to create watches. Together they infuse the brand with cutting-edge fashion appeal and attitude.

Barouh was raised in a family dedicated to the watch and diamond trades in the 1940s. When he followed in his father's footsteps, he added his own flair and updated creativity to the mix. In 1985, he moved his family to Miami, Florida, and established Michele Watches—named after his daughter. He began selling his collection in Latin America and later developed a branding and marketing strategy to bring Michele Watches to the US market.

In fall 2000, Michele Watches made a splash on the scene with its jeweled fashion timepieces. The unusual Michele Watches Collection focuses on fashion-forward styling, sophistication and quality. Indeed, the brand was born on the philosophy of offering a level of worldliness and fashion intermixed with a sense of marked difference. The first collection was the CSX-Diamond Collection—a fusion of sport and sparkle combining a steel case with a diamond bezel, mother-of-pearl dial and colorful interchangeable straps. The series was an immediate hit and within a year the brand was developing new interpretations and extensions of the line.

Within two years, Michele Watches witnessed an enormous increase in brand recognition around the world. By fall of 2002, it was one of the top-selling brands of diamond watches by leading luxury American retailers including Neiman Marcus, Bloomingdale's, Saks Fifth Avenue, Nordstrom, and Barneys.

Additionally, the Hollywood Foreign Press Association honored Michele Watches when it selected the brand's watches for the 2002 Presenter's Gift Box for the Golden Globe Awards. Today, Michele Barouh is Creative Director. In addition to working with retailers in all of the brand's key markets around the world, she has developed the Michele Watches website and has worked with her father and brother to develop a comprehensive merchandising and marketing strategy.

All Michele Watches timepieces are designed with the utmost attention paid to every detail of workmanship and presentation. Because the Michele Watches collection is designed to offer an array of expressions, moods and personalities, color and materials are vital. All cases are crafted of stainless steel and are finished in either a high-polish or with 23-karat rose- or yellow-gold plating.

Designs and styles are available to match all occasions and new collections are regularly unveiled to keep the brand a step ahead of the world's changing fashions. The interchangeable watchstrap is a key factor in the success of the Michele Watches collection. A diamond watch that is casually chic with a colorful alligator strap can be transformed into evening elegance in just moments with a change of strap.

Michele Watches collections use a variety of top-notched materials for straps, including farmed lizard, alligator, varnished lacquer leathers, grosgrain, denim, and silicon. Soft grain leather, ostrich, silk, and horsehair are other materials used in straps to create additional fashion statements. Bracelet watches are also available in either polished solid stainless steel or plated in a 23-karat gold finish.

Many of the timepieces feature iridescent mother-of-pearl dials in a painter's palette of colors. Other watches feature colorful enamel dials, often etched or embossed with subtle designs to add extra depth and detail.

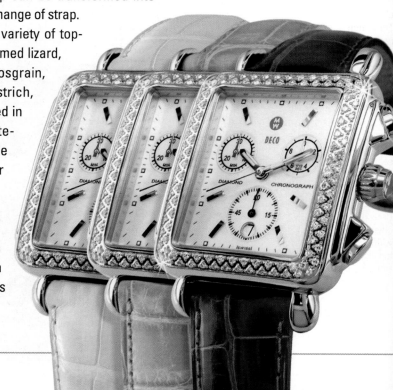

HIGHLIGHTS

- Michele Watches offers a variety of collections that are always evolving. One of its newest series is the Coquette Collection. It features a gently curved stainless steel elongated case, is pillow-shaped and is handset with more than 150 diamonds. This watch offers a sweep-second subdial at 6:00 and houses a Swiss movement that is water resistant to 3atm.

- There is also a Coquette Collection with a high-polished steel case rather than a diamond-adorned case. This watch makes a daring statement of retro beauty, especially when paired with exciting, colorful lizard or grosgrain straps.

- Other important new lines include the CSX Petite series (26mm in diameter)—evolved from the brand's very first watch launch—and the Deco line of cushion-cornered square watches.

- The Urban collection offers a barrel-shaped case bedecked in diamonds. There is also an Urban Steel Chrono with chronograph and calendar functions.

MONTRES ALLISON

a young company with cutting-edge designs, Montres Allison® creates timepieces of distinction. Drawing on a wealth of experience and turning to the finest movement manufacturers, Montres Allison has built a reputation amongst watch connoisseurs for its inspiring styling and technical function.

It was about a half a dozen years ago that Terry L. Allison II, a watch retailer and founder of an important internet community for wristwatch enthusiasts, turned his sights to creating watches under his own name. While Allison had been designing watches on the side for years, he had not pursued this avenue. Until **1997** when he initiated the Montres Allison concept and began designing watches in earnest. It was his goal to create bold timepieces that embodied modernity and top technology and offered wearers something different.

In **2000**, the first Montres Allison watches were unveiled. These timepieces, called Jour et Nuit, were tonneau-shaped watches made from solid steel. In **2001**, the company launched a collection of complex calendar watches, and in **2002** premiered the Jitana collection. Additionally, the brand has unveiled a series of complex watch models that offer bold alternatives in design.

While Montres Allison is headquartered in Colorado, the brand has locations in Switzerland and Hong Kong.

Montres Allison

Primarily, Montres Allison watches house exclusive movements embellished in-house by the company, or built on ETA Swiss-made movements. Watches are crafted not only in 18-karat gold, but also in steel, copper and even brass.

Design and styling is key at Montres Allison, where round and retro-styled tonneau watches steal center stage. Among the key collections are Jitana, which was named for Terry L. Allison II's young daughter. This series of tonneau-shaped timepieces features automatic movements, color-coordinated straps and brilliant-hued dials for drama and beauty. Exceptional in their design, the Jitana Series watches feature dual timezone functions, sun/moon indicators, and a beautiful aperture at 6:00 displaying the balance wheel with a tourbillon-style bridge.

The Energie collection of round watches with stepped cases also features complex automatic movements with added features and functions.

TOP
The Evolution watch is a tonneau-shaped timepiece.

BOTTOM
The Energie collection of round stepped-cased watches house automatic movements.

TOP LEFT
Terry L. Allison II, founder,
Montres Allison luxury
timepieces.

TOP RIGHT
Montres Allison Ciclone
with second timezone
at 12:00.

RIGHT
Jessica Stiles, Montres
Allison spokesperson.

BOTTOM
The Uragano is crafted
of solid copper and the
balance wheel and
tourbillon style bridge
are visible at 6:00.

HIGHLIGHTS

- Continually creating new timepieces, Montres Allison
  has unveiled several complex pieces. Among them is the
  Evolution—a tonneau-shaped watch with link bracelet
  and mechanical movement.

- Montres Allison is unique in creating beautiful
  timepieces such as the Uragano of solid copper.

- While complicated watches have been a mainstay in
  the Montres Allison line, the company now takes its
  mastery of craftsmanship a step further and designs its
  own tourbillon.

MONTRES ALLISON

SLAATHAUG MASTER CALENDIERE   REF. MA 200.102

Movement: mechanical, automatic winding, MA 200.102.
Functions: sun/moon; day; date; month; seconds; hours; minutes; 24 hour.
Case: stainless steel, two-piece tonneau-shaped case; anatomically curved case; 34mm wide x 41mm long, 14mm deep; curved crystal; back fastened by four screws.
Dial: white, guilloché, printed Arabic numerals.
Indications: sun/moon at 6; 24 hour at 6; day at 9; month at 12; date at 3.

Bracelet: stainless steel, signed stainless steel clasp.
Price: $20,995
Notes: only 200 individually numbered pieces created.

TOURBILLON II   REF. MA 200.1032

Movement: mechanical, manual wind, MA 200.103.
Functions: hours; minutes; tourbillon mechanism.
Case: 18K white-gold, two-piece tonneau-shaped case; anatomically curved case; 37mm wide x 41mm long, 14mm deep; curved crystal; back fastened by four screws; display back.
Dial: black, matte, hand printed.

Indications: hours; minutes.
Strap: signed black alligator, signed 18K white-gold deployant clasp.
Also available: platinum case, sterling silver case, stainless steel case.
Price: $99,995

CICLONE   REF. MA 200.105

Movement: mechanical, automatic winding, modified MA 200.101.
Functions: second time zone; hours; minutes.
Case: stainless steel, two-piece tonneau-shaped case; anatomically curved case; 37mm wide x 41mm long, 14mm deep; curved crystal; back fastened by four screws; display back.
Dial: silver, guilloché, Arabic numerals.

Indications: second time zone at 12; center hours and minutes.
Strap: black leather, signed stainless steel deployant clasp.
Also available: platinum case, sterling silver case, stainless steel case, copper case.
Price: $6,995

URAGANO   REF. MA 200.106

Movement: mechanical, automatic winding, modified MA 200.101.
Functions: sun/moon; hours; minutes.
Case: stainless steel, two-piece tonneau-shaped case; anatomically curved case; 37mm wide x 41mm long, 14mm deep; curved crystal; back fastened by four screws; display back.
Dial: blue, guilloché, Arabic numerals.

Indications: sun/moon at 12; center hours and minutes.
Strap: black leather, signed stainless steel deployant clasp.
Also available: platinum case, sterling silver case, stainless steel case, copper case; maroon dial.
Price: $6,995

RESERVE DE MARCHE
REF. MA 200.107

Movement: mechanical, automatic winding, MA 200.107.
Functions: power-reserve indicator; second time zone; date; hour; minutes; seconds.
Case: stainless steel, two-piece tonneau-shaped case; anatomically curved case; 37mm wide x 41mm long, 14mm deep; curved crystal; back fastened by four screws; display back.
Dial: antique yellow guilloché, Arabic numerals.
Indications: power reserve at 12; date at 3; second time zone at 6; center hours; minutes; seconds.
Strap: brown leather, signed stainless steel deployant clasp.
Also available: platinum case, sterling silver case, stainless steel case, copper case.
Price: $6,995

ENERGIE
REF. MA 200.108

Movement: mechanical, automatic winding, MA 200.107.
Functions: power-reserve indicator; second time zone; date; hour; minutes; seconds.
Case: stainless steel.
Dial: silver guilloché, matte gold background, Arabic numerals.
Indications: power reserve at 12; date at 3; second time zone at 6; center hours; minutes; seconds.
Strap: black leather, signed stainless steel deployant clasp.
Also available: platinum case, sterling silver case, stainless steel case, copper case.
Price: $6,995

EVOLUTION
REF. MA 200.115

Movement: mechanical, automatic winding, ETA 2824-2.
Functions: date; hours; minutes; seconds.
Case: stainless steel, two-piece tonneau-shaped case; anatomically curved case; 34mm wide x 41mm long, 14mm deep; curved crystal; back fastened by four screws; display back.
Dial: beige with mother-of-pearl inlay.
Indications: date; hours; minutes; seconds.
Strap: brown leather with stainless steel deployant clasp.
Also available: platinum case, sterling silver case, stainless steel case, copper case.
Price: $6,995

JITANA DEUX
REF. MA 200.117

Movement: mechanical, automatic winding, MA 200.117.
Functions: sun/moon; second time zone; hours; minutes; seconds.
Case: stainless steel, two-piece tonneau-shaped case; anatomically curved case; 34mm wide x 41mm long, 14mm deep; curved crystal; back fastened by four screws; display back.
Dial: black guilloché, Arabic numerals.
Indications: sun/moon at 3; second time zone at 9; center hour/minute; small seconds below center.
Strap: black alligator, signed stainless steel deployant clasp.
Also available: platinum case, sterling silver case, stainless steel case, copper case; wood-grain dial, rose-gold dial, blue dial, white mother-of-pearl dial.
Price: $6,995

OLIVIER ROUX

a true artist, Olivier Roux unites his astute talents for hand engraving with his enthusiasm for aesthetic and technical mastery to unveil an unusual collection of timepieces. Drawing on themes of ancient mythology and deities, Roux has created exceptionally intriguiging works of art and technology.

Born in Geneva in **1964**, Olivier Roux was trained as an engraver at one of Geneva's finest workshops. In **1984**, at the young age of 20, Roux started his own business engraving various objects of art. Restless in spirit, Roux decided to travel and in **1989** he took off to experience the world. For three years, he traveled the globe and was inspired by a variety of techniques and concepts. In **1992**, he joined an engraving work-shop run by several associates and, for the ensuing years, he produced works of art independently.

Still, he was driven by a desire to bring his ideas and work to fruition under his own name. He developed his own series of engravings and, in **2001**, realized his long-held personal ambition and launched his own line of hand-engraved timepieces. Each of his watches evokes a sense of human nature, geography and cultural diversity that constitutes the richness of our global environment.

Montres Olivier Roux's collection includes models named for Egyptian, Greek, Roman and Aztec gods and goddesses. Each piece is hand engraved and created in very limited numbers. Roux handcrafts in each of the three main colors of gold and the motifs he utilizes for engraving include arabesques, curves, stylized lines and geometrics that shimmer in light and offer dramatic depth.

OLIVIER ROUX

Passionate and enthusiastic about his work—which is more of a love than an occupation—Roux hand engraves the gold cases of his watches with the utmost attention to detail. Etching out the hard gold surfaces and working in relief techniques that date back to the 1700s and 1800s, Roux has deftly revived this fine art of embellishment.

In addition to their beautiful engravings, some of Roux's watches also feature enameling and diamonds. Each watch is fitted with a top-quality leather strap and houses supreme automatic movements. With the exception of the mechanical chronograph models, each watch houses a 21-jeweled movement.

Watches that revolve around the Egyptian themes include Maet (goddess of truth, order and justice) and Nouf (named for the goddess of the sky). Maet is crafted in 18-karat red gold and features a face ornamented with guilloché patterns. The bezel is set with 98 Top Wesselton diamonds. Nouf, crafted in 18-karat gray gold, features black enamel set within nearly a carat of exquisite Top Wesselton VVS quality diamonds.

Drawing inspiration from Greek mythology, Roux has created Athena (goddess of wisdom, science and art), Circe (named for the goddess of magic), Helios (god of the sun and light) and Kronos (god of time). Athena is crafted in 18-karat yellow gold and features an enameled bezel that is tobacco in color. Circe is elegantly crafted in 18-karat gray gold with a white dial. The entire case and case-to-bracelet attachment is engraved with starburst-like Greek designs.

LEFT
Named for the famed Greek goddess Athena, this elegant 18-karat yellow-gold watch features an enameled case.

BOTTOM (from left)
Inspired by the ancient Egyptians, this Nouf watch is named for the goddess of the sky and features exquisite hand-enameled art work with diamonds.

Inspired by Aztec cultures, the Tialoc (named for the god of rain and vegetation) features an elegant wheat and grain motif engraved on the 18-karat gray-gold case.

Circe, named for the Greek goddess of magic, is elegantly hand engraved with a Grecian design.

Crafted in 18-karat red gold, the Maet watch features a guilloché dial and is set with .78 carats of diamonds.

TOP LEFT

Called the Chronograph Column-Wheels, this mechanical watch houses a Valjoux 71 movement that is hand finished with the Côtes de Genève seal on its bridges.

RIGHT

Crafted in red gold, the Chronograph Automatic watch is decorated with a guilloché dial and a hand-engraved stylized motif.

HIGHLIGHTS

■ In addition to the exceptional gold engraved timepieces that comprise his main collection of watches, Roux has unveiled several stunning new models. Perhaps top among them is an 18-karat white-gold watch called Luxury Watch. The exquisite timepiece is set with 1,021 Top Wesselton VVS quality diamonds weighing four carats. The watch dial and case-to-bracelet attachments are also set with diamonds and there is a double row of diamonds on the outer edge of the case. The inner portion of the case is meticulously engraved with a spectacular floral pattern.

■ Two chronograph watches have also been introduced. One is the exceptional Chronograph Automatic, crafted in 18-karat red gold and decorated with a guilloché dial. The case of the watch is hand etched and engraved with a unique design of stylized lines and shapes.

■ The Chronograph Column-Wheels watch houses a mechanical Valjoux 71 chronograph movement and features bridges that are hand chased with the Côtes de Genève pattern and circular graining. This watch, crafted in 18-karat white gold, features a hand-guillochéd dial and an engraved pattern of geometric lines. It features a sapphire caseback.

OMEGA

this Swiss watch company has been making instruments of precision and beauty since its inception 155 years ago. Indeed, Omega was one of the first brands to create chronographs and chronometers and was a leader in timing Olympic Games early in the 20th century.

Omega landed on the moon in the 1960s, and continues to be involved not only in the U.S. space program, but also in sports timing, auto and yacht racing and in expeditions and explorations—and its timepieces keep pace to the tiniest fraction of a second.

In its world-renowned Speedmaster series, Omega recently unveiled the Speedmaster Broad Arrow limited-edition watch. Based on the first model in the Speedmaster series, this newest addition uses an exclusive, completely new Omega chronograph movement. Developed by Omega and produced for the company by Frédéric Piguet, the new caliber is a self-winding COSC-certified chronometer with column-wheel chronograph mechanism. The special limited-edition Broad Arrow models feature the hand of the original Speedmaster watch, and house a platinum rotor with an 18-karat gold Speedmaster medallion. The watch features an enamel dial and is limited to just 99 pieces in each color of gold. There is also a skeletonized version crafted in a platinum case and produced in a series of 21 pieces.

Omega has unveiled a new version of the Speedmaster Professional Chronograph—still the only watch ever worn on the moon. The movement of the new model is the Caliber 861, originally implemented in the Speedmasters. However, it employs the latest technical standards. Additionally the design of the moon watch retains the same classic look it had in the 1960s, with black dial and luminous markers and hands. Today's Speedmaster Professional line is enhanced by a version

TOP CENTER

This 18-karat gold Speedma Broad Arrow limited-edition watch features an enamel d with tachometer reading. It is created in 99 pieces of yellow, red and white gold.

FAR LEFT

The Omega Speedmaster Professional watch was first flight-qualified by NASA for manned space flight missions 1965. Its timeless design rema intact. The new version house a mechanical hand-wound chronograph, luminous hands and markers and a hesalite crystal that will not shatter int pieces if broken.

BOTTOM LEFT

The limited-edition Speedma Broad Arrow is created in tw versions. This model is craft in platinum and features a skeleton movement. It house the Omega 3221 self-winding COSC-certified chronometer movement with platinum roto and 18-karat gold medallion. Only 21 pieces of this model be created.

BELOW

Omega unveils the Constella 50th Anniversary watch in th models for men, three for women. All of these watche house self-winding mechani chronometer movements.

384

ABOVE

The Constellation Quadra Chrono watch is designed in a steel case and is available with or without a diamond-set case.

RIGHT

top

Celebrating its involvement with the most anticipated yacht race in the world, Omega unveils the America's Cup Chronograph in steel and in titanium. It houses the exclusive new Omega caliber 3303 self-winding column-wheel chronograph movement.

center

Omega's revolutionary Co-Axial escapement is used for the first time in a column-wheel chronograph movement. This watch is also an officially certified chronometer and offers 55 hours of power reserve.

bottom

The Limited Edition 2002 Museum Collection watch is based on the 1951 Omega Cosmic watch and offers multiple calendar functions.

BOTTOM RIGHT

Omega's My Choice Constellation Mini watch is now available in steel with diamond and comes in a variety of mother-of-pearl dials, including pink, blue and white.

with a scratch-resistant sapphire crystal and transparent sapphire case-back—revealing the movement that bears the inscription, "The first and only watch worn on the moon."

In its more elegant Constellation collection, Omega offers a host of versatile new models. The Constellation 50th Anniversary watch was unveiled in 2002 and the series includes three ladies' models and three men's models in steel or gold, each engraved with the words "Constellation—50 Years" on the caseback. Dial colors include black, cream and silver and are embossed with the Omega logo.

Also new is the striking Omega Quadra watch line. With its square design and sporty accents, the chronograph watch comes in a variety of models and colors. New versions of the My Choice Constellation Mini also have been unveiled, with elegant mother-of-pearl dials complemented by color-coordinated straps or elegant bracelets. New chronometer models, including a Co-Axial Chronograph crafted in either steel or 18-karat rose gold, have also joined the De Ville Co-Axial series. This marks the first time a chronograph watch has been fitted with a Co-Axial escapement.

HIGHLIGHTS

- The Omega America's Cup Chronograph is crafted in either steel or titanium, features a unidirectional-rotating bezel with ring in black aluminum or brushed steel. The watch features large luminous hour markers and hands, chronograph totalizers and a date window. The screw-in crown is equipped with an O-ring gasket and decompression ring and the watch is fitted with a helium escape valve. The self-winding column-wheel chronograph is water resistant to 300 meters.

- In its Museum Collection, Omega recently unveiled a redesign of its first-ever Omega watch with calendar. The second watch in Omega's Museum series, the Limited Edition 2002 piece is based on a 1951 Omega Cosmic watch with multiple calendar functions. The watch is crafted in 18-karat red gold and features a domed antireflective sapphire crystal. The stunning square watch features a black dial with 18-karat rose-gold hands, markers and moonphase display.

PANERAI

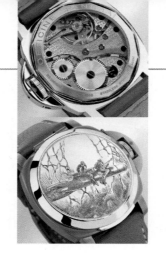

a deft blend of Italian styling and Swiss technology, Panerai has been a consistent leader in the world of professional timing instruments for more than 140 years. Indeed, when Guido Panerai founded his company in Florence in 1860, it was with the commitment to build professional timekeepers more so than pocket watches. His early work led to many patents in the timekeeping and optics fields. In the early 1930s, Panerai established a close relationship with the Royal Italian Navy and began supplying the soldiers with precision pocket watches and aiming sights for torpedoes. During World War II, Panerai supplied Radiomir watches to the Royal Italian Navy—firmly establishing itself as a leader in precision timing.

In 1993, after 50 years of creating watches exclusively for the commandos of the Royal Italian Navy, Panerai offered its timepieces to the world at large with limited editions of the Luminor. The precision watches were recognized for their performances under extreme situations and were eagerly sought by collectors. In 1997, the Richemont Group purchased Panerai and evolved the brand, adding new products upholding Panerai's tradition and increasing its worldwide presence.

Panerai's successful oversized timepieces are based on the Luminor and Radiomir, and each exists in the three key Panerai collections: Historical, Contemporary and Special Editions. In the Historical Collection, Panerai has unveiled the Luminor 44mm watch with its own new hand-wound mechanical movement. Guaranteed water resistant to 300 meters but tested to 400 meters, this exceptional watch is cased in either steel or titanium and has a transparent caseback to allow viewing of the engraved movement.

In its Contemporary Collection, Panerai has added some complexities. The Panerai Radiomir watch, pure and elegant in its simplicity, is now available in two sizes: 40mm and 42mm. Fitted with an automatic mechanical GMT/Alarm movement, the watch is now available in polished stainless steel. Also new to the Contemporary Collection is the Luminor Power Reserve watch. Available in two sizes in titanium or steel, this watch offers a power reserve of 42 hours. It houses the exclusive OP1X caliber movement from Panerai with 21 jewels, and is COSC certified. Another new model is the

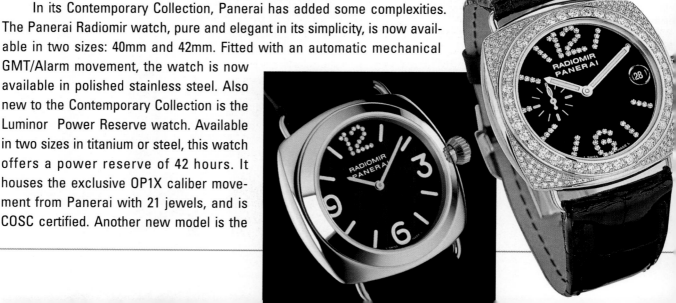

Luminor Marina Gold watch—created in 18-karat gold with a slight pink tinge—the first Panerai Luminor to have a gold case. Formed from a single block of precious metal, the case is 44mm in diameter, is COSC certified and is produced in a limited edition of just 150 pieces.

In its Special Editions Collection, Panerai has added the Luminor Marina 1950 watch-a magnificent 47mm timepiece that pays tribute to the first of its type unveiled in 1950. Perfectly legible under water, the watch conforms to its earlier counterpart with a dial consisting of two superimposed layers and a bridge device that is protected by trademarks. The COSC-certified chronometer watch offers a power reserve of 56 hours and is crafted in steel. It will be produced in a symbolic 1,950 pieces over a two-year period.

Also in the Special Editions Collection is the exceptional Luminor Blackseal watch that links past, present and future. The watch features a brushed steel cover that is engraved with two Italian frogmen in action on their human torpedo—an image that also appears on the dial of the watch. The engraving is executed entirely by hand by Panerai's skilled craftsmen.

HIGHLIGHTS

■ Panerai has formed an alliance with Mercedes-AMG (supplier of high-performance automobiles) and has developed two new chronographs specifically for the company. The two Luminor Chrono creations reflect their pedigree designs with dials that instantly evoke the AMG's dashboard instruments and are easily readable. One version is crafted in brushed titanium and polished steel and houses a high-precision automatic mechanical movement. The COSC-certified chronometer chronograph is fitted with an integrated bracelet and is created in an edition of only 100 pieces. The second version is even more exclusive—produced in an edition of just 55 pieces. Also fitted with an automatic mechanical movement, the certified chronometer is produced in 18-karat white gold.

■ At the 2002 Laureus World Sports Awards—which paid tribute to athletes internationally—Panerai was a supporter of the Laureus Regatta/Panerai Trophy sailing event. For the occasion of the competition, Panerai created a limited-edition Luminor GMT Regatta 2002 with second time zone. Only 300 pieces of this ocean chronometer will ever be made.

PARMIGIANI FLEURIER

Parmigiani is a brand dedicated to creating horological masterpieces that excel in both beauty and technology. A master watchmaker and world-renowned restorer of antique timepieces, Michel Parmigiani has set some of the highest standards in watchmaking for himself and his team of experts—standards that define the brand and set it apart from others.

Relatively young in the world of watchmaking, Parmigiani established his company in **1975** as an independent restoration business. Within just a few years, his reputation for excellence and his penchant for perfection made him one of the most sought-after watchmakers. Some of the world's finest brands turned to Parmigiani to create private-label watches for them. In **1995**, Michel Parmigiani was awarded the Prix GAIA for his activities and research in the horological field.

It was in **1996** that Parmigiani unveiled the first collection of timepieces to bear his name. The Parmigiani Fleurier line consisted of ladies'and men's watches, as well as several clocks, a few unique timepieces and a Grande Complication, which underscored his dedication to the fine Swiss watchmaking heritage.

Parmigiani's collection was very well received by connoisseurs around the world for its technical expertise, advanced craftsmanship and sublime elegance. Each year since the inception of the brand, Parmigiani has unveiled striking new watches ranging from chronometers to complicated watches such as the minute repeater and tourbillon. Still, he remains steadfast in his commitment to perfection. Every watch is handmade in his workshops in Fleurier and—ensuring exclusivity—only a few thousand timepieces are created annually.

In the classically elegant Toric collection of round time-pieces defined by the engraved godroons of its bezel, Parmigiani has added several impressive new models. Top among them are the Toric Perpetual Calendar Retrograde and the Repeater GMT. The Toric Perpetual Calendar Retrograde, previously in the collection, has been completely redesigned and now houses the first perpetual calendar movement manufactured entirely by Parmigiani. Using as a base the automatic mechanical Caliber 331, which was launched in 2001, the new movement incorporates additions that enable moonphase indication accurate to within 57 seconds in each lunar cycle. The discrepancy is thus reduced to only one day every 120 years.

The Toric Minute Repeater GMT chimes the hours, quarters and minutes on two gongs. It also features a second time-zone indicator and the date. The watch features an original second-time and calendar adjustment two-push- piece system developed by Parmigiani that is easy to use.

Parmigiani has also added models to the very harmoniously curved Form collection. The Forma Hebdomadaire, created to spark a contemporary flair within the Parmigiani line, features an extended, reshaped, larger curved case with longer case-to-bracelet attachments. The dial, inspired by Fibonacci's Golden Rule of numbers in nature, features a sub-second's dial that also incorporates the date aperture. This watch is crafted only in steel. The Forma Grande and Piccola collections essentially consist of the two sizes of Forma cases ensconced with varying degrees of diamonds. In their completely adorned versions, the Forma Piccola has 486 diamonds on the case, and the Forma Grande features 563 diamonds weighing nearly four carats.

TOP LEFT

The Toric Minute Repeater GMT watch is crafted in 18-karat rose gold or in platinum. The watch features a second time-zone indicator and date hand, in addition to chiming the hours, quarters and minutes on two separate gongs.

CENTER

The Forma Grande and Piccola Joaillerie watches are adorned with varying degrees of diamonds. When totally diamond-bedecked, the Piccola model features approximately 3 carats of diamonds; the Forma Grande, features nearly four carats. Each watch is crafted in 18-karat yellow, rose or white gold.

Michel Parmigiani has formed an alliance with the house of Bugatti, bringing together the aspirations of two great names devoted to the research of a perfect artistic and technical symbiosis.

While Bugatti is in the process of creating the fastest sports car in the world (the EB16.4 Veyron with 1001 horsepower and 16 cylinders), Parmigiani Fleurier has perfected a world-premiere mechanical timepiece for the brand.

The Parmigiani Fleurier Bugatti wristwatch was inspired by automobile technology. The case is designed specifically to make the movement visible. The movement has its bridge and constituent parts arranged on a horizontal axis rather than a vertical one, enabling the wearer to view the wheelwork like a cross-section diagram. This original idea, initially formulated by the very inventive watchmaker Vincent B rard, has made possible the successful outcome of a revolutionary horological concept.

Developing an ingenious system in design and operation, Parmigiani seals the association between the two houses by integrating both logos on the dial of the Parmigiani Fleurier Bugatti watch. What's more, the dial is not placed on the top of the watch, as usual, but vertically on the front of the case, making it easy to read while driving.

Parmigiani has also added to the elegant Basica collection with striking new dials. Crafted in solid 18-karat gold, the new dials of the Basica Primavera are satin finished with a sunray pattern and a translucent lacquer of pink, blue, amber or tea. Michel Parmigiani has reworked the appliqué Arabic numerals for the Basica Primavera with a curvaceous art-nouveau inspiration.

TOP LEFT

Crafted in 18-karat white or rose gold, the Toric Quantième Perpetual Retrograde watch houses Parmigiani's 332 automatic mechanical movement equipped with additional perpetual calendar retrograde 290 module with 22-karat solid gold oscillating weight.

TOP RIGHT

The Toric Chronograph 2003, crafted in all three colors of gold and in platinum, displays new dials completely redesigned. Shown here, the new Blu Lavanda color.

BOTTOM

Extraordinary in its design, the Parmigiani Fleurier Bugatti watch offers a full look at the movement within. Crafted in 18-karat white gold, it houses the 370 transverse hand-wound mechanical movement with 10 days of power reserve. The watch features six sapphire crystals and is water resistant to 30 meters.

TORIC WESTMINSTER   REF. PF004184

Movement: manual-winding, 25101, regulated in 5 positions; caliber 12'''; 27.6mm; 3 Hz; 21,600 vph; 42 jewels; 75-hour power reserve; hand-chamfered and polished bridges and mechanisms; Côtes de Genève decoration; 18K pink-gold, rhodium plated.

Functions: hour, minute, second by index; second GMT time zone; Westminster melody chimes at hours, quarters and minutes on four gongs by means of four strike-hammers; tourbillon rotating once each minute; balance wheel with timing screws.

Case: 18K gold (Ø 42mm), set with a real sapphire cabochon; cambered front sapphire crystal, flat back crystal; double-fluted bezel; hand-engraved identification number on the back. Water resistant to 3atm.

Dial: black minutes and seconds, red on the bezel; gold oval cartouche; blued steel Javeline hour and minute hands; blued steel index second hand.

Strap: alligator leather, square scales, black; gold buckle with tongue.

TORIC QUANTIÈME PERPÉTUEL RETROGRADE   REF. PF000474

Movement: automatic, 33201 caliber, 13 ''', 32 jewels, 28,800 vph, balance spring with micrometer screw regulation, 22 K gold rotor, engraved and personalized by hand. Mounted and finished by hand, decorated with a Côtes de Genève pattern and beveled.

Functions: hour, minute; perpetual calendar (date, day, month, year, moonphase).

Case: 18K white-gold, three-piece case (Ø 40.5mm, thickness 11.0mm); curved sapphire crystal; bezel with double hand-engraved knurling; white-gold crown with natural sapphire cabochon; knurled back attached by 6 screws, displaying the movement through a sapphire crystal. Water resistant to 3atm.

Dial: solid gold, engine-turned (guilloché) with "grain d'orge" pattern, eggshell color; applied white-gold bands and logo; printed minute track; white-gold Javeline hands.

Indications: four-year cycle at 12; moonphase at 6; center month and day of the week; date with arrow-shaped center retrograde hand.

Strap: crocodile leather; white-gold clasp.

Also available: in pink gold; with anthracite dial.

TORIC QUANTIÈME PERPÉTUEL RÉTROGRADE   REF. PF000471

Movement: automatic, 33201 caliber, 13 ''' , 32 jewels, 28,800 vph, balance spring with micrometer screw regulation, 22 K gold rotor, engraved and personalized by hand. Mounted and finished by hand, decorated with a Côtes de Genève pattern and beveled. **Functions:** hour, minute, second; perpetual calendar (date, day, month, year, moonphase).

Case: 18K pink-gold, three-piece case (Ø 40.5mm, thickness 11.0mm); curved sapphire crystal; bezel with double hand-engraved knurling; pink-gold crown with natural sapphire cabochon; knurled back attached by 6 screws, displaying the movement through a sapphire crystal. Water resistant to 3atm.

Dial: solid gold, engine-turned (guilloché) with "grain d'orge" pattern, anthracite color; applied white-gold bands and logo; printed minute track; white-gold Javeline hands.

Indications: four-year cycle at 12; moonphase at 6; center month and day of the week; date with arrow-shaped center retrograde hand.

Strap: crocodile leather; pink-gold clasp.

Also available: in white gold; with eggshell dial.

TORIC QUANTIÈME PERPÉTUEL RÉTROGRADE   REF. PF000471

The Perpetual Calendar Retrograde has been completely redesigned so as to receive the first perpetual calendar movement manufactured entirely by Parmigiani. The movement adopts the Parmigiani Fleurier automatic 331caliber, launched in 2001, as a base with some modifications (332 caliber) and incorporates the additional plate of the 290 Perpetual Calendar which is also manufactured at the workshops at Fleurier.

The Toric Perpetual Calendar Retrograde unveils a new face. Its eggshell or anthracite-colored 18K gold dial is guilloché, with applied white-gold measuring scales and an oval logo. The new version would not have come into existence if its technical elements were not enhanced.

A function previously absent in Parmigiani Fleurier wristwatches, the precision moonphase indication, makes its appearance in this new model. Parmigiani Fleurier workshops use a train of supplementary gears for an indication based on a duration of 29 days, 12 hours and 45 minutes, resulting in an excess of only 57 seconds after a lunar cycle. The discrepancy is thus reduced to only one day every 120 years.

TORIC MINUTE REPEATER GMT — REF. PF000462

Movement: mechanical, manual-winding, Christophe Claret 251 caliber. Côtes de Genève decorated and beveled.
Functions: hour, minute, small second; second time zone; 24 hours; minute repeater.
Case: 18K pink-gold, three-piece case (Ø 42.0mm, thickness 13.2mm), curved sapphire crystal; bezel with double hand-engraved knurling; repeater slide mounted on the middle; pink-gold crown with natural sapphire cabochon and oval pusher with case protection; back fastened by 5 screws, displaying the movement through a sapphire crystal. Water resistant to 3atm.
Dial: solid gold, eggshell color, engine-turned (guilloché) with a basket pattern, white-gold flange; applied white-gold cabochon markers, 6 and 12 Arabic numerals, and logo; printed minute track; white-gold Javeline hands.
Indications: 24-hours second time zone time at 3; small seconds at 9; date with center half-moon hand on the flange.
Strap: crocodile leather, pink-fold clasp.
Also available: in platinum.

TORIC MINUTE REPEATER GMT — REF. PF000462

Invented to enable the exact time to be known in complete darkness, in the days when light was only provided by ephemeral candles, the Minute Repeater chimes the hours, quarters and minutes on two gongs. Parmigiani Fleurier pays tribute to the creative spirit of that era by creating this magnificent, complex mechanical timepiece, combined for the first time with second time zone indication and date display. Thus the owner can, at will, activate the slide of the Minute Repeater positioned on the case middle at 9 o'clock and hear the time struck, as well as checking the time in the selected zone on the counter at 3 o'clock on the dial, or the date indicated by a central hand on a circular white gold area with a scale of 31 days. Wanting to introduce a modern touch to this mechanism, Michel Parmigiani has devised an original way of adjusting the GMT and calendar functions. Two pushers are positioned on the case at 2 and 4 o'clock. Simply by pressing them, the adjustment of the respective indications of the date and the second time zone is carried out. The winding crown set with a real cabochon sapphire is used to set the time of the central hour and minute hands in the usual manner, while the small-seconds dial is at 9 o'clock.

TORIC CHRONOGRAPH 2003 — REF. PF000000

Movement: mechanical, automatic-winding, 190 caliber; with 22K gold rotor. Hand-chamfered bridges and mechanisms with Côtes de Genève decoration.
Functions: hour, minute, second; date; chronograph function with 30-minute counter and 12-hour counter.
Case: platinum; winding crown set with a genuine cabochon sapphire; sapphire crystal cambered on the front and flat on the caseback. Water resistant to 3atm.
Dial: 18K gold dial with "grain d'orge" guilloché, blue lavender color with black counters; Parmigiani Javeline hour and minute hands in 18K gold.
Indications: chronograph seconds; small seconds; minute counter and hour counter hands in nickel-plated steel.
Also available: in four colors: in platinum with blue lavender dial; in yellow gold with white dial; in white gold with black silvered dial; in pink gold with black gilded dial.

BASICA PRIMAVERA DIAMONDS 37MM — REF. PF000460

The Basica collection of wristwatches with its sweetly elegant lines now provides a reflection penetrated by a new light. The simple, generous roundness of its curves is distinctive of the timeless Parmigiani Fleurier style. The dials of the Basica Primavera have a deep, clear brilliance with a penetrating luminosity. Like all Parmigiani Fleurier dials, they are made of solid 18K gold. This noble metal is brush-finished with a sunray pattern and a translucent lacquer of the desired shade is then delicately applied: pink, blue, amber or tea. The Basica Primavera collection also incorporates the constant aesthetic attention Michel Parmigiani pays to every detail. The applied Arabic numerals have been entirely reworked with an Art-nouveau inspiration. Their new, generous, slender curves give a new look to the passing hours and give the finishing touch to the immediately recognizable classic style of Parmigiani Fleurier. Available in two sizes (in pink yellow or white gold), with a sapphire back enabling the finish of its polished chamfered bridges with Côtes de Genève decoration to be admired, the Basica has an automatic movement certified Chronometer (COSC), with an oscillating weight of 18K gold and a power reserve of 72 hours.

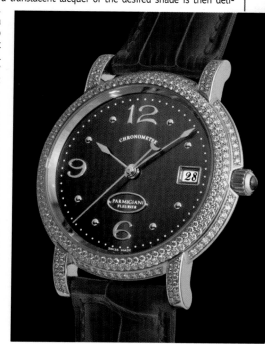

PARMIGIANI FLEURIER

BASICA PRIMAVERA 32,5MM   REF. PF000452

Movement: mechanical, automatic-winding, 340 caliber (Frédéric Piguet 1150 cal. base), 72-hour power reserve, 29 jewels, 28,800 vph; balance spring regulation by micrometer screw. 18K gold rotor. Mounted and finished by hand, Côtes de Genève decorated and beveled. Certified chronometer (COSC).
Functions: hour, minute, second; date.
Case: 18K pink-gold, three-piece case (Ø 32.5mm, thickness 8mm), curved sapphire crystal; pink-gold crown with natural sapphire cabochon and oval pusher with case protection; snap-on back displaying the movement through a sapphire crystal. Water resistant to 3atm.

Dial: solid gold, tea-color enameled; applied white-gold markers and Arabic numerals; logo with white-gold rim; printed minute track; white-gold Javeline hands.
Indications: date at 3 with white-gold rim.
Strap: crocodile leather, pink-fold clasp.
Also available: in yellow gold, amber dial; in white gold, pink or blue dial. Standard version: yellow gold, pink gold, ivory or black dial with Arabic or Roman numerals; in white gold, porcelainized or black dial with Arabic or Roman numerals; in jewel version.

FORMA GRANDE JOAILLERIE   REF. PF005706

Movement: mechanical, automatic-winding, 331 manufactured caliber (11'''1/2, 3.5mm thick), double winding barrel; 55-hours autonomy, 32 jewels, 28,800 vph; balance spring with micrometer screw regulation; 22K gold rotor, engraved by hand. Bridges and pillar-plate in alpaca. Mounted and finished by hand, decorated with Côtes de Genève and circular graining patterns and beveled.
Functions: hour, minute, second; date. **Case:** 18K pink-gold, two-piece case (size 41.0 x 34.0mm, thickness 9.0mm), rectangular cambered on all sides, brilliant pavé;

antireflective curved sapphire crystal; partly recessed pink-gold crown with deep grooves; knurled back attached by 6 gold screws, displaying the movement through a sapphire crystal. Water resistant to 3atm.
Dial: solid gold with white mother of pearl cover; 12 in pink gold with set brilliant; logo with pink-gold rim; blued-steel skeleton Delta Parmigiani hands.
Indications: date at 6 with pink-gold rim.
Strap: crocodile leather; pink-gold clasp with set brilliants.
Also available: with bracelet; in yellow gold: in white gold, strap or bracelet. Without brilliants, with silvered or black dial.

FORMA HEBDOMADAIRE   REF. PF005717

Movement: manual-winding, 110 manufactured caliber (13'''x10'''), in tonneau shape; 8-days power reserve; 28 jewels; balance spring with micrometer screw regulation and swan-neck spring. Bridges and pillar-plate in alpaca. Mounted and finished by hand, decorated with Côtes de Genève pattern and beveled. **Functions:** hour, minute, small second; date; power reserve.
Case: stainless steel, two-piece case (size 54.0 x 37.5mm, thickness 11.4mm),

rectangular cambered on all sides; antireflective curved sapphire crystal; back attached by 6 screws, displaying the movement through a sapphire crystal. Water resistant to 3atm.
Dial: solid gold, silvered, grained finish, subdial decorated with circular beads; applied rhodium-plated gold markers (12 Arabic numeral); bands with circular beads and with black rim and rhodium-plated gold cabochon: all applied on the printed minute track; blued-steel skeleton Delta Parmigiani hands.
Indications: date and small seconds at 6; power reserve at 12.
Strap: crocodile leather; steel clasp.
Also available: with black dial.

FORMA HEBDOMADAIRE   REF. PF005716

First launched in 2001, the Forma collection is acquiring a new aesthetic and mechanical dimension this year. While the classic Forma stimulated senses by its harmonious curves of classic elegance, the Forma Hebdomadaire impresses by its authority. Created to give the Parmigiani Fleurier collection a different, more contemporary look, the original curves of the Forma are the fruit of a quest: a search for perfect coherence and proportions between attachments, caseband and bracelet. The watch's

rich, sensual plasticity is reminiscent of nature's flowing lines. In perfect symbiosis with the body, the Forma hugs the curves of the wrist; no harshness interrupts its rounded smoothness to the touch. With a fine sense of proportions and a light touch, Michel Parmigiani intensified the richness of Forma's lines. He extended and reshaped its curved outline, redrawing the volumes of its attachments derived from a spiral. The result is a new case size, larger than the two previous ones, and one that Parmigiani Fleurier for the first time decided to make in an unfailing metal, steel, as an immutable carapace. The very high technology level required for the complex development of its multiple volumes enhances its precious qualities still further.

FORMA PICCOLA JOAILLERIE   REF. PF005711

Movement: mechanical, automatic-winding, 145 manufactured caliber (Frédéric Piguet 6.15 caliber), 40-hours autonomy, 29 jewels, 21,600 vph. Mounted and finished by hand, decorated with Côtes de Genève and circular graining patterns and beveled.
Functions: hour, minute.
Case: 18K yellow-gold, two-piece case (size 33.0 x 24.0mm, thickness 10.0mm), rectangular cambered on all sides, brilliant pavé; antireflective curved sapphire crystal; partly recessed gold crown; back attached by 4 gold screws, displaying the movement through a sapphire crystal. Water resistant to 3atm.
Dial: solid gold with white mother-of-pearl cover; 12 in gold with set brilliant; logo with pink-gold rim; blued-steel skeleton Delta Parmigiani hands.
Bracelet: yellow gold with set brilliants on the outer links; recessed clasp.
Also available: with strap; in pink gold: in white gold, strap or bracelet. Without brilliants, with silvered or black dial.

FORMA PICCOLA JOAILLERIE   REF. PF005714

Through the subtle and methodical quest for harmonious proportion under the aegis of the Golden Rule, the curved sides of the Forma are perfect for welcoming the sumptuousness of light. The ample curves of the caseband, constituent parts of the original form of the wristwatch, were not to be compromised. The setting of precious stones was not to alter the harmony of the curves in any way. Michel Parmigiani reworked his drawings at length, seeking to respect his original design in every detail while working out the precise diameter of each diamond. The two sizes of the Forma in gold are now available in completely or partially jewel-set versions, covered with many hundreds of precious stones. It is only this very complex setting of a very large number of diamonds on the caseband that has made it possible to create the Grande and Piccola Forma collection. The definition resulting from the restricted diameter of the diamonds reveals the aesthetic richness of the piece. The Forma Piccola has 250 diamonds (2,915 carats) on the caseband in its partially set version, while the completely set version has a total of 486 diamonds (1,454 carats) on the caseband and attachments.

IONICA "8 DAYS"   REF. PF000469

Movement: mechanical, manual-winding, 110 manufactured caliber (13'''x10'''), in tonneau shape, 8-days power reserve, 28 jewels; balance spring with micrometer screw regulation and swan-neck spring. Mounted and finished by hand, decorated with Côtes de Genève pattern and beveled.
Functions: hour, minute, small second; date; power reserve.
Case: 18K pink-gold, three-piece case (size 45.0 x 36.0mm, thickness 10.8mm), rectangular cambered on all sides; curved mineral glass; bezel with double hand-engraved knurling; pink-gold crown with natural sapphire cabochon; knurled back attached by 8 gold screws, displaying the movement through a sapphire crystal. Water resistant to 3atm.
Dial: solid gold, silvered, covered with pink mother of pearl; applied pink-gold Arabic numeral and logo; pink-gold Javeline hands.
Indications: date at 3; small seconds at 6; power reserve at 12 with applied pink-gold sector.
Strap: crocodile leather; pink-gold clasp.
Also available: in yellow or white gold; in platinum. With eggshell-color or anthracite dial: in yellow, pink or white gold or platinum.

IONICA "8 DAYS"   REF. PF000470

Contrasting the iron law of the market and following the certainly more expensive and complex way of the best watchmaking tradition for his Ionica tonneau, Michel Parmigiani choose to create "his" tonneau-curved movement (while today commercial logics impose the use of round standard movements also for shaped models).
As a result, we have now manufacture caliber 110 of Parmigiani Fleurier.
The construction by separate bridges, which must take into account the tension exerted by the main spring dimensioned for a power reserve of 8 days, is really beautiful.
In line with the best tradition are also the balance-spring regulator system with micrometer adjustment and regulator spring (swan-neck shaped).

PATEK PHILIPPE

arguably the finest watchmaker in the world, this legendary brand has built its legacy and unparalleled reputation on a philosophy dedicated to technical excellence and creative genius. Perhaps no other watchmaker can claim such an illustrious past.

Indeed, since its inception in **1839**, when Antoine Norbert de Patek founded Patek, Czapek & Co with Francois Czapek, this brand has created some of the world's most astounding exclusive and limited-edition complicated timepieces. It was in **1844** that Patek met and became lifelong friends with Jean Adrien Philippe who had developed the first keyless watch two years earlier. In **1845**, the two men formed Patek & Co., which was renamed Patek Philippe in **1851**. The union of these two brilliant horologists led to multiple developments in the world of watchmaking. The brand quickly became one of the most sought-after names in the world, with such notables as Queen Victoria, Madame Curie, Rudyard Kipling and Albert Einstein donning Patek Philippe watches.

In **1932**, the Stern family (makers of exquisite watch dials) took over the ownership of this prestigious brand. Following in the brilliant footsteps of its founding fathers, the Sterns managed Patek Philippe with vigilance. Indeed, the company has been family owned and operated ever since and has consistently remained on the cutting edge of research, development and innovation. Patek Philippe holds more than 60 patents and has unveiled such complex marvels as the world's most complicated pocket watch and one of the most complicated wristwatches ever built—the Sky Moon Tourbillon (Ref. 5002, launched in **2001**).

In typical Patek Philippe style, the most recent watches it has unveiled to the world are masterpieces of art and technology, of beauty and sophistication. Top among them is the spectacular Sky Moon Ref. 5102 wristwatch. Crafted in 18-karat white gold, this astronomical wonder depicts the night sky of the northern hemisphere and traces the angular progression of the stars. It also displays the moonphases and the angular positions of the moon.

Two years in the making (on the heels of more than eight years of development for its predecessors, the Star Caliber and the Sky Moon Tourbillon), the Ref. 5102 Sky Moon wristwatch houses a complex astronomical movement that consists of 301 components. The complicated display system relies on three separate stacked sapphire crystal disks that rotate at different speeds to depict their information.

In addition to offering the time, the moon and star placement, the lunar orbit and moonphases, this watch indicates the mean solar time, time of meridian passage of Sirius and time of meridian passage of the moon. Annual production of the Sky Moon is restricted due to the enormous effort involved in crafting, assembling and regulating this feat of horology. It is estimated that no more than 30 pieces will be created per year.

TOP

Ref. 5074 Minute Repeater with perpetual calendar houses an exclusive chiming mechanism with two cathedral gongs that are twice as long as conventional ones and are crafted of a steel alloy developed by Patek Philippe.

BOTTOM LEFT

From the Twenty-4 Petite collection, these 18-karat rose-gold and white-gold models feature diamonds to varying degrees: lining the complete length of the case and bracelet; bordering the case only.

BOTTOM RIGHT

The self-winding movements of Ref. 5074 and Ref. 5079 are based on Patek Philippe's caliber R27, which has a 22-karat-gold mini rotor integrated in the plate.

HIGHLIGHTS

- A true master of complications, Patek Philippe has unveiled two minute-repeater watches with unique cathedral gongs. The newest cathedral chime repeater watches are: Ref. 5074, which incorporates a perpetual calendar and 24-hour subsidiary dial; and Ref.5079, which features a strikingly elegant hand-enameled white dial.

  - Ref. 5074 houses the R27Q caliber—one of the most complicated movements ever made. Comprised of 467 parts, the movement houses a 22-karat-gold rotor and supports three subsidiary dials on the watch face.

  - For women, Patek Philippe continues in its tradition of creating striking timepieces with diamond accents. Among the newest watches are several diamond-adorned Twenty-4® watches in a petite size. There is also a haute joaillerie Twenty-4 watch in either 18-karat white or yellow gold set with approximately eight carats of diamonds on the bracelet and case.

CALIBER 16.250

Manual-winding movement, autonomy of 38 hours. Geneva Seal. **Functions:** hours, minutes. **Shape:** round. **Diameter:** 16.00mm (7′′′). **Thickness:** 2.50mm. **Jewels:** 18 (escape wheel with end-stones). **Balance:** smooth. **Frequency:** 28,800 vph. **Balance-spring:** flat, with "Triovis" index and micrometer screw regulation device.

Shock-absorber system: Incabloc. **Notes:** the pillar-plate is decorated with a circular-graining pattern, the bridges are decorated with a Côtes de Genève pattern and beveled. Noticeable on the balance bridge is the special "Triovis" index and the balance spring stud holder allowing the regulation of the oscillations of the balance without disturbing the alignment of both the roller-table and the escapement line. **Derived caliber:** 16.250 PS LU (16.250 with small seconds and moonphase; diameter: 16.30mm, thickness: 2.95mm, 115 components).

CALIBERS 175 AND 177

Manual-winding movement, autonomy of 43 hours. Geneva Seal. **Functions:** hours and minutes. **Shape:** round. **Diameter:** 20.80mm (9′′′1/4). **Thickness:** extra-thin, 1.77mm. **Jewels:** 18 (escape wheel with end-stones).

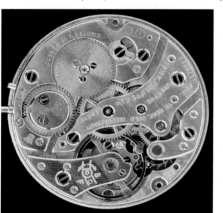

Balance: Gyromax, diameter: 7.40mm, in beryllium bronze, with 4 regulation inertia-blocks. **Frequency:** 18,000 vph; Caliber 177: 21,600 vph. **Balance-spring:** flat. **Shock-absorber system:** Kif. **Notes:** the pillar-plate is decorated with a circular-graining pattern, the bridges are decorated with a Côtes de Genève pattern and beveled. At present, only Caliber177/02 is produced; it has the same technical features as the 175, differing only in its vibration per hour datum.

CALIBER 215

Manual movement, autonomy of 44h. Geneva Seal. **Functions:** hours, minutes. **Shape:** round. **Diameter:** 21.50mm (9′′′1/2). **Thickness:** 2.55mm. **Jewels:** 18 (escape wheel with end-stones). **Balance:** Gyromax, with 8 regulation inertia-blocks. **Frequency:** 28,800 vph. **Balance-spring:** flat. **Shock-absorber system:** Kif.

Notes: pillar-plate decorated with a circular-graining pattern, bridges decorated with a Côtes de Genève pattern and beveled. **Derived calibers:** 215 PS (215 with small seconds); 215 PS FUS 24H (215 PS with two time zones with fast correction and 24 hours; diameter: 21.90mm, thickness: 3.35mm, 178 components).

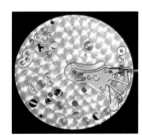

CALIBER 215 PS FUS 24H

This movement equips the Travel Time and Calatrava Travel Time models. It allows the display of two time zones by two different hour hands. When this function is not needed, the second hour hand may remain completely hidden behind the first one. The mechanisms added on the dial side of the pillar-plate allow controlling of the second hour hand simply by pressing down two pushers to make it move forward or backward in hourly increments. Furthermore, a protection device prevents the mechanism from being damaged by simultaneous pressure exerted on both pushers. The colors of the hands, including the 24-hour hand, help to immediately distinguish local time (burnished hand like the hour hand actuated by the pushers) and home time (gold colored) with the corresponding hand remaining fixed.

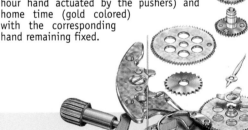

CALIBER 28-20/220

Manual-winding movement, autonomy of 240 hours (10 days), with two series-mounted winding barrels. Geneva Seal. **Functions:** hours, minutes, small seconds; power reserve. **Shape:** rectangular. Size: 28.00x20.00mm. **Thickness:** 5.05mm. **Jewels:** 29 (9 in gold settings and escape wheel with end-stones). **Balance:** Gyromax, with 8 regulation inertia-blocks. **Frequency:** 21,600 vph. **Balance-spring:** flat. **Shock-absorber system:** Kif. **Notes:** pillar-plate decorated with a circular-graining pattern; bridges are decorated with a Côtes de Genève pattern and beveled. Officially certified "chronometer" (COSC). **Above:** the dial-side view of the movement provided with the 10-days feature shows the wheelwork of the power-reserve display (it has its pivot at the center of the clear-colored great wheel); below, the particular positioning of the jewels of the regulating organ and escapement on the pillar-plate are visible. The jewels are positioned in a slightly hollowed area in a sinusoid shape, including the balance jewel (recognizable by the shock-absorber spring) on one side and the escape-wheel jewel (with the ninth gold setting which is not visible on the main side of the movement) on the other side. On the right is the hour-setting system with a rocking spring and setting-lever, all brushed and beveled. From here, a gear cascade (under a bridge fastened by two screws) transmits motion from the winding—stem to the center hour—and minute wheels.

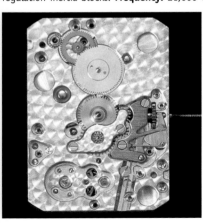

PATEK PHILIPPE

CALIBER 240 PS (THE PHOTOGRAPH REPRESENTS THE BASIC CALIBER 240)

Basic caliber: 240 (without small seconds).
Automatic-winding movement, autonomy of 48 hours; off-center 22-karat gold micro-rotor mounted on a ball bearing. Geneva Seal.
Functions: hours, minutes, small seconds (off-center between 4 and 5).
Shape: round. **Diameter:** 27.00mm (12′′′). **Thickness:** extra-thin, 2.40mm.
Jewels: 27 (escape wheel with end-stones).
Balance: Gyromax, with 8 regulation inertia-blocks.
Frequency: 21,600 vph.
Balance-spring: flat.
Shock-absorber system: Kif.
Notes: the pillar-plate is decorated with a circular-graining pattern, the micro-rotor and bridges are decorated with a Côtes de Genève pattern and beveled.

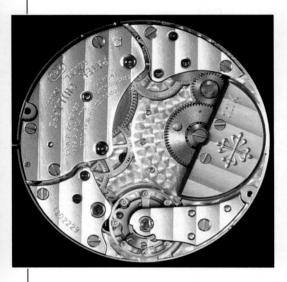

Derived calibers: 240 Q (240 + perpetual calendar module and 24 hours), s. photograph bottom; 240 SC (240 with center seconds); 240 PS IR ML4 (240 PS with power reserve and moonphase—diameter: 31.00mm, thickness: 3.85mm); 240 PS IRM LU (like 240 PS IR ML4 with date with coaxial hand without moonphase—s. photograph on front page above on the left); 240/188 (240 with world time indication—s. photograph on the right and below).

CALIBER 240 PS (THE PHOTOGRAPH REFERS TO THE BASIC CALIBER 240)

On the dial-side view it is possible to notice the bearing supporting the micro-rotor; the latter is housed inside the movement. With respect to conventional rotors, this solution allows obtaining automatic calibers of rather reduced thickness. The jewel between 4 and 5 supports the pivot of the small-seconds hand in the PS version.

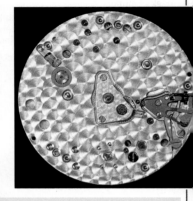

CALIBER 240/188 (DIAL SIDE)

Dial-side view of Caliber 240/188. Among the mechanisms added on the pillar-plate for the world-time indication, there is the special big L-shaped lever (occupying the upper side and partly the left side). This lever, controlled by a pusher (visible on the drawing below) allows correcting the relevant indications on the dial in a synchronized way: the reference town disc, 24-hour disc and local-time hand. They move forward simultaneously by one step for each point of pressure exerted on the pusher. During this operation the minute hand keeps its position.

CALIBER 240 Q (SIDE OF THE MODULE "PERPETUAL CALENDAR WITH 24 HOURS")

Basic caliber: 240. Automatic-winding movement, autonomy of 38/48 hours, 275 components; off-center 22-karat gold micro-rotor mounted on a ball bearing. Geneva Seal. **Functions:** hours, minutes; perpetual calendar until 2100 (date, day, month, leap year, moonphase, with 4 fast correctors); 24 hours.
Shape: round. **Diameter:** 27.50mm (12′′′). **Module diameter:** 30.00mm (13′′′1/2). **Thickness:** 3.88mm.
Jewels: 27 (escape wheel with end-stones).
Balance: Gyromax, with 8 regulation inertia-blocks. **Frequency:** 21,600 vph. **Balance-spring:** flat. **Shock-absorber system:** Kif.
Notes: the module and the 4-year cycle cam are decorated with a circular-graining pattern, the bridges and levers are brushed and beveled.

The pillar-plate is decorated with a circular-graining pattern, the micro-rotor and bridges are decorated with a Côtes de Genève pattern and beveled. The same module is combined with Caliber R 27 PS (automatic-winding repeater), thus originating Caliber R 27 Q (automatic repeater with perpetual calendar).

CALIBER 240/188

To regulate a Patek Philippe watch with World time indication for the first time, it is sufficient to press down the pusher until the local time-zone reference-city is set to 12; then, with the crown pulled out, to set the hands at the local time. (The watch in the photograph indicates 10 p.m. i.e., the 22nd hour on the 24-hour disc.) After its initial setting, the watch will automatically indicate the time in all 24 zones. Anyway, the real novelty of this World time Patek consists of the possibility of changing the time-zone time together with the other indications on the 24-hour disc by using the same pusher. In case of a journey to Tokyo, for instance, it is sufficient to set the destination city's name to 12—the hour hand and the 24-hour ring will be perfectly adjusted according to the local time.

CALIBER 240 PS IRM C LU

Patek Philippe defines some of its watches as "small complications"; among which are the three models presently housing the Caliber 240 PS IRM C LU. As a modification of the former version (without date and provided with a hand adjustable to the exact full-moon phase when it occurs; 242 elements), on the dial it displays small seconds (PS), power reserve (IRM), analogue date (C) and moonphase (LU). With respect to the basic caliber 240 PS, mechanisms for additional indications were added and the two independent correctors for date and moonphase (NB: on every watch, such corrections should always be made as far as possible from midnight). Furthermore, this mechanism has the following sizes: diameter: 31mm and thickness: 3.98mm; it uses 29 jewels and consists of 265 elements.

CALIBER 315 SC

Automatic-winding movement, autonomy of 50 hours; 21-karat gold center rotor, mounted on a ball bearing. Geneva Seal. **Functions:** hours, minutes, center seconds; date (with fast corrector).
Shape: round. **Diameter:** 27.00mm (11'''1/2). **Embedding diameter:** 27.60mm. **Thickness:** 3.22mm. **Jewels:** 29 (escape wheel with end-stones).
Balance: Gyromax, with 8 regulation inertia-blocks.
Frequency: 21,600 vph. **Balance-spring:** flat.
Shock-absorber system: Kif.
Notes: the pillar-plate is decorated with a circular-graining pattern, the bridges are decorated with a Côtes de Genève pattern and beveled, the rotor is decorated with a concentric circle pattern with an engraved Calatrava cross.
Derived calibers: 315 SQR (315 SC + 126 perpetual calendar module with retrograde date, 368 components; diameter: 28.00mm, thickness: 5.25mm, 31 jewels, autonomy of 38/48 hours); 315 SQA 24H (315 SC with annual calendar (date, day, month) and 24 hours); 315 SQA IRM LU (315 SC with annual calendar (date, day, month, moonphase) and power reserve); 330 SC (315 SC with date-disc positioned inside; thickness: 3.50mm); 330 SC IZR (330 SC with power reserve, 240 components, 30 jewels, autonomy of 48 hours).

CALIBERS 315 SC AND 330 SC (DIAL SIDE)

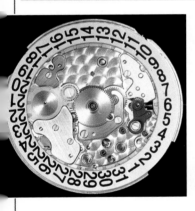

In a dial-side view, the standard version of Caliber 315 SC (s. photograph above) shows the wheel and mobile element of the date change at 9. Another striking feature is the finish of the calendar bridges: brushing, circular graining and beveling.
Caliber 330 SC (s. photograph below) differs only by the presence of a date-disc with a smaller diameter and, hence, positioned inside the perimeter. This difference allows positioning of the date window on the dial in a more centralized place.
With respect to the calibers adopted formerly, i.e. 310 SC and 335 SC (two-way winding rotor, smooth balance, 28,800 vph), Patek Philippe succeeded in obtaining the maximum power intensity at half the total time by using a winding system based on a one-way rotating rotor. Thus, it is possible to eliminate the frictions and dead times occurring during the inversion of the rotor rotation and mostly due to the presence of the supplementary device devoted to this function, i.e. the inverter. Furthermore, the performance of the Gyromax balance allows reducing the frequency to 21,600 vph without worsening the precision of the whole movement.

CALIBER 315 AND ITS DERIVATIVES

The "exploded" view of this movement allows appreciating above all what is normally hidden behind different bridges, the gear train, i.e. the organs transmitting the motive force from the winding barrel to the escapement and further to the balance. The outer part (yellow) of the winding barrel transmits motion, through its spring, to the balance by engaging the pinion of the big intermediate wheel and, through the subsequent wheels, to the seconds and escape wheels. The latter transmits, each time one of its teeth is freed by the pallets, an impulse (again through the pallets) that allows the balance to maintain the amplitude of its oscillations unchanged, thus overcoming even very small frictions that could stop it in a very short time. The structure of this movement allows the seconds hand to take over the motion from an additional wheel driven by the intermediate wheel, while in other cases it is also possible to position the seconds wheel at the center, by placing the relevant hand directly onto it. Lifting the balance-bridge, it is possible to appreciate the Gyromax balance, virtually present in all the versions and characterized by using 8 regulation inertia-blocks that make the use of an index superfluous.

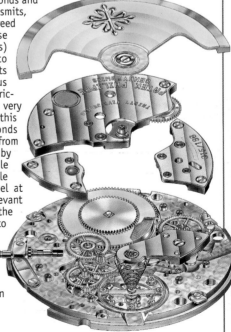

PATEK PHILIPPE

CALIBER 315 SQA IRM LU (ANNUAL CALENDAR)

Thanks to the introduction of this complication, it was possible to near the performances of a perpetual calendar (here the manual date-correction must be initiated once a year, to pass from the 28th or 29th of February to the 1st of March), but with an extremely simplified mechanical construction. The real "brain" of this system is the small wheel provided with five projections, indicated within the circle. These projections "decide"—by engaging a feeler lever (under the same wheel)—the correct date change at the end of the months with 31 days (feeler lever on the circumference of the tooth bases) or 30 days (feeler lever on the projections, as on the drawing), except for the month of February that would be of 30 days without manual correction. The simplification of the annual calendar mechanism allowed realizing a module functioning almost exclusively by toothed wheels and gears, thus excluding rocking bars and levers which would otherwise

be necessary for the correct functioning of a perpetual calendar.
The original version is Caliber 315 SQA 24H (patent N° CH685585 G, March 1, 1996—the first day of its first annual cycle), features the basic caliber 315 SC and the annual calendar module 198 with digital date display and digital 24 hours at 6, analogue day and month respectively at 10 and 2; with respect to the base, it has 316 elements, autonomy of 48 hours, 35 jewels, diameter: 30.00mm, thickness: 5.22mm.

CALIBER R 27 PS (MINUTE REPEATER)

Automatic-winding movement, autonomy of 48 hours; 22-karat gold off-center micro-rotor mounted on a ball bearing. Geneva Seal.
Functions: hours, minutes, small seconds; double-tone minute repeater.
Shape: round.
Diameter: 28.00mm (12'''1/2). **Embedding diameter:** 27.60mm.
Thickness: 5.05mm.
Jewels: 39 (escape wheel with end-stones).
Balance: Gyromax, with 8 regulation inertia-blocks.
Frequency: 21,600 vph.
Balance-spring: flat.
Shock-absorber system: Kif.
Notes: the pillar-plate is decorated with a circular-graining pattern, the bridges

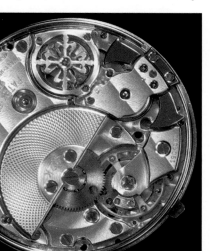

are decorated with a Côtes de Genève pattern and beveled, the micro-rotor, included within the movement's total thickness is guilloché engraved, the Calatrava cross is skeletonized and gilded.
Derived calibers: R 27 Q (R 27 PS without small seconds + perpetual calendar module, 24 hours, visible in Caliber 240 Q on the previous pages; thickness: 6.90mm); R 27 PS-QR (R 27 PS + 126 perpetual calendar module with retrograde date, visible below).

CALIBER R 27 PS (MINUTE REPEATER)

Caliber R 27 PS, dial-side view. The repeater gears are visible in this image. At 11 is the 14-toothed rack for the minute strokes. Below the minutes reel at the center of the movement is the minutes volute (with four bowed arms), almost hiding the smaller sized quarters volute (spiral-shaped, stepped). Also visible nearby is the hours volute, on the left below.
The functioning of a repeater mechanism depends on a series of feeler levers (one respectively for the hours, quarters and minutes) and on their positions on these volutes (representing a very memory of the sonnerie mechanism). When the sonnerie mechanism is actuated by the cursor positioned on the case side, the positions of said levers determine the number of strokes.
It is because of the mechanical complexity of the whole that a repeater represents one among the most expensive complications in horology.

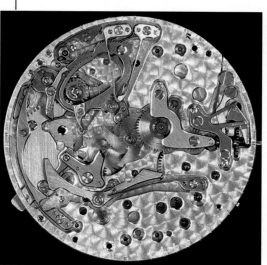

Besides that, the complication of Caliber R 27 PS constitutes a highly refined technical solution, as all of the repeater mechanisms are housed on the same pillar-plate and not on an additional module. For this reason, a manufacturer is obliged to design the movement as a whole.

CALIBER R 27 PS-QR (MINUTE REPEATER, PERPETUAL CALENDAR)

Basic caliber: R 27 PS. Automatic movement, autonomy of 48 hours; 22-karat gold off-center micro-rotor mounted on a ball bearing. Geneva Seal.
Functions: hours, minutes, small seconds; perpetual calendar (retrograde date, day, month, leap year, moonphase with 4 fast correctors); minute repeater. **Shape:** round. **Diameter:** 28.00mm (12'''1/2). **Embedding diameter:** 27.60mm. **Thickness:** 6.98mm. **Jewels:** 39 (escape wheel with end-stones). **Balance:** Gyromax, with 8 regulation inertia-blocks. **Frequency:** 21,600 vph. **Balance-spring:** flat. **Shock-absorber system:** Kif.
Notes: pillar-plate decorated with a circular-graining pattern, bridges decorated with a Côtes de Genève pattern and beveled, micro-rotor included within the movement's total thickness, guilloché engraved, Calatrava cross skeletonized and gilded. The **126 module** includes the mechanisms of a perpetual

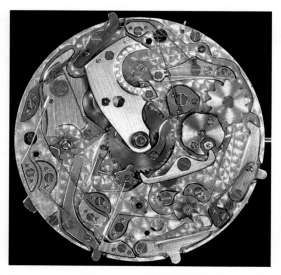

calendar with date display by retrograde hand. Below 12 there is a 4-point star wheel for the digital indication of the four-year cycle (leap year included); at 2 and 9 there are the wheels for the month and day-of-the-week indications through windows. The same perpetual calendar module is also used for the basic calibers RTO 27 PS-QR (repeater, tourbillon, manual-winding perpetual calendar) and 315 SQR (automatic-winding perpetual calendar).

CALIBER RTO 27 PS (TOURBILLON, MINUTE REPEATER)

Manual-winding movement, autonomy of 48 hours. Geneva Seal.
Functions: hours, minutes, small seconds; minute repeater.
Shape: round.
Diameter: 28.00mm (12'''1/2). **Embedding diameter:** 27.60mm.
Thickness: 6.55mm.
Jewels: 28.
Balance: Gyromax, with 8 regulation inertia-blocks and tourbillon device with an antimagnetic carriage turning once in a minute.
Frequency: 21,600 vph.
Balance-spring: Breguet.
Notes: the pillar-plate is decorated with a circular-graining pattern, the bridges are decorated with a concentric circle pattern and beveled, the Calatrava is cross is skeletonized and gilded. This movement consists of approximately 400 components, 84 of which belong exclusively to the tourbillon.
Derived calibers: RTO 27 PS-QR (RTO 27 PS + 126 perpetual-calendar module with retrograde date; 8.58mm, 506 components, autonomy of 38/48 hours).

CALIBER CH 27-70 Q (CHRONOGRAPH, PERPETUAL CALENDAR)

Manual-winding movement, autonomy of 50/60 hours, 353 components. Geneva Seal.
Functions: hours, minutes, small seconds; perpetual calendar (date, day, month, leap year, moonphase with 4 fast correctors); 24 hours; chronograph with two counters (center seconds, 30 minutes).
Shape: round.
Diameter basic movement: 27.00mm (12''').
Diameter module: 30.00mm (13'''1/2).
Thickness: 7.20mm.
Jewels: 24 (escape wheel with end-stones).
Balance: Gyromax, with 8 regulation inertia-blocks. **Frequency:** 18,000 vph.
Balance-spring: Breguet.
Shock-absorber system: Kif.
Notes: pillar-plate decorated with a circular-graining pattern, bridges are decorated with a Côtes de Genève pattern and beveled.
Derived calibers: CHR 27-70 Q (CH 27-70 Q with split-second chronograph feature).
Caliber CH 27-70 (diameter 27.00mm), the newest among Patek Philippe's chronographs, a simple manual-winding chronograph with two counters.

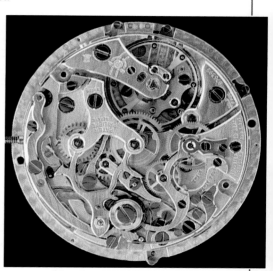

CALIBER CHR 27-70 Q (SPLIT-SECOND CHRONOGRAPH, PERPETUAL CALENDAR)

Manual-winding movement, autonomy of 50/60 hours, 407 components. Geneva Seal.
Functions: hours, minutes, small seconds; perpetual calendar (date, day, month, leap year, moonphase with 4 fast correctors); 24 hours; split-second chronograph with two counters (chronograph center seconds and minutes).
Shape: round.
Diameter basic movement: 27.00mm (12''').
Diameter module: 30.00mm (13'''1/2).
Thickness: 8.86mm.
Jewels: 28 (escape wheel with end-stones).
Balance: Gyromax, with 8 regulation inertia-blocks.
Frequency: 18,000 vph.
Balance-spring: Breguet.
Shock-absorber system: Kif.
Notes: pillar-plate decorated with a circular-graining pattern, bridges decorated with a Côtes de Genève pattern and beveled. The perpetual calendar module, visible in the photograph on the right, is the same as the one of Caliber CH 27-70 Q.

CALIBER CH 27-70 Q (DIAL SIDE)

There are two classes of perpetual calendars: with a 48-month and a 12-month cam. Visible among the different components visible in the photograph (next to the winding crown) is the year cam (four-year cycle) subdivided into four 12-month sequences; among the notches determining the duration of the month of February (the four deepest notches), the shortest one represents a leap-year February. To separate the month and year indications, a series of gears transmits motion to a 12-toothed wheel (just above) by reducing its rotation speed by a quarter with respect to the year cam.
Seen on the left is the 7-toothed star wheel related to the window displaying the day of the week.
At 6 is the pivot of the moonphase disc, whose indication is extremely accurate. After one year, the variation with respect to the real datum is only 11 minutes and 47 seconds. In other words, the watch will function for approximately 122 years before the overall variation will total one day. The same perpetual-calendar module is used also with Caliber CHR 27-70 Q, split-second chronograph with perpetual calendar.

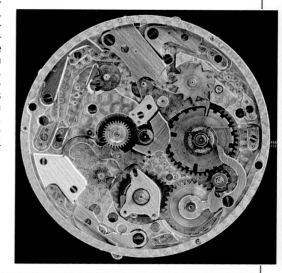

PERRELET

recognized by his peers as one of the greatest watchmakers of the 18th century, Abraham-Louis Perrelet was respected as an inventor and brilliant artisan. Creating the world's first automatic watch more than 230 years ago, Perrelet was way ahead of his time. Today, the company that bears his name carries on in his tradition.

Born into a humble family in **1729**, Abraham-Louis Perrelet demonstrated astute mechanical inclinations at a very early age. As an adolescent, he helped his father build watchmaking tools and developed a passion for the profession. At the age of 20, he struck out on his own and in **1749** began watchmaking in the Neuchâtel mountains.

Perrelet invented a multitude of important tools for the watchmaking industry and began creating escapements and other components that demonstrated his keen abilities. Over the years he was master to some of the finest watchmakers in history, including Abraham-Louis Breguet. Longing to perfect the methods of timekeeping, Perrelet regularly searched for solutions to contemporary problems. In **1770**, in a stroke of genius, he invented the world's first automatic watch. It was his vision to add to the watch movement a freely oscillating weight whose energy would automatically wind the main spring. Perrelet's automatic watch was a highly sophisticated product and proved to be the forerunner of several inventions of the late **18**th century.

Abraham-Louis's grandson, Louis-Frédéric emigrated to Paris and soon became the official watchmaker to Kings Louis XVIII, Charles X and Louis-Philippe. He was awarded at least four gold medals at French Trade Fairs in the **1820**s and **1830**s. According to the Fair's official record in **1839**, he was the inventor of the split-seconds chronograph (patented in **1827**).

His son Louis was also official watchmaker to King Louis-Philippe and ran the family workshop from **1854** until **1870**. In all, five generations of Perrelet watchmaking would span a total of three centuries.

In **1995**, Flavio Audemars—an industrialist within the watch and microtechnique industry in the south of Switzerland—reinstated the Perrelet name in style. Establishing the brand in an historic building in Neuchâtel, Perrelet SA was founded. The brand created only automatic watches and adopted the motto "Tradition and Innovation." That same year, Perrelet presented its first timepieces to the world—watches that housed a unique double rotor. Perrelet has since built an entire collection of double-rotor watches, including a Skeleton model unveiled in **1999**.

THIS PAGE

LEFT
A series of elegant pocket watches made by Abraham-Louis Perrelet around 1780.

BOTTOM
Flavio Audemars is Perrelet's president and founder of the company.

FACING PAGE

Released internationally in 2002, the Rectangle Royale Paris features the "Clous de Paris" motif on the dial.

TOP
Hearts define the elegant styling of this Lady Coeur design.

LEFT
Diamonds adorn the upper rotor of these Lady Tempest watches. Dials are crafted of natural mother of pearl and accented with diamond markers.

The unique winding system of Perrelet's 1995 automatic timepieces was powered by two connected rotors. One rotor is positioned traditionally on the bridge side of the movement, and the other is on the dial side where surplus energy is stored. Since the mid-1990s, Perrelet has developed another system that allows for complications to be integrated into the watches.

Every Perrelet double-rotor watch features one exquisite viewable rotor. Either hand engraved or set with diamonds, the highly decorated top rotor is a main attraction of Perrelet watches, one that demonstrates the brand's keen craftsmanship. Every detail of Perrelet watches is meticulously designed and produced. Top rotors are crafted in 18-karat white, yellow or rose gold and a serial number is engraved on each timepiece. Crystals feature double-sided anti-glare sapphires, and the markers and hands are applied carefully on the dial.

Perrelet's fine collection includes both round and rectangular watches. Within the round-cased

watches are the Lady Coeur, the Lady Tempest, the Classic, and the Chronograph Grand Maitre. The Lady Coeur automatic watch features elegantly feminine styling. The upper rotor, visible on the dial, is decorated with 18-karat gold hearts. To further enhance the motif, a single heart is set at 6:00 on a red, blue, green or gray sunburst dial.

Similarly, the Lady Tempest collection is also resolutely feminine. Its dials are crafted of pale pink, blue or white mother of pearl, and the 18-karat gold top rotor is set with varying degrees of diamonds depending on the model.

The Classic model from Perrelet perpetuates the characteristics of elegance and refinement. Dials are either brushed anthracite or antique silver, and the rotors are made of gold that is color-coordinated with the case. The Chronograph Grand Maitre features the rotor at 12:00 and three counters on the dial. There is also a square date window at 4:00. The chronograph is offered with either a silver, titanium, copper or blue dial with alligator strap or bold steel bracelet.

There is also the very special LeLocle round automatic watch with double rotor. This superb watch is fitted with Perrelet's caliber 181 with date and is crafted in 18-karat gold with color-coordinated gold top rotor. The transparent caseback is engraved with "LeLocle" and the series number of the watch.

A B O V E
The Classic houses Perrelet's PR3H-2000 movement and features an upper rotor in 18-karat gold to match the case.

T O P   R I G H T
The Chronograph Grand Maitre is a technical feat for Perrelet. It features chronograph with three counters plus the date, which is linked to Perrelet's patented double-rotor system.

R I G H T
The stunning LeLocle collection pays tribute to the Swiss watchmaking town where Abraham-Louis Perrelet lived for many years.

PERRELET

Perrelet's stylish rectangular watches are immediately recognizable in design.

The Rectangle Royale is crafted in steel. It houses the Perrelet PR3H-2000 movement with date. The upper rotor is crafted in 18-karat white gold. This watch is offered with silver, blue, titanium or sand-colored dial.

From this initial series, the Lady R was born. Crafted in smaller dimensions, the striking watch comes in a variety of combinations. The dials are crafted in rose, blue, black or natural mother of pearl and are enhanced by diamond markers. The top rotor of the Lady R is set playfully with 49 diamonds for added elegance. Perrelet has also created versions with diamond-set bezels for ultimate shimmer. The Lady R is available with a fabric strap or with an elegant link bracelet.

The Rectangle Royale Chronograph with its majestic dimensions (40mm x 34mm) emulates the period in the brand's history when Louis-Frédéric Perrelet (Abraham-Louis's grandson) opened his shop in Paris and made watches for the kings of France.

ABOVE

The Rectangle Royale Chronograph shown here features luminescent numerals and square subdials for sporty appeal.

RIGHT

Housing the 165 caliber based on a Dubois Depraz movement, this Rectangle Royale Chronograph features embossed Asian-inspired commas as markers and round subdials for the chronograph counters.

HIGHLIGHTS

■ Building on its highly successful Rectangle Royale line, Perrelet has unveiled new models that scintillate the senses.

■ The Perrelet Rectangle Royale Paris automatic watch houses Perrelet's caliber 180 in its steel case. Again paying homage to Louis-Frederic Perrelet's craftsmanship of watches for French kings, the Rectangle Royale Paris features an engine-turned anthracite or silver dial with a "Clous de Paris" décor.

■ Another masterpiece of distinction is the Rectangle Royale Chronograph. This impressive watch is crafted in steel and houses the Perrelet 165 caliber based on a Dubois Depraz movement.

■ The Rectangle Royale Chronograph is presented with two different dial designs. One features the round rotor at 12:00 and three round chronograph subdials. The hour markers are Asian-inspired commas and are embossed on the dial. This version is available in silver or an unusual ochre-colored dial.

■ The second version of the Rectangle Royale Chronograph features a sportier dial in black, anthracite or blue. It features luminescent numbers and rectangular subdials for the chronograph counters that reflect the case design.

PERRELET

RECTANGLE ROYALE CHRONOGRAPHE

Movement: mechanical, automatic-winding, Perrelet 165 caliber (ETA 2892A2 caliber base + Dubois Dépraz chronograph module). Patented double rotor.
Functions: hour, minute, small second; chronograph with 3 counters.
Case: stainless steel, three-piece case (size 42 x 36mm, thickness 13mm), rectangular with cut angles, brushed and polished finish; antireflective flat sapphire crystal; rectangular pushers; back attached by 8 screws, displaying the rotor through an antiglare sapphire crystal. Water resistant to 3atm.
Dial: silvered, grained; white-gold micro-rotor at12; subdials decorated with circular beads with glossy black crowns and silver and red printed indications; printed bent markers and railway minute track; luminescent bâton hands.
Indications: small second at 3; hour counter at 6; minute counter at 9; center seconds; minute track.
Strap: crocodile leather, hand-stitched; steel clasp.
Also available: with steel bracelet; with black, anthracite, blue, silver or okra dial; with rectangular subdials.

EXCEPTION RECTANGLE ROYALE LIMITED EDITION

Movement: automatic-winding, Perrelet 180 caliber. Patented double rotor.
Functions: hour, minute, second; date. **Case:** 18K yellow-gold, three-piece case (size 39.5 x 33.5mm, thickness 9.3mm), rectangular with cut angles, brushed and polished finish; antireflective flat sapphire crystal; back attached by 8 screws, displaying the rotor through an antiglare sapphire crystal. Water resistant to 3atm. **Dial:** silvered, grained; center white-gold micro-rotor; printed Roman numerals and minute track; luminescent bâton hands. **Indications:** date at 6. **Strap:** crocodile leather, hand-stitched; yellow-gold clasp.
Also available: with black dial, 30 pieces; pink gold, black or ivory dial, 30 pieces each version; white gold, black or blue dial, strap or bracelet, 100 pieces each dial type.

RECTANGLE ROYALE PARIS

Movement: mechanical, automatic-winding, Perrelet 180 caliber. Patented double rotor.
Functions: hour, minute, second.
Case: stainless steel, three-piece case (size 36 x 30mm, thickness 9.4mm), rectangular with cut angles, brushed and polished finish; antireflective flat sapphire crystal; back attached by 8 screws. Water resistant to 3atm.
Dial: anthracite, guilloché with Clous de Paris pattern; center white-gold micro-rotor; applied square and printed bâton markers; luminescent Railway hands.
Strap: crocodile leather, steel clasp.
Also available: with silvered dial; with bracelet. Mother-of-pearl dial (s. photograph).

RECTANGLE ROYALE PARIS

Movement: mechanical, automatic-winding, Perrelet 180 caliber. Patented double rotor.
Functions: hour, minute, second.
Case: stainless steel, three-piece case (size 36 x 30mm, thickness 9.4mm), rectangular with cut angles, brushed and polished finish; antireflective flat sapphire crystal; back attached by 8 screws. Water resistant to 3atm.
Dial: pink mother of pearl; center white-gold micro-rotor; applied cabochon and drop-shaped markers Alpha hands.
Bracelet: stainless steel; steel fold-over clasp.
Created as a limited editions of 30 numbered pieces.
Also available: bezel with brilliants, rotor with brilliant pavé, prune-color dial.

410

GRAND MAÎTRE CHRONOGRAPHE

Movement: mechanical, automatic-winding, Perrelet PR.6H-2000 caliber (ETA 2892A2 caliber base + Dubois Dépraz 2021 chronograph module). Patented double rotor.
Functions: hour, minute, small second; chronograph with 3 counters.
Case: stainless steel, three-piece case (Ø 40mm, thickness 13mm), brushed and polished finish; antireflective flat sapphire crystal; oval pushers; snap-on back displaying the rotor through an antiglare sapphire crystal. Water resistant to 3atm.
Dial: rosé, brushed with a sun pattern; white-gold micro-rotor at12; subdials decorated with a guilloché basket pattern with silvered crowns; applied Roman numerals; open burnished leaf-style hands.
Indications: small second at 3; date between 4 and 5; hour counter at 6; minute counter at 9; center seconds; minute track with divisions for 1/5 of a second.
Bracelet: stainless steel; recessed steel fold-over clasp.
Also available: with alligator leather strap; with black, silver, titanium, copper or blue dial.

EXCEPTION PLATINUM 21

Movement: mechanical, automatic-winding, Perrelet 181 caliber. Patented double rotor; the rear rotor is chased and open. **Functions:** hour, minute, second; date.
Case: platinum, three-piece case (Ø 40mm, thickness 9.5mm); antireflective flat sapphire crystal; crown with sapphire cabochon; snap-on back. Water resistant to 3atm.
Dial: anthracite gray, brushed with a sun pattern; center white-gold numbered micro-rotor; applied Roman numerals and rhombic markers; Poire style hands; minute track.
Indications: date at 6 with chased white-gold rim.
Strap: crocodile leather, hand-stitched; steel clasp.
Note: created as a limited editions of 21 pieces numbered on the rotor.

LE LOCLE

Movement: mechanical, automatic-winding. Patented double rotor; the rear rotor is engraved with the emblem of Le Locle town.
Functions: hour, minute, second, date.
Case: 18K pink-gold, three-piece case (Ø 40mm, thickness 9.5mm); antireflective flat sapphire crystal; knurled middle; snap-on back. Water resistant to 3atm.
Dial: glossy black; center pink-gold micro-rotor; emblem of Le Locle town at 6; white printed Arabic numerals with luminescent dots on top; skeleton Pomme hands; printed railway minute track.
Indications: date at 6 with magnifying lens.
Strap: alligator leather, hand-stitched; pink-gold clasp.
Also available: in yellow gold, white dial: in steel, white or black dial. . "Classic": pink gold, anthracite dial, alligator leather strap; yellow gold, antique-style silver dial, alligator leather strap or bracelet; white gold, antique-style silver or anthracite dial, alligator leather strap; steel, antique-style silver or anthracite dial, alligator leather strap or bracelet.

LADY TEMPEST - LADY COEUR

Movement: automatic-winding. Patented double rotor; the rear rotor is chased.
Functions: hour, minute, second. **Case:** stainless steel, three-piece case (Ø 30mm, thickness 9.3mm); antireflective flat sapphire crystal; snap-on back. Water resistant to 3atm. **Dial:** sky-blue mother of pearl; center white-gold micro-rotor with brilliant pavé; applied markers, 6 in Arabic numerals, logo at 12, 8 in brilliants; leaf-style hands. **Strap:** lizard skin, hand-stitched; pink-gold clasp. **Also available:** with bracelet; black or rosé dial.
Without brilliants: in steel, natural mother of pearl, sky-blue, black or rosé dial, lizard skin strap or steel bracelet; in yellow gold, natural mother of pearl or rosé dial, lizard skin strap.
Lady Coeur (small pict.): steel with blue, red, green or gray enameled dial, lizard skin or velvet strap, bracelet; steel and yellow gold with blue, red or green enameled dial, or steel and pink gold with gray enameled dial: lizard skin or velvet strap, steel bracelet; yellow or pink gold with blue, red or green enameled dial, lizard skin or velvet strap.

QUINTING

mystery and beauty have lured man and woman alike since the dawn of time. Quinting watches possess a mystique that is perhaps one of the most alluring qualities of all timepieces on the market today: they are transparent from front to back.

The realization of a transparent watch had long been the dream of engineer René Quinting. Fascinated by the world of mechanics, by the inner workings of timepieces, by the hands and wheels of watches, Quinting embarked on a quest to bring the concept of skeleton watches to an all-new level. In **1993**, he established his own company and set about achieving his goal.

With the help of two trained engineers and an electrotechnical engineer, Quinting realized his dream after six years of intense research and development. Indeed, the two engineers contributed greatly to the creation of the final product and the electrotechnical engineer, Pascal Berclaz, infused the company with the financial backing to bring the watch's concept to reality.

In **1999**, Quinting unveiled its first Mystery Transparent watch to the world. It received multiple honors and recognition and was an immediate hit with collectors. In **2000**, Berclaz purchased the brand and determined to develop the Mystery Transparent watch into a full-range series of high-tech timepieces.

As chairman of Quinting, Berclaz brought the brand to the **2002** World Watch and Jewelry Fair in Basel with a complete collection of watches—nearly a dozen models in all, including chronographs bedecked in diamonds and gemstones.

TOP LEFT
Crafted in steel with
white dial accents
and a black leather
strap, this new Quinting
Mystery watch displays
time only.

CENTER
Blue accents transform
this modern Quinting
Mystery watch into a
stylistic statement. It is
crafted in steel in the
smaller 43mm version.

Inspired by the technology that powers Cartier's Mystery Clocks, Quinting watches are a complex feat of mechanical strategy and innovative thinking. Essentially, each Quinting watch houses a patented mechanical movement with four motors that are mounted inside the external rim of the case—hidden from view. From these motors, the hands are driven by a system of mobile sapphire crystals, each of which has peripheral teeth and a central staff to rotate uniformly and smoothly.

There are six transparent mobile sapphires—one each for the hours, minutes, date, and one each for the chronograph hours, minutes and seconds. Additionally, there are six stationary sapphires which hold the assemblage together. All of the crystals have been specially treated to achieve a total antireflective effect. Because of these multiple layers, Quinting timepieces are naturally extra-thick—a feature made less noticeable by the oversized diameters of the watchcases.

The caseback of Quinting watches consist of an engraved ring made of scratch-resistant enamel. The ring carries the individual series number of the hand-assembled piece. Quinting watches are offered in 43mm or 47mm models, and are crafted in either steel, 18-karat gold or platinum. Special versions offer diamond- and gemstone-set bezels and diamond inner rings.

TOP LEFT

Contemporary and appealing this Quinting Mystery Chronograph is crafted in 18-karat gold and is set with diamonds and sapphires.

TOP RIGHT

Red spices up the hours, minutes and seconds of this 47mm Quinting Mystery watch that is crafted in 18-karat gold. This chronograph watch also comes in blue.

RIGHT

The Quinting Mystery Chronograph watches are offered with either a leather strap or a totally integrated link bracelet.

HIGHLIGHTS

- In addition to the highly successful Quinting Mystery Chronograph watches, the brand has unveiled several time-only models. Elegantly designed with futuristic styling, the new 3-hand transparent watch versions feature boldly polished cases, dots as hour markers and a choice of either Arabic or Roman numerals.

- Some of the 3-hand transparent watches feature inner rings of color, coordinated with colored numerals and colored straps for alluring appeal. Among the colors offered are red, blue, purple, white, and black.

- Quinting has also been working quietly on an all-new mechanical Quinting Mystery watch, which it plans to release on the market sometime in late 2003.

RAYMOND WEIL

f or more than 25 years, RAYMOND WEIL has created masterpieces of time, art and elegance which express the creative desires of our times. RAYMOND WEIL gathers inspiration from works of art and music, cleverly embodying these premises with a passion enviable amongst some of the best-known Swiss watchmakers.

Since its founding by Raymond Weil in **1976**, this Geneva-based watch company has been an enigmatic leader due to the creation, design and color-intensive elements in its designs. Using all that modern technology has to offer, RAYMOND WEIL has never settled for anything less than impeccable product quality.

Most of the RAYMOND WEIL collections draw their inspiration from major musical works such as Parsifal—the brand's signature collection—Don Giovanni and Othello. Each of these collections reflects RAYMOND WEIL's love for classical music, the opera and the arts.

In **1982**, the talented and passionate Raymond Weil welcomed Olivier Bernheim into the family business. Instrumental in opening new markets and making structural and transitional changes within the company, Bernheim is now president and CEO of the company.

Since its inception, RAYMOND WEIL has produced elegant and cutting-edge timepieces. In **1983**, RAYMOND WEIL launched the incredibly successful, classically elegant Amadeus collection, dedicated to Mozart. Several years later, the bold Othello was introduced and in **1988**, the stunning color-stained-crystal Traviata watch made its debut. Indeed, the Traviata timepieces were so sophisticated and striking in their use of color and style that RAYMOND WEIL was soon recognized as a leader in technical and aesthetic design.

RAYMOND WEIL unveiled the Parsifal collection of steel and 18-karat gold watches in **1991**. This most celebrated collection continues to make its mark as a true virtuoso. Valiant, powerful and refined, the Parsifal is a timepiece of symmetry and harmony.

Throughout the late **1980**s and into the **1990**s, RAYMOND WEIL grew to be one of Switzerland's most important watch influences. Indeed, the vision of RAYMOND WEIL can be summed up in just a few words: creation, innovation and evolution—each of which is a permanent element in the brand's professional code of ethics.

RAYMOND WEIL

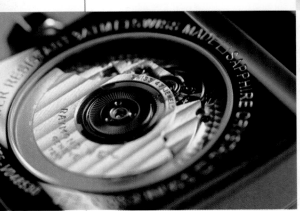

Adhering to a constant quest for perfection, RAYMOND WEIL continually unveils impeccable works of craftsmanship and beauty. Insistent that technical prowess remains supreme, RAYMOND WEIL has harmoniously blended tradition and modernity, technology and art into each timepiece.

One such exceptional collection is the Don Giovanni series. Recently, RAYMOND WEIL launched an unusual version of the Don Giovanni chronograph watch and the new creation dominates the collection with its extraordinary dimension and splendid execution.

The daring Don Giovanni Cosi Grande watch is the result of combined research into new ideas and solutions in watchmaking. A phenomenal creation of complexity in design and technical aesthetics, the Don Giovanni Cosi Grande is a mechanical chronograph with automatic winding. Hand-assembled by RAYMOND WEIL's finest watchmakers, the chronograph includes the traditional functions of start, stop, restart, and return to zero, and offers a 30-minutes counter and a 12-hours counters.

The Don Giovanni Cosi Grande watch is crafted in steel and features a curved rectangular case of extreme dimensions. It is 50mm long by 37.6mm across and is fitted with a domed sapphire crystal with antireflection treatment. Water resistant to 30 meters, the watch features a transparent caseback to view the mechanism.

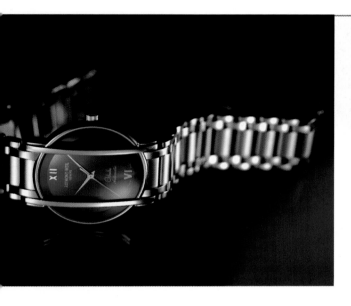

In 2001, RAYMOND WEIL gave the Othello collection—first unveiled to the world in 1986—a stunning relaunch. The rebirth of Othello captures the very essence of the innovative spirit of the brand. With a calm and discreet design that emphasizes strength of character and uncompromising beauty, Othello is equally daring and mysterious.

The round, thin case features a slightly curved sapphire crystal that charms and fascinates. The depth of the dark blue dial bordered by a midnight-blue bezel is tirelessly captivating, and the two thin steel bars that stretch from top to bottom across the sapphire crystal add unparalleled depth and dimension.

Sophisticated and intriguing, the new Othello collection is a profound expression of individuality. In addition to the enticing midnight-blue Othello, RAYMOND WEIL has also unveiled two splendid new versions of the Othello in 18-karat gold. Called the Othello OR collection, the sleek watches are crafted in either yellow or rose gold and in typical Othello style feature two vertical bars of gold sliced across the curved crystal of the watch—a strikingly bold and innovative design.

The Othello OR Jaune line is crafted in 18-karat yellow gold with a cognac dial. The bars are set with 46 diamonds for scintillating effect. The Othello OR Rose collection is crafted in 18-karat rose gold with a dial influenced by burgundy reflections. These elegant watches embody the pioneering and inventive design spirit of the brand.

HIGHLIGHTS

- Focusing on mechanical excellence, RAYMOND WEIL has developed the Tradition Mecanique watch. Housed in a sleek, round steel case, the automatic timepiece features a white dial set with Roman numerals and date at 3:00. The watch is equipped with a subseconds dial at 6:00 and offers a transparent caseback to reveal the mechanical hand-assembled movement.

- In the Parsifal collection the brand has unveiled the Aspiration Chronograph Automatic. Crafted in 18-karat gold or steel, the watch is offered in a variety of models—including a diamond-adorned version for women. It is water resistant to 100 meters and features a date window at 12:00. The Parsifal is also now available in five mini models in gold, bedecked with diamonds.

- In true RAYMOND WEIL style, the brand has also launched an innovative new corporate identity based on a "Time to ..." concept. The message in advertising and marketing campaigns revolves around "time to celebrate" for the Parsifal models; "time to create" for the Othello collection; and "time to dream" for the Don Giovanni series.

RICHARD MILLE

designed around a concept of high-performance and advanced technologies unique to Richard Mille, this brand's watches offer radical styling with an emphasis on perfection and luxury. Selecting the tourbillon as his launch timepiece and taking it steps further—ensuring chronometer status and perfection of use—Richard Mille has unveiled a watch unlike any other.

A veteran in the watch industry, Richard Mille began his career in **1974** as a commercial director for one of the world's largest watch companies, where he remained for 20 years. In **1994**, Mille joined the renowned house of Mauboussin and for four years acted as CEO in different capacities. In **1998**, Mille resigned as president and CEO of Mauboussin's watch division and opted to strike out on his own. Initially, Mille consulted with a number of companies about their watch development, including Audemars Piguet, Repossi and Baccarat. In fact, he created and developed the Baccarat watch, which was just launched in late **2002**.

At the same time, Mille was developing his own timepiece. Inspired by the perfection found in the automotive and aviation industries, and impressed with high-tech mechanical objects, Mille vowed to create a performance timepiece. His designs were incomparable in standards and incorporated a specially developed tourbillon escapement. The innovative technical choices applied to the design of this sophisticated watch required thousands of hours to develop. For more than a year, Mille designed and redesigned his watch until he had achieved perfection.

For extensive periods, he subjected his timepieces to rigorous testing and fine-tuning to ensure precision and reliability. Finally, in **2001**, Mille was ready to begin production of his watches. The first watch was the Tourbillon RM 001, launched in August **2001**. It was followed that same year with the Tourbillon RM 002—an evolution of the first watch featuring a titanium plate and function indicator. In **2002**, Mille unveiled the Tourbillon RM 003 with dual-time indicator. Indeed, Mille has a number of exciting new inventions in the works with plans for expansion.

Richard Mille timepieces offer a very different conceptual approach in the luxury watch field. It is Mille's goal to be to the watch industry what Ferrari and Mc Laren are to the automotive field—technologically advanced, innovative and performance oriented. Indeed, the image of Mille is anything but typical. The timepieces produced by this brand are the results of a very talented team of engineers working in an ultra-modern production workshop to serve as strong 21st century concept.

The Richard Mille watch is an object of relentless reliability and bold difference. All of the components have been manufactured from scratch and many are totally integrated. Every detail of the Richard Mille watches have been the subject of extreme scrutiny. Each movement contains 267 components—the production of which require more than 20,000 mechanical operations. Even the tiny titanium screws used in the watch undergo twenty or more operations before meeting Richard Mille's approval.

The main elements of the movement—including the flexible tourbillon and barrel bridges—have been specially studied and tested to achieve a high level of shock resistance. Richard Mille has developed a special, rapidly rotating spring barrel that is designed to ensure a smooth power flow by improving the slippage between turns. Additionally, the brand has created a new escapement design that is aimed at reducing friction. Indeed, all aspects of the research and development of the Richard Mille watch has been designed to achieve remarkable performance while preserving significant power reserve. Richard Mille has also worked with Audemars Piguet/Renaud & Papi to develop the use of nano-robots to implement certain processes.

The materials used for Richard Mille watches are high-tech, including titanium, ceramic (for the cap jewel on the tourbillon) and ARCAP (an alloy with superb mechanical properties of endurance and resistance to distortion). Cases are luxuriously hand milled of 18-karat gold or platinum, and no casing ring is required in the integrated production of the watch. In terms of design, comfort is key. The watch has an ergonomically curved case and lateral ribs for extra strength.

TOP
A side view of the newest Tourbillon RM 003.

BELOW
A drawing of Mille's Tourbillon RM 003.

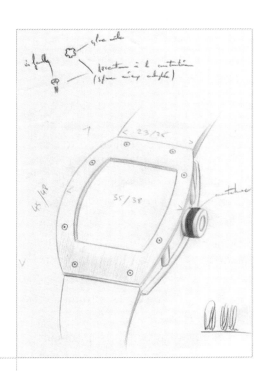

HIGHLIGHTS

■ In addition to the technical characteristics of Richard Mille
watches—many of which represent major advances in watchmaking
technology—the timepieces, nevertheless, are all hand finished in
the tradition of haute horology.

■ While the first tourbillons unveiled in 2001 were immediate hits,
Richard Mille has rolled out a new tourbillon, the Tourbillon RM 003,
with dual time-zone indicator and has plans for watches that do
not include the tourbillon escapement.

■ In 2003, the new models are to include a Chronograph RM 004 and
an Automatic Caliber.

■ By the year 2004, Richard Mille plans to include ladies' timepieces in
its collection.

■ It is the brand's five-year goal to produce
between 3,000 and 5,000 units per year and to
remain exclusive with no more than 100 retailers
authorized worldwide to distribute Richard Mille
timepieces.

RICHARD MILLE

TOURBILLON DOUBLE FUSEAU

Movement: mechanical, manual winding, Richard Mille 003-1 caliber.
Functions: hour, minute, tourbillon, torque indicator, second time zone display, power reserve. **Case:** 18K white-gold, 3-piece tonneau-shaped anatomically curved case (size 37.8 x 39mm, thick. 14.3mm), brushed finish with polished profiles; curved sapphire crystal, antireflective on both sides; crown with coaxial pusher for the winding, neutral and hour setting positions; rectangular pusher with case protection at 9 for the selec-

tion of the GMT time; back fastened by 4 screws, displaying the movement through an antireflective sapphire crystal.
Dial: translucent, with white printed Arabic numerals; applied and luminescent cabochon markers on the first flange with minute track printed by electro-erosion; printed minute track with numeric progression on the second flange.
Indications: power reserve between 10 and 11; torque indicator between 1 and 2; second time zone at 3 with translucent disc; winding crown position at 4.
Strap: leather with through reinforcement fastened by the case screws; white-gold tongue buckle.
Versions: titanium, pink or white gold, platinum. All with rubber strap.

TOURBILLON DOUBLE FUSEAU

This extraordinary watch represents a well conceived and perfectly realized masterpiece, combining the high technology levels of today's horology and automotive industries, from which it draws some functional and technical-aesthetic solutions. Richard Mille gives his first work a well defined shape, by taking advantage from his passions and thorough knowledge of business management acquired through his experience as a manager at Mauboussin and

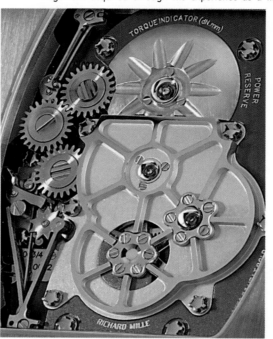

Repossi. His creation, a concentrate result of high technology, is far from the criteria of classical horology, being deeply marked by motive details. The presence of stud bolts (through screws) connecting casebacks and bezels through the thin-walled case middles is perhaps the most apparent characteristic feature at first sight. Yet this is not the only particular solution and improvement realized – there are also several important technical innovations introduced into mechanical horology. The barrel cover is designed as a "diaphragm spring", typical for automotive clutches, but the inside turned ribs are conceived in such a way as to reduce friction between the spring and walls of the barrel.

TOURBILLON DOUBLE FUSEAU

This sector of the movement, i.e. the winding barrel, received further attention. At first sight, on the dial one may immediately notice the displays related to the power reserve indication and the actual strength of the spring (torque indication). These devices are matched by optimized inside parameters, such as the unwinding speed of the spring and the velocity of manual winding. Further interesting details are: the eccentric screws fastening the

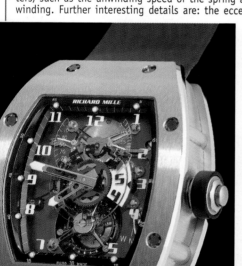

barrel cover and the material used for the shaft – Chronifer, a stainless, antimagnetic and hardenable alloy without nickel content.
Eccentric screws offer an improved behavior during maintenance operations. This advantage is also met by other components as the result of a new approach to the conception and construction of movements.

TOURBILLON DOUBLE FUSEAU

A further example of how accurately assistance operations were solved by technical innovations is to be found in the innovatory hour setting device. This can be actuated through the selector coaxial with the winding crown (winding – idle – hour setting positions, provided with a hand indicator on the dial between 4 and 5). It is mounted on a small dedicated module and may be repaired or completely replaced by offering easy access from the rear side,

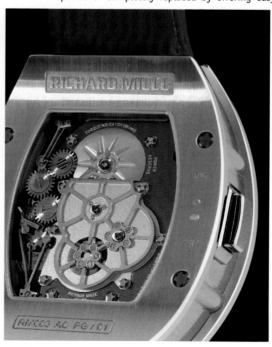

without any need to remove the closing bridge. The latter, that closes the movement, is in Arcap, an alloy assuring a higher rigidity of the whole made up of pillar-plate and bridges. It shows some resemblance with the cover of the timing chain system of racing cars. Of course, in our case – where eyes claim for aesthetics – milled areas are shot-blasted and the raised parts (such as stiffening ribs) are black-polished by hand. All the bigger screws (for bridges and cases) are in titanium and have special heads with star-shaped grooves in order to assure a better control of the fastening strength. They have a longer duration and resist better accidental troubles during mounting or disassembling operations.

TOURBILLON

Movement: mechanical, manual winding, with tourbillon device, Richard Mille 002-1 caliber.

Functions: hour, minute, torque indicator, power reserve.

Case: 18K white-gold, 3-piece tonneau-shaped anatomically curved case (size 45 x 37.8mm, thick. 12.5mm), brushed finish with polished profiles; curved sapphire crystal, antireflective on both sides; crown with coaxial pusher for the winding, neutral and hour setting positions; back fastened by 4 screws, displaying the movement through an antireflective sapphire crystal.

Dial: translucent, with white printed Arabic numerals; applied and luminescent cabochon markers on the first flange with minute track printed by electro-erosion; printed minute track with numeric progression on the second flange.

Indications: power reserve between 10 and 11; torque indicator between 1 and 2; second time zone at 3 with translucent disc; winding crown position at 4.

Strap: leather with through reinforcement fastened by the case screws; white-gold tongue buckle.

Versions: titanium, pink or white gold, platinum. All with rubber strap.

TOURBILLON

As far as the tourbillon device is concerned, i.e. the heart of all of the realizations by Richard Mille, including the split-second chronograph that is still at a prototype stage, its diameter totals 12.30 millimeters, the two-arm balance has a diameter of 10 millimeters and a frequency of 21,600 vibrations per hour. It is in Glucydur and equipped with a spring in Elinvar and a shock-absorber system of the Kif Elastor type. Furthermore, it works according to the variable inertia principle, with four adjustment screws and, therefore, without any regulator device. This solution offers the advantage of assuring a very accurate adjusting, needing less maintenance work and higher resistance in case of shocks.

It is housed within a titanium carriage with end-stone in ceramic material that reduces wear considerably. The settings of the main jewels (there are 23 jewels in total) are in gold. The whole movement is 6.35 millimeter thick, 30.20 millimeter high and 28.60 millimeter wide.

TOURBILLON

Movement: mechanical, manual winding, with tourbillon device, Richard Mille 002-1 caliber.

Functions: hour, minute, torque indicator, power reserve.

Case: pink gold, 3-piece tonneau-shaped anatomically curved case (size 45 x 37.8mm, thick. 12.5mm), brushed finish with polished profiles; curved sapphire crystal, antireflective on both sides; crown with coaxial pusher for the winding, neutral and hour setting positions; back fastened by 4 screws, displaying the movement through an antireflective sapphire crystal.

Dial: translucent, with white printed Arabic numerals; applied and luminescent cabochon markers on the first flange with minute track printed by electro-erosion; printed minute track with numeric progression on the second flange.

Indications: power reserve between 10 and 11; torque indicator between 1 and 2; second time zone at 3 with translucent disc; winding crown position at 4.

Strap: leather with through reinforcement fastened by the case screws; pink-gold tongue buckle.

Versions: titanium, pink or white gold, platinum. All with rubber strap.

TOURBILLON

In conclusion, the particular solutions adopted for the movement finish are also worthwhile mentioning.

As far as the movement-blank is concerned, all of the bevels of component edges, angles and rims, including those having a locking function, are polished by hand. Milling is performed with a final brushing operation by the shot-blasting technique. For the burnishing of sight surfaces the PVD method was adopted.

Steel parts show a shot-blasted background, the inner part of the thickness is brushed, bevels and upper surfaces are polished by hand.

The ends of milled profiles are honed and polished, pivots are burnished by a rolling process.

Wheels undergo a hollow beveling operation with a diamond grinding wheel as well as a circular surface smoothing process. Before cutting out teeth, wheels are gilded and finally they are further finished by hand in order to assure their indeformability and performance.

RGM

Crafting with a passion for fine timepieces and a dedication to old-world techniques, American watchmaker Roland G. Murphy has created a line of automatic and manual-wind watches that can rival Switzerland's finest.

A Swiss-trained watchmaker residing in Lancaster, Pennsylvania, Murphy has been creating watches since the mid 1980s when he worked for one of Switzerland's large watch companies. It was his dream to build his own timepieces and to make his mark in America's watchmaking history. In the early 1990s, he began his quest to design and produce his own timepieces.

The first RGM watches were unveiled to the world in 1993—mechanical masterpieces crafted in exclusive, limited editions. His timepieces were met by collectors and connoisseurs with great enthusiasm and for the past decade, Murphy has been designing and producing timepieces that hold true to his commitment to mechanical precision.

All RGM watches are assembled in Lancaster, and each demonstrates Murphy's stringent attention to detail. Cases are unique—designed by Murphy and produced in Switzerland exclusively for him. Dials are artistically finished and hand guilochéd, and often blued-steel hands are used. Murphy crafts in platinum, 18-karat gold, or steel.

Technical complications and functions are important features of the RGM line. Murphy's collection boasts power-reserve timepieces, perpetual calendars, minute repeaters, automatic chronographs with moonphase displays, and tourbillons.

RGM creates fewer than 400 watches per year—a testament to the time and effort of one man. Indeed, Murphy creates his timepieces with true dedication. He designs watches that he loves and finds a global audience that shares his tastes and appreciates his fine craftsmanship. One of the few watchmakers in the

TOP CENTER
Offering hour, minute, second and date function, this Classic Automatic watch is crafted in stainless steel and features a sapphire crystal and displays caseback. The solid silver dial is hand engraved.

LEFT
This Classic Automatic watch is crafted in solid 18-karat rose gold and features a hand-engraved silver dial. The movement is automatic with an 18-karat gold hand-engraved rotor.

BOTTOM LEFT
Crafted in stainless steel, this Power Reserve watch with date indicator is part of the William Penn collection. It houses an RGM/Jaquet tonneau-shaped manual-wind movement with 22 jewels and featuring the Côte de Genève finish on its bridges and plates. The dial is silvered solid gold.

BOTTOM RIGHT
This Power Reserve Moonphase watch, part of the William Penn collection, is available in either stainless steel or 18-karat rose gold. The RGM/Jaquet movement is tonneau-shaped and the watch features a sapphire caseback for viewing of the intricate engraving.

world to offer custom service and personal attention, Murphy is easily reached by his clientele and admirers by phone or email—a tradition he intends to preserve so that RGM watch owners may speak directly to the man who created their timepieces.

It is this attention to the needs and desires of the consumers, along with the strict attention to the most intricate details of watchmaking, that have made Murphy an icon of America's watchmaking future.

HIGHLIGHTS

- RGM loves to create custom-made, high-quality timepieces designed to the customer's specifications.

- RGM watch repair and restoration is the service center in the United States for several Swiss watch brands. The brand's repair and restoration expertise applies to both antique and modern mechanical watches. As a producer of complicated timepieces, RGM is able to draw on its own resources to handle most any challenge from manual-wind to automatic watches to complications including chronographs, perpetual calendars, minute repeaters, or tourbillons. Whether a 150-year-old pocket watch, vintage watch, or modern Rolex chronometer, a customer's timepiece is always in good hands at RGM.

- RGM will introduce a special new caliber at the 2003 World Watch and Jewelry Fair in Basel, Switzerland.

RGM

WATCH COMPANY

ROGER DUBUIS

just eight years old, Roger Dubuis has come full circle. With the opening of its glass-ensconced workshops and the employment of a multitude of talents, Roger Dubuis is today a complete Manufacturer.

In 1995, Sogem SA began as a partnership between master watchmaker Roger Dubuis and business entrepreneur and watch lover Carlos Dias. Production of watches began that very same year. While Dubuis had been a watchmaker for some of the finest brands in the world for more than 40 years, he had become restless. It was his dream to create an incredibly different timepiece collection—one based on the premise of tradition but with a vision of the future.

The first timepieces launched by Dubuis in 1996 were housed in round cases and called Hommage, in honor of the original spirit of watchmaking. The second collection featured the sophisticated square-cambered Sympathie case. The sizes and shapes of these watches garnered Dubuis great attention, and he went on to develop two impor-

tant calibers of his own: the RD28 and the RD98 mechanical movements. In the ensuing years, Dubuis unveiled the MuchMore collection of oversized rectangular watches, changed its Sogem name to Manufacture Roger Dubuis SA, and increased its collection to include complications.

In 2002, the brand opened its own workshops. Three stories tall, the enormous glass and steel structure houses everything from the tooling and heavy machinery to the actual gemsetting and watchmaking stations. The

Manufacture Roger Dubuis SA embodies the original concepts of the Dubuis watch line perfectly: futuristic vision and preservation of tradition. Every Dubuis watch is created in a handmade, exclusive edition of just 28 individually numbered pieces.

FACING PAGE

TOP LEFT

This GoldenSquare watch is an instantaneous perpetual calendar with five windows and a second time-zone indicator.

BOTTOM CENTER

Housing the RD98 caliber, this manually wound GoldenSquare case offers hours, minutes and a small seconds dial at 9:00.

THIS PAGE

TOP LEFT

From the Sympathie collection, this square-cambered case houses a three-retrograde-hand caliber RD5799 movement that is decorated with the Côtes de Genève pattern. The watch offers jumping retrograde hour and date, and dragging retrograde minute.

TOP CENTER

The Sympathie Chronograph houses the RD56 movement with column wheel and manual-wind mechanism.

FAR RIGHT

From the MuchMore collection, this exquisite watch features a hand-enameled dial representing the continent of Europe. Only 28 pieces will ever be created and each is unique in its painting.

BOTTOM LEFT

From the TooMuch collection this striking watch features a case set with 84 pink sapphires and a dial set with 28 pink sapphires of a deeper shade.

BOTTOM RIGHT

This LadyTooMuch precious gem watch is set with 309 diamonds on the case, 36 diamonds on the dial, and 27 diamonds on the strap. It houses a mechanical movement that is water resistant to 3atm.

HIGHLIGHTS

- In constant search of new technical challenges, Dubuis has created an instantaneous perpetual calendar with five windows. The RD29 movement employs a new method of display that offers the week, date and month in a triple window at 12:00. The leap-year cycle is shown through a fourth window, and a fifth window depicts day and night. This watch also has a second time-zone function that displays moonphases. The complication consists of 240 components. First crafted in the GoldenSquare collection, the watch is available this year.

- In its Sympathie collection, a three-retrograde watch makes its debut. More than a year in development, the automatic mechanical movement of this piece consists of 126 parts. The glistening mother-of-pearl and guilloché dial displays the jumping hours and date hands together, offset by a dragging minute hand.

- Diamonds and gemstones now adorn the double-strapped LadyTooMuch collection. In a new haute joaillerie series, cases are encrusted with either colorless or black diamonds, blue or pink sapphires, or emeralds—with each bearing the Geneva Hallmark of excellence.

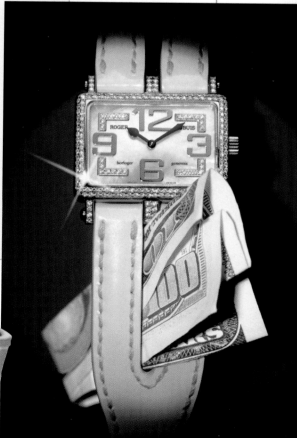

ROLEX

One of the most famous names in watchmaking, Rolex has enjoyed international success for nearly a century thanks to its grand watchmaking skills and extraordinary marketing prowess.

Founded by Hans Wilsdorf, Rolex made international headlines in 1926 with its famed Oyster watch. Billed as the first water-resistant watch, the Oyster's case proved to be impervious to water when Mercedes Gleitze wore the watch while swimming the English Channel. A patented wonder, the Oyster laid the groundwork for future high-tech watches from Rolex.

Decade after decade since, Rolex has been on the cutting edge when creating chronographs and chronometers of distinction. Chuck Yeager wore a Rolex on his wrist when he broke the speed of sound barrier in 1947 and Sir Edmund Hillary wore a Rolex when he climbed Mt. Everest in 1953. Over the ensuing decades, a host of athletes and Olympic contenders made Rolex their watch brand of choice.

Today, Rolex continues to produce the Oyster—offering a wide selection of models for men and women including the Datejust and the Perpetual. Additionally, Rolex offers the Cosmograph Daytona, Yacht Master, Submariner, Explorer and GMT Master II collections of superb functional instruments—each of which gains new models regularly.

First unveiled in 2001, the Oyster Lady-Datejust has several new models—each equipped with Rolex's own caliber self-winding mechanisms and offering a host of impressive mother-of-pearl dials on either 18-karat gold or platinum cases. Each new addition to Rolex's extensive collection bears witness to the brand's watchmaking expertise and aesthetic abilities.

Among the new Lady-Datejust models are versions with chocolate or black mother-of-pearl dials, as well as some with creamy pastel dials of blue, pink and pale green. Many of the new timepieces are adorned with varying degrees of diamonds on the dial, bezel, case, and bracelet. In fact, Rolex has unveiled a dazzling 18-karat yellow- or white-gold Lady-Datejust that is totally bedecked with diamonds—from dial to bezel to case, to bracelet. In the Datejust 34mm, Rolex offers an 18-karat white-gold bracelet with a double row of diamonds on the bezel and a diamond-adorned dial.

HIGHLIGHTS

- This past year, Rolex put renewed emphasis on its Cellini collection of timepieces. Top among them is the Cellinium— a work of classic elegance. Crafted in platinum, this exclusive timepiece is fitted with a black crocodile strap and a mother-of-pearl guillochéd dial with small seconds hand at 6:00.

- Rolex has added to the Cellissima white-gold collection of timepieces. Among the new watches is a stunning tonneau-shaped watch with elongated case alternating between polished metal and diamond accents. The case is set with 222 diamonds for sparkling appeal. Also new is a round Cellissima version, whose white-gold case is bedecked with more than 100 diamonds on the lugs.

- Rolex offers a touch of cosmic influence with its latest Cosmograph Daytona watch with meteorite dial accented by a flaming red seconds hand and red accents on the chronograph.

ROLEX

OYSTER PERPETUAL COSMOGRAPH DAYTONA   REF. 116519

Movement: mechanical, automatic-winding, Rolex 4130 caliber of own manufacture; 72 hours autonomy, Glucydur balance with "Microstar" micrometer regulation, 44 jewels, 28,800 vibrations per hour, Breguet balance spring. Officially certified chronometer (COSC).
Functions: hour, minute, small second; chronograph with three counters.
Case: 18K white-gold, three-piece case (Ø 40mm, thickness 12.5mm), polished

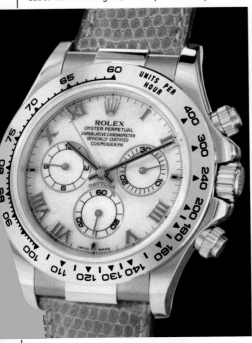

and brushed finish; sapphire crystal; fixed bezel with engraved tachometer scale; white-gold screw-down crown with three-fold gasket and case protection; screw-down pushers; screwed-on back. Water resistant to 10atm.
Dial: pink mother of pearl, counter crowns with white-gold rims; applied white-gold Roman numerals; white-gold bâton hands.
Indications: minute counter at 3; small second at 6; hour counter at 9; center second counter; minute track with divisions for 1/5 of a second.
Strap: lizard skin; white-gold fold-over clasp.
Also available: with turquoise, green chrysoprase, yellow mother of pearl dial and lizard skin strap in matching colors.

OYSTER PERPETUAL DATE YACHT-MASTER ROLESIUM   REF. 168622

The waterproof Yacht Master is realized with three case sizes: large - diameter 40 millimeters, medium - diameter 34 millimeters, small - diameter 29 millimeters. Medium size models come with traditional dials showing steel, blue, white or champagne-color backgrounds or the white reflexes of mother of pearl, also combined with markers made of precious stones.
The name of the Rolesium model, shown in the photograph, is added to the tra-

ditional versions in yellow gold or stainless steel with gold and indicates the steel alloy with the same name, used by the Genevan House for some models of the past.
Today, the name Rolesium defines a new interpretation of the most recent Rolex model, characterized by the combination of stainless steel for case and bracelet with platinum for bezel and dial.
Also available: Ø 40mm Ref. 16622; Ø 29mm Ref. 169622.

OYSTER PERPETUAL DAY-DATE   REF. 118206

Movement: mechanical, automatic-winding, caliber Rolex 3155. Officially certified chronometer (COSC).
Functions: hour, minute, second; day and date.
Case: platinum, three-piece case (Ø 36mm, thickness 12.4mm); sapphire crystal with "Cyclope" magnifying glass on the date; polished bombé bezel; white-gold screw-down crown with double gasket; screwed-on back. Water resistant to 10atm.

Dial: ice blue with sun pattern; applied white-gold Roman numerals; printed railway minute track; white-gold bâton hands.
Indications: date at 3; day at 12.
Bracelet: Superpresident platinum, polished and brushed finish; recessed fold-over clasp with embossed logo.
Also available: with brilliant markers; in yellow gold with champagne dial and brilliant markers; in pink gold with pink dial and brilliant markers; in white gold with silvered or coppered dial and brilliant markers. Oyster bracelet: in yellow gold with brilliant markers; in pink gold with brilliant markers; in white gold with brilliant markers.

OYSTER PERPETUAL DAY-DATE   REF. 118209

Movement: mechanical, automatic-winding, 3155 Rolex caliber. Officially certified chronometer (COSC).
Functions: hour, minute, second, day and date.
Case: 18K white-gold, three-piece case (Ø 36mm, thickness 12.4mm); sapphire crystal with "Cyclope" magnifying glass on the date; polished white-gold bombé bezel; white-gold screw-down crown with double gasket; screwed-on back. Water resistant to 10atm.

Dial: copper with sun pattern; applied white-gold Roman numerals; white printed railway minute track; white-gold bâton hands.
Indications: date at 3; day at 12.
Bracelet: Oyster white gold with polished and brushed finish, fold-over clasp.

OYSTER PERPETUAL LADY DATEJUST REF. 79165

Movement: mechanical, automatic-winding, 2235 Rolex caliber. Officially certified chronometer (COSC).
Functions: hour, minute, second; date.
Case: 18K pink-gold, three-piece case (Ø 26mm, thickness 10.5mm); sapphire crystal with "Cyclope" magnifying glass on the date; bombé bezel; pink-gold screw-down crown with double gasket; screwed-on back. Water resistant to 10atm.
Dial: black; applied pink-gold Arabic numerals; printed railway minute track; pink-gold bâton hands.
Indications: date at 3.
Bracelet: Oyster pink gold with polished and brushed finish; fold-over clasp.
Also available: in yellow gold with Oyster bracelet; in stainless steel and yellow gold with Oyster bracelet; with Jubilé bracelet.

OYSTER PERPETUAL LADY DATEJUST REF. 79239

Movement: mechanical, automatic-winding, 2235 Rolex caliber. Officially certified chronometer (COSC).
Functions: hour, minute, second; date.
Case: 18K white-gold, three-piece case (Ø 26mm, thickness 10.5mm); sapphire crystal with "Cyclope" magnifying glass on the date; knurled bezel; lugs with set diamonds; white-gold screw-down crown with double gasket; screwed-on back. Water resistant to 10atm.
Dial: beige mother of pearl; applied white-gold Roman numerals; white-gold bâton hands.
Indications: date at 3.
Bracelet: Superpresident white gold with polished and brushed finish; recessed fold-over clasp with embossed logo.
Also available: in yellow gold; other jewel versions.

OYSTER PERPETUAL DATEJUST REF. 78248

The Rolex 2235 caliber is used for the Datejust family with its 30 millimeter diameter. This automatic movement, provided with 29 jewels, is characterized by the "Microstar" balance in Glucydur (a copper-beryllium alloy) with an adjustment device acted by the screws positioned on the external perimeter, ensuring a micrometer precision rate. Other outstanding features are: the Parechoc shock absorber, a Breguet balance spring; its frequency is equal to 28,800 vibrations per hour. The photograph shows a precious piece realized entirely in 18K yellow-gold with a gold tone mother of pearl dial; engine-turned (guilloché) peripheral ring with hours in Roman numerals, at 12 a five-pointed crown. The President bracelet is characterized by numerous small-sized links that make the whole seem particularly smooth.
Also available: with Oyster or Jubilé bracelet; in steel with pink dial, Oyster bracelet.

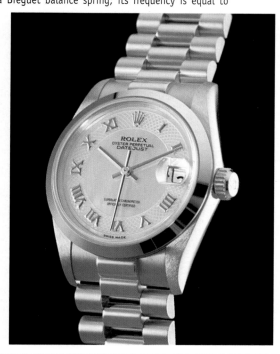

CELLINI BASKET REF. 5320/9

Movement: mechanical, manual-winding, Rolex 1602 caliber.
Functions: hour, minute.
Case: 18K white-gold, three-piece case, in square curved shape (size 34x31.5mm; thickness 6.5mm); jointed lugs; white-gold crown; snap-on back.
Dial: mother of pearl; applied white-gold square markers with set brilliants; white-gold Régate hands.
Strap: ostrich skin; white-gold clasp.
Also available: other versions on request.

Scatola del Tempo
SIMPLY THE BEST

Scatola del Tempo winding watch boxes are the most luxurious, technically advanced equipment available in which to preserve and protect the most important timepiece collections.

The world's most astute watch collectors and the most avid watch lovers recognize that the care of their expensive and exclusive timepieces is in itself an art. For this very reason, the owners of Scatola del Tempo—watch connoisseurs themselves—developed the ultimate container in which to keep the world's finest watches.

This original watch box was the first that fully met the requirements of modern collectors and is the only one that assures top-level quality standards. Its birth dates back to the end of the 1980s and is due neither to a mere marketing choice nor to a diversification logic of a business already operating in this sector. On the contrary, Scatola del Tempo is a result of the will and initiative of a collector who wanted a watch holder suitable for the quality level of the models he himself owned. Finally he resolved to construct it himself, having access to local handicraft and by using only first-quality materials. After building a very limited series of such boxes, some of which he shared with good friends, quite soon he received requests for additional pieces. Thus a lively example of classic Italian product, appreciated and well known on five continents, was generated almost spontaneously. Now it is sold in all of Europe's capital cities, as well as on the islands of the Pacific Ocean.

SCATOLA DEL TEMPO

The reasons for such success are simple, but not taken for granted. Scatola del Tempo is based on an essential principle: none of its constructive details can be left to chance or be underestimated. From the ergonomic design of the boxes to the exquisite silks for linings, to the mechanics of fastenings and the outer leather finish, each element is chosen with deliberate precision and finely finished. Scatola del Tempo—always on the cutting edge—was the first Manufacture to create and produce boxes with internal rotors for winding watch movements. While others have followed, collectors must make a careful assessment with respect to similar products offered at the same price or even for much less.

In fact, the realization of Scatola del Tempo's rotors was achieved by directly cooperating with some of the most famous Houses of Swiss horology (including Patek Philippe, which uses these for its perpetual calendars) and by focusing essentially on the following four basic parameters: rotational speed; turning direction of the rotor; number of revolutions per hour; and time interval of functioning of the rotor in one day.

All the mechanical parts are produced in St.Imier (top), as well as the motors of the rotors. Instead, final assembling, internal and external finishing of the boxes, as we as final testing and quality control, all take place in Italy (bottom; Mr. Sandro Colariet Scatola del Tempo's creator and owner, in a relax mome in Barzanò).

1RT Pendulette
The 1RT Pendulette is one of the newest creation from Scatola del Tempo. Slightly smaller than the original 1R the Pendulette possesses several important innovation The first of these innovation is a completely new electro ic system, which controls th rotation. After it is turned ON the Pendulette will rotate fo exactly 1,300 revolution per day, stopping in exactly the same position it was when i began. (If the unit is turned OFF before the 1.300 revolution cycle is complete, it wil still stop in exactly the same position as when it was first started.) Another innovation the cylinder housing, with a precisely engineered groove which holds the spring-load watch holder. The spring-loading mechanism makes easy to put virtually any size watch on the holder. It is powered by standard LR-20 alkaline batteries, which las at least one year under normal use.

One of the brand's most recent creations is the prestigious 32RT model, designed for great collectio or specialized shops.

The new 18RT-RA is provided with a patented opening device.
Details of the box include t exceptional level of finishe and the sophisticated engineering of electronic and m chanical elements.

These guidelines are essential due to the fact that the watch must be wound but not over-wound, i.e. it must work in optimal conditions and no organ must be uselessly stressed. Furthermore, the choice of the motor is also based on its reduced magnetic field, in such a way as not to jeopardize the functioning of the balance-spring. Finally, all of the mechanical components are tested for accuracy.

All of them are produced in Switzerland by adopting the same tolerance standards and machines used to produce tourbillon carriages or the pillar-plates of minute repeaters. Scatola del Tempo watch boxes are exquisite objects of unwatched detail.

FRONT PAGE

3RTM

The rotor of the La Scatola del Tempo, in the Squelette model, combines in an irrepeatable manner, an extreme mechanical perfection toghether with a design of great emotional impact.
All models of La Scatola del Tempo are sold in the best watchmaker's shops-jewelries worldwide.

THIS PAGE

7RT

First quality materials, leathers tanned with natural methods, silk woven directly in the same factory and all parts skilfully manufactured by hand all over the production cycle.These are the particulars that make La Scatola del Tempo a unique "object" of its kind, impossible to replicate.

The boxes with Rotory Mechanism

These devices, designed for automatic movement wristwatches (particularly useful for perpetual calendars) substitute the wrist's movement to keep the watches wound regularly. The S.C.S. & C. Scatola del Tempo has, for several years, produced special containers with one or more rotating supports run by an electronic micro-motor that supplies the movement with ideal winding. The traditional models offer ten different re-winding programs, making it possible to simulate one's own activity level through a program selector placed inside the battery holder. Each program specifies a set schedule (considering the natural habits of people who wear the watches by day and set them down at night) of so many hours of rotations in both directions. Starting from the setting "0" there is a gradual lessening in the number of running hours but an increase in the number of rotations. The indications show, besides on-off, the state of the batteries (both automatic LED signal on the exterior, and a dial indicator on the back activated by a button) and the stand-by power. By using a 6-volt transformer in the jack, one may eliminate the batteries. However, rotors using alkaline batteries will work for more than one year for all models.

9 RTRA

The man is the protagonist in the entire manufacturing cycle.

The scrupulous care put in the finishing guarantees a very high quality standard, known and appreciated all over the world. A person purposely assigned to the finishing of the rotors at St. Imier (CH).

FRONT PAGE

TOP LEFT

1RTSL

Box for keeping one automatic watch wound, in black. Made of nylon and black leather with an opening with a gold-colored metal ring making the watch visible, this article has a very good price.

TOP CENTER

Trousse

Tool box with utensils produced by Bergeon, a Swiss company, for the care of one's watches.

TOP RIGHT

1RT

Box for keeping one automatic watch wound. Black, natural leather, red.
In the one-watch box the selection of the rotation direction (clockwise, suitable for almost all automatics, or counter clockwise as some need) can be made by using a selection-slide on the front of the rotor.

CENTER

3RT

Box for keeping three automatic watches wound, in black, leather, red. It is available in the Squelette version with briar-wood base and the motor gears visible in black polished brass.

Technical specifications

Exterior structure: Evaporated beech wood covered in natural organic tanned leather.

Interior: flexible polyurethane resin, differentiated density, covered in jacquard silk in paisley design or in leather. The internal structure can hold perfectly the specified number and size of watches. Each place provides the necessary space for the winding crown and any possible push-pieces for other functions.

Clasp: in gilded brass, marked and numbered by hand.

Each piece is entirely handmade by craftsmen; the hardware has received anti-magnetic treatment.

BOTTOM

2A
Box for two watches with leather straps or flexible bracelets. Black, natural leather, red.

1P
Men's jewelry box for travel, black with space for one watch and accessories (cuff links, rings, lighters, pens, etc.)

1A
Box for one watch with leather strap or flexible bracelet. Black, natural leather.

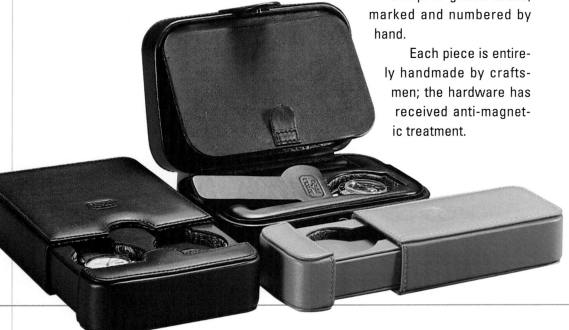

4+4 RA
Briar-wood box for four
watches with leather
strap plus four with rigid
bracelet.

4+4SP
Travel box for eight
watches with leather
strap or flexible
bracelet.
Black, natural leather,
red.

The "SdT" Watch

The name of this chronograph refers to the
name of this Italian company, a leader in the
production of precious leather cases for
watches, considering taste and quality that
are particularly modern as well as formal and
functional choices of definite class.
Chronograph with automatic movement
(Valjoux cal. 7750) with three counters and
date. Steel case with screw-down crown and
screwed-on caseback, water resistant to 10
atm. Dial with Arabic numerals and sword-
style hands with red/sky-blue "SdT" logo,
counters and flange with tachymeter scale
contrasting the black background. Calfskin
strap and case with electronic rotational
winding system programmed at 1,200 revolutions in 24 hours, the basic piece of Scatola
del Tempo in Barzanò, an old hamlet in the
Province of Lecco in Northwest Italy.

TOP LEFT

Treasure Box CO
Travel jewelry box for women. Red, blue.

TOP RIGHT

Small pen case
Holds six pens and comes in black, natural leather and red.

4A
Travel box for four watches with leather strap or flexible bracelet. Black, natural leather, red.

CENTER

4P
Men's accessories case for four watches with leather strap and accessories (cuff links, rings, lighters, pens, etc.).
Black, natural leather.

BOTTOM LEFT

Pen case
The large size model holds 24 pens and is available in red.

BOTTOM RIGHT

Pen case
The medium size model carries 12 pens and comes in black, natural leather, red.

TAG HEUER

e douard Heuer was passionate about precision. When he founded his workshop in 1860, he had only one aim: taking time measurement to greater heights. Since then, the company has always been in the avant-garde of watchmaking, whether in terms of technology, the choice of materials or design.

From the first patent for a chronograph mechanism in **1882** to the **2002** Geneva GP de l'Horlogerie awarded Micrograph F1 combining timekeeping and chronograph functions; from the first stopwatch measuring 100ths of a second (**1916**) to the first analog display quartz chronograph (**1983**), not forgetting the Chronomatic, first automatic chronograph movement with a microrotor (**1969**), TAG Heuer wrote some of the greatest chapters in watchmaking history.

This mastery is reflected in the impressive number of patents making TAG Heuer one of the key references in Swiss Made watchmaking know-how. For 143 years, the company has confirmed its initial vocation: producing watches that constantly challenge the frontiers of precision, reliability and aesthetics.

That is why the TAG Heuer philosophy is symbolized by the slogan "Swiss Avant-Garde since 1860."

TAG HEUER

The Micrograph F1: a unique combination of prestige, performance and innovation from TAG Heuer.

Eighty-eight years after the mythical Micrograph, TAG Heuer innovates again in 2002 by creating the Micrograph F1, a unique instrument combining the qualities of a prestigious watch with the functions of a high-performance professional timekeeping instrument.

Stemming directly from the brand's expertise in the field of top-level sports timekeeping, this watch provides specific car race timing functions in addition to the traditional hour, date, alarm and dual time-zone functions. The Micrograph F1 allows to measure non-stop a race track time up to 1/100th of a second, memorizing and ranking each lap timing with the lap number in order to perfectly store and analyze all the race data and the best lap. The Micrograph F1 boosts a high-end digital screen and anti-reflective sapphire crystal.

This unique movement, developed by the research and development of TAG Heuer, is produced in Switzerland.

The 2002 Design Watch Prize at the Grand Prix d'Horlogerie de Genève

To optimize the readability of the timekeeping, TAG Heuer designed the Micrograph F1 with large and clear square digits on a high-quality liquid crystal display protected by an anti-reflective sapphire. The pure square shape of the case frames logically the display: for TAG Heuer, the design must be first determined by the function. The TAG Heuer Micrograph F1 has won the 2002 Design Watch Prize at the Grand Prix d'Horlogerie de Genève.

Epitomizing the avant-garde spirit of TAG Heuer, the Kirium line launched in 1997 made its mark on the history of watch design.

In four years, Kirium has become one of the brand's flagship lines.

TAG Heuer now presents the Kirium Formula 1 Chronograph, an advanced technology timepiece combining the unique design of the series with an extraordinary set of functions.

The only TAG Heuer chronograph capable of measuring time to within 1/100th of a second, the Kirium Formula 1 Chronograph is packed with technological feats: it offers no less than seven specific functions.

One of the prime features of this digital chronograph is to provide a double time display: analog version, the hour, minute and seconds hands glide smoothly over an understated black dial; digital mode, the otherwise invisible chronograph functions appear. A chronograph with two faces provides a radically innovative time read-off.

The LINK Calibre 36 chronograph: an unprecedented encounter between the prestige of a sportschronograph and the ultimate precision of the Calibre 36 movement.

In Tiger Woods' honour, and to celebrate the partnership with the greatest golfer of all time, TAG Heuer introduces the LINK Calibre 36 chronograph: this exceptional automatic movement enables time measurement to the nearest 1/10th of a second. No other automatic movement in the world can reach a higher level of precision. This performance is made possible by the high frequency of the movement, oscillating at 36,000 vibrations per hour. It is certified by the Swiss Official Chronometer Testing Institute, which entitles the LINK Calibre 36 chronograph to be called a Chronometer.

With these Timepieces, TAG Heuer takes sport chronographs into another time sphere, in which ultra-precise mechanisms merge with the power of an incredibly avant-garde design .

TAG HEUER

Classics: the myths and adventures of modern times

Ever further, ever faster. The progress of today's world is inseparable from the measurement of time. TAG Heuer develops its innovations and pays tribute to the technical revolutions of the twentieth century by projecting its creativity and look into the new millennium.

TAG Heuer's Classics are prestigious sport watches and chronographs icons, born in the 30's, 50's and 70's decades. Later, they still live on, timeless, in everyone's mind-watchmaking expertise in its purest form. Refinement, technical virtuosity, inventive genius-the Classics embody the great modern saga of the industry. As well as the passion of sportsmen and the glory that goes to victors, the Classics are the ultimate in their class and honor four prestigious names known around the world: Monaco, Carrera, Monza-and now Autavia. This re-engistered brand icon has won its place as a must have in the highly restricted circle of the Classics series.

Carrera Chronograph: a tribute to an exceptional race

In 1964, Jack Heuer paid a connoisseur's tribute to this legendary race of which his friends Ricardo and Pedro Rodriguez had told him so much in Sebring. He decided to name the newly developed chronograph for his father's workshops in Switzerland Carrera. This unusual model featured an unusual sloping surface around the dial rim, used for the graduated 1/5th of a second scale. Another legend had been born.

Carrera is the name of the Mexican odyssey created in 1950 to celebrate the completion of the Panamerican highway linking the two hemispheres, the North and the South, Alaska and the Tierra del Fuego: the Carrera Panamericana Mexico.

The functional and understated design have been carefully safeguarded, with only a few subtle changes: the case is now fitted with a delicately hollowed sapphire crystal, a technique formerly reserved for strictly limited series. Its dial comes in three versions: in black or velvety silver, it is a perfect match for a black or brown alligator strap: the racing version fitted with three silver-ringed counters is teamed with a perforated black leather strap reminiscent of driving gloves.

Autavia: the never-ending legend

Autavia, comprised of the two words Automobile and Aviation.
1933. Aeroplanes and automobiles are equipped with the legendary Autavia dashboard. 1963. Autavia becomes a chronograph-wristwatch that is adopted six years later by an ace race car driver, Jo Siffert.

The Autavia dashboard is 70 years old, and the Autavia chronograph is turning 40. A double birthday in homage to precision watchmaking—and prestige. Its strength: the TAG Heuer Caliber 11 movement. Includes vital tachometer on the fixed bezel.

TAG Heuer's view of ergonomics: live every day in harmony with the future. Hence the tonneau-shaped case, with its crown placed at 9:00. Two timers—the seconds timer at 3:00, the minutes timer at 9:00—are very easy to read. Two dials. The first: the silver opaline dial combined with black timers and blue hands. The other: the black dial with silver timers and orange hands. Hand-set appliqué indexes, water-resistance to a depth of 50 meters, and scratch-proof convex sapphire crystal.

Autavia is made in man's likeness—as interpreted by TAG Heuer. A talent for invention and a taste for sports, with that special chic that sets the gentleman apart: unmistakable signs of heroes of the road, sea and sky. Heroes forever.

Monza Calibre 36, ultimate precision:

When the chequered flag came down on the 1971 Formula 1 Italian Grand Prix in Monza, just 1/100th of a second separated the winner, Peter Gethin, from his closest rival, Ronnie Peterson.

In honour of the legendary Milanese track, and the closest finish ever in the history of F1 racing, TAG Heuer is proud to announce Monza Calibre 36, a chronograph designed to measure short times in tenths of a second. It relies on a pendulum oscillating at a frequency of 36,000 vibrations per hour. No automatic chronograph can offer a greater level of precision.

Fitted with a hand sewn strap in black or brown crocodile skin with a folding steel buckle, the Monza Calibre 36 chronometer is certified by the Contrôle Officiel Suisse des Chronomètres, Switzerland's official chronometer inspection body. So TAG Heuer has joined the exclusive circle of watchmakers with expertise in high-precision automatic movements. With this chronograph, stamped with the seal of a motoring legend, TAG Heuer builds a bridge between two ages marked by the same passion.

TOP RIGHT

Autavia Caliber 11. The absolute mastery of time and speed; the art of chronograph.

LEFT

Jo Siffert, wearing the original model of Autavia chronograph.

BOTTOM RIGHT

Monza Calibre 36. An icon of the 30's, with the 1/10th second automatic chronogaph.

TAG HEUER

The 2000 Aquagraph:
a unique chronograph to dive in total security

Twenty years after the 2000 series was developed to meet divers' expectations, TAG Heuer presents the 2000 Aquagraph: a revolutionary automatic chronograph with unique functions, a high-tech model designed for professional diving with the collaboration of professional divers .

Because a watch is not only indispensable when diving, but actually vital, the TAG Heuer 2000 Aquagraph has been designed as a constant point of reference, the last operational indicator when all other instruments have stopped.

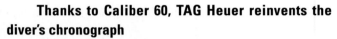

Thanks to Caliber 60, TAG Heuer reinvents the diver's chronograph

In the silence of the ocean depths, the 2000 Aquagraph becomes one with the diver's body: its heart beats to the rhythm of an automatic-winding mechanical movement, Caliber 60, which ensures that the watch runs smoothly even in the most extreme conditions.

But Caliber 60 is above all a unique automatic movement which displays the chronograph minute hand in the center of the dial and not on a subdial or counter. This enables obvious and instant read-off of the minutes being timed.

When moving through the different decompression levels, the diver can set the chronograph and, thanks to the pushbuttons that are functional to depths of 500 meters, can thus view at a glance the number of minutes elapsed.

The ultimate security "autoblock" bezel

Another remarkable innovative feature of the 2000 Aquagraph is an ultra-secure unidirectional-turning bezel. To ensure maximum security when diving, TAG Heuer has developed a unique and patented autolock turning bezel system which avoids any risk of the diver turning it accidentally in either direction. Thus, even if his arm hits a rock, the reference points cannot be thrown out and the diver can thus enjoy unrestricted freedom of movement.

A genuine chronograph for professionals

In addition to Caliber 60 and the autolock turning bezel, the 2000 Aquagraph is guaranteed water-resistant to 500 meters. It also comprises a screw-locked crown with safety indicator and an automatic helium valve for dives requiring hyperbaric chambers.

HIGHLIGHTS

■ In 2002, TAG Heuer was acclaimed by the media for its innovations (Micrograph Formula 1, Link Caliber 36, Link Searacer, 2000 Aquagraph, new Carrera chronograph ...) and its communication initiatives (new "What are you made of ?"advertising campaign, new website, itinerant boutique,...).

■ The brand has been honored by its champions, sources of inspiration for the designers and makers of TAG Heuer's famed sportswatches and eyewear:

- Marion Jones — Best woman athlete of the year, track and field star, 5 Olympic medals Sydney 2000, winner of the Golden League and the World Cup 2002
- Sarah Fisher — Best woman driver of the year, winner of MPDA and "Caschi d'Oro" and "Discovery GP" 2002 for her Indy Racing results including pole position
- Tiger Woods — Best World Golfer of the year (US PGA)
- Sébastien Bourdais — Formula 3000 FIA World Champion and 2003 Cart driver in Newman-Hass Team
- Nick Dougherty — Best rookie of the Golf Volvo Tour (European PGA) 2002
- David Coulthard — Winner of the Formula One Monaco Grand Prix, the icon of prestigious motoracing and 2003 West McLaren-Mercedes Team driver
- Kimi Raikkonen — Best young Formula One driver 2002 and 2003 West McLaren-Mercedes Team driver
- Peter Holmberg — Match Races 2002 World Champion (Swedish tournament)
- Chris Dickson — Finalist of the Louis Vuitton Cup, Oracle BMW racing team
- Jacques Villeneuve — Formula One World champion and Indy 500 winner

■ These male and female champions from the worlds of track, motor racing, and golf provide TAG Heuer with superior inspiration and requirements to design and craft the most high-performance and prestigious timepieces in their class.

TAG HEUER

KIRIUM CHRONOGRAPH — REF.CL5110.BA0700

Movement: mechanical, automatic winding, TAG Heuer Caliber 17, Chronometer certified by the Swiss Official Chronometer Testing Institute (COSC).
Functions: hour, minute, second, date, chronograph with 3 counters.
Case: stainless steel, three-piece fine-brushed case (Ø 43.5mm, thickness 13.2mm); curved sapphire crystal; fine-brushed counter, clockwise-turning bezel, with luminescent marker and engraved minute track, for the calculation

of diving times; screw-in crown with case protection, with micro gasket preventing water and dust infiltration; screwed-on caseback. Water resistant to 20atm.
Dial: black; luminescent applied round steel markers; printed minute track on the flange; skeletonized rhodium-plated hands with luminescent tips.
Indications: small second at 3; hour counter at 6; minute counter at 9; date at 4.

KIRIUM FORMULA ONE — REF. CL111A.FT6000

Movement: quartz, digital and analog, based on ETA E20 caliber. **Functions:** analog hour, minute and second; LCD numeric display hour, minute, second and date; chronograph 1/100th; countdown, daily and calendar alarm; second time zone; perpetual date; back-lit dial. **Case:** stainless steel, three-piece brushed case (Ø 43.3mm, thickness 14.3mm); curved sapphire crystal with antireflection treatment; fine-brushed unidirectional turning bezel, with luminescent marker and engraved minute

track, for the calculation of diving times; helicoydal polished crown providing access to the 7 functions, with case protection, with micro gasket preventing water and dust infiltration; screwed-on caseback. Water resistant to 20atm.**Dial:** LCD numeric display, specifically developed by TAG Heuer, black dial with back light, luminescent painted hour markers, skeletonized rhodium-plated hands with luminescent tips. **Bracelet:** vulcanized rubber bracelet, with folding buckle, perfectly integrated into the case. The insertion of polyamide, reinforced with glass fiber, guarantees excellent quality for the integration of the bracelet into the head. **Also available:** with fine-brushed steel, with polished case; fold-over clasp with double safety device.

KIRIUM CHRONOGRAPH TI5 — REF. CL1181.FT6000

Movement: quartz, ETA 251.262. **Functions:** hour, minute, second, date, chronograph with 3 counters. **Case:** titanium grade 5, three-piece polished case (Ø 42.85mm, thickness 12.7mm); curved sapphire crystal with antireflection treatment; polished unidirectional turning bezel, with luminescent marker and engraved minute track, for the calculation of diving times; screw-in crown with case protection, with micro gasket preventing water and dust infiltration;

screwed-on caseback. Water resistant to 20atm.
Dial: carbon fiber dial; luminescent round markers; printed minute track on the flange; skeletonized rhodium-plated hands with luminescent tips.
Indications: 1/10th of a second counter at 2; small second at 6; hour counter at 10. **Bracelet:** vulcanized rubber bracelet, with titanium grade 5 polished folding buckle, perfectly integrated into the case. The insertion of polyamide, reinforced with glass fiber, guarantees excellent quality for the integration of the bracelet into the head. **Also available:** in fine-brushed titanium grade 5. Man's size watch with quartz movement, case in titanium with polished finish.

LINK CHRONOGRAPH — REF. CT5111.BA0550

Movement: mechanical, automatic winding, TAG Heuer Caliber 16. Chronometer certified by the Swiss Official Chronometer Testing Institute (COSC).
Functions: hour, minute, second, date, chronograph with 3 counters.
Case: stainless steel, three-piece fine-brushed case (Ø 41.90mm, thickness 15.43mm); curved sapphire crystal; fine-brushed counter-clockwise-turning bezel, with luminescent marker and engraved minute track, for the calculation of diving

times; screw-in crown with case protection, with micro gasket preventing water and dust infiltration; screwed-on caseback. Water-resistant to 20atm.
Dial: black; counter decorated with circular beads pattern; applied bâton marker with luminescent dots; tachymeter scale printed on the flange; luminescent rhodium-plated bâton hands.
Indications: small second at 9; hour counter at 6; minute counter at 12; date at 3.
Bracelet: brushed steel; fold-over clasp with double safety device.
Also available: with blue or silvered dial; in fine-brushed steel. Man's size with quartz movement, steel with polished and/or fine-brushed finish, silvered, blue, white and black dial.

LINK CALIBER 36   REF. CT511B.BA0564

Movement: mechanical, automatic winding, TAG Heuer Caliber 36; 1/10th of a second rating precision guaranteed by high frequency of movement: 36,000 vph; the oscillating weight is decorated with a Côtes de Genève (Geneva Waves) vertically striped pattern; power reserve of minimum 50 hours. Chronometer certified by the Swiss Official Chronometer Testing Institute (COSC). **Functions:** hour, minute, second, date, chronograph with 3 counters. **Case:** stainless steel, three-piece polished

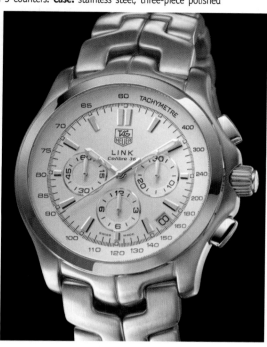

and fine-brushed case (Ø 41.9mm, thickness: 14.48mm), scratch-resistant sapphire crystal, glare-proof on both sides, polished fixed bezel, shaped pushbuttons, transparent caseback in scratch-resistant sapphire crystal. Water resistant to 20atm. **Dial:** opalescent silvered dial, sand-blasted faceted hour markers, spiral-decorated applied counters, monochrome transferred logo, faceted skeleton hands, LINK Caliber 36 printed at the bottom of the monochrome logo TAG Heuer. **Indications:** date at 4; hour counter at 6; small second at 9; minute counter at 3. **Bracelet:** fine-brushed LINK steel bracelet, clasp with pushbuttons incorporated within the link. **Also available:** black dial with fine-brushed fixed bezel.

LINK   REF. WT141J.BA0561

Movement: quartz, ETA 956.112.
Functions: hour, minute, second, date.
Case: stainless steel, three-piece polished case (Ø 29.8mm, thickness 9.55mm); curved sapphire crystal; polished unidirectional turning bezel, set with 53 Top Wesselton (VVS) for a total of about 0.25 carats; screw-down crown with case protection, with micro gasket preventing water and dust infiltration; screwed-on caseback. Water resistant to 20atm.
Dial: white mother of pearl set with 11 Top Wesselton (VVS) diamonds for a total of about 0.06 carats; luminescent rhodium-plated bâton hands.
Indications: date at 3.
Bracelet: polished stainless steel; fold-over clasp with double safety device.
Also available: with blue/gray mother-of-pearl dial.

2000 EXCLUSIVE CHRONOGRAPH   REF. CN2111.BA0339

Movement: mechanical, automatic winding, TAG Heuer Caliber 16.
Functions: hour, minute, second, date, chronograph with 3 counters.
Case: stainless steel, three-piece case (Ø 44mm, thickness 14.6mm), brushed and polished finish; flat sapphire crystal; unidirectional turning dodecagonal bezel, with 6 polished hold riders, luminescent marker and engraved minute track, for the calculation of diving times; screw-in crown with case protection; screwed-on caseback. Water resistant to 20atm.
Dial: black with Clous de Paris pattern; applied faceted bâton markers with luminescent dots, counters decorated with circular beads pattern; tachometer scale printed on the flange; luminescent rhodium-plated bâton hands. **Indications:** date at 3; hour counter at 6; small second at 9; minute counter at 12.
Bracelet: stainless steel, brushed finish with polished and brushed central links; fold-over clasp with double safety device.
Also available: with metallic blue or silvered dial. Man's size with quartz movement, steel with polished and fine-brushed finish, black, silvered and blue dial.

2000 EXCLUSIVE   REF. WN2111.BA0332

Movement: Mechanical, automatic winding, TAG Heuer Caliber 5.
Functions: hour, minute, second, date.
Case: stainless steel, three-piece case (Ø 41.7mm, thickness 11.2mm), brushed and polished finish; flat sapphire crystal; unidirectional turning dodecagonal bezel, with 6 polished hold riders, luminescent marker and engraved minute track, for the calculation of diving times; screw-in crown with case protection; screwed-on caseback. Water resistant to 20atm.
Dial: silvered with Clous de Paris pattern; applied faceted bâton markers with luminescent dots; applied Arabic numerals; printed railway minute track with luminescent dots at quarters; luminescent steel bâton hands.
Indications: date at 3.
Bracelet: stainless steel, brushed finish with polished and brushed central link; fold-over clasp with double safety device.
Also available: with metallic blue and black dial. Man's size with quartz movement, black, white and translucent blue dial.

TAG HEUER

AUTAVIA   REF. CY2110.BA0775

Movement: mechanical, automatic winding, TAG Heuer Caliber 11.
Functions: hour, minute, second, date, chronograph with 2 counters.
Case: stainless steel, three-piece polished and fine-brushed case (Ø 41.2mm, thickness 13.45mm), scratch-resistant sapphire crystal, crown at 9:00; protected elliptical pushers with 8 facets; screwed-on caseback. Tachymeter on fixed bezel. Water resistant to 5atm.

Dial: white dial with two black counters, applied faceted bâton markers, with luminescent hour-markers; printed railway minute track; luminescent rhodium-plated bâton hour and minute hands, blue chronograph's hand.
Indications: small second at 3; date at 6; minute register at 9.
Bracelet: stainless steel with steel folding clasp with push buttons.
Also available: with black dial, two white counters and orange-red chronograph's hand.

CARRERA RACING   REF. CV2113.FC6182

Movement: mechanical, automatic winding, TAG Heuer Caliber 17.
Functions: hour, minute, second, date, chronograph with 3 counters.
Case: stainless steel, three-piece polished and fine-brushed case (Ø 39mm, thickness 13.5mm), scratch-resistant sapphire crystal, fluted crown; screwed-on caseback. Water resistant to 5atm.
Dial: black dial with three silver-ringed counters, applied faceted rhodium-plated bâton markers, with luminescent hour-markers; printed railway minute track; luminescent rhodium-plated bâton hour and minute hands.

Indications: small second at 3; date at 4; hour counter at 6; minute register at 9.
Bracelet: black calfskin perforated leather strap with polished steel folding clasp with safety push buttons.
Also available: with black or silvered dial and/or black or brown calfskin leather strap.

MONACO STEVE MCQUEEN   REF. CW2113.FC6183

Movement: mechanical, automatic winding, TAG Heuer Caliber 17.
Functions: hour, minute, second, date, chronograph with 2 counters.
Case: stainless steel, three-piece polished and fine-brushed case (size 40.4 x 38.5mm, thickness 13mm), curved Plexiglas, semi-recessed crown; protected elliptical pushers with 8 facets; caseback fixed with 4 screws. Water resistant to 3atm.

Dial: metallic blue dial with sun pattern, applied faceted rhodium-plated bâton markers, with luminescent dots; 2 square silvered registers; printed minute track; luminescent rhodium-plated bâton hour and minute hands, red chronograph's hands.
Indications: small second at 3; date at 6; minute register at 9.
Bracelet: blue genuine crocodile leather strap with polished steel folding clasp with safety push buttons.
Also available: with black and silvered dial and/or black or brown crocodile strap or black or brown calfskin leather strap.

MONACO GOLD   REF. CW5140.FC8144

Movement: mechanical, automatic winding, TAG Heuer Caliber 17, Chronometer certified by the Swiss Official Chronometer Testing Institute (COSC).
Functions: hour, minute, second, date, chronograph with 3 counters.
Case: 18K yellow-gold, three-piece polished and fine brushed case (size: 40.4 x 38.5mm, thickness: 13mm), curved Plexiglas, semi-recessed crown; protected elliptical pushers with 8 facets; caseback fixed with 4 screws. Water resistant to 3atm.

Dial: silver with sunray effect; applied faceted 18K yellow-gold-plated bâton markers with luminescent hour-markers; luminescent 18K yellow-gold-plated bâton hour and minute hands; printed minute track.
Indications: small second at 3; date and hour counter at 6; minute register at 9.
Bracelet: full-grain black genuine crocodile leather strap with standard buckle in solid 18K polished yellow gold.
Also available: with brown crocodile leather strap.

MONZA CALIBER 36   REF. CR5111.FC6175

Movement: mechanical, automatic winding, TAG Heuer Caliber 36; 1/10th of a second rating precision guaranteed by high frequency of movement: 36,000 vph; the oscillating weight is decorated with a Côtes de Genève (Geneva Waves) vertically striped pattern; power reserve of minimum 50 hours. Chronometer certified by the Swiss Official Chronometer Testing Institute (COSC). **Functions:** hour, minute, second, date, chronograph with 3 counters. **Case:** stainless steel, three-piece polished and fine-brushed case (Ø 41.2mm, thickness 13.4mm), scratch-resistant sapphire crystal, glare-proof on both sides, large and fluted pull-motion polished crown; transparent caseback in scratch-resistant sapphire crystal, fixed with 4 screws. Water resistant to 5atm.

Dial: silvered base intricately engraved with sectors of guilloché; 9 hand-applied Arabic numerals, luminescent hour-markers and luminescent rhodium-plated bâton hands, printed minute track.
Indications: small second at 9; date at 6; hour counter at 6; minute counter at 3.
Bracelet: full-grain hand-sewn genuine crocodile leather strap with polished steel folding clasp with safety push buttons.
Also available: with black dial and/or brown crocodile strap.

MONZA WATCH   REF. WR2110.FC6164

Movement: mechanical, automatic winding, TAG Heuer Caliber 6.
Functions: hour, minute, second, date.
Case: stainless steel, three-piece polished and fine-brushed case (Ø 37.5mm, thickness 10.1mm), scratch-resistant sapphire crystal, large and fluted pull-motion polished crown. Water resistant to 5atm.
Dial: black with 10 faceted rhodium-plated bâton markers and 2 applied Arabic numerals, luminescent hour-markers and luminescent rhodium-plated bâton hands; printed minute track.
Indications: small second at 6; date at 4.
Bracelet: full-grain black crocodile leather strap with polished steel folding clasp with safety push buttons.
Also available: with brown crocodile strap.

ALTER EGO GOLD   REF. WP1443.BG0755

Movement: quartz.
Functions: hour, minute.
Case: 18K yellow-gold, two-piece polished case (Ø 25mm, thickness 7.15mm), convex sapphire crystal, off-centered crown at 4 with case protection; back fixed with 6 screws. Water resistant to 10atm.
Dial: white mother of pearl with 12 Top Wesselton (VVS) diamond indexes 1mm in diameter for a total of about 0.053 carats; specific architecture with raised flange between the hour markers; thin and elegant 18K yellow-gold-plated hands.
Indications: none.
Bracelet: 18K yellow-gold polished finish with massive folding buckle; butterfly opening with push-button feature.

ALTER EGO RIVER OF DIAMONDS   REF. WP131L.BA0755

Movement: quartz.
Functions: hour, minute.
Case: stainless steel, two-piece polished case (Ø 29mm, thickness: 7.7mm) set with 52 Top Wesselton (VVS) diamonds 1.7mm in diameter for a total of 1.04 carats; convex sapphire crystal; off-centered crown at 4 with case protection; back fixed with 6 screws. Water resistant to 10atm.
Dial: white mother of pearl with 12 Top Wesselton (VVS) diamonds, 4 of 1.1mm in diameter and 8 of 1mm in diameter, for a total of about 0.059 carats; specific architecture with raised flange between the hour markers; thin and elegant rhodium-plated hands.
Indications: none.
Bracelet: stainless steel polished finish set with 234 Top Wesselton (VVS) diamonds for a total of about 2.574 carats, massive folding buckle, butterfly opening with push-button feature.

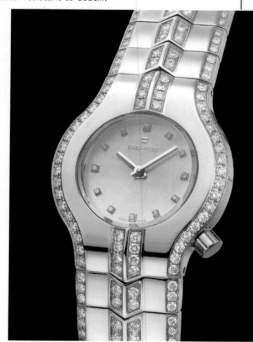

TechnoMarine

The revolutionary TechnoMarine brand is synonymous with the words elegant, fashionable, trend setting and timeless. The innovative watch company that first combined plastic and diamonds to create an entirely new breed of timepieces has made its way onto millions of wrists in just five short years and continues to design timepieces that are interchangeable and easily worn with both bathing suits and ball gowns.

TechnoMarine founder Franck Dubarry possessed a love for all things water inspired since his youth. By the time he headed off to college, this avid sportsman had begun SCUBA diving and mastered the sports underwater fishing, sailing and surfing. Dubarry aspired to live life to the fullest—and that aspiration is evident in his timepieces he has created.

In **1999**, Dubarry broke the barrier between a sports chronograph and an elegant watch by combining the unimaginable—a plastic gel strap with a diamond bezel and the TechnoMarine brand was born. It was Dubarry's vision to evolve his company into a full lifestyle brand based on his mantra—designs that embody the best that life, sea and land have to offer. Indeed, by incorporating the two mismatched elements of rubber and diamonds, Dubarry paved the way for a new generation of time keepers. He continues to take the combination of diamonds and plastic to the next level with designs like the diamond-embedded gel strap of the XS Lady, and the revolutionary shaped Wave, inspired by the natural movement of the ocean.

TechnoMarine has gained a reputation as a pioneer brand in the watch industry known not only for its innovative designs, but also for its technological precision and superior craftsmanship. Since its inception, TechnoMarine has expanded its distribution to over six continents and has evolved to include more than 300 styles. In **2001**, the brand divided those models into two separate divisions: TechnoMarine (which includes upscale styles from $700 to $20,000 retail); TechnoMarine Sport (with watches priced at $700 or less).

THIS PAGE

ABOVE
Faithful to its brand identity TechnoMarine introduces its new Jewelry Collection. These Polo bracelets come in white- or yellow-gold pavé set on colored leather bands.

LEFT
The XS Lady watch is crafted of steel and is water resistant to100 meters. Its dial features silver numerals and 8 full-cut diamonds set on a mother-of-pearl dial. The watch is sold with a gel strap intertwined with 36 full-cut diamonds.

BELOW
TechnoMarine founder, Franck Dubarry.

FACING PAGE

CENTER
Crafted in steel, this TechnoSquare Chrono Diamond watch offers date indicator and times to 1/10th of a second. The watch houses an ETA movement and is set with 124 full-cut diamonds.

BOTTOM RIGHT
This TechnoSquare MAG Chrono Automatic watch crafted in stainless steel. Water resistant to 100 meters, it features a lacquered two-toned dial.

TECHNOMARINE

TechnoMarine's success can also be attributed to the versatile nature of its watches and consistently unique design qualities. As an expression of Dubarry's passion for design and shape, the Wave has become his latest vision of a jeweled timepiece. In tribute to the ocean, TechnoMarine created a sophisticated yet versatile symbol of curvaceous beauty. This decadent, tasteful and undeniably feminine Swiss watch is water resistant to 30 meters—yet features 722 full-cut diamonds totaling 5.6 carats. The Wave is available with two interchangeable straps (one satin and one leather) and is just the first of many new additions to the TechnoMarine lines.

Evolved from the TechnoDiamond Collection, the XS Lady takes the combination of diamonds and plastic to the next level with a unique diamond-embedded gel strap—housing 36 full-cut white diamonds. There are an additional 88 full-cut white diamonds surrounding the stainless steel case. TechnoMarine would never consider designing a timepiece that could not be worn in the water, so the timepiece is water resistant to 100 meters.

TechnoMarine's impressive portfolio of designs also includes four new undeniably extravagant timepieces: the TM Pavé, TechnoLady Chrono Pavé, TechnoSquare Chrono Pavé and the Butterfly Pavé. All of the Pavé timepieces are extraordinarily grand. The TM Pavé has a circular rotating bezel covered with 136 full-cut diamonds arranged in a bead setting, and a full diamond pavé dial embedded with 143 full-cut diamonds. With a Swiss movement, chronograph, and date indicator, the TM Pavé has all of the functions of a precision watch with the durability of a stainless steel case and water resistance of up to 200 meters. The TechnoLady Chrono Pavé's functions have all the advantages of a chronograph, but in a smaller sized watch for a woman. This mini chrono's sleek design is accentuated by 260 full-cut diamonds, an entirely diamond-pavé face and a diamond bezel. It can be worn interchangeably on both lizard and gel bands. The TechnoSquare Chrono Pavé is a dazzling timepiece with 336 full-cut diamonds encrusted throughout the entire 18-karat rose-gold case. This Swiss movement is also a chronograph with a date indicator. The Butterfly Pavé watch stands out from the rest thanks to its unique shape, which is adorned with 184 full-cut white diamonds around the face. All of these stunning timepieces are unique expressions of individuality and beauty.

TechnoMarine recently introduced its largest timepiece ever, the XS MAG. The oversized square case, the avant-garde styling, and the square mini-dial with stylized numerals make a statement on the wrist of any wearer. The cutting-edge design is combined with technical features and is housed in a stainless steel case resistant to water and air pressure, thermal heights and chemical treatments.

In addition to TechnoMarine's unconventional timepieces, the brand also offers classic, contemporary designs like the TechnoSquare MAG, which features a modern two-toned face, a Swiss movement and is water resistant up to 100 meters. It is available with an automatic movement on a stainless steel bracelet with a transparent caseback.

New and exciting modifications have been made to a few of the favorites in the TechnoMarine Sport collection including the TMY, TM Apnea and LadySport. New dials and colors continue to make these timepieces three of the most desirable styles in the collection.

P LEFT

y named the Red Square,
chronograph watch
sures time to 1/10th of a
nd and offers a date
ator. Housed in a steel
e, the watch is water
stant to 100 meters.

P CENTER

TechnoSquare MAG
no Quartz watch features
quered two-tone dial and
ld with an alligator strap
a gel strap.

P RIGHT

iculously set with 136
cut diamonds arranged in
ad setting, this TM Pavé
onograph is housed in a
l case that is water
stant to 200 meters.

GHT CENTER

Diva Full Pavé chronograph
ch is crafted in 18-karat
and features 445 full-cut
e diamonds weighing 3.3
ts. Water resistant to 50
ers, the watch features a
phire crystal and a full-pavé
ond dial with mother-of-
rl subdials.

TTOM RIGHT

Elegante is a large
angular pendant, with a
ond pavé grid, framing
interchangeable jean,
ic leather or black pony
rts.

TTOM CENTER

se yellow- and white-gold
st rings are part of the new
hnoMarine Jewelry
ection and are full-pavé
interchangeable lizard
ds.

HIGHLIGHTS

- In 2003, Franck Dubarry is introducing TechnoMarine's first jewelry collection. TechnoMarine's brand identity is built on two strengths: creative design and the one-step-ahead factor.

- Focusing on the concept of interchangeability, the Jewelry Collection will offer consumers the option of customizing each piece of jewelry to best fit their moods and styles. The Jewelry Collection is not focused on one specific style, but on several diverse designs for rings, earrings, bracelets and necklaces.

- Pieces such as the Lola ring will include a diamond-pavé band that slips easily onto interchangeable colored gel rings and can be worn with the matching earrings. Twist ring—available in full pavé or steel with a pyramid-cut amethyst or blue topaz—can be worn with interchangeable lizard bands. The Elegante, a large rectangular pendant with a diamond pavé grid, is offered with interchangeable neckstraps including denim, exotic leather or black pony inserts. The collection also includes gold and diamond-pavé "Polo" and "ID Baby" bracelets.

- In addition to the interchangeable pieces, Dubarry has designed three magnificent rings made of turquoise, sparkling blue topaz, sugilite, amethyst, smoked quartz, and diamonds.

- The TechnoMarine Jewelry Collection is in select retail locations around the world as of spring 2003. With TechnoMarine's first Jewelry Collection, Dubarry takes another step toward achieving his vision of evolving TechnoMarine into a full lifestyle brand.

- In 2003, TechnoMarine will launch a full collection of accessories: eyewear, pens and stylized knives dedicated to TechnoMarine's taste for innovative design.

TECHNOMARINE

TECHNOLADY CHRONO DIAMOND PAVÉ   REF. DTLCPP

Movement: Swiss ETA G15.211.
Functions: hour, minute, small second at 6:00. Chronograph 1/10 second.
Chronograph: second in the center; 1/10 second at 2:00; minute at 10:00.
Case: stainless steel 316 L.
Bezel: unidirectional rotating bezel with 128 full-cut white diamonds. 0.85 carats.

Crystal: mineral.
Size: 33mm.
Water resistant: 660 ft/200 meters.
Dial: full-pavé white diamonds.
Bracelet: one lizard strap with stainless steel buckle and one gel strap with standard stainless steel buckle.
Packaging: brown wooden box with turquoise leather lining.
Warranty: 1 year.
Price: available upon request.

TM PAVÉ   REF. DTMPWP

Movement: Swiss ETA G10.711
Functions: hour, minute, small second at 6:00. Chronograph 1/10 second.
Chronograph: second in the center; 1/10 second at 2:00; minute at 10:00.
Case: stainless steel 316 L.
Crystal: mineral.
Size: 37.5mm.

Water resistant: 660 ft/200 meters.
Dial: full-pavé with 143 full-cut white diamonds and pink counters.
Bracelet: one genuine crocodile strap with stainless steel buckle and one gel strap with standard stainless steel buckle.
Also available: full-pavé with white diamonds and white counters (ref. DTMP-WW); full-pavé with black diamonds and light blue counters (ref. DTMPBB).
Packaging: brown wooden box with turquoise leather lining.
Warranty: 1 year.
Price: available upon request.

TECHNOLADY CHRONO DIAMOND   REF. DTLC07

Movement: Swiss ETA G15.211.
Functions: hour, minute, small second at 6:00. Chronograph 1/10 second.
Chronograph: second in the center; 1/10 second at 2:00; minute at 10:00.
Case: stainless steel 316 L.
Bezel: unidirectional rotating bezel with 128 full-cut white diamonds arranged in a bead setting, 0.85 carats.

Crystal: mineral.
Size: 33mm.
Water resistant: 660 ft/200 meters.
Dial: white mother-of-pearl with pink Arabic numerals.
Bracelet: one lizard strap with stainless steel buckle and one gel strap with standard stainless steel buckle.
Also available: black mother-of-pearl (ref. DTLC-02); white mother-of-pearl with white Arabic numerals (ref. DTLC-05); white mother-of-pearl with blue Arabic numerals (ref. DTLC-01).
Packaging: brown wooden box with turquoise leather lining.
Warranty: 1 year.
Price: available upon request.

TECHNODIAMOND TM   REF. DTMWW

Movement: Swiss ETA G10.711. **Functions:** hour, minute, small second at 6:00. Chronograph 1/10 second. **Chronograph:** second in the center; 1/10 second at 2:00; minute at 10:00. **Case:** stainless steel 316 L.
Bezel: unidirectional rotating bezel with 136 full-cut diamonds, 1.17 carats.
Crystal: mineral. **Size:** 37.5mm. **Water resistant:** 660 ft/200 meters.
Dial: white mother-of-pearl with 8 diamond hour indexes and white subdials.

Bracelet: one genuine alligator strap with stainless steel buckle and one gel strap with standard stainless steel buckle.
Also available: black diamonds on unidirectional bezel and white mother-of-pearl dial with white counters (ref. DTMBB); white and black diamonds on unidirectional bezel and white mother-of-pearl dial with white counters (ref. DTMBW); white diamonds on unidirectional bezel and white mother-of-pearl dial with blue jean counters (ref. DTMJW); white diamonds on unidirectional bezel and white mother-of-pearl dial with mauve counters (ref. DTMMW).
Packaging: brown wooden box with turquoise leather lining.
Warranty: 1 year.
Price: available upon request.

TECHNOSQUARE MGM CHRONO   REF. TSCM02

Movement: Swiss ETA 251.272.
Functions: hour, minute, small second at 6:00. Chronograph 1/10 second.
Chronograph: second in the center; 1/10 second at 2:00; minute at 10:00.
Case: stainless steel 316 L. **Crystal:** sapphire. **Size:** 38 x 48mm, curved 6:00-12:00. **Water resistant:** 330 ft/100 meters.
Dial: lacquered black with Arabic numerals.
Bracelet: one genuine alligator leather band with white stitching with stainless steel buckle with double tongue and one gel strap with standard stainless steel buckle.
Also available: two-toned lacquered dial in blue (ref. TSCM-01); two-toned lacquered dial in mauve (ref. TSCM-09); two-toned lacquered dial in rhodium (ref. TSCM-15); two-toned lacquered dial in orange (ref. TSCM-19); two-toned lacquered dial in silver and black (ref. TSCM-25); two-toned lacquered dial in chocolate (ref. TSCM-26).
Packaging: brown wooden box with turquoise leather lining.
Warranty: 1 year.
Price: available upon request.

TECHNOSQUARE CHRONO   REF. DTSCWW

Movement: Swiss ETA 251.471. **Functions:** hour, minute, small second at 6:00. Chronograph 1/10 second. **Chronograph:** second in the center; 1/10 second at 2:00; minute at 10:00.
Case: stainless steel 316 L; 124 full-cut white diamonds on top and bottom parts and 68 full-cut white diamonds around the face. **Crystal:** sapphire, curved 6:00-12:00. **Size:** 32 x 43mm.
Water resistant: 330 ft/100 meters. **Dial:** mother-of-pearl dial with white diamond indexes.
Bracelet: one genuine alligator strap with stainless steel buckle and one gel strap with standard stainless steel buckle.
Also available: white mother-of-pearl dial and black lacquered numbers (DTSC-01); white mother-of-pearl dial and lilac lacquered counters—Lilac numbers (DTSC-03); black dial and silver lacquered counters—Pink numbers (DTSC-08); silver lacquered dial and counters—Silver numbers (DTSC-14); purple lacquered dial and counters—Silver numbers (DTSC-09); white dial and burgundy lacquered counters—Burgundy numbers (DTSC-15); black lacquered dial and counters—Silver numbers (DTSC-16); white lacquered dial and counters -Silver numbers (DTSC-25); white lacquered dial and counters—Turquoise numbers (DTSC-26). **Packaging:** brown wooden box with turquoise leather lining. **Warranty:** 1 year. **Price:** available upon request.

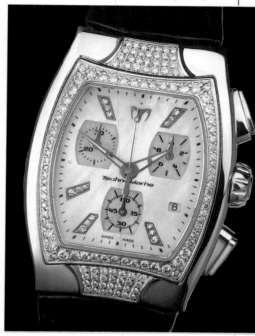

XS LADY   REF. DXSL02

Movement: Swiss ETA 902.002. **Functions:** hour, minutes.
Case: stainless steel 316 L with 88 full-cut white diamonds, 0.85 carats.
Crystal: sapphire. **Size:** 24 x 38mm. **Water resistant:** 330 ft/100 meters.
Dial: black mother-of-pearl dial with silver Arabic numerals and 8 full-cut white diamonds.
Bracelet: integrated gel strap combined with 36 full-cut white diamonds and stainless steel buckle.
Also available: navy mother-of-pearl dial with silver Arabic numerals and 8 full-cut white diamonds (ref. DXSL-01); silver mother-of-pearl dial with silver Arabic numerals and 8 full-cut white diamonds (ref. DXSL-05); lilac mother-of-pearl dial with silver Arabic numerals and 8 full-cut white diamonds (ref. DXSL-09); sky blue mother-of-pearl dial with silver Arabic numerals and 8 full-cut white diamonds (ref. DXSL-11); electric blue mother-of-pearl dial with silver Arabic numerals and 8 full-cut white diamonds (ref. DXSL-21).
Packaging: brown wooden box with turquoise leather lining.
Warranty: 1 year.
Price: available upon request.

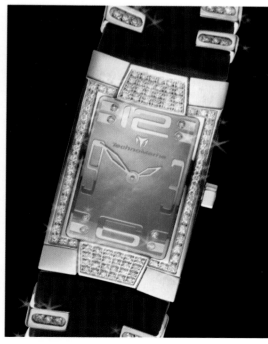

XS MGM   REF. XSCM02

Movement: Swiss ETA 251.272.
Functions: hour, minute, small second at 6:00. Chronograph 1/10 second.
Chronograph: second in the center; 1/10 second at 2:00; minute at 10:00.
Case: stainless steel 316 L.
Crystal: sapphire. **Size:** 34.5 x 47mm. **Water resistant:** 330 ft/100 meters.
Dial: lacquered black with stylized numerals.
Bracelet: leather strap with stainless steel double-tongue buckle.
Also available: yellow lacquered dial (ref. XSCM-04); silver lacquered dial (ref. XSCM-05); orange lacquered dial (ref. XSCM-19); petrol lacquered dial (ref. XSCM-21); blue lacquered dial (ref. XSCM-01).
Packaging: brown wooden box with turquoise leather lining.
Warranty: 1 year.
Price: available upon request.

TECHNOMARINE

DIVA WHITE GOLD FULL PAVÉ   REF. DTPWG

Movement: Swiss ETA 251.272.
Functions: hour, minute, small second at 6:00. Chronograph 1/10 second.
Chronograph: second in the center; 1/10 second at 2:00; minute at 10:00.
Case: 18K white-gold with 445 full-cut white diamonds, 3.30 carats (case and dial).
Crystal: sapphire. **Size:** 40mm. **Water resistant:** 5atm/50 meters.

Dial: full-paved diamonds with mother-of-pearl sub-dials.
Bracelet: one genuine crocodile strap with 18K gold butterfly buckle and one gel strap with standard stainless steel buckle.
Also available: 18K rose-gold case and dial with white diamonds (ref. DTPRG).
Packaging: brown wooden box with turquoise leather lining.
Warranty: 1 year.
Price: available upon request.

DIVA ROSE GOLD FULL PAVÉ   REF. DTPRG

Movement: Swiss ETA 251.272.
Functions: hour, minute, small second at 6:00. Chronograph 1/10 second.
Chronograph: second in the center; 1/10 second at 2:00; minute at 10:00.
Case: 18K rose-gold with 445 full-cut white diamonds, 3.30 carats (case and dial).
Crystal: sapphire. **Size:** 40mm. **Water resistant:** 5atm/50 meters.
Dial: full-paved diamonds with mother-of-pearl subdials.

Bracelet: one genuine crocodile strap with 18K gold butterfly buckle and one gel strap with standard stainless steel buckle.
Also available: 18K white-gold case and dial with white diamonds (ref. DTPWG).
Packaging: brown wooden box with turquoise leather lining.
Warranty: 1 year.
Price: available upon request.

TECHNOSQUARE CHRONO ROSE GOLD PAVÉ   REF. DTSCPR

Movement: Swiss ETA 251.471.
Functions: hour, minute, small second at 6:00. Chronograph 1/10 second.
Chronograph: second in the center; 1/10 second at 2:00; minute at 10:00.
Case: 18K rose-gold with 336 full-cut white diamonds, 3.22 carats.
Crystal: sapphire, curved 6:00-12:00. **Size:** 32 x 43mm.
Water resistant: 5atm/50 meters.

Dial: Sunray finished.
Bracelet: one genuine alligator strap with 18K gold buckle and one gel strap with standard stainless steel buckle.
Also available: 18K white-gold case with white diamonds on sunray-finished dial (ref. DTSCPW).
Packaging: brown wooden box with turquoise leather lining.
Warranty: 1 year.
Price: available upon request.

BUTTERFLY PAVÉ   REF. BYSD05

Movement: Swiss ETA 980.163. **Functions:** hour, minute, small second at 6:00. Swiss made. **Case:** stainless steel 316 L; bezel set with 184 full-cut diamonds, 1.75 carats. **Crystal:** sapphire, curved 6:00-12:00. **Size:** 37.5mm. **Water resistant:** 5atm/50 meters.
Dial: lacquered, of silver color with silver Arabic numerals.
Bracelet: integrated leather band with standard stainless steel buckle.

Also available: 18K rose-gold case and dial with white diamonds (ref. DTPRG).
Packaging: brown wooden box with turquoise leather lining.
Warranty: 1 year.
Price: available upon request.

RED SQUARE — REF. RSCQ02

Movement: ETA G10-71A.
Functions: hour, minute, small second at 6:00. Chronograph 1/10 second.
Case: stainless steel 316 L.
Crystal: mineral, curved.
Size: 40 x 50mm.
Water resistant: 330 ft/100 meters.
Dial: lacquered black with Arabic numerals.
Bracelet: leather strap with stainless steel buckle.
Also available: gray lacquered dial (ref. RSQC-06); silver lacquered dial (ref. RSCQ-05); blue lacquered dial (ref. RSQC-11); black and white lacquered dial (ref. RSCQ-25).
Packaging: black and aluminum box.
Warranty: 1 year.
Price: available upon request.

RED SQUARE — REF. RSCQ05

Movement: ETA G10-71A.
Functions: hour, minute, small second at 6:00. Chronograph 1/10 second.
Case: stainless steel 316 L.
Crystal: mineral, curved.
Size: 40 x 50mm.
Water resistant: 330 ft/100 meters.
Dial: lacquered silver with Arabic numerals.
Bracelet: leather strap with stainless steel buckle.
Also available: gray lacquered dial (ref. RSQC-06); black lacquered dial (ref. RSCQ-02); blue lacquered dial (ref. RSQC-11); black and white lacquered dial (ref. RSCQ-25).
Packaging: black and aluminum box.
Warranty: 1 year.
Price: available upon request.

TMY CHRONO ON STEEL BAND — REF. TMY02M

Movement: OS60.
Functions: hour, minute, small second at 6:00 (on/off). Chronograph 1/20 second.
Chronograph: second in the center; 1/20 second at 6:00; hour at 9:00; minute at 12:00.
Case: stainless steel 316 L.
Bezel: Engraved unidirectional rotating.
Crystal: mineral.
Size: 40mm.
Water resistant: 660 ft/200 meters.
Dial: lacquered black with metal inserts.
Bracelet: stainless steel bracelet with butterfly buckle.
Also available: white lacquered dial (ref. TMY-05); red lacquered dial (ref. TMY-07); dark blue lacquered dial (ref. TMY-11); yellow lacquered dial (ref. TMY-14); light blue lacquered dial (ref. TMY-21); chocolate lacquered dial (ref. TMY-26); silver lacquered dial (ref. TMY-22).
Packaging: black and aluminum box with screwdriver.
Warranty: 1 year.
Price: available upon request.

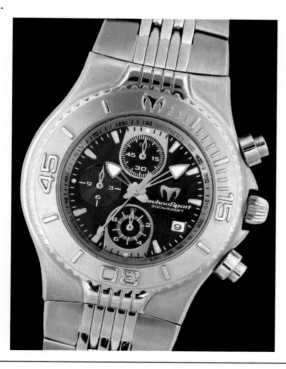

TMY CHRONO — REF. TMY02

Movement: OS60.
Functions: hour, minute, small second at 6:00 (on/off). Chronograph 1/20 second.
Chronograph: second in the center; 1/20 second at 6:00; hour at 9:00; minute at 12:00.
Case: stainless steel 316 L.
Bezel: engraved unidirectional rotating.
Crystal: mineral.
Size: 40mm.
Water resistant: 660 ft/200 meters.
Dial: lacquered black with metal inserts.
Bracelet: one leather strap and one gel strap, both with stainless steel buckle.
Also available: white lacquered dial (ref. TMY-05); red lacquered dial (ref. TMY-07); dark blue lacquered dial (ref. TMY-11); yellow lacquered dial (ref. TMY-14); light blue lacquered dial (ref. TMY-21); chocolate lacquered dial (ref. TMY-26); silver lacquered dial (ref. TMY-22).
Packaging: black and aluminum box with screwdriver.
Warranty: 1 year.
Price: available upon request.

TIFFANY & CO.

tiffany is synonymous with tradition and sophistication. Since its founding in 1837, this great House has been internationally acclaimed as a premier silversmith and jeweler. Also, since the 1870s when Tiffany unveiled its first watches, the brand has produced some of the finest pocket watches, stopwatches and wristwatches under its legendary name.

In **1851**, Charles Lewis Tiffany became the first retailer in America to sell Patek Philippe watches. Later, Patek Philippe assisted Tiffany by acting as a private watchmaker for the company for a short time. In the **1870s**, Tiffany established its own watchmaking facility in Geneva, and the brand's affluent, elegant gold watchcases were praised for their aesthetic beauty. In **1866**, in pursuit of technical excellence, the brand unveiled the Tiffany Timer stopwatch, which was used extensively for engineering purposes as well as for timing sporting events.

At the **1876** Philadelphia World's Fair, Tiffany received special recognition for gemstone watches. The company's fate as a prolific watchmaker was forever sealed. In the ensuing decades, the brand received gold medals and awards for a host of other timepieces.

A century later in **1983**, Tiffany introduced the Atlas® collection of watches, based on the unique design of the Atlas clock built by the brand's founder. Since then, Tiffany & Co. has unveiled the Tesoro luxury sports watch (1987) and the T150 Limited Edition timepiece created in **2001** by Patek Philippe to celebrate the 150th anniversary of the original partnership. Today, Tiffany continues its fine tradition of unveiling timepieces with character.

TIFFANY & CO.

Celebrating its heritage in fine style, Tiffany & Co. has unveiled the new Tiffany Mark™ collection of elegant timepieces. Inspired by some of the original Tiffany pocket watches, the all-new Tiffany designs reinforce the company's reputation for style and excellence. Two different shapes define the collection—each with a layered construction that yields sublime proportion and definitive integrity.

The round Tiffany Mark watch features five layers in its case design, and the Tiffany Mark coupe—features four layers. Each is hand assembled to emulate the venerable 19th century Tiffany pocket watches. Crafted in platinum, 18-karat gold or stainless steel, the Tiffany Mark watch collection features elegant hands, and numerals so slender that, at first glance, they appear to be "marks" rather than gracefully elongated Roman numerals.

To personalize the watch, Tiffany offers a number of variations. There are two different sized cases and each is fitted with a genuine alligator strap. The 18-karat gold version and the stainless steel model are also available with a flexible seven-row bracelet that is composed of 118 individual curved pieces for ergonomic appeal and comfort. The line is comprised of seven different movements, all hand assembled with superb Swiss craftsmanship to Tiffany's exacting standards.

Elegance is a trademark of this legendary company—one that translates beautifully in this Mark watch.

BOTTOM
The Tiffany Mark collection is available with seven different movements. Cases come in two sizes.

466

HIGHLIGHTS

- Representing a company milestone, Tiffany & Co. unveils the extraordinary Tiffany Mark collection—inspired by its pocket watches from the 1800s.

- At its worldwide introduction, the Tiffany Mark wins a limelight position on the brand's timeline of fine watch designs.

- Tiffany & Co. turned to master watchmaker Girard-Perregaux for the tourbillon movement in its Tiffany Mark platinum Tourbillon watch.

- In typical style, the legendary House opted to offer the collection with a choice of seven different Swiss movements. Each watch is water resistant to five atmospheres.

- Among the fine mechanical movements are a hand-wound mechanical; an automatic watch with self-winding mechanism; a full-calendar watch that offers the month, date, day and phases of the moon; a chronograph; a regulator; and a tourbillon. There is also a quartz resonator, battery-powered movement.

TOP LEFT

These Mark watches feature elegant, applied Roman numerals, and the round watch offers date at 3:00.

TOP RIGHT

Tiffany's designers worked diligently to develop the ergonomic 118-piece bracelet that is offered with the Mark watches. The strap models feature top-quality leather.

RIGHT

This elegant Mark watch features a classic regulateur dial. The hours are read from the subdial at 12:00, the minutes are read off of the main octagonal dial and the seconds are at 6:00.

BOTTOM

This antique Tiffany pocket watch demonstrates the brand's long-standing relationship with the world of luxury timekeeping.

ULYSSE NARDIN

this exceptional watchmaking company creates some of the most exquisite and elaborate time-pieces on the market today—a tradition it has honored for more than 150 years.

Founded in 1846, Ulysse Nardin has been awarded 18 coveted gold medals and has garnered more than 4,000 awards over the past century and a half for its superb craftsmanship and technology. However, it is the technology introduced by the brand over the past 20 years that has propelled Ulysse Nardin to the forefront of true innovation in watchmaking.

Under the vigilant eye of owner Rolf Schnyder, the brand has enjoyed global attention for these introductions of the past two decades. Regularly, Schnyder has turned to world-renowned inventor, scientist and watchmaker, Dr. Ludwig Oechslin, to execute ideas that heretofore were unheard of in wristwatches. Among the shining stars emanating from this cooperation are the famed Trilogy of Time series (including an astrolabium, planetarium and tellurium wristwatch) and the multi-patented Freak watch (with 8-day tourbillon carousel and no hands or dial).

Indeed, Ulysse Nardin has demonstrated leadership in the creation of complicated watches and chronometers time and again by regularly turning out technical masterpieces that triumph in the field of innovation and precision. Most recently, the company unveiled the first Westminster Carillon Tourbillon Jaquemarts Minute Repeater watch. Named for Genghis Khan—one of the world's greatest conquerors and Mongolian rulers from the 12th and 13th centuries—the complex musical timepiece boasts powerful accomplishments both inside and out.

The term Jaquemarts refers to the moving figures on a watch, clock or other timepiece, and is often interchangeable with the term automaton. In this incredible watch, the hand-carved 18-karat gold figures on the black onyx dial (which represent a warrior on horseback, two sword fighters and a musician) move in synchronization with the sound of the gongs of the carillon. A pinnacle of art and traditional watchmaking, the Genghis Khan watch features the Westminster chiming carillon. The Westminster chime pat-

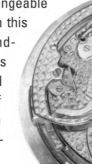

ABOVE
Rolf Schnyder.

LEFT
The Genghis Khan watch is the first timepiece to include Westminster Carillon, tourbillon, jaquemarts and minute repeater.

BOTTOM LEFT
A close-up look at details of the Genghis Khan.

BELOW
Genghis Kahn automatic movement.

tern has four gongs that sound the time. When the repeater is activated, the tiny hammers within the watch chime the hour, the minutes and the quarter hours—each producing a different sound. As the time is sounded, the dial figures move accordingly: the sword fighters move with the hour sound, the horse rider thrusts his spear into the minute indicator ring for the minutes, and the musician moves with the quarters.

The manually wound movement also houses a tourbillon escapement for extreme precision. The Genghis Khan will be created in a limited edition of just 30 pieces in 18-karat rose and 30 pieces in 18-karat white gold—released over the next six to eight years and retailing for approximately $400,000 each.

HIGHLIGHTS

- Ulysse Nardin recently unveiled the Christopher Columbus Set in a limited edition of 25 pieces in rose gold and 100 pieces in stainless steel. Each set it individually numbered and comes in an exclusive mahogany box. The set consists of three watches: the Marine Chronometer 1846; the Marine Diver Chronometer 1846; the Annual Calendar Chronograph.

- The Marine Chronometer 1846 is a COSC-certified mechanical timepiece crafted with a power reserve of approximately 42 hours and offering a date indicator and subseconds hand.

- The Marine Diver 1846 watch houses a self-winding mechanical movement with a solid white-gold rotor and 42 hours of power reserve. The watch is COSC certified and water resistant to 300 meters.

- The Marine Annual Calendar Chronograph watch features screw-down crown and pushers, antireflective sapphire crystal and full chronograph functions. It also offers a tachometer to measure speed over a distance of 1,000 meters.

VACHERON CONSTANTIN

among the world's most venerable watch companies, Vacheron Constantin has been creating luxury watches, uninterrupted, for nearly two and a half centuries. Arguably the oldest Geneva-based brand still in operation, Vacheron Constantin was founded in 1755 by Jean-Marc Vacheron and François Constantin—master watchmakers with the strictest codes of perfection.

Today, this esteemed brand continues to follow its founding fathers' creeds of innovation and excellence. In its Geneva workshops, the brand creates its own calibers and timepieces—watches of stature that range from mechanical wonders to dazzling diamond designs.

Most recently, the company unveiled a very unusual timepiece in honor of the brand's 247th anniversary. The To-and-Fro Calendar watch features a to-and-fro, 31-day calendar mechanism that is visible from both the front and the back of the watchcase. Part of the Complications line, the watch is crafted in a platinum case that is water resistant to 30 meters. The self-winding movement features a power reserve of 38 hours that can be observed in action.

The dial plate of the watch has been cut out significantly to reveal the main features of the day-of-the-week display and the to-and-fro date calendar mechanisms.

A work of art, only 247 pieces of the To-and-Fro Calendar watch will ever be built—each bearing its production and limited-series numbers engraved on the caseback. The remarkable movement of this watch, Vacheron Constantin's Caliber 1126 R31, features 36 jewels and its mainplates display the Côtes de Genève decorative pattern.

Also new to the Complications line, Vacheron Constantin has unveiled a Perpetual Calendar watch of distinction. By combining a perpetual calendar with a 31-day retrograde calendar, Vacheron Constantin has demonstrated its superior watchmaking skills. The new timepiece is

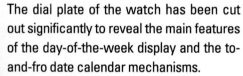

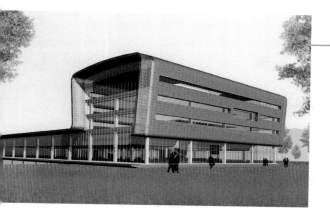

FACING PAGE

TOP LEFT
The Power Reserve watch from the Complications collection features a new dial with lined guilloché pattern.

BOTTOM LEFT
Remarkably different with its skeletonized dial plate, this To-and-Fro Calendar watch houses a self-winding movement with day of the week display, to-and-fro date calendar mechanism, and offers more than 38 hours of power reserve.

BOTTOM RIGHT
Crafted in either platinum or in 18-karat rose gold, the Perpetual Calendar Retrograde watch features a 31-day retrograde readout.

THIS PAGE

TOP LEFT
Vacheron Constantin's new Manufacture will house the company's workshops, headquarters and museum.

TOP CENTER
These designs from the 1972 collection feature the famed asymmetrical case in either 18-karat yellow or white gold and an all-new Milanese mesh bracelet.

TOP RIGHT
One of the Commemorative pieces in the 1972 series, this watch is called Sound.

BOTTOM
The Patrimony received the award for the Extra-Slim category in the Geneva Watchmaking competition.

crafted either in platinum or in 18-karat rose gold with a transparent caseback for viewing of the automatic movement. The dial is elegantly decorated with the Clous de Paris guilloché design.

The brand has also updated the star of its Complications collection—the Power Reserve. Essentially, Vacheron Constantin improved the dial's legibility with larger numerals and easier to read subdials, and enhanced its appearance with a textured guilloché. The Power Reserve is crafted in 18-karat yellow gold and houses an automatic movement.

Vacheron Constantin has also added significantly to its Les Essentielles collection, with a particular emphasis on the 1972 series. This successful asymmetrical watch is now adorned with a braided 18-karat white- or yellow-gold shimmering Milanese Mesh bracelet that underscores the watch's distinctive geometric appeal. This knitted metal fabric is composed of interlaced gold wire that is incredibly supple to the touch. The women's 1972 watch design has been adorned further with a row of sparkling brilliant-cut diamonds on the case.

HIGHLIGHTS

■ In celebration of the 30th anniversary of the 1972 timepiece design, Vacheron Constantin turned to Parisian styling for a new and distinguished series of 60 limited-edition watches. The company has produced 30 18-karat white-gold watches and 30 18-karat pink-gold watches—each featuring a diamond-set bezel and a diamond pavé dial. Since Paris had originally recognized the watch's exceptional merits 30 years ago, Vacheron Constantin wanted to include the haute couture city in its creation of the anniversary pieces. The company went to the Parisian house of Lesage for its exceptional threads, fabrics, beads and spangles that were to be the essence of the straps for the new series. The result is a stunning series of very different timepieces.

■ For the second year in a row, Vacheron Constantin won the Grand Prize of Geneva for watchmaking design. The award was given in the Extra-Slim Watch category for Vacheron Constantin's Patrimony watch, which is fitted with the caliber 1003 movement that barely measures 1.64mm from front to back and 20mm across.

■ Vacheron Constantin has begun building its new Manufacture in Geneva—signaling a major step for the brand. The new site will house Vacheron Constantin's workshops, international headquarters and museum. The building was designed by French-Swiss architect Bernard Tschumi, who won the commission in an international architectural competition sponsored by Vacheron Constantin.

VACHERON CONSTANTIN

MALTE CHRONOGRAPH PERPETUAL CALENDAR   REF. 47112

Movement: mechanical, manual-winding, 1141 QP caliber (Lemania base + calendar module), 21 jewels, 18,000 vph. **Functions:** hour, minute, small second; perpetual calendar (date, day, month, year, moonphase); chronograph with two counters. **Case:** platinum, three-piece, brushed and polished case (Ø 39mm, thickness 13.6mm); curved sapphire crystal; 4 correctors on the middle; rectangular white-gold pushers; back attached by 4 screws, displaying the movement through a sapphire crystal and provided with a hinged cover (with inside surface fastened by 3 screws, removable for personalization). Water resistant to 3atm.
Dial: silvered; zones decorated with circular beads; applied white-gold Roman numerals, bâton markers and logo; white-gold bâton hands.
Indications: year between 1 and 2; minute counter at 3; moonphase (with engraved white-gold disc) and date at 6; small seconds at 9; day and month below 12; center second counter; minute track with divisions for 1/5 of a second and five-minute progression.
Strap: alligator leather, hand-stitched; platinum clasp.
Also available: in yellow gold.

MALTE PERPETUAL CALENDAR   REF. 47031

Movement: mechanical, automatic-winding, 1126 QPR caliber, autonomy 40 hours, 36 jewels, 28,800 vph.
Functions: hour, minute; perpetual calendar (date, day, month, year, four-year cycle); chronograph with two counters.
Case: 18K pink-gold, three-piece, brushed and polished case (Ø 39mm, thickness 11.9mm); curved sapphire crystal; 4 correctors on the middle; pink-gold crown; back attached by 6 screws, displaying the movement through a sapphire crystal and provided with a hinged cover. Water resistant to 3atm.
Dial: silvered, guilloché; zones decorated with circular beads; applied pink-gold Roman numerals, bâton markers and logo; printed minute track; pink-gold bâton hands.
Indications: four-year cycle at 3; month between 4 and 5; four-digit year display at 6; day between 7 and 8; date with arrow-shaped burnished-gold retrograde center hand.
Strap: alligator leather, hand-stitched; pink-gold clasp.
Also available: platinum.

MALTE RÉGULATEUR DUAL TIME   REF. 42005

Movement: mechanical, automatic-winding, Vacheron Constantin 1206 caliber. 18K yellow-gold rotor. Officially certified chronometer (COSC).
Functions: hour, minute, small second; date; second time-zone time; 24 hours.
Case: 18K yellow-gold, three-piece polished and brushed case (Ø 38.5mm, thickness 11mm); antireflective curved sapphire crystal; 1 date corrector on the middle; gold crown and pusher for the independent adjustment of the second time-zone time; back fastened by 6 screws, displaying the movement through a sapphire crystal (with inside surface fastened by 3 screws, removable for personalization). Water resistant to 3atm.
Dial: silvered; center zone decorated with circular beads; applied gold logo; printed railway minute track with applied square markers and five-minute progression; gold bâton hands.
Indications: off-center hours at 12 with printed Roman numerals; center seconds; small seconds and date at 5; second time-zone 24-hour display at 9.
Strap: alligator leather, hand-stitched; gold clasp.
Also available: in white gold.

MALTE GRANDE DATE   REF. 42015

Movement: mechanical, automatic-winding, Vacheron Constantin 1204 caliber. 18K yellow-gold rotor. Officially certified chronometer (COSC).
Functions: hour, minute, second; date.
Case: 18K white-gold, three-piece case (Ø 38mm, thickness 9.8mm); antireflective curved sapphire crystal; white-gold crown; back fastened by 6 screws, displaying the movement through a sapphire crystal. Water resistant to 3atm.
Dial: silvered; center printed Arabic numerals; applied white-gold logo; printed railway minute track; gold bâton hands.
Indications: big-sized date in a window at 6.
Strap: alligator leather, hand-stitched; white-gold clasp.
Also available: with black dial; in yellow gold with silvered dial.

MALTE GRANDE CLASSIQUE   REF. 81500

Movement: mechanical, manual-winding, Vacheron Constantin 1400 caliber (9'''). Entirely designed and realized by the House. 40-hour autonomy, 20 jewels, 28,800 vph, end-stone on the escape-wheel, micrometer screw regulation of the balance-spring. Decorated with circular graining and Côtes de Genève patterns and beveled. Hall-marked by the Geneva Seal.

Functions: hour, minute, small second.

Case: 18K pink-gold, three-piece case (Ø 35.5mm, thickness 7.6mm); curved sapphire crystal; bezel with set brilliants; pink-gold crown; back fastened by 4 screws, displaying the movement through a sapphire crystal. Water resistant to 3atm.

Dial: silvered; guilloché with a wave pattern, zone decorated with circular beads; pink-gold bâton markers and logo; printed minute track; pink-gold bâton hands.

Indications: small seconds at 6.

Strap: alligator leather, hand-stitched; pink-gold clasp.

Also available: in yellow or white gold. Ref. 81000 without brilliants, in yellow gold; pink or white gold.

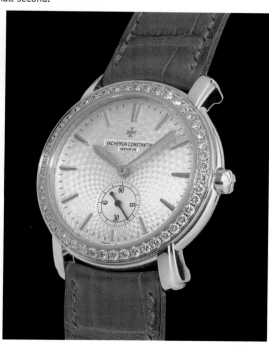

MALTE POWER RESERVE, MOONPHASE   REF. 83500

Movement: mechanical, manual-winding, end-stone on the escape-wheel, micrometer screw regulation of the balance-spring.

Functions: hour, minute; power reserve; moonphase.

Case: 18K white-gold, three-piece case (Ø 33mm, thickness 8.8mm); curved sapphire crystal; bezel with set brilliants; white-gold crown; back fastened by 4 screws, displaying the movement through a sapphire crystal. Water resistant to 3atm.

Dial: sky-blue mother-of-pearl, guilloché; markers with set brilliants, applied white-gold Roman numerals and logo; printed railway minute track; white-gold bâton hands.

Indications: moonphase at 9; power reserve between 11 and 12.

Strap: alligator leather, hand-stitched; white-gold clasp.

Also available: in yellow or pink gold. Without brilliants, in yellow, pink or white gold.

ROYAL EAGLE CHRONOGRAPH   REF. 49145/339A

Movement: mechanical, automatic-winding, 1137 caliber (Frédéric Piguet 1185 caliber).

Functions: hour, minute, small second; date; chronograph with 3 counters.

Case: stainless steel, three-piece tonneau-shaped anatomically curved case (size 39 x 36mm, thickness 13.2mm); antireflective curved sapphire crystal; trapezoid pushers; back fastened by 8 screws. Water resistant to 5atm.

Dial: silvered; recessed subdials decorated with circular beads; printed Arabic numerals, applied white-gold logo; luminescent white-gold bâton hands.

Indications: minute counter at 3; small seconds at 6; hour counter at 9; big date at 12; center seconds; minute track with luminescent markers at quarters.

Bracelet: brushed and polished steel, double fold-over safety clasp.

Also available: with leather strap.

ROYAL EAGLE DAY-DATE   REF. 42008

Movement: mechanical, automatic-winding, 1206 QSSL caliber. Balance with 28,800 vph. Officially certified chronometer (COSC).

Functions: hour, minute, small second; day and date.

Case: stainless steel, three-piece tonneau-shaped anatomically curved case (size 39 x 36mm, thickness 13.2mm); antireflective slightly curved sapphire crystal; trapezoid pushers; back fastened by 8 screws. Water resistant to 3atm.

Dial: silvered; two subdials decorated with circular beads; printed Arabic numerals, applied gold logo; luminescent gold bâton hands.

Indications: date at 3; small seconds at 6; day at 9.

Strap: alligator leather, hand-stitched; gold clasp.

Also available: in white gold.

VERSACE

One of the most incredible legends of our time, Versace is a name respected around the world. Established by Italian Gianni Versace, the company is an icon of fashion and design.

Versace started his business in 1978 with the help of his brother Santo. A prolific designer with a dream to have his own collection, Versace had a talent and creative spirit that propelled him to global success in a very short time. His creations were bold, daring designs that constantly challenged the norm. His designers offered vibrant colors, elegant accents and incredible cuts. Not only did Versace shine in the world of fashion, but the company also delved into the realm of accessories, fragrance, home décor, jewelry and timepieces—all with gusto.

Since 1997, following the untimely death of Gianni, the Versace brand has been run by his sister, Donatella Versace, who had been intimately involved since the company's inception. Keeping the Versace spirit alive and infusing new innovations, Donatella propelled the brand to new heights in couture and jewelry and watches.

The timepiece collection is a brilliant mix of women's and men's watches that combine color, fashion-forward design and technical excellence. The collection consists of four key lines, including the Greca (a rectangular watch with architectural inspirations), the Fifth (a contemporary geometric series), the Madison (distinctive round watches with unusual case-to-bracelet attachments), and the Character (a square, angled watch contoured to fit the wrist). All of the collections feature timepieces that are adorned with diamonds and gemstones to varying degrees.

All Versace watches are made in Switzerland according to strict codes of excellence. Included in the collection are automatics, date watches and chronographs of distinction. Color plays a very important role in Versace timepieces, with many adorned with vivid blue straps of python, leather and microfiber. Bracelets are equally as alluring, with striking chain links that integrate harmoniously with the watch designs.

Among the newest timepieces are the Character with chronograph and expansions to the recently unveiled Versace on Fifth series of watches. The Chrono on Character is a large square watch with a sapphire crystal and

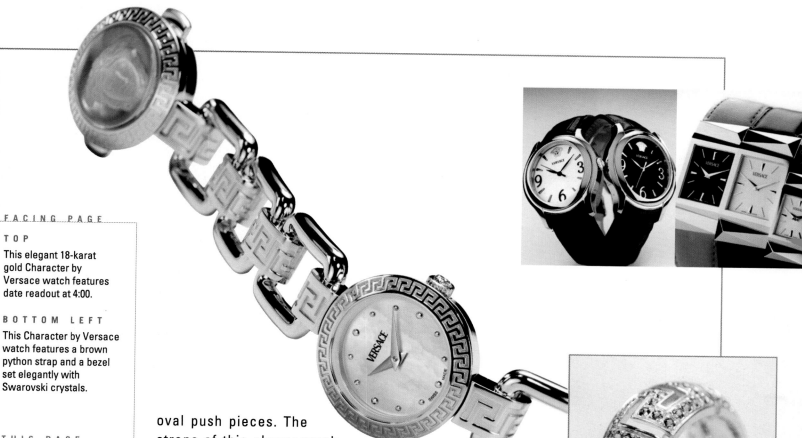

FACING PAGE

TOP

This elegant 18-karat gold Character by Versace watch features date readout at 4:00.

BOTTOM LEFT

This Character by Versace watch features a brown python strap and a bezel set elegantly with Swarovski crystals.

THIS PAGE

TOP LEFT

This Versace on Corniche watch features an open-linked bracelet with Greek motif finished with a pink crystal center stone on the clasp.

TOP RIGHT

left

For these elegant Bond watches, Versace turned to Arabic numerals and markers for a more modern appeal.

right

These Rodeo watches are crafted of stainless steel or gold plating.

FAR RIGHT

From the Greca line, this Sapho by Versace ring is set with 59 sapphires.

BOTTOM RIGHT

This Versace on Landmark watch is crafted of polished steel and engrave with the Greca freeze pattern. It is finished with a dial sporting the Medusa head.

oval push pieces. The straps of this chronograph watch are created in an unusual microfiber that is particularly impervious to water and other elements. The watch is water resistant to 30 meters.

New pieces have joined the distinguished Versace on Fifth collection of elegant watches with curved, rectangular cases and t-shaped case-to-bracelet attachments. Among the new models are diamond-adorned versions in steel, as well as colorful versions on lizard straps.

HIGHLIGHTS

- Among the new Versace pieces are the Versace on Corniche and Versace on Landmark. The Corniche piece is a stunning open-worked bracelet watch with round case and Greca decoration around the clasp—which features a center stone of yellow, pink or blue quartz.

- The Versace on Landmark watch is rectangular and crafted in polished steel with either an ivory or black dial. The head of the Medusa logo is on the dial in sterling silver at 12:00.

- Versace carriers its elegant designs from timepieces through to its collection of writing instruments and jewelry. Its new Vaso jewelry collection is geometrical in design and features a Versace interpretation of Greek symbols. One of the newest designs is a Sapho Greca ring that features diamonds, and either blue, yellow or pink sapphires or tsavorites on the band. An accompanying bracelet and earrings are available.

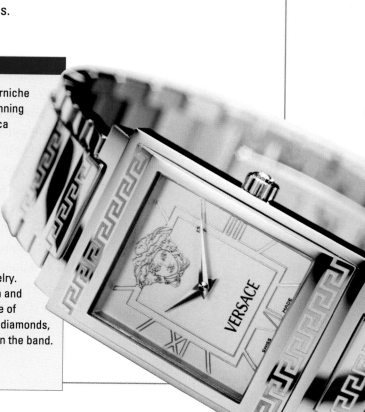

ZANNETTI

t he house of Zannetti differentiates itself by creating watches that are out of the ordinary. Being different is the imperative of our modern life, where we continuously chase the usual names and the usual shapes. Years ago, in order to distinguish one's self, it was enough to choose the expensive items and places to visit. Now, things have changed. Even in the haute couture range, many things have become monotone and overly popular—seen too many times in throbbing advertising messages. Therefore, in order to wear something authentic, it must be something that stands out from the chorus. Zannetti has succeeded in joining wisdom and manual work to create absolutely unique objects—objects with the best technology available today and guaranteeing the highest level of quality. These are the two characteristics that have always distinguished Zannetti's production all over the world.

The House makes limited pieces of sublime quality, using sophisticated complex designs. The true key of distinction is to leave traces in time. Like in a kaleidoscope of shapes and colors, the dials, cases and movements of Zannetti's unusual timepieces are richly decorated—all of them contributing to a unique effect. Considering their constructive complexity, Zannetti watches are absolutely impossible to copy. All Zannetti watches start out in the traditional way, beginning with a main design sketched by hand that defines the "personality" of the watch. The second step is to work on the details: the study of the functionalities of every model, including the position of the movement, or the activation of the push buttons. Then the utmost attention is paid to the type and quality of the decorations and finishing.

Some prototypes are made in order to verify the aesthetic and technical choices before passing into production. The big difference between Zannetti and other haute de gamme brand names resides essentially in the fact that the House continuously works its cases entirely by hand. Therefore the engravings are not fruit of a pantograph, maybe computerized, but the result of one skillful craftsman, equipped with patience and a sharp burin that realizes the watches one by one, following a certain outline but always varying piece to piece. The same rules are also applied to the base-relief workings, the dials, the crowns, the push buttons, and the lunette.

All are refined by hand, and the intricate differences in the final results are noticeable. The Zannetti watch is absolutely unique, and while everyone may not necessarily recognize it, a true Connoisseur of watches and valuables will recognize it immediately—a small difference, but the true essence of haute horology. Zannetti is not a brand defined by marketing strategies. Riccardo Zannetti, being a caring person, takes into consideration the happiness that marks the lives of those who choose his creations. Perhaps this is the reason he succeeds so well in understanding and interpreting the requirements of his clients. This today is truly a symbol of distinction.

HIGHLIGHTS

- Every single model in the Zannetti production is numbered progressively, and comes with an international guarantee. Additionally, every collection is realized in a limited series—a necessity in order to respect the quality controls without making compromises.

- Every model is designed personally by Riccardo Zannetti, who then follows the entire production cycle.

- The materials used for the collections are multiple. The cases are hand crafted in yellow or white gold, or in versions of stainless steel or palladium.

- The dials, which are also refined by hand, are crafted of gold, silver or mother of pearl, and are always further personalized and refined by hand during their creation.

- The best mechanics and movements, made in Switzerland, are used. They are then further personalized by hand with simple engravings on the rotor and bridges.

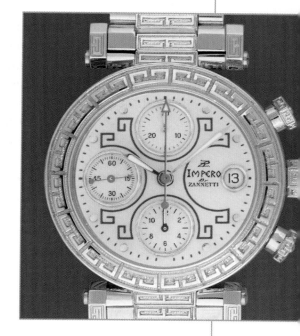

ZENITH

In the beginning was time. And time became noble matter, aspiring towards the ultimate goal—ZENITH. Was the name given to the brand inspired by the sheer limits of the night sky? Tales of such, over time, have nearly achieved the status of legend, but invariably arose from a real event.

Georges Favre-Jacot, as the story goes, went out into the famed Jura Mountains one evening in **1865** while in the grips of a feverish search for a name for his new outstanding caliber. There, the 22-year-old watch inventor found inspiration in an exalting moment at the end of a long and taxing day. The night-blue firmament, as seen on the lunar disks of the classical ChronoMaster designs today, provided the backdrop for the clusters of stars forming the Milky Way and a multitude of constellations. The chill of early spring was bracing and his attention naturally focused on the brightest point on the celestial dome—the luminous Polar Star at the zenith. An association of ideas and a moment of illumination, plus a few strides back to his office, produced the six capital letters of ZENITH, marked by a nib on vellum parchment and later etched into the platinum of the fine calibers made by the watchmaking firm. Fate had intended that a name able to conjure up an entire philosophy should be displayed above the door of the establishment, and not simply on the bridges of completed watch movements.

By **1875**, ZENITH had developed pocket watches, clocks and pendulum clocks, and was creating navigating instruments for the navy. Always rising to the challenge of producing a watch that is both attractive and accurate, ZENITH uses the finest machines and employs the skills of only the most disciplined craftsmen dedicated to the work they produce.

To date, ZENITH has won 1,565 first prizes for its innovative prowess and ZENITH is one of the rare watchmakers able to produce a number of chronograph calibers with column wheels and integrated self-winding systems within the movement of an extra-flat watch—which can also be adapted to include a number of additional complications. Faithful to the spirit of Favre-Jacot and harmoniously reconciled with the modern world, ZENITH has established an impressive tradition of unveiling outstanding watches with movements produced in the same watchmaking center.

Now part of a tradition dating back more than 138 years, at least thirty different calibers had been created before the most famous one appeared in **1969**. The chronograph caliber El Primero ran at the high frequency of 36,000 vibrations per hour—with thirteen lines and only 6.50mm thick—and featured an integrated self-winding system. The caliber stands as a reference around the world, and is identified by a traditional serial number and its special name, a distinctive feature for ZENITH.

In **1994**, ZENITH unveiled the ultra-slim Elite movement—still highly utilized today. In **2001**, ZENTIH returned to its roots by inventing new calibers and, in **2002**, the brand unveiled four new movements, 14 new models and an impressive 52 new references.

"Proportion is a question of millimeters."

Such involvement and commitment, at every stage of development and production, obviously enhances the image of ZENITH as a creative source of new ideas. Such ideas are expressed as intelligent interpretations of the performance achieved by the celebrated El Primero chronograph, while also offering functional variations on the Elite movement—challenging time itself and generations past and future.

It is a rare luxury to be able to create an individual universe, to be able to put a name to the dials and movements created, thus enhancing the exclusive aura of collections of timepieces noted for their sheer perfection, in every tiny detail. A watch is an entity in its own right. The image it conveys must express perfection and its presentation must surpass all limits.

A simple glance is all that is needed: the case, whether gold or stainless steel, polished and individually assembled, will catch a glint of light and the focal point will be on the hands. The delicate hands used in ZENITH watches are cut from gold leaf, or stainless steel, finished and mounted with great care; they must never come into contact with the fine "guilloché" finish of the face, or with the Roman or Arabic numerals carefully applied by hand. These hands are the outer sign of the inner life of the movement, the first manifestation of the value of time choreographed in a circular dance. ZENITH watches are perfectly balanced and the supreme refinement extends to the leather straps and metal bracelets.

*"Beauty is
the splendor
of truth."*

The straps are cut from carefully selected sections of alligator skin, with fine, even scales; the leather is dyed with non-allergic vegetable coloring, hand-finished in saddle-stitch and fitted with a triple-folding clasp made from heat-forged gold or stainless steel. The metal bracelets, born of fire, are carefully and slowly assembled, with each link being polished or satin-buffed, then riveted to the next one. It is a painstaking exercise, and the flexible motion of each link is closely checked for optimal comfort.

Luxury as an intrinsic part of everyday routine is a leitmotif for ZENITH, where, inside the workshops, watches are made and assembled with complete devotion, and each part is methodically checked. Such prestigious timepieces are the fruit of the experience and skills of experts, trained by the finest masters, perpetuating the centuries' old tradition, and offering eloquent proof of Plato's statement: Beauty is the splendor of truth.

TOP LEFT

Le Grand Remorqueur (1923), Fernand Léger. The secret of the most audacious works of art is to combine tradition and modernity.

BOTTOM

With true beauty that comes with authenticity, timepieces made by ZENITH craftsmen express the ineffable joy experienced when extending the scope of life.

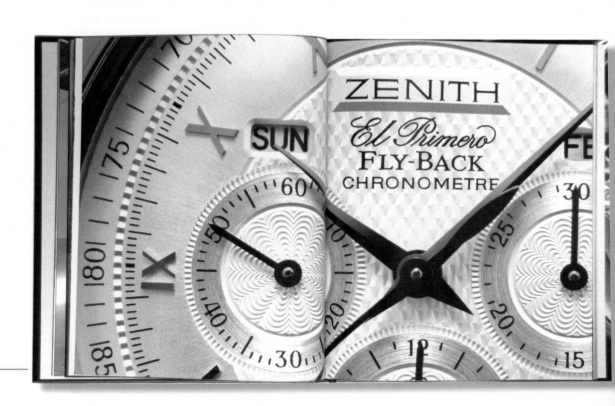

GRANDE PORT-ROYAL EL PRIMERO

HIGHLIGHTS

■ In 2002, ZENITH unveiled four bold new movements to further enhance its significant collection. The brand also launched 14 new models representing an impressive 52 new references.

■ ZENITH has launched a new publicity campaign to mark the company's vigor and emphasis on technical prowess and excellence. In the campaign, beauty, simplicity and truth take center stage. The ChronoMaster El Primero, Grande Class Elite and Port Royal El Primero are majestically captured in an instant of time by the keen eye of photographer Kanji Hishi. The detail of the dial, the design of the case, and the complexity of the movement are the stars of the campaign.

■ ZENITH has unveiled a book for lovers of objects of art. *The Collection, Volume II*, highlights the 2002-2003 models in the ChronoMaster, Class and Port-Royale lines—all of which are equipped with the legendary Elite or El Primero movements.

ZENITH

GRANDE CHRONOMASTER EL PRIMERO GT   REF. 03.1240.4001/01.C495

Movement: automatic, Zenith New El Primero caliber 4001. White-gold rotor, engine-turned (guilloché) with a "grain-d'orge" pointed pattern. Officially certified chronometer(COSC). **Functions:** hour, minute, small second; full calendar (date, day, month, moonphase); fly-back chronograph with 3 counters. **Case:** 18K white-gold, three-piece case (Ø 42, thickness 13.1mm), cambered sapphire crystal, antireflective coating on both sides; 2 correctors on the middle; 18K white-gold oval push-

buttons and crown; back fastened by 6 screws, displaying the movement through a sapphire crystal. Water resistant to 3atm. **Dial:** silvered, guilloché with a "grain-d'orge" pointed pattern, cambered, brushed hour ring and subdial crowns, white-gold triangular markers and Roman numerals applied by hand, white-gold Régate hands. **Indications:** month at 2; 30-minute counter at 3; date between 4 and 5; 12-hour counter and moonphase at 6; small second at 9; day at 10; center second counter with a precision of 1/10 of a second; minute track with divisions for 1/5 of a second; tachometer scale. **Strap:** Louisiana alligator leather, white-gold triple deployment buckle. **Also av.:** yellow or pink gold; stainless steel with stainless steel rotor; platinum (on request).

GRANDE CHRONOMASTER EL PRIMERO XT   REF. 18.1250.4009/01.C495

Movement: automatic, Zenith New El Primero caliber 4009. Rose-gold rotor, engine-turned (guilloché) with a "grain-d'orge" pointed pattern. Officially certified chronometer (COSC). **Functions:** hour, minute, small second; full calendar (date, day, month, moon ages); fly-back chronograph with 3 counters. **Case:** 18K rose-gold, three-piece case (Ø 43, thickness 13.5mm), cambered sapphire crystal, antireflective coating on both sides; 2 correctors on the middle; 18K rose-gold oval push-buttons

and crown; back fastened by 6 screws, displaying the movement through a sapphire crystal. Water resistant to 3atm. **Dial:** silvered, guilloché with a "grain-d'orge" pointed pattern, cambered, brushed hour ring and subdial crowns, rose-gold Roman numerals applied by hand, rose-gold Régate hands. **Indications:** month at 2; 30-minute counter at 3; date between 4 and 5; 12-hour counter and analog moon ages at 6; small second at 9; day at 10; center second counter with a precision of 1/10 of a second; minute track with divisions for 1/5 of a second; tachometer scale. **Strap:** Louisiana alligator leather, rose-gold triple deployment buckle. **Also available:** yellow or white gold; stainless steel with stainless steel rotor; platinum (on request).

CHRONOMASTER EL PRIMERO DIAMONDS   REF. 43.0240.410/09.C501

Movement: automatic, Zenith El Primero caliber 410. White-gold rotor set with 35 diamonds, engine-turned (guilloché) with a "grain-d'orge" pointed pattern. Officially certified chronometer (COSC). **Functions:** hour, minute, small second; full calendar (date, day, month, moonphase); chronograph with 3 counters. **Case:** 18K white-gold, three-piece case (Ø 40, thickness 13mm), cambered sapphire crystal, antireflective coating on both sides; bezel with two rows of set brilliants (144 stones, 1.43 carats); 2 correctors on the middle;

white-gold oval push-buttons and crown; back fastened by 6 screws, displaying the movement through a sapphire crystal. Water resistant to 3atm. **Dial:** silvered, guilloché with a "grain-d'orge" pointed pattern, cambered, brushed hour ring and subdial crowns, white-gold triangular markers (12 Roman numeral) applied by hand and 6 in brilliants; burnished gold-leaf style hands (coloring obtained by galvanic plating). **Indications:** month at 2; 30-minute counter at 3; date between 4 and 5; hour 12-counter and moonphase at 6; small second at 9; day at 10; center second counter with a precision of 1/10 of a second; minute track with divisions for 1/5 of a second; tachometer scale. **Strap:** python skin, white-gold triple deployment buckle. **Also available:** with pink, black or mother-of-pearl python skin strap.

CHRONOMASTER SQUELETTE   REF. 30.0240.410.92.C497

Movement: automatic, Zenith El Primero caliber 410SQ. Yellow-gold skeleton rotor. Officially certified chronometer (COSC).
Functions: hour, minute, small second; full calendar (date, day, month, moonphase); chronograph with 3 counters.
Case: 18K yellow-gold, three-piece case (Ø 40mm, thickness 13.5mm), cambered sapphire crystal, antireflective coating on both sides; 2 correctors on the

middle; yellow-gold oval push-buttons and crown; back fastened by 6 screws, displaying the movement through a sapphire crystal.
Dial: skeletonized, chased, gilded; subdials anthracite with grained pattern, printed and gilded; yellow-gold Régate hands.
Indications: month at 2; 30-minute counter at 3; date between 4 and 5; 12-hour counter and moonphase at 6; small second at 9; day at 10; center second counter with a precision of 1/10 of a second; minute track; tachometer scale.
Strap: python skin, yellow-gold triple deployment buckle.

GRANDE CLASS EL PRIMERO   REF. 65.0520.4002/01.C492

Movement: automatic, Zenith New El Primero caliber 4002. Rotor engine-turned (guilloché) with a "grain-d'orge" pointed pattern. Officially certified chronometer (COSC).
Functions: hour, minute, small second; date; chronograph with two counters.
Case: 18K white-gold, three-piece case (Ø 44mm) curved sapphire crystal, antireflective coating on both sides; oval push-buttons; steel crown; snap-on back displaying the movement through a sapphire crystal. Water resistant to 3atm.
Dial: black with a grained pattern, cambered; rhodium-plated brass pointed markers and Arabic numerals; rhodium-plated brass Régate hands; printed minute track.
Indications: 30-minute counter at 3; date between 4 and 5; 12-hour counter at 6; small second at 9; center second counter with a precision of 1/10 of a second; minute track with divisions for 1/5 of a second; tachometer scale.
Strap: Louisiana alligator leather, 18K white-gold triple deployment buckle.

GRANDE CLASS EL PRIMERO   REF. 03.0520.4002/21.C492

Movement: automatic, Zenith New El Primero caliber 4002. Rotor engine-turned (guilloché) with a "grain-d'orge" pointed pattern. Officially certified chronometer (COSC).
Functions: hour, minute, small second; date; chronograph with two counters.
Case: stainless steel, three-piece case (Ø 44mm), curved sapphire crystal, antireflective coating on both sides; oval push-buttons; steel crown; snap-on back displaying the movement through a sapphire crystal. Water resistant to 3atm.
Dial: black with a grained pattern, cambered; rhodium-plated brass, pointed markers and Arabic numerals; rhodium-plated brass Régate hands; printed minute track.
Indications: 30-minute counter at 3; date between 4 and 5; 12-hour counter at 6; small second at 9; center second counter with a precision of 1/10 of a second; minute track with divisions for 1/5 of a second; tachometer scale.
Strap: Louisiana alligator leather, stainless steel triple deployment buckle.

CLASS EL PRIMERO SPORT   REF. 03.0510.400/04.C491

Movement: automatic, Zenith El Primero caliber 400. Officially certified chronometer (COSC).
Functions: hour, minute, small second, date, chronograph with 3 counters.
Case: stainless steel, three-piece case (Ø 40mm, thickness 12.8mm), cambered sapphire crystal, antireflective coating on both sides; oval push-buttons; snap-on back, displaying the movement through a sapphire crystal. Water resistant to 5atm.
Dial: silvered, cambered, zones decorated with circular beads; luminescent Arabic numerals, luminescent rhodium-plated brass Régate hands.
Indications: 30-minute counter at 3; date between 4 and 5, 12-hour counter at 6; small second at 9; center second counter with a precision of 1/10 of a second; minute track with divisions for 1/5 of a second; tachometer scale.
Strap: Louisiana alligator leather, stainless steel triple deployment buckle.
Also available: with stainless steel bracelet; with black dial and luminescent Arabic numerals.

CLASS ÉLITE DUAL TIME   REF. 03.1125.682/02.C490

Movement: automatic, extra flat, Zenith Elite 682 caliber.
Functions: hour, minute, small second, date, second time zone.
Case: stainless steel, three-piece case (Ø 39mm, thickness 9.7mm), curved sapphire crystal, antireflective coating on both sides; second time-zone corrector by a rectangular pusher at 10; snap-on back, displaying the movement through a sapphire crystal. Water resistant to 3atm.
Dial: silvered, cambered, brushed hour ring, center disc engine-turned (guilloché) with a "grain-d'orge" pointed pattern, subdial guilloché with a shell pattern and brushed crown; rhodium-plated pointed markers and Arabic numerals applied by hand; printed minute track; rhodium-plated brass Régate hands.
Indications: date at 3; small second at 9; second time-zone with arrow-shaped center hand in burnished brass with skeleton tip.
Strap: Louisiana alligator leather, stainless steel triple deployment buckle.
Also available: in yellow, pink or white gold.

ZENITH

CLASS ÉLITE RESERVE DE MARCHE   REF. 18.1125.685/01.C490

Movement: automatic, extra flat, Zenith Elite 685 caliber.
Functions: hour, minute, small second, date, power reserve.
Case: 18K rose-gold, three-piece case (Ø 37mm, thickness 9.3mm), curved sapphire crystal, antireflective coating on both sides; snap-on back, displaying the movement through a sapphire crystal. Water resistant to 3atm.
Dial: silvered, cambered, brushed hour ring, center disc engine-turned (guilloché) with a "grain-

d'orge" pointed pattern, subdial guilloché with a shell pattern and brushed crowns; rose-gold triangular and pointed markers and Arabic numerals applied by hand; printed minute track; rose-gold Régate hands.
Indications: power-reserve indicator at 2; small second at 9, date between 4 and 5.
Strap: Louisiana alligator leather, rose-gold triple deployment buckle.
Also available: in yellow or white gold or stainless steel.

CLASS ÉLITE   REF. 17.1125.680/02.C490

Movement: automatic, extra-flat, Zenith Elite 680 caliber.
Functions: hour, minute, small second, date.
Case: 18K yellow-gold, three-piece case (Ø 37mm, thickness 7.9mm), curved sapphire crystal, antireflective coating on both sides; snap-on back, displaying the movement through a sapphire crystal. Water resistant to 3atm.
Dial: silvered, cambered, brushed hour ring, center disc engine-turned (guilloché) with a "grain-

d'orge" pointed pattern, subdial guilloché with a shell pattern and crown with a grained pattern; gold-plated brass pointed markers and Arabic numerals applied by hand; printed minute track; gold-plated brass Régate hands.
Indications: date at 3; small second at 9.
Strap: Louisiana alligator leather, yellow-gold triple deployment buckle.
Also available: in pink or white gold; in stainless steel.

GRANDE PORT ROYAL EL PRIMERO RECTANGLE REF. 03.550.400/21.C492

Movement: automatic, Zenith El Primero caliber 400. Officially certified chronometer (COSC).
Functions: hour, minute, small second; date; chronograph with 3 counters.
Case: stainless steel, two-piece case (size 40 x 36mm, thickness 13mm), curved sapphire crystal, antireflective coating on both sides; rectangular push-buttons; back fastened by 6 screws, displaying the movement through a curved

sapphire crystal. Water resistant to 5atm.
Dial: black with central damier, brushed hour ring; subdials decorated with circular beads; silvered raised painted Arabic numerals, 6 and 12 applied raised pointed markers in rhodium-plated brass; luminescent rhodium-plated brass Railway hands.
Indications: 30-minute counter at 3; date between 4 and 5; 12-hour counter at 6; small second at 9; center second counter with a precision of 1/10 of a second; minute track with divisions for 1/5 of a second; tachometer scale.
Strap: Louisiana alligator leather, stainless steel triple deployment buckle.
Also available: with silvered dial; with bracelet.

GRANDE PORT ROYAL EL PRIMERO   REF. 03.550.400/01.M550

Movement: automatic, Zenith El Primero caliber 400. Officially certified chronometer (COSC).
Functions: hour, minute, small second, date, chronograph with 3 counters.
Case: stainless steel, two-piece case (size 40 x 38mm, thickness 13mm), curved sapphire crystal, antireflective coating on both sides; rectangular push-buttons; back fastened by 6 screws, displaying the movement through a curved sapphire

crystal. Water resistant to 5atm.
Dial: silvered, with central damier, brushed hour ring; subdials decorated with circular beads; silvered raised painted Arabic numerals; 6 applied raised pointed in rhodium-plated brass; luminescent burnished brass Railway hands.
Indications: 30-minute counter at 3; date between 4 and 5; 12-hour counter at 6; small second at 9; center second counter with a precision of 1/10 of a second; minute track with divisions for 1/5 of a second; tachometer scale.
Bracelet: stainless steel; stainless steel triple deployment buckle.
Also available: with black dial; with strap.

CALIBER 410 EL PRIMERO

Caliber 410 contains 354 components, 277 of which differ, and is shown here in a dial-side view. Visible are the full calendar gears and discs. At 3 is the chronograph minutes hand, at 6 the chronograph hours hand, at 9 the small seconds, and at the center the pivot of the chronograph seconds hand. As is true for the whole movement, the calendar is completely integrated with the basic pillar-plate. This certainly represents one of the keys for the success of El Primero: a complete integration of watch mechanism, chronograph function and automatic-winding system, allowing a reduction of its thickness to less than 2mm, i.e. less than the average size of most automatic chronographs.

MOVEMENTS 4001 AND 4009 EL PRIMERO

Caliber 13 ''' - **Diameter:** 30mm - **Height:** 7.55mm. 356 parts. **Jewels:** 31.
Frequency: 36,000 vph. **Power reserve:** over 50 hours.
Measures short time intervals to a 10th of a second.
Automatic winding in both directions.
Mechanical movement manufactured, assembled and decorated by hand.
COSC certified.
Chronograph functions coordinated by the column-wheel.
*Functions 4001:
Hour; Minute; Small second; 30-minute counter; 12-hour counter; sweep second hand; date; day; month; phases of the moon.
*Functions 4009:
Hour; Minute; Small second; 30-minute counter; 12-hour counter; sweep second hand; date; day; month; ages of the moon.

MOVEMENT 4002 EL PRIMERO

Caliber 13 ''' - **Diameter:** 30mm - **Height:** 6.5mm.
337 parts. **Jewels:** 31.
Frequency: 36,000 vph.
Power reserve: over 50 hours.
Measures short time intervals to a 10th of a second.
Automatic winding in both directions.

Mechanical movement manufactured, assembled and decorated by hand. COSC certified.
Chronograph functions coordinated by the column-wheel.

Functions: Hour; Minute; Small second; 30-minute counter; seconds hand in the center; date.

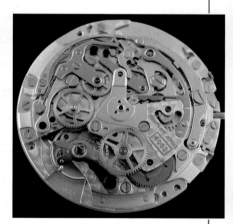

MOVEMENT 682 ELITE

Extra-flat automatic movement with second time zone.
Caliber 11 ''' 1/2, **Diameter:** 25.6mm.
Jewels: 26.
Frequency: 28,800 vph.

Extra-flat movement.
Shockproof device.
Index assembly with fine adjustment.
Power reserve: over 50 hours.
Central rotor on ball bearings.
Automatic winding in both directions.

Mechanical movement manufactured, assembled and decorated by hand.

Functions: Hour; Minute; Small Second; date; second time zone.

MOVEMENT 685 ELITE

Extra-flat automatic movement with power-reserve indicator.

Caliber 11 ''' 1/2 - **Diameter:** 25.6mm - **Height:** 4.48mm.
180 parts. **Jewels:** 38.

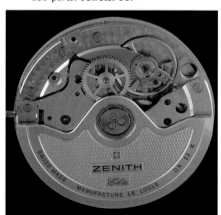

Frequency: 28,800 vph.
Power reserve: over 50 hours.
Automatic winding in both directions.

Mechanical movement manufactured, assembled and decorated by hand.

Functions: Hour; Minute; Small second; date; power-reserve indicator.

A. LANGE & SÖHNE
Altenberger Strasse 15
D-01768 Glashütte in Sachsen
Germany
Tel: 49 35053 485 41

ARNOLD & SON
The British Masters SA
23, Avenue Leopold-Robert
2300 La Chaux-de-Fonds,
Switzerland
Tel: 41 32 910 90 62

AUDEMARS PIGUET
1348 Le Brassus
Switzerland
Tel: 41 21 845 14 00

BAUME & MERCIER
61, Route de Chêne
1211 Geneva 29
Switzerland
Tel: 41 22 707 31 31

BEDAT & C°
45, Rue Agasse
1211 Geneva 29
Switzerland
Tel: 41 22 718 01 88

BERTOLUCCI
16, B Champs-Montants
2074 Marin, Switzerland
Tel: 41 32 756 75 00

BLANCPAIN
6, Chemin de l'Etang
1094 Paudex, Switzerland
Tel: 41 21 796 36 36

BOUCHERON
Luxury Goods International S.A.
2, Monruz
2002 Neuchâtel
Switzerland
Tel: 41 32 729 60 20

BREGUET
1344 L'Abbaye, Switzerland
Tel: 41 21 841 90 90

BREITLING
Case Postale 1132
2540 Grenchen
Switzerland
Tel: 41 32 654 54 54

CARTIER INTERNATIONAL
51, Rue Pierre Charron
75008 Paris, France
Tel: 33 1 40 74 62 07

CÉDRIC JOHNER.SA
28, Route de Pressy
1253 Vandoeuvres
Switzerland
Tel: 41 22 750 82 13

CHARLES OUDIN
8, Place Vendôme
75001 Paris, France
Tel: 33 1 40 15 99 00

CHARRIOL
1227 Prospect Street
La Jolla CA 92037 USA
Tel: 858 454 0011

CHAUMET
12, Place Vendôme
75001 Paris, France
Tel: 33 1 44 77 24 00

CHOPARD
8, Rue de Veyrot
1217 Meyrin-Geneva 2
Switzerland
Tel: 41 22 719 31 31

CHRISTIAN DIOR
8, Rue Fourcroy
75017 Paris, France
Tel: 33 1 44 29 36 36

CHRONOSWISS
Elly Staegmeyr Strasse 12
D-80999 München, Germany
Tel: 49 089 892 60 70

CLERC
2, Rue Charles Bonnet
1206 Geneva, Switzerland
Tel: 41 22 731 79 31
Tel USA: 800 840 1447

CONCORD
35, Rue de Nidau
2501 Bienne, Switzerland
Tel: 41 32 329 34 00

DANIEL JEANRICHARD
14, Cernil-Antoine
2301 La Chaux-de-Fonds
Switzerland
Tel: 41 32 925 70 50

DAVID YURMAN
501 Madison Avenue
New York NY 10022 USA
Tel: 212 593 1122

de GRISOGONO
176 bis. Route de St. Julien
1228 Plan-les-quates,
Switzerland
Tel: 41 22 317 10 80

de WITT
28, Route de Pressy
1253 Vandoeuvres
Switzerland
Tel: 41 22 750 82 13

DELANEAU
29/31, Route de l'Aéroport
1215 Geneva 15, Switzerland
Tel: 41 22 799 53 53

DUBEY & SCHALDENBRAND
7, Industries
2316 Les Ponts-de-Martel
Switzerland
Tel: 41 32 937 14 30

EBEL
113, Rue de la Paix
2301 La Chaux-de-Fonds
Switzerland
Tel: 41 32 912 31 23

EBERHARD & CO
12, Riva Paradiso
6900 Lugano
Switzerland
Tel: 41 91 993 26 01

FRANCK MULLER
22, Rue de Malagny
1294 Genthod, Switzerland
Tel: 41 22 959 88 88

FRANÇOIS-PAUL JOURNE
17, Rue de l'Arquebuse
1204, Geneva, Switzerland
Tel: 41 22 322 09 09

FRÉDÉRIQUE CONSTANT S.A.
39, Rue Peillonnex, Chene-Bourg
1225 Geneva, Switzerland
T: 41 22 860 04 40

GEORGES V
Rue de Grand-Chêne 7
1002 Lausanne, Switzerland
Tel: 41 21 329 05 52

GEVRIL
23 Dover Terrace
Monsey NY 10952 USA
Tel: 845 425 9882

GIRARD-PERREGAUX
1, Place Girardet
2301 La Chaux-de-Fonds
Switzerland
Tel: 41 32 911 33 33

GLASHÜTTE ORIGINAL
Altenberger Strasse, 1
D-01768 Glashütte in Sachsen
Germany
Tel: 49 35053 462 31

GOLDPFEIL SA
8, Rue Ceard
1204 Geneva, Switzerland
Tel: 41 22 317 79 80

GRAHAM
The British Masters SA
23, Avenue Leopold-Robert
2300 La Chaux-de-Fonds
Switzerland
Tel: 41 32 910 90 62

GUCCI TIMEPIECES
Luxury Goods International S.A.
2, Rue de Monruz
2002 Neuchâtel
Switzerland
Tel: 41 32 723 06 06

HARRY WINSTON
82, rue de Lausanne
1202 Geneva, Switzerland
Tel: 41 22 716 29 00

HERMÈS
Erlenstrasse 31A
2555 Brügg, Switzerland
Tel: 41 32 366 70 50

HUBLOT
44, Route de Divonne
1260 Nyon 2, Switzerland
Tel: 41 22 362 19 70

**INTERNATIONAL WATCH CO.
(IWC)**
Baumgarten Strasse, 15
8201 Schaffhausen
Switzerland
Tel: 41 52 635 65 65

JAEGER-LECOULTRE
8, Rue de la Golisse
1347 Le Sentier, Switzerland
Tel: 41 21 845 02 02

JEAN-MAIRET & GILLMAN
11, Chemin du Petray
1222 Visenaz, Switzerland
Tel: 41 22 855 07 60

L. LEROY
Y. Parc SA
Rue Galilée 15
1400 Yverdon-les-Bains
Switzerland
Tel: 41 24 423 93 00

LÉONARD
41A, Route de Chêne
1208 Geneva, Switzerland
Tel: 41 22 700 73 53

LOCMAN
Piazza G. da Verrazzano, 7
57034 Marina di Campo (LI)
Tel: 39 05 6597 90 02

LONGINES
2610 Saint Imier, Switzerland
Tel: 41 32 942 45 25

MICHELE WATCHES
20201 NE 16th Place
Miami FL 33179 USA
Tel: 305 650 9771

MONTRES ALLISON
1548 Karlann Drive
Golden CO 80403 USA
T: 303 582 5217

OLIVIER ROUX SA
28, rue du Grand Bureau
1227 Carouge-Geneva
Switzerland
Tel: 41 22 301 24 94

OMEGA
96, Rue Stampfli
2500 Bienne 4, Switzerland
Tel: 41 32 343 95 80

PANERAI
Via Ludovico di Breme, 44/45
20156 Milan, Italy
Tel: 39 02 302 61

PARMIGIANI FLEURIER
Rue du l'Hopital 33
2114 Fleurier, Switzerland
Tel: 41 32 862 66 30

PATEK PHILIPPE
141, Chemin du Pont du Centenaire
1211 Geneva 2, Switzerland
Tel: 41 22 884 20 20

PERRELET
2, rue du Tresor
2000 Neuchâtel, Switzerland
Tel: 41 32 721 33 43

QUINTING
Chemin Clos Belmont, 2
1208-Geneva
Switzerland
Tel: 41 22 718 78 80

RAYMOND WEIL S.A.
Avenue Eugène-Lance 36-38
1211 Genève 26
Switzerland
Tel: 41 22 884 00 55

RGM
590 Centerville Road, #130
Lancaster PA 17601 USA
Tel: 717 653 9799

**RICHARD MILLE
HOROMETRIE S.A.**
11 Rue du Jura
2345 Les Breuleux Jura
Switzerland
Tel: 41 32 959 43 53

ROGER DUBUIS
12, Avenue Industrielle
1227 Geneva
Switzerland
Tel: 41 22 827 49 49

ROLEX
3/7, Rue François Dussaud
1211 Geneva, Switzerland
Tel: 41 22 308 22 00

SCATOLA DEL TEMPO
Via del Mille, 17
23891 Barzanò, Italy
Tel: 39 03 921 1481

TAG HEUER
14a, Avenue des Champs-Montants
2074 Marin, Switzerland
Tel: 41 32 755 60 00

TECHNOMARINE
2915 Biscayne Boulevard
Miami FL 33137 USA
Tel: 305 438 0880

TIFFANY & CO
727 Fifth Avenue
New York NY 10022 USA
Tel: 800 526 0649

ULYSSE NARDIN
3, Rue du Jardin
2400 Le Locle
Switzerland
Tel: 41 32 931 56 77

VACHERON CONSTANTIN
1, Rue des Moulins
1204 Geneva
Switzerland
Tel: 41 22 310 32 27

VERSACE PRECIOUS ITEMS
GV Distribution
645 Fifth Avenue, 12 Floor
New York NY 10022 USA
Tel: 1 212 813 0190

ZANNETTI
Via Monte d'Oro, 18/19/20
00186 Rome, Italy
Tel: 39 06 687 6651

ZENITH
34, Rue des Billodes
2400 Le Locle
Switzerland
Tel: 41 32 930 62 62